THE ROSETTA STONE.
This basalt slab is inscribed with a copy of the bilingual Decree promulgated by the whole of the priesthood of Egypt assembled at Memphis, in the ninth year of the reign of Ptolemy V Epiphanes (B.C. 196), to celebrate the first commemoration of the coronation of the king, who was not crowned until the eighth year of his reign. The decree is written in two forms of Egyptian writing, *i.e.*, hieroglyphic and demotic, and in Greek; it enumerates the good works of the king, and orders that additional honours be paid to him and his ancestors. B.M. No. 24.

THE MUMMY

A Handbook of Egyptian Funerary Archaeology

E. A. WALLIS BUDGE

SECOND EDITION
REVISED & GREATLY ENLARGED

DOVER PUBLICATIONS, INC., New York

Published in Canada by General Publishing Company, Ltd., 30 Lesmill Road, Don Mills, Toronto, Ontario.
Published in the United Kingdom by Constable and Company, Ltd.

This Dover edition, first published in 1989, is an unabridged republication of the second, revised and enlarged, edition as published by the Cambridge University Press (Cambridge, England) in 1925 (the first edition appeared in 1893). For reasons of space, a number of plates have been moved to different locations in the present edition, but the original numerical sequence of plates has been retained despite anomalies of location.

Manufactured in the United States of America
Dover Publications, Inc., 31 East 2nd Street, Mineola, N.Y. 11501

Library of Congress Cataloging-in-Publication Data

Budge, E.A. Wallis (Ernest Alfred Wallis), Sir, 1857–1934.
The mummy.

Reprint. Originally published: 2nd ed. Cambridge : University Press, 1925.
Includes bibliographical references and index.
1. Egypt—Antiquities. 2. Funeral rites and ceremonies—Egypt. 3. Mummies—Egypt. I. Title.
[DT61.B916 1989] 932 88-31011
ISBN 0-486-25928-5

DEDICATED

TO THE MEMORY OF

JOHN PEILE, LITT.D.

MASTER OF

CHRIST'S COLLEGE

CAMBRIDGE

A mark of gratitude & regard

PREFACE

In the year 1892, on the recommendation of J. H. Middleton, Slade Professor of Fine Art in the University of Cambridge, the Syndics of the Fitzwilliam Museum commissioned me to make a Catalogue[1] of the Egyptian Antiquities preserved in that Institution. When the Catalogue was printed, Professor Middleton and Professor Robertson Smith were of the opinion that the detailed descriptions of the antiquities should be prefaced by an Introduction, of sufficient length to contain a summary of the history of Egypt, with a list of the cartouches of the principal kings and a series of short chapters, containing such information as would enable the student to use the Catalogue with advantage, and at the same time acquire the principal facts concerning Egyptian funerary archaeology. As a result of the suggestions as to what the Introduction should contain, the manuscript of it grew longer and longer, and when the question of printing arose the Syndics of the Cambridge University Press decided that the Introduction must be printed as a separate volume.

The collection of Egyptian antiquities in the Fitzwilliam Museum was in 1892 comparatively small, and many classes of funerary antiquities were not represented in it. When it was decided to print the Introduction in a separate volume Professor Middleton and Professor Robertson Smith asked me to include in it descriptions of the objects essential for an Egyptian funeral from good typical examples in the British Museum. I therefore added many paragraphs on the amulets and other objects which formed the equipment of mummies, on the various kinds of coffins, sarcophagi and tombs in which the mummy was laid, and on the furniture found in Egyptian tombs generally.

Whether the possibility of preserving the body for an indefinite period was suggested to the predynastic Egyptians by the sight of the unchanged forms of their dead after years of interment (which may have been due to the dryness of the soil, as some have thought), or whether they wrapped it in skins of beasts or reed mats, or, in dynastic times, embalmed it as the result of their unbroken and ineradicable belief in a future life and immortality, matters little. The fact remains that the preservation of the body was the chief end

[1] *A Catalogue of the Egyptian Collection in the Fitzwilliam Museum, Cambridge*. Cambridge University Press 1893.

and aim of every Egyptian who wished to attain to everlasting life. And it is to the cult of the dead, the predominant feature of which was the preservation of the mummy, that we owe most of our knowledge of the Egyptians for a period of about 5000 years. The papyri buried with mummies instruct us concerning the Egyptian Religion; the scenes, sculptured or painted on the walls of the corridors and chambers in the tombs in which they were laid, enable us to reconstruct the history of the daily life of the Egyptians; and the inscriptions and objects found in the graves and tombs supply us with exact information as to their raids and wars, trade and commerce, professions and handicrafts, avocations and amusements, and their religious and social institutions. Egypt lives again through her dead, *i.e.* her mummies, and, as the INTRODUCTION which I wrote dealt chiefly with the equipment of mummies, it was decided to call it when in published form *The Mummy*, and to add as an explanatory title *Chapters on Egyptian funereal Archaeology*. The book was published by the University Press, Cambridge, in the early autumn of 1893. The first edition was exhausted in a few months, and a reprint was issued in the following winter; many of the Chapters were translated into Arabic and published in periodicals and newspapers in Egypt, and, if their editors could have obtained electrotypes of the illustration blocks, an Arabic translation of the complete work would have been printed in Cairo.

As years passed the discoveries of natives and Europeans in Egypt made the rewriting of the section of *The Mummy* that dealt with the history of Egypt necessary, and many of the purely archaeological paragraphs were found to need revision and expansion. I had collected much new material and was contemplating a new edition of the book, revised and enlarged, when the War broke out and so the idea was dropped. In 1923 I raised the question of a new edition with the Syndics of the Cambridge Press, and was rejoiced to hear from their Secretary, Mr. S. C. Roberts, that they were prepared to consider the matter favourably. I had thought of retaining all the illustrations in the first edition of *The Mummy* and as much of the letterpress as possible; but I learned that during the War the stereotype plates had been requisitioned by the Government and melted down for military purposes. Thus it became necessary to rewrite the book, and to supplement such illustrations as were worth reproducing with a series of new black-and-white ones and half-tone plates. Thanks to the friendly help and courtesy of Mr. Roberts and the technical assistance of Mr. W. Lewis, Printer to the University, arrangements were quickly made, and the present edition of *The Mummy* is the result.

The section dealing with the History of Egypt has been rewritten and the same may be said of the List of the royal Cartouches. Important discoveries have been made in Egypt during the thirty-two years which have elapsed since they were written, and it is now possible to give a nearly connected account of the history of the country from the late Neolithic to the Roman Period. Comparatively little has been done to clear away the difficulties that beset every attempt to formulate a system of Chronology, chiefly because the Egyptians were not skilled chronographers, and all the evidence obtainable from the inscriptions indicates that, under the New Empire at least, they possessed very little exact information about the early history of their country. It seems probable that the beginnings of dynastic civilization are to be placed somewhere in the fourth millennium before Christ; when the Neolithic Period began and ended is unknown. No exact dating is possible before the seventh century B.C. And if we are to believe, as some authorities do, that the Sumerian and Egyptian civilizations were related intimately and were derived from a common source, we must place the beginnings of the dynastic civilization of Egypt in the later rather than the earlier centuries of the fourth millennium before Christ.

As concerning the List of Cartouches given herein, the addition of the Horus names and Nebti names was considered to be unnecessary, for most of them are given in my *Book of the Kings of Egypt*, 2 vols., London, 1908, and also, with much additional information, in Gauthier's *Le Livre des Rois d'Égypte*, Paris, 1907–17. Many Nesubâti and Son-of-Rā names have been added, and thanks to the labours of the American excavators at Nûrî and other places near the ruins of Napata, the capital of the earlier native Nubian kingdoms in the Egyptian Sûdân, it has been possible to include those of the successors of Tanutâmen. The history of the period of Dynasties XXII–XXIV is obscure, and the order of the succession of their kings is doubtful.

The somewhat lengthy Chapter on the Rosetta Stone has been reprinted with a few additions, for a handy summary of the facts connected with the history of the decipherment of the Egyptian hieroglyphs is as necessary now as when the Chapter was written. The facts collected by Dean Peacock and printed in his *Life of Thomas Young*, London, 1855, and the extracts from contemporary letters and papers on the subject given by Leitch in his edition of the

Miscellaneous Works by the late Thomas Young, London, 1855, prove that the work of Young on the hieroglyphs and that of Åkerblad on Demotic were of far more importance than is usually attributed to them. Young was the first to realize the phonetic character of Egyptian hieroglyphs, and he was the first to obtain the correct values of several of them. Champollion adopted his methods and used his values, without acknowledgment, and those who were unacquainted with the facts assigned to him the honour and credit due to Young. Many modern writers on Egyptology seem never to have read the facts summarized by Dean Peacock, and therefore repeat the mistake made by their predecessors a century ago. In like manner the valuable service which Lepsius rendered to Champollion's system is usually ignored in modern times. By his "Lettre à M. le Professeur I. Rosellini sur l'Alphabet Hiéroglyphique" (see *Annali dell' Instituto Archeologico di Roma*, vol. IX, 1837) Lepsius gave to it the coherence which it lacked and set it on a sure foundation.

Many of the sections of *The Mummy* in which the various classes of antiquities are described have been either rewritten or expanded, *e.g.* the section on the Scarab. Thanks to the labours of Fabre and his study of the habits of the *scarabaeus sacer* it is now possible to harmonize the statements about it made by classical writers, and to show why some of the Fathers of the Church, and the Gnostics, both pagan and Christian, regarded it as a symbol of Christ. Many new sections have been added, *e.g.* Obelisks, Shrouds, Spirit Houses, Foundation Deposits, Wands, Draughts, Hypocephali, etc. During my years of service in the British Museum I kept a list of all the reasonable questions put to me by members of the public, who were seeking information about Egyptian "anticas" either as collectors or as students of Egyptology. Many of these I answered in the *Guides* to the various Galleries and Rooms, and the answers to a great many others are given in the present work. With two great branches of Egyptian Archaeology, viz. Art and Architecture, I have made no attempt to deal, because I possess no special knowledge of these subjects. It seems to me that, in order to discuss these subjects satisfactorily, a writer on them must posses not only a knowledge of Egyptian, Western Asiatic, and Mediterranean Island Art and Architecture generally, but also much technical knowledge. And he should possess naturally the intuition and sympathy that will enable him to understand and to interpret to others the effect that the ancient craftsman intended to produce on those who saw his work. The professional Egyptologist is far too busy with his texts to deal adequately with Egyptian Art, even supposing that he is endowed by nature with the necessary qualifications. Much excellent work has been done for Egyptian Art and Architecture by Perrot and Chipiez (*A History of Art in Ancient Egypt*, 2 vols., London, 1883), by Prisse d'Avennes (*Histoire de l'art Égyptien*, Paris, 1878–9), by Maspero (*Ars una species mille, Histoire générale de l'art. Égypte*, Paris, 1912), and by Jean Capart (*L'art Égyptien*, Paris, 1909–11; *Les Débuts de l'Art en Égypte*, Brussels, 1904; *Leçons sur l'Art Égyptien*, Liége, 1920), but very much more remains to be done, especially in connection with proving or disproving the alleged relationship of the Art and Architecture of Mesopotamia with the Art and Architecture of Egypt. Mr. E. Bell's *Architecture of Ancient Egypt*, London, 1924, affords much solid information about Egyptian Architecture, and forms a useful introduction to Capart's great work *L'Art Égyptien*, of which the first volume has already appeared (Brussels, 1924); the section *L'Architecture* will be indispensable to every student.

In this enlarged edition of *The Mummy* seventy-five "black-and-white" illustrations and thirty-nine plates, containing about 194 reproductions (from specially made photographs) of typical objects in the British Museum, are given. These objects, as well as those described throughout the book, have been chosen from the National Collection, because the British Museum is open to the public for several hours daily, to say nothing of Sundays, and collectors and students can see and study the objects exhibited there without let or hindrance.

My thanks are due to the Trustees of the British Museum for permission to photograph the fine series of Egyptian antiquities reproduced on the Frontispiece and Plates I–XXXVIII, and for the copies of some of the early funerary objects and stelae published by them in *Hieroglyphic Texts from Egyptian Stelae, &c., in the British Museum*, London, 1911–25. For lists of works dealing with Egyptian History and Archaeology generally, the reader is referred to the excellent classified Bibliography published in *The Cambridge Ancient History*, vols. I–III, Cambridge, 1923 f.

E. A. WALLIS BUDGE

48 BLOOMSBURY STREET,
BEDFORD SQUARE, W.C. 1
September 19, 1925

CONTENTS

LIST OF PLATES

LIST OF ILLUSTRATIONS IN THE TEXT

THE MUMMY

THE LAND OF EGYPT

EGYPT lies in the north-east corner of the continent of Africa, and is joined to Asia by the Isthmus of Suez. It is bounded on the north by the Mediterranean Sea, on the east by a barren desert and the Red Sea, on the south by the Sûdân, and on the west by the Libyan Desert. The Peninsula of Sinai and the Oases[1] were not parts of Egypt proper, and were only acquired by conquest. Egypt, in fact, consists of nothing but the Nile and the lands that are watered by its main stream and branches. The **soil of Egypt** is a thick layer of sedimentary deposits which have been laid down upon the surface of a great mass of crystalline rocks. In the deepest part of it this layer has a depth of 110 feet, and authorities on Nile irrigation think that it has been deposited at the rate of 4 inches in a century.[2] Attempts have been made to date objects by the depths at which they have been found in it, but all such calculations are useless, because stone and metal objects work their way through the mud more easily than those made of pottery and lighter materials. Some bronze figures in the British Museum, which when dredged up were assigned to a period several thousand years B.C., are now known to belong to the Saïte or Ptolemaïc Period. In early dynastic times Egypt was that portion of the Nile Valley that lay between the Mediterranean Sea and Sun-t (Syene) and Abu, the Elephant Island; to-day the northern boundary of Egypt is the Island of Faras, a few miles to the north of Wâdî Ḥalfah. The Egyptians gave many names to their land, but the commonest was **Kam-t**, , *i.e.*, the "Black," because of the dark colour

[1] The Principal Oases were Sîwah (Jupiter Ammon), Al-Khârgah (Great Oasis), Dâkhlah (Little Oasis), Farâfrah, Baharîyah, Uaḥ-t, Sekhet-ḥemam.

[2] *I.e.*, the layer has taken 33,000 years to make.

of the soil; the deserts on each side of the Nile were spoken of as **Ṭesher-t**, , *i.e.*, the "Red," because of the lighter colour of the sand and stones. Another old name for Egypt was **Ta-merȧ**, , or , or . In pre-dynastic times the country between Syene and Memphis was called "Land of the South," , *i.e.*, **Upper Egypt**, and that between Memphis and the Mediterranean Sea was called "Land of the North," , *i.e.*, **Lower Egypt**. The **Delta** is, strictly speaking, the triangular island enclosed by the Rosetta and Damietta arms of the Nile and the Mediterranean Sea. These two Egypts are referred to frequently in the inscriptions as **Taui**, , or , or , or , or , or , *i.e.*, the **Two Lands**. The Hebrews called the whole country **Mizraim** (Gen. x, 6), and many think that this dual form refers to the Two Lands, *i.e.*, the South and the North. The Greek name Αἴγυπτος is probably derived from an ancient native name of Memphis, **Ḥekaptaḥ**, , in Coptic ⲉⲕⲉⲡϯⲁ. From this Greek form came the Latin **Aegyptus**, and later our **Egypt**. Naville suggests that the name Egypt is derived from Ageb, , and that the country was the "land of the flood," *i.e.*, the Inundation, which was poured out over the whole land by the Flood-god Ageb, . Maṣr مصر, the Arab name for Cairo, means to many Muslims all Egypt, and it is probable that Ḥekaptaḥ did the same to the old inhabitants of the country.

From the earliest times Egypt was divided into a series of districts, which the Egyptians called *ḥesp* and the Greeks νόμος, ro **Nome**. Each nome had its own god, or totem, its chief city, its chief temple, and its own worship and feasts and sacred objects, animate and inanimate; and the portions of it that were cultivated regularly, or at intervals, and the canals, were all carefully watched over by the central administration in the capital of the nome. The boundaries of these nomes remained practically unchanged for thousands of years. The number of the nomes given in Egyptian lists is forty-two, like that of the Assessors in the Judgment Hall of Osiris—twenty-two in Upper and twenty in Lower Egypt. Classical writers give varying numbers. Diodorus, who says the nome dates from the time of Sesostris, gives their number as thirty-six (I, 54), Pliny, who calls them *praefecturas oppidorum* (V, 9, 9), gives their number as forty-five, and some writers enumerate forty-seven. The Greeks divided Egypt into three parts—Upper, Central and Lower. Central Egypt appears to have been the district between the Thebaïd and the Delta. It was called **Heptanomis,** and its seven nomes were Memphites, Herakleopolites, Crocodilopolites, Aphroditopolites, Oxyrhynchites, Cynopolites and Hermopolites. The Great and the Lesser Oases were considered to be parts of Heptanomis. For the Egyptian lists of nomes see Brugsch, *Dict. Géog.*, p. 1358 ff., and Rochemonteix, *Mémoires Miss. Française*, tom. X, p. 329 ff.; also see Ptolemy, *Geographia*, IV, 5, ed. Mercator, pp. 105–108. Modern Egypt is divided into fourteen Provinces, of which eight are in Upper and six are in Lower Egypt. Each has its own capital, which is generally situated on or quite near to the ancient capital of one of the great nomes of Ancient Egypt. Each Province is divided into districts, some of which represent the smaller nomes of Pharaonic times.

THE NOMES OF EGYPT

UPPER EGYPT

	Nome		Capital	
1.		Ta-sti		Ab (*Elephantine*)
2.		Uthes-Ḥer		Ṭeb (*Apollinopolis Magna*)
3.		Nekhen (?)	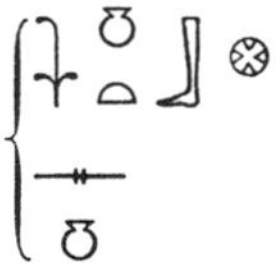	Nekheb (*Eileithyiaspolis*) or Sen (*Latopolis*)
4.		Uas	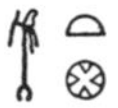	Uas or Åpt (*Thebes*)
5.		Ḥerui		Qebt (*Coptos*)
6.		Tchaus (?) Åati (?)	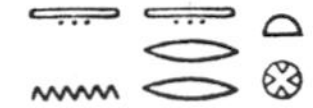	Ta-en-terr (*Tentyris*)
7.		Seshesh (?) Hu (?)	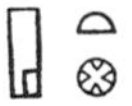	Ḥet (*Diospolis Parva*)

	Nome	Capital
8.	ABETCH (TA-UR ?)	Teni or Åbṭ (*This*) (*Abydos*)
9.	KHEM (?) MEN (?)	Åpu (*Panopolis*)
10.	UATCHIT	Ṭebu (*Aphroditopolis*)
11.	SET	Shâsḥetep (*Hypselis*)
12.	ṬUF (?)	Nutenthbak (*Hierakonpolis*)
13.	ATEF-KHENT	Sauṭ (*Lykopolis*)
14	ATEF-PEḤU	Qes (*Cusae*)
15.	UN	Khmenu (*Hermopolis*)
16.	MAḤETCH	Ḥebnu (. . . .)
17.	ÅNPU (?)	Kasa (*Kynonpolis*)
18.	SEPA	Ḥet-Benu (*Hipponus*)
19.	BUTCHAMUI (?) UABU	Per-matchet (*Oxyrhynchus*)
20.	NĀRT-KHENT	Ḥenensu (*Herakleopolis* ***Magna***)
21.	NĀRT-PEḤU	Smen-Ḥer (*Nilopolis ?*)
22.	MATEN	Tepâḥ (?) (*Aphroditopolis*)

LOWER EGYPT

	Nome		Capital	
1.		ÅNEB-ḤEṬCH		Men-nefer (*Memphis*)
2.		ṬUAU	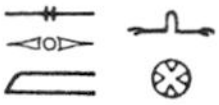	Sekhem (*Letopolis*)
3.		ÅMENT (?)		Åmu Nutent-Ḥap (*Apis*)
4.	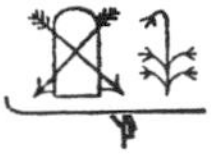	SÅPI-SHEMĀ	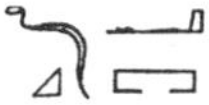	Tcheqā (. . . .)
5.	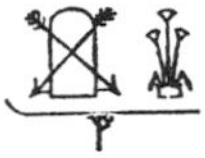	SÅPI-MEḤ		Sait (*Saïs*)
6.		KAKHAS (?)	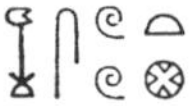	Khasuu (*Xoïs*)
7.		. . . -ÅMENTI		Senti-nefer (*Metelis*)
8.		. . . -ÅBTI		Thekut (*Succoth*) Per-Tem (*Pithom*) (*Sethroe ?*)
9.		ANTCHTI ĀTI (?)		Per-Åsår-neb-Ṭeṭ (*Busiris*)
10.	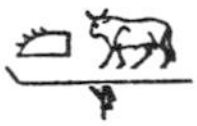	KAM-UR		Ḥet-ta-ḥeråb (*Athribis*)
11.	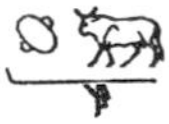	ḤESEB- . . .		Per-maqa Kaḥebes (*Kabasos*)
12.		THEB- . . .		Theb-netert (*Sebennytos*)
13.		ḤEQ-ĀNTCH		Ånu (*Heliopolis*)

	Nome	Capital
14.	Khent-Åb	Tchān (*Tanis*)
15.	Tcheḥuti	Per-Tcheḥuti (*Hermopolis*)
16.	Ḥat-meḥit	Per-Ba-neb-Ṭeṭ (*Mendes*)
17.	Beḥṭ	Pa-Khen-en-Åment (*Diospolis*)
18.	Åmu-khent	Per-Bast (*Bubastis*)
19.	Åmu-peḥu	Per-Uatchit (*Buto*)
20.	Sepṭ . . . (?)	Peges (*Phakussa*)

DISTRICTS OF NUBIA (Kenstt).

1.	Peḥ-Qenus	2.	Mârâu-t (Meroë)
3.	Nâpata (Jabal Barkal)	4.	Petenḥer (Pontyris)
5.	Panebes (Pnups)	6.	Tauatch (Autoba)
7.	Behen (Boôn)	8.	Atefti (Tasitia)
9.	Nehau (Noa)	10.	Meḥi (Meae)
11.	Maāmaā (Ibrîm)	12.	Bak (Kubbân ?)
13.	Ḥe-t-Khent	14.	Palek, Coptic ⲠⲒⲖⲀⲔ, Philae

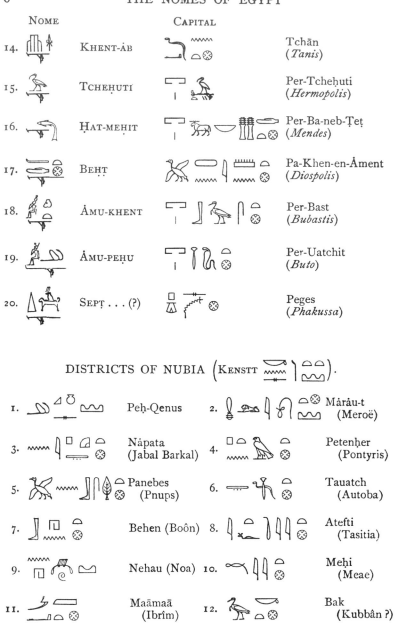

THE NILE

It has been well said that the Nile is Egypt, and Egypt is the Nile. The Nile is the maker of Egypt, for it and its two great tributaries, the Blue Nile and the Atbarâ, have brought down the life-giving mud from Abyssinia and the Eastern Sûdân that is now the soil of Egypt. The Egyptians called the Nile **Ḥep,** 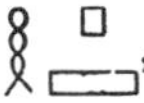, or **Ḥāp,** 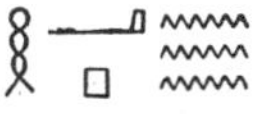 and **Ḥāpi,** , but it has been suggested[1] that the original form of the name is **Ḥepr,** . As to its meaning, some would connect it with the root *ḥāp,* "to hide," and would regard Ḥep or Ḥāpi as the "hidden river," but this is improbable, and the true derivation of the name is unknown. It is doubtful if the early dynastic Egyptians knew the source of the river or the real cause of the annual Inundation. Under the XIIth dynasty the existence of the Atbarâ and the Blue Nile was probably known to them, and it is possible that they may have heard of Lake Ṣânâ in Abyssinia and of one or two of the great Lakes in Central Africa, but the course of the White Nile must have been unknown to them. Some assume that the men of the caravans which brought copper from the copper-producing district of Tanganyika may have passed on to the Nubians information about the great Lakes that filtered down into Egypt, and this is quite possible. The origin of the Greek and Roman name Νεῖλος, Nilus, is, like that of the Egyptian name, unknown. The Arabs reproduce the name under the form An-Nîl النّيل. Some connect "Nile" with the Hebrew נַחַל and others with *Nîl,* the plant from which indigo is derived. The god of the Nile was called **Ḥāpi,** and he was said to be self-begotten and to be the father of all the gods who lived in the Great World-Ocean which surrounded the world; and like other great gods, Rā, Åmen, Kheperà, etc., he was called "One." The Nile, which watered Egypt and formed the chief source of life of the whole country, was at one period believed to come direct from the World-Ocean, and to enter Egypt through a cavity which lay between two rocks on or near the Island of Elephantine. Herodotus calls the mountains Krôphi and Môphi, which names probably represent the Egyptian words "Qer-Ḥāpi" and "Mu-Ḥāpi." Though in the famous Hymn to Ḥāpi in Sallier Papyrus II (Brit. Mus. No. 10182) it is said that figures of the god cannot be sculptured in stone, and that images of him do not exist, we find that drawings of him are given on papyri, and that there are sculptured figures

[1] *Aeg. Zeitschrift,* Bd. 47, p. 163 ff.

of him in existence; compare the quartzite sandstone statue of him, which was made for Prince Shashanq, in the British Museum (South Eg. Gallery, No. 766). He is represented in the form of a man with a woman's breast, and wearing a cluster of water plants on his head. He carries in front of him an offering table loaded with food and drink of all kinds, and the bodies of water-fowl hang by his side. The plant worn by the Nile-god of the North was the lotus , and that by the Nile-god of the South the papyrus . Under the New Empire the Vignettes in the Book of the Dead represent the shrine and throne of Osiris as placed on the waters of the celestial Ocean Nenu, or Nu; and in late times the Nile was said to be Osiris himself, whose seed fecundated the soil of Egypt, which was at the same time identified with Isis.

The true cause of the Inundation was known to Aristotle, who attributed it to the melting of the snow on the mountains in Central Africa and the rains in Abyssinia (see Partsch, *Ueber das Steigen des Nil*, Leipzig, 1900). Eratosthenes considered the great Equatorial Lakes to be the source of the Nile, and Ptolemy the geographer held the same view. The first map in which the general arrangement of the Lakes is shown is that of F. Pigafetta, of Vicenza, a military engineer (born 1533, died 1603), which was published in 1580. The source of the Blue Nile was seen by Pedro Paez in 1615, by Jeronimo Lobo in 1626, and by Bruce in 1772. Salîm, an Egyptian officer, ascended the White Nile as far as Gondokoro about 1840. Lake Victoria was discovered by J. H. Speke in 1858; Sir William Garstin showed that this was the true source of the Nile, and not the Kagera River, as Kandt claimed (see his *Caput Nili*, Berlin, 1904, and Garstin's *Report*, Egypt No. 2, 1904). Lake Albert was discovered by Baker on March 16, 1864, and Lake Albert Edward by Stanley in 1875. The "White Nile" is the part of the Nile between Lake Nô and Kharṭûm; from Lake Nô to Lake Albert the Nile is called "Baḥr al-Jabal," and from Lake Albert to Lake Victoria the "Victoria Nile" or the "Somerset River." The Blue Nile, or Abâî, the Astapos of Strabo, joins the White Nile 1,560 miles from Lake Victoria, and the Atbarâ, the Astaboras of Strabo, joins it at Ad-Damar.

The **Cataracts** are six in number. No. 1 is between Aswân-Philae, No. 2 ends a few miles south of Wâdî Ḥalfah, No. 3 is at Ḥannek, No. 4 at Adramîyah, No. 5 at Wâdî al-Ḥamâr, and No. 6 at Shablûkah. The length of the Nile is about 3,470 miles.[1]

[1] For a good account of the discovery of the Nile see Johnston, H., *The Nile Quest*. On the Nile generally see Sir W. Garstin's great *Report* on the Lake Area, etc., and Lyons, *Physiography of the River Nile*, Cairo, 1906; the map of the Nile Basin published by the Survey Department in Cairo in 1908 is the best in existence.

Model of an Egyptian House. Predynastic Period. B.M. No. 35505.

Green slate object sculptured with a hunting scene. Predynastic Period. B.M. No. 20790.

Earthenware vase in the form of a box decorated with figures of oryxes, etc. Predynastic Period. B.M. No. 32639.

1 

1 Dried body of an Egyptian of the Neolithic Period. B.M. No. 32751.

2 

2 **Earthenware** seated figure of a youth of the Neolithic Period. B.M. No. 50945.

THE ANCIENT EGYPTIANS

THE attempts made hitherto to identify the **race** to which the ancient Egyptian belonged have not been crowned with success, but it must be admitted that the subject is one of very great difficulty. The pre-dynastic mummies, by which alone we can gain any idea of the physical form of the primitive Egyptian, have been examined and dissected and commented upon by the professional anatomist and craniologist, but the different results which the experts obtain from the same specimens compel the archaeologist to regard them as inconclusive. And the same may be said of the statements that they make about dynastic mummies. The dried bodies and bones from the graves at Naḳâdah give us an idea of the physical form and characteristics only of the better-class folk who lived in that district in the late Neolithic Period, for only they were " buried "; but of the great mass of the working and peasant classes, who were not " buried," they tell us nothing. And it is the same in the case of the mummies of the Dynastic Period, which were of kings or priests or high officials; only the better-class folk were " buried " in brick and stone maṣṭabahs, pyramids and rock-hewn tombs, and what the people of the " lower orders " were like in the Delta and Middle and Upper Egypt we do not know. I am assuming that the Delta had been formed, and that men were settled in it and on both banks of the Nile from the First Cataract to the Mediterranean Sea. The primitive Egyptian—I mean the man who laid the foundations of the religious beliefs of the pre-dynastic and dynastic Egyptians, but not necessarily of their kings and rulers—was, I believe, an African. But from the earliest period his lands must have been invaded by peoples from the east and the west, and the north and the south, and his rulers seem, more often than not, to have been foreigners. The inhabitants of the Nile Valley, from Uganda to the Mediterranean Sea, were from time immemorial a very mixed people, even as they are to-day, and for the greater number of the theories about their relationships and their migration, which have been propounded by the scientific experts, I have not succeeded in finding any foundation. Thus Erich Schmidt, as a result of his measurements of Egyptian skulls, identified three main types—the pure Egyptian, the Nubian, and a mixture of both. Among the brachycephalic skulls he distinguished the brachycephalic Egyptian and the brachycephalic Nubian.[1] Ripley says, " From the Semites in the Canary Islands, all across northern Africa,

[1] *Aeg. Zeitschrift*, Bd. XXXVI, p. 114, and see Stahr, *Die Rassenfrage im antiken Aegypten*. Virchow's views are stated in the *Sitzungsberichte* of the Berlin Academy, 1888, p. 767 f.

to central Arabia itself, the cephalic indices of the nomadic Arabs agree closely. They denote a head form closely allied to that of the long-headed Iberian race, typified by the modern Spaniards, South Italians and Greeks. It was the head form of the ancient Phoenicians and Egyptians also, as has recently been proved beyond all question."[1] According to Dr. Elliot Smith the " Proto-Egyptian man was 5 feet 5 inches in height, and his woman nearly 5 feet; he was of slender build, and had dark hair, dark eyes and a bronzed complexion. His skull was long and narrow and his forehead narrow and slightly bulging. His cheeks were narrow and their bony supports flattened, his nose small, and broad and flattened at the bridge, his chin pointed, his jaw weak, and his teeth of moderate or small size."[2] As the writer of these statements is a professional anatomist the archaeologist can only record them without comment, and hope that all such assertions are more correct than many of the statements which anatomists, craniologists and anthropologists make on archaeological subjects. According to Jéquier, who has studied all the available material and is qualified to discuss it, the indigenous Egyptians closely resembled the peoples who settled among them, and they were of comparatively sturdy build, with light complexions, and hair that varied in colour from fair to black; and their skulls were dolichocephalic, like those of the Berbers, and they resembled neither Semites nor Negroes.[3]

The archaeological evidence available suggests that among the earliest invaders of Egypt from the west in the Pre-dynastic Period were the **Libyans,** who, entering Middle Egypt, brought with them a civilization that was somewhat similar to that of the peoples of Europe in the Neolithic Period, and was of a higher class than that of the Egyptians. The natives of the deserts on the east bank of the Nile (**Hamites**) also invaded the cultivated lands of the Egyptians, and their kinsfolk in Arabia and the countries beyond it to the east found it necessary to follow their example from time to time. The **indigenous people** were a non-warlike race, and were content to act as hewers of wood and drawers of water to the invaders, who seized what they wanted and held it by force of arms. Some of the invaders who came into Egypt from the east by way of the Wâdî Ḥammâmât appear to have been skilled in the art of working in metal, and the native armed with flint weapons went down before the metal battle-axe, club and dagger. At some time or other, probably during the Pre-dynastic Period, numbers of people from the east who possessed a civilization similar to that of the

[1] Ripley, *The Races of Europe*, p. 387. His references for this statement are Bertholon, 1892, p. 43; Sergi, *The Mediterranean Race*, 1897a, Chap. I; and Fouquet, 1896 and 1897, on the basis of de Morgan's discoveries.

[2] *Ancient Egyptians*, p. 47 ff.

[3] See the *Bulletin de la Société Neuchâteloise de Géographie*, 1912, p. 127 f.

Sumerians—they may even have been Sumerians—found their way into Egypt. They brought with them superior processes in the arts and crafts, and their religion was of a higher character than that of the Egyptians, and their gods were represented in human forms.[1] It was their influence that caused the Egyptians of a later date to give human bodies to their bird gods, animal gods, and reptile gods. It seems that these invaders first made their way into Upper Egypt, and that having settled themselves there they invaded other parts of the country, both in the south and in the north, and that wherever they went they imposed their sovereignty on the natives. It is probable that the Followers, or Servants, of Horus, whose exploits are related in the great text at Edfû, are none other than these foreigners. Their success was due entirely to the Mesenu, or workers in metal, who accompanied them, and who were armed with great copper harpoons.[2] The copper from which they were made[3] may have been mined in the great copper district near Tanganyika. Another set of invaders entered Egypt at a very early period, probably before the union of the South and the North under Menȧ. These were Semites, and they came into Egypt by the caravan roads through Syria and Palestine, and little by little gained power and influence, especially in the Delta. Many came as traders pure and simple, but there must always have been there a considerable number of Semitic refugees driven thither by famines or by the desire for more favourable conditions of existence. With the Negro the Egyptian is in no way connected. The original physical and mental characteristics of the indigenous Egyptians were modified temporarily as the result of intermarriages with their conquerors, but I am assured by competent authorities that no amount of alien blood has so far succeeded in destroying the fundamental characteristics, both physical and mental, of the "dweller on the Nile mud," *i.e.*, the *fallâḥ*, or tiller of the ground, who is to-day what he has ever been. Left to himself he would never have conquered the Sûdân and Western Asia, and without the initiative and superior brains of the foreigner he would never have built the pyramids and the temples and tombs which have excited the wonder and admiration of the civilized world for thousands of years. But there is in the indigenous Egyptian a persistence which has made him outlast all the great nations who have subjugated him, and Artîn Pâshâ may have been right when he said that the *fallâḥ* would still be digging in the mud of Egypt when the British soldier had ceased to be.

[1] See Wiedemann, *Der Tierkult der alten Aegypter*, p. 27 ff., and *Muséon*, New Series, tom. VI, p. 113 ff.

[2] See Maspero, *Études de Mythologie*, tom. II, p. 313 f.; and Sethe, *Aeg. Zeitschrift*, Bd. LIV, p. 50 f.

[3] See Naville, *Archives Suisses*, tom. I, p. 54 f.

EGYPTIAN CHRONOLOGY

EGYPTIAN chronology is a subject that is full of difficulty, and in spite of all the elaborate essays that have been written about it by Lepsius, Bunsen, Champollion-Figeac, Brugsch and Meyer, no system of chronology that is generally accepted by Egyptologists in England, France and America has yet been formulated. The truth is that the facts necessary for constructing a correct scheme of chronology are wanting, and the Egyptians themselves afford little help in overcoming the difficulty. It has been assumed that there was a Palaeolithic Period in Egypt, but when it began no man can say; two trustworthy authorities think that it ended about B.C. 10,000, but whether it came to an end abruptly as the result of some natural or artificial calamity, or whether it merged gradually into the Neolithic Period, is not known. It is assumed, and probably correctly, that the succeeding waves of civilization of the Neolithic Period lasted a few thousand years, and then, possibly under the influence of foreign invaders and settlers, the last one merged into the civilization known as "dynastic." But no one knows how long these various waves of pre-dynastic civilization lasted, or when the merging took place. The duration of these civilizations need not trouble us, but the date of the merging is very important, if it can be discovered, especially if it helps us to find out when the unification of Egypt under a king took place.

One of the principal objects of every student of Egyptian Chronology is to find out when the first king of the first dynasty began to reign. The native monuments do not help us in any way, and on this point the famous Palermo Stele[1] fails us. When complete this Stele was a rectangular diorite slab, measuring about 7 feet by 2 feet, which was inscribed on both sides with the annals of a large number of pre-dynastic kings and of the kings who reigned from the time of the unification of Egypt until about the middle of the Vth dynasty. The names of the pre-dynastic kings were probably about 120 in number, but only nine (two mutilated) are preserved; the length of the period during which they reigned is unknown; some think that the evidence that can be deduced from the Stele justifies them in stating that the reigns of the kings of the first three dynasties occupied a period of 500 years. This would be very important if the date of the first year of the first king of Egypt

[1] This fragment of a large slab is preserved in the Museum at Palermo; hence its name. It was first published by Pellegrini in the *Archivio Storico Siciliano*, New Series, 20th year, pp. 297–316, with 3 plates, but its real importance was first pointed out by Schäfer in the *Abhandlungen der könig. Preus. Akad.* for 1902, and the system of dating by years named after events, as was the custom at one time in Babylonia, was first recognized by Maspero (*Revue Critique*, 1899 and 1901). See also Naville, *Recueil des Travaux*, tom. XXV, pp. 1–10, and Gauthier, *Le Musée Égyptien*, tom. III, p. 29 ff.

were known, but this the Stele does not tell us. And none of the other native monuments, viz., the King Lists on the Tablet of Ṣakkârah,[1] the Tablets of Abydos,[2] the Tablet of Karnak,[3] and the King List on papyrus at Turin,[4] gives us any help in this respect. Much useful and quite valuable information on Egyptian Chronology generally we owe to the List of Egyptian Dynasties compiled by the priest Manetho, who flourished in the reign of Ptolemy II Philadelphus. He arranged the kings of Egypt in dynasties and gave the names and the number of kings in each dynasty, together with the lengths of their reigns and the sum total of the years of each dynasty. It is the fashion for some to decry the work of Manetho, because his figures have been garbled by generations of copyists, but without it the King Lists of Lepsius and Meyer would have been far less correct and useful than they are. Like all chronographers and historians, both ancient and modern, he could only use such materials as were available; where they were trustworthy his statements are generally correct, where they were not his information is faulty. But Manetho does not help us to fix the date when the first king of the first dynasty began to reign, and the Egyptians themselves did not know it.

The first competent man in modern times to attempt to ascertain this was Lepsius, who set out carefully all the evidence on the subject available to him in his *Chronologie der Aegypter*,[5] Berlin, 1849. Bunsen discussed the matter tentatively in *Aegyptens Stelle*, Hamburg, 1845, but being unable to make use of the hieroglyphic texts did nothing to remove its difficulty. He appears to have relied on the chronological scheme which Champollion-Figeac published in his *Égypte Ancienne*, Paris, 1835, p. 269, and which Lepsius proved to be impossible in his invaluable *Königsbuch*, which appeared at Berlin in 1858, about the time when Bunsen was publishing further volumes of his work at Hamburg. Champollion-Figeac gave as his date for the Ist dynasty B.C. 5867, for the XIIth B.C. 3703, and for the XVIIIth B.C. 1822, but Lepsius assigned to these dynasties the dates of B.C. 3892, B.C. 2380, and B.C. 1591, respectively, and Bunsen's dates were B.C. 3623, B.C. 2755, and B.C. 1625, respectively.

[1] It contains 50 royal names, including that of Rameses II, and 8 are wanting; for an illustration of it see Budge, *Hist. Egypt*, Vol. I, p. 121 ff.

[2] The larger is in the temple of Osiris at Abydos, where it was discovered by Dümichen in 1864; it contains the names of 75 kings arranged in chronological order, the last being the name of Seti I. The Second King List of Abydos, when complete, contained the names of 52 kings; it was found by Bankes at Abydos in 1818 and is now in the British Museum (No. 592). For the remaining names see Budge, *B.M. Guide to Sculpture*, p. 163.

[3] It gives the names of several kings of the XIth and XIIIth–XVIIth dynasties, but is useless for chronological purposes.

[4] See Lepsius, *Auswahl*, pll. 3–6, and Meyer, *Aeg. Chronologie*, Berlin, 1904.

[5] It may be mentioned, in passing, that Egyptian hieroglyphic types were used for the first time in this volume.

Ten years later Mariette, probably influenced by Champollion-Figeac's scheme, assigned the date of B.C. 5004 to the Ist dynasty,[1] and in 1878 Wilkinson proposed B.C. 2320,[2] but the idea uppermost in the mind of the latter was to make Egyptian chronology harmonize with that given by Archbishop Ussher to ancient nations printed in our English Bibles at that period. Brugsch, adopting as a general principle that 100 years should be allowed for every three consecutive reigns, suggested B.C. 4400 as the date for the Ist dynasty, and B.C. 1700 for that of the XVIIIth.[3] Many felt that Brugsch's dates were reasonable and probable, and accepted them provisionally, feeling sure that the last words on Egyptian chronology had not been spoken. The above facts show clearly the difficulty of the subject. The differences in the results obtained by different scholars were due in the first place to the fact that they had no common reliable data on which to base their enquiries, and in the second to the failure of the Egyptians to keep records that were historical or chronological in our sense of the word. A general idea of the probable length of the period of dynastic civilization can be obtained from the monuments, but the data do not exist from which to make a detailed scheme of chronology.

Some of the modern writers on the subject, more notably Meyer, think that a system which is *approximately* correct can be evolved by assuming that the ancient Egyptians were acquainted with and made use of the **Sothic Period.** The oldest year known in Egypt consisted of 12 months, each containing 30 days, and its use for magical purposes survived until the beginning of the New Kingdom. The Egyptians found out at a very early period that the true year contained more than 360 days, and in the Pyramid Text of Pepi II reference is made to the gods who were born (*i.e.*, their birthdays took place) on the five days that the Egyptians added to the year.[4] The year of 360 days was divided into three seasons, each containing four months, which were called Akhet, Pert and Shemu. According to Meyer, Akhet began on July 19th, Pert on November 16th, and Shemu on March 16th and ended on July 13th. Then followed the epagomenal days, or five days added to the year. This may be called the vague or wandering year, for as the year of 365 days was shorter than the true year by nearly a quarter of a day, it would work backward through all the months of the year until the first day of the wandering year would coincide with the first day of the solar year. The Egyptians must have found out this fact at a very early period, and have realized that when a sufficient number of vague

[1] *Notice des Principaux Monuments*, Paris, 1869, p. 15.
[2] *Ancient Egyptians*, ed. Birch, 1878, Vol. I, p. 28 ff.
[3] *Egypt under the Pharaohs*, ed. 1880, pp. 341–346.

[4] , Pepi II, l. 754 (ed. Sethe, Vol. II, p. 472).

years had passed the midwinter festivals would be celebrated in the height of summer. The Annual Inundation of the Nile controlled their agricultural operations, and so for all practical purposes the vague year was sufficient. It has been assumed that at one period unknown the Egyptians decided to make their year begin about the time of the Inundation, and that at another unknown period they declared its first day to be that on which the star Sept,  (Sothis, Sirius or the Dog-star), rose heliacally, *i.e.*, with the sun. The interval between one rising of Sirius and the next would be a solar year and would contain nearly 365¼ days, *i.e.*, would be nearly a quarter of a day longer than the vague year. Supposing that the first day of the vague year and the first day of the solar year fell on the same day, 1,461 vague years or 1,460 solar years must pass before the same thing could happen again. Now Censorinus, a Roman grammarian, wrote a work entitled *De Die Natali* about A.D. 238, and dedicated it to his patron, Quintus Caerellius, as a birthday gift.[1] In this he discusses (xviii, 10) the Egyptian year, which, he says, is reckoned from the first day of the month of Thoth, and he says that the first day of the year in which he was writing was the first day of the month of Thoth, and was the equivalent of the VIIth day of the Kalends of July, or June 25th. He adds that this was also the case 100 years before (A.D. 139), when the equivalent of the first day of Thoth was the XIIth day of the Kalends of August, or July 21st, on which day the Dog-star Sirius is wont to rise. This statement is taken to mean that a Sothic Period ended on July 21st (July 20th according to Meyer), and therefore the one before that ended in B.C. 1321–20, and the one before that in B.C. 2781–80, and the one before that in B.C. 4238–37. And, because there are three[2] instances in the texts in which the date of the rising of Sirius is expressed in terms of the vague year, Meyer and others have assumed that the Egyptians were acquainted with and used the Sothic Period. But there is no evidence that they did. The whole Sothic Period theory rests on the words of Censorinus and on the assumption of Meyer, which is based on them. Nowhere in the hieroglyphic texts is there any mention of such a period. And with the annual Inundation to guide the Egyptians in their

[1] The modern editions of his work by O. Jahn and F. Hultsch are very handy, but Lindenbrog's edition, issued in 1614, with commentary, is still a very valuable book.

[2] The first is found in the Ebers Papyrus, and is to the effect that the New Year Festival was celebrated on the 9th day of the 11th month of the 9th year of Åmen-ḥetep I, which fell on one of the four years B.C. 1550–49 to 1547–46, according to Meyer. From the second (Brugsch, *Thesaurus*, p. 363a) Meyer deduces that Thothmes III reigned from May 3rd, B.C. 1501, to March 17th, 1447, and from the third he concludes that the 7th year of Usertsen III fell in the period B.C. 1882–81, 1879–78, and the first in the period B.C. 1888–87 to 1885–84 (see his *Nachträge zu Aegyptischen Chronologie*, Berlin, 1908, p. 18).

agricultural affairs such a period would be wholly unnecessary. Mr. Cecil Torr has discussed the difficulties that are in the way of accepting it from the point of view of the mathematician,[1] and as far as I know his objections to the acceptance of Meyer's datings have not been satisfactorily disposed of. Some Egyptologists have accepted Meyer's theories, but many reject them. And even among those who accept his calculations there are some who disagree with his theory that the Dynastic Period of Egyptian History lasted for less than three Sothic Periods, and that the Calendar was introduced into Egypt B.C. 4241. Thus Petrie says that this date must be pushed back a whole Sothic Period[2] of 1,460 years, the effect of which would be to make Usertsen III to reign about B.C. 3300. Brugsch, whose knowledge of the texts was unsurpassed, and who had thoroughly sifted all the mathematical and astronomical evidence that had been brought forward by Riehl and Mahler, says that in the second century of our Era the reckoning by vague years with the Sothic years in the background first acquired an importance that they had certainly never possessed at a remote period of antiquity. And quoting with approval Krall's remarks in his *Stud. zur Gesch. d. alt. Aeg.* I, he goes on to say that both the Sothic Period and the Phoenix Period were a discovery of the second century that followed the celebration of the recovery from illness of the Emperor Antoninus Pius on July 20th, A.D. 139, in which year the fixed and the movable first day of Thoth fell on the same day. To the chronographers of that period who occupied themselves with the works of Manetho on the History of Egypt, the Sothic Period appeared to offer the most suitable assistance in fixing the great intervals of time of a defective Era by means of easily calculated figures.[3] The truth is that Brugsch distrusted the results obtained by the astronomers and mathematicians because of the variations in the results obtained by the different authorities from the same data.[4] So many dates, which were declared by their advocates to have been " ascertained astronomically " and to be " absolutely certain," have been proved by facts to be wholly wrong, that we are bound to conclude that mathematicians, like archaeologists, sometimes make mistakes.

Brugsch was well acquainted with all that could be said in favour of the Sothic Period, and, as he was convinced that the use of the

[1] *Memphis and Mycenae*, p. 57.

[2] *Researches in Sinai*, London, 1906, Chap. XII ; *Historical Studies*, p. 10 ff.

[3] Den damaligen Chronographen, welches ich mit dem manethonischen Werke über die Geschichte Aegyptens beschäftigten, erschien die Sothisperiode als das geeignetste Hülfsmittel, die grossen Zeitabschnitte einer mangelden Aera durch leicht berechenbare Zahlen zu fixiren. *Die Aegyptologie*, Leipzig, 1891, p. 357 ; and see Brugsch, *Thesaurus*, p. 203.

[4] See Nicklin's valuable and instructive paper on this point in the *Classical Review*, Vol. XIV, 1900, p. 148.

vague year by the Egyptians was inseparable from the knowledge of a fixed solar year, he made no attempt to make use of it in his scheme of chronology. Had he thought that it was known to the Egyptians he would certainly have discussed it when he dealt in his *Aegyptologie* (p. 353) with the effort made to reform the Calendar by Euergetes I, B.C. 238. In fixing the dates of the dynasties he, like Lepsius, though in a lesser degree, was influenced by Manetho's King List and, judging by archaeological evidence, he made the intervals between the VIth and XIIth and between the XIIth and the XVIIIth dynasties too long. The dates that he and others have assigned to the Ist dynasty depend upon the numbers of the years that they have assigned to these two intervals. But these dates—Lepsius B.C. 3892, Bunsen B.C. 3623, Lieblein B.C. 3893, Brugsch B.C. 4455 or B.C. 4400, Meyer B.C. 3315, Breasted B.C. 3400, Hall B.C. 3500—are only INDEXES to the opinions of those who propose them, and it is quite possible that every one of them is wrong in point of actual fact. The material for fixing with certainty the date of the Ist dynasty does not exist at present. But the dates proposed are valuable, for they show that each scholar, with the exception of Brugsch, believes that the civilization that we know from the monuments existed in Egypt under the first king of the Ist dynasty must be placed *somewhere* in the fourth millennium B.C. Similarly, the dates proposed for the XIIth dynasty—Lepsius B.C. 2380, Bunsen B.C. 2755, Lieblein B.C. 2268, Brugsch B.C. 2466, Hall B.C. 2212 (?),[1] Meyer and Breasted B.C. 2000—show that all these scholars place the civilization that flourished under the XIIth dynasty in the third millennium B.C., and the greater number of them in the second half of it. But the material for fixing the date of the first year of the reign of Åmenemḥat I, the first king of the dynasty, does not exist.

The length of the period of the rule of the Hyksos, which came between the XIIth and XVIIIth dynasties, is still a vexed question, but when we come to the XVIIIth dynasty itself the chronology has surer foundations, and dates can be fixed with a considerable degree of certainty. This fact we owe chiefly to the information derived from the Tall al-'Amârnah Tablets. From one of these we learn that Ashur-uballiṭ, King of Assyria, corresponded with Åmenḥetep III and Åmenḥetep IV, Kings of Egypt. The Assyriologists, who have abundant chronological and historical material on which to base their statements, say that Ashur-uballiṭ reigned from B.C. 1370–1340.[2] According to this Åmenḥetep III and Åmenḥetep IV must have reigned in the first half of the XIVth century B.C. Hall gives the date of the accession of Åmenḥetep IV as *circa* B.C. 1380.[3] The

[1] *Cambridge Ancient History*, Vol. I, p. 173.

[2] See the comparative list of Egyptian, Babylonian, Assyrian, Hittite and Mitannian kings in Hall, *History of the Near East*, p. 262.

[3] *Cambridge Ancient History*, Vol. I, p. 173.

dates of the reigns of Thothmes III and Ȧāḥmes I have been fixed by him at B.C. 1501 and B.C. 1580 respectively; and thus trustworthy chronology begins in Egypt with the XVIIIth dynasty. It is a remarkable fact that long before astronomical dates and Babylonian and Assyrian synchronisms were known Lepsius had assigned B.C. 1591 as the date for the beginning of the XVIIIth dynasty, Bunsen B.C. 1625, and Lieblein B.C. 1490; and for the end of the dynasty Brugsch had set down B.C. 1400. These scholars derived their conclusions from the archaeological evidence of the monuments, which they used to control the statements of Manetho. This is no place to describe their treatment of the intervals between the VIth and XIIth and XIIth and XVIIIth dynasties, which the reader will find fully discussed in Hall's *Ancient History of the Near East*, VIth edition, 1924. Some of his conclusions will not be universally accepted, but being both an archaeologist and a trained historian he is able to classify and arrange the various kinds of evidence that have to be considered, and to estimate the full value of each and its bearing upon the period that he is treating. His decisions on chronology are not those of a mere excavator or a student of Egyptology from books, but those of a man who has lived for many years with the great collections of Egyptian antiquities in the British Museum, and whose duties have made it necessary for him to handle them daily. His principal dates are as follows :—

Beginning of the Old Kingdom	B.C. 3500(?)
Great Pyramid Built (IVth dynasty)	B.C. 3050(?)
End of the Old Kingdom (VIIIth dynasty) ..	B.C. 2400(?)
Middle Kingdom (XIth dynasty)	B.C. 2375(?)
Beginning of XIIth dynasty	B.C. 2212(?)
End of XIIth dynasty	B.C. 2000(?)
End of Middle Kingdom .. .. *circa*	B.C. 1580

XVIIIth dynasty—

Ȧāḥmes I	B.C. 1580
Ȧmenḥetep (Amenōphis) I	B.C. 1559
Thothmes I	B.C. 1539
Thothmes II	B.C. 1514
Ḥatshepsut (Queen)	B.C. 1501–1479
Thothmes III	B.C. 1501–1447
Ȧmenḥetep II	B.C. 1447–1421
Thothmes IV	B.C. 1421
Ȧmenḥetep III	B.C. 1412
Ȧmenḥetep IV (Ȧakhunȧten)	B.C. 1380
Smenkhkarā	B.C. 1362
Tutānkhȧmen	B.C. 1360
Ȧi	B.C. 1350
Ḥeremḥeb	B.C. 1345–1321

XIXth dynasty—

Rameses I ..	.. .. ..	*circa*	B.C. 1321
Seti I ..	.. .. ..	,,	B.C. 1320
Rameses II ..	.. .. ..	,,	B.C. 1300
Menephthah	.. .. ..	,,	B.C. 1234
Åmenmeses	.. .. ..	,,	B.C. 1225
Rameses Sa Ptaḥ ..	.. ..	,,	B.C. 1223
Seti II ..	.. .. ..	,,	B.C. 1215

XXth dynasty—

Setnekht ..	.. .. ..	,,	B.C. 1205
Rameses III	.. .. ..	,,	B.C. 1204
Rameses IV	.. .. ..	,,	B.C. 1172
Rameses V ..	.. .. ..	,,	B.C. 1166
Rameses VI	.. .. ..	,,	B.C. 1162
Rameses VII	.. .. ..	,,	B.C. 1159
Rameses VIII	.. .. ..	,,	B.C. 1157
Rameses IX	.. .. ..	,,	B.C. 1156
Rameses X ..	.. .. ..	,,	B.C. 1136
Rameses XI	.. .. ..	,,	B.C. 1130

XXIst dynasty— *Thebans.*

Ḥerḥer ..	.. .. ..	,,	B.C. 1100
Pinetchem I	.. .. ..	,,	B.C. 1055
Menkheperrā	.. .. ..	,,	B.C. 1043
Pinetchem II	.. .. ..	,,	B.C. 995
Pasebkhānu II	.. .. ..	,,	B.C. 979

Tanites.

Nesibanebṭeṭ	.. .. ..	,,	B.C. 1100
Pasebkhānu I	.. .. ..	,,	B.C. 1095
Åmenemȧpt	.. .. ..	,,	B.C. 1043
Sa-Åmen ..	.. .. ..	,,	B.C. 995
Ḥer-Pasebkhānu	.. .. ..	,,	B.C. 977

XXIInd and XXIIIrd dynasties—

The order of the succession of the kings of these dynasties is doubtful, and the arrangement here given is that suggested by Daressy and Gauthier, which is tentatively accepted by Hall. See the table facing page 516 of the VIth edition of his *Ancient History*, London, 1924.

Shashanq I	.. .. ..	*circa*	B.C 947
Osorkon I ..	.. .. ..	,,	B.C. 925
Teklet I ..	.. .. ..	,,	B.C. 889
Osorkon II ..	.. .. ..	,,	B.C. 880
Shashanq II	.. .. ..	,,	B.C. 850
[Hersaast ..	.. .. ..	,,	B.C. 850]
[Petabast ..	.. .. ..	,,	B.C. 836]

Auput	*circa* B.C.	825
Shashanq III	,, B.C.	818
[Teklet II	,, B.C.	812]
[Osorkon III	,, B.C.	778]
Pimai	,, B.C.	766
Shashanq IV	,, B.C.	763
[Teklet IV	,, B.C.	755]
[Ruṭāmen	,, B.C.	745]
Osorkon IV	,, B.C.	725
XXVth dynasty—		
Piānkhi (the Great)	,, B.C.	721
XXIVth dynasty—		
Tafnekht	,, B.C.	720
Bakenrenef	,, B.C.	718–712
XXVth dynasty—		
Shabaka	,, B.C.	715
Shabataka	,, B.C.	700
Taharq	,, B.C.	689
Tanutȧmen	,, B.C.	663
XXVIth dynasty—		
Psemtek I	,, B.C.	663
Nekau (Necho)	,, B.C.	609
Psemtek II	,, B.C.	593
Uaḥȧbrā	,, B.C.	588
Ȧāḥmes II	,, B.C.	569
Psemtek III	,, B.C.	526
Persian Conquest	,, B.C.	525

OUTLINE OF THE HISTORY OF EGYPT

THREE great Periods may be distinguished in Egyptian History: the Palaeolithic Period, the Neolithic Period and the Dynastic Period. The duration of the first is unknown, but competent authorities who have studied palaeolithic sites and remains in Egypt think that it ended about B.C. 10000. If this be so the Neolithic Period and the Dynastic Period must together have lasted nearly 10,000 years, for the latter ended with the submission of Egypt to Alexander the Great. The unification of Upper and Lower Egypt under Menȧ, according to the lowest computation, took place somewhere in the fourth millennium before Christ. But the evidence of the Stele of Palermo (see p. 12) shows that at least 120 kings reigned over Lower Egypt before this event, and we are assuming very little when we say that there were kings reigning in both

A "Spirit house." B.M. No. 32610.

Painted buff-coloured vase of the Predynastic Period with perforated lugs.
B.M. No. 36328.

Red granite statue of Betchmes, a royal kinsman. IIIrd dynasty. B.M. No. 171.

Painted limestone seated figure of Neferhi. IIIrd or IVth dynasty. B.M. No. 24714.

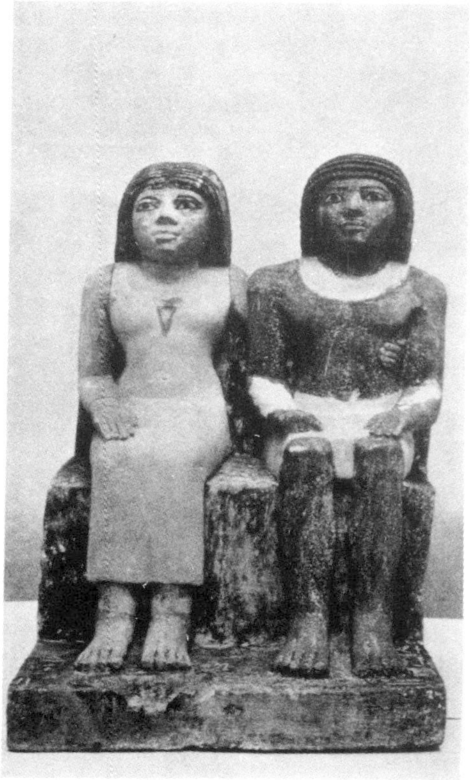

Painted limestone figures of Katep and his wife Ḥetepḥeres. IVth dynasty. B.M. No. 1181.

Upper and Lower Egypt about B.C. 5000. A thousand years later the Egyptians had reached the comparatively high level of civilization that is made known to us by the contents of the graves of the late Neolithic Period. They made reed mats with great skill and were expert potters, although they were unacquainted with the potter's wheel, and their flint tools and weapons prove them to have been masters in the art of flint working. The discovery of copper objects in some graves of the late Neolithic Period shows that they possessed some knowledge of working in metals, and there is abundant proof that they were able to make vessels in stone as well as in earthenware. They were adepts in making flat figures of animals and birds (some with inlaid eyes), which, according to some authorities, they used as slabs on which to rub down a mineral material for use as eye-paint. They buried their dead in shallow oval graves, the bodies having been first sun-dried or even smoked, as is the custom still in many parts of Africa. The body was wrapped in a reed mat or skin of an animal, perhaps a gazelle or a bull, and with it were placed pots containing food of some kind, and flint knives, spear-heads and other weapons to enable the deceased to defend himself against the attacks of foes or savage animals. The neolithic Egyptians worshipped many gods, perhaps totems, and various animals, and each district had its own god and sacred animal. It is clear that they believed in a future existence, perhaps even in immortality as we understand the word. Life in the next world was to them a continuance of life in this; what a man was here that would he be there. Passages in the Pyramid Texts and in the Theban Recension of the Book of the Dead suggest that among some primitive Egyptians the bodies of the dead were sometimes dismembered, sometimes decapitated and sometimes burnt. In pre-dynastic times the dead were buried in the pre-natal position on their left sides, with the hands placed before their faces and their chins almost touching their knees.[1] Women of quality were buried in the same position. No example of a pre-dynastic Egyptian being buried at full length is known to me. Whether the Egyptians of the late Neolithic Period had discovered the art of writing is doubtful, but their decorated pottery made at that time shows that they had attained very considerable skill in drawing figures of animals and birds, symbols of their gods, palisades, etc. The ability to draw figures of natural and artificial objects accurately appears to be one of the fundamental characteristics of the indigenous Egyptian, and it probably accounts for the persistence of the hieroglyphs in religious and ceremonial inscriptions down to the very end of the Dynastic Period. In any case the system of writing that was in use under the kings of the Ist dynasty was based upon the results of the efforts of their neolithic predecessors.

[1] See the authorities mentioned in the paragraphs on the Egyptian Tomb.

The above statements about the Neolithic Egyptians are based upon evidence derived from the graves of the people of the South, or Upper Egypt, who from time immemorial have differed in many ways from the inhabitants of Lower Egypt and the Delta. The southerners were, comparatively speaking, shut in, and their country could only be invaded by foreigners who were obliged to cross barren wastes and deserts before they reached the Nile. The northerners were more accessible, and it was easy for the peoples of the Mediterranean and the tribes of the Eastern Desert and the peoples of Palestine and Syria to reach the Delta. And the conditions of life being easier in the fertile lands of the Delta there must always have been there more settlers from abroad than in Upper Egypt. There must have been frequent fights between the South and the North, and the rivalry between the King of the South, *Nesut* or *Ensut*, and the King of the North, *Bȧt*,[1] did not cease until Men, or Menȧ, the legendary Menes, a King of the South, vanquished the King of the North and united the two kingdoms under his rule. Probably this was not effected as the result of a single battle, but only after a long struggle which lasted for years. The Stele of Palermo has preserved the names of seven pre-dynastic kings, viz., Ska, Khaāu, Tau, Thesh, Neheb, Uatchāntch and Mekha, but the names of Menȧ's predecessors, with the exception of "the king of the South, Ȧp", and the "Horus Ru", are unknown.

Manetho, a priest of Sebennytus, who flourished in the reign of Ptolemy II Philadelphus, wrote a History of Egypt which is now lost, but versions of his list of the kings of Egypt have been preserved in the works of Eusebius and Julius Africanus. In these King-Lists the kings are grouped in **dynasties**, the reason for which is unknown. The 30 dynasties are divided into three groups, viz., dynasties I–XI, dynasties XII–XIX and dynasties XX–XXX, and these correspond roughly with the Old Kingdom, Middle Kingdom and New Kingdom. That the Egyptians did not divide their kings into dynasties is proved by the Tablet of Ṣaḳḳârah and the Tablets of Abydos.

THE OLD KINGDOM

The First Dynasty. From This.

The first king of this dynasty and the unifier of the two Egypts seems to have been **Narmer**, (to call him by his "Horus name"[2]), who adopted, as "King of the South and North,"

[1] is usually said to represent a bee, but some entomologists think that the insect here drawn is a hornet or wasp.

[2] See the remarks that precede the list of cartouches in this book.

Sculptured Green Stone Ceremonial Palette of Narmer

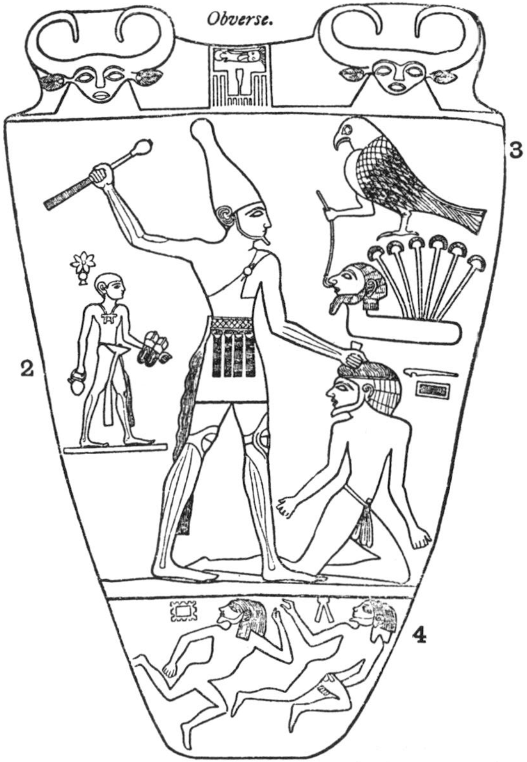

1. Narmer, wearing the White Crown, slaughtering an enemy by smashing his skull with a club having a stone head.
2. The king's sandal bearer.
3. The king, in the form of a hawk, leading captive 6,000 prisoners of the land of Ua.
4. Slaughtered enemies.

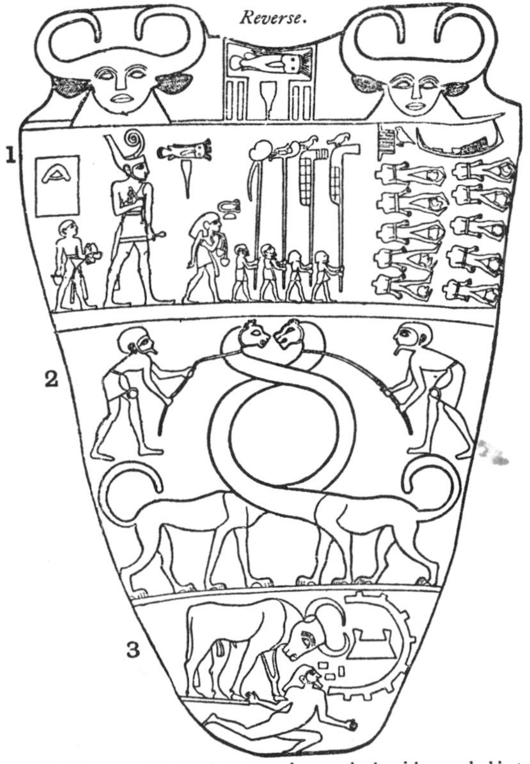

1. Narmer, with attendants carrying standards with sacred objects on them, going to inspect decapitated enemies.
2. Hunters lassoing animals with elongated intertwined necks.
3. The king, in the form of a bull, breaking into a fortress of the enemy.

the title MEN, or MENÀ, , , which Manetho turned into **Menes.** He was a mighty warrior, and the latest historians, Hall[1] and Petrie,[2] give his date at *c.* B.C. 3500 and B.C. 5546 (!) respectively; the latter makes him reign more than forty years. The most striking monuments of his reign are the inscribed mace-head at Oxford, on which he recorded the capture of enormous numbers of men and cattle, and the so-called green stone "Palette" at Cairo, which is sculptured with scenes commemorating his conquests in the Delta. Assuming that Narmer was the first king of this dynasty, his successor was a king whose Horus name was **Āḥa,** the "Fighter," and whose Nebti name was **Men.** Narmer seems to have had no Nebti name, and if this be so it would follow that Āḥa was the first dynastic king to be Lord of Upper and Lower Egypt. The hieroglyphs which read Nebti are , and they represent Nekhebit, the Vulture-goddess of Nekhen, the old capital of Upper Egypt, and Uatchit, the Uraeus-goddess of Per-Uatchit (Buto). Apparently Narmer did not conquer the district the capital of which was Nekhen, and if this be so the absence of a Nebti name in his inscriptions is accounted for. Āḥa was buried in a brick-built tomb at Abydos, and the ebony plaques found in it prove that in his reign the Egyptians were able to arrange hieroglyphs in such a way as to form sentences with connected meanings. The influence under which they acquired this faculty seems to have been of foreign origin; some think it was European and others Mesopotamian or Syrian. A wife of Āḥa was called **Netḥetep** or Neith-ḥetep, who was a votary of the goddess of Saïs, or a native of her city. Āḥa was succeeded by **Khent, or Tcher,** , or , and he was followed by a king whose Horus name was **Tcha** , and whose Nebti name was **Tcheser**; the former is the Àtet , and the latter the Àta of the King-List of Abydos. Mernet, or Mer-Neith, the wife of Tcha, was probably the mother of **Ṭen,** , the next king. The Nesu-bàt name of this king is , which has usually been read **Semti,** but the reading Khaskheti has also been proposed. The scribe who made the draft for the list of Kings in the temple of Seti I at Abydos erred and transcribed the signs by *Ḥesepti* (meaning the "two nomes," and not the "two lands"), which is the original of **Usaphais**, the king's name according to Manetho. Semti was a great king, and the objects that were found in his tomb at Abydos attest his glory and power. His

ĀḤA

[1] *Cambridge Ancient History,* Vol. I, p. 267.
[2] *History,* p. 10.

nobles were rich and luxurious, and the ivory carver, the workers in gold and in stone, and skilled handicraftsmen of all kinds produced examples of their work that command our admiration to-day. His fame lasted through succeeding centuries, and we find him mentioned in the Medical Papyrus at Berlin (Brugsch, *Recueil* II, pl. xcix), the Ebers Papyrus (pl. 103, l. 2); and the composition or redaction of one of the Chapters of the Book of the Dead (LXIV) is assigned to the period of his reign (Brit. Mus. Papyrus of Nu, sheet 13; Lepsius, *Todtenbuch*, pl. 53; Naville, *Todtenbuch*, Vol. II, p. 139; Budge, *Chapters of Coming Forth by Day*, Vol. I (text), p. 145). The inscribed ivory and ebony tablets found in his tomb contain records of important events of his reign and incidentally supply much information about the civilization of his time. Some of these record the name of the "seal-bearer of the King of the North,"

No. 1.

No. 2.

No. 1. Wooden tablet of Semti enumerating the events of one of the years of his reign, viz., celebration of a festival at which the king danced before his god, the building of a sanctuary, etc.

No. 2. Tablet with a representation of Semti slaughtering an enemy.

one Ḥemaka, , who was the Viceroy, or Chancellor or Wazîr of the King in Lower Egypt.

The successor of Semti was **Merpeba,** whose Horus name was Āntchȧb, ; later tradition associated his name prominently with Memphis, but the objects found in his tomb at Abydos afford us little information about him. The next king bore the Horus name of **Smerkha[t]**, , and Manetho gives **Semempses** as his personal name. The scribes of the XIXth dynasty were puzzled by the sign (or signs) for his personal name, which appeared in the list from which they were copying, and they drew the figure of a man holding a stick before him and advancing in a threatening attitude, . This sign is usually read " Ḥui " or " Nekhti," but neither of these words can possibly be the original of the Semempses of Manetho. It is now assumed that the sign in the list from which the scribes were copying was , which is read **Shemsu,** , and means " Follower " (of some god) ; this word is perhaps the original of the Semempses of Manetho. The objects found in his tomb at Abydos tell us nothing about the events of his reign, and but for the three figures of this king which are sculptured on the rock-tablet at Wâdî Maghârah in the Peninsula of Sinai nothing would be known of the invasion of this country by the Egyptians. The king no doubt wanted the control of the mines whence came copper and the beautiful green stone 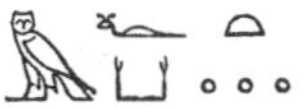 *mefkat* (malachite), which the Egyptians of all periods prized so highly. The last king of the dynasty was **Qā,** 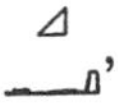, whose Nebti name was **Sen,** . The scribes of the XIXth dynasty could not read correctly the signs , and thus we find on the Abydos List , Qebḥ, and on the Tablet of Ṣaḳḳârah , Qebḥu. The Greek Lists give for this king's name Bieneches, Bienthes and Vibestes.

The Second Dynasty. From This.

The kings of this dynasty were nine in number, and the statue No. 1 at Cairo (published by Grébaut in *Le Musée Égyptien*, pl. xiii) shows that the first three were **Ḥetepi-sekhemui,** 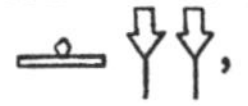, who some think was the Betchau,[1] , of the Abydos List and the Boethos of Manetho, **Nebrā Kakau** (Kaiechos), and **Enneter** with the Nesu-bȧt name of Ba-en-neter, the Binothris of Manetho. Kakau is said to have established (re-established ?) the worship of the Apis Bull at Memphis, the Mnevis Bull at Heliopolis, and the Ram of Mendes, animals that had probably been worshipped in these towns from time immemorial. The introduction of the name of Rā into his name proves that the influence of the priests of this foreign Sun-god at Heliopolis was already very considerable. In the time of Enneter " it was decided that women might

[1] Hall thinks that Betchau is a misreading by the ancient scribes of the Horus name of Narmer, *Cambridge Ancient History*, Vol. I, p. 267.

hold the imperial government,"[1] which suggests that the old African matriarchal system, which had probably been in abeyance, was re-established. Of **Uatchnes,** the fourth king, nothing is known, except that he appears to represent the Tlas of Manetho.[2] The next king, according to the Abydos List, was **Senṭȧ,** , the Sethenes of Manetho, but the monuments mention a king of this period whose Horus name was **Sekhem-ȧb,** which is written 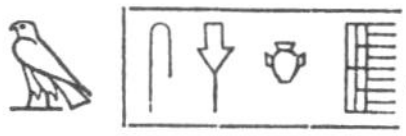. But according to some[3] this king had a second Horus name, **Perenmaāt** , and he is remarkable as possessing a name as the representative of Set, the god of evil, viz., **Perȧbsen** 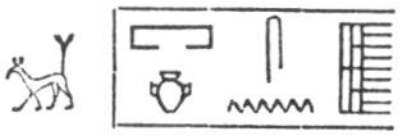. Some regard Sekhem-ȧb and Uatchnes as one and the same king; of King Senṭȧ nothing is known. The next king, **Karā,** the Chaeres of Manetho, of whom nothing is known, was succeeded by **Neferkarā,** in whose time "the Nile flowed with honey during eleven days."[4] According to the King-Lists the last two kings of this dynasty were **Nefer-ka-Seker** 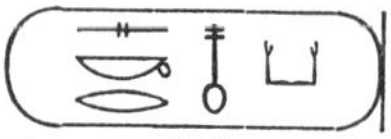, the Sesochris of Manetho, "whose height was five cubits and his breadth three,"[5] and **Ḥutchefa**; some writers identify the former with Khā-Sekhem and the latter with Khā-sekhemui, but these are probably one and the same king, the founder of the IIIrd dynasty. It is important to note the early appearance of the name of the god Seker in the royal name Nefer-ka-Seker. Seker was the god of Death of the inhabitants of Memphis, and his name survives in a disguised form in "Ṣaḳḳârah," by which name the modern Egyptians call the district that represents the great necropolis of Memphis.

The Third Dynasty. From Memphis.

The first king of this dynasty was **Khā-sekhem,** 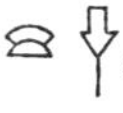, who later called himself **Khā-sekhemui,** ; the first form of his name is that which he adopted as the representative of Horus, and the second shows that he considered himself to be the successor

[1] Cory, *Ancient Fragments,* ed. Hodges, p. 113.
[2] For Hall's theory about this name see *Cambridge Ancient History,* p. 275.
[3] Petrie, *History* (revised edition, 1923), p. 33.
[4] Cory, *Ancient Fragments,* p. 113.
[5] *Ibid.,* p. 113.

of both Horus and Set. His personal name was **Besh.**[1] Some think that Khā-sekhem and Khā-sekhemui were two distinct kings, and that the former was Nefer-ka-Seker and the latter Ḥutchefa of the King-Lists. Others think that Khā-sekhem is the Tchatchai or Bebi of the King-Lists, and the Necherophes of the Greek Lists. According to Manetho, "in his time the Libyans revolted from the Egyptians; but on account of an unexpected increase of the moon, they surrendered themselves for fear."[2] Since the inscription on a statue of the king states that as a result of his fighting in the North, *i.e.*, Lower Egypt, he slew 47,209 of the enemy, it is clear that Khā-sekhem and Necherophes are one and the same king. His queen was called Enmaāthāp, a name that shows she was associated with the cult of Apis at Memphis, and she was the mother of Tcheser. A large number of objects bearing the names of Khā-sekhem were found by Mr. Quibell at Hierakonpolis, but the king himself was buried at Abydos. According to Petrie (p. 37) the tomb building measured 223 by 54 feet, and the chamber that was intended to hold the body was built of stone and measured 17 by 10 by 6 feet. The chambers close by contained vases in stone and copper, flint and copper weapons, jars of various shapes and sizes, grain, etc.

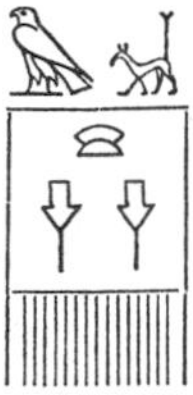

KHĀ SEKHEMUI

Khā-sekhemui was succeeded by his son **Tcheser,** , or **Tchesersa,** , whose Horus name was Khatneter, 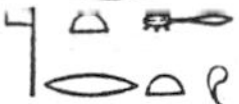. He built the so-called **Step Pyramid** at Ṣaḳḳârah.[3] This remarkable building, which may have covered the king's tomb, is nearly 200 feet high, and was probably surmounted by a shrine containing the figure of a god, perhaps in animal form. This building may be compared with the "stepped towers" and stupas and topes which have been built in India and the neighbouring countries from time immemorial. Manetho says[4] that "Tosorthros," *i.e.*, Tcheser, was called Asclepius (*i.e.*, Aesculapius) by the Egyptians for his medical knowledge, and that he built a house of hewn stones and greatly patronized writing. There is no evidence in the texts that Tcheser was called either Aesculapius or Imḥetep, the famous Egyptian demi-god with whom the Greek god of medicine was, at a later period, identified. But there is proof that Tcheser's architect was called Imḥetep and that he was famed for his wisdom[5] and great knowledge of medicine.[6] Under the New Kingdom he

[1] It is written thus 

[2] Cory, *op. cit.*, p. 113.

[3] Specimens of the green-glazed faïence tiles which lined two of the chambers under the building may be seen in the British Museum, No. 2437 ff.

[4] Cory, *op. cit.*, p. 113.

[5] Thus in the XIth dynasty, Ȧntef couples his name with that of Ḥertataf.

[6] See Budge, *Gods of the Egyptians*, Vol. I, p. 522 ff., and Sethe, *Imhotep*, Leipzig, 1902.

was worshipped as a god, and many bronze figures of him are to be seen in our great museums.[1] In Memphis, which was the chief seat of his cult, he was declared to be the son of Ptaḥ and the goddess Sekhmit. An inscription cut on a granite boulder on the Island of Saḥil in the First Cataract states that a terrible famine occurred in Egypt in the reign of Tcheser because the Nile ceased to rise for seven years. The statement may be a fact, but the inscription was composed during the Ptolemaïc Period, probably by the priests of the local god of the First Cataract, with the view of enhancing their own importance.[2] The king's maṣṭabah tomb was discovered at Bêt Khallâf by Garstang in 1891 ; it is built of brick and is about 300 feet long and 150 feet wide. Little is known of the reign of Tcheser, but it seems that he was very active as a builder, and that he was the first king of Egypt to erect the "stepped tower," which later took the form of a true pyramid.[3] The reliefs at Wâdî Maghârah show that he maintained the control of the Egyptians over the copper mines in Sinai. From the Westcar Papyrus (ed. Erman, Berlin, 1890) we learn that Tcheser was interested in magic, and that his chief Kher-ḥeb was a man of remarkable learning and possessed great skill in the working of magic. The same document mentions King Nebka, whose place in the IIIrd dynasty cannot be fixed with certainty.

Tcheser's successor was probably the king whose Horus name was **Sanekht,** , and whose tomb was discovered by Garstang at Bêt Khallâf. The Egyptian and Greek King-Lists give the names of several kings, Tetȧ (Åtet), Setches, Tcheser-teta and Åḥtes, but nothing is known of them. The last king but one of this dynasty was **Ḥuni,** who, according to the Prisse Papyrus (pl. i, l. 7), was the predecessor of Seneferu, and is probably to be identified with the Neferkarā of the Abydos List and the Kerpheres of Manetho. The last king of this dynasty was **Seneferu,** and under his rule the power of Egypt waxed great, and the Peninsula of Sinai and a portion of the Egyptian Sûdân were added to her territories. The reliefs on the rocks at Wâdî Maghârah proclaim his conquest of the country, and his invasion of the Sûdân must have been on a very comprehensive scale, for the Stele of Palermo states that he brought back from that country 7,000 living prisoners and 200,000 cattle, large and small. He built a fleet of ships which were not less than 150 feet in length,[4] and lighters or cargo boats, each of which was

[1] *E.g.*, Brit. Mus. 27357 and 579.

[2] The Egyptian text with an English translation will be found in Budge, *Legends of the Gods*, London, 1912, p. 120.

[3] In 1924 Mr. C. J. Firth, of the Cairo Museum, excavated some remarkable stone buildings close by the Step Pyramid ; in some of the chambers were fluted stone pillars.

[4] Reckoning the cubit at 18 inches. But if the large cubit of 20 inches is intended the ships were 166⅔ feet in length.

manned with a crew of 16 men. The ships sailed to the Syrian coast, and one year 40 of them, loaded with cedar wood from Lebanon, arrived in Egypt ; some of this wood was used in making the doors of the king's palace. This palace was divided into two parts, in accordance with the fact that Seneferu was lord of the Two Egypts, the South and the North, and each part had its gate with an appropriate title. The king also built 35 houses, but no details of their construction or use are given ; the mines of Sinai supplied the copper, Mount Lebanon the cedar wood, the quarries of Ṭurah the stone, and the Sûdân the labourers. Seneferu built the monument that is commonly called by Europeans the **pyramid of Mêdûm** and by the natives Al-Haram al-Kaddâb, *i.e.*, the False (or Lying) Pyramid. Its general appearance recalls that of a Babylonian ziggurat. It is in three stages and is about 115 feet high. It was opened by Maspero in 1881 and was subsequently excavated by Petrie, who entered the sepulchral chamber. One of the stone pyramids at Dahshûr is also supposed to have been built by Seneferu. He was one of the first to use a " Horus of gold " name, . The chief wife of Seneferu was called Merit-tefs, . After her husband's death she passed under the honourable protection of the two great kings Khufu (Cheôps) and Khāfrā (Chephren). In the reign of Seneferu died Methen, a scribe and high administrative official in Lower Egypt ; he was buried in a maṣṭabah tomb near the " stepped tower " of Tcheser. With the death of Seneferu the Archaic Period of Egyptian History came to an end and the era of mighty buildings in stone begins.

The Fourth Dynasty. From Memphis.

According to Manetho the first king of the IVth dynasty was **Sōris,** in Egyptian **Shaȧru** , but nothing is known about him. His successor was **Khufu**, or Khnemu Khufu, the Suphis of Manetho and the Cheôps of Herodotus, who will be for ever famous as the builder of the largest of the three great **Pyramids**[1] **of Gîzah** (for details see the section on Egyptian Tombs). The pyramid was probably connected by means of a causeway with a funerary temple in which the liturgies for the dead king were recited, but it is doubtful if this temple is

[1] The word pyramid is perhaps derived, through the Greek, from the Egyptian PEREMUS, , which is said by some to mean the *slope* of a pyramidal building, and by others the vertical height. See *Aeg. Zeit.*, 1874, p. 148.

represented by the so-called **Temple of the Sphinx**,[1] as some have supposed. It seems that all the resources of the king and all the energies of his people were devoted to the building of this pyramid, which was to contain the king's tomb, for there is no evidence to show that Khufu made any attempt to "enlarge the borders" of Egypt by means of wars of conquest. A figure of King Khufu in ivory is preserved in the British Museum. **Ṭeṭefrā**, the successor of Khufu, reigned but a few years, and he was followed by **Khāfrā**, or Chephren, the Suphis of Manetho. He built a great pyramid side by side with that of Khufu, but it was a little smaller, and the lower parts of its sides were cased in granite. The funerary temple, like that of Khufu, was on the east side, and a slightly raised embankment led from it to the granite and limestone building which is commonly called the "temple of the Sphinx." When Mariette excavated this temple (or perhaps gate) in 1853 he found at the bottom of a pit in one of the chambers seven statues of Khāfrā, and we may therefore assume that he built it. Near this temple stands that mysterious monument the **Sphinx**, in Egyptian Ḥu , which was at once the symbol of the god Ḥer-em-ȧakhut, , *i.e.*, "Horus on the horizon" (the Harmakhis of the Greeks), and of the king, the earthly representative of this god.[2] An inscription found by Mariette[3] in the temple of Isis near the pyramid of Khufu states that Khufu built (rebuilt ?) this temple of Isis, and some have supposed that it was he who had the spur of rock carved into the form of a man-headed lion and parts of it filled up with masonry to make the contour of the body more perfect. Others take the view that the Sphinx is a pre-dynastic monument, but this theory has no foundation. Between the paws of the Sphinx is a long inscription of Thothmes IV, which seems to associate the monument with Khāfrā, but the cartouche—if indeed there be one—is broken, and the inscription itself is a "pious fraud" that was composed at a late period by the priests of the temple there who wished to enhance the importance of the object of their cult. The name of the king who made the Sphinx is unknown, and modern Egyptologists know as little about its history as did the Egyptians under the New Kingdom. It is possible that if the whole monument were entirely cleared of sand some information about its age might be obtained. The reign of Khāfrā is remarkable for a wonderful development in the skill of architects and workers in stone, and

[1] This building lies a little to the S.E. of the Sphinx, and is about 150 feet square; the hall measures 60 feet by 30 feet, and contains 10 pillars, and the narrow part of the temple measures 80 feet by 25 feet, and contains 6 pillars.

[2] The Sphinx is hewn out of the living rock, and is about 150 feet long; the head is 30 feet long, the face 14 feet wide; the paws are 50 feet long, and the total height of the monument is 70 feet.

[3] For the text see *Monuments Divers*, pl. 53.

the diorite statue of the king now in the Cairo Museum is probably the finest work of any Egyptian sculptor.

Khāfrā was succeeded by **Menkaurā,** the Mencherês of Manetho, who built a great pyramid, which was cased in granite, side by side with those of Khufu and Khāfrā. But the resources of the royal house must have become reduced, for Menkaurā's pyramid is less than half as high as those of his two great predecessors.[1] No wars of conquest were undertaken by him, and the building of his pyramid seems to have exhausted his energies. Some versions of the Rubrics of Chapters XXXB and LXIV state that these important sections of the Book of the Dead were "found" by Ḥerṭaṭaf at Khemenu (Hermopolis), the city of Thoth, whilst on a tour of inspection of the temples of Egypt. Variant versions ascribe the "finding" of these Chapters to the reign of Semti, a king of the Ist dynasty. Menkaurā was succeeded by **Shepseskaf**, of whom practically nothing is known, and the two or three other kings of the dynasty were unimportant. Manetho mentions Ratoeses, Bicherês, Sebercherês and Thamphthis as the last kings of the dynasty, but the Tablet of Ṣaḳḳârah only gives us Sebekkarā, who may be Sebercherês. Of portrait figures in wood made under the IVth dynasty the most striking is undoubtedly the so-called **Shêkh al-Balad.**

The Fifth Dynasty.

Under the IVth dynasty the priests of Rā of Heliopolis, a form of the Sun-god of foreign (probably Syrian) origin, consolidated their power considerably, and their influence was strong enough to make all the kings of that dynasty after Khufu insert the name of Rā in their Nesu-bȧt names. The kings of the Vth dynasty did not come from Elephantine, as Manetho says, but from Heliopolis, and the first of them, **Userkaf,** the Usercheris of Manetho, was high priest of Rā. He and **Saḥurā** and **Kakaȧ** were the sons of Userrā, a priest of Rā, by his wife Ruṭ-ṭeṭeṭ, and all three reigned over Egypt. It was a dogma of the priesthood of Rā at that time that Userkaf and his brothers were begotten by Rā himself, who visited Userrā's wife and companied with her, and that the King of Egypt was in very truth the "son of Rā." As such he must add a **fifth name** to his names as (1) Horus, (2) the Horus of gold, (3) the lord of Nekhen and Per-Uatchit, and (4) as the King of the South and the North. From this time onward every king of Egypt, whether of Egyptian origin or not, called himself the "son of Rā." In later days, when Ȧmen, or Ȧmen-Rā, became the King of the Gods, it was asserted by his priesthood that the god assumed the human form of a man and begot the king of Egypt. Alexander

[1] *I.e.*, 215 feet as against 451 and 450 feet.

the Great owed his success in Egypt to the fact that the god of the Oasis of Sîwah acknowledged him to be his son.

Userkaf seems to have opened up communication with the Northern Sûdân or Nubia, for his name has been found on several rocks in the First Cataract. His successor, **Saḥurā,** who was probably unable to control the caravan roads to the South, sent an expedition to Punt by sea, in order to obtain *ȧnti* and other vegetable ingredients for balsams, unguents and perfumes, which were employed in funerary and other ceremonies. The exact position of Punt is unknown, but it lay probably a little to the south of Somaliland. The expedition was very successful, for, according to the Palermo Stele, the Egyptians brought back in their ships 80,000 bundles of *ȧnti* (myrrh), 6,000 bars (?) of white-coloured gold, and 2,600 pieces of precious wood (ebony ?). The rocks of Sinai show that he made an expedition to the region of the copper mines, and he is represented as smashing the skull of a typical native in the usual fashion. The Palermo Stele shows that as a result of this expedition his officers brought back 6,000 [pieces of turquoise stone]. Saḥurā built a pyramid at Abuṣîr, which was connected with a tower gate by a causeway about 650 feet long; from this a second causeway led to his funerary temple.

The reigns of Nefer-ȧrikarā, Shepseskarā, Neferfrā and Khāneferrā, the successors of Saḥurā, were unimportant, and the next king, **Enuserrā,** or Userenrā, whose son-of-Rā name was **Ȧn,** is known chiefly by the pyramid and funerary temple which he built at Abuṣîr, near the pyramid of Neferȧrikarā Kakaȧ.[1]

Passing over **Menkauḥeru** (the Mencherês of Manetho), whose reign was unimportant, we come to **Ṭeṭkarā Ȧssȧ** (the Tarcherês of Manetho), who succeeded in opening up communication with the south viâ Syene and the First Cataract. According to a letter[2] of Pepi II, a king of the VIth dynasty, which he sent to Ḥerkhuf, a great shêkh of the caravans that traded between Elephantine and the remote countries of the Sûdân, King Ȧssȧ sent an expedition to the Sûdân under the leadership of a high official called Ba-ur-Ṭeṭ, who brought back a dwarf[3] from Punt and was handsomely rewarded. The working of the copper mines in Sinai went on vigorously, and as the name of Ȧssȧ appears on the rocks in the Wâdî Ḥammâmât, it would seem that the military and mercantile traffic between the Nile and the Red Sea passed through this Valley, which offered a short route to Sinai, Punt and other countries to the south of Egypt. The last king of the Vth dynasty was **Unȧs,** who was buried in the

[1] The funerary temples, with their short pyramids, or "sun stones," set on mounds like truncated pyramids were excavated and described by Borchardt in 1907–13.

[2] See *Aeg. Zeit.*, 1893, pp. 65–73, and Sethe, *Urkunden*, Bd. I, pp. 120–131.

[3] *Ṭeng*, .

Façade and "false door" from the tomb of Ptaḥ-shepses, high priest of Memphis, who flourished in the reigns of Menkaurā and his successors. IVth dynasty. B.M. No. 682.

Bronze table of offerings, with its vessels complete, which was made for the Kher-ḥeb of Abydos, called Ȧṭenȧ. VIth dynasty. B.M. No. 5315.

Model of a granary of the Old Kingdom; by the side of the stairway leading to the roof is a model of the guardian with his grain measure beside him. VIth dynasty. B.M. No. 21804.

small pyramid, about 60 feet high, which he built at Ṣaḳḳârah. Ptaḥ-ḥetep, the great Wazîr and author of the famous Book of Moral Precepts which bears his name, flourished in the reign of Ȧssȧ. The walls of the two largest chambers and of two of the corridors are covered with hieroglyphic inscriptions deeply cut in the stone and inlaid with green paste. These inscriptions are of the greatest importance, for they throw much light on the manners and customs and religion of the primitive inhabitants of the country. They contain incantations and other magical texts which were to be recited for the benefit of the dead king in the Other World. Some of these were composed in the Pre-dynastic Period, and the scribes of the period found it difficult to understand them. The remainder seem to have been the work of the priests of Rā and to have been introduced into Egypt when they succeeded in establishing the cult of this foreign god in the country. The tomb of Unȧs is the earliest tomb that contains these texts, and it is somewhat surprising that they were not cut on the walls of the chambers and corridors of the pyramids of Khufu, Khāfrā and Menkaurā.

The Sixth Dynasty. From Memphis.

The reigns of the first two kings[1] of this dynasty, **Tetȧ** and **Userkarā Ȧti,** were unimportant, and details of them are wanting. Tetȧ built a pyramid near that of Unȧs, and it contains hieroglyphic texts of the class described above. The greatest king of the dynasty was **Meri-Rā Pepi I,** the Phios of Manetho, who strengthened the power of Egypt in the Sinaitic Peninsula and worked the quarries of Ḥammâmât, Ḥetnub and Elephantine. He succeeded in coming to an arrangement with the local chiefs of Elephantine, who helped him not only to obtain large quantities of granite from the quarries at Aswân, but assisted his expeditions to the South when they came to the southern frontier of Egypt. In all his affairs—domestic, military and commercial—Pepi I was assisted materially by the great soldier and statesman called **Unȧ.** This great man raised an army of Sûdânî men and with them fought and conquered on several occasions the confederation of nomad tribes in the Eastern Desert and in the region of the Cataracts, and so rendered his caravans safe from attack by them. Unȧ also defeated the desert tribes who lived to the north-east of the Delta and southern Palestine. The exploits and triumphs of Unȧ, which, fortunately, he has recorded in the biography that was found[2] in his tomb at Abydos by Mariette, are, substantially, the history of his master's reign. The arts and crafts flourished under Pepi's rule, and the building of large tombs by priests, officials and nobles in all parts of Egypt

[1] Manetho begins this dynasty with Othoēs, and says that he was killed by his guards.

[2] The stele on which it was inscribed is now in the Cairo Museum.

gave occupation to workers in stone and copper, etc., of all kinds. The skill of the worker in copper[1] is well illustrated by the figures of the king and his son that Quibell found in pieces at Hierakonpolis and are now in the Cairo Museum. The figure of the king is over 6 feet in height, and that of his son a little more than 3 feet, and the eyes in both heads are inlaid with obsidian.

The pyramid of Pepi I is at Ṣaḳḳârah, and the walls of its chambers are covered with hieroglyphic texts of a magical and religious character.

Pepi I was succeeded by his eldest son **Merenrā I Meḥtiemsaf** (the Menthesuphis of Manetho), whose mother was one of two sisters, each of whom was called Ānkhnes-Merirā, daughters of the governor of the nome of This. He came to the throne when quite young and only reigned 5 years (7 according to Manetho). His chief interest lay in developing relations with the Nubian and Sûdânî kings, about whose countries he must have heard much from Unȧ. On his accession he appointed this distinguished man to be governor of the South, and the relations between the Egyptian Court and the nobles of Elephantine became so cordial that Merenrā visited the Gate of the South in the last, *i.e.*, the fifth year of his reign, and, presumably, inspected the works in the granite quarries, and received the homage of the chiefs of Matchai, Ȧrthet and Uauat. Unȧ, having been born in the reign of Tetȧ, was superseded, probably on account of his age, by the Egyptian Ḥerkhuf, who, with the help of the shêkhs of the caravans at Elephantine, made three journeys to the countries that lay in the Sûdân far to the south. On his last journey the gifts that he brought back for the king were so numerous that 300 asses were needed to transport them to Elephantine. Merenrā died in the fifth year of his reign and was buried in the pyramid at Ṣaḳḳârah, which the natives call "Haram as-Sayyâdîn" (the Pyramid of the Hunters). The tomb was plundered in the Middle Ages, and the head of the mummy was broken off the body and the lower jaw smashed. The king's remains are in the Cairo Museum (No. 3017), in the case that contains some of the bones of Unȧs.

Merenrā I was succeeded by his half-brother **Neferkarā Pepi II** (Phiôps) who, according to Manetho, began to reign at the age of six and died aged 100 years. Ḥerkhuf made another journey to the Southern Sûdân, probably in the first year of the reign of Pepi II, and returned laden with the products of the South and with a pygmy from the "land of the spirits," who knew how to perform the dances of the gods of his country. When this was reported to the king he wrote a letter dated the 15th day of the third month of the first season of the second year of his reign and ordered him to bring the pygmy to his Court without delay, and he promised to give him a greater reward, if he did so, than that with which King

[1] The analysis given in the official *Guide* (the edition of 1915, p. 85) is: copper 58·50 per cent., tin 6·557 per cent., carbonate of copper 34 per cent.

Ȧssȧ had rewarded his chancellor, Ba-ur-ṭeṭ, who also had brought a pygmy from the South to Memphis. The king said that he desired "to see the pygmy more than all the products of Sinai and Punt." We may assume that Ḥerkhuf obeyed his lord and received his reward. The roads to the South being thus opened, the Egyptians proceeded first to extend their influence and later to manifest their power in the Northern Sûdân. And there is no doubt that the expeditions that they sent into the Northern Sûdân under the VIth dynasty prepared the way for the conquest and later occupation of that country under the XIIth dynasty. Details of the reign of Pepi II are wanting, but it seems that the king and his officials devoted themselves chiefly to the development of foreign trade and of the industries that were associated with the cult of the dead. It also appears that much of the power possessed by the Pharaohs of the Vth dynasty slipped from the hands of Pepi II, for when he died the kingdom broke up and every great noble throughout the country became a law to himself. Pepi II was buried in his pyramid at Ṣaḳḳârah, which much resembles that of his half-brother Merenrā I. It was opened at the expense of Mr. John Cook in 1881 by Maspero, who was buried by a fall of masonry in one of the chambers, and was only dug out with the greatest difficulty by E. Brugsch Bey (later Pâshâ) and the workmen.

Of **Merenrā II Meḥtiemsaf,** the Menthesuphis of Manetho, who says that he reigned one year, and **Netaqerti,** the last two kings of the dynasty, nothing is known. The latter is called Nitôcris by Manetho, who speaks of him as "the most handsome woman of her time, of a fair complexion." He goes on to say that she built the third pyramid; but Netaqerti was a king and not a queen. His prenomen was Menkarā, and this Manetho confused with Menkaurā, the name of the actual builder of the third pyramid.

The reign of Pepi II was followed by a period of anarchy and destruction, and it is possible that the Libyans and Syrians and nomads from the East invaded the country. Although the Turin Papyrus and the native King-Lists supply the names of over twenty "kings" who were supposed to have ruled over Egypt and to have formed the VIIth and VIIIth dynasties of Manetho, none of them was a Pharaoh in the old sense of the word. According to Manetho the **Seventh Dynasty,** from Memphis, consisted of 70 kings who reigned 70 days, and the **Eighth Dynasty,** also from Memphis, of 27 kings,[1] the total of whose reigns was 146 years. Such power as these Memphite kinglets (whether native or foreign) possessed was snatched from their hands by the feudal lords of Ḥensu, or Ḥennsu,  (Palermo Stele ), the חָנֵס of

[1] Their names will be found in the list of royal names at the end of this section.

Isaiah and the Herakleopolis of the Greeks.[1] Of these lords Manetho makes two dynasties, the **Ninth** and the **Tenth.** To each he attributes 19 kings, and says that the total of the lengths of their reigns was 594 years. The first king of the IXth dynasty was one **Khati I,** whom Manetho calls Achthoês and describes as worse than any of his predecessors. " He did much harm to all the inhabitants of Egypt, was seized with madness, and killed by a crocodile " (Cory, *op. cit.*, p. 116). Some think that this Khati was the king whose prenomen, Nebkaurā, is mentioned in the story of the "Eloquent Peasant." Other kings of this dynasty known from the monuments are **Khati II,** with the prenomen of Åbmerirā, the author of the famous " Teaching " which is extant in papyri in St. Petersburg, and **Khati III** and **Khati IV,** with the prenomens Uaḥkarā and Kamerirā. The kings of Herakleopolis were acceptable neither to the Egyptians of the Delta nor to those of Upper Egypt proper. They received much support from the princes of Siût (Asyût or Cynopolis), and three of these princes, Khati I, Tefabȧ and Khati II, rendered them assistance of a military character on various occasions. It is probable that the first great prince of Siût was established in his chieftainship by a king of Herakleopolis, but whether he was or not, his successors gave loyal assistance to the Herakleopolitans. Khati II was a contemporary of Kamerirā, and his fleet and his bowmen made him a valuable ally by land and by river. On one occasion Kamerirā was obliged to flee from his capital and seek asylum with Khati II at Siût. Khati II collected his fleet and his army and sailed down to Herakleopolis and re-established Kamerirā in his kingdom.[2] But meanwhile the power of the princes of Thebes was becoming great, and there came a day when they marched to the north and overthrew the forces of the princes of Siût and the king of Herakleopolis, and so became masters of Upper Egypt, with Thebes as their capital. With the downfall of the princes of the North the Old Kingdom came to an end.

The Eleventh Dynasty. From Thebes.

The **founder** of this dynasty was one **Åntef-ā,** *i.e.*, Åntef " the Great," who on his stele in the Cairo Museum calls himself Erpā and Ḥa, and great chief of the nome of Thebes, and says that he did the will of the king as Keeper of the Gate of the South, and that he was the support (or pillar or prop) of him that gave life to the Two Lands (*i.e.*, Egypt). He was also the " president of the

[1] In Assyrian 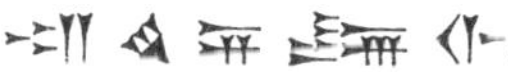, in Coptic ϩⲛⲏⲥ, and in Arabic اهناس Ahnâs.

[2] The inscriptions are published by Griffith, *Inscriptions of Siût and Dêr Rîfeh*, London, 1889, and translated by him in *Bab. and Or. Record*, Vol. III, and Maspero, *Revue Critique*, 1889, p. 410 ff.

priests." The name of his king is not given, but he was, of course, a Herakleopolitan. The fact that Ȧntef is called "the Great" shows that his predecessors in his office bore the name of Ȧntef. At some time in his life unknown to us this Ȧntef-ā, prince of Thebes, adopted the Horus name of Uaḥ-ānkh, , and called himself , king of the South and North, and extended his dominion as far north as Siûṭ. The southern boundary was Edfû. The stele on which he describes his conquests and his establishment of a "Gate of the North" is dated in year 50, but it is doubtful if he was king of Egypt for 50 years. Of his successor **Ȧntef-ā II,** who adopted Nekhtnebtepnefer, , as his Horus name, nothing is known. He was succeeded by a series of kings, each of whom bore the son-of-Rā name of Menthuḥetep, but the order in which they reigned is doubtful. The first of them, **Menthuḥetep I Ḥer Sānkhȧbtaui,** finally overthrew the power of the Herakleopolitan kings and their allies the princes of Siûṭ, and thus became king of Egypt. **Menthuḥetep II Nebkherurā,** whom some identify with **Menthuḥetep Nebḥaprā,**[1] made himself the overlord of **Ȧntef-ā III,** who seems to have been a rival claimant for the throne, and his rule extended northwards to Memphis and beyond. He also brought the Nubian tribes into subjection. He is famous as the builder of the remarkable funerary temple and pyramid at Dêr al-Baḥarî which were excavated by Naville and Hall in 1903–7. Of his successor **Menthuḥetep III Sānkhkarā** very little is known. During his reign a high official called Ḥenu organized an expedition to Punt to fetch myrrh and other products of the South. He, with an armed escort of 3,000 men, made his way to the Red Sea by way of the Wâdî Hammâmât, and they dug twelve wells and three tanks in the desert which supplied the force with water in abundance. He built a ship and despatched it to Punt, and on his way back to the Nile he dug out a number of blocks of stone in the quarries of the Valley and took them to the Nile to be hewn into statues of the king for the temple. According to some the XIth dynasty ended with Menthuḥetep III. But the monuments mention other Menthuḥeteps, namely **Menthuḥetep Nebtauirā** and **Menthuḥetep Sekhā · · · t-rā**; the first is known from inscriptions in the Wâdî Hammâmât, and the second from a fragment found at Dêr al-Baḥarî by Naville. The modern historians of Egypt disagree as to the position of the former in the dynasty,

[1] Petrie makes them two distinct kings. In some cartouches we have the sign  which can be read *Kheru* or *ḥap*, and in others we have  *ḥap*, which can only be read *ḥap*. The question is complicated by the two different Horus names.

and the latter they do not take into consideration at all. Breasted calls the former Menthuḥetep IV, and places him at the end of the dynasty; Hall wishes to "telescope" him into Menthuḥetep I Sānkhȧbtaui; and Petrie follows Breasted in calling him Menthuḥetep IV, but makes him No. 7 in the dynasty, and places him before Menthuḥetep III Sānkhkarā, whom he makes No. 9 in the dynasty and calls Menthuḥetep V. Menthuḥetep Nebtauirā sent his Wazîr Ȧmenemḥat to the Wâdî Ḥammâmât to quarry blocks of stone for a sarcophagus and cover, and the inscriptions of both king and official record the successful performance of the mission. Ȧmenemḥat says that he took ten thousand men with him, and if this statement be a fact, it is impossible to believe that such an army was necessary for the carrying out of what must after all have been a comparatively small quarrying operation. The god Menu apparently approved of the mission, for he made himself manifest, and the birth of a kid, and heavy rain, falling when it was urgently needed, were regarded as lucky portents.[1] Manetho says that the XIth dynasty consisted of 16 Theban Kings, among whom was **Ammenemes.** He, it seems certain, was no other than the Ȧmenemḥat mentioned above, and was probably Ȧmenemḥat I, the first king of the XIIth dynasty. If this be so Nebtauirā would appear to have been the last king of the XIth dynasty.

The Middle Kingdom

The Twelfth Dynasty. From Thebes.

The monuments show that this dynasty consisted of eight kings: four bore the name of Ȧmenemḥat, three the name of Usertsen, or Senusrit, and the eighth was called Sebekneferurā. **Ȧmenemḥat I,** whose name suggests that he was a follower of **Ȧmen,** the chief local god of Thebes, in whose honour he founded a temple, supported by his armed followers, removed the dependants of the Menthuḥetep kings from his path and seized the throne. The priests of Ȧmen, a very ancient god, whose cult is known to have existed under the IInd dynasty, were more powerful than those of Menthu at Hermonthis, and therefore an Ȧmenemḥat and not a Menthuḥetep became king. Ȧmenemḥat was an able and vigorous king, and as a result of his firm rule and wise foresight the material prosperity of the country increased greatly. The quarries in the Wâdî Ḥammâmât and Ṭurah were worked diligently, and the greatest temples in Upper and Lower Egypt were repaired, and in some cases rebuilt. He reduced the great tribes of Nubia and the

[1] The inscriptions were published by Lepsius, *Denkmäler*, Bd. II, Bl. 149, but more fully by Golénischeff in his *Epigraphical Results of an Excursion to Wâdî Ḥammâmât*, pp. 65–79 and pll. I–XVIII, St. Petersburg, 1887.

Northern Sûdân[1] to subjection, and overcame all his enemies, both native and foreign. Choosing neither Thebes nor Memphis he built himself a fortified palace called Åthet Taui, 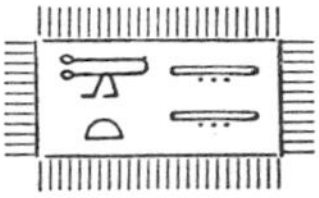 *i.e.*, " Conqueror of the Two Lands," on the west bank of the Nile, about 30 miles to the south of Memphis. The king's policy in dealing with the nobles of the country is well illustrated by the inscription of Khnemuḥetep at Bani Ḥasan, which shows that Åmenemḥat was strong, wise and just. Towards the close of his life an attempt was made one night, through the connivance of the palace officials, to murder him, but he either slew or put to flight his would-be assassins.[2] Probably as a result of this incident he associated his son Usertsen I (Sen-Usrit) with him in the rule of the kingdom. He built his pyramid Qa-nefer, , at Al-Lisht, probably near his fortified palace ; he reigned in all 30 years. Shortly before his death his son and co-regent was conducting a campaign in the Western Delta, and with him was a young officer called Sanehat. When news reached the prince that his father was dead, he at once returned to substantiate his claim to the throne. But in the mind of Sanehat the news struck terror, and watching his opportunity he hid himself in the brushwood, and then fled from the army, and got out of the country into Palestine as fast as he could. He had many adventures, nearly died of thirst, was rescued by the nomads, and married a woman of quality and became a great shêkh. He won great fame and riches by slaying an insolent and arrogant mighty man of war of the Goliath type. The reason why Sanehat took to flight when he heard of the king's death is not clear ; it has been suggested that he was a son of Åmenemḥat I, and was afraid that he might be put to death. The story of Sanehat was very popular among the Egyptians.[3]

Åmenemḥat I was succeeded by his son **Usertsen I** (Sen-Usrit[4]), who reigned for 45 years, 10 of which he was co-regent with his father, and 3 co-regent with his son. Manetho calls him " Sesonchôsis," with the variant " Sesortôsis," from which " Sesostris " was evolved.

[1] The American excavations at Dafûfah, near the Island of Arḳô, a little to the south of the Third Cataract, proved that the fort there was held by Åmenemḥat I, and by Pepi II of the VIth dynasty.

[2] The king describes the attack in his " Teaching," a XIXth dynasty copy of which is preserved in the Brit. Mus. Papyrus Sallier II. Many parts of it have been translated by Maspero, Amélineau, Erman, Griffith and others.

[3] The hieratic text was published by Lepsius, *Denkmäler*, Abth. VI, Bll. 104–7. The best translations are those of Erman, *Aus den Papyrus*, pp. 14–29, and Gardiner, *Die Erzählung des Sinuhe*, Leipzig, 1904.

[4] These words seem to mean " Brother (or associate) of Usrit," 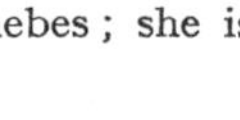, or , a form of the goddess Isis worshipped at Thebes ; she is mentioned in Chapters CX and CXLV of the Book of the Dead.

In this reign the old copper mines in Sinai were reopened and new ones worked, and many temples were repaired. Usertsen I refounded the great temple of Ȧnu (Heliopolis) and had a description of his work cut upon a stele which was set up in it.[1] One of the two obelisks, with metal pyramidions, which he set up in front of it is still standing, and is 65 feet high.[2] He sent an expedition into Nubia under the leadership of Ȧmeni, who was buried at Bani-Ḥasan, and the great chiefs of Elephantine who owned the caravans that traded between their town and the South assisted the royal forces. Some of them, *e.g.*, Sarenput, marched with them so far as the modern town of Dongola. An Egyptian fort and temple were built at Buhen (Wâdî Ḥalfah), and Haptchefa, an Egyptian, was appointed governor of the district round about the modern town of Karmah, at the head of the Third Cataract. This district is called Kas, , and is the Kûsh, or Cûsh, of the Bible. The object of such expeditions, or raids, as they ought to be called, was to obtain gold and slaves and the products of the South, even as it was in the days of Seneferu. An Egyptian officer was sent also to the Oasis of Khârgah in the Western Desert to extend the authority of Pharaoh over the peoples of the Oases, and to take tribute from the caravans that traded with Dâr Fûr and Kordofân. The king's pyramid at Al-Lisht was excavated in 1908–14 by the Metropolitan Museum of New York, and 10 large statues of him were found in it.

Ȧmenemḥat II, the Ammanemês of Manetho, who says that he was slain by his eunuchs, reigned about 35 years, including 3 as co-regent with his father and 3 with his son. No military expeditions were undertaken during this reign, but the mines of Sinai were worked by a large colony of Egyptians at Sarâbît al-Khâdim, for whose benefit a temple to the goddess Hathor was erected. Several great officials were sent to the Sûdân to fetch gold, precious stones, etc., and fortified rest-houses were built by the Egyptians for the protection of the men who brought the gold to Elephantine. It is probable that most of them were by the river, at least as far as Buhen (Wâdî Ḥalfah). Some officials were sent to Punt viâ the Wâdî Ḥammâmât, and thus the Egyptian Sûdân was being regularly opened up in two directions. Ȧmenemḥat II built a pyramid called Kherp, 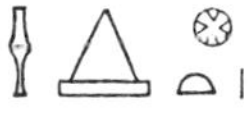, at Dahshûr, which was excavated by De Morgan.

Usertsen II (Sen-Usrit) reigned 19 years, during 3 of which he was co-regent with his father. Like his father he continued the

[1] A copy of the opening lines of it is preserved on a leather roll now in Berlin; see Stern in *Aeg. Zeit.*, 1874, p. 85 ff.

[2] His obelisk at Begig, now fallen, is 46 feet in length; see Lepsius, *Denkmäler*, Abth. II, Bl. 119.

" peaceful penetration " of the Sûdân by fostering trade with the South, and the import of gold into Egypt in his reign was very considerable. In the sixth year of his reign 37 Āmu, or nomads of the Eastern Desert (Semites), brought a gift of *mestchemut* , *i.e.*, antimony (Coptic ⲥⲧⲏⲙ), for eye-paint; the scene of the presentation is depicted on the walls of the tomb of Khnemuḥetep at Bani-Ḥasan. Usertsen II built a pyramid at the mouth of the great canal leading to the Fayyûm at a place now called Al-Lâhûn. It was built of sun-dried bricks cased with stone, and was opened by Mr. G. W. Fraser. About a mile and a-half from the ruins of this pyramid, at Kahûn, are the ruins of the town in which the workmen who built the pyramid lived; here were found several important, but fragmentary, papyri and many fragments of Minoan pottery.[1]

Usertsen III (Sen-Usrit) reigned about 38 years and effected the annexation of Nubia and of the Egyptian Sûdân so far as the head of the Second Cataract. In the eighth year of his reign he cleared out, repaired and enlarged the old canal which had been made in the First Cataract by Unȧ in the VIth dynasty, thus doing away with a difficult and time-wasting " portage." He carried out three or four very lucrative campaigns in Nubia and built the famous fortresses at Samnah and Kummah, on rocky eminences overlooking the Nile, about 30 miles south of Wâdî Ḥalfah. He fortified Jazîrat al-Malik (Uronarti), where Crowfoot and Budge discovered the great red granite inscribed royal stele which they took to Kharṭûm in 1906, and many other places in the Second Cataract, especially Matûḳah and Mirgissi. He despised the natives, whom he describes in his inscriptions as " cowardly and mean-spirited," and he boasts that he reaped the crops which they had sown, and stopped their wells, and slew their cattle, and carried off their women. And he prohibited any " Black " from passing Samnah and Kummah except for trading purposes. The Sesostris of later tradition, of whom Usertsen III was no doubt the original, is said to have been a mighty traveller, and to have conquered all Asia in nine years, and Europe so far as Thrace. But the monuments show that all his expeditions were in Nubia, and that only once did one of his officers, Khusebek by name, invade any other country. This official made a raid into Palestine, but its object seems to have been booty, not conquest. The pyramid built by Usertsen III at Dahshûr was excavated by De Morgan in 1894; outside the enclosing wall of the pyramid he found the royal funerary cedar-wood boat, which was about 30 feet long, and was broad enough to hold a double line of rowers and a sledge. Some have identified Usertsen III, or " Lachares," with the Nachares of Christian chronographers, in whose reign the patriarch Abraham is said to have visited Egypt.

[1] On this pottery see Hall in *Cambridge Ancient History*, Vol. I, p. 307

Ȧmenemḥat III, the greatest king of the XIIth dynasty, reigned about 48 years, and is called " Lamares " by Strabo. No great wars of conquest or raids for booty were undertaken by him, but he devoted himself to increasing the material prosperity of his country. Art, sculpture and architecture flourished under his powerful protection, and the monuments prove that his building operations continued throughout his reign. The quarries in Sinai were worked and vast quantities of stone were quarried in the Wâdî Ḥammâmât, Crocodilopolis and Ṭurah. He carried out great works in connection with the irrigation of the country. He increased the area watered by the old canal now called Baḥr Yûsuf[1] by means of a huge embankment, and reclaimed a large quantity of land from the bed of the great depression in the limestone which was known as **Lake Moeris.** The Birkat al-Ḳurûn in the western Fayyûm is all that is left of Lake Moeris, which, it has now been shown, was not an artificial lake, as Herodotus thought. Lake Moeris was said to be 150 miles in circumference and to have an area of 750 miles, and to be 50 paces deep ; the surface of Birkat al-Ḳurûn is 150 feet below sea-level,[2] and its cubic contents are equal to 1,500,000,000 cubic metres. Ȧmenemḥat III had records kept of the height reached by the waters of the Nile at Samnah and Kummah, and these show that the river-level was 26 feet higher during the Inundation than it is at the present time. These are dated in years 3, 5, 7, 9, 14, 15, 22, 23, 24, 30, 32, 37, 40, 41 and 43 of the king's reign, and they may have been connected in some way with regulating the inflow of water into Lake Moeris. He built the great temple which Herodotus (II, 148), Strabo (XVII, 37) and Diodorus (I, 5) call the **Labyrinth.** This was nothing but the large temple dedicated to Sebek, the Crocodile-god, which he built to the south of his pyramid tomb,[3] now known as the **Pyramid of Hawârah**[4]; this is said to have stood between the entrance to the Fayyûm and Crocodilopolis (Arsinoë) and to have had an area measuring 1,000 feet by 800 feet. The remains of the temple were used in building the railway ! The king set up two great statues of himself, each about 40 feet high, not in the middle of Lake Moeris, as Herodotus thought, but close by. The remains of the pedestals on which they were placed existed a few years ago, and were called by the natives **Pharaoh's Chairs** (*Kirasi al-Fir'aûn*). The sphinxes which Mariette found at Ṣân (Tanis), and believed to be the work of the Hyksos,

[1] It leaves the Nile a little to the north of Asyûṭ and, passing through a gap in the Libyan mountains, enters the Fayyûm after a course of about 200 miles.

[2] The average level of Lake Moeris was 80 feet above the Mediterranean Sea.

[3] Opened by Petrie in 1889 ; for a description of the king's wonderful tomb see *Kahun, Gurob and Hawara*, p. 12.

[4] Petrie, *Hawara*, pp. 5 and 6.

were undoubtedly made for Åmenemḥat III.[1] That the face of the Sphinx at Gîzah is a portrait of this king is not so certain. The Teaching of Seḥetepȧbrā was written during the reign of Åmenemḥat III.

The reigns of **Åmenemḥat IV** and **Sebekneferurā,** the last monarchs of this dynasty, were unimportant ; the latter, a woman, is called " Skemiophris " by Manetho. The monuments mention **Ḥer,** a king with the prenomen of Auȧbrā, who must have reigned, probably as a co-regent, with Usertsen III or Åmenemḥat, about this time, and also an **Usertsen** with the prenomen of Seneferȧbrā.

The Thirteenth Dynasty from Thebes and the Fourteenth Dynasty from Xoïs.

Manetho says that the Theban kings of the XIIIth dynasty were 60 in number, and that they reigned 453 years, and that the Xoïte kings of the XIVth dynasty were 76 in number, and that they reigned 184 or 484 years. The King-Lists and other monuments supply the names of about 108 kings who reigned during the period between the end of the XIIth dynasty and the beginning of the first Hyksos dynasty (the XVth), and it is possible that scarabs may supply a good many more, but very few of these kings had the right to assume the title of , " King of the South and North." When death removed the wise head and strong hand of Åmenemḥat, all the great nobles in Egypt knew that he could have no real successor, and each proceeded to assert his independence and to usurp authority. At Thebes the families of the Åntefs and the Menthuḥeteps and the Åmenemḥats probably put forward claimants to the throne, and the nomarch of Lower Egypt no doubt did the same, and it is more than probable that there were two or more nobles who called themselves " King of the South and North " at the same time. Manetho's totals of the years of the reigns of these " kings " must be too high, but at present there is no evidence available to correct them. When Åmenemḥat III died he left Egypt rich and prosperous, for all the gold in the Sûdân and the Eastern Desert was at his disposal. In fact, Egypt was well worth plundering, and all her enemies were well aware of this fact, and not many scores of years can have passed before the people were robbed of their wealth, and they were reduced to the state of subjection to which they were accustomed when there was no really powerful central authority in Egypt.

The first king of the XIIIth dynasty was a Theban called **Khutauirā Ugaf** (?) 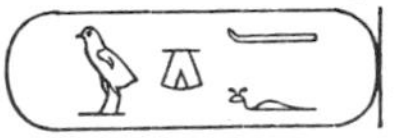, but nothing is known of his reign or why he was permitted to ascend the throne. The

[1] This is proved by Golénischeff in *Recueil*, XV, p. 131 ff.

next king who exercised any real power was **Sekhemkhutauirā Sebekḥetep I,** whose name is found on the rocks at Samnah in connection with the registers of the heights of the Nile during the Inundations of the first four years of his reign. There were several kings called Sebekḥetep, whose true sequence cannot be stated, and **Sebekemsaf** and **Sebekemsauf**; all these were votaries of the Crocodile-god Sebek and they may have belonged to the family of Ȧmenemḥat III, the founder of Crocodilopolis. Sebekḥetep II was succeeded by **Neferḥetep,** who took the prenomen of Khāsesheshrā, the son of the priest Ḥaānkhf by the princess Kema, . His wife was called Senseneb, and he had four children. He was a zealous votary of Osiris, and he established the worship of this god at Abydos in accordance with the information on the subject that he derived from a perusal of the rolls of papyri in the library of the great temple at Heliopolis.[1] He seems to have had a co-regent in his brother, who became **Sebekḥetep III,** with the prenomen Khāneferrā. Sebekḥetep III was the greatest king of the dynasty, and his rule extended from the northern Delta to the foot of the Fourth Cataract. He built a temple on the Island of Argo (Arḳaw or Argaw), near Dongola, and had two statues of himself, each about 24 feet high, quarried to set up before it.[2] The temple suggests that there was an Egyptian garrison near to protect the caravans from the South and to receive the gold which came from there. The granite statue of **Sekhemuatchtauirā** in the British Museum was found near this place. Among the kings of the XIVth dynasty, who were said to come from Xoïs,[3] were **Mermashāu,** who ruled from Tanis, where two statues of him were found among the ruins of the temple of Ptaḥ, and **Neḥsi** or **Rāneḥsi,** who also seems to have ruled from Tanis. These were probably contemporaries of the earlier Theban kings of the XIIIth dynasty. Among the last kings of the XIIIth dynasty must come **Ȧntef-ā Herḥermaāt-sesheshrā, Ȧntef-ā** his brother, **Ȧntef-ā Upmaātsesheshrā,** and **Ȧntef-ā Nubkheperrā.** The monuments show that the last of these possessed considerable power in Egypt, and his tomb is mentioned in the Abbott Papyrus. The principal document of his reign is a decree inscribed on a door-jamb at Coptos,[4] which orders the expulsion of a priest of Menu from the temple of this god and the sequestration of his stipend, and forbids the employment of his sons in any priestly capacity. The delinquent Tetȧ, the son of Menuḥetep, had, in some way unspecified, acted disloyally and

[1] The stele recording the fact was published by Mariette, *Catalogue*, tom. II, pl. 28 ff.

[2] They were quarried on the Island of Tombos near Karmah.

[3] Khasu , Coptic ⲥϧⲱⲟⲩ, the Sakhâ سخا of the Arabs.

[4] For the text see Petrie, *Coptos*, pl. VIII.

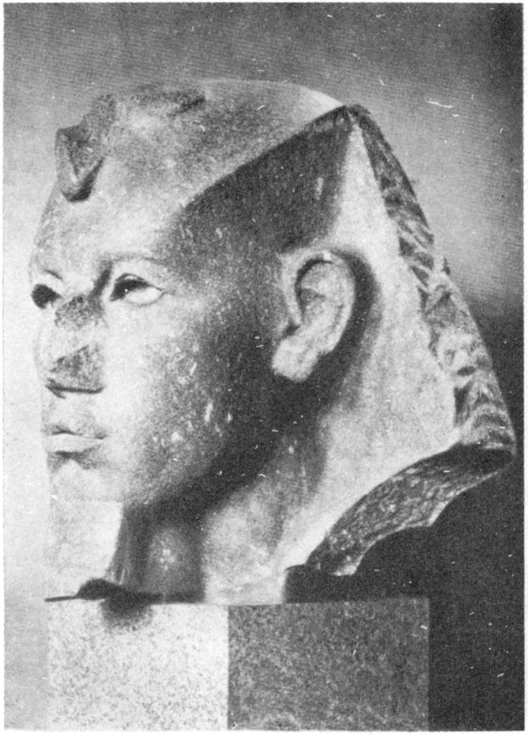

Head of a colossal statue of Ȧmenemḥat III, a king of the XIIth dynasty, which was usurped by Osorkon II, about B.C. 866. B.M. No. 1064.

Red granite statue of Sekhem-uatch-taui-Rā, a king of the XIIIth or XIVth dynasty. From Arko in the Egyptian Sûdân. B.M. No. 871.

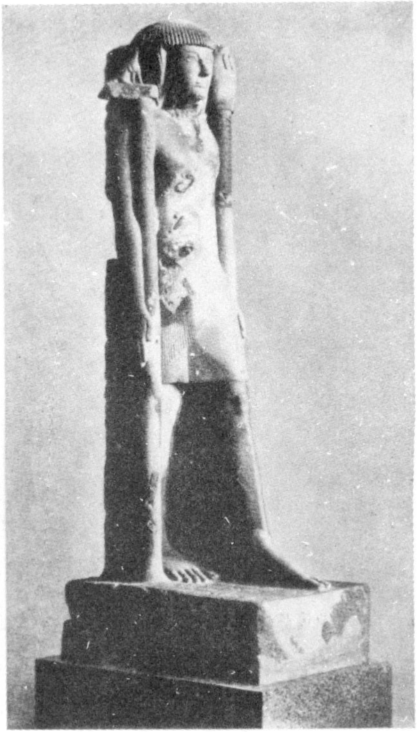

Flint agglomerate statue of Khā-em-Uast, eldest son of Rameses II. XIXth dynasty. B.M. No. 947.

Limestone statue of Queen Teta-shereṭ, an ancestress of Ȧāḥmes I, the founder of the XVIIIth dynasty. B.M. No. 22558.

Granite lion dedicated to the temple of Sulb by Tutānkhȧmen (about B.C. 1400) in memory of "his father" Ȧmenḥetep III. It was found at Jabal Barkal, whither it seems to have been taken by Ȧmen-Ȧsru, about 1000 years later. XVIIIth dynasty. B.M. No. 34.

treasonably against his god and king. Another king who reigned towards the end of the XIIIth dynasty was **Khentcher,** whose prenomen was Enmaātrāenkhā (?) 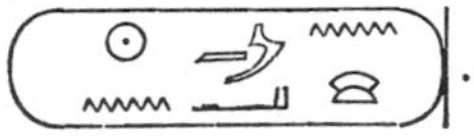.

The Fifteenth and Sixteenth Dynasties. Hyksos.

The rule of the Kings of the XIIIth and XIVth dynasties was brought to an end by the invasion of Egypt through her north-east frontiers by a confederation of nomad tribes that made their way into the Delta and destroyed the temples and burned the towns and enslaved the people. The native documents, of course, say nothing about these people, though they are referred to in later inscriptions as the "filthy ones," . Manetho calls them **Hykshos,** or "Shepherd-Kings," and Josephus **Hyksos,** adding the same explanation of the name as Manetho. The form of the name given by Manetho represents the Egyptian  , Ḥequ Shasu, *i.e.*, "Shasu-Chiefs," but in this we no doubt see the plural form of the equivalent of the title that the Hyksos king Khian adopted as his own, , Ḥeq semtu,[1] "Prince of the deserts." Manetho knew quite well that the desert folk were nomads,  *shasu,* and that they were shepherds by profession, but robbers of caravans whenever they had an opportunity. There were Semites of many kinds among them, men from Sinai and Palestine, and Syrians. But the host that invaded the Delta and occupied it must have had among them men with military training who were armed with effective weapons and probably led by officers skilled in the arts of war, who were determined to occupy the Delta and rule the country. No mere confederation of nomad tribes bent on plunder could have done what they did. Manetho says the kings of the XVth dynasty were of Phoenician or Canaanitish origin, but some authorities think that they were Syrians supported by Aryans, and that they invaded Egypt with chariots and horses, to which the Egyptians were strangers. Manetho gives the names of six of these kings, viz., Salatis, Beon (or Bnon), Pachnan (or Apachnas), Staan, Archlês (or Assis) and Aphôbis[2] (or Apôphis). They ruled from Memphis,

[1] Budge, *History of Egypt*, Vol. III, 1902, p. 138. 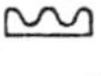 is now read *khas-t* 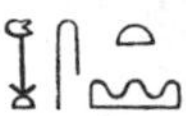, and the form  is known. Thus we have ; see *Aeg. Zeit.*, Bd. 45, p. 140.

[2] The Rhind Papyrus (Brit. Mus., No. 10058) was written in the reign of Aphôbis (Ȧpepȧ I).

the old capital, and from Avaris, , Ḥe-t Uār, a new capital which they founded in the Eastern Delta. When the invaders were settled in the Delta, little by little they began to assume titles like the old Pharaohs, and we find that one of them, whom Manetho calls "Aphôbis," in Egyptian **Åpepå,**  **(I)** enclosed his name in a cartouche and adopted the prenomen Āuserrā as King of the South and North. Another king of the same name adopted a Horus name, Seḥeteptaui, , " Pacifier of the Two Lands," and he and many others called themselves " son of Rā." One of the most important of the Hyksos kings was **Khian,**  (the Iannas of Manetho), whose names are found on the basalt lion weight in the British Museum (No. 987), which George Smith, the Assyriologist, purchased in Baghdâd, and on a statue discovered by Naville at Bubastis.[1] Mariette discovered at Ṣân (Tanis) a stele[2] mentioning a king called **Nubti,** with the prenomen of Setāpeḥti, and stating that he reigned 400 years before Rameses II ; but some think that Nubti was the god Set, and that the period is mythological. The names of a great many Hyksos kings and princes are known from scarabs, but it is impossible to arrange them chronologically at present ; some of the names are manifestly Semitic, but the greater number of them are not.[3] The exact length of the reigns of the Hyksos is unknown, but it probably did not exceed 200 years.

The Seventeenth Dynasty.

According to Manetho the Hyksos kings of this dynasty were 43 in number, and they reigned 151 years ; the Theban kings were also 43 in number, and they reigned 151 years. These statements have no historical value. The monuments make it quite clear that the Theban kings were in subjection to the Hyksos, for remains found at Gebelên prove that these hated foreigners were the *de facto* lords of Upper Egypt. The American excavators at Dafûfah, near Karmah, at the head of the Third Cataract, found that the " Plain of Potsherds "[4] was covered with masses of pottery of the Hyksos Period, and on the north side of Dafûfah they found a " Hyksos cemetery." The question which now arises naturally is,

[1] On the vase cover inscribed with this king's name found by Sir A. Evans at Knossos ; see the *Annual* of the British School at Athens, Vol. VII, p. 65.

[2] Described by de Rougé in *Rev. Arch.*, tom. IX, 1864, and figured in Budge, *History of Egypt*, Vol. III, p. 157.

[3] For lists see Newberry, *Scarabs*, p. 150 ff. ; Budge, *Book of Kings*, Vol. I, p. 93 ff.

[4] See the *Bulletin*, Boston, December, 1915, p. 71.

Was this pottery taken there by trading caravans from the North in the ordinary way of business, or was it made there by the people who formed a Hyksos colony in that great and ancient Sûdânî trading-centre ?[1] The cemetery suggests the existence of a Hyksos colony, governed by Hyksos officials. Be this as it may, the only Theban kings of the XVIIth dynasty are: **Tauā Seqenenrā I,** whose tomb is mentioned in the Abbott Papyrus[2]; **Tauāā Seqenenrā II,** whose tomb is mentioned in the same papyrus; **Tauāqen Seqenenrā III,** who was killed in fighting against the Hyksos[3]; **Kames,** who was probably the son of Tauāqen, and **Senekhtenrā.** The Hyksos contemporary of Tauāqen was one of the kings called Ȧpepȧ, or Rā-Ȧpepi , as we know from the Papyrus Sallier I (Brit. Mus. No. 10185). This document states that Rā-Ȧpepi wrote to Tauāqen from Avaris complaining that the hippopotami in the sacred lake at Thebes made so much noise, both by day and by night, that he was unable to sleep, and he called upon him to let huntsmen deal with the noisy beasts. The text suggests, too, that Rā-Ȧpepi wished the Theban king to introduce the worship of the Hyksos god Sutekh, 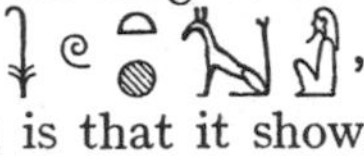, into Thebes. The chief value of this composition is that it shows that Rā-Ȧpepi was the overlord of Tauāqen. What answer Tauāqen sent to Avaris is not known, but it seems that war broke out between the Hyksos and the Egyptians in his reign, and that with his head almost battered to pieces he died fighting for the independence of his people. The war was continued by **Kames,** his son by Queen Tetȧsheret, but nothing is known of his acts, and, though his reign was short, he seems to have made his rule effective so far as Herakleopolis, perhaps even beyond. He married his sister Ȧāḥḥetep, the daughter of Tetȧsheret, whose family seems to have belonged to Khemenu (Hermopolis), and probably consolidated his kingdom by so doing. Of their sons, one called **Senekhtenrā** reigned for a year or two, but nothing is known about him.

The New Kingdom

The Eighteenth Dynasty. From Thebes.

The Hyksos were conquered and driven out of Egypt by **Ȧāḥmes (I)**, the Amôs, Amâses or Amôsis of Manetho, the son of Kames and Ȧāḥḥetep, who was the founder of the XVIIIth dynasty. The story of the expulsion of the Hyksos is told by Ȧāḥmes, whose

[1] Specimens of Hyksos pottery are exhibited in the British Museum; see *Guide to the 4th, 5th and 6th Egyptian Rooms*, p. 257.

[2] Maspero, *Enquête*, p. 20.

[3] His mummy was found at Dêr al-Baḥarî.

father, Baba, had fought in the wars under Tauāqen (Seqenen-Rā III). He was a native of Nekheb (Al-Kâb), and was made captain of a war-boat at an early age. He was present at the capture, by Åāḥmes I, of Avaris, the Hyksos capital in the Eastern Delta, and was on several occasions rewarded with gifts of gold and slaves. He followed the king in the pursuit of the Hyksos to Sharuhen (mentioned in Joshua xix, 6), and witnessed the capture of that city. A namesake and fellow-citizen, Åāḥmes-pen-Nekheb, describes a further pursuit of the Hyksos by the king, who pushed his forces through Palestine and invaded Southern Syria. Åāḥmes I also sent an expedition into Nubia and reduced the tribes between Al-Kâb and Elephantine and the Nubians to subjection. With a portion of the spoil obtained by his successful warfare he endowed the temple of Åmen at Karnak, and so laid the foundation of the great wealth and power of the priesthood of Åmen, or Åmen-Rā, " King of the gods " at Thebes.

Åmenḥetep I, the Amenôphthis of Manetho, sent an expedition to raid Nubia and re-established the Egyptian frontier in the south at Kash, in the Third Cataract, and captured the captain of the Blacks and appointed an overlord for their country. He also raided a district of Libya and a portion of Syria, and returned with much spoil, a portion of which he devoted to rebuilding the temple of Åmen and endowing the priesthood thereof. The incorporation of the name of Åmen in his name proclaims the influence of the priesthood of Åmen over his family and their devotion to this god. Åmenḥetep's predecessor had been a votary of the Moon-god Åāḥ, and the god's name formed part of his own.

Tcheḥutimes (Thothmes I), the Tuthmôsis of Manetho, married Princess Åāḥmes 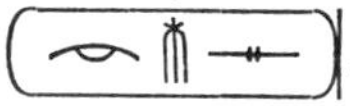, and thus consolidated his claim to the throne; his mother was called Senseneb. He at once appointed a viceroy over Lower and Upper Nubia, who bore the title " Prince of Kash (Cush)," and caused records of his accession to be cut on the rocks at Buhen and other parts of Nubia. In the second year of his reign he set out for Nubia, taking with him the two officers called Åāḥmes (Amasis), who had served under his predecessors, and, according to the story of one of them, he engaged in the fight personally and slew his antagonist. He built a fort on the Island of Tombos near the head of the Third Cataract, and in the stele which he set up there he boasts that his kingdom extends from this point to the Euphrates, a river which, up to that time at all events, he had never seen. He returned to Thebes with the body of the Nubian chief, whom he had slain, hanging head downwards from the bows of his boat. He next led an expedition into Syria and marched as far north as the country of the great rivers (Naharina), and took many prisoners and obtained great spoil. His captains Åāḥmes, the son of Baba, and Åāḥmes-pen-Nekheb, performed splendid acts of personal bravery, and one brought into the king's camp a chariot and horses and the charioteer, and the other a chariot and a horse and 21 hands which he had cut off from his prisoners' bodies! Thothmes I set up a stele somewhere in Syria to commemorate his victories, and it was seen by Thothmes III. He devoted a large share of his spoil to the repairs of the temples throughout the land, and he built a splendid pylon at Karnak in the temple of Åmen, and set up two granite obelisks there in honour of Åmen-Rā. These, the successors of the "sun-stones" of Heliopolis, probably mark the fusion of Åmen, the old god of Thebes, with Rā, the foreign Sun-god of Heliopolis. Thothmes I also rebuilt and refurnished the temple of Osiris at Abydos.

Thothmes II, the Chebrôs or Chebron of Manetho, was the son of Thothmes I by Princess Mutnefert. He had been co-regent with his father, just as had been his half-brothers Uatchmes and Åmenmes and his half-sister Ḥatshepsut, who were the offspring of Thothmes I by Queen Åāḥmes. Uatchmes and Åmenmes died before Thothmes I, and when this king died Thothmes II and Ḥatshepsut had equal claims to the throne, so they married each other and reigned jointly. The above statements rest upon the facts which, it seems to the present writer, may be legitimately deduced from the evidence of the monuments. But some think that Thothmes I had one son, called Thothmes, by his wife Princess Åāḥmes, and another son, also called Thothmes, by a lady of inferior birth whose name was Åset. Thothmes, son of Åset, they say, compelled Thothmes I to abdicate and became the king whom we know as Thothmes III. He married Ḥatshepsut, and the two reigned jointly for a few years, then Thothmes III, having dissociated Ḥatshepsut from the rule of the kingdom, had her name cut out of the monuments. Then Thothmes, the son of Princess Åāḥmes, overthrew Thothmes, the son of Åset, who was reigning, and re-established his father Thothmes I as co-regent, and also cut out Ḥatshepsut's name from the monuments. When Thothmes I died, Thothmes, son of Princess Åāḥmes, reigned alone; on his death Thothmes, son of Åset, resumed his reign and, the breach between himself and his half-sister being patched up, he remarried Ḥatshepsut and they reigned jointly. When Ḥatshepsut died he became sole king. This theory, which was first propounded by Sethe,[1] has few, if any, facts to support it, and is contradicted by the general evidence of the monuments of the period. It has been adopted by Breasted,[2] who, however, in his *History* (p. 267), frankly states that his "reconstruction is not without difficulties." Elsewhere, in a book published in the same year as his *History* (1906), he says that Sethe's explanation

[1] See his *Untersuchungen*, I, Leipzig, 1896, pp. 1–58, and *Aeg. Zeit.*, Bd. XXXVI, p. 24 f.

[2] "A New Chapter in the Life of Thothmes III," published in Sethe's *Untersuchungen*, Vol. II, Leipzig, 1900.

"is the first, and thus far the only scientific study of the problem employing and reckoning with all the materials."[1] Sethe's arguments about the mutilation and recutting of Ḥatshepsut's name on the walls of her temple at Dêr al-Baḥarî are wholly rejected by Naville,[2] who knows more about that building than any other man. Von Bissing has shown[3] that Sethe's principal assumptions are wholly unfounded, and Hall's remarks[4] reveal the unsoundness of the arguments that Sethe and Breasted have adduced in support of their theory.

During the reign of Thothmes II the Nubians again rebelled, and raided the Egyptian caravans and made incursions into Egyptian territory. An Egyptian army marched into Nubia, pillaging, burning and destroying as it went, and an inscription at Aswân says that every male was killed, with the exception of one of the sons of the Prince of Kash, who, with his family, was taken prisoner, bound in fetters, and brought before the king, who set his feet upon his body. The usual loot was brought back to Thebes, and the god Åmen received his share. In this reign the Egyptians made a raid into Retenu, or Northern Syria, and captured so many prisoners that their general, Åāḥmes-pen-Nekheb, was unable to count them.

Ḥatshepsut, who adopted the prenomen of **Maātkarā** (the Amensis or Amersis of Manetho), married her half-brother, Thothmes II, and, when he died, became Queen of Egypt. She had been associated by her father, Thothmes I, with himself in the rule of the kingdom, and the experience that she had thus gained, coupled with her great natural ability and forceful personality, made her rule effective. Her husband seems to have been a weakling, both mentally and physically, and the government of the country fell somewhat naturally into her capable hands. She seems to have been a prototype in most ways of Ṣâliḥ Ayyûb's slave-woman, the famous Shajar ad-durr, who held courts, presided over councils, and attended to the discipline of the army, until the arrival of her lord's heir, Tûrânshâh.[5] Ḥatshepsut sent a fleet of five ships to Punt, and their commander, Neḥsi, brought back large quantities of myrrh, "green gold," spices for incense, ebony, boomerangs, eye-paint, leopard skins, and a number of apes and dog-headed baboons. The reception of the Egyptians by Paruhu, , Prince of Punt, was most friendly. The great architect, Senmut, built for Ḥatshepsut the famous temple with three terraces, called Tcheser Tcheseru, at Dêr al-Baḥarî, and on its walls she caused to be

[1] *Ancient Records*, Vol. II, p. 53.
[2] *Aeg. Zeit.*, Bd. XXXV, p. 30 ff., and Bd. XXXVII, p. 48 ff.
[3] *Aeg. Zeit.*, Bd. XLI, p. 126.
[4] *Ancient History*, pp. 286, 287.
[5] Her story is well told by Lane-Poole in his *Egypt in the Middle Ages*, p. 237 ff.

sculptured a series of reliefs depicting the principal events of this expedition. Another series of reliefs in this temple illustrated the fiction of her being begotten by Åmen-Rā, King of the gods, who was held to have consorted with her mother in the form of a man. Ḥatshepsut caused herself to be represented in male form, with a beard, and in masculine attire, for she believed herself to be a counterpart of the god Åmen, and in her inscriptions masculine pronouns and verbal forms are used in speaking of her. She was a loyal servant of Åmen, and enriched his temple, and set up there four mighty granite obelisks[1] to the glory of her god and the memory of her father, Thothmes I. They were quarried at Aswân by Senmut and brought to Thebes in seven months—a wonderful piece of work. Ḥatshepsut rebuilt and repaired many of the temples in Egypt, and devoted a large portion of the spoil and tribute that came to her to their endowment. Under her patronage the arts and crafts flourished, and though there is no evidence that she conducted any wars of conquest, none of the frontiers of Egypt was thrust back during her reign.

Thothmes III, the Misaphris or Misphragmuthôsis of Manetho, was the son of Thothmes II and Queen Åset (Isis), and nephew and, perhaps, husband of Queen Ḥatshepsut, with whom he reigned as co-regent for about 21 years. Though as co-regent he had the rank and titles of the King of Egypt, he possessed no real power, for his aunt ruled absolutely, even as she had ruled when she was co regent with Thothmes II. As soon as Ḥatshepsut was dead Thothmes determined to make the peoples of Western Asia, who had promptly refused to pay tribute to Egypt and had declared themselves independent, to submit again to Egyptian supremacy. In the 22nd year of his reign (which included the years of his co-regency) he set out on his first expedition to Syria, defeated a confederation of Asiatics, and besieged and captured the town of Megiddo, and returned to Egypt with an enormous amount of spoil. Expeditions followed in the 24th, 25th, 29th, 30th, 31st, 33rd, 34th, 35th, 36th, 37th, 38th, 39th, 40th, 41st, and 42nd (?) years of his reign, but it was the earlier expeditions that made him master of all Northern Syria and the country to the east of the Euphrates. In the 30th year of his reign he captured Kadesh, Simyra, and Arvad, and two years later he set up a tablet at Ni, 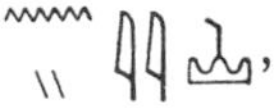, side by side with that of Thothmes I, to mark the limit of the Egyptian Empire to the East in Western Asia. Whilst in this country Thothmes III hunted elephants, and his general, Åmenemḥeb, says that he helped his master to capture 120 of them, , and that on one occasion he saved the king's life by cutting off the trunk

[1] One of these is still standing.

of an elephant which was attacking him. The account of these campaigns, which was most carefully written day by day on a leather roll by the scribe Thânni, shows that Thothmes III was a good tactician and military administrator, a bold and fearless general, and the narratives of his acts and deeds recorded on many monuments prove that he was the greatest of all the kings who sat on the throne of Pharaoh. As a conqueror and statesman the only other Egyptian king who can possibly be compared with him is Usertsen (Sen Usrit) III, and this opinion was shared by the Egyptians themselves, for at Jabal Dôshah, in the Sûdân, the two names are cut side by side. Towards the close of his life Thothmes III sent his soldiers into Nubia, where the great tribes had revolted. In the 50th year of his reign he set out for the Sûdân, and in passing through the First Cataract he ordered the old canal, which had been made under the VIth dynasty, to be cleared out. He went on to Buhen (Wâdî Ḥalfah) and, presumably, to Samnah, beyond Sarras, where he ordered a temple to be built in honour of Usertsen III. On his return to Egypt he passed through the canal in the Cataract, and about four years later he died. His expeditions in Western Asia broke the power of the Prince of Kadesh and his powerful allies, and the amount of spoil, gifts and tribute that Thothmes brought back to Egypt as the result of them can hardly be imagined. His tribute from Nubia must have been very great, and the gifts that he received from Cyprus and the neighbouring countries were not inconsiderable. A large proportion of his spoil he devoted to the enlargement of the great temple of Âmen and the endowment of the priests, and the great colonnade[1] built by him at Karnak proves that he was as great a builder as he was soldier. He rebuilt and repaired all the great temples of Egypt, he built a fort in the Lebanon mountains, and founded the great temple at Ṣulb on a plain on the left bank of the Nile in the Third Cataract. He set up four great obelisks at Thebes ; one is on the hill of the Lateran in Rome, one in New York, one on the Thames Embankment, and a part of the fourth is in Constantinople. Thothmes III was buried in the Valley of the Tombs of the Kings, and his tomb was discovered by Loret in 1898. The best summary of his conquests is found on a large stone stele, which was originally set up in the great temple of Âmen at Karnak and is now in the Egyptian Museum in Cairo ; it was discovered by Mariette and published by him in his *Album*, pl. 32, and in his *Karnak*, pl. 11. Many translations of it exist.

Âmenḥetep II, the Amenôphis of Manetho, was the son of Thothmes III, and for a short time before his father's death he had been his co-regent. When Thothmes III died the peoples of Western Asia revolted, declined to pay their annual tribute to Egypt, and declared themselves independent. Âmenḥetep set out at once to

[1] It is about 150 feet long, 50 feet wide, and has 50 columns and 32 rectangular pillars.

crush the rebellion, and defeated the enemy at Shemshu-Åtum; he led his troops in person and captured many prisoners and horses with his own hand. He then marched on and crossed the Orontes, and a little later he captured seven rebel chiefs in their country of Takhisa. Continuing his march he came to Ni, where he was warmly welcomed, and soon after, probably at Akathi, the chiefs of Mitanni[1] paid tribute and submitted to him. Whether he marched into the country of Mitanni, which lay along the middle Euphrates, is doubtful, but somewhere near the place where he stayed his advance he set up a memorial tablet, as Thothmes III and Thothmes I had done at Ni. His expedition, or rather raid, into Syria procured for him much loot in the shape of 1,650 *ṭeben*[2] of gold, 210 horses, 300 chariots, hundreds of chiefs and 240 of their wives, and a very large amount of copper.[3] With the spoil which the king obtained in Upper Rethenu he brought back the bodies of the seven chiefs whom he had slain in Takhisa, and he sailed up the Nile with them suspended from the bows of his royal barge. Six of the bodies were hung upon a gateway at Thebes, and the seventh he sent up to Napata, to be hung on the city wall, so that all men might know throughout Egypt and Nubia and Kash that he had conquered the rebels in Western Asia. The mention of Napata in his inscriptions shows that he was master of the Sûdân as far as the foot of the Fourth Cataract, but there is reason to believe the influence of Egypt extended nearly as far south as the modern town of Kharṭûm. He built or rebuilt temples at Amâda and Elephantine and carried out works at Karnak and Memphis and Heliopolis. His mummy was found in his tomb by Loret in 1899.

Åmenḥetep II was succeeded by his son, **Thothmes IV,** the Tuthmôsis of Manetho. According to the legend cut on the great granite stele between the paws of the Sphinx he owed his throne to the good offices of Ḥeremåakhu, the god who is symbolized by the Sphinx at Gîzah, *i.e.*, to the powerful priesthoods of Memphis and Heliopolis. Be this as it may, he made an expedition into Northern Syria early in his reign and returned laden with spoil, and he gratified the priesthood of Åmen at Thebes by bringing back great logs of cedar wood from Lebanon to make a new sacred boat for the god. For some reason, which is not quite clear, unless we suppose that he was troubled by the trend of events that he saw taking place in Northern Syria, Thothmes IV sent to Artatama, king of Mitanni and grandfather of Tushratta, and asked for his daughter to wife, and he had to make his request seven times before the

[1] The kingdom of Mitanni only lasted 75 years. Seven of its kings are known, viz., Saushshatar, Artatama I, Shutarna I, Tushratta, Artatama II, Shutatarra, and Mattiuaza. The Mitannian language was non-Semitic.

[2] The *ṭeben* = between 90 and 91 grammes. Ten *ṭeben* of gold would represent about £105 of our money.

[3] 500,000 *ṭeben* (about 44⅘ tons).

Mitannian king granted it.[1] In due course the Princess of Mitanni came to Egypt, probably with a suitable escort of nobles and ladies, and there seems to be little doubt that she brought with her the religious beliefs that caused so much trouble in Egypt in later days. Her native name is not known, but she seems to have been called **Mutemuȧa,**  , in Egyptian, and she became the mother of the next king, Ȧmenḥetep III. Thothmes IV, encouraged by the counsel of Ȧmen, made an expedition, in the eighth year of his reign, into Nubia, where the tribes had revolted on a large scale. What he did there exactly cannot be stated, for nearly one-half of the inscription on a rock in the First Cataract, which tells the story of it, is destroyed. But we may assume that the rebellion was put down in the usual way, and that when a sufficient number of the natives had been killed the remainder brought as gifts to the king slaves, male and female, gold and other Sûdânî produce, which the king took back to Thebes. His reign was too short (nine years or so) for the completion of any great building work, but he did one remarkable thing at Thebes, for he finished the work on the great granite obelisk, now known as the Lateran Obelisk, which Thothmes III had left incomplete at his death, and set it up. He added columns of text on the sides of the central dedication texts of Thothmes III, and from those on the south side of it we learn that the obelisk lay on its side unfinished for 35 years.

Ȧmenḥetep III, the Hôros of Manetho and the **Memnon** of Greek writers, was the son of Thothmes IV by the Mitannian princess to whom the Egyptians gave the name of Mutemuȧa. The official fiction, which is illustrated by the bas-reliefs on the walls of the temple of the Southern Apt (*i.e.*, the Temple of Luxor), is that he was begotten by Ȧmen, who took the form of a man and companied with Queen Mutemuȧa. In the fifth year of his reign a rebellion broke out in the country south of the Third Cataract (now the Dongola Province) and Ȧmenḥetep, employing the Nubian regiments which his viceroy Merimes had enrolled, marched to the South and defeated the rebels utterly. About 300 of them were killed and their hands cut off, and 750 of them were taken prisoners. Having reduced the natives to subjection he went southwards on what may be regarded as an exploring expedition, but, as the positions of the places which he mentions, Ḥuā, Kheskhet and Unshek, cannot be located, we do not know how far south he went. When in the Dongola Province it would be easy for him to march by the old caravan route to the place called Matammah, nearly opposite Shindî, on the Nile, and the Qebḥu-Ḥer, or Pool of Horus, where he set up his memorial stele, may be the famous Gakdûl Wells. From

[1] See the Tall al-'Amârnah tablet, Berlin, No. 24 (ed. Winckler, p. 51).

this time to the end of his reign the Egyptian viceroys collected the tribute from Kash and the countries to the south and transmitted it yearly to Thebes. Ȧmenḥetep III made several expeditions into Western Asia, but these were to all intents and purposes "royal progresses." The great kings of Babylon, Mitanni, and Assyria, and the chiefs of Palestine and Syria, and even Cyprus, were on the most cordial terms with him, and it is clear from the evidence of the letters in cuneiform found at Tall al-'Amârnah[1] that many of them regarded him not only as their overlord but also as their friend. Vassal states paid their tribute regularly and, with the riches of Western Asia and the Sûdân pouring into her coffers, Egypt became the most wealthy and prosperous country in the world. All the Mesopotamian peoples remembered that the blood of a Mitannian princess ran in the veins of Ȧmenḥetep III, and that he was their kinsman, and not a foreigner. The pleasure that he took in their lion hunts endeared him to the Euphratean shêkhs, and he strengthened the tie between them and himself by marrying one, if not two, of the daughters of Kadashman Harbe, king of Babylon, and the Mitannian princesses Tatumkhipa, daughter of Tushratta, and Gilukhipa, daughter of Shutarna. His "great chief wife" was Queen Tī, 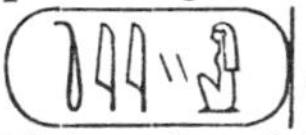, the Te-i-e 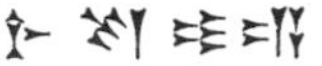 of the Tall al-'Amârnah Tablets, daughter of Iuȧa and Thuȧa, who appear to have been people of good position in life, and he coupled her name with his own in all documents. It is clear that she was an able woman, and maintained her influence over the king all his life. Ȧmenḥetep III was a great builder. All the great quarries were worked actively in his reign, and he built:—the oldest part of the Serapeum at Ṣaḳḳârah, a great pylon, etc., at Karnak, the Temple of Luxor, the great temple on the west bank of the Nile, with the famous "**Colossi** of Memnon," a temple at Al-Kâb, a temple at Elephantine, a temple at Sadêngah in the Sûdân in honour of Tī, his great Queen, and the magnificent sandstone temple at Ṣulb, before which were placed the granite lions now in the British Museum. He joined the Temples of Karnak and Luxor by an avenue with rows of kriosphinxes on each side, and to please Tī he made a great ornamental lake, 3,700 cubits long and 700 cubits broad, on the west bank of the Nile, which is now probably represented by the Birkat Habû. As the official son of Ȧmen he made splendid gifts to the temple of the god at Karnak, and in this capacity was actually worshipped as a god at Ṣulb in the Sûdân. But he supported the cult of Ȧten, of whom his wife Tī was a votary, as we see from the

[1] The story of the finding of these tablets is told in my *Nile and Tigris*, Vol. I, p. 140. The texts are published by Bezold and Budge, *The Tell el-Amarna Tablets in the British Museum*, London, 1892, and Winckler and Abel, *Der Thontafelfund*, Berlin, 1889, 1890; the best translations are those of Knudtzon, *Die el Amarna-Tafeln*, Leipzig, 1907.

great scarab[1] commemorating the making of her lake. The wealth of Egypt in his reign was incalculable, for Egypt was then the trading centre of the known world, and Åmenḥetep III spent the royal revenue right royally on magnificent buildings, sculpture and statuary, and on beautiful things of every kind ; he was the *Roi Soleil* of all craftsmen, designers and artists. He was a liberal and tolerant ruler, fond of pomp and ceremony, and pleasure and excitement, but bold and courageous withal. The Asiatics loved Thothmes III, the slayer of 120 elephants, and Åmenḥetep III, the slayer of 102 lions during the first ten years of his reign and of 96 wild cattle out of a herd of 190 in the second year of his reign, was a man entirely after their own heart. During the last half of his reign Åmenḥetep III made no journey into Western Asia, and the Hittites took the opportunity of seizing some of Egypt's possessions there. They were helped by a number of nomad tribes, and at length Åmenḥetep III was obliged to send troops to drive out the invaders. The mistake he made was in not going himself. The revolt was put down, and peace restored, but the decay of Egypt's power in Western Asia had begun, and the rebels only waited for the king's death to declare their independence.

Åmenḥetep IV was the son of Åmenḥetep III by Queen Tī ; he reigned about 17 years and died probably before he was 30,[2] though the same authority who says that his mummy is that of a man of 25 or 26 also says that he may have lived until he was 36 ![3] Thus the anatomical evidence about his age is neither conclusive nor definite. At what age Åmenḥetep IV began to reign is not known, but it was before he was fifteen ; his wife **Nefertiti** was his half-sister, being the daughter of his father by a Mesopotamian woman. He also inherited his father's wife Tatumkhipa, , the daughter of Tushratta, king of Mitanni.[4] As a child he imbibed religious ideas and beliefs which were not in accordance with native Egyptian theology, and under the tuition of Åi, the husband of his nurse, and the influence of his mother Tī, who seems to have been the *de facto* ruler of the country during the last years of her husband's life and the early years of her widowhood, he adopted the cult of Åten. It is clear that he was clever and unusually precocious, and fearless and courageous in giving effect to his convictions at all costs, and the monuments show that his obstinacy was great. In the early years of his reign he built a Benben House, 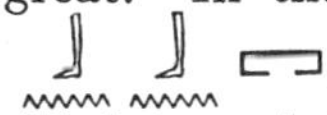, *i.e.*, a solar sanctuary in his temple of Gem-Åten at Thebes, and this provoked the enmity of the priests

[1] On the five classes of great scarabs made to commemorate great events in the king's life see the section SCARABS in this book.

[2] See Dr. Elliot Smith's remarks in Davis, *The Tomb of Queen Tiyi*, London, 1910.

[3] Elliot Smith, *Tutankhamen*, London, 1923, p. 84.

[4] See Budge, *History of Egypt*, Vol. IV, p. 128.

of Ȧmen. In the sixth year of his reign he publicly declared his adhesion to the cult of Ȧten, *i.e.*, of the actual physical sun, and in his religious madness he rejected all the non-solar gods of his country, among them being the god Ȧmen. Utterly regardless of the fact that the whole social life of his capital was bound up in the cult of Ȧmen, he disbanded the priests of Ȧmen and confiscated the revenues of their god, thereby bringing chaos into his country. He had the name of Ȧmen and the word for "gods," , cut out from the monuments. There was no god but Ȧten, he said, and though this divine name was a very old one in Egypt, his dogmas concerning his Ȧten were wholly abominable to the Egyptians generally. Finding life unbearable at Thebes, he departed to a place about 300 miles to the north, and on the plain on the east bank of the Nile, which measures about 3 miles by 5 miles, he founded his City of God and new capital, which he called "Ȧakhutenȧten," *i.e.*, the "Horizon of Ȧten."[1] The plain on the west bank was also made a part of his capital, and he set up fourteen stelae, or "boundary stones," to mark its limits. And he gave himself a new name, "Ȧakhunȧten," which may mean something like "Ȧten is content." This done he made himself high priest of Ȧten, with the ancient title of Ur-maa, , "the Great Seer," and set to work to promulgate his views among his adherents, whom from time to time he rewarded lavishly. He built Ȧten temples in Nubia, Hermonthis, Thebes, Memphis, and one in Syria, and a certain number of interested officials imbibed his "Teaching," which is set forth in the well-known hymn to Ȧten. Satisfied with his religion and happy in his domestic circle,[2] he passed several years in playing the priest and directing the choral services in his temple, and the religious dances, and the acrobatic performances in which his followers delighted. Meanwhile the power of Egypt was waning rapidly in Western Asia, for the kings of Mitanni and Babylon and Assyria realized quickly that the king of Egypt was only a fanatical priest and no warrior, and before the death of Ȧmenḥetep IV Western Asia was lost to Egypt. Of the last years of his reign we know nothing, but he appointed **Sākarā,** who married his eldest daughter, Merit-Ȧmen, co-regent, and soon after died and was buried in a rock-hewn tomb on the east bank of the Nile. His character and religion have formed the subjects of extravagant eulogies by some and of sharp criticism by others, but if anatomical authority be correct he is entitled to our sympathy. For "The peculiar features of Akhenaton's head and face, the grotesque form assumed by his legs and body, no less than the eccentricities of his behaviour

[1] Within a few years after its founder's death this city fell into decay, and its ruins are now known generally as "Tall al-'Amârnah."

[2] His family consisted of seven daughters.

and his pathetic failure as a statesman, will probably be shown to be due to his being the subject of a rare disorder, only recently recognized by physicians, who have given it the cumbrous name of Dystocia adiposo-genitalis. One of the effects of this condition is to delay the process of the consolidation of the bones."[1]

The reign of **Sākarā,** the successor of Åmenḥetep IV, was short and unimportant, and he was followed by **Tutānkhåten,** who had married Ānkhesenpaåten, the third daughter of Åmenḥetep IV. His genealogy is uncertain, but he calls Åmenḥetep III his father in his inscription on the granite lion from Ṣulb, and it is probable that his statement is literally true. As soon as he became king he changed his name to **Tutānkhåmen** (his wife also changed hers to Ānkhesenpa-Åmen) and relinquished the feeble attempt which he had made to perpetuate his father-in-law's religion. He re-established the worship of Åmen, re-appointed his priests, made good what was ruined, and restored the name of Åmen in every important building from Memphis to Napata. He had a gold figure of Åmen cast for the sanctuary, and figures of Åmen and Ptaḥ made of gold and inlaid with precious stones, and new figures of the other gods were made for him and placed in their ruined shrines. In other words he restored to the priests of Åmen the property which his father-in-law had stolen from them and their god. The singing men and women and dancers and acrobats who were employed in the services of Åten were brought by him to Thebes, and when he had " purified " them he made them servants in the House of Åmen and in his own palace. This act of clemency was greatly appreciated by the Egyptians. During his short reign of five or six years he received the tribute of the Sûdân, and his faithful servant Ḥui[2] would have us believe that the Syrians also sent him gifts and tribute.[3] Of the circumstances of the death of Tutānkhåmen nothing is known, but he was probably still a young man when he died. And, judging by the state of confusion in which Lord Carnarvon and Mr. Carter found his funerary furniture in the tomb which they opened in the Valley of the Tombs of the Kings in Western Thebes, his death was untimely and unexpected. He seems to have been succeeded by the " divine father " **Ȧi,** , who had married Tī, the " chief nurse who had reared the god," *i.e.*, Åmenḥetep IV, . His reign was very short and no

[1] Elliot Smith, *Tutankhamen*, p. 84.

[2] See the reproductions of the scenes in his tomb in Lepsius, *Denkmäler*, Abth. III, Bll. 115–118 and 301–306, and the texts in Brugsch, *Thesaurus*, p. 1133 ff.

[3] The sole trustworthy authority for the acts of Tutānkhåmen is the great stele which he set up at Karnak, and which was discovered by Legrain in 1905. For the text see *Recueil de Travaux*, Vol. XXIX, 1907, pp. 162–173. A summary of its contents is given in my *Tutānkhåmen*, London, 1923, p. 3 ff.

Cast in bronze of the head of a portrait-statue of Tutānkh-âmen in the Egyptian Museum in Berlin; it is exhibited in the British Museum.

Seated figures of Khāmuast and his wife. XVIIIth dynasty. B.M. No. 2301.

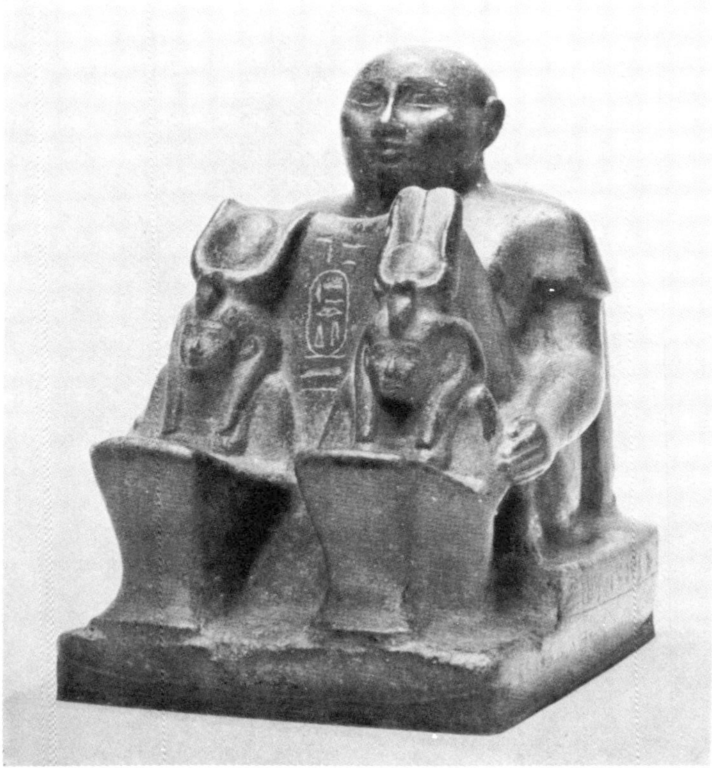

Seated figure of Ḥarua, an official of Queen Åmenårṭas holding figures of Hathor and Tefnut. XXVIth dynasty. B.M. No. 46699.

Statue of Isis and Osiris dedicated by Sha-shanq, an official of the high priestess of Åmen at Thebes. XXVIth dynasty. B.M. No. 1162.

details of it are known. He possessed two tombs, one at Åakhuten-åten and another at Thebes; he was buried in the latter, and his fine granite sarcophagus is still in it.

After Acherres, or Ancheres, who is presumably Åmenḥetep IV, Manetho gives as kings Rathos, Khebres, and Akherres, and next Armesses, or Armais; in this last-named we probably have **Ḥerem-ḥeb,** the successor of Åi. This wise and astute man was a native of Alabastronpolis, , in Upper Egypt, and a member of a family whose god was Åmen. According to an inscription at Turin[1] he was begotten by Åmen (like Ḥatshepsut and Åmenḥetep III), who clothed him with the "skin of the god." He was nominally a follower of Åten, and held command in the Delta under Åmen-ḥetep IV, with whom he was a favourite. He performed successfully some important business in Syria for this king, and was advanced from office to office until he became the "chief mouth" in Egypt and the deputy, or Wazîr, of the king. Under Tutānkh-åmen he became the *de facto* ruler of Egypt. The priests of Åmen made him marry Princess Mutnetchemet, a kinswoman of Nefertiti and Åmenḥetep IV, and as they had determined to make him king the marriage gave him a legal claim to the throne. When Åi died Ḥeremḥeb was taken to Thebes and crowned king, and he at once re-established the worship of Åmen on the old lines. He repaired the temples, filled the shrines with the sacred figures and objects of worship, endowed the temples and priests, and provided for the cleaning and maintenance of the sacred buildings. Ḥeremḥeb undertook no great wars of conquest, but at some time in his life he must have taken prisoner a number of chiefs of the Mediterranean or Syrian peoples, whose names are found at Karnak. He also directed a raid or campaign in Nubia to collect tribute, and he offered to Åmen gifts from Punt, to which country he sent an expedition. He was a wise and a just ruler, and spent the whole of his reign in righting wrongs, dispensing justice, removing fraud and corruption from the public services, and in bettering the condition of the people. This is proved by the Code of Laws which he had cut upon a huge stele about 16 feet 6 inches high and 10 feet wide and set up at Karnak, where it was discovered by Maspero in 1882.[2] When Ḥeremḥeb was an official over the Delta he had a tomb made for himself at Ṣaḳḳârah, and from it came the doorposts and stele in the British Museum.[3] But when he was king he had the usual rock-hewn tomb made for him in the Valley of the Tombs of the Kings, and this was opened and cleared out by Mr. Ayrton in

[1] See Birch, *Trans. Soc. Bibl. Arch.*, Vol. III, p. 486.

[2] For the text see Bouriant, *Recueil*, tom. VI, p. 41 ff.; Davis and Maspero, *The Tombs of Harmhabi and Touatānkhamanou*, London, 1912, p. 45 ff.; and Müller's translation in *Aeg. Zeit.*, 1888, p. 70 ff.

[3] Northern Egyptian Gallery, Nos. 461–463.

1908.[1] According to an inscription published by Birch[2] the actual reign of Ḥeremḥeb was 21 years, but in later times it seems to have been the custom to reckon the years of his reign from the death of Åmenḥetep IV, and the inscription of Mes, an official of Rameses II, actually speaks of the 59th year of the reign of Ḥeremḥeb.

In Manetho's list of the kings of the XVIIIth dynasty he makes a Rameses to be the successor of Ḥeremḥeb, but as this king was no other than the Rameses I of the monuments and the founder of a new dynasty, he is here made the first king of the XIXth dynasty.

The Nineteenth Dynasty. From Thebes [Memphis (?)].

The circumstances under which **Rameses I** ascended the throne are not known. He seems not to have been a kinsman of Ḥeremḥeb, but though there is no evidence that royal blood ran in his veins, it is probable that he had some legal claim to the throne. His devotion to Åmen is proved by the great Hall of Columns which he began to build at Karnak, and he may have owed his throne to the influence of the priesthood of Åmen, who supported his claim, whatever it was. He was well advanced in years when he began to reign, and too old to conduct campaigns personally, but he sent his son Seti to raid Nubia and collect tribute in the usual way, and, in the second year of the reign of Rameses, Seti set up a stele at Buhen (Wâdî Ḥalfah) to record his father's conquest of the country and his endowment of the temple at Buhen. That year Rameses died, and he was succeeded by Seti, the first king of this name on the throne of Egypt. The giving of this name " Seti " to his son suggests that Rameses I was a native of Lower Egypt, where Set was king of the gods, as Åmen-Rā was at Thebes. According to ancient mythological tradition Horus ruled Upper Egypt and Set the Delta, the former being the god of Good and the latter the god of Evil. In later times Set, or Setesh, became a Warrior-god, and as Sutekh was well known to Hittites and other peoples of Western Asia. **Seti I,** the follower of Set, calls himself Merenptaḥ, or " beloved of Ptaḥ," the great god of Memphis, which also suggests that the Delta was the home of the family of Rameses I. In the first year of his reign he marched against the Shasu people, and when they were defeated he attacked Northern Syria and captured a city called Kadesh, and conquered the Hittites, whose king was called Mursil (II), and the Amorites, and collected great spoil from all the chiefs throughout the country. He fought like the god Bāl, , *i.e.*, Baal, and his onset was like a flame of fire (lightning ?). Åmen of

[1] For a full description of it see the publication of T. Davis mentioned on p. 61, note 2.
[2] *Inscriptions in the Hieratic and Demotic Character*, pl. 14.

Thebes was not forgotten, and cedar wood for a new barge for him was brought back from Lebanon. Seti carried a great quantity of spoil to Thebes for presentation to Åmen, and during the celebration of the great festival he slaughtered a number of prisoners before the god. But Seti went no more into Western Asia, and he made a treaty with Mursil II, king of the Hittites, just as one of the kings of the XVIIIth dynasty had done with Shubbiluliuma (Sapalul), Mursil's predecessor. Either before or immediately after his Asiatic campaign, Seti I defeated the Libyans in Western Egypt and took from them much spoil, of which Åmen at Thebes received his share.

Having finished his wars Seti devoted his attention to the temples throughout Egypt. The great mines were opened and supplied material for their rebuilding or repair, and Seti, by sinking wells on the desert routes, succeeded in working the gold mines in the Eastern Desert and those near the Red Sea. He built the famous temple, which Strabo calls the "Memnonium," at Abydos, and placed in it the great King-List containing the names of the 76 kings whom he wished to commemorate. The bas-reliefs in this temple are masterpieces of Egyptian sculpture. He set up 79 columns in the Hall of Columns at Karnak, and built his funerary temple in Western Thebes, and made a wonderful rock-hewn tomb for himself in the Valley of the Tombs of the Kings. The series of bas-reliefs at Karnak which illustrate his campaigns in Western Asia and Libya form a magnificent record of his reign and are of great value. He died after a reign of about 19 years and was buried at Thebes, and his mummy was found at Dêr al-Baḥarî; his splendid alabaster sarcophagus is in Sir John Soane's Museum in Lincoln's Inn Fields.

Rameses II, the Rapsakes or Rampsês of Manetho, was the son of Seti I by Queen Tuȧa' , and when his father died he succeeded in removing his elder brother from his path and seizing the throne. He was over 30 years of age when he succeeded; he reigned about 67 years, and was a centenarian when he died. He married many wives, and reckoned his children by scores. He consolidated his position by going to Thebes and securing the support of the priests of Åmen and by continuing the building of the temple of Seti I at Abydos, and by restoring the tombs of the earlier kings at Abydos. Realizing that much gold would be necessary for carrying out his plans, he had wells dug in the desert between the Nile and the gold mines in the Wâdî al-'Alâḳi, and as water was found we may assume that the mines were regularly worked for some years at least. At the same time the Egyptians raided the Egyptian Sûdân and obtained much spoil; his two sons, Åmenḥerunamif and Khāmuast, assisted him in this work. Some of the painted bas-reliefs in the little rock temple at Bêt al-Walî, near Kalâbshah in Nubia, illustrate his raids in Nubia. In the fourth year of his reign he conducted a campaign in Palestine and Phoenicia, and so began his great attempt to win back for Egypt the countries which Thothmes III had conquered and added to her possessions. Memorials of this campaign are the three stelae which Rameses II had cut on the rocks near the mouth of the Dog River (Nahr al-Kalb) near Bêrût. In the fifth year of his reign Rameses II broke the treaty which his father had made with Mursil II, king of the Hittites, and collecting his forces—Egyptians, Sûdânî soldiers, and dwellers on the sea coast—marched into Phoenicia. Mursil II collected troops from his allies in the east, north and west, and his mighty host marched down the Valley of the Orontes to meet the Egyptians.

The Egyptian troops were divided into four regiments, which were named after the gods Åmen, Rā, Ptaḥ and Sutekh, respectively. When the two armies were near Kadesh on the Orontes, Rameses II, deceived by two Hittite spies who had been sent by Mursil II to tell him that the Hittite army was concentrated near Aleppo, marched on to Kadesh. Suddenly the Hittites, who were drawn up on the north of Kadesh, fell upon the Egyptians, who were unprepared, and succeeded in driving a wedge into the regiment of Rā and breaking it into two parts, and the Egyptian camp was captured by them. When Rameses, who was himself engaging the Hittites elsewhere, heard of this, he changed front, drove back in hot haste, retook the camp, and then fought his way through the enemy's formations, and in a most wonderful way succeeded in rejoining his army. A general attack on the enemy by the Egyptians followed, and the Hittites were beaten and put to flight. Many of them fled to the river and were drowned, and Mursil II, collecting his scattered forces, retreated; but the Egyptians were unable to follow up the advantage they had gained, and Rameses II returned to Egypt, apparently having failed to capture Kadesh.[1] The narrative by Rameses II of the battle sounds somewhat bombastic, but it is quite clear that it was the personal bravery of the king that gave the Egyptians the victory. On the death of Mursil II his son Mutallu reopened hostilities, and for 10 or 12 years Rameses II was actively engaged in battle with him, neither the Hittites nor the Egyptians gaining a decisive advantage. Khattusil (III), the Khetasar of the Egyptian texts, a son and successor of Mutallu, realizing that he could not drive the Egyptians out of Palestine, proposed a peace, and a Treaty of peace and alliance was drawn up as between equals,

[1] The hieroglyphic text that gives the Egyptian account of the battle will be found in Maspero's *Recueil*, tom. VIII, p. 126 ff., and the hieratic text of Pentaurt's account in Birch, *Select Papyri*, Vol. I, pll. XXIV–XXXIV; see also de Rougé, *Le Poème de Pentaour*, Paris, 1856. Good summaries will be found in Breasted's *Battle of Kadesh*, where a reconstruction of the battle is given, and in Hall, *History of the Near East*, p. 360.

in which Rameses and Khattusil undertook never to invade each other's territory. From this Treaty[1] it is clear that 15 years of almost constant fighting had in no way benefited either the Egyptians or the Hittites, and the former had to abandon finally all hope of regaining the countries in Western Asia which Thothmes III had conquered and of further tribute from Syria. Thirteen years later Rameses married a daughter of the Prince of Kheta, and she appears in a relief at Abu Simbel under the name of Urmaāneferurā.

In the years following his wars Rameses devoted himself to repairing the temples of Egypt, and in every building he touched he took care that his name should occupy a prominent position. He "usurped" the monuments in a shameless fashion, and as a result of his restorations the names of the founders in many cases disappear entirely. His greatest work is the famous rock-hewn temple, 185 feet long, at Abu Simbel, in Nubia, in which he was worshipped as a god. In front of this he set up four colossal granite statues of himself, each about 60 feet in height; close by it he built the temple of Hathor, with six statues, four of himself and two of his wife Nefertȧri-mertenmut. He made Tanis his capital and lived there. He practically rebuilt that city, and the gods Sutekh and Bār (Baal) and other Syrian and Hittite gods were worshipped in its temples. The Stele of 400 years suggests that the city was founded by Nubti, a Hyksos king. Rameses built at Thebes the Ramesseum, which Diodorus calls the "Tomb of Osymandyas," and Strabo the "Memnonium,"[2] and completed the Hall of Columns, and made additions to the Temple of Luxor, in front of which he set up several statues of himself and two granite obelisks, each about 80 feet high. According to Exodus i, 11, he built the city of Pithom, the ruins of which are now called Tall al-Maskhuṭah, in the Eastern Delta. Rameses appears to have been an arrogant, self-assertive and vain man, full of brute courage in his early manhood, and obstinate and determined. His charging the Hittites almost single-handed at the Battle of Kadesh was a splendid exploit, but he does not appear to have been a good tactician or a good soldier or statesman. He added no territory to Egypt, and during his long reign his country steadily declined. His mummy was found at Dêr al-Baḥarî and was unrolled by Maspero on June 1st, 1886.

Merenptaḥ (Menephthah), the Ammenephthes of Manetho, was the son of Rameses II by Queen Ȧstnefert; he was co-regent with his father for several years, and was no longer a young man when he ascended the throne. During the first four years of his

[1] It was drawn up in Egyptian and Hittite, and the Hittite version, judging from the tablets found at Boghaz Kyöi, was written in cuneiform. The Egyptian text has been edited and skilfully handled by Müller in *Mittheil. Vorderas. Ges.*, Bd. V, No. 5, and both the Egyptian and cuneiform texts are discussed by Gardiner and Langdon in *Jnl. Eg. Arch.*, Vol. VI, p. 179 ff.

[2] The colossal but very ugly statue of himself which he set up there was 60 feet high, and weighed at least 885 tons.

reign the Libyans seized some of the Oases and other Egyptian territories and became so bold that they invaded the suburbs of Memphis and Heliopolis. They were assisted by several Mediterranean peoples,[1] and even Europeans from the mainland, and their object was to occupy the Delta permanently. In the fifth year of his reign Merenptaḥ fortified his cities and collected a great army and set out to do battle with the Libyans and their allies. The armies met at Perȧr-t, , a place probably near the Wâdî Naṭrûn, and the Libyan host was led by Maraiui, , the son of Ṭeṭ, king of Libya. Cheered by a dream in which Ptaḥ gave him a sword, and a consciousness of the good-will of Ȧmen of Thebes and of Set, the god of the Delta, Merenptaḥ attacked the enemy boldly, and according to the Egyptian chronicler fearful carnage ensued. The battle raged for six hours and the Egyptians slew the enemy by thousands. The king of Libya fled, casting away his arms and sandals and garments as he went, and his camp fell into the hands of the king of Egypt. Over 6,000 Libyans were slain and their bodies mutilated, 9,376 were made prisoners, and among the spoil were 9,111 swords, 126 horses, 120,314 weapons of various kinds, etc. The battle was decisive and the Egyptian victory complete. Merenptaḥ had crushed the rebellion that broke out in Palestine soon after the death of Rameses II and, having overcome all his foes, he determined to set up a stele to commemorate his conquests. He took the large stele which Ȧmenḥetep III had set up in his temple in Western Thebes, and on its back he had engraved the text which is now generally known as the "Hymn of Victory," and which is a useful supplement to his historical inscriptions at Karnak. He had this stele taken to his funerary temple, where it was found by Petrie in 1896.[2] Special interest was aroused in the text because the **Israelites,** , are mentioned for the first time in an Egyptian inscription, and the monument has therefore been called the **Israel Stele.** Merenptaḥ says in it that the princes [everywhere] grovel before him and do homage to him, that the Nine Nations of the Bow (Nubians) are crushed, Libya is laid waste, Kheta has been pacified, Canaan is brought to misery, Ascalon and Gezer have been captured, Inuama has been annihilated, the Israelites

[1] The identifications first made by de Rougé have been amplified and discussed by H. R. Hall in his *Oldest Civilization of Greece*, p. 173, and in the *Annual of the British School at Athens*, Vol. VIII, p. 173, and in his *Ancient History*, p. 377. His latest views on the *Peoples of the Sea* will be found in the Memorial Volumes of Champollion and Ramsay.

[2] For the text see Spiegelberg, *Aeg. Zeit.*, Bd. XXXIV, p. 1 ff., and his subsequent edition of it in Petrie, *Six Temples*, pll. 13 and 14. Valuable notes on it were given by Müller in Maspero's *Recueil*, Vol. XX, p. 31 ff.

are wasted and have no seed, and Khal (Palestine) has become the widow[1] of Egypt. The mention of the Israelites in Merenptaḥ's Hymn of Victory has a bearing on one of the theories about **the Exodus** which has been widely held. According to it the Exodus took place in the reign of Merenptaḥ (Rameses II being regarded as the " Pharaoh of the oppression ") and he was the king who was said to have been drowned[2] in the Sea of Reeds, יַם־סוּף, which early Christian tradition identified with the Red Sea. But if the Israelites were settled in Palestine and were conquered by Merenptaḥ, it is quite clear that they cannot have left Egypt during his reign and arrived in Palestine after 40 years' wandering in the desert. Though there are many points in favour of the view that the Exodus took place in Merenptaḥ's reign, the evidence concerning an earlier occupation of Palestine by the Hebrews, which is supplied chiefly by the Tall al-'Amârnah tablets, shows that it must be abandoned. And it also makes it nearly certain that the Khabiru and the Sa-Gaz peoples, who laid Canaan waste in the reign of Åmenḥetep and took possession of the country, were the Hebrews and the mixed desert tribes who joined them. There must have been some incident in the history of the house of Jacob which gave rise to the story of the Exodus as we have it in the Bible, but exactly what it was no man can say. The narrative in the Book of Exodus was written long after the event by one who only knew of it by hearsay or tradition and who was ignorant of the geography of the Isthmus of Suez. The character of his story is stamped once and for all by his statement that there went out " 600,000 on foot *that were* men, beside children. And a mixed multitude went up also with them ; and flocks and herds, *even* very much cattle " (Exodus xii, 37, 38). Josephus seems to have regarded the expulsion of the Hyksos as the Exodus of the Bible, but this was probably due to racial vanity and his desire to prove that the ancestors of his nation were at one time kings of Egypt.[3] The fact seems to be that the original story of the Exodus, whatever it was, has been so mishandled by editors and scribes that it is no longer recognizable, but the local colour that still survives convinces me that an Exodus of some kind did actually take place. The account of the **Route of the Exodus** in the Book of Exodus is as difficult to understand as the story of

[1] Here there is a play on the word for " widow " and the name of the country.

[2] His mummy was found at Dêr al-Baḥarî and is now in the Museum in Cairo. Those who believed that he was drowned declared that his body was recovered from the sea, and that it bore on it physical indications that he had been drowned.

[3] The various theories about the time of the Exodus have been discussed and analysed by Peet, *Egypt and the Old Testament*, London, 1922, and the *pros* and *cons* are set forth clearly by Hall, *Ancient History*, p. 404 ff. It is possible that a number of Semites fled from Egypt on the death of Rameses II, and that their flight was regarded as an exodus by later Jewish writers.

the Exodus itself, and has been the subject of much controversy, for the writer was ignorant of the geography of the Isthmus of Suez and the Peninsula of Sinai and of the physical conditions of the neighbouring country generally. The literature on the subject is considerable, but the two principal theories about the route of the Israelites after leaving Egypt are well set forth by Naville (*Jnl. of Eg. Arch.*, Vol. X, 1924, p. 11) and Peet (*Egypt and the Old Testament*, London, 1922).

On the death of Merenptaḥ a period of anarchy began. The first king who succeeded him was **Ȧmenmeses,** a man of the people, who had neither right nor claim to the throne. The length of his reign is unknown. He was succeeded by **Seti II Merenptaḥ** and **Saptaḥ Merenptaḥ,**[1] but the order of the reigns of these two kings is doubtful. It is probable that Seti II followed Saptaḥ Merenptaḥ. Saptaḥ married Ta-Usrit, who is probably the Thuôris of Manetho, and if this be so this Queen must in later times have been regarded as a woman of outstanding ability. Saptaḥ reigned at least six years, during which the Nubian tribute was duly paid. His funerary temple and that of his queen were excavated by Petrie in 1896. The mummy of the king was found in the tomb of Ȧmenḥetep II. The queen's tomb was usurped by Seti II. The last king of the dynasty was Seti III Merenptaḥ, who had been appointed "Prince of Kash" by Saptaḥ, but his reign was short, and however capable he may have been as a ruler of "naked Blacks" he failed to benefit Egypt during his reign. He had no legal successor, and when he died the great nobles fell to quarrelling among themselves, and as each did what he pleased, there being no central authority to control them, the country fell into a state of confusion almost unparalleled. A certain Syrian official in Egypt watched his opportunity and, having made himself Dictator, ruled the Egyptians in a cruelly despotic fashion. Rameses III, in describing the condition of the country before he came to the throne, calls this man "**Ȧrsu,** , a Syrian,"[2] , but whether Ȧrsu is a proper name, or an abusive epithet, or two words meaning that the Syrian "made himself," as Spiegelberg thinks, is not decided. The Syrian was overthrown by **Setnekht,** who appears to have been a kinsman of Rameses II; he ascended the throne and reigned for about one year. On his death he was succeeded by his son Rameses III.

The Twentieth Dynasty.

Rameses III, the Rhampsinitos of Herodotus,[3] the son of Setnekht, reigned 31 years. In the early years of his reign a great confederation of peoples from Philistia, Cyprus, Crete and the

[1] In the inscriptions at Wâdî Ḥalfah he is called RAMESSU SAPTAḤ.
[2] In the Great Harris Papyrus, ed. Birch, pl. 75, l. 4.
[3] See Wiedemann, *Herodots Zweites Buch*, Leipzig, 1890, p. 445.

northern shores of the Mediterranean Sea attacked Egypt by land and by sea, but Rameses fought them on land with his army, and on sea with his ships, and gained a great victory. About 12,000 of their dead warriors were mutilated, and a great number of prisoners and spoil were taken. Fired by his success, Rameses led his army into Phoenicia and Syria, and was vain enough to try to repeat the exploits of Thothmes and to try to regain Egypt's lost possessions in those countries, but the expedition was a failure in spite of the spoil which he brought back to Egypt. Soon after his return the Libyans again attacked Egypt, but Rameses defeated them and slew about 2,175 of them. Among the spoil were 1,205 men and their commander and five officers, swords of extraordinary length, bows, quivers, chariots and horses and asses, and much cattle. A little later he marched against the tribes who lived in and about Mount Seir and had revolted, and reduced them to subjection. The remaining years of his reign he spent in developing the commerce of his country, and Egypt gained more from trade during his reign than she could have obtained by conquest. Rameses maintained two fleets, one in the Red Sea and one in the Mediterranean Sea, and thus was able to protect native mercantile shipping in both seas. To assist the caravans travelling to and from Syria he built a great reservoir and sank a well at Āina, and enclosed it with strong walls. He developed the copper and malachite mines of Sinai, he encouraged the trade between Egypt and the East viâ the canal from Memphis and the Red Sea, and his ships sailed freely to the Somali Coast and Punt and the ports of Arabia that were frequented by ships from the Far East. His wealth made it easy for him to treat his subjects generously, and as there was no brigandage in the country it was possible "for an Egyptian woman to walk fearlessly whithersoever she pleased, for neither man nor woman among the people would molest her" (Harris Papyrus, pl. 78, ll. 9–12). His benefactions to the great priesthoods were magnificent in character, and to the temples of Thebes, Heliopolis and Memphis, he gave, among other things, 113,433 men, 490,386 oxen, 1,071,780 aruras of land, 514 vineyards and orchards, 88 boats, 160 towns in Egypt and 9 in Palestine, 324,750 bundles of fodder, 71,000 bundles of flax, 426,965 water-fowl, 2,382,650 sacks of fruit, 353,919 fat geese, 5,279,552 bushels of corn, 6,272,431 loaves of bread. He built the so-called "Pavilion" and the great temple of Madînat Habû at Thebes; a beautiful little palace in the old Hyksos town of Tall al-Yahûdîyah in the Delta, and a splendid tomb in Western Thebes, commonly known as Bruce's Tomb and the Tomb of the Harper. For the conspiracy to dethrone him see Devéria, *Le Papyrus Judiciaire*, Paris, 1868. Rameses III was followed by a series of 9 kings, each of whom bore the name of Rameses. **Rameses IV** was co-regent with his father for 4 years. He built a road from the Nile to the Red Sea, and among the 8,368 workmen and others were 800

Āperu, , whom some have identified as Hebrews. He was entirely in the hands of the priesthood of Ȧmen and gave lavishly to their god. **Rameses V** reigned about 4 years, and the reigns of **Rameses VI–VIII** were unimportant. **Rameses IX,** who reigned about 18 years, instituted a prosecution of the robbers who were pillaging the royal tombs and breaking up their mummies; the papyrus giving an account of their doings is in the British Museum[1] (Abbott Papyrus No. 10221). **Rameses X** continued the prosecution of the tomb robbers. **Rameses XI** is perhaps the king referred to in the Story of the Possessed Princess of Bekhten, and during the reign of **Rameses XII** the high priest of Ȧmen, Ḥer-Ḥer, sent Unuȧmen to Lebanon to fetch cedar wood to make a new barge for Ȧmen.[2] As each of these Rameses kings reigned, more and more power passed into the hands of the priests of Ȧmen, and when, after a reign of about 28 years, Rameses XII died, Ḥer-Ḥer, the high priest of Ȧmen, seized the throne and called himself king of all Egypt. But neither he nor his successors were acknowledged in the Delta, and the nobles there set up a dynasty of kings of their own. At the same time a great merchant prince in the Delta, called Nesibanebṭeṭ, proclaimed himself king of Lower Egypt. Thus we have, for the XXIst dynasty, kings at Thebes and kings at Tanis, though Manetho only recognizes "seven Tanite kings." The Priest-kings of Thebes were: **Ḥer-Ḥer, Pinetchem I, Menkheperrā, Pinetchem II** and **Pisebkhānu II**; the kings of Tanis were **Nesibanebṭeṭ, Pisebkhānu I, Ȧmenemȧpt, Saȧmen** and **Ḥer-Pisebkhānu.**[3] Ḥer-Ḥer and Nesibanebṭeṭ, the Smendes of Manetho, were contemporaries. Pinetchem I, the Nefercherês of Manetho, son of the high priest Piānkh, married Maātkarā, daughter of Pisebkhānu I, the Psusenês of Manetho, and Pinetchem II and Saȧmen were contemporaries. Ȧmenemȧpt is probably the Amenophthis of Manetho, but Osorchor and Psinaches are difficult to identify. Osorchor may represent Neterkheperrā, a part of the prenomen of Saȧmen. The reigns of all these kings are historically unimportant, and the monuments afford little information about them. Our knowledge of the reigns of the Priest-kings at Thebes is derived chiefly from the dockets that they inscribed on the royal mummies, which they were compelled to remove from their tombs to hiding-places at Dêr al-Baḥarî and in the tomb of Amenḥetep II and elsewhere. The dockets supply the dates when the mummies were repaired or removed, and give, in each case, the name of the king who undertook this pious work.

[1] See Birch, *Select Papyri*, Vol. II, pll. 1–8; Chabas, *Mélanges*, tom. II; Maspero, *Une Enquête Judiciaire*, Paris, 1871; and Newberry, *Amherst Papyri*, p. 24.

[2] For the text and translations see Golénischeff in Vol. XXI of Maspero's *Recueil*, and Erman in *Aeg. Zeit.*, Bd. XXXVIII, p. 1 ff.

[3] It was probably a daughter of this king whom Solomon married.

The Twenty-Second Dynasty. From Bubastis.

On the death of Pisebkhānu II the throne was seized by **Shashanq (I)**, or **Sheshenq,** a man of Libyan descent, whose grandfather had married Meḥtenusekh, high priestess of Åmen. Shashanq made his son **Auput** high priest of Åmen, and some think that the descendants of Ḥer-Ḥer then migrated to Napata, where they attempted to establish the cult of their god Åmen on the lines which they had followed at Thebes. Auput continued the work of repairing and removing the royal mummies, a work pleasing to Åmen of Thebes. Shashanq is the **Shishak** of Manetho and of I Kings xiv, 25, II Chron. xii, 2, 5, 7, 9, and the principal event in his life was his invasion of Palestine and the capture of Jerusalem, which took place probably in the 16th year of his reign and in the 5th year of the reign of Rehoboam. He carried off much gold and silver, and the shields and bucklers of Solomon, and the golden quivers which David had taken from the king of Zobah. He returned to Egypt in triumph and had an account of the campaign cut upon the walls of the second pylon at Karnak. Here he gives a list of 133 districts and towns in Palestine which he had conquered.

Shashanq I was succeeded by his son **Osorkon (I),** the Osorthôn of Manetho, who married Maātkarā, the daughter of Pisebkhānu, the last king of the XXIst dynasty. Champollion identified him with "Zerah the Ethiopian," who invaded Palestine with one million men and 300 chariots (II Chron. xiv, 9 ff.) and was defeated by Asa, king of Judah. Of **Teklet (I),** the son and successor of Osorkon I, nothing of importance is known. **Osorkon II** built the great Festival Hall of the Temple of Bast at Bubastis (Pibeseth), on the site of the sanctuary of the temple which had been built there by Pepi I, a king of the VIth dynasty; it was excavated by Naville in 1887–89. The relations between Palestine and Egypt in the reign of Osorkon II were friendly, but he had no great authority anywhere outside Egypt. Some have identified him with Zerah the Ethiopian (II Chron. xiv, 9) and, relying on the statement made by Shalmaneser III (B.C. 859–824)[1] that there were 1,000 men of the Muṣrai () present at the Battle of Ḳarḳara (B.C. 854), have said that the king of Egypt sent a force to help the Khatti and their allies against the king of Assyria. But the "Muṣrai" were natives of a district near Khatti land, and not Egyptians. The reign of Osorkon II is memorable because of a very high inundation of the Nile, which in the third year of his reign flooded the temple of Karnak to the depth of several feet. The remaining kings of this dynasty, **Shashanq II, III and IV** (?), **Teklet II** and **Pamai,** were unimportant, and their correct order has not been satisfactorily decided. For the arguments see Gauthier, *Livre des Rois*, tom. III, p. 351.

[1] See the King-List in *Guide to the Assyrian and Babylonian Antiquities*, 3rd edition, p. 254.

The Twenty-Third Dynasty. From Bubastis.

The first king of this dynasty was **Peṭabast,** the Petoubatês of Manetho, who reigned about 23 years. He ruled Upper Egypt and Thebes, for the descendants of the Priest-kings forsook Thebes when Shashanq I united the South and the North, and migrated to Napata, which had been the capital of Egypt's Nubian Kingdom since the time of Åmenḥetep III, and began to reign as they had reigned at Thebes. Later Peṭabast seems to have appointed a viceroy, perhaps the high priest of Åmen, over Thebes, called **Auput-meri-Amen,** who styles himself , "King of the South and the North," for in an inscription[1] on the quay wall at Thebes the 16th year of the reign of Peṭabast is made equivalent to the 2nd year of the reign of this Auput. In the 19th year of Peṭabast the name of a high priest of Åmen, and not that of Auput, is given. Peṭabast figures in a historical romance written in demotic which has been edited by Krall.[2] Peṭabast was succeeded by **Osorkon III,** who reigned about 20 years, but his rule over Thebes was interrupted by a great invasion of Nubians, who were incited thereto by the priests of Åmen at Napata. The king of Napata at that time was **Piānkhi,** son of Kashta and the Egyptian princess Shepenupt, the daughter of Osorkon III. In the twenty-first year of his reign Piānkhi heard that **Tafnekht,** a great noble of Saïs, having overcome all the opposition of the chiefs in the Delta and part of Upper Egypt, had made himself, to all intents and purposes, King of Egypt. He was supported by the priesthoods of Ptaḥ of Memphis and Rā of Heliopolis; and his power was great, and Osorkon III was unable to suppress him. Piānkhi, seeing that his authority and possessions in Upper Egypt, over which he claimed sovereignty so far north as Herakleopolis, were jeopardized, determined to reduce Tafnekht, and forthwith set out on his great expedition to Egypt. In less than one year the rebel chiefs submitted to him and paid him tribute, and even Tafnekht took an oath of allegiance to him, his gods being witnesses for the sincerity of his words. Piānkhi returned to Napata laden with spoil, and set up in the temple of Åmen a huge granite stele, on which was inscribed a detailed account[3] of his expedition into Egypt, and of the splendid success which he had achieved. The narrative is usually clear and is couched in simple words, and it gives the impression that Piānkhi, though a fierce fighter, was a generous foe and a man who would take no mean

[1] Discovered and published by Legrain, *Aeg. Zeit.*, Bd. XXXIV, p. 111 ff.

[2] In Vol. VI of the Collection of the Archduke Rainer.

[3] The text was first published by Mariette, *Monuments Divers*, pll. 1–6; a handy edition of it, with an English translation, will be found in Budge, *Annals of Nubian Kings*, p. 1 ff. For other English translations see Breasted, *Ancient Records*, Vol. IV, p. 418; Brugsch, *Egypt under the Pharaohs*, Vol. II, p. 240.

advantage of a stricken enemy. His sincere reverence for his god, his respect for Nemlet's wives and daughters, and his royal rage when he found that his horses had suffered from want of food, proclaim the piety, courtesy and compassion of this great Nubian warrior. Osorkon III, who had submitted to Piānkhi, was permitted to renew his rule over Thebes, and with one Teklet he founded a chapel there. Manetho includes in the XXIIIrd dynasty two kings called **Psammus** and **Zêt,** saying that they reigned 10 and 31 years respectively. These kings have not yet been identified from the monuments. Some think Psammus was the son of Osorkon III, which is possible. As to Zêt, several identifications have been proposed,[1] and Lauth and Hall think he may be Kashta, the grandfather of Tirhaḳah.[2]

The Twenty-Fourth Dynasty. From Saïs.

The only king of this dynasty was Bakenrenef, who assumed as his prenomen Uaḥkarā 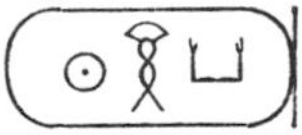, which the Greeks corrupted into **Bocchoris** ; he was the son of Tafnekht of Saïs, whose revolt brought Piānkhi into Egypt, and reigned six years. Diodorus says (I, 34) he was one of the six lawgivers of Egypt,[3] with a powerful mind and a weak body ; Aelian thought little of him.[4] Manetho says that in his reign a sheep spoke, and Aelian says that this sheep had eight legs,[5] two tails, two heads, and four horns. Krall found a reference to this sheep in a demotic papyrus.[6] Eusebius says that Bocchoris was burnt alive (Mai and Zohrab, *Chron. Armen.*, pp. 104, 318).

The Twenty-Fifth Dynasty. Nubians.

The first of the three kings of this dynasty was **Shabaka,** the Sabbakôn of Manetho, who reigned about 12 years. He was a contemporary of Sargon II, king of Assyria (B.C. 722–705), and some think that Sib'e, 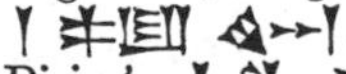, the TURDAN, or Egyptian commander, and the Pi-ir-'u , *i.e.*, Pharaoh, who paid tribute to Sargon II, and the So סוא of II Kings xvii, 4, and Shabaka are one and the same person. But the Assyrians, at least in Ashurbanipal's time, were quite familiar with Shabaka's name, which they wrote Sha-ba-ku-u, 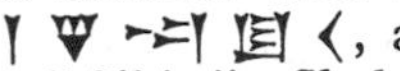, and there seems no reason why it should appear as " Sib'e." Shabaka must

[1] They are summarized in my *History of Egypt*, Vol. VI, p. 116.

[2] Hall, *Ancient History*, p. 491.

[3] The other five being Mnevis, Sasyches, Sesostris, Amasis and Darius, the father of Xerxes.

[4] *De Nat. Animalium*, XI, xi (ed. Didot, p. 191).

[5] "A lamb with eight legs has been born on a South Wales farm."—*Times*, March 24th, 1916, p. 5.

[6] See his *Grundriss*, p. 151, and his *Festgaben für M. Büdinger*, p. 3 ff.

have had communications with Sargon II, for two seals stamped with his name were found at Nineveh.[1]

Shabaka was succeeded by his son **Shabataka,** who reigned 12 years. When Sennacherib, king of Assyria (B.C. 705–681), attacked Palestine in his third campaign, he scattered and put to flight at the Battle of Altaḳu (the Eltekeh of Joshua xix, 44) the countless host of bowmen and chariots and horses, which the king of Milukhkhi had sent to oppose him. He captured the sons of the king of Egypt, took Altaḳu and Tamna, and then besieged and captured Jerusalem. Very little information about Shabataka is given by the monuments, and how he died is not known, but an ancient tradition says that after he had reigned 12 years he was murdered by Tirhâḳâh because he had allowed his troops to be defeated at the Battle of Altaḳu.

Taharqa, the Tirhâḳâh of the Bible and Tarkos of Manetho, succeeded Shabataka, and reigned about 25 years (B.C. 689–663); some interesting details of his early life are given on a stele which he set up at Tanis.[2] He built a rock-hewn temple at Jabal Barkal (Napata) about 120 feet long, with a porch and a courtyard, and several smaller sanctuaries in the "Holy Mountain." Two colossal statues of Bes decorate the pillars of the hypostyle hall. At Thebes he repaired and added to several of the old buildings. All the histories of Egypt state that during his reign Sennacherib set out to invade Egypt, and Josephus (*Antiquities* X, i, 4–5) says that he was engaged in besieging Pelusium, but that when he heard that Tirhâḳâh was marching against him he departed from Egypt. Josephus goes on to say that when Sennacherib returned to Jerusalem he found that God had smitten his army with a pestilence, and that 185,000 men died on the first night. He also repeats the story of Herodotus to the effect that field mice ate up the bows and quivers and the leathern handles of the shields of the Assyrians, and that the next morning, when they were in full flight, many of them fell. It is clear that Josephus, relying on the Bible narrative, believed that Sennacherib's army of 185,000 men was miraculously destroyed in a single night. Now it is obvious that this disaster could not have happened to Sennacherib's host during the campaign when he captured Jerusalem and returned to Nineveh in triumph, for that campaign was highly successful. Therefore historians have been driven to assume that Sennacherib undertook a second campaign that was specially directed against Egypt, but thanks to the researches[3] of Mr. Sidney Smith, of the British Museum, we now know that Sennacherib never made this assumed second expedition, and that

[1] See Bezold, *Catalogue*, p. 1784.

[2] See Birch, *Monuments of the Reign of Tirhakah*, in *Trans. Soc. Bibl. Arch.*, Vol. VII, p. 194 ff.

[3] See Smith, Sidney, *Babylonian Historical Texts*, London, 1924, Section I, the *Esarhaddon Chronicle*, p. 1 ff., plates 1 and 2.

the king whose army was destroyed was not Sennacherib, but Esarhaddon, and that the destruction of that army was caused by a STORM, and not by field mice or pestilence. The proof of this statement is obtained from a chronological tablet, No. 25091, in the British Museum, which describes the Egyptian campaigns of Esarhaddon. This tablet says :—

> In the 6th year (of Esarhaddon's reign, B.C. 675) the troops of Assyria went to Egypt, they fled before a great storm.
>
> In the 7th year (B.C. 674) on the 8th Adar, the troops of Assyria fought against the city *Sha amelie*.

Now the Babylonian Chronicle merely says concerning B.C. 675 that "The Assyrian went to Egypt," and does not mention a storm. It goes on to say that in the 7th year of Esarhaddon (B.C. 674) the army of Assyria fought against Egypt ; in the tenth year (B.C. 671) Esarhaddon took Memphis ; its king (Tirhâḳâh) escaped, but his brother was taken prisoner and the city was looted. In the twelfth year (B.C. 669) Esarhaddon went to Egypt, " fell sick on the way and died on Marcheswân 10th." The Babylonian Chronicle mentions the expedition of B.C. 675, but the recently translated tablet shows why it was without results. Having ordered the investment of Jerusalem and Tyre, Esarhaddon marched against Pelusium,[1] Egypt's chief fortress on her north-east frontier. He was overtaken by a storm—that is to say, the terrible *habûb*, which is really a sand blast driven by a desert wind travelling 60 or 70 miles an hour, that suffocates man and beast, and tears up tents and buries an encampment in an hour or two. The number of the men who perished as given in the Bible must be an exaggeration, but as the storm wrecked Esarhaddon's plans for the year his army must have suffered severely. In 671 he captured Memphis, received the submission of the nobles, and having appointed twenty governors to rule the provinces of his new kingdom, returned to Nineveh. Soon after his departure Tirhâḳâh appeared again in Egypt, drove out the governors appointed by Esarhaddon, and, having entered Memphis, proclaimed himself king of all Egypt. Hearing of these doings Esarhaddon, in the twelfth year of his reign (B.C. 669), set out again for Egypt, probably with the intention of punishing Tirhâḳâh, but he died on the way.

Esarhaddon was succeeded by Ashurbanipal (B.C. 668–626), who, as soon as he heard of the deposition of Esarhaddon's governors, set out for Egypt and, having defeated Tirhâḳâh's forces at Karbaniti, occupied Memphis. Tirhâḳâh fled a second time, probably to Thebes. Ashurbanipal sent a force up the Nile to Thebes, whereupon Mentuemḥat, the governor, submitted, and Tirhâḳâh fled to Napata. Ashurbanipal recalled and re-appointed the governors

[1] Smith, *op. cit.*, p. 10.

who had been appointed by his father,[1] and returned to Nineveh with great spoil. At once Tirhâḳâh reappeared, and plotted the destruction of the Assyrian garrison in Egypt with Sharruludari, governor of Tanis, Nekau, governor of Saïs, and others. The plot was discovered, and when Ashurbanipal heard of it he sent another army to Egypt; the revolt was crushed mercilessly, and Sharruludari and Nekau were sent in chains to Nineveh. The former was put to death there, but Nekau was pardoned and entreated honourably, and sent back to Egypt loaded with gifts, and his son, to whom the Assyrian name of Nabûshezibani was given, was made governor of Athribis. A few years later Tirhâḳâh died, and we may note that in an inscription found at Karnak he claims sovereignty over Khati Land, Assyria, Libya, Western Asia and the Eastern Deserts.

Tirhâḳâh was succeeded, B.C. 663, by **Tanutâmen,**[2] "lord of the two horns," , a Nubian who had been his co-regent for some years. Under the inspiration of a dream[3] he marched into Egypt, seized Memphis, and slaughtered the Assyrian garrison. Nekau of Saïs was killed, but his son Psemtek escaped to Assyria. When these things were reported to Ashurbanipal in Nineveh he set out for Egypt, and when Tanutâmen heard of his arrival he fled to Thebes. The chiefs of the Delta promptly submitted to Ashurbanipal, who left Memphis and followed Tanutâmen to Thebes. Tanutâmen then fled to Kipkipi (Ḳepqepa ?), and Thebes fell into the hands of the Assyrians, who plundered temples and houses alike, and stripped the city of everything that had value and could be carried away. They then burnt the city and left it a smoking ruin, and they carried off so much spoil, to say nothing of men, women and children and horses, that the king himself says that he returned to Nineveh with " a full hand." Thebes never recovered from the punishment that Ashurbanipal inflicted upon it.

The Twenty-Sixth Dynasty. From Saïs.

The first king of this dynasty was **Psemtek (I),** or Psammitichos, the son of Nekau, the governor of Saïs who had been pardoned by Ashurbanipal, and he reigned 54 years, counting from the time when

[1] For their names and cities see Smith, G., *History of Assurbanipal*, p. 48 ff.; *Aeg. Zeit.*, 1872, p. 29 ff.; Steindorff, *Beiträge zur Assyriologie*, Vol. I, p. 595 ff. A list of names in cuneiform, with their probable Egyptian equivalents, will be found in Budge, *History of Egypt*, Vol. VI, p. 172.

[2] I have shown in my History of Egypt (Vol. VI, p. 165) that the Assyrian transcript of this name is TAN-DA-MA-NI-E; Tanutâmen was a nephew of Tirhâḳâh.

[3] A copy of the text made from a cast of the stele recording it which was found at Jabal Barkal is given by Budge, with an English translation in *Annals of Nubian Kings*, p. 71 ff. The text was first published by Mariette, *Mon. Div.*, pl. 7.

he was reinstated by the king of Assyria. He married Shepenupt, a daughter of Piānkhi, and so legalized his claim to the throne of Egypt. His daughter Nitaqert (Nitocris) was adopted by Shepenupt, a sister of Tirhâḳâh, and thus was able to inherit her property legally. He obtained the throne by the help of Ionian and Carian mercenaries. He trusted to the garrisons that he had established at Elephantine, Pelusium, Daphnae and Marea to protect his country against the Nubians, Arabians and Libyans, and devoted himself to the development of the commerce of Egypt. He built the large side-gallery to the Serapeum at Ṣaḳḳârah. A great revival of art and sculpture took place in his reign, and the best works of the Old Kingdom were chosen as models. In 612, two years before the death of Psemtek I, the **Fall of Nineveh** took place; we owe the discovery of this fact to Mr. C. J. Gadd, of the British Museum.[1]

Psemtek I was succeeded by his son **Nekau,** the Pharaoh Nechoh of II Kings xxiii, 29, II Chron. xxxv, 20, and Jeremiah xlvi, 2, who reigned at least 16 years. He maintained a large army, which contained many Greeks and Carians, and he encouraged commerce in every way, keeping one fleet of ships in the Mediterranean and another in the Red Sea. He tried to remake the old canal which ran from Memphis to the head of the Gulf of Suez, but though he employed 120,000 men on the work he did not finish it.[2] Early in his reign he collected a large army and marched into Palestine and, having vanquished Josiah, king of Judah, in the Battle of Megiddo, became practically master of the country. A few years later he went up to Carchemish to fight against the Babylonians and Medes,[3] who were led by Nebuchadrezzar II, and was utterly defeated and obliged to retreat in hot haste to Egypt.

Psemtek II, son of Nekau, is said to have made an expedition into Nubia, and to have reached the town of Kerkis, near Wâdî Ḥalfah, but the monuments say little about him. The famous Greek inscription on the broken statue of Rameses II at Abu Simbel dates from his reign.[4]

Uahȧbrā, the Hophra of Jeremiah xliv, 30, and the Apries of the Greeks, succeeded Psemtek II and reigned 19 years. He made an expedition into Phoenicia and captured Tyre and Sidon, but he gave no effective help to Zedekiah in Jerusalem, and the city was taken by Nebuchadrezzar II. Apries sent by request a number of Egyptians to help the chief Adikran against the Cyrenaeans, but as a result of their defeat and slaughter by the Cyrenaeans a rebellion broke out in Egypt, the people declaring that Apries had wilfully

[1] For the text and translation of the Babylonian Chronicle see his *Fall of Nineveh*, London, 1923.

[2] It was finished by Darius I, was re-dug by Trajan in the IInd century A.D., and repaired or re-dug by ʻAmr ibn al-ʻÂṣ about A.D. 640.

[3] See Gadd, *The Fall of Nineveh*, p. 7, note 1.

[4] See Krall, *Grundriss*, p. 177; Wiedemann, *Aeg. Gesch.*, p. 631 f.

sent their countrymen to death. Apries sent a general called Ȧāḥmes (Amasis) to quell the rebellion, but the rebels proclaimed him king, and Apries was obliged to make him his co-regent. A few years later Apries collected an army of mercenaries and attacked Amasis, but he was defeated and was eventually murdered by his own followers.[1] There is no proof that Nebuchadrezzar II invaded Egypt, either during the reign of Apries or of his successor.

Ȧāḥmes (Amasis) **II,** the successor of Apries, reigned 44 years. He married Tentkheta, and became by her the father of Psemtek III, and was the official husband of Ānkhnesneferȧbrā, the high priestess at Thebes. During his long reign he repaired many of the temples in all parts of Egypt, especially at Thebes, Abydos, Memphis and Saïs. He founded Naukratis, near Saïs, and the city became practically a Greek state ; the trade between Egypt and the outer world flourished exceedingly, the Delta becoming the clearing-house of the Western World.

Psemtek III, the Psammacherites of Manetho, reigned six months ; very few monuments of his reign exist, and they tell us nothing about his reign. He sent an army, which consisted chiefly of mercenaries, to withstand Cambyses at Pelusium, but the Egyptians were beaten, and many of them turned and fled to Memphis. Cambyses sent an envoy to make terms with them, but they attacked his boat and killed him, and tore the crew limb from limb. Cambyses then came to Memphis, and 2,000 Egyptians were slain to satisfy his vengeance. Psemtek III was deposed, but Cambyses entreated him kindly until Cambyses was told that he was conspiring against him, and then he had Psemtek put to death. Egypt then became, like Babylonia and Assyria, a province of the Persian Empire.

The Twenty-Seventh Dynasty. Persians.

Cambyses, the son of Cyrus, reigned from B.C. 529–521. He went from Memphis to Saïs in the Western Delta, where lived a friend and supporter, the priest Utchaḥerresenet, , who conducted him about the city and interested him in the history of the goddess Neith of Saïs and her temple, and obtained from him authority to eject the foreigners who had settled in her holy precincts. The temple was purified, its priests reinstated and its revenues restored, and Cambyses was present at the reconsecration of the temple and, like a Pharaoh of old, publicly worshipped the goddess.[2]

[1] See Daressy in Maspero's *Recueil,* tom. XXII, p. 1 ff. Breasted says that Daressy's French translation is " nine-tenths conjecture " ; see *Ancient Records,* Vol. IV, p. 509.

[2] The inscription relating these facts is cut on a statue of Utchaḥerresenet in the Vatican ; for the literature see Wiedemann, *Aeg. Geschichte,* p. 667, and for a translation see Brugsch, *Egypt under the Pharaohs,* Vol. II, p. 293 f. ; a summary made from the text will be found in my *History of Egypt,* Vol. VII, p. 44 f.

With the consent of Cambyses, Utchaḥerresenet re-organized the affairs of the Delta, and with such success that Darius the Great applied to him for advice and counsel. Cambyses occupied Egypt as far as Elephantine, and he sent expeditions to the country south of the Fourth Cataract, and to the Oasis of Jupiter Ammon (Sîwah). The army which he sent from Thebes to Sîwah was overwhelmed by a terrible *habûb*, or sand storm, and was never more heard of. Some writers on Egypt, ignorant of the physical conditions of the Western Desert, and knowing nothing of the " moving sand-hills," regard this story as a fable. But Egyptian and Turkish military annals are full of reports of disasters of the kind and, to the writer's personal knowledge, a caravan of 700 camels with a military force was lost through a *habûb* between Korosko and Abu Ḥamad, and only two men escaped to tell the tale. A defeat of Cambyses in the Sûdân seems to be mentioned in the Annals of Nastasen,[1] where his name is given as , K-M-B-S-U-Ṭ-N-T; the objections to Schäfer's identification of the name are not well founded.

Darius I, the Great (B.C. 521–485), arrived in Egypt about B.C. 517. He was wise and tolerant in his rule over Egypt; he adopted the rank and style of the Pharaohs, and supported the religious institutions of the country, and endowed a college for the priests at Saïs. He completed the clearing out of the old Nile–Red Sea Canal, which had been begun by Nekau, and along its course set up stelae with inscriptions recording the fact in Egyptian, Persian, Susian and Babylonian. He repaired the temple of Ptaḥ at Memphis, and built a sandstone temple to Åmen in the Great Oasis, or the Oasis of Khârgah. It was about 150 feet long and 60 feet wide, and had three pylons. On the wall of the second chamber is cut a wonderful Hymn to Åmen as the One God, of whom all other gods are forms.[2]

Xerxes I, the Great (B.C. 485–465), succeeded in quelling the revolt that had broken out under the direction of **Khabbasha** , who was probably burnt or flayed alive, and tradition says that Xerxes ruled the country harshly. The monuments tell us nothing about his reign; examples of the alabaster vases inscribed with his name in Egyptian, Persian, Susian and Babylonian are to be seen in the British Museum.

Artaxerxes I (B.C. 465–424) did not adopt Egyptian titles like his father, but was content to have a transcription of his name

[1] For the text and a German translation see Schäfer, *Regierungsbericht des Königs Nastesen*, Leipzig, 1901; English renderings will be found in my *Egyptian Sûdân*, Vol. II, p. 97 ff., and *Annals of Nubian Kings*, p. 140 ff.

[2] See Birch, *Trans. Soc. Bibl. Arch.*, Vol. V, pp. 293–302; Brugsch, *Reise*, 1878.

enclosed within a cartouche and to call himself " Pharaoh the Great," . Hardly any trace of his long reign of 41 years is found in Egypt.

Darius II (B.C. 424–404) is known in Egypt chiefly by his inscription on the walls of the temple of Åmen which Darius I built at Al-Khârgah.

The Twenty-Eighth Dynasty.

Of **Amyrteos,** the only king of this dynasty mentioned by Manetho, nothing is known from the monuments.

The Twenty-Ninth Dynasty. From Mendes.

The nobles who seized the opportunity of calling themselves " kings of the South and the North," and compose Manetho's XXIXth dynasty, were: **Naifāuruṭ** (Nepherites) **I,** who made his son Nekhtnebf his co-regent; **Hagr** (Achôris), who repaired some of the temples of Thebes; and **Psamut** (Psammuthis), who carried out repairs at Karnak. Of Manetho's **Nepheritis** (II) and **Muthis** nothing is known.

The Thirtieth Dynasty. From Sebennytus.

Nekhtḥerḥeb, the Nektanebês of Manetho, repaired many of the temples in Egypt and built a temple at Bahbit al-Ḥajârah in honour of Horus, and a small temple by the Serapeum. He set up two obelisks before the temple of Ptaḥ, and these and his great inscribed stone sarcophagus are in the British Museum.[1] He reigned 18 (?) years, and was succeeded by **Tcheḥer,** the Teôs of Manetho, who reigned 2 years, and who repaired the temple of Khensuḥetep at Thebes. **Nekhtnebf,** the Nektanebos of Manetho, reigned at least 17 years. He was a great builder, and remains of his works are found in nearly all the great temples of Egypt. He attempted to withstand the Persians, who were attacking Pelusium under Artaxerxes II (B.C. 404–359), but the Egyptians were defeated and Nekhtnebf retreated with the remnant of his army to Memphis. Seeing that one after another the cities in the Delta were submitting to the Persians, he quietly abdicated his kingdom and fled to Nubia. Thus ended the reign of the last native king of Egypt. Artaxerxes II plundered the country and returned to Persia with great spoil. Under **Artaxerxes III** (B.C. 359–338), **Arses** (B.C. 338–336), and **Darius III** (B.C. 336–331) Egypt again became a province of Persia.

Alexander the Great (B.C. 356–323) defeated Darius at the **Battle of Issus** (B.C. 332), and came to Memphis, where he was acclaimed as the saviour of the country. He legalized his sovereignty

[1] The famous Metternich stele was set up in his reign; see Golénischeff, *Die Metternichstele*, Leipzig, 1877.

over the country by paying a visit to the Oasis of Jupiter **Ammon**, where the god Ȧmen acknowledged him to be his son, and therefore the lawful king of Egypt. He founded the city of **Alexandria** (B.C. 322) near the old town of Rāqeṭi, , Coptic ⲣⲁⲕⲟϯ. On the death of Alexander, when his kingdom was divided, Egypt fell to the share of Ptolemy Lagus, who administered the country in the name of Alexander's half-brother and son **Philip Arrhidaeus** and **Alexander II** of Egypt. The former never set foot in Egypt, and the latter, who was brought there when he was a child of six, was murdered seven years later, and Ptolemy Lagus became king of Egypt under the title of **Ptolemy I**[1] **Soter I** (B.C. 304). He founded the **Alexandrian Library** and Museum and introduced the worship of **Serapis. Ptolemy II Philadelphus** (B.C. 287) founded the cities of Berenice and Arsinoë and built the **Pharos** of Alexandria. In his reign the **Septuagint** was compiled and **Manetho** wrote a History of Egypt. **Ptolemy III Euergetes I** (B.C. 246) began to build the Temple of Edfû. He added a day to the year every fourth year, thus anticipating **Leap-year. Ptolemy IV Philopator I** (B.C. 222) built a hall to the temple of Ȧrqȧmen (Ergamenes) at Dakkah, defeated Antiochus the Great at the Battle of Raphia, and inaugurated elephant hunts in the Sûdân. **Ptolemy V Epiphanes** (B.C. 205). The **Rosetta Stone** is inscribed with a bilingual copy of the Decree which the priests passed at Memphis in the ninth year of his reign. **Ptolemy VI Philometor I** (B.C. 173). **Ptolemy VII** took the title of **Euergetes** (II). **Ptolemy VIII Eupator**—cartouches wanting. **Ptolemy IX Philopator II** or Philopator Neos—cartouches wanting. **Ptolemy X Philopator III** (also Philometor II) took the title of **Soter** (II). **Ptolemy XI Alexander I** took the title of **Philometor** (III). **Ptolemy XII Alexander II**—cartouches wanting. **Ptolemy XIII Philopator IV Philadelphus II, Ptolemy XIV** and **Ptolemy XV**—cartouches wanting. **Ptolemy XVI** was the son of Cleopatra and Julius Caesar, and was called Caesarion.

After the death of Antony and Cleopatra **Egypt became a Roman Province (B.C. 30),** under the rule of a Prefect. **Nero** (A.D. 54–60) sent two centurions into the Sûdân to report on the country generally. **St. Mark** arrived in Alexandria about A.D. 70. **Trajan** (A.D. 98) re-opened the Nile and Red Sea Canal. **Hadrian** (A.D. 117) visited Egypt twice. **Decius** (A.D. 249) persecuted the Christians. **Diocletian** (A.D. 284) abandoned Nubia and subsidized the Blemmyes and the Nobadae; he persecuted the Christians, and the Coptic **Era of the Martyrs** begins with the first year of his reign. "Pompey's Pillar" was set up in his reign. **Marcianus**

[1] The principal monuments of the Ptolemies in Egypt are described in my *History of Egypt*, Vols. VII and VIII.

(A.D. 450–457) invaded Nubia, chastised the Blemmyes and Nobadae, and made them agree to keep the peace for 100 years. In the first half of the VIth century **Silko,** king of the Nobadae, embraced Christianity; his capital is now called Old Dongola. **Justinian** (A.D. 527–565) sent Narses to close the temples at Philae and to suppress the worship of Isis and Osiris. Narses confiscated the revenues of the temples and carried off the gold statues of the gods to Constantinople. **Chosroës,** the Persian, invaded Egypt in 619 and held the country for 10 years. Owing to the desertion from the Persians of the Arab tribes, who had attached themselves to **Muḥammad the Prophet** (born at Al-Makkah August 20th, 570, died in June, 632), **Heraclius** was able to defeat the Persians in Syria and so again became master of Egypt. In 640 **'Amr ibn al-'Âṡ,** general of 'Umar the Khalîfah, conquered Egypt, and the country became a province of the newly founded Arab Empire. The first Arab capital was Al-Fusṭât, near Babylon, and the second was Al-Ḳahîrah (Cairo), which was founded in 969. The Turks, under Salîm, conquered Egypt in 1516–17, and Egypt became a Pashalik of the Turkish Empire. **Sa'îd Pâshâ** (1854) built railways in the Delta, and under him the digging of the **Suez Canal** was begun; the canal was opened in 1869. In 1882 the British bombarded Alexandria, and after the Battle of Tall al-Kabîr (September 13th) occupied Cairo. On November 18th, 1914, a British Protectorate over Egypt was proclaimed, and on December 19th the Khedive, 'Abbâs II, was deposed, and the suzerainty of Turkey came to an end. On the same day Prince Ḥusên Kamâl was proclaimed Sulṭân of Egypt. In the "Declaration to Egypt" dated Cairo, February 28th, 1922, the first principle laid down is "The British Protectorate over Egypt is terminated and Egypt is declared to be an independent sovereign state."

LIST OF THE NESUBÀTI AND SON OF RĀ NAMES OF THE PRINCIPAL KINGS OF EGYPT

UNDER the earliest dynasties the king of Egypt possessed four "strong names," or rather titles: 1. The **Horus**-name, *i.e.*, his name as the successor of Horus, which was indicated by ; 2. The **Nebti**-name, as the chosen one of Nekhebit and Uatchit, the Mother-goddesses of Upper and Lower Egypt respectively, which was indicated by ; 3. The **Horus-of-gold**-name, which was indicated by [1]; 4. The **Nesu-bàti**-name, *i.e.*, his name as king of the

[1] Reading uncertain.

South (Nesut , later Nesu) and king of the North (Bȧti), which was indicated by . When the priests of Rā gained supreme power under the IVth and Vth dynasties they made the king adopt a **fifth name** as the **Son of Rā** . The Horus-name was written in a rectangular frame called SEREKH , which some think means "royal house," and others "banner," but there is reason for saying that the *serekh* represents a funerary building, and that the name in it is the king's "cognizance," and the name of his Ka. The drawing given here gives a good idea of its general form, and the name inside it, NEB MAĀT, "Lord of Truth," is the Horus name of Seneferu, the last king of the IIIrd or first king of the IVth dynasty. The Nesubȧti and Son-of-Rā names are written inside an oval , which is commonly called **cartouche**[1] (*i.e.*, cartridge), a word derived through the French from the Italian *cartoccio*. It is probable that this oval, or "elliptical ring," was originally circular in form, like the hieroglyphic which represents a cylindrical seal being rolled over the mud which is to receive the impression. The connection between the cartouche and the seal seems obvious. In the following list it is only possible to give a selection of the names of each king.[2]

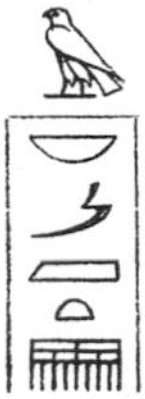

PRE-DYNASTIC KINGS: 1. KINGS OF LOWER EGYPT

1. 
. . . . pu.

2. 
Ska.

3. 
Khaȧu (?).

4. 
Tȧu.

5. 
Thesh.

6. 
Neheb (?).

7. 
Uatchnār(?).

8. 
Mekha.

9. 
. . . a.

[1] The use of this word in this sense was inaugurated by Champollion.
[2] For a list of all the royal names see Budge, *The Book of the Kings of Egypt*, 2 vols., London, 1908, and Gauthier, *Livre des Rois*, Paris, 1916 ff.

2. Kings of Upper Egypt

10. 

Nār-mer.

11. 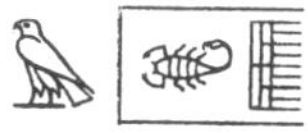

Tchar (?).

Dynastic Kings: Dynasty I

12. 

Menȧ, Men (Menes).

13. 

Ȧtet I. Ȧtet II.

14. 

Ȧtet III.

15. 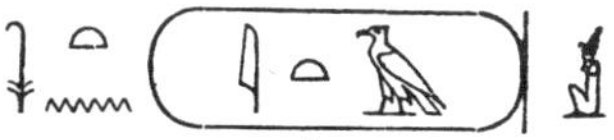

Ȧta.

16. 

Ḥesepti (?). Semti.

17. 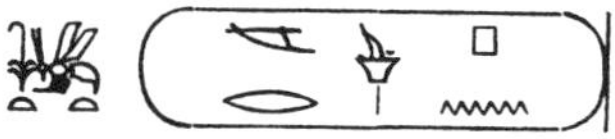

Merpeba.

18. 

Ḥui or Nekhti.

19. 

Qebḥu.

Dynasty II

1. 

Baiuneter.

2. 

Batchau.

3. 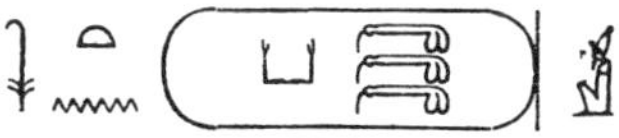

Kakau.

4. 

Banneter.

5. 

Uatchnes.

6. 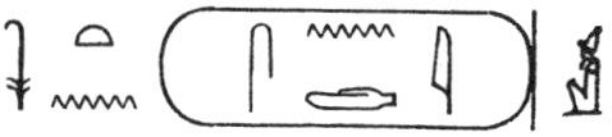

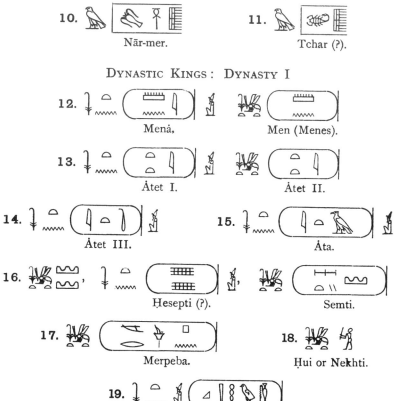

Senṭȧ.

7. 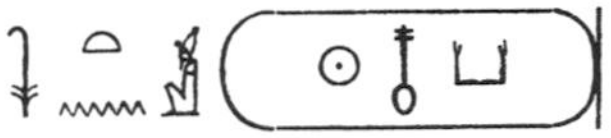
Neferkarā I.

8. 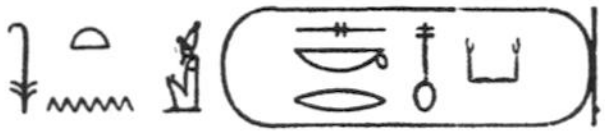
Neferkaseker.

9. 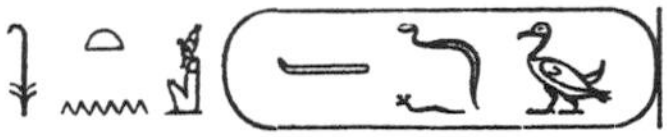
Ḥutchfa.

10. 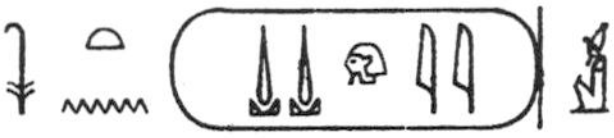
Tchatchai.

11. 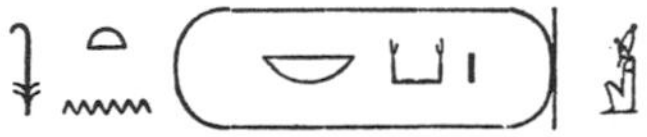
Neb-ka I (Nebkarā I ?).

DYNASTY III

1. 
Tcheser I.

2. 
Tcheser II (Åtet IV ?).

3. 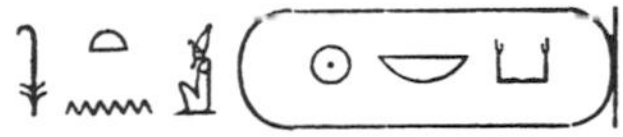
Nebkaıā II.

4. 
Setches.

5. 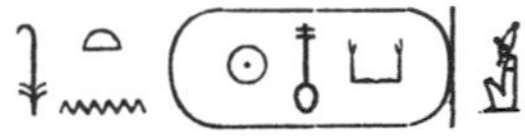
Neferkarā II.

6. 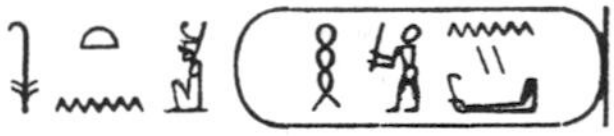
Ḥuni.

DYNASTY IV

1. 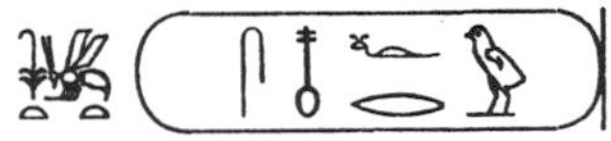
Seneferu.

2. 
Khufu (Cheops).

3. 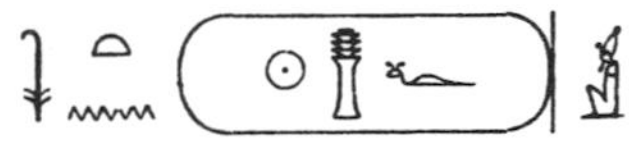
Ṭeṭefrā.

4. 
Khāfrā.

5. 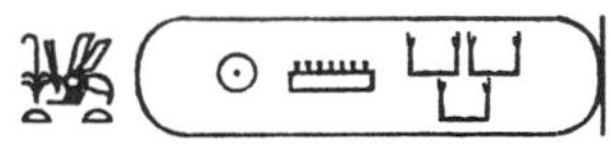
Menkaurā.

6. 
Shepseskaf.

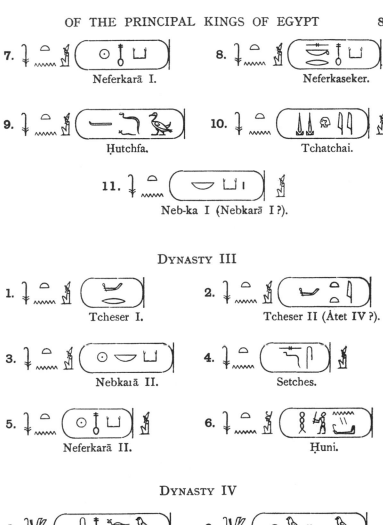

DYNASTY V

1. Userkaf. 2. Saḥurā.

3. Neferårikarā I.; Var. Kakaå.

4. Shepseskarā. 5. Neferfrā.

6. Enuserrā. Ån I.

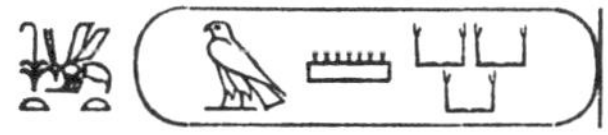

7. Menkauḥer.

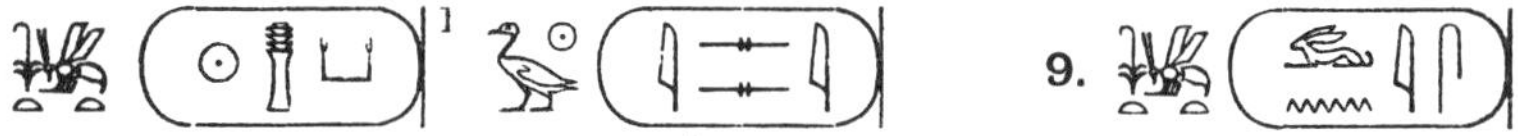

8. Ṭeṭkara.[1] Åssā. 9. Unås.

DYNASTY VI

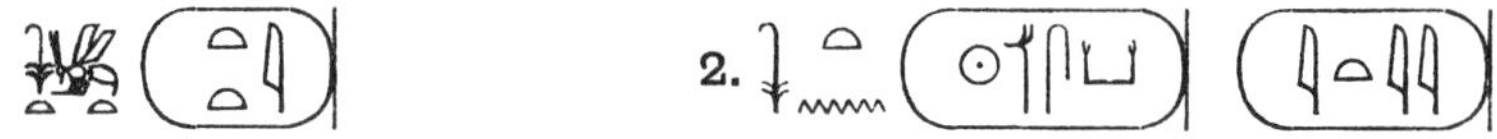

1. Åtet V. 2. Userkarā I. Åti I.

3. Merirā. Pepi I.

4. Merenrā I. Meḥtiemsaf I.

[1] Variant 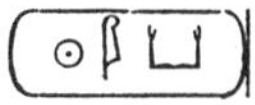 Maātkarā I.

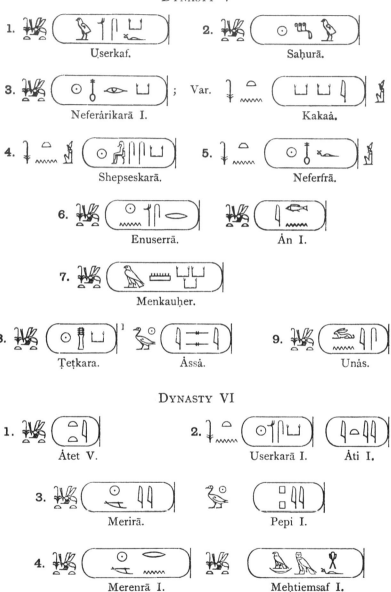

5. 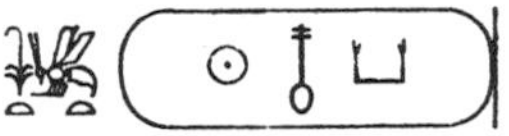

Neferkarā III.

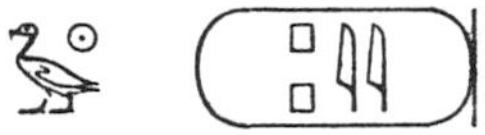

Pepi II.

6. 

Merenrā II Meḥtiemsaf.

7. 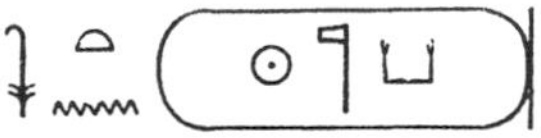

Neterkarā.

8. 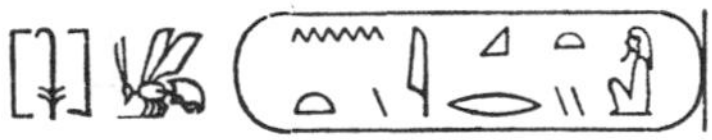

Netȧqerti.

Dynasties VII (?) and VIII

1. 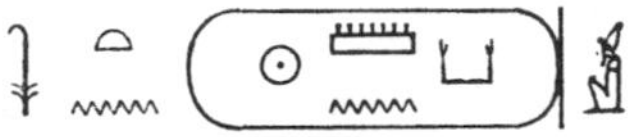

Menkarā.

2. 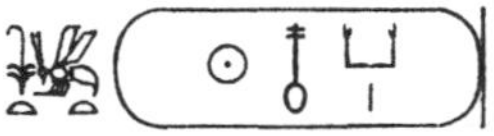

Neferkarā IV.

3. 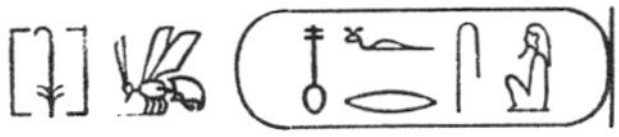

Nefres.

4. 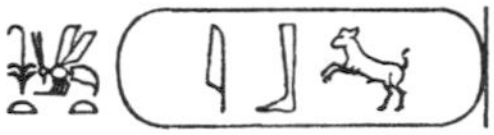

Ȧb (?).

5. 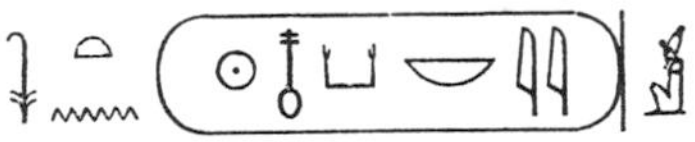

Neferkarā V Nebi.

6. 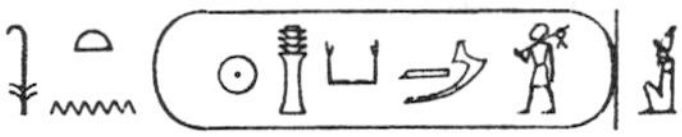

Ṭeṭkarā II Maā . . .

7. 

Neferkarā VI Khenṭu.

8. 

Merenḥer I.

9. 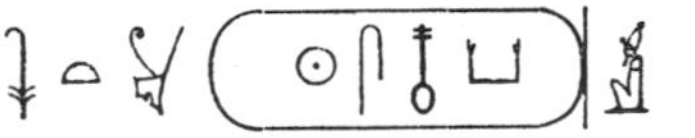

Seneferkarā I.

10. 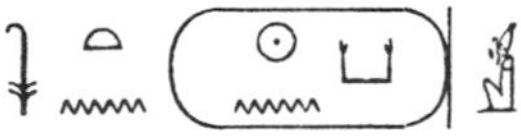

Nekarā I.

11. 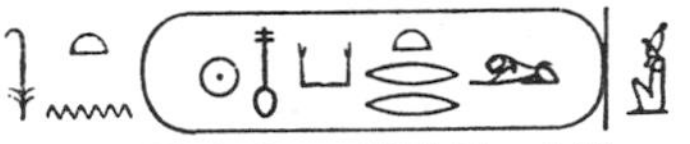

Neferkarā VII Terrl (?).

12. 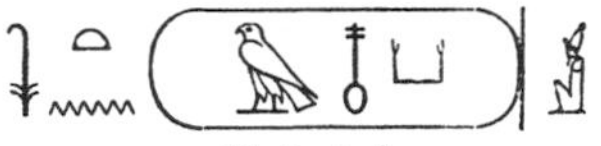

Neferkaḥer.

13. 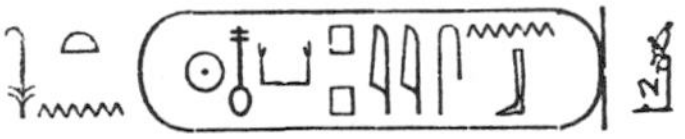

Neferkarā VIII Pepi III Senb.

14. 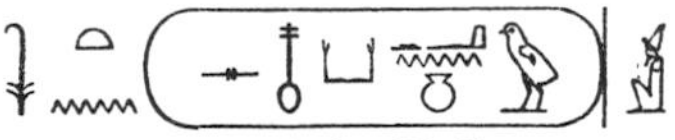

Seneferka II Ānnu.

15. 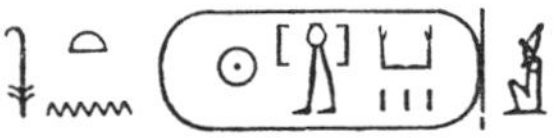

Ȧnkaurā (?).

16. 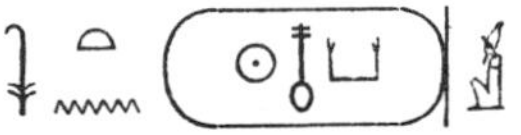

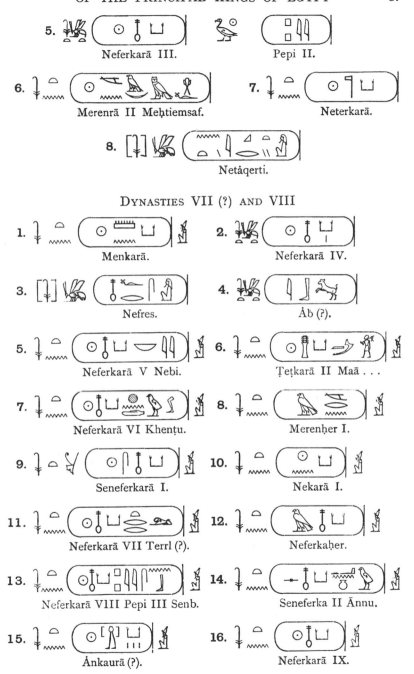

Neferkarā IX.

17. 
Neferkauḥeru.

18. 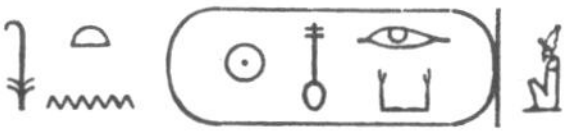
Neferårikarā.

19. 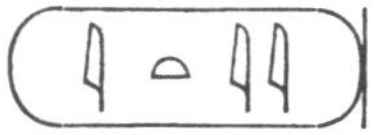
Åti II.

20. 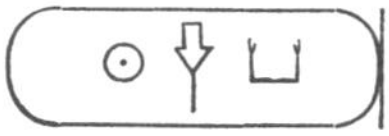
Sekhemkarā I.

21. 
Iemḥetep.

22. 
Uatchkarā.

DYNASTIES IX AND X

1. 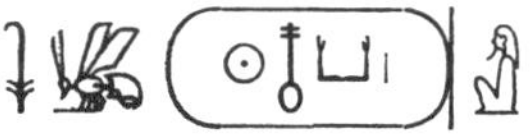
Neferkarā X.

2. 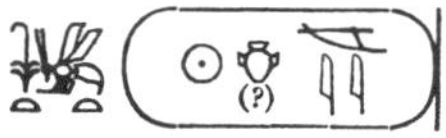
Åbmerirā.

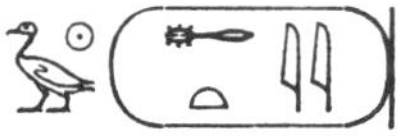
Khati.

[Names of five kings wanting here.]

3. 
Meriåāḥ (?).

4. 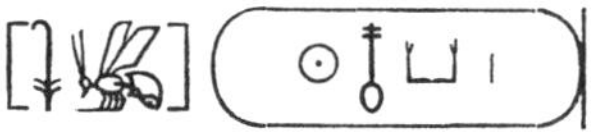
Neferkarā XI.

5. 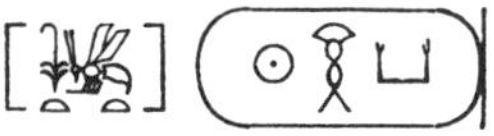
Uaḥkarā I.

Khati II.

6. 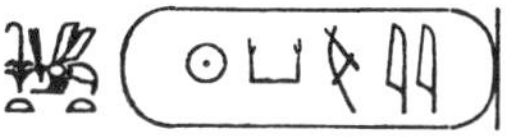
Kamerirā II.

7. 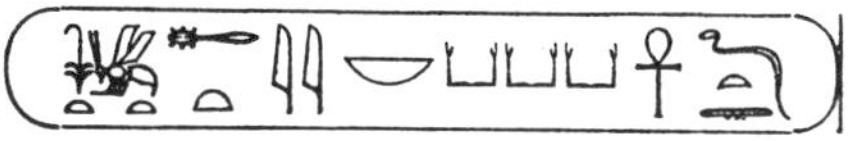
Khati Nebkau.

To this period probably belong :—

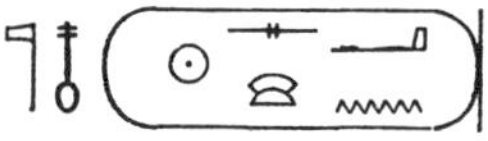
Skhānrā.

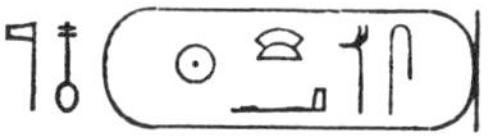
Khāuserrā I.

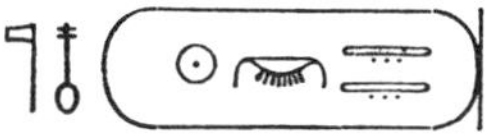
Nubtauirā.

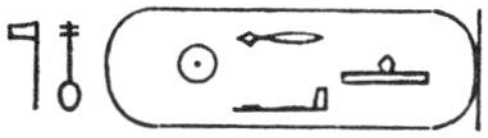
Āaḥeteprā I.

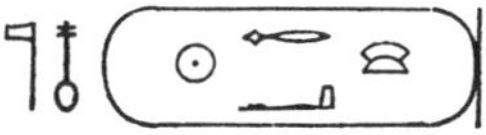
Āakhārā.

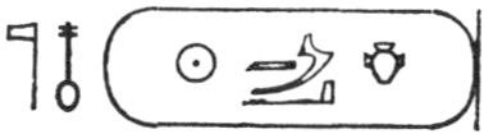
Maāåbrā.

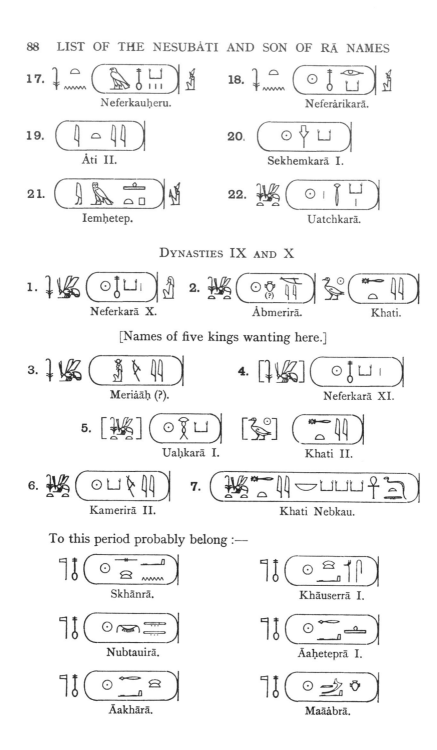

Dynasty XI

1. , Ȧntef I, the great Erpā.

2. 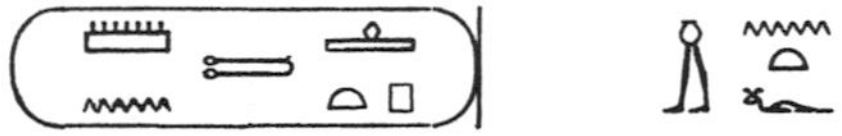

Menthuḥetep I. Ȧntef II (?).

3. , Uaḥ ānkh.)

Ȧntef III (?).

4. , Nekht-neb-tep-nefer.)

Ȧntef IV.

5. 

Qakarā I. Ȧntef V (?).

6. 

Sānkhȧbtaui. Menthuḥetep II.

7. 

Nebḥeprā. Mentuḥetep III.

8. 

Ȧntef VI (?).

9. 

Nebtauirā. Menthuḥetep IV.

10. 

Sānkhkarā. Menthuḥetep V.

DYNASTY XII

1. 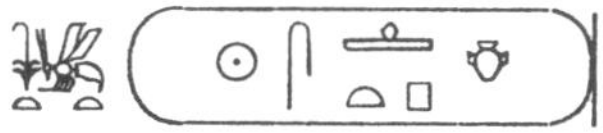 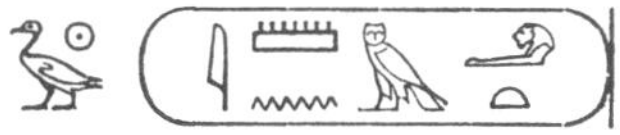

Seḥetepȧbrā I. — Ȧmenemḥat I.

2. 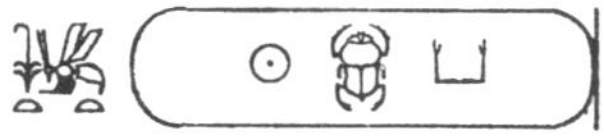 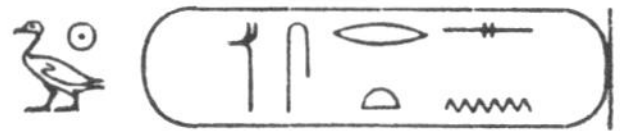

Kheperkarā I. — Usertsen (Sen-Usrit (?)) I.

3.  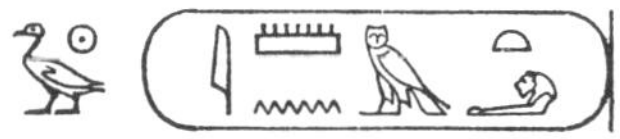

Nubkaurā. — Ȧmenemḥat II.

4. 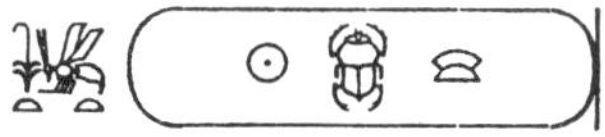 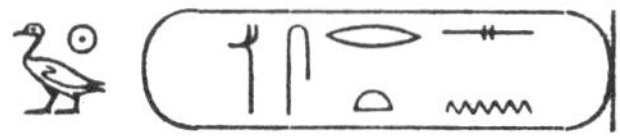

Kheperkhārā. — Usertsen (Sen-Usrit (?)) II.

5.  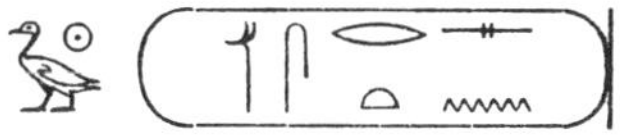

Khākaurā. — Usertsen (Sen-Usrit (?)) III.

6.  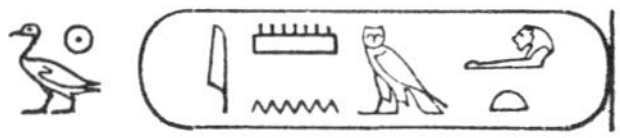

Enmaātrā. — Ȧmenemḥat III.

7. 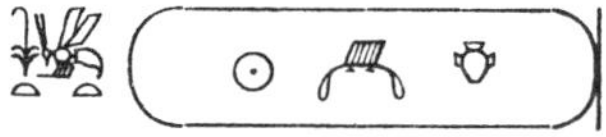 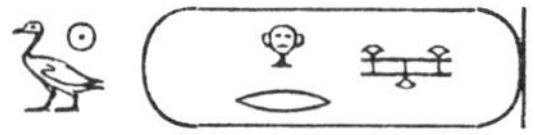

Auȧbrā. — Ḥer.

8. 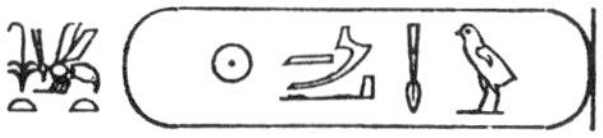 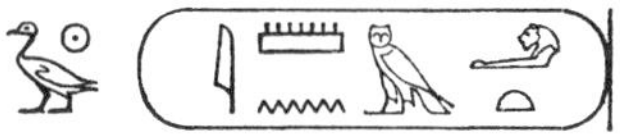

Maākherurā. — Ȧmenemḥat IV.

9.  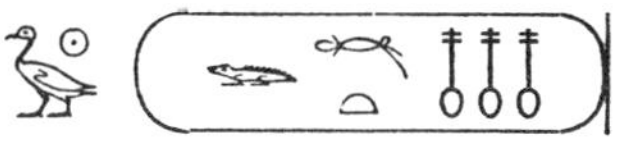

Sebekneferurā. — Sebekshetṭneferu.

10. 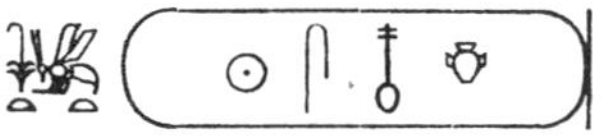 

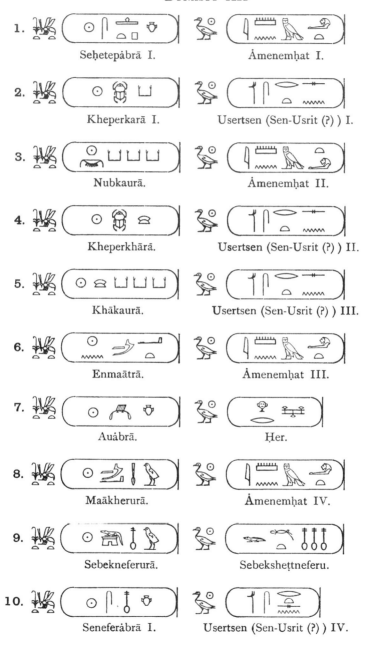

Seneferȧbrā I. — Usertsen (Sen-Usrit (?)) IV.

DYNASTY XIII

1. 

Khutauirā. Ugaf (?).

2. 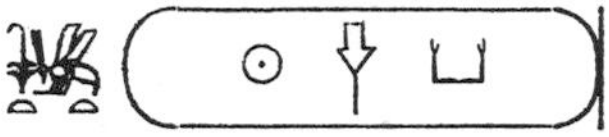

Sekhemkarā.

(Horus name, .)

3. 

Sesheshkarā. Ȧmenemḥat VI (?) Senbf.

4. 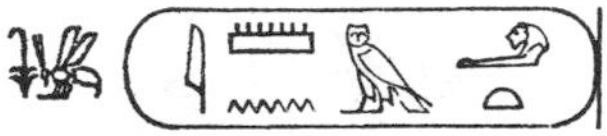

Ȧmenemḥat VII (?).

5. 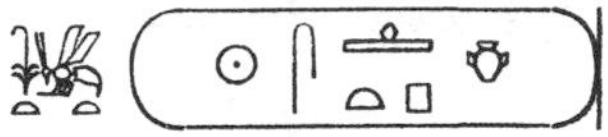

Seḥetepȧbrā II.

6. 

Ȧufni.

7. 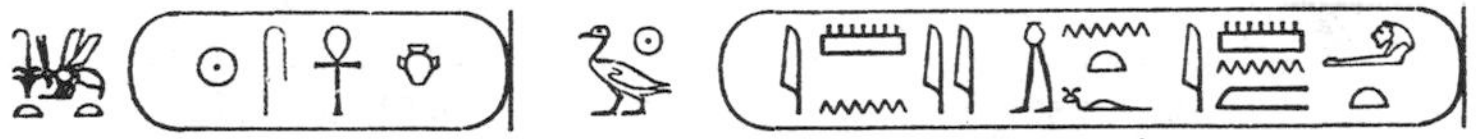

Sānkhȧbrā. Ȧmeni Ȧntef VII (?) Ȧmenemḥat VIII.

8. 

Smenkarā.

9. 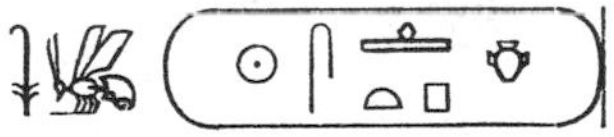

Seḥetepȧbrā.

10. 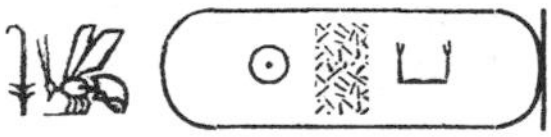

. . . karā.

11. 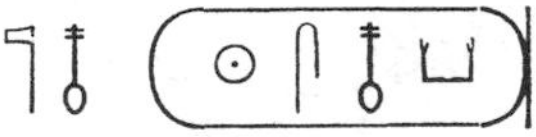

Seneferkarā II.

12. 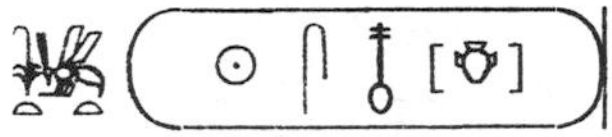

Seneferȧbrā II.

13. 

Netchemȧbrā.

14. 

Sebekḥetep I (?).

15. 

Rensenb.

16. 

Auȧbrā.

17. 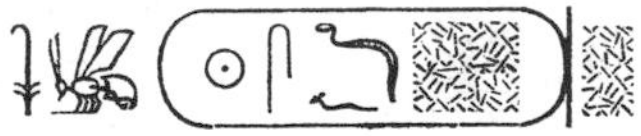

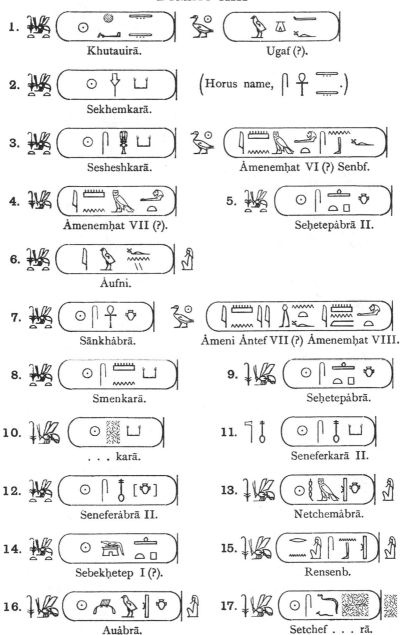

Setchef . . . rā.

18. 

Sekhemkhutauirā Sebekḥetep II. Ȧmenemḥat Sebekḥetep.

19. 

Usrkarā II.

20. 

Smenkhkarā. Mer-mashāu.

21. 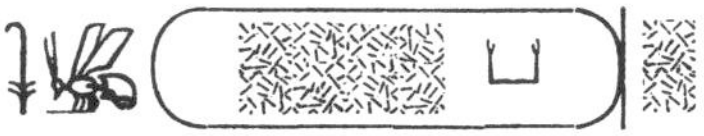

. . . .

22. 

Ka Set-Rā (?). Ka Set-Rā (?).

23. 

Sekhemsuatchtauirā. Sebekḥetep III.

24. 

Khāsesheshrā. Neferḥetep I.

25. 

Ḥetḥersa (Sa-Hathor).

26. 

Khāneferrā. Sebekḥetep IV.

27. 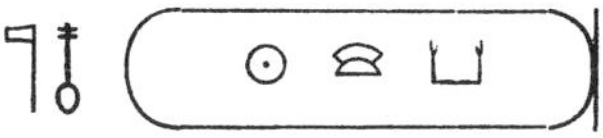

Khākarā.

28. 

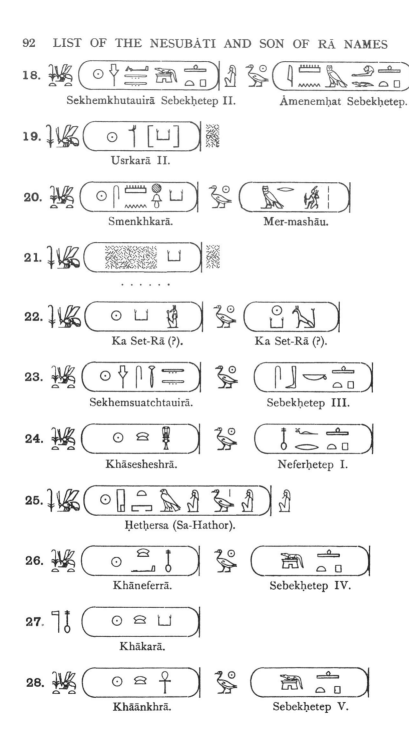

Khāānkhrā. Sebekḥetep V.

29. 

Khāḥeteprā. Sebekḥetep VI.

30. 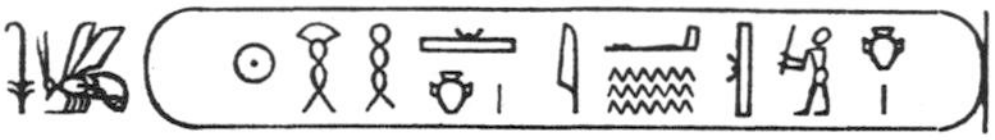

Uaḥȧbrā I. Ȧāȧb.

31. 

Merneferrā. Ȧi I.

32. 

Merheṭeprā I. Ȧn.

33. 

Merḥeteprā II. Sebekḥetep VII.

34. 

Sānkhenrā Senbtu (?).

35. 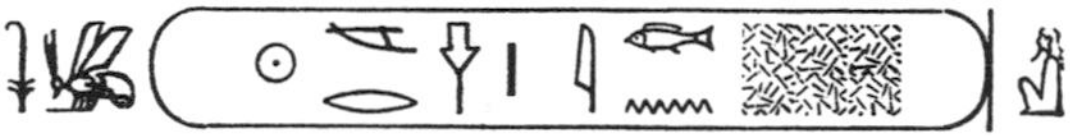

Mersekhemrā Ȧn . . . . . .

36. 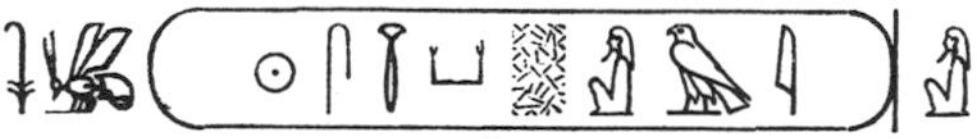

Suatchkarā Ḥeruȧ.

37. 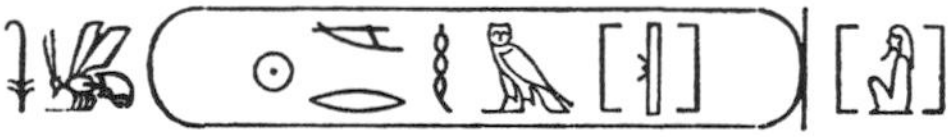

Mernetchemrā.

38. 

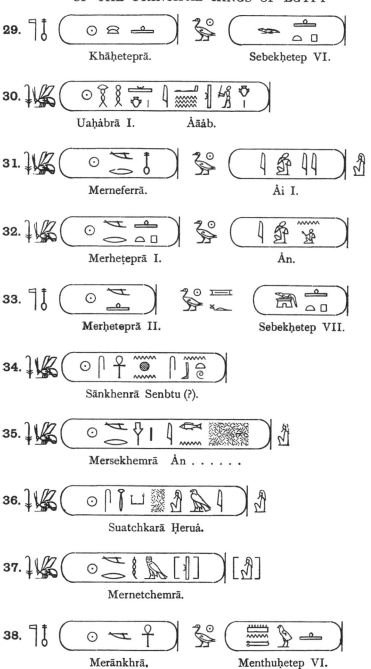

Merānkhrā. Menthuḥetep VI.

39. 

Merkheperrā.

40. 

Merkaurā. Sebekḥetep VIII.

41. 

Ṭeṭneferrā. Ṭaṭaumes.

42. 

Nebmaātrā I.

43. 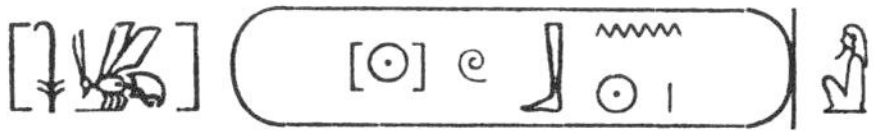

Ubenrā I.

44. 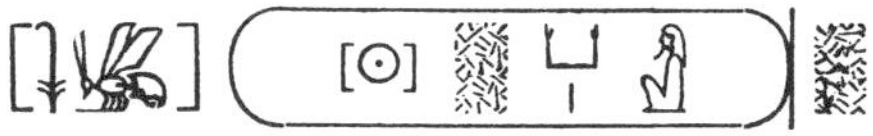

. . . . . karā.

45. 

Nebmaātrā II.

46. 

Ṭeṭānkhrā. Mentuemsaf.

47. 

Neḥsi. Neḥsi (the "Black").

48. 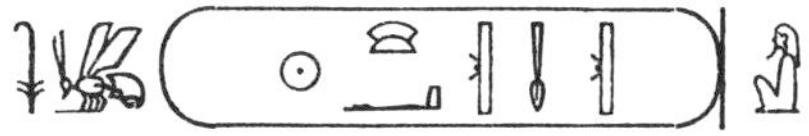

Khākherurā.

49. 

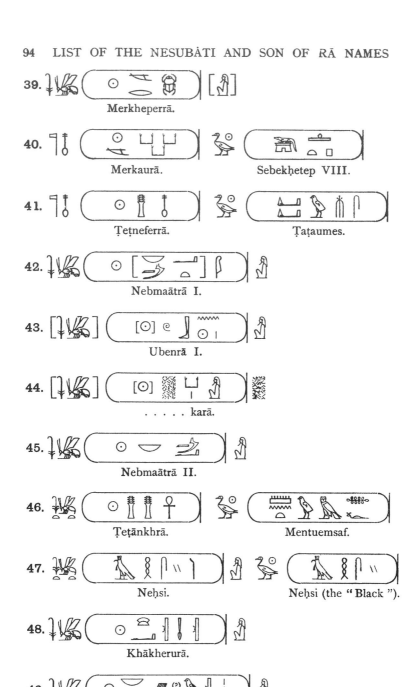

Nebfaurā.

The following kings probably belong to the XIIth dynasty :—

1. 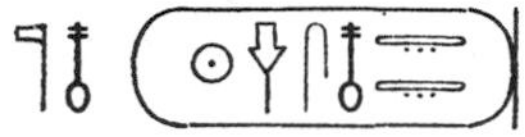

Senefertauirā Sekhem.

2. 

Mersekhemrā II.

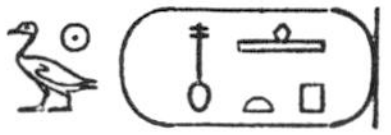

Neferḥetep II.

3. 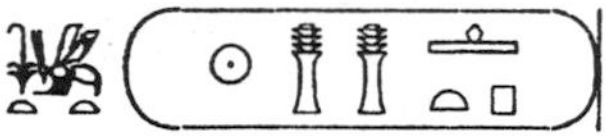

Ṭetḥeteprā.

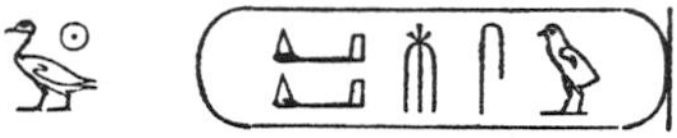

Ṭaṭamesu II.

4. 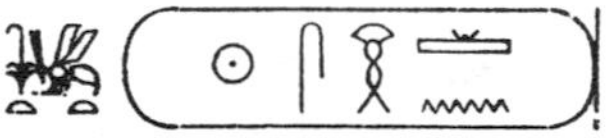

Suaḥenrā.

Senbmȧȧu.

DYNASTY XIV (TURIN PAPYRUS)

1. 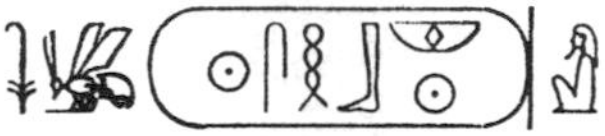

Seḥebrā.

2. 

Mertchefarā.

3. 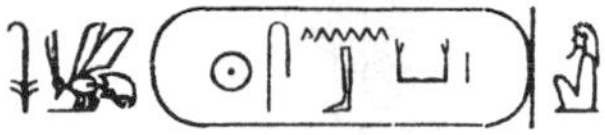

Senbkarā.

4. 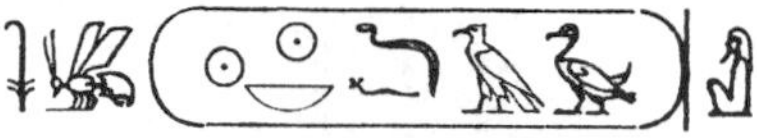

Nebtchefarā I.

5. 

Ubenrā II.

6. 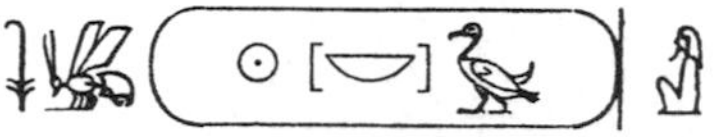

Nebtchefarā.

7. 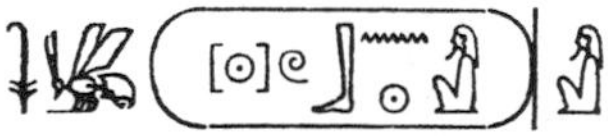

Ubenrā III.

8. 

Autȧbrā.

9. 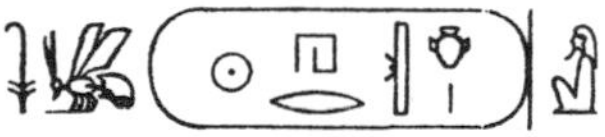

Herȧbrā.

10. 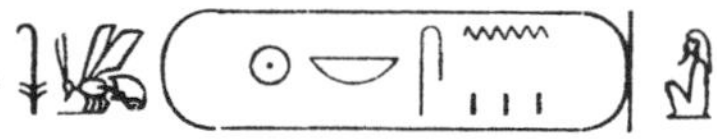

Nebsenrā.

11. 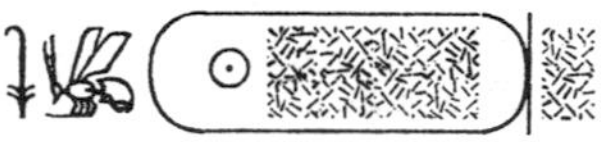

. . . . . . rā.

12. 

Sekheperenrā.

13. 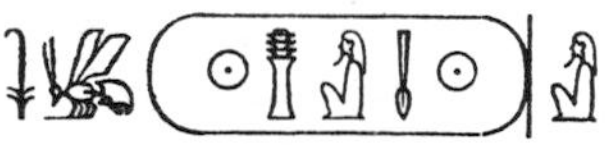

Ṭeṭkherurā.

14. 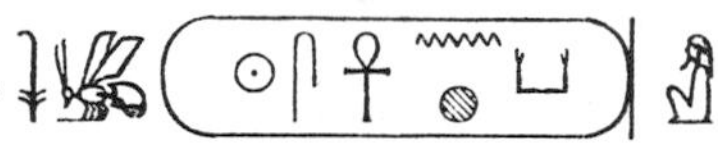

Sānkhkarā.

15. 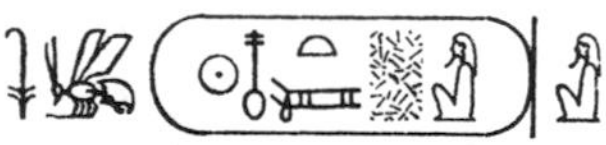

Nefertem . . . rā.

16. 

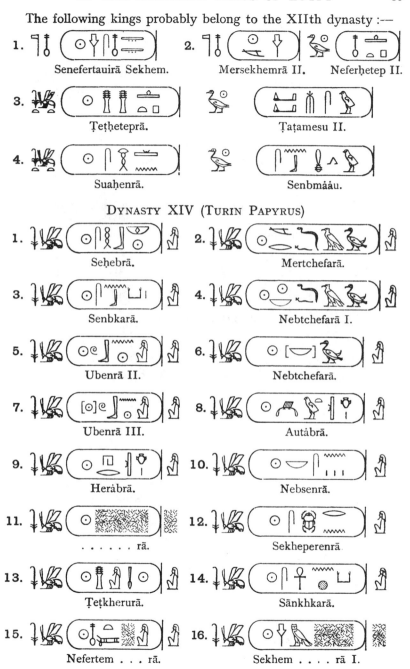

Sekhem . . . . rā I.

17. 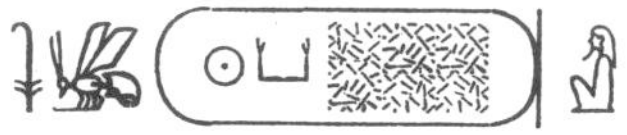

Ka . . . . . rā.

18. 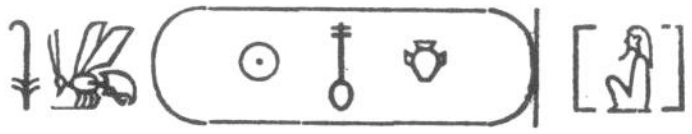

Neferåbrā.

19. 

Å . . . . . rā.

20. 

Khā . . . . rā.

21. 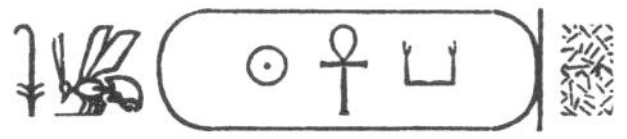

Ānkhkarā.

22. 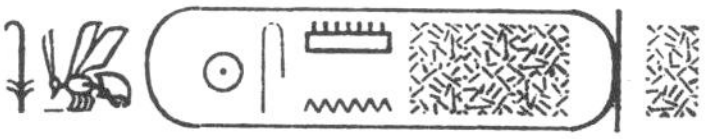

Smen . . . . rā.

23. 

Mersekhemrā.

24. 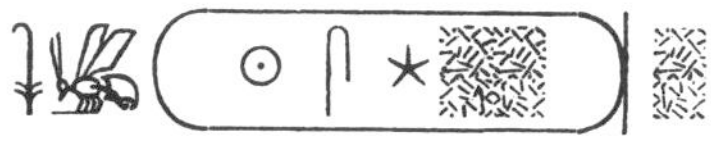

Seba . . . . rā.

25. 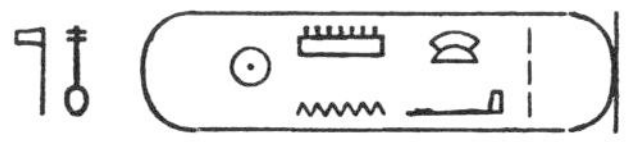

Menkhāurā.

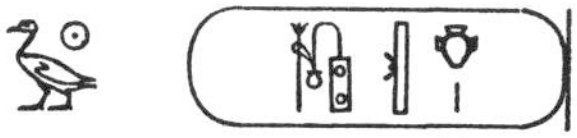

Seshåb (?).

To this period probably belong :—

,

Sebkai,

, and

Khuåqer,

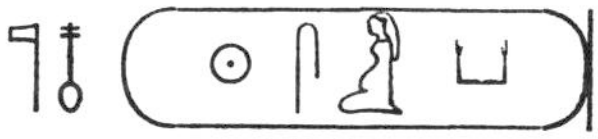

Sebakkarā.

Dynasties XV and XVI

In the Turin Papyrus all the Nesubåt names of the kings are broken, but the personal names of two kings are legible, viz.,  Ānatå and  Bebnum (?). The following names of Hyksos kings are derived from the monuments :—

1. 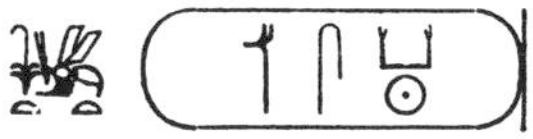

Userkarā III.

Khentcher.

2. 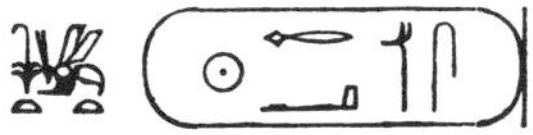

Āauserrā.

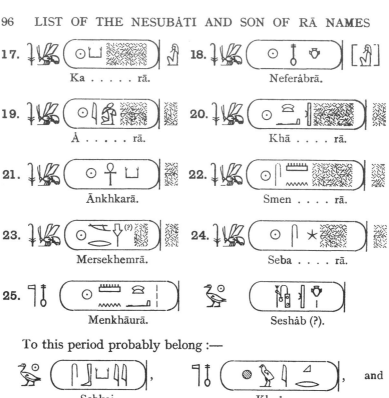

Åpepå.

3. 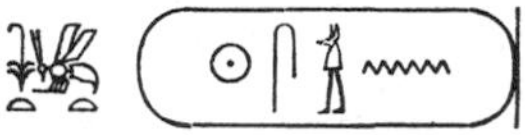
Suserenrā.

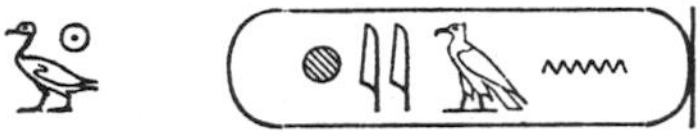
Khian.

4. 
Nebkhepeshrā.

Åpep.

5. 
Āārqrā.

6. 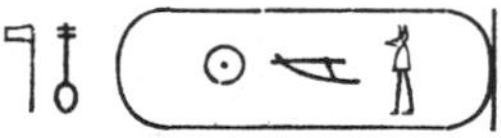
Meruserrā.

Iābeqher.

7. 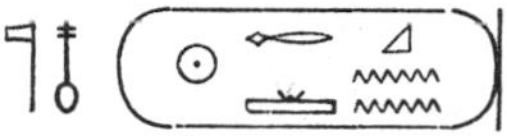
Āaqenrā.

Åpepȧ.

The following kings probably reigned during the Hyksos Period :—

1. 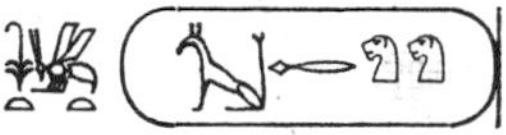
Āapeḥtiset.

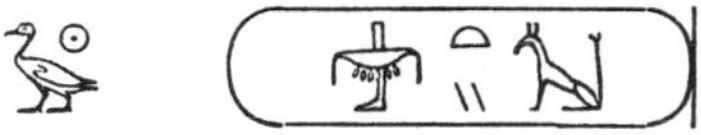
Nubti.

2. 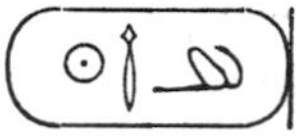
Āapeḥrā.

3. 
Āaneterrā.

4. 
Āaḥeteprā II.

5. 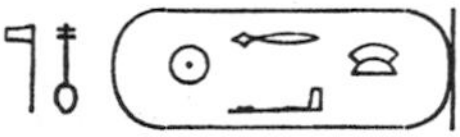
Āakhārā II.

6. 
Uatchkarā.

7. 
Nubkarā.

8. 
Nebṭeṭrā.

9. 
Nub . . . rā.

10. 
Nekarā II.

11. 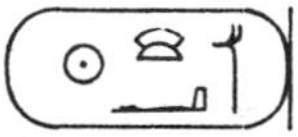
Khāuserrā II.

12. 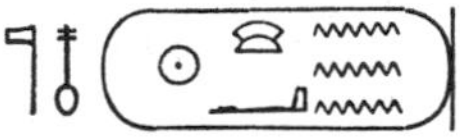
Khāmurā (?).

13. 
Kasetrā.

14. 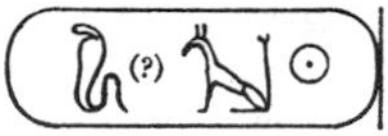
. . . setrā.

15. 
Semqen.[1]

16. 
Ānther.

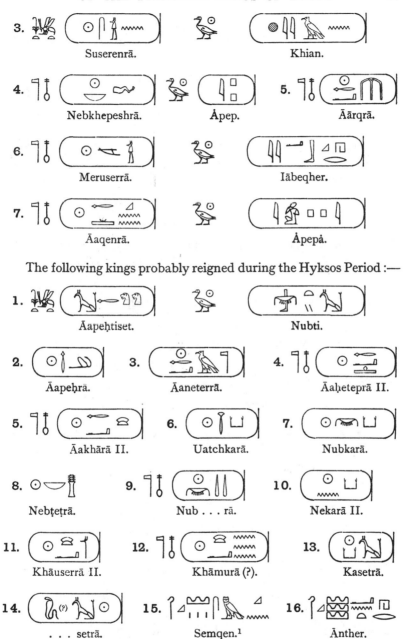

[1] His title was "governor of the deserts."

17. 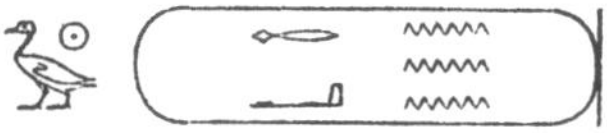
Āamu.

18. 
Iāpeqher.

19. 
Iāmu.

20. 
Ipeqḥer.

21. 
Uatcheṭ.

22. 
Seket (?).

23. 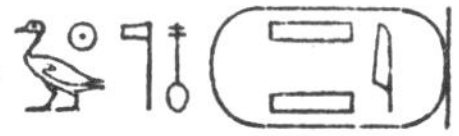
Sheshȧ.

24. 
Qar.

Dynasty XVII

The names of all the kings of the XVIIth dynasty in the Turin Papyrus, save two, are mutilated, viz.,  Nebȧriaurā, and 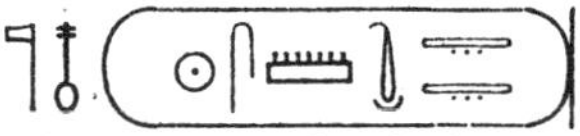 Smentauirā. The following kings, whose names are derived from the monuments, probably belong to the XVIIth dynasty :—

1. 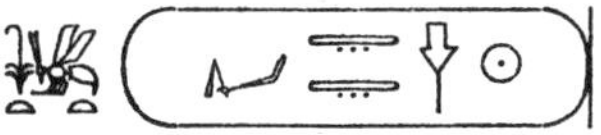 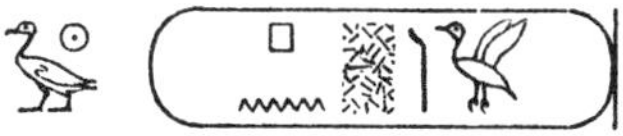
Khutauisekhemrā. Pen . . . .

2. 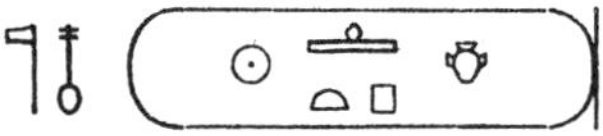 
Ḥetepȧbrā. . . . . Ḥernetchtef.

3. 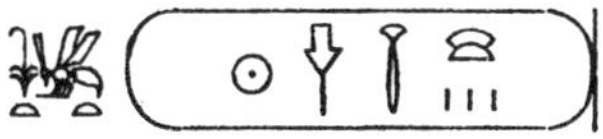 
Sekhemuatchkhāurā. Sebekemsaf.

4.  
Sekhemsheṭṭauirā. Sebekemsauf II.

5.  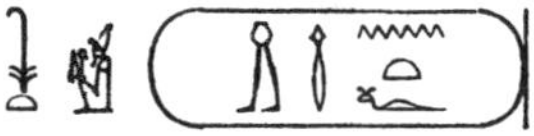
Sesheshrāherḥermaā. Ȧntef VIII Āa.

6. 

Sesheshrāupuemmaā.

Ȧntef IX Āa.

7. 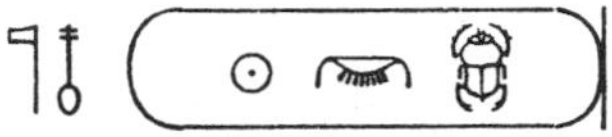

Nubkheperrā.

Ȧntef X Āa.

8. 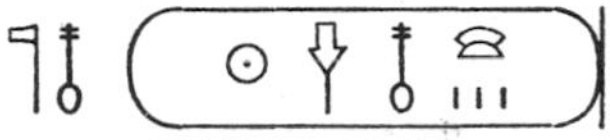

Sekhemneferkhāurā.

Upuatuemsaf.

9. 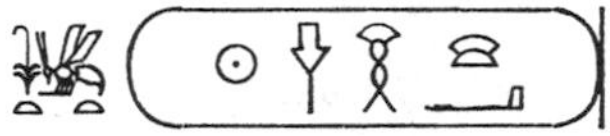

Sekhemuaḥkhārā.

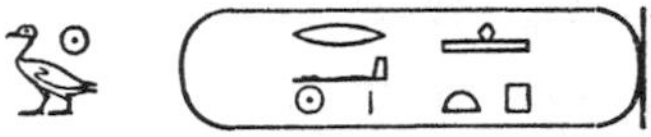

Rāḥetep.

10. 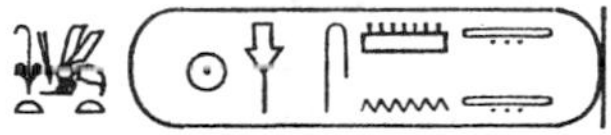

Sekhemsmentauirā.

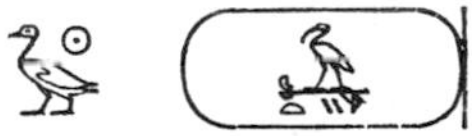

Tcheḥuti.

11. 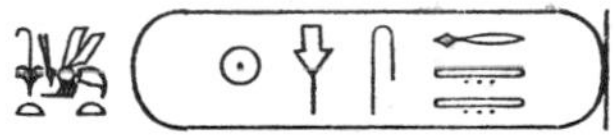

Sekhemrāsāataui.

12. 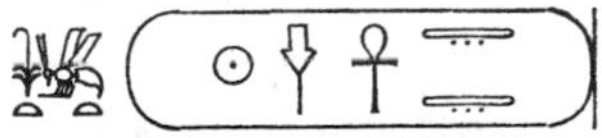

Sekhemrāānkhtaui.

13. 

Rāmessusertaui.

14. 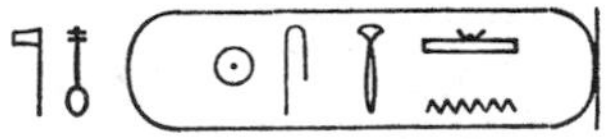

Suatchenrā I.

15. 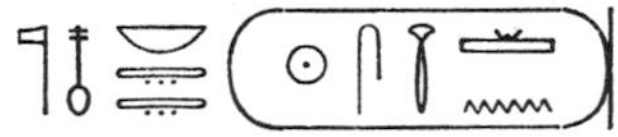

Suatchenrā II.

16. 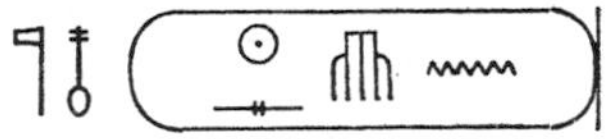

Skhentenrā.

17. 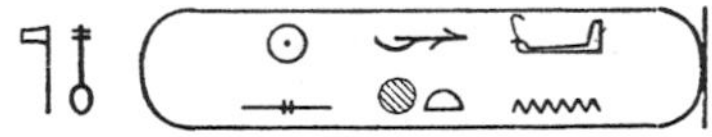

Senekhtenrā.

18. 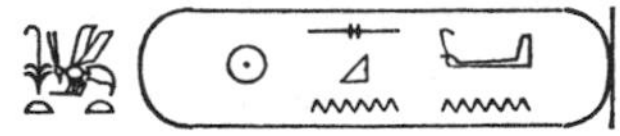

Seqenenrā I.

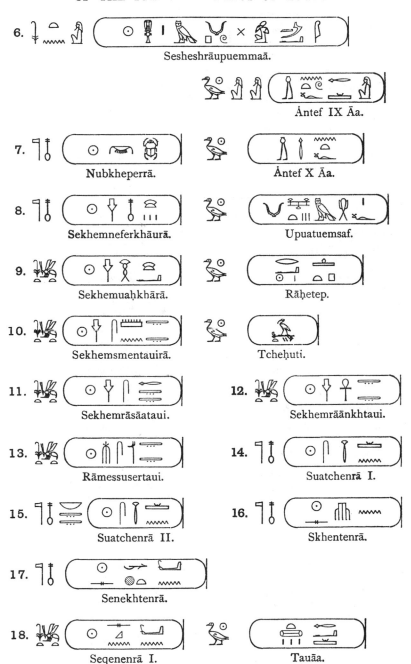

Tauāa.

19. 

Seqenenrā II. — Tauāa Āa.

20. 

Seqenenrā III. — Taāaqen.

21. 

Uatchkheperrā. — Kames.

Dynasty XVIII

1. 

Nebpeḥtirā. — Ȧāhmes I.

2. 

Tcheserkarā. — Ȧmenḥetep I.

3. 

Āakheperkarā. — Tcheḥutimes I.

4. 

Āakheperenrā. — Tcheḥutimes II.

5. 

Maātkarā. — Ȧmen's consort, Ḥatshepsut

6. 

Menkheperrā. — Tcheḥutimes III.

7. 

Āakheperurā. — Ȧmenḥetep II.

8. 

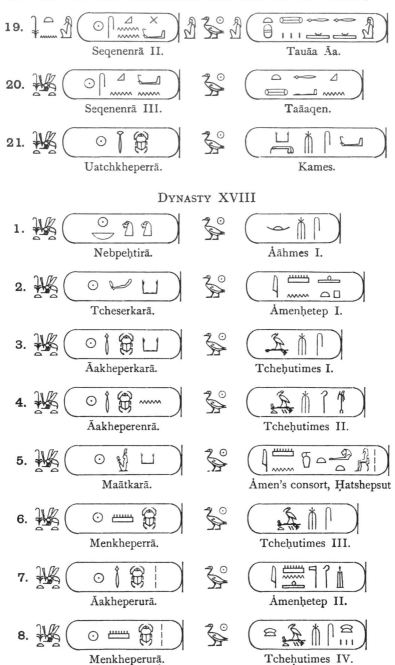

Menkheperurā. — Tcheḥutimes IV.

9. 

Nebmaātrā. — Åmenḥetep III.

10. 

Neferkheperurā Uāenrā. — Åmenḥetep IV.

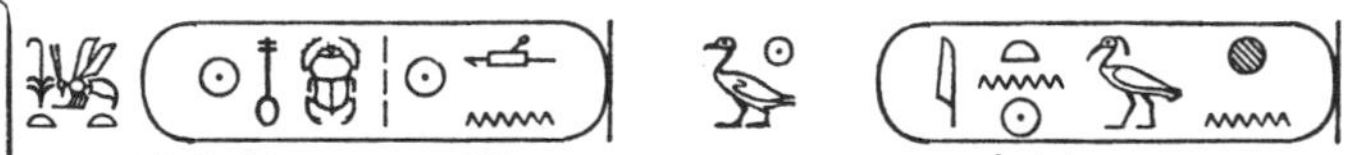

Neferkheperurā Uāenrā. — Åakhuenåten.

11. 

Ānkhkheperurā. — Sāakarā Tcheserkheperu.

12. 

Kheperunebrā. — Tutānkhåmen.

13. 

Kheperkheperurāårimaāt. — Åi.

14. 

Tcheserkheperurā. — Åmenemḥeb, beloved of Horus.

Dynasty XIX

1. 

Menpeḥtirā. — Rāmessu I.

2. 

Menmaātrā. — Seti I, beloved of Ptaḥ.

3. 

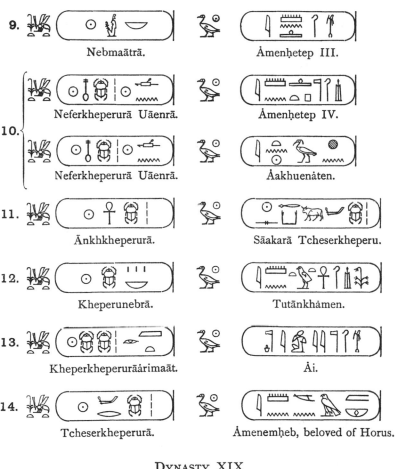

Usrmaātrā I Setepenrā. — Rāmeses II, beloved of Åmen.

4. 

Baenrā Mer-en-neteru. — Merenptaḥ I.

5. 

Menmārā Setepenrā. — Åmenmeses.

6. 

Userkheperurā Meriàmen. — Seti II Merenptaḥ II.

7. 

Åakhuenrā Setepenrā. — Merenptaḥ Saptaḥ.

8. 

Årsu a Syrian.

Dynasty XX

1. 

Userkhāurā Setepenrā. — Setnekht meri Åmenrā.

2. 

Usermaātrā II meri Åmen. — Rāmeses III.

3. 

Usermaātrā III Setepen Åmen. — Rāmeses IV.

4. 

Usermaātrā IV Sekheperenrā. — Rāmeses V meri Åmen.

5. 

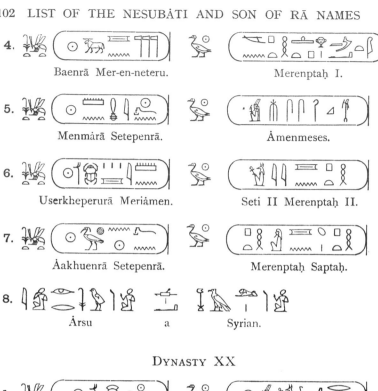

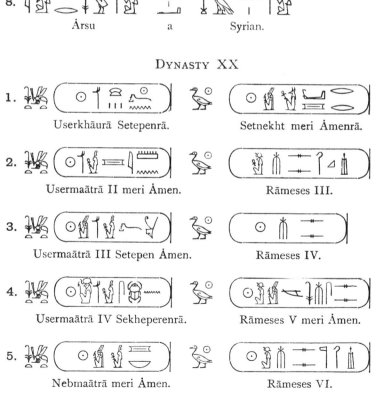

Nebmaātrā meri Åmen. — Rāmeses VI.

6. 

Usermaātrā V Setepenrā meri Åmen. — Rāmeses VII Divine emanation, governor of Ån.

7. 

Usermaātrā VI Åakhuenåmen. — Rāmeses VIII meri Åmen.

8. 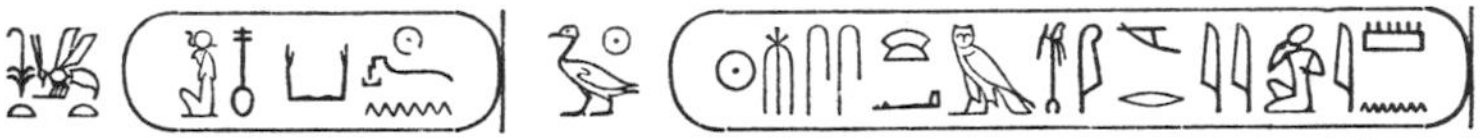

Neferkarā XI Setepenrā. — Rāmeses IX Khāem Uast meri Maāt Åmen.

9. 

Khepermaātrā Setepenrā. — Rāmeses X Åmenḥer khepesh-f.

10. 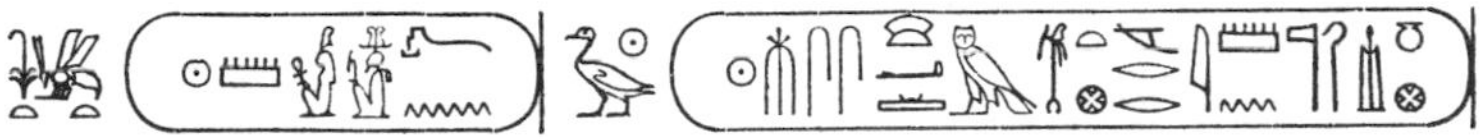

Menmaātrā II Setepenptaḥ. — Rāmeses XI.

11. 

Sekhāenrā meri Åmen. — Rāmeses XII Saptaḥ II.

DYNASTY XXI—(*a*) HIGH PRIESTS OF ÅMEN

1. 

Ḥeriḥer I, Priest first of Åmenrā, king of the gods.

2. 

First priest of Åmen. — Ḥeriḥer II Saåmen.

3. 

Paiānkh.

4a. 

Painetchem I (as high priest).

4b. 

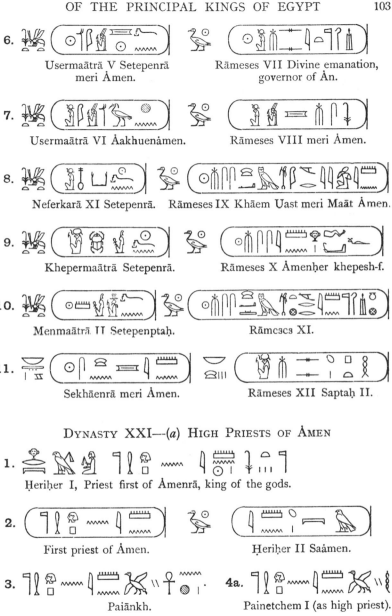

Kheperkhārā Setepenåmen. — Painetchem I meri Åmen (as king).

5. 

Tcheṭ-khensu-åuf-ānkh.

6. 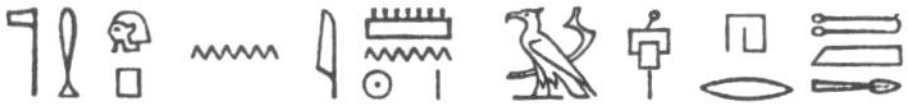

Masaherth.

7. 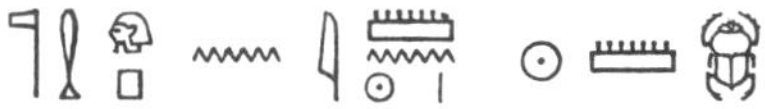

Menkheperrā II (as high priest).

8. 

Menkheperrā II (as high priest and king).

9. , as king 

Painetchem

10. 

Tåakheperurā I Setepenrā. Pasebkhān.

11. , high priest of Åmen-Rā, and son of Shashanq I.

Åuapet.

DYNASTY XXI—(*b*) KINGS OF TANIS

1. 

Hetchkheperrā Setepenrā. Nesbanebṭeṭ (Smendes).

2. 

Taåkheperurā Setepenrā. Pasebkhān I.

3. 

Kheperkhārā Setepenåmen. Pasebkhān II.

4. 

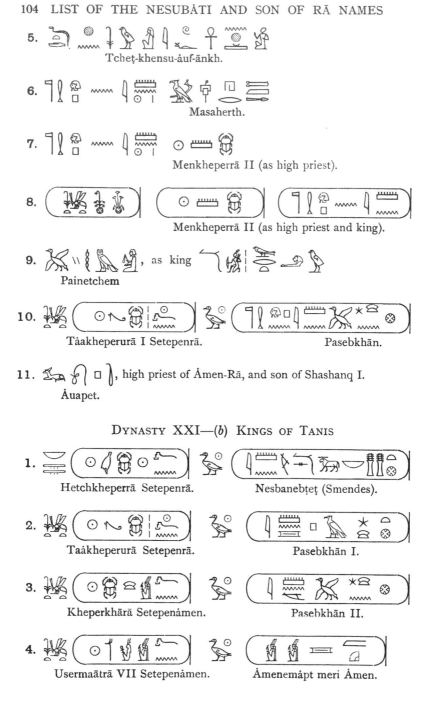

Usermaātrā VII Setepenåmen. Åmenemåpt meri Åmen.

5. 

Neterkheperrā Setepenȧmen. Saȧmen meri Ȧmen.

6. 

Āakheperrā Setepenȧmen. Pasebkhān III meri Ȧmen.

Dynasty XXII

1. 

Ḥetchkheperrā Setepenrā. Shashanq I meri Ȧmen (Shishak).

2. 

Sekhemkheperrā Setepenrā. Uasarken meri Ȧmen (Osorkon I).

3. 

Usermaātrā. Thekletȧ I.

4. 

Usermaātrā Setepenȧmen. Uasarken meri Ȧmen (Osorkon II).

5. 

Ḥetchkheperrā Setepenȧmen. Ḥersaȧst meri Ȧmen.

6.  [1]

Sesheshkheperrā Setepenrā. Shashanq meri Ȧmen.

7. 

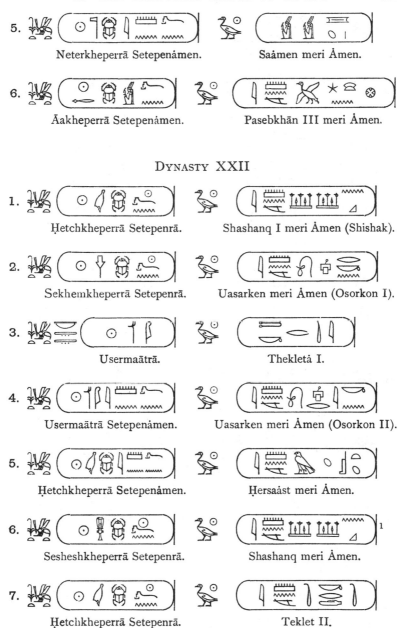

Ḥetchkheperrā Setepenrā. Teklet II.

[1] Gauthier doubts the existence of this king (*Livre des Rois*, tom. III, p. 351).

8. 

Usermaātrā Setepenȧmen. Shashanq II (?) meri Ȧmen.

9. 

Usermaātrā meri Ȧmen. Shashanq III (?) meri Ȧmen.

10. 

Usermaātrā Setepenȧmen. Pamȧi meri Ȧmen, son of Isis.

11. 

Āakheperurā. Shashanq IV (?).

Dynasty XXIII (Contemporary with Dynasty XXII)

1. 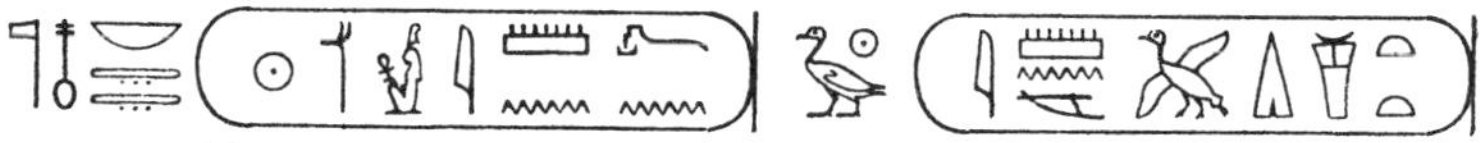

Usermaātrā Setepenȧmen. Paṭabast I.

2. 

Usermaātrā Setepenȧmen. Uapeth meri Ȧmen, son of Bast.

3. 

Usermaātrā Setepenȧmen. Uasarken III meri Ȧmen, son of Isis.

4. 

Usermaātrā Setepenȧmen. Theklet III meri Ȧmen, son of Isis.

5. 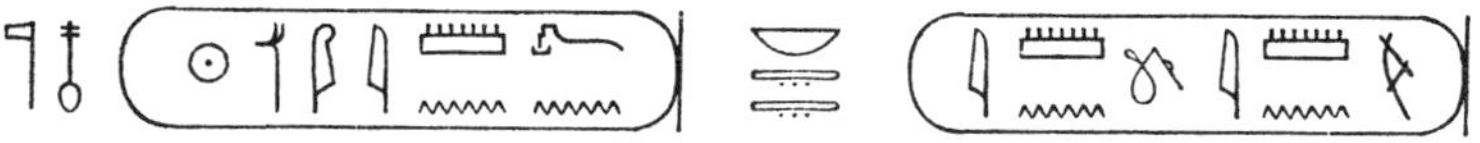

Usermaātrā Setepenȧmen. Ruṭȧmen meri Ȧmen.

6. 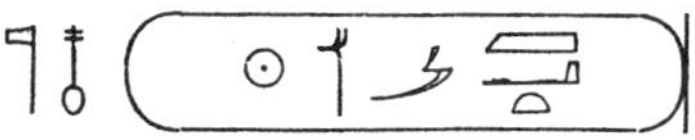 . . . .

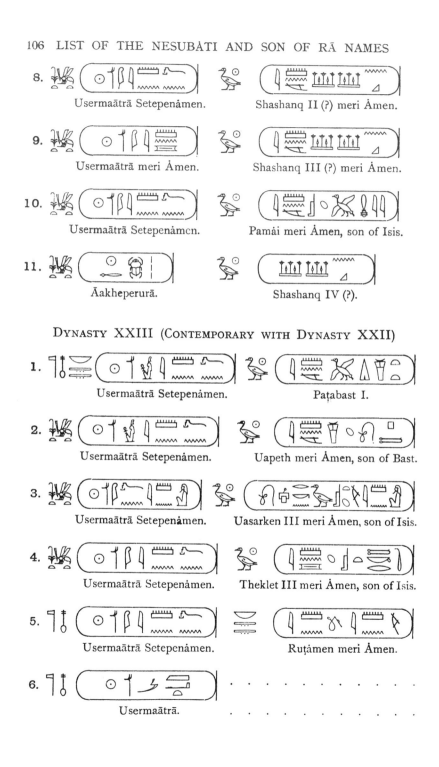

Usermaātrā. . . . .

Among the miscellaneous local rulers of this period were :—

1. 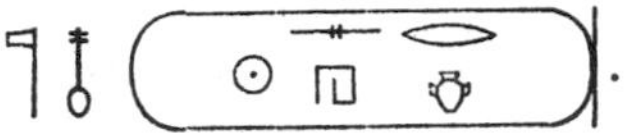

Seherȧbrā Peṭabast.

2. 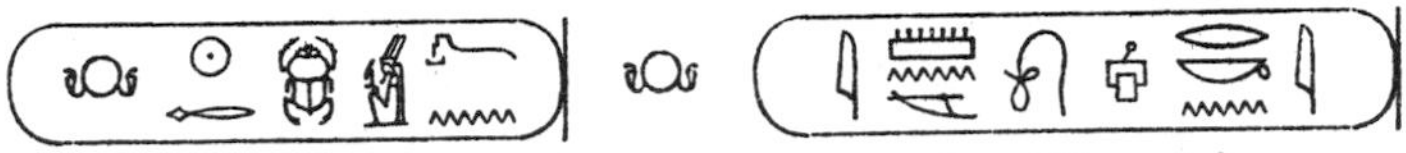

Āakheperrā Setepenȧmen. Uasarken IV meri Ȧmen.

3. 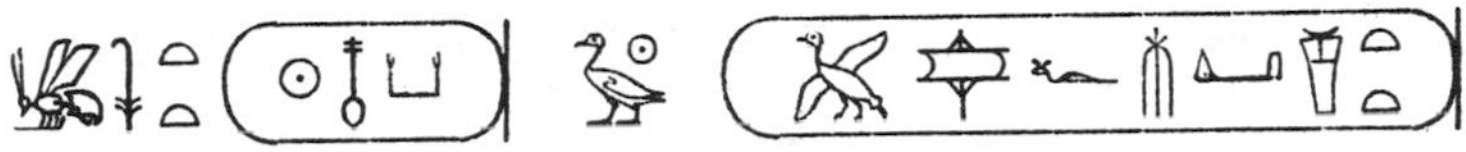

Neferkarā. Patabastt . . . . . .

4. 

Kheperkhārā Khānefer. Tcheḥutiemḥat.

5. 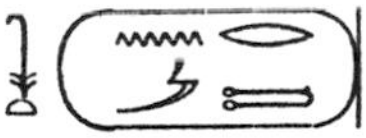

Nemareth.

6. 

Ȧupeth.

7. 

Pakameri.

8. 

Uasneterrā Setepenrā. Shashanq V.

9. 

Menkheperrā. Menirā.

Dynasty XXIV (Contemporary with the Nubians)

1. 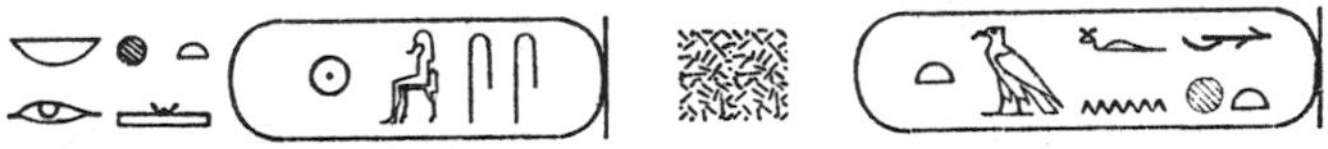

Shepsesrā. Tafnekht.

2. 

Uaḥkarā. Bakenrenf.

3. 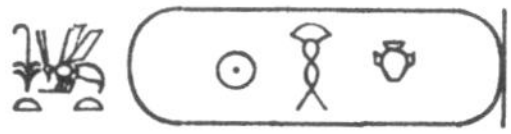

Uaḥȧbrā.

4. 

Nebakau (?).

5. 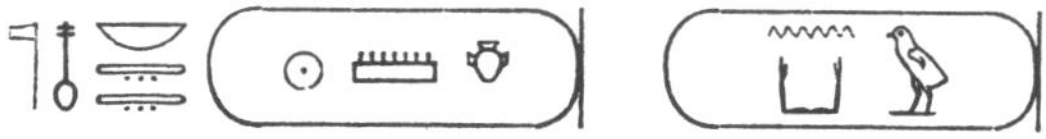

Menȧbrā. Nekau.

Dynasty XXV—Nubians

1. 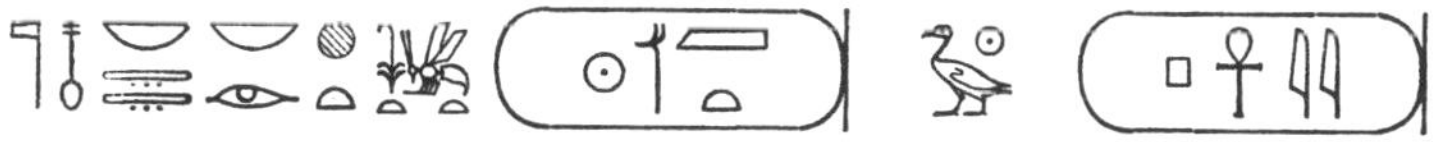

Usermaātrā. Pānkhi I meri Ȧmen.

2. 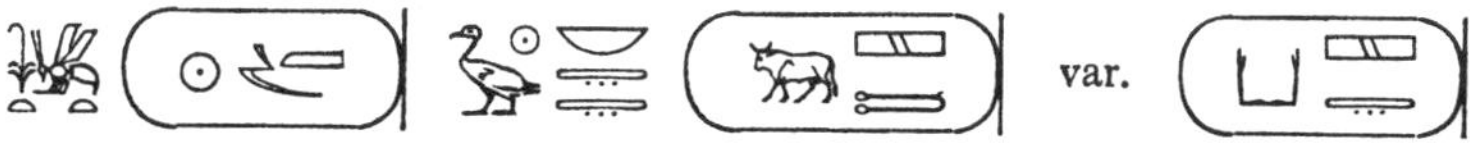

Maātrā (?). Kasht. var. Kashta.

3. 

Neferkarā. Shabaka.

4. 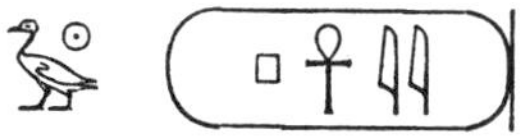

[Prenomen unknown.] Pānkhi II.

5. 

Ṭeṭkaurā. Shabataka.

6. 

Akhurā Nefer-Tem. Tahlq (Tirhȧḳȧh).

7. 

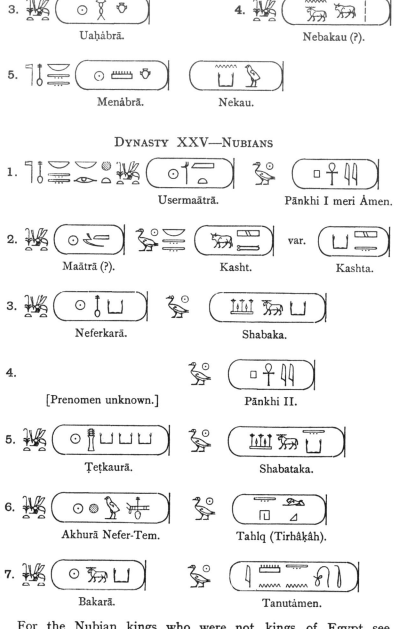

Bakarā. Tanutȧmen.

For the Nubian kings who were not kings of Egypt see pp. 115, 120 f.

Dynasty XXVI

1. 

Uaḥȧbrā. Psemthek I.

2. 

Uhemȧbrā. Nekau II.

3. 

Neferȧbrā. Psemthek II.

4. 

Ḥāāȧbrā. Uaḥȧbrā (Apries).

5. 

Khnemȧbrā. Ȧāḥmes (son of Neith).

6. 

Kaānkhenrā. Psemthek III.

Dynasty XXVII—Persians

1. 

Mesutrā. Kambȧthet (?).

var. 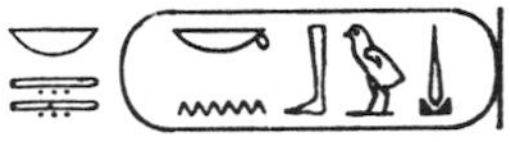

Kanbutcha (Cambyses).

2. 

Steturā. Ȧntriush.

var. 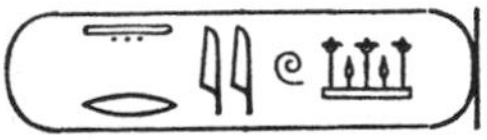

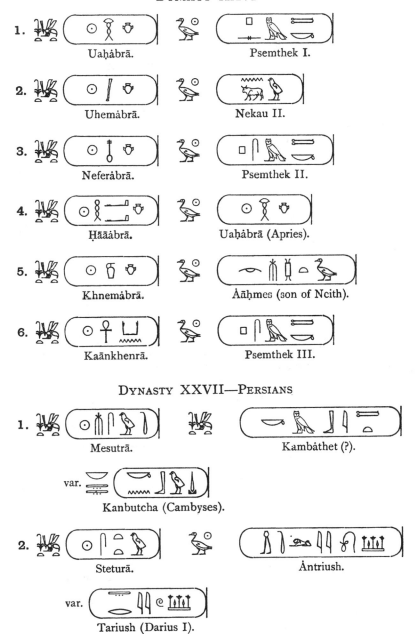

Tariush (Darius I).

3. 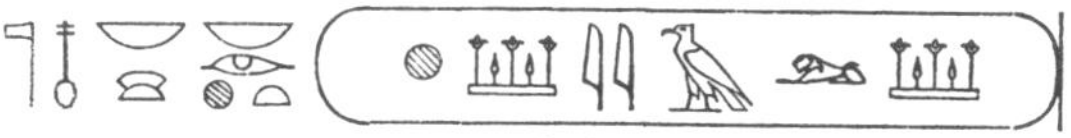

Khshiarsh (Xerxes I).

var. 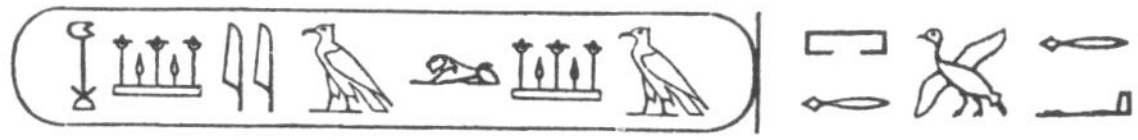

Khshiarsh. Pharaoh, the Great.

4. 

Artakhshashs (Artaxerxes I).

var. 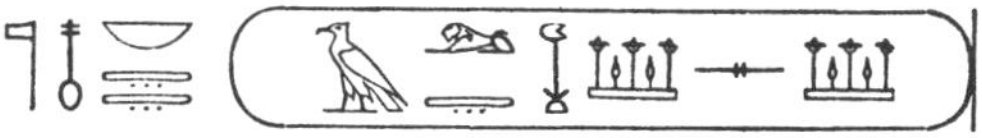

5. 

Meri Åmenrā. Åntriush (Darius II).

Dynasty XXVIII

Manetho states that the XXVIIIth dynasty was of Saïte origin, but according to him it consisted of one king only, Ἀμυρταῖος (or Ἀμύρτεος), who reigned six years. No Egyptian monument of this king has come down to us, and his name in Egyptian is not known. The various theories on the subject are well summarized by H. Gauthier, *Livre des Rois*, tom. IV, premier fasc., p. 158.

Dynasty XXIX

1. 

Baenrā meri neteru. Naifāuiruṭ (Nepherites).

2. 

Khnemmaātrā. Heqri (?) Achôris. Heqer.

3. 

Userrā Setepenptaḥ. Psamut (Psamouthis).

No monuments of Mouthis and Nepherites (II ?), the last two kings of this dynasty, according to Manetho, have hitherto been identified, and the Egyptian originals of these names are unknown.

Dynasty XXX

1. 

Senetchemȧbrā Setepenȧmen. Nekhtḥerḥeb meri Rā (?).

2. 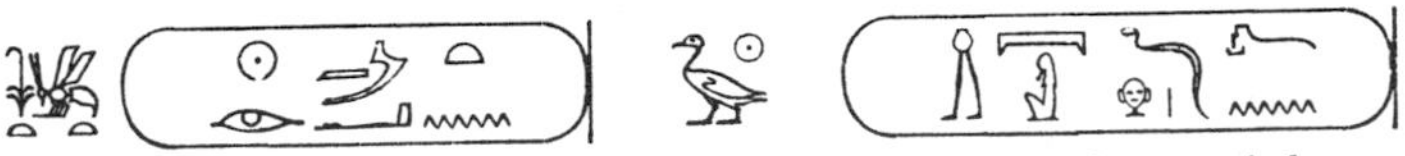

Ȧrimaātenrā. Tcheḥer Setepenȧnḥer.

3. 

Kheperkarā. Nekhtnebf.

Dynasty XXXI

According to Manetho this dynasty consisted of three Persian kings, Ὦχος, Ἀρσῆς and Δαρεῖος, whose total reigns lasted for a period of from about 10 to about 15 years. No monument bearing the name either of Ochus or Arsês is known, and the only mention of Darius III is found in a demotic papyrus in the Louvre (see Revillout, *Chrest. démotique*, p. 296, and Revillout, *Revue Égyptologique*, tom. I, p. 2). The following king was probably a contemporary of Artaxerxes III, Ochus, or of his successor Arsês, but his reign may have coincided with that of Darius III :—

Senenentanen Setepenptaḥ. Khababasha (?).

Macedonians

1. 

Setepenrā meriȧmen. Alksȧnṭrs (Alexander the Great).

2. 

Setepenrā meriȧmen. Plipus (Philip Arrhidaeus).

3. 

Ḥāāābrā Setepenȧmen. Ȧlksȧnṭrs (Alexander II).

var. 

, Pharaoh, Alexander, the son of Alexander.

PTOLEMIES

1.  Ptolemy I,

Setepenrā meriȧmen Pṭlmis.

with the titles  netch = Soter, and  khshḥtrp Satrap.

2.  Ptolemy II,

Userkarā meriȧmen Ptlumis.

with the title  "brother-loving" (Philadelphus).

3. 

{Flesh and bone of the two brothers.} Setepenrā Sekhemānkhenȧmen.

Ptulmis, ever-living, beloved of Ptaḥ.

Ptolemy III, with the title  "the well-doing god" (Euergetes I).

4. 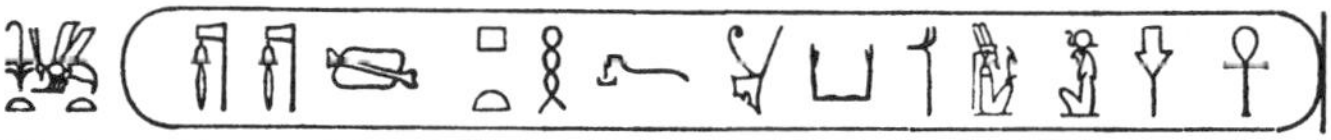

{Flesh and bone of the two well-doing gods.} Setepenptaḥ Userkarā Sekhemānkh-Ȧmen.

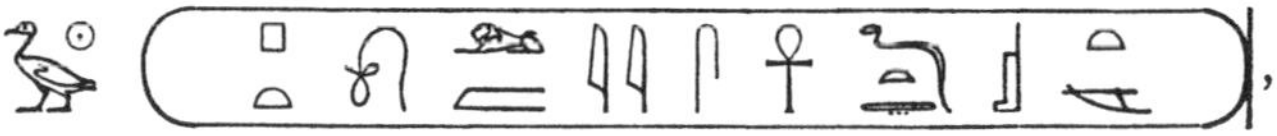,

Ptulmis, ever-living, beloved of Isis.

Ptolemy IV, with the title  "father-loving god" (Philopator).

5. 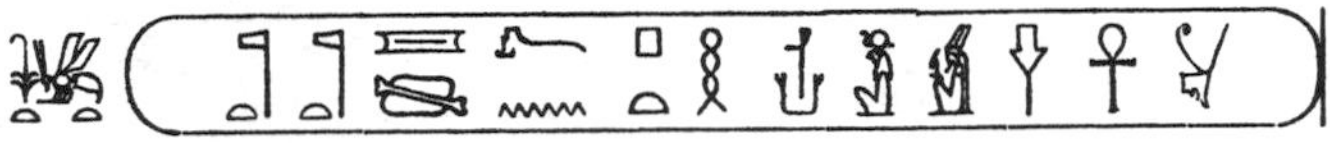

{Flesh and bone beloved of the two Father-gods.} Setepenptaḥ Userkarā Sekhemānkhen-Ȧmen.

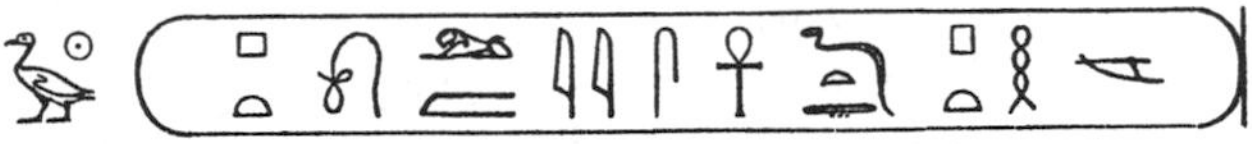,

Ptulmis, ever-living, beloved of Ptaḥ.

Ptolemy V, with the title "the god who appears" (Epiphanes).

6. 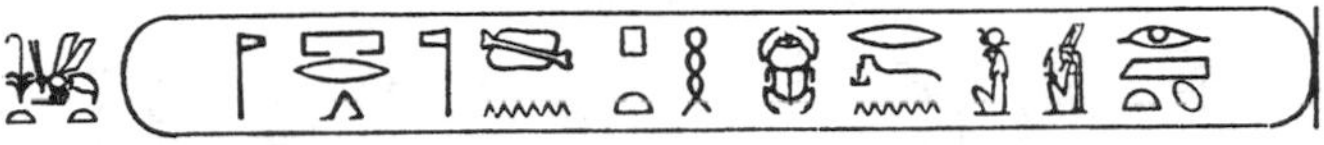

{Flesh and bone of the two gods who appeared.} Setepenptaḥkheperȧ Ȧrimaātrāȧmen.

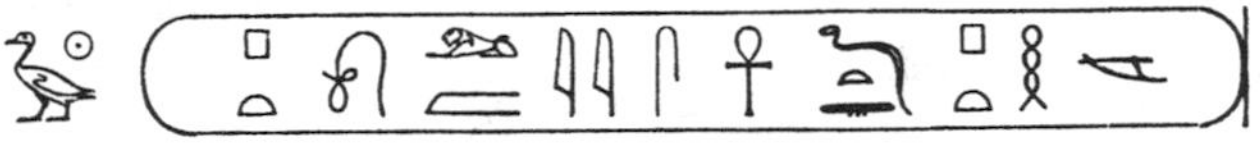,

Ptulmis, ever-living, beloved of Ptaḥ.

Ptolemy VI, with the title "the god loving his mother" (Philometor).

7. 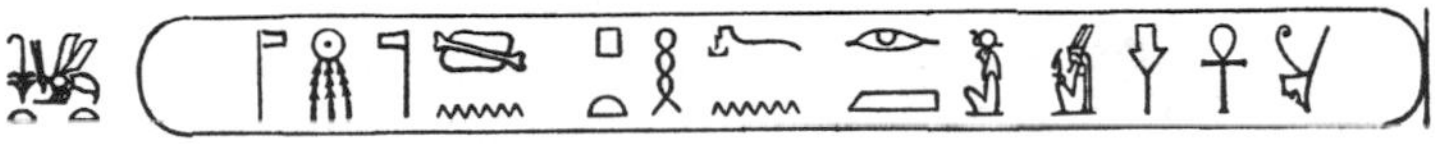

{Flesh and bone of the two gods who appeared.} Setepenptaḥ Ȧrimaātrā Sekhemānkhen-Ȧmen.

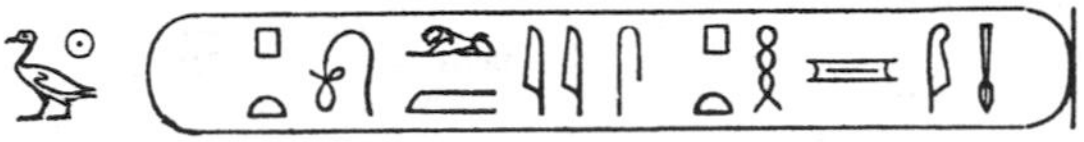 Ptolemy VII,

Ptulmis, beloved of Ptaḥ.

with the title "the well-doing god" (Euergetes II).

8. Πτολεμαῖος Εὐπάτωρ, or Ptolemy VIII Eupator. Cartouches for this king have not been found, but the title Eupator is rendered by  and . See Gauthier, *Livre des Rois*, tom. IV, p. 340.

9. Φιλοπάτωρ Νέος, or Ptolemy IX Philopator II. Cartouches for this king have not been found, but the titles Neos Philopator are rendered by  "the god, the youth, loving his father."

10. ,

{Flesh and bone of the well-doing god (Euergetes), beloved of his mother, the well-doing goddess, the Avenging Lady.} {Setepenptaḥ, Ârimaātrā, Sekhemānkhȧmen.}

i.e., Ptolemy X Philopator II (or Philometor, 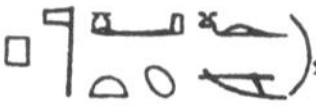), with the title , "the god who delivers" (Σωτήρ). His Son-of-Rā name was 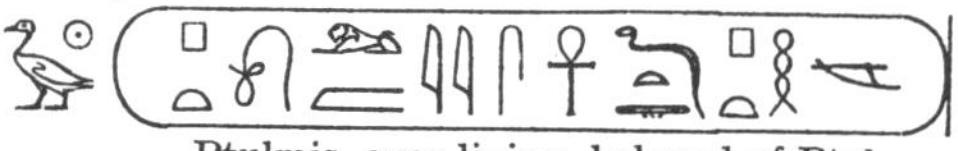

Ptulmis, ever-living, beloved of Ptaḥ.

11. 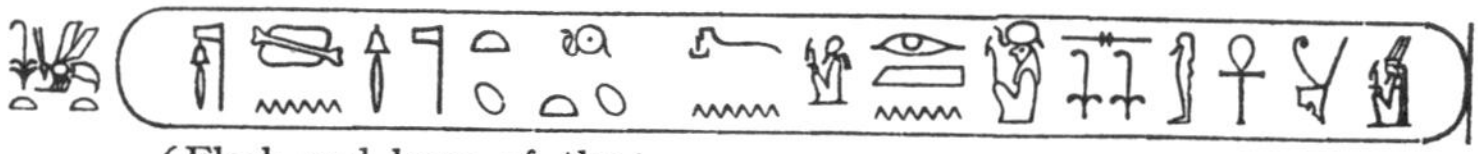

{Flesh and bone of the well-doing god and the well-doing goddess Rāt.} {Setepenptaḥ, Ârimaātenrā, Senenānkhenȧmen.}

,

Ptulmis, who is called Alexander, the ever-living, the beloved of Ptaḥ.

i.e., Ptolemy XI Alexander I, with the title  "the god loving his mother" (Philometor).

12. Ptolemy XII Alexander II. The cartouches of this king have not been found.

13. 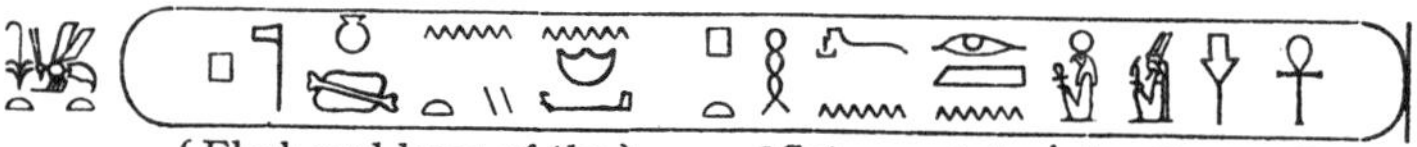

{Flesh and bone of the god who saves.} {Setepenptaḥ, Ârimaātenrā, Sekhemānkhȧmen.}

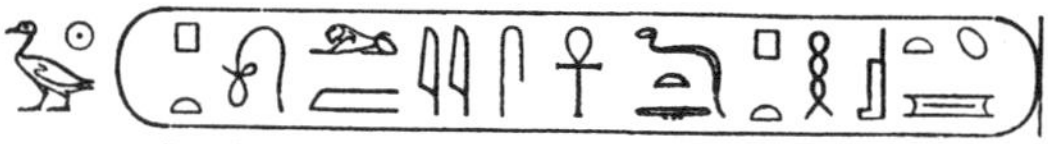, *i.e.*, Ptolemy XIII

Ptulmis, ever-living, beloved of Ptaḥ and Isis.

with the titles 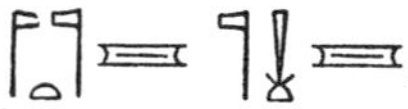, "lover of the two divine fathers" (Philopator III), and "brother lover" (Philadelphus II).

14. 

Klaupatra (Cleopatra VII), goddess, loving her father (Philopator)

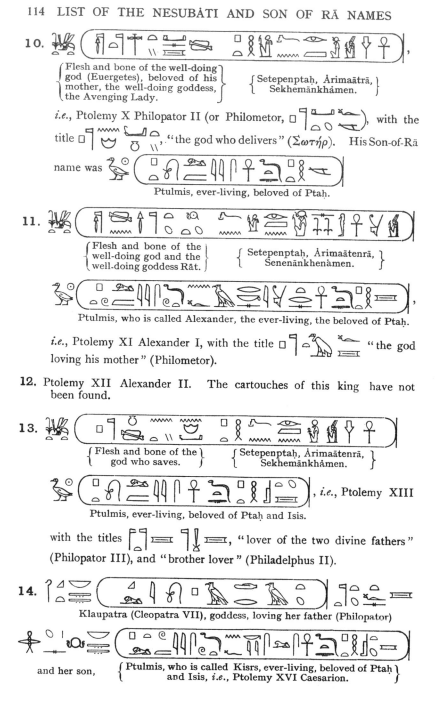

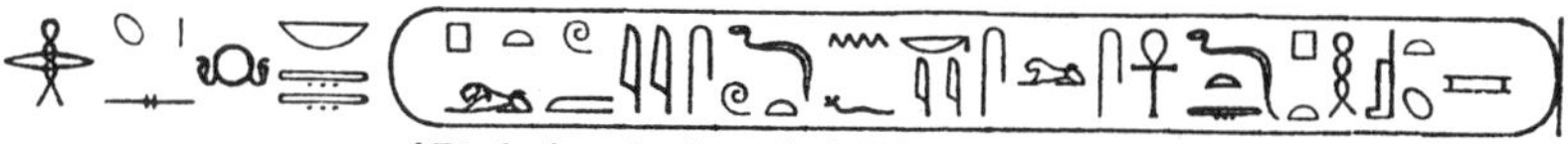

and her son, {Ptulmis, who is called Kisrs, ever-living, beloved of Ptaḥ and Isis, *i.e.*, Ptolemy XVI Caesarion.}

KINGS OF NORTHERN NUBIA, CONTEMPORARIES OF THE PTOLEMIES

1. 

Ṭetiàmen, Tàaānkhrā, Àrqàmen, ever-living, beloved of Isis.
i.e., Ἐργαμένης, the contemporary of Ptolemies II, III and IV (?).

2. 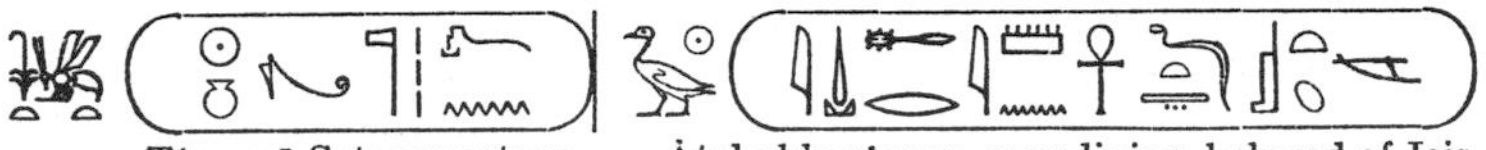

Tàaenrā-Setepenneteru, Àtchakharàmen, ever-living, beloved of Isis.
His date is uncertain.

On the two kings Harmakhis and Ānkhmakhis, who are only known from demotic papyri, and for the literature, see Gauthier, *op. cit.*, tom. IV, p. 425 ff.

ROMANS

CAESAR AUGUSTUS

1. 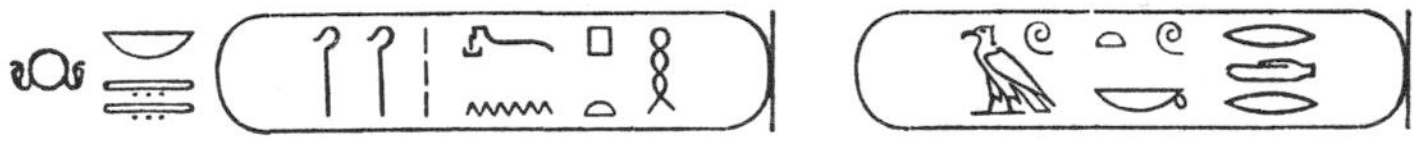

Ḥeqḥequ Setepenptaḥ   Autukrṭr (Autokrator)

Kisras (Caesar), ever-living, beloved of Ptaḥ and Isis.

TIBERIUS CAESAR AUGUSTUS

2. 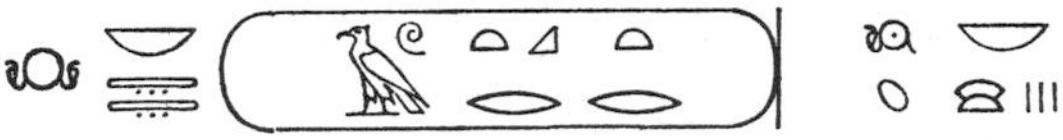

Autokrator

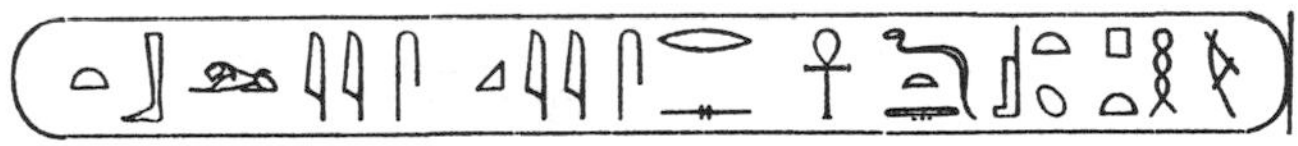

{Tebris / Tiberius}   Kisrs / Caesar   {ever-living, beloved of Ptaḥ and Isis.}

GAIUS CAESAR AUGUSTUS GERMANICUS [CALIGULA]

3. 

Ḥeqḥequ Autokrator, beloved of Ptaḥ and Isis,

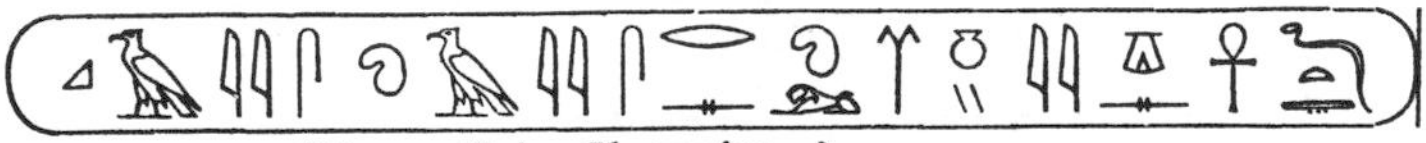

{Caesar Gaius Kermnigs, / Germanicus,} ever-living.

Tiberius Claudius Caesar Augustus Germanicus

4. 

Ḥeqḥequ Autokrator, beloved of Ptaḥ and Isis,

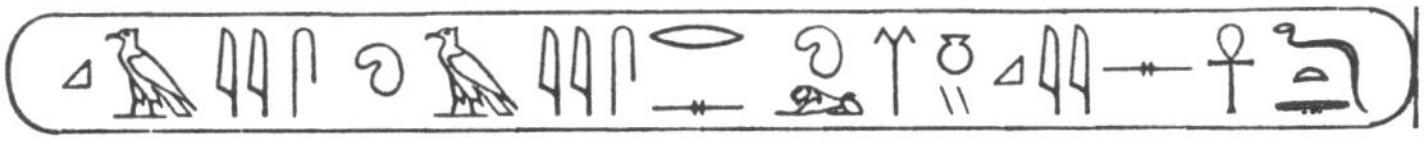

{Kais / Gaius} {Kaisrs / Caesar} {Krmnikis, / Germanicus,} ever-living.

Nero Claudius Caesar Augustus Germanicus

5. 

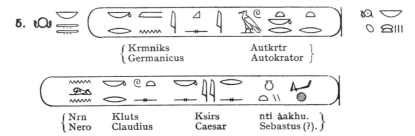

{Krmniks / Germanicus} {Autkrtr / Autokrator}

{Nrn / Nero} {Kluts / Claudius} {Ksirs / Caesar} {nti âakhu. / Sebastus (?).}

Servius Livius Augustus Sulpicius Galba

6. 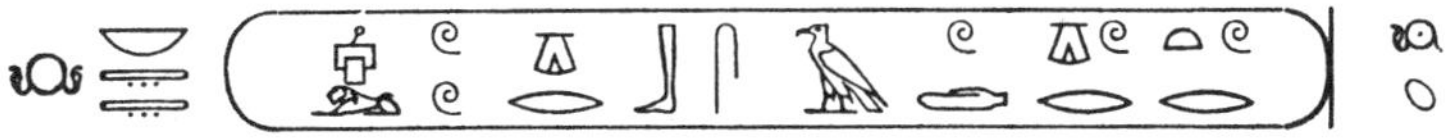

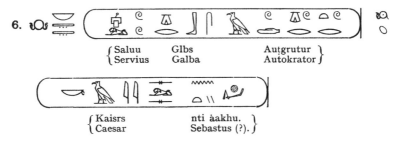

{Saluu / Servius} {Glbs / Galba} {Auṭgrutur / Autokrator}

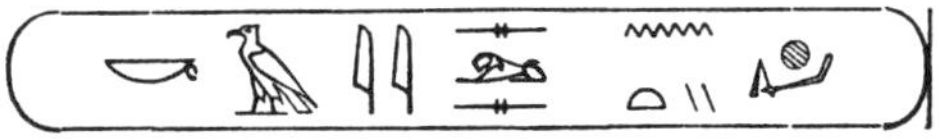

{Kaisrs / Caesar} {nti âakhu. / Sebastus (?).}

Marcus Salvius Otho (Othon)

7. 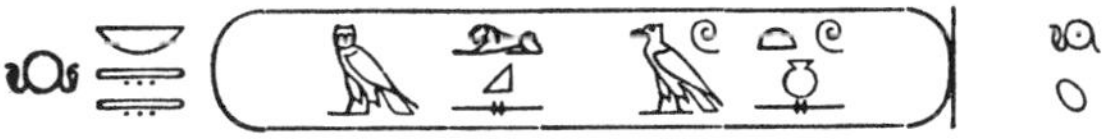

{Mrks / Marcus} {Autuns / Othon}

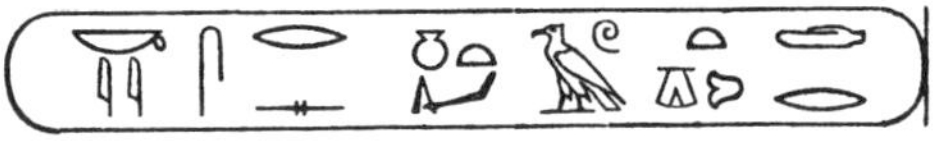

{Kisrs / Caesar} {Autgrtr. / Autokrator.}

Caesar Augustus Vespasian

8. 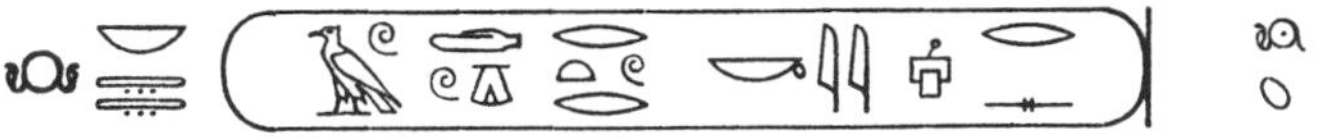

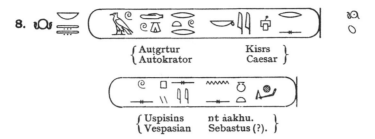

{Autgrtur / Autokrator} {Kisrs / Caesar}

{Uspisins / Vespasian} {nt àakhu. / Sebastus (?).}

Titus Caesar Vespasian Augustus

9. 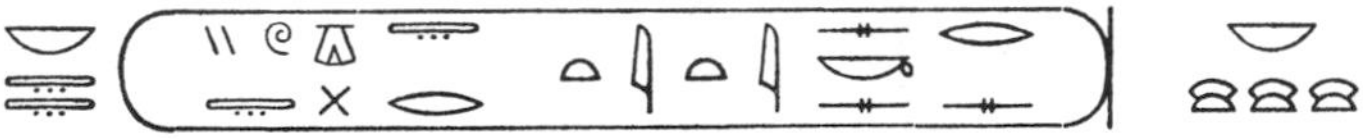

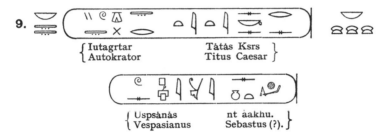

{Iutagrtar / Autokrator} {Tàtàs Ksrs / Titus Caesar}

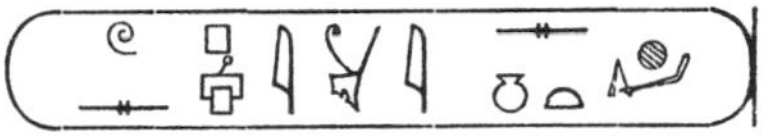

{Uspsànàs / Vespasianus} {nt àakhu. / Sebastus (?).}

Caesar Domitian Augustus Germanicus

10. 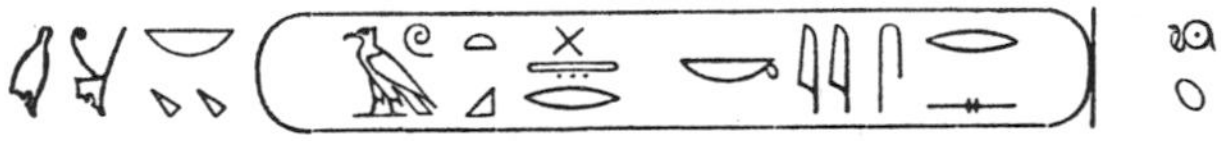

Autokrator Caesar

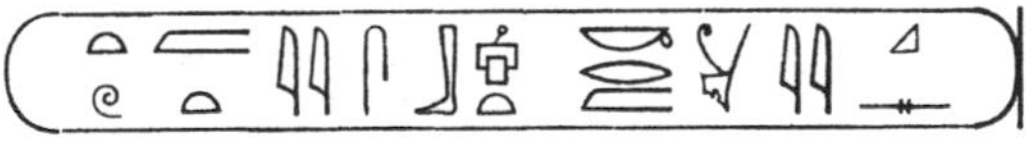

{Tumti Sebst / Domitian Sebastus} {Krmniks. / Germanicus.}

Caesar Nerva Augustus

11. 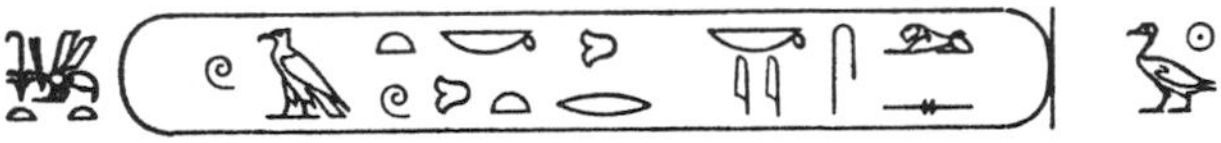

Autokrator Caesar

{Neruàs / Nerva} {nt àakhu. / Sebastus (or Augustus).}

Caesar Nerva Trajan Augustus Germanicus

12. 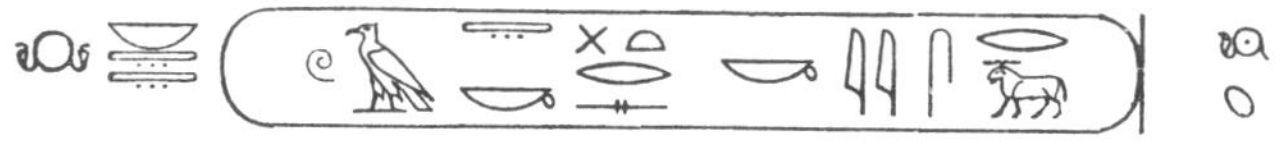

Autokrator Caesar

{ Trins / Trajan } { nti åakhu. / Augustus. }

Caesar Trajan Hadrian Augustus

13. 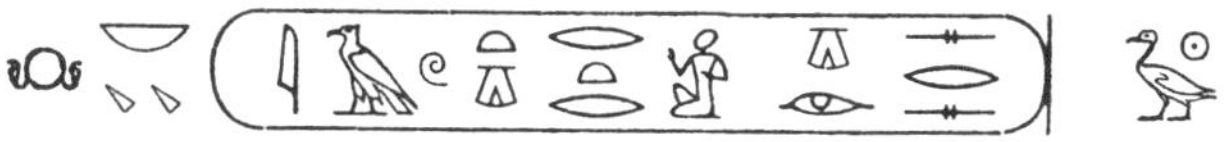

Autokrator Caesar

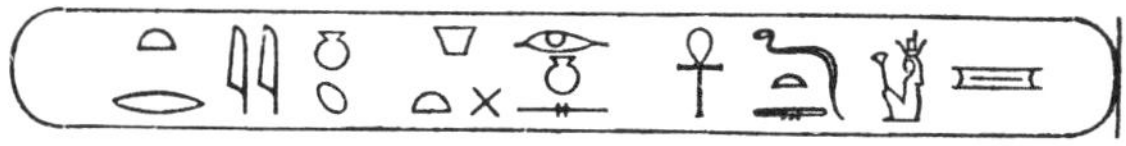

{ Trins / Trajan } { Atrins / Hadrian } { ever-living, beloved / of Isis. }

Titus Aelius Hadrian Antoninus Augustus Eusebes

14. 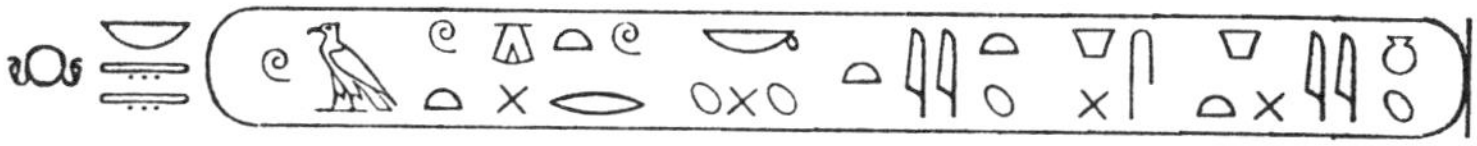

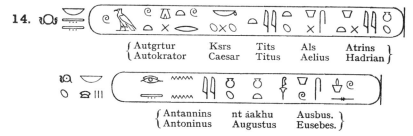

{ Autgrtur / Autokrator } { Ksrs / Caesar } { Tits / Titus } { Als / Aelius } { Atrins / Hadrian }

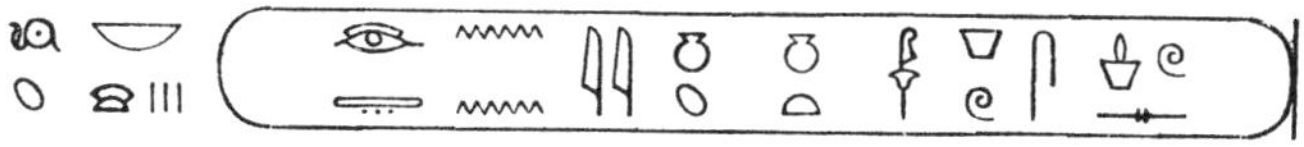

{ Antannins / Antoninus } { nt åakhu / Augustus } { Ausbus. / Eusebes. }

Lucius Aurelius Verus Augustus

15. 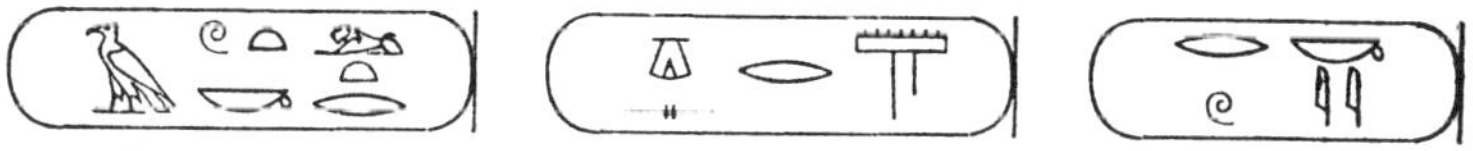

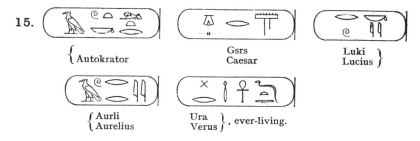

{ Autokrator } { Gsrs / Caesar } { Luki / Lucius }

{ Aurli / Aurelius } { Ura / Verus }, ever-living.

MARCUS AURELIUS ANTONINUS AUGUSTUS

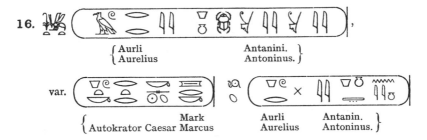

16. 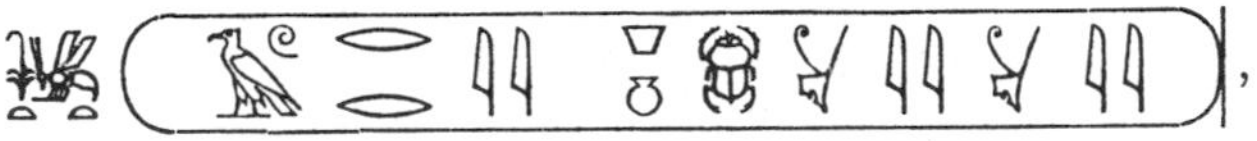

{Aurli / Aurelius} Antanini. / Antoninus.}

var. 

{Mark / Autokrator Caesar Marcus} Aurli / Aurelius Antanin. / Antoninus.}

MARCUS AURELIUS COMMODUS ANTONINUS

17. 

Autokrator Caesar

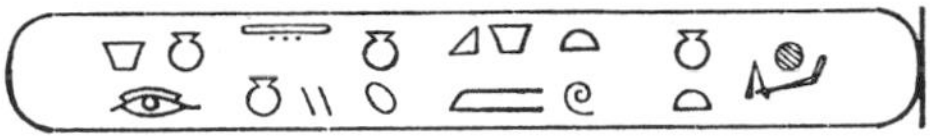

{Antanins / Antoninus} Kamtu / Commodus nt åakhu. / Augustus.}

18. PUBLIUS HELVIUS PERTINAX } Cartouches wanting.

19. GAIUS PESCENNIUS NIGER JUSTUS }

LUCIUS SEPTIMIUS SEVERUS PERTINAX

20. 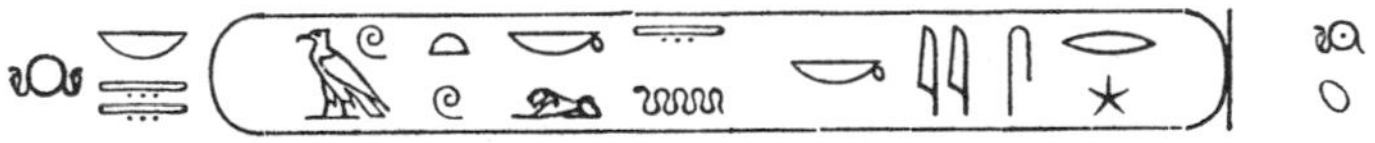

Autokrator Caesar

{Sauri / Severus} nti åakhu. / Augustus.}

MARCUS AURELIUS ANTONINUS (CARACALLA)

21. 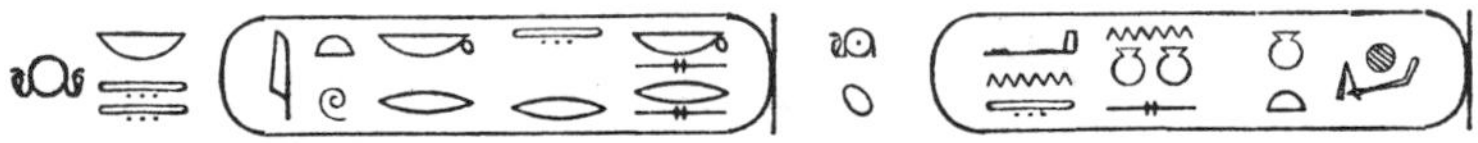

Autokrator Caesar Antoninus Augustus.

Publius Septimius Geta Augustus

22. 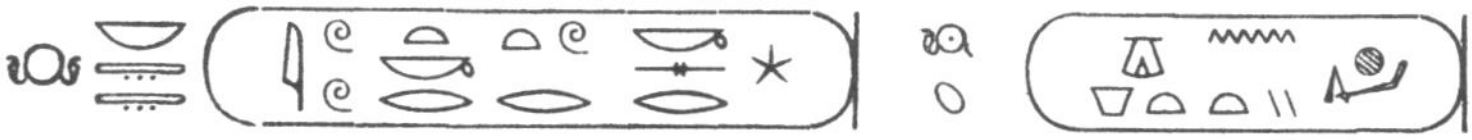

Autokrator Caesar {Gat nti åakhu. / Geta Augustus.}

23. Marcus Opellius Severus Macrinus
24. Marcus Aurelius Antoninus (Elagabalus)
25. Marcus Aurelius Severus Alexander
26. Gaius Julius Verus Maximinus
27. Marcus Antonius Gordianus

(23–27: Cartouches wanting.)

Marcus Julius Philippus

28. 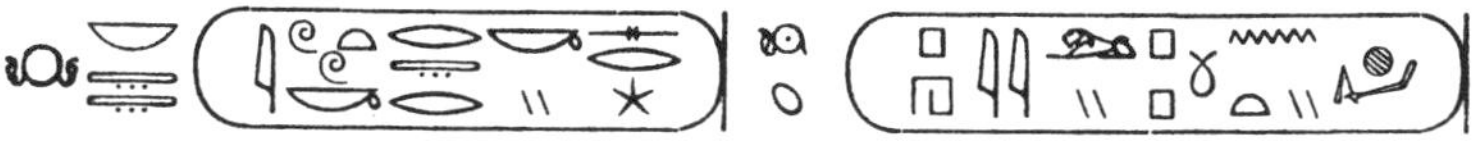

Autokrator Caesar {Philipps nti åakhu. / Philip Augustus.}

Gaius Mersius Quintus Traianus Decius

29. 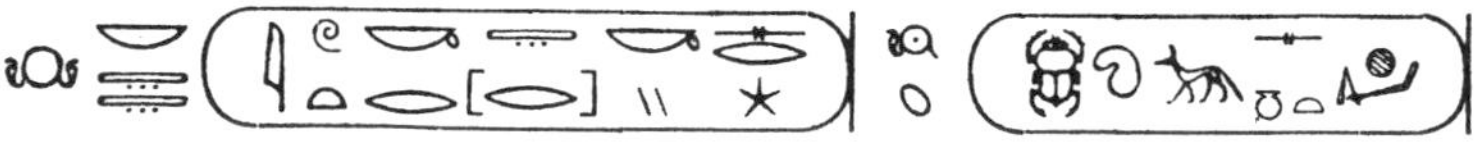

Autokrator Caesar {Takis nti åakhu. / Decius Augustus.}

Kings of Napata (Southern Nubia)

1. 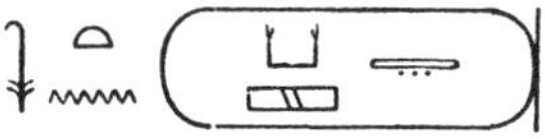

Kashta.

2. 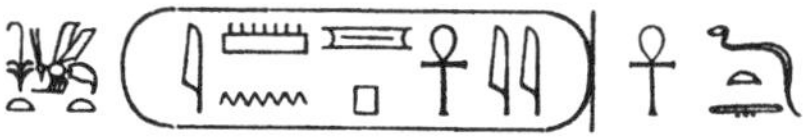

Pānkhi meri Åmen.

3. 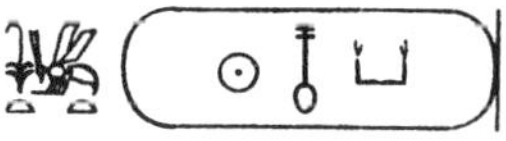

Neferkarā

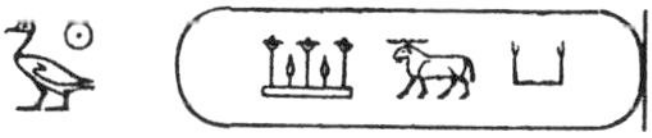

Shabaka.

4. 

Ṭeṭkarā

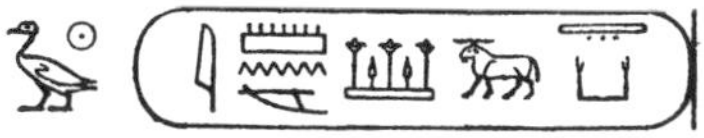

Shabataka meri Åmen.

5. 

Akhunefertem — Tahrq (or Tarhq) = Tirhâḳâh.

6. 

Bakarā — Tanutȧmen.

7. 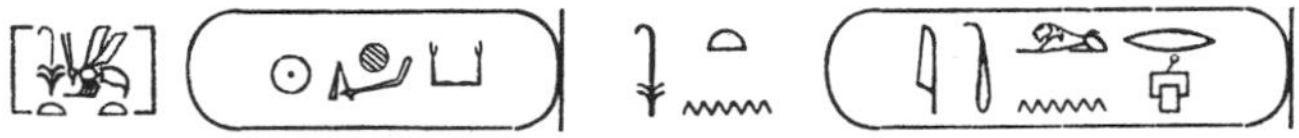

Akhukarā — Atlnersa.

8. 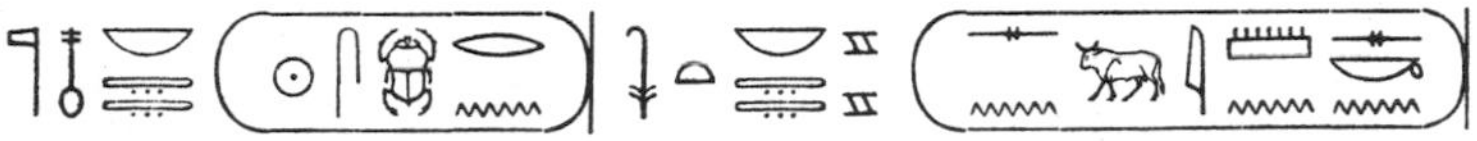

Sekheperenrā — Senkaȧmenseken.

9. 

Ānkhkarā — Ȧnlȧmen.

10. 

Merkarā — Ȧspelta.

11. 

Uatchkarā — Amtlq.

12. 

Sekhemkarā — Malneqen.

13. 

Neferkarā — Nelmāi (?).

14. 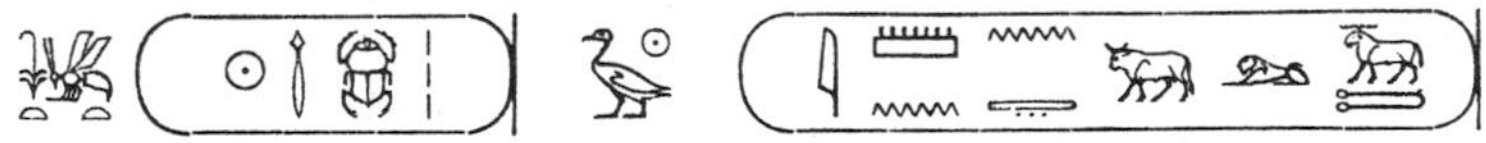

Ākheperurā — Netaklabathȧmen.

15. 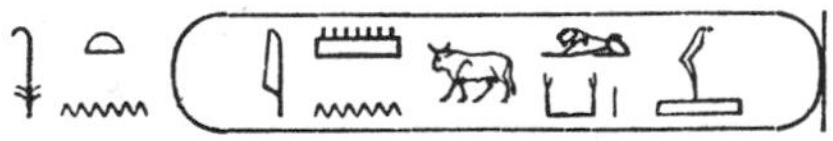

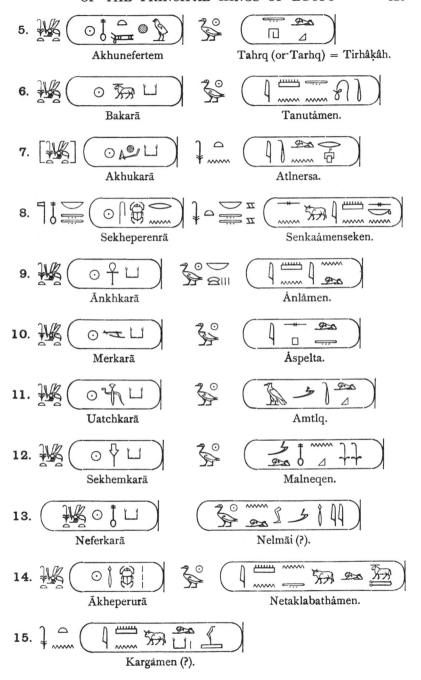

Kargȧmen (?).

16. 

Setepkarā — Åstabarqāmen.

17. 

Segerḥtauirā — Åsāsnuāq (?).

18. 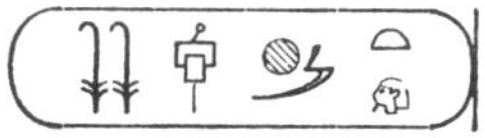

Nasakhmat (?).

19. 

Kheperkarā — Maluibåmen (?).

20. 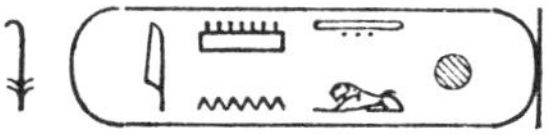

Talakhåmen.

21. 

Neferåbrā — Ḥerinutårekåmen.

22. 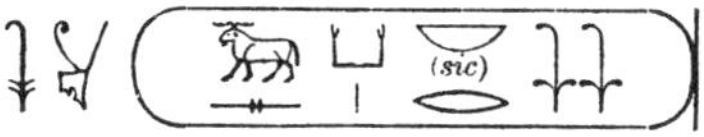

Baskakeren.

23. 

Ḥersaåtef — Sameriåmen.

24. 

Åkhertn — Pānkalaru (?).

25. 

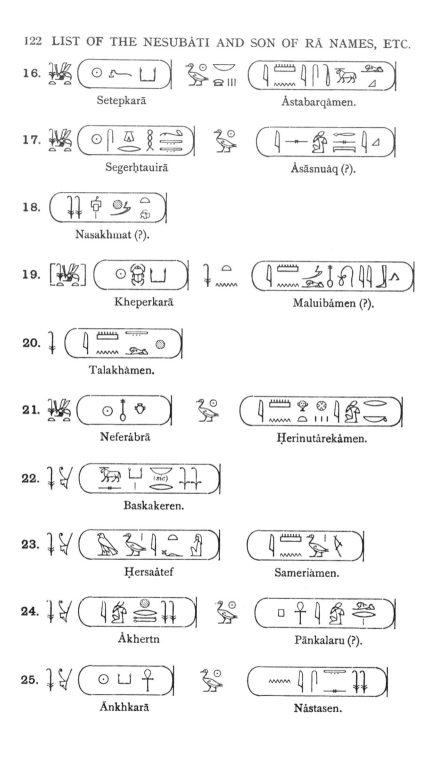

Ānkhkarā — Nåstasen.

THE DECIPHERMENT OF THE EGYPTIAN HIEROGLYPHS—THE ROSETTA STONE AND THE OBELISK FROM PHILAE

THE famous " Stone " in the British Museum (Southern Egyptian Gallery, No. 24), which is now universally known as the **Rosetta Stone,** was accidentally discovered at a spot near the town of Rashîd, or Rosetta, in the Western Delta. The fortunate finder was M. Boussard,[1] or Bouchard, a French Officer of Engineers, who was engaged in strengthening Fort St. Julien in August, 1799. This fort stood on the west bank of the Rosetta arm of the Nile, exactly opposite Jazîrat al-Khaḏrah, about half-way between Burg Sa'îr and Jazîrat Warshî. The spot where the Stone was found marks the site of the temple of Bolbitine, which was probably dedicated to the god Tem in the reign of king Nekhtḥerḥeb, or Nektanebus I, who reigned about B.C. 378. The Stone was taken to the house of Gen. Menou in Alexandria, who had it carefully packed up in cotton cloth and matting, and claimed it as his personal property. After the capitulation of Alexandria all the antiquities which had been collected in Cairo by Napoleon ready for despatch to Paris were surrendered, according to Article XVI of the Treaty of Capitulation, to Gen. Hutchinson, who ordered them to be sent to London. Among the antiquities surrendered was the Rosetta Stone, which Gen. Menou refused to give up, declaring that it was his private property. When Gen. Hutchinson heard this he sent a detachment of artillerymen and a "devil cart " to Maj.-Gen. H. Turner, and ordered him to take possession of the Stone. This was done without delay, and Gen. Turner embarked with it on board the frigate " Égyptienne," which the British had captured in the harbour at Alexandria, and arrived at Portsmouth in February, 1802. With the consent of the Secretary of State the Stone was taken to the rooms of the Society of Antiquaries of London, where it remained until it was removed to the British Museum. In April the Rev. S. Weston read a translation of the Greek text before the Society, and in July the Council ordered four casts of the Stone to be made, and one each to be sent to the Universities of Oxford, Cambridge, Edinburgh and Dublin.

In its present state the Rosetta Stone is an irregularly shaped slab of compact black basalt which measures about 3 ft. 9 in. by 2 ft. 4½ in. by 11 in., and the top corners and the right-hand bottom corner are wanting. It is inscribed with 14 lines of hieroglyphic text, 32 lines of demotic and 54 lines of Greek. The inscription on the Stone is **bilingual,**[2] and is written

[1] He attained the rank of " General," and was alive in 1814.

[2] The Rosetta inscription has been often called trilingual and compared to the Bihistûn Inscription ; but in the former there are only two languages, though three forms of writing are employed, while in the latter there are three distinct languages.

in Egyptian and in Greek. The Egyptian portion is in hieroglyphs and also in demotic characters.

We may arrive at an idea of the original size of the Rosetta Stone by comparing the number of lines upon it with the number of those upon the **Stele of Canopus,** which is also inscribed in hieroglyphic, demotic and Greek, and measures 7 ft. 2 in. by 2 ft. 7 in. by 1 ft. 2 in., and is inscribed with 36 lines of hieroglyphs, 73 lines of demotic writing, and 74 lines of Greek. The demotic inscription is on the edge of the stele, and seems to have been overlooked by Lepsius when he was preparing his edition of the hieroglyphic and Greek texts. This stele was set up at Canopus in the ninth year of the reign of **Ptolemy III Euergetes I (B.C. 247–222),** to record the decree made at Canopus by the priesthood, assembled from all parts of Egypt, in honour of the king. It records the great benefits which he had conferred upon Egypt, and states what festivals are to be celebrated in his honour, and in that of Berenice, etc., and, like the Rosetta Stone, concludes with a resolution ordering that a copy of this inscription in hieroglyphs, Greek and demotic, shall be placed in every large temple in Egypt. Now the Rosetta Stone is inscribed with 32 lines of demotic, and the Stele of Canopus with 73; but as the lines on the Rosetta Stone are rather more than double the length of those on the Stele of Canopus, it is pretty certain that each document is of about the same length. The Stele of Canopus has 74 lines of Greek to 54 on the Rosetta Stone, but as the letters are longer and wider, it is clear from this also that the Greek versions occupied about the same space. Allowing then for the difference in the size of the hieroglyphic characters, we should expect the hieroglyphic inscription on the Rosetta Stone to occupy 14 or 15 lines. When complete the stele must have been about 12 inches longer than it is now, and the top was probably rounded and inscribed, like that of the Stele of Canopus, with a winged disk, having pendent uraei, that on the right wearing , the crown of Upper Egypt, and that on the left , the crown of Lower Egypt; by the side of each uraeus, laid horizontally, would be 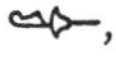, and above  *ta ānkh,* "giver of life."

The inscriptions on the Rosetta Stone form a version of the Decree of the whole priesthood of Egypt, assembled in solemn conclave at Memphis to do honour to **Ptolemy V Epiphanes,** king of Egypt **(B.C. 196),** written in hieroglyphs, demotic and Greek. A complete facsimile[1] of them was published by the Society of

[1] Other facsimiles are given in Lepsius, *Auswahl,* Bl. 18, and in Arundale and Bonomi, *Gallery of Antiquities,* pl. 49, p. 114.

Antiquaries[1] in 1802, and copies were distributed among the scholars who were anxious to undertake the investigation of the texts. The hieroglyphic text has been translated by Brugsch in his *Inscriptio Rosettana*, Berlin, 1851 ; by Chabas, *L'Inscription hiéroglyphique de Rosette*, Paris, 1867 ; by Sharpe, *The Rosetta Stone in hieroglyphics and Greek*, London, 1871 ; by Birch, *Gallery of Antiquities*, p. 114 ; and by Mahaffy, *Empire of the Ptolemies*, pp. 316–327. The demotic text has been studied by M. de Sacy, *Lettre à M. Chaptal sur l'inscription égypt. de Rosette*, Paris, 1802 ; by Åkerblad, *Lettre à M. de Sacy sur l'inscription égypt. de Rosette*, Paris, 1802 ; by Young, *Hieroglyphics* (collected by the Egyptian Society, arranged by Dr. T. Young, 2 vols., fol., 100 plates, 1823–1828), pl. X ff. ; by Brugsch, *Die Inschrift von Rosette nach ihrem ägyptisch-demotischen Texte sprachlich und sachlich erklärt*, Berlin, 1850 ; by Salvolini, *Analyse Grammaticale Raisonnée de différents textes des anciens Égyptiens*, Vol. I., *Texte hiéroglyphique et démotique de la pierre de Rosette*, Paris, 1836 [this work was never finished] ; by de Saulcy, *Analyse Grammaticale*, Vol. I, pt. I, Paris, 1845 ; by de Rougé, *Lettre à M. de Saulcy* (*Revue Arch.*, 1847, pp. 321–343) ; by Revillout, *Chrestomathie Démotique*, 1880 ; and by Hess, *Der Demotische Teil der Dreisprachigen Inschrift von Rosette*, 1902. The Greek text has been edited in *Vetusta Monumenta*, Vol. IV, pll. VIII and IX ; and *Description de l'Égypte*, tom. V, pll. V–VII ; by Lepsius, *Auswahl*, pll. XVIII and XIX ; Heyne, *Commentatio in inscriptionem graecam monumenti trinis titulis insigniti ex Aegypto Londinum apportati*, in tom. XV of *Comment. Soc. R. Sc. Gött.*, pp. 260–280 ; Ameilhon, *Éclaircissements sur l'inscription grecque du monument trouvé à Rosette*, Paris, 1803 ; Bailey, *Hieroglyphicorum Origo et Natura*, Cambridge, 1816 ; Drumann, *Commentatio in inscriptionem prope Rosettam inventam*, Regiomont, 1822 ; and Drumann, *Historisch-antiquarische Untersuchungen über Aegypten, oder die Inschrift von Rosette aus dem Griechischen übersetzt und erläutert*, Königsberg, 1823 ; Lenormant, *Essai sur le texte grec de l'inscription de Rosette*, Paris, 1842 ; Letronne, *Recueil des inscriptions grecques et latines d'Égypte*, Paris, 1842 ; and by Franz in Boeckh, *Corpus Inscriptionum Graecarum*, t. III, 1853, p. 334 ff., No. 4697, etc. The complete hieroglyphic, demotic and Greek texts, together with transliterations and English translations and facsimiles, will be found in Budge, *The Decrees of Memphis and Canopus*, Vols. I–III, London, 1904. This work is out of print. A good and cheap autotype facsimile of the Stone, with a few pages of letterpress by myself, was published by the Trustees of the British Museum in 1914, price sixpence. The glass was removed and the Stone was

[1] The Greek version of the decree of the Egyptian Priests in honour of *Ptolemy the Fifth*, surnamed *Epiphanes*, from the stone inscribed in the sacred and vulgar Egyptian and the Greek characters, taken from the French at the surrender of Alexandria. London, 1802. Nichols.

levelled and grey powder was carefully dusted into the inscriptions. A day when the light was most suitable was waited for and the photograph was taken by Mr. D. Macbeth, who had mounted his camera on a scaffold immediately above the Stone. The reproduction on the Plate opposite is, for its size, one of the best ever made.*

Contents of the Decree of the priests at Memphis.—The inscriptions upon the Rosetta Stone set forth that Ptolemy V Epiphanes, while king of Egypt, (1) consecrated revenues of silver and corn to the temples; (2) that he suppressed certain taxes and reduced others; (3) that he granted certain privileges to the priests and soldiers; (4) that when, in the eighth year of his reign, the Nile rose to a great height and flooded all the plains, he undertook, at great expense, the task of damming it in and directing the overflow of its waters into proper channels, to the great gain and benefit of the agricultural classes; (5) that he remitted taxes; (6) that he gave handsome gifts to the temples, and (7) that he subscribed to the various ceremonies which were carried on in them. In return for these gracious acts the priesthood assembled in the great temple of Ptaḥ at Memphis decreed that a statue of the king should be set up in a conspicuous place in every temple of Egypt, and that each should be inscribed with the name and titles of **Ptolemy, the saviour of Egypt.** Royal apparel was to be placed on each statue, and ceremonies were to be performed before each three times a day. It was also decreed that a gilded wooden shrine, containing a gilded wooden figure of the king, should be placed in each temple, and that these were to be carried out with the shrines of the other kings in the great panegyrics. It was also decreed that ten golden crowns of a peculiar design should be made and laid upon the royal shrine; that the birthday and coronation day of the king should be celebrated each year with great pomp and rejoicing and feasting; that the first five days of the month of Thoth should each year be set apart for the performance of a festival in honour of the king; and finally that a copy of this decree, engraved upon a tablet of hard stone in hieroglyphic, demotic and Greek characters, should be set up in each of the temples of the first, second and third orders, near the statue of the ever-living Ptolemy. It was formerly supposed that the Greek portion of the inscriptions was the original document, and that the hieroglyphic and demotic versions were merely translations of it, but many reasons have been adduced for thinking that the original draft was in demotic, especially as neither the hieroglyphic nor the Greek version really represents the exact meaning of many of the carefully thought-out phrases of the demotic text.

Although it is nearly certain that, without the aid of the Greek inscription found on the socket of an obelisk at Philae, and the hieroglyphic inscription found on the obelisk which belonged to that socket, the hieroglyphic alphabet could never have been recovered from the Rosetta Stone, still it is around this wonderful document that all the interest in the decipherment of the Egyptian hieroglyphs clings. For many hundreds of years the interest of the learned of all countries has been excited by the hieroglyphic inscriptions of Egypt, and the theories propounded as to their contents were legion. Speaking broadly, the references to this subject by classical authors[1] are not very satisfactory; still there are some remarkable exceptions, which will be referred to presently. Inasmuch as the names of Roman emperors, as late as the time of Decius, were written in hieroglyphs, it follows that the knowledge of this subject must have been possessed by someone, either Greek or Egyptian, in Egypt. "For a hundred and fifty years after the Ptolemies began to reign, the Egyptian hieroglyphics appear to have been commonly used, and the Egyptians were not prohibited from making use, so far as it seemed requisite, according to ritual or otherwise appropriate, of the native language and of its time-hallowed written signs."[2] Little by little, however, the Greek language displaced the Egyptian among the upper classes, and the writing in common use among the people, called to-day "demotic" or "enchorial," and anciently "epistolographic," completely usurped the place of the "hieratic" or cursive form of hieroglyphic writing. Even the abbreviated texts from the Book of the Dead which became common in the Graeco-Roman Period were often written in demotic, and much of the fiction of that time was written in demotic. The Egyptians seem to have forgotten the fact that the "words of the god," , were held by their ancestors to be holy. Although the Greeks and Romans appear not to have studied the hieroglyphs thoroughly, only repeating generally what they were told about certain signs, nevertheless writers like Herodotus, Diodorus Siculus, Strabo, Hermapion, Chaeremon, Clemens Alexandrinus, and Horapollo, contribute information on this subject of considerable value.

To **Hecataeus** of Miletus,[3] who visited Egypt between B.C. 513–501, we owe, through **Herodotus,** much knowledge of Egypt, and he must be considered the earliest Greek writer upon Egypt. **Hellanitus** of Mytilene, B.C. 478–393, shows in his Αἰγυπτιακὰ that he has some accurate knowledge of the meaning of some hieroglyphic words.[4] **Democritus** wrote upon the hieroglyphs of Meroë,[5] but this work is lost. **Herodotus** says that the Egyptians used two quite different kinds of writing, one of which is called sacred

[1] See Gutschmid, "Scriptorum rerum Aegyptiacarum Series," in *Philologus*, Bd. X, Göttingen, 1855, SS. 712 ff.

[2] Mommsen, *Provinces of the Roman Empire*, Vol. II, p. 243.

[3] See "De rerum Aegyptiacarum scriptoribus Graecis ante Alexandrum Magnum," in *Philologus*, Bd. X, S. 525.

[4] See the instances quoted in *Philologus*, Bd. X, S. 539.

[5] Περὶ τῶν ἐν Μερόῃ ἱερῶν γραμμάτων. Diogenes Laertius, *Vit. Democ.*, ed. Isaac Casaubon, 1593, p. 661.

(hieroglyphic), the other common[1] (demotic). **Diodorus** says that the Ethiopian letters are called by the Egyptians "hieroglyphs."[2] **Strabo,** speaking of the obelisks at Thebes, says that there are inscriptions upon them which proclaim the riches and power of their kings, and that their rule extends even to Scythia, Bactria, and India.[3] **Chaeremon** of Naucratis, who lived in the first half of the Ist century after Christ,[4] and who must be an entirely different person from Chaeremon the companion of Aelius Gallus (B.C. 25), derided by Strabo,[5] and charged with lying by Josephus,[6] wrote a work on Egyptian hieroglyphs,[7] *περὶ τῶν ἱερῶν γραμμάτων*, which has been lost. He appears to have been attached to the great library of Alexandria, and as he was a "sacred scribe" it may therefore be assumed that he had access to many important works on hieroglyphs, and that he understood them. He is mentioned by Eusebius[8] as *Χαιρήμων ὁ ἱερογραμματεύς*, and by Suidas,[9] but neither of these writers gives any information as to the contents of his work on hieroglyphs, and we should have no idea of what manner of work it was but for the extract preserved by **John Tzetzes** (Τζέτζης, born about A.D. 1110, died after A.D. 1180). Tzetzes was a man of considerable learning and literary activity, and his works[10] have value on account of the lost books which are quoted in them. In his *Chiliades*[11] (Bk. V, line 395) he speaks of *ὁ Αἰγύπτιος ἱερογραμματεὺς Χαιρήμων*, and refers to Chaeremon's *διδάγματα τῶν ἱερῶν γραμμάτων*. In his Exegesis of Homer's Iliad he gives an extract from the work itself, and we are able to see at once that it was written by one who was able to give his information at first hand. This interesting extract was first brought to the notice of the world by the late Dr. Birch, who published a paper on it in the *Transactions of the Royal Society of Literature*, Vol. III, second series 1850, pp. 385–396. In it he quoted the Greek text of the extract, from the edition of Tzetzes' *Exegesis*, first published by Hermann,[12]

[1] Καὶ τὰ μὲν αὐτῶν ἱρά, τὰ δὲ δημοτικὰ καλέεται. Herodotus, II, 36, ed. Didot, p. 84.

[2] Diodorus, III, 4, ed. Didot, p. 129.

[3] Strabo, XVII, 1, § 46, ed. Didot, p. 693.

[4] According to Mommsen he came to Rome, as tutor to Nero, in the reign of Claudius. *Provinces of Rome*, Vol. II, pp. 259, 273.

[5] Γελώμενος δὲ τὸ πλέον ὡς ἀλαζὼν καὶ ἰδιώτης. Strabo, XVII, 1, § 29, ed. Didot, p. 685.

[6] *Contra Apion*, I, 32 ff. On the identity of Chaeremon the Stoic philosopher with Chaeremon the ἱερογραμματεύς, see Zeller, *Hermes*, XI, s. 431.

[7] His other lost work, Αἰγυπτιακά, treated of the Exodus.

[8] *Praep. Evang.*, v, 10, ed. Gaisford, t. 1, p. 421.

[9] *Sub voce* Ἱερογλυφικά.

[10] For an account of them see Krumbacher, *Geschichte der Byzantinischen Literatur*, München, 1891, pp. 235–242.

[11] Ed. Kiessling, Leipzig, 1826, p. 191.

[12] Draconis Stratonicensis Liber de Metris Poeticis. Joannis Tzetzae Exegesis in Homeri Iliadem. Primum edidit . . . . . God. Hermannus, Lipsiae, 1812.

and added remarks and hieroglyphic characters illustrative of it, together with the scholia of Tzetzes, the text of which he emended in places. As this extract is so important for the history of the study of hieroglyphs, it is given here, together with the scholia on it, from the excellent edition of the Greek text, by Lud. Bachmann, *Scholia in Homeri Iliadem*, Lipsiae, 1835, pp. 823, § 97, and 838, with an English translation.

Ὅμηρος δέ, παιδευθεὶς ἀκριβῶς δὲ πᾶσαν μάθησιν ἐκ τῶν συμβολικῶν Αἰθιοπικῶν γραμμάτων, ταῦτά φησιν· οἱ γὰρ Αἰθίοπες στοιχεῖα γραμμάτων οὐκ ἔχουσιν, ἀλλ' ἀντ' αὐτῶν ζῷα παντοῖα, καὶ μέλη τούτων καὶ μόρια· βουλόμενοι γὰρ οἱ ἀρχαιότεροι τῶν ἱερογραμματέων τὸν περὶ θεῶν φυσικὸν λόγον κρύπτειν, δι' ἀλληγορικῶν καὶ συμβόλων τοιούτων καὶ γραμμάτων τοῖς ἰδίοις τέκνοις αὐτὰ παρεδίδουν, ὡς ὁ ἱερογραμματεὺς Χαιρήμων φησί·

1. *καὶ ἀντὶ μὲν χαρᾶς, γυναῖκα τυμπανίζουσαν ἔγραφον·*
2. *ἀντὶ λύπης, ἄνθρωπον τῇ χειρὶ τὸ γένειον κρατοῦντα, καὶ πρὸς γῆν νεύοντα·*
3. *ἀντὶ δὲ συμφοράς, ὀφθαλμὸν δακρύοντα·*
4. *ἀντὶ τοῦ μὴ ἔχειν, δύο χεῖρας κενὰς ἐκτεταμένας·*
5. *ἀντὶ ἀνατολῆς, ὄφιν ἐξερχόμενον ἔκ τινος ὀπῆς·*
6. *ἀντὶ δύσεως, εἰσερχόμενον·*
7. *ἀντὶ ἀναβιώσεως, βάτραχον·*
8. *ἀντὶ ψυχῆς, ἱέρακα· ἔτι καὶ ἀντὶ ἡλίου καὶ θεοῦ·*
9. *ἀντὶ θηλυγόνου γυναικός, καὶ μητρὸς καὶ χρόνου καὶ οὐρανοῦ, γῦπα·*
10. *ἀντὶ βασιλέως, μέλισσαν·*
11. *ἀντὶ γενέσεως καὶ αὐτοφυῶν καὶ ἀῤῥένων, κάνθαρον·*
12. *ἀντὶ γῆς, βοῦν·*
13. *λέοντος δὲ προτομὴ πᾶσαν ἀρχὴν καὶ φυλακὴν δηλοῖ κατ' αὐτούς·*
14. *οὐρὰ λέοντος, ἀνάγκην·*
15. *ἔλαφος, ἐνιαυτόν·*
16. *ὁμοίως καὶ ὁ φοίνιξ·*
17. *ὁ παῖς δηλοῖ τὰ αὐξανόμενα·*
18. *ὁ γέρων, τὰ φθειρόμενα·*
19. *τὸ τόξον, τὴν ὀξεῖαν δύναμιν· καὶ ἕτερα μύρια· ἐξ ὧν Ὅμηρος ταῦτά φησιν· ἐν ἄλλῳ δὲ τόπῳ, εἴπερ αἱρεῖσθε, ἰδὼν ἐκ τοῦ Χαιρήμονος, καὶ τὰς τῶν γραμμάτων αὐτῶν ἐκφωνήσεις Αἰθιοπικῶς εἴπω.*

" Now, Homer says this as he was accurately instructed in all learning by means of the symbolic Ethiopian characters. For the Ethiopians do not use alphabetic characters, but depict animals of all sorts instead, and limbs and members of these animals; for the sacred scribes in former times desired to conceal their opinion about the nature of the gods, and therefore handed all this down to their own children by allegorical methods and the aforesaid symbols and characters, as the sacred scribe Chaeremon says."

1. " And for *joy*, they would depict a woman beating a tambourine."

[The drum or tambourine was used in the temples for festival services, and a woman beating a tambourine is the determinative of the words *seger*, " to beat a tambourine," and *ṭekhennu.*]

2. " For *grief*, a man clasping his chin in his hand and bending towards the ground."

[A man, seated, with his hand to his mouth, is the determinative of the word *khaȧnȧu*, " grief." A seated woman with head bent and hands thrown up before her face, is the determinative of *ḥat*, " to weep."]

3. " For *misfortune*, an eye weeping."

[The weeping eye is the determinative of the common word *rem*, " to weep."]

4. " For *want*, two hands stretched out empty."

[Compare *ȧt*, " not to have," " to be without." Coptic ⲁⲧ.]

5. " For *rising*, a snake coming out of a hole."

[Compare = *per*, " to come forth, to rise " (of the sun).]

6. " For *setting*, [the same] going in."

[Compare = *āq*, " to enter, to set " (of the sun).]

7. " For *vivification*, a frog."[1]

[The frog *ḥefnu*, means 100,000, hence fertility and abundance of life. See also the description of the frog used as an amulet in the section " Amulets."]

8. " For *soul*, a hawk ; and also for *sun* and *god*."

[Compare *ba*, " soul," *neter*, " god," and *Ḥer*, " Horus " or " the Sun-god."]

[1] But compare Horapollo (ed. Leemans, p. 33), Ἄπλαστον δὲ ἄνθρωπον γράφοντες, βάτραχον ζωγραφοῦσιν.

9. "For a female-bearing woman, and *mother* and *time* and *sky*, a vulture."

[*mut*, "mother," is the common meaning of a vulture, and at times the goddess Mut seems to be identified with *nut*, "the sky." Horapollo says that the vulture also meant "year" (ed. Leemans, p. 5), and this statement is borne out by the evidence of the hieroglyphs, where we find that = *renpit*, "year."]

10. "For *king*, a bee."

[Compare *nesu-bȧt*, "king of the North and South."]

11. "For *birth* and *natural growth*, and *males*, a beetle."

[The beetle *Kheperȧ* was the emblem of the god *Kheperȧ* , who is supposed to have created or evolved himself, and to have given birth to gods, men, and every creature and thing in earth and sky. The word means "to become," and in late texts *kheperu* may be fairly well rendered by "evolutions." The meaning *male* comes, of course, from the idea of the ancients that the beetle had no female. See the section SCARAB.]

12. "For *earth*, an ox."

[*ȧḥet* means field, and *ȧḥ* means "ox"; can Chaeremon have confused the meanings of these two words, similar in sound ?]

13. "And the fore part of a lion signifies *dominion* and *protection* of every kind."

[Compare *ḥa*, "chief, that which is in front, duke, prince."]

14. "A lion's tail, *necessity*."

[Compare *peḥ*, "to force, to compel, to be strong."]

15, 16. "A stag, *year*; likewise the *palm*."

[Of the stag meaning "year" I can give no example. The palm branch or *renpit*, is the common word for "year."]

17. " The boy signifies *growth*."

[Compare , which is the determinative of words meaning " youth " and juvenescence.]

18. " The old man, *decay*."

[Compare , the determinative of  *àau*, " old age."]

19. " The bow, the *swift* power."

[The Egyptian word for bow is  *peṭ*. Compare  *peṭ*, " to run, to flee away."]

" And others by the thousand. And by means of these characters Homer says this. But I will proceed in another place, if you please, to explain the pronunciation of those characters in Ethiopic fashion, as I have learnt it from Chaeremon."[1]

In another place[2] Tzetzes says, " Moreover, he was not uninitiated into the symbolic Ethiopian characters, the nature of which we will expound in the proper places. All this demonstrates that Homer was instructed in Egypt," *ναὶ μὴν οὐδὲ τῶν Αἰθιοπικῶν συμβολικῶν γραμμάτων ἀμύητος γέγονε, περὶ ὧν ἐν τοῖς οἰκείοις τόποις διδάξομεν ὁποῖα εἰσί. καὶ ταῦτα δὲ τὸν Ὅμηρον ἐν Αἰγύπτῳ παιδευθῆναι παραδεικνύουσι*, and upon this the scholia on Tzetzes say :—*Περὶ τῶν Αἰθιοπικῶν γραμμάτων Διό[δωρος] μὲν ἐπεμνήσθη, καὶ μερικῶς εἶπεν, ἀλλ' ὥσπερ ἐξ ἀκοῆς ἄλλου μαθὼν καὶ οὐκ ἀκριβῶς αὐτὸς ἐπιστάμενος [εἰ] καί τινα τούτων κατέλεξεν ὥσπερ ἐν οἷς οἶδε παῤῥησιάζεται. Χαιρήμων δὲ ὁ ἱερογραμματεὺς ὅλην βίβλον περὶ τῶν τοιούτων γραμμάτων συνέταξεν. ἅτινα, ἐν τοῖς προ[σφόροις] τόποις τῶν Ὁμηρείων ἐπῶν ἀ[κρι]βέστερον καὶ πλατυτέρως ἐρῶ.*[3] " Diodorus made mention of the Ethiopian characters and spoke particularly, yet as though he had learnt by hearsay from another and did not understand them accurately himself, although he set down some of them, as though he were talking confidently on subjects that he knew. But Chaeremon the sacred scribe compiled a whole book about the aforesaid characters, which I will discuss more accurately and more fully in the proper places in the Homeric poems." It is much to be regretted that Chaeremon's work, if he ever fulfilled his promise, has not come down to us.

One of the most valuable extracts from the works of Greek and Roman writers on Egypt is that from a translation of an

[1] Hermann, p. 123, ll. 2–29 ; Bachmann, p. 823, ll. 12–34.

[2] Hermann, p. 17, ll. 21–25 ; Bachmann, p. 755, ll. 9–12.

[3] Hermann, p. 146, ll. 12–22 ; Bachmann, p. 838, ll. 31–37.

Egyptian obelisk by **Hermapion**, preserved by Ammianus Marcellinus;[1] unfortunately, however, neither the name of Hermapion's work nor the time in which he lived is known. This extract consists of the Greek translation of six lines of hieroglyphs: three lines are from the south side of the obelisk, one line from the east side, and a second and a third line from the other sides. A comparison of the Greek extract with any inscription of Rameses II on an obelisk shows at once that Hermapion must have had a certain accurate knowledge of hieroglyphs; his translation of the lines, however, does not follow consecutively. The following examples will show that the Greek, in many cases, represents the Egyptian very closely. *Λέγει Ἥλιος βασιλεῖ Ῥαμέστῃ· δεδώρημαί σοι ἀνὰ πᾶσαν οἰκουμένην μετὰ χαρᾶς βασιλεύειν, ὃν Ἥλιος φιλεῖ* = 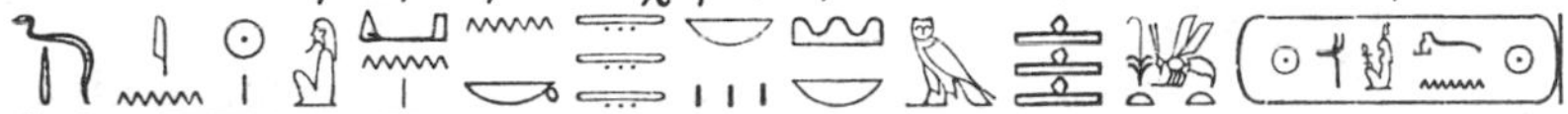  "Says Rā, I give to thee all lands and foreign countries with rest of heart, O king of the North and South, Usr-maāt-Rā-setep-en-Rā, son of the Sun, Rameses, beloved of Åmen-Rā." *Θεογέννητος κτιστὴς τῆς οἰκουμένης* =  "born of the gods, possessor of the two lands" (*i.e.*, the world). *Ὁ ἑστὼς ἐπ' ἀληθείας δεσπότης διαδήματος, τὴν Αἴγυπτον δοξάσας κεκτημένος, ὁ ἀγλαοποιήσας Ἡλίου πόλιν* =  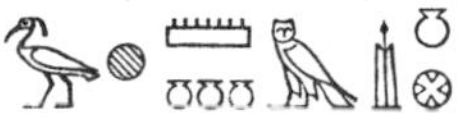 "[the mighty bull], resting upon Law, lord of diadems, protector of Egypt, making splendid Heliopolis with monuments." *Ἥλιος θεὸς μέγας δεσπότης οὐρανοῦ* =  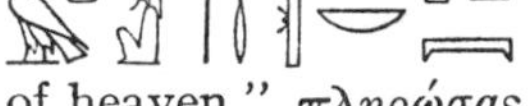 "Says Rā Harmakhis, the great god, lord of heaven," *πληρώσας τὸν νεὼν τοῦ φοίνικος ἀγαθῶν, ᾧ οἱ θεοὶ ζωῆς χρόνον ἐδωρήσαντο* = 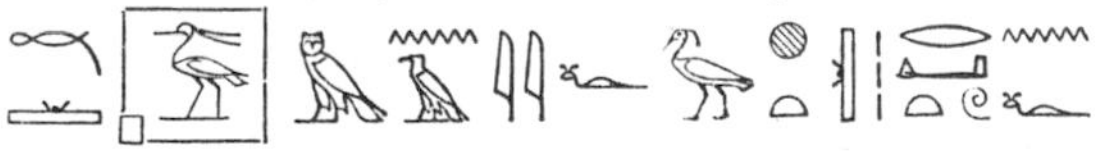  "filling the temple of the *bennu* (phœnix) with his splendours, may the gods give to him life like the Sun for ever," etc.

The Flaminian obelisk, from which the Egyptian passages given above are taken, was brought from Heliopolis to Rome by Augustus, and placed in the Circus Maximus,[2] whence it was dug out; it now stands in the Piazza del Popolo at Rome, where it was

[1] Liber XVII, 4.

[2] Qui autem notarum textus obelisco incisus est veteri, quem videmus in Circo, etc. Ammianus Marcellinus, XVII, 4, § 17. It seems to be referred to in Pliny, XXXVI, 29.

set up by Pope Sixtus V in 1589.[1] This obelisk was originally set up by Seti I, whose inscriptions occupy the middle column of the north, south, and west sides; the other columns of hieroglyphs record the names and titles of Rameses II who, in this case, appropriated the obelisk of his father, just as he did that of Thothmes III. The obelisk was found broken into three pieces, and in order to render it capable of standing up, three palms' length was cut from the base. The texts have been published by Kircher, *Oedipus Aegyptiacus*, tom. III, p. 213; by Ungarelli, *Interpretatio Obeliscorum Urbis*, Rome, 1842, p. 65 *sqq.*, plate 2; and by Bonomi, who drew them for a paper on this obelisk by the Rev. G. Tomlinson in *Trans. Royal Soc. Lit.*, Vol. I, Second Series, p. 176 ff. For an account of this obelisk see Zoega, *De Origine et Usu Obeliscorum*, Rome, 1797, p. 92.

The next Greek writer whose statements on Egyptian hieroglyphs are of value is **Clement** of Alexandria, who flourished about A.D. 191–220. According to Champollion, " un seul auteur grec, . . . a démêlé et signalé, dans l'écriture égyptienne sacrée, les élémens phonétiques, lesquels en sont, pour ainsi dire, le principe vital[2] . . . Clément d'Alexandrie s'est, lui seul, occasionnellement attaché à en donner une idée claire; et ce philosophe chrétien était, bien plus que tout autre, en position d'en être bien instruit. Lorsque mes recherches et l'étude constante des monuments égyptiens m'eurent conduit aux résultats précédemment exposés, je dus revenir sur ce passage de Saint Clément d'Alexandrie, que j'ai souvent cité, pour savoir si, à la faveur des notions que j'avais tirées d'un examen soutenu des inscriptions hiéroglyphiques, le texte de l'auteur grec ne deviendrait pas plus intelligible qu'il ne l'avait paru jusque-là. J'avoue que ses termes me semblèrent alors si positifs et si clairs, et les idées qu'il renferme si exactement conformes à ma théorie de l'écriture hiéroglyphique, que je dus craindre aussi de me livrer à une illusion et à un entraînement dont tout me commandait de me défier."[3] From the above it will be seen what a high value Champollion placed on the statements concerning the hieroglyphs by Clement, and they have, in consequence, formed the subject of various works by eminent authorities. In his *Précis* (p. 328) Champollion gives the extract from Clement with a Latin translation and remarks by Letronne.[4] Dulaurier in his *Examen d'un passage des Stromates de Saint Clément d'Alexandrie*, Paris, 1833, again published the passage and gave many explanations of words in it, and commented learnedly upon it. (See also Bunsen's *Aegyptens Stelle*, Bd. I, p. 240, and Thierbach, *Erklärung*

[1] For a comparative table of obelisks standing in 1840 see Bonomi, "Notes on Obelisks," in *Trans. Royal Soc. Lit.*, Vol. I, Second Series, p. 158.

[2] *Précis du Système hiéroglyphique des anciens Égyptiens*, Paris, 1824, p. 321.

[3] *Précis*, p. 327.

[4] See also *Œuvres Choisies*, tom. I, pp. 237–254.

auf das Aegyptische Schriftwesen, Erfurt, 1846.) The passage is as follows :—

αὐτίκα οἱ παρ' Αἰγυπτίοις παιδευόμενοι πρῶτον μὲν πάντων τὴν Αἰγυπτίων γραμμάτων μέθοδον ἐκμανθάνουσι τὴν ἐπιστολογραφικὴν καλουμένην, δευτέραν δὲ τὴν ἱερατικήν, ᾗ χρῶνται οἱ ἱερογραμματεῖς, ὑστάτην δὲ καὶ τελευταίαν τὴν ἱερογλυφικήν, ἧς ἡ μέν ἐστι διὰ τῶν πρώτων στοιχείων κυριολογική, ἡ δὲ συμβολική. τῆς δὲ συμβολικῆς ἡ μὲν κυριολογεῖται κατὰ μίμησιν, ἡ δ' ὥσπερ τροπικῶς γράφεται, ἡ δὲ ἄντικρυς ἀλληγορεῖται κατά τινας αἰνιγμούς, ἥλιον γοῦν γράψαι βουλόμενοι κύκλον ποιοῦσι, σελήνην δὲ σχῆμα μηνοειδὲς κατὰ τὸ κυριολογούμενον εἶδος, τροπικῶς δὲ κατ' οἰκειότητα μετάγοντες καὶ μετατιθέντες, τὰ δ' ἐξαλλάττοντες, τὰ δὲ πολλαχῶς μετασχηματίζοντες χαράττουσιν. Τοὺς γοῦν τῶν βασιλέων ἐπαίνους θεολογουμένοις μύθοις παραδιδόντες ἀναγράφουσι διὰ τῶν ἀναγλύφων, τοῦ δὲ κατὰ τοὺς αἰνιγμοὺς τρίτου εἴδους δεῖγμα ἔστω τόδε. τὰ μὲν γὰρ τῶν ἄλλων ἄστρων διὰ τὴν πορείαν τὴν λοξὴν ὄφεων σώμασιν ἀπείκαζον, τὸν δὲ ἥλιον τῷ τοῦ κανθάρου, ἐπειδὴ κυκλοτερὲς ἐκ τῆς βοείας ὄνθου σχῆμα πλασάμενος ἀντιπρόσωπος κυλίνδει. φασὶ δὲ καὶ ἑξάμηνον μὲν ὑπὸ γῆς, θάτερον δὲ τοῦ ἔτους τμῆμα τὸ ζῷον τοῦτο ὑπὲρ γῆς διαιτᾶσθαι, σπερμαίνειν τε εἰς τὴν σφαῖραν καὶ γεννᾶν, καὶ θῆλυν κάνθαρον μὴ γίνεσθαι.[1]

" For example, those that are educated among the Egyptians first of all learn that system of Egyptian characters which is styled EPISTOLOGRAPHIC ; secondly, the HIERATIC, which the sacred scribes employ ; lastly and finally the HIEROGLYPHIC. The hieroglyphic sometimes speaks plainly by means of the letters of the alphabet, and sometimes uses symbols, and when it uses symbols it sometimes (*a*) speaks plainly by imitation, and sometimes (*b*) describes in a figurative way, and sometimes (*c*) simply says one thing for another in accordance with certain secret rules. Thus (*a*) if they desire to write *sun* or *moon,* they make a circle or a crescent in plain imitation of the form. And when (*b*) they describe figuratively (by transfer and transposition without violating the natural meaning of words), they completely alter some things and make manifold changes in the form of others. Thus, they hand down the praises of their kings in myths about the gods which they write up in relief. Let this be an example of the third form (*c*) in accordance with the secret rules. While they represent the stars generally by snakes' bodies, because their course is crooked, they represent the sun by the body of a beetle, for the beetle moulds a ball from cattle dung and rolls it before him. And they say that this animal lives under ground for six months, and above ground for the other portion of the year, and that it deposits its seed in this globe and there engenders offspring, and that no female beetle exists."

[1] *Clem. Alex.,* ed. Dindorf, tom. III, *Strom.* lib. v, §§ 20, 21, pp. 17, 18.

From the above we see that Clement rightly stated that the Egyptians had three kinds of writing—epistolographic, hieratic and hieroglyphic. The epistolographic is that kind which is now called "demotic," and which in the early days of hieroglyphic decipherment was called "enchorial." The hieratic is the kind commonly found on papyri. The hieroglyphic kind is described as, I. *cyriologic*, that is to say, by means of *figurative phonetic characters*, *e.g.*, *emsuḥ*, "crocodile," and II. *symbolic*, that is to say, by actual representations of objects, *e.g.*, "goose," "bee," and so on. The symbolic division is subdivided into three parts: I. *cyriologic by imitation, e.g.*, , a vase with water flowing from it represented a "libation"; II. *tropical, e.g.*, , a crescent moon to represent "month," , a reed and palette to represent "writing" or "scribe"; and III. *enigmatic, e.g.*, , a beetle, to represent the "sun."[1] In modern Egyptian Grammars the matter is stated more simply, and we see that hieroglyphic signs are used in two ways: I. Ideographic, II. Phonetic. *mu*, "water," is an instance of the first method, and *m-s-u-ḥ*, is an instance of the second. Ideographic signs are used as *determinatives*, and are either *ideographic* or *generic*. Thus after *mȧu*, "cat," a cat is placed, and is an *ideographic* determinative; but , heaven with a star in it, written after *gerḥ*, is a *generic* determinative. Phonetic signs are either *Alphabetic* as *a*, *b*, *k*, or *Syllabic*, as *men*, *khen*, etc.

Porphyry the Philosopher, who died about A.D. 305, says of Pythagoras[2]:—

Καὶ ἐν Αἰγύπτῳ μὲν τοῖς ἱερεῦσι συνῆν καὶ τὴν σοφίαν ἐξέμαθε, καὶ τὴν Αἰγυπτίων φωνήν, γραμμάτων δὲ τρισσὰς διαφοράς, ἐπιστολογραφικῶν τε καὶ ἱερογλυφικῶν καὶ συμβολικῶν, τῶν μὲν κοινολογουμένων κατὰ μίμησιν, τῶν δὲ ἀλληγορουμένων κατά τινας αἰνιγμούς.

"And in Egypt he lived with the priests and learnt their wisdom and the speech of the Egyptians and three sorts of writing, epistolographic and hieroglyphic and symbolic, which sometimes speak in the common way by imitation and sometimes describe one thing by

[1] Champollion, *Précis*, p. 278.
[2] Porphyry, *De Vita Pythagorae*, ed. Didot, § 11, p. 89, at the foot.

another in accordance with certain secret rules." Here it seems that Porphyry copied Clement inaccurately. Thus he omits all mention of the Egyptian writing called "hieratic," and of the subdivision of hieroglyphic called "cyriologic," and of the second subdivision of the symbolic called "tropic." The following table, based on Letronne, will make the views about hieroglyphic writing held by the Greeks plain :—

Herodotus, Diodorus and the inscription of Rosetta divide Egyptian writing into two divisions

- I. The common, called
  - δημοτικά and δημώδη by Herodotus and Clement,
  - ἐγχώρια by the inscription of Rosetta,
  - ἐπιστολογραφικά by Clement of Alexandria and Porphyry.
- II. The sacred, divided by Clement into
  - 1. Hieratic, or the writing of the priests.
  - 2. Hieroglyphic composed of
    - *a.* Cyriologic, by means of the first letters of the alphabet.
    - *b.* Symbolical comprising the
      - *a.* Cyriological by imitation.
      - *b.* Tropical or metaphorical.
      - *c.* Enigmatical.

The next writer of importance on hieroglyphs is **Horapollo,** who towards the close of the IVth century of our era composed a work called Ἱερογλυφικά ; this book was translated into Greek by one Philip, of whom nothing is known. Wiedemann thinks that it was originally written in Coptic, which, in the Middle Ages, was usually called "Egyptian," and not in ancient Egyptian.[1] In this work are given the explanations of a number of ideographs which occur, for the most part, in Ptolemaïc inscriptions ; but, like the list of those given by Chaeremon, no *phonetic* values of the signs are given. Nevertheless the list is of considerable interest. The best edition of Horapollo is that of Conrad Leemans,[2] but the text was edited in a handy form, with an English translation and notes by Samuel Sharpe and Dr. Birch, by J. Cory, in 1840.

In more modern times the first writer at any length on hieroglyphs was Athanasius **Kircher,** the author of some ponderous works[3] in which he pretended to have found the key to the hieroglyphic inscriptions, and to translate them. Though a man of

[1] *Aegyptische Geschichte,* p. 151. The sepulchre of Gordian was inscribed in *Egyptian.* "Gordiano sepulchrum milites apud Circeium castrum fecerunt in finibus Persidis, titulum hujus modi addentes et Graecis, et Latinis, et Persicis, et Judaicis, et Aegyptiacis literis, ut ab omnibus legeretur." Erasmus, *Hist. Rom. Scriptorum,* Basle, 1533, p. 312, at the top.

[2] Horapollinis Niloi Hieroglyphica edidit, diversorum codicum recenter collatorum, priorumque editionum varias lectiones et versionem latinam subjunxit, adnotationem, item hieroglyphicorum imagines et indices adjecit C.L. Amstelod., 1835.

[3] *Obeliscus Pamphilius, ... Hieroglyphicis involuta Symbolis, detecta e tenebris in lucem asseritur,* Rome, 1650, fol. *Oedipus Aegyptiacus,* hoc est, universalis hieroglyphicae veterum doctrinae, temporum injuria obolitae instauratio. Rome, 1652–54. Tom. I–IV, fol.

great learning, it must be plainly said that, judged by scholars of to-day, he would be considered an impostor. In his works on Coptic[1] there are, no doubt, many interesting facts, but mixed with them is such an amount of nonsense that Jablonski says, touching one of his statements, "Verum hic ut in aliis plurimis fucum lectoribus fecit Jesuita ille, et fumum vendidit"; from the same writer, also, Kircher's arrogant assertions called forth the remark, "Kircherus, in quo semper plus inest ostentationis, quam solidae eruditionis."[2] It is impossible to understand what grounds Kircher had for his statements and how he arrived at his results; as for his translations, they have *nothing* correct in them. Here is one taken at random from *Oedipus Aegyptiacus*, tom. III, p. 431, where he gives a translation of an inscription (A) printed on the plate between pp. 428 and 429. The hieroglyphs are written on a Ptaḥ-Seker-Osiris figure and read :—

tcheṭ ȧn Ȧsȧr Khent Ȧmentt neter āa neb

"*Saith Osiris, at the head of the underworld, god great, lord of*

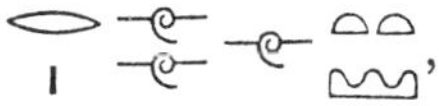
, etc.

Re-stau

Re-stau (i.e., *the passages of the tomb*),"

and his translation runs :—"Vitale providi Numinis dominium, quadruplicem Mundani liquoris substantiam dominio confert Osiridis, cujus unà cum Mendesio foecundi Numinis dominio, benefica virtute influente, omnia quae in Mundo sunt, vegetantur, animantur, conservantur." Other writers on hieroglyphs whose works Kircher consulted were John Peter Bolzanius **Valerianus**,[3] and **Mercati**,[4] but no good results followed their investigations. In the year 1770 Joseph **de Guignes** determined the existence of groups of characters having determinatives,[5] and four years later he published his *Mémoire*,[6] in which he tried to prove that the epistolographic and symbolic characters of the Egyptians were to be found in the Chinese characters, and that the Chinese nation was nothing but an Egyptian

[1] *Prodromus Coptus*, Rome, 1636; *Lingua Aegyptiaca restituta*, Rome, 1643.

[2] Jablonski, *Opuscula*, tom. I, ed. Water, 1804, pp. 157, 211.

[3] *Hieroglyphica, seu de sacris Aegyptiorum aliarumque gentium litteris Commentariorum libri VII, duobus aliis ab eruditissimo viro annexis*, etc., Basil., 1556.

[4] *Degli Obelischi di Roma*, Rome, 1589.

[5] Essai sur le moyen de parvenir à la lecture et à l'intelligence des Hiéroglyphes égyptiens. (In *Mémoires de l'Académie des Inscriptions*, tom. XXXIV, pp. 1–56.)

[6] *Ibid.*, tom. XXXIX, p. 1 ff.

colony. In 1797 **Zoega** made a step in the right direction, and came to the conclusion[1] that the hieroglyphs were letters and that the cartouches contained royal names. A few years later **Silvestre de Sacy** published a letter on the inscriptions on the Rosetta Stone,[2] and the work of this learned man was soon after followed by that of Åkerblad who, in a letter to M. de Sacy,[3] discussed the demotic inscription on the recently discovered Rosetta Stone, and published an alphabet of the demotic characters, from which a large number were adopted in after times by Young and Champollion. It would seem that Åkerblad never gained the credit which was due to him for his really good work, and it will be seen from the facts quoted in the following pages how largely the success of Young's labours on the demotic inscription on the Rosetta Stone depended on those of Åkerblad.

But side by side with the letters of de Sacy and Åkerblad and the learned works of Young and Champollion, there sprang into existence a mass of literature full of absurd statements and theories written by men having no qualifications for expressing opinions on hieroglyphic matters. Thus the **Comte de Pahlin,** in his *De l'Étude des Hiéroglyphes,*[4] hesitated not to say that the inscription on one of the porticoes of the Temple at Denderah contained a translation of the hundredth Psalm, composed to invite all people to enter into the house of the Lord. The same author said that to produce the Books of the Bible, which were originally written on papyri, it was only necessary to translate the Psalms of David into Chinese and to write them in the ancient characters of that language.[5] **Lenoir** considered the Egyptian inscriptions to contain Hebrew compositions,[6] and **Lacour** thought that they contained Biblical phrases.[7] Worse than all these wild theories was the belief in the works of the Kircher school of investigators, and in the accuracy of the statements made by **Warburton,**[8] who, it must be confessed, seems to have recognized the existence of alphabetic characters, but who in no way deserves the praise of **Bailey,** the Cambridge prize essayist, "Vir singulari quodam ingenii acumine praeditus, Warburtonus; qui primus certe recentiorum ad rectam harum rerum cognitionem patefecit viam."[9]

1 *De Usu et Origine Obeliscorum*, Rome, 1797, fol., p. 465.

2 *Lettre au citoyen Chaptal, au sujet de l'Inscription égyptienne du Monument trouvé à Rosette,* Paris, 1802.

3 *Lettre sur l'Inscription égyptienne de Rosette,* Paris, 1802.

4 Published at Paris in 5 vols., 1812.

5 *Lettres sur les Hiéroglyphes,* Weimar, 1802.

6 In *Nouvelle explication des Hiéroglyphes,* Paris, 1809–10, 4 vols.; and *Nouveaux Essais sur les Hiéroglyphes,* Paris, 1826, 4 vols.

7 See his *Essai sur les Hiéroglyphes égyptiens,* Bordeaux, 1821.

8 In his *The Divine Legation of Moses demonstrated, to which is adjoint an Essay on Egyptian Hieroglyphics,* London, 1738, 2 vols.

9 *Hieroglyphicorum Origo et Natura,* Cambridge, 1816, p. 9.

Young and Champollion

Here naturally comes an account of the labours of **Young** and **Champollion,** two men who stand out pre-eminently as the true discoverers of the right method of decipherment of Egyptian hieroglyphs. As much has been written on the works of these *savants,* and as some have tried to show that the whole merit of the discovery belongs to Young, and others that it belongs to Champollion, it will not be out of place here to summarize the actual facts which can now be put together about the value of the labours of each; a few details concerning the lives of these remarkable men may also be given.

Thomas Young was born at Milverton, in Somersetshire, on June 13th, 1773. His parents were both members of the Society of Friends. At the age of two he could read fluently, and before he was four he had read the Bible through twice. At the age of six he learnt by heart in six weeks Goldsmith's *Deserted Village.* When not quite seven years of age he went to a school, kept by a man called King, at Stapleton, near Bristol, where he stayed for a year and a half. In March, 1782, when nearly nine years of age, he went to the school of Mr. T. Thompson, at Compton, in Dorsetshire, where he remained four years. Here he read Phaedrus's Fables, Cornelius Nepos, Virgil, Horace expurgated by Knox, the whole of Beza's Greek and Latin Testament, the First Seven Books of the Iliad, Martin's Natural Philosophy, etc., etc. Before leaving this school he had got through six chapters of the Hebrew Bible. About this time he learnt to use the lathe, and he made a telescope and a microscope, and the Italian, Persian, Syriac, and Chaldee languages all occupied his attention. From 1787 to 1792 he was private tutor to Hudson Gurney, at Youngsbury, in Hertfordshire, where he seems to have devoted himself to the study of English, French, Italian, Latin, Greek, Hebrew, Chaldee, Syriac, Samaritan, Arabic, Persian, Turkish, and Ethiopic, as well as to that of Natural Philosophy, Botany, and Entomology. In 1792 Young began to study Medicine and Anatomy in London, and in 1793 he entered St. Bartholomew's Hospital as a pupil. In 1798 Young received a splendid bequest from his uncle, Dr. Brocklesby, consisting of his house in Norfolk Street, Park Lane, his library, his prints, his pictures, and about £10,000 in money; hence he was free to form his own scheme of life. In May, 1801, he discovered the undulatory theory of light, and his paper on this subject was read before the Royal Society in the November following; in the same year he accepted the office of Professor of Natural Philosophy at the Royal Institution. In 1802 he was appointed Foreign Secretary of the Royal Society. In 1803 he read a paper before the Royal Society, and was elected a Fellow the following year (balloted for and elected, June 19th). Shortly after he attended medical lectures in

Edinburgh and Göttingen, and he subsequently went to Cambridge, where he took the degree of Bachelor of Medicine (1803), and afterwards that of Doctor of Physic (1808). The attention of Young was called to Egyptian inscriptions by Sir W. E. Rouse Boughton, who had found in a mummy case at Thebes a papyrus written in cursive Egyptian characters, and to a notice of this which Young prepared for his friend he appended **a translation of the demotic text of the Rosetta Stone.** As the details of his studies on the Rosetta Stone belong to the history of the decipherment of Egyptian hieroglyphs, they are given further on. The reader who wishes to understand Young's position, and to know what exactly he contributed towards the decipherment of Egyptian hieroglyphs, should read Dean Peacock's account of it in Leitch's *Life of Thomas Young*, Vol. III, London, 1845, pp. 258–344. Here he will find a collection of dated letters from Young and Champollion which put the relations of these two great men in their true light, and supply a series of facts which are usually suppressed by the friends of Champollion.

In 1816 Young was appointed Secretary to a Commission for ascertaining the length of the seconds pendulum, for comparing French and English standards, etc., and in 1818 he was appointed Secretary of the Board of Longitude and Superintendent of the Nautical Almanac. In 1825 he became Medical Referee and Inspector of Calculations to the Palladium Insurance Company. In 1826 he was elected one of the eight foreign Associates of the Academy of Sciences at Paris. In February, 1829, he began to suffer from repeated attacks of asthma, and by the April following he was in a state of great weakness; he died on May 10th, not having completed his fifty-sixth year. An excellent steel engraving of Young, by R. Ward, from a picture by Sir Thomas Lawrence, P.R.A., forms the frontispiece to his life by Dean Peacock, which, according to J. J. Champollion-Figeac, " exprime fidèlement la douceur, la grâce, les traits d'une figure toute rayonnante d'intelligence."[1]

Jean François Champollion, surnamed **le Jeune,** was born at Figeac on December 23rd, 1790. As a boy he made rapid progress in classical studies, and he devoted himself at the same time to botany and mineralogy; at a very early date, however, he showed a natural taste for oriental languages and, like Young, was, at the age of thirteen, master of a fair knowledge of Hebrew, Syriac and Chaldee.[2] In 1807 his brother, J. J. Champollion-Figeac, brought him to Paris and caused him to be admitted to the Cours de l'École des Langues Orientales, and introduced him to Silvestre de Sacy. Soon after

[1] *Lettre au Directeur de la Revue Britannique au sujet des Recherches du Docteur Young*, Paris, 1857, p. 11.

[2] On the subject of Champollion's studies at Grenoble see *Chroniques Dauphinoises*, par A. Champollion-Figeac, tom. III, pp. 153, 156, 157–238.

his arrival in Paris Champollion turned his attention to the study of the hieroglyphic inscription on the Rosetta Stone, but his powerful friend de Sacy advised the elder brother to warn the younger off a study which *ne pouvait donner aucun résultat.* In 1812 (1809 ?) he was nominated Professor of Ancient History to the faculty of Letters at Grenoble, where he still carried on his oriental studies. When he arrived in Paris he found that the older Egyptologists maintained that hieroglyphs were a symbolic language and, seeking to verify this theory, he wasted a year. He sketched out a plan for a large work on Egypt in several volumes, and the first part of it appeared at Grenoble in 1811, entitled *Introduction* ; it was never sold, for only about thirty copies were printed, but it appeared, without the analytical table of Coptic geographical names, under the title *L'Égypte sous les Pharaons,* 8vo., 2 vols., 1814.

About this time (May 19th, 1814) Young, in England, was studying the texts on the Rosetta Stone, and had actually made a translation of the demotic section, making use of the results obtained by de Sacy and Åkerblad. Whatever may be said as to Champollion's ignorance of Young's results, it is quite certain that he must have known of those of Åkerblad, and we know (see p. 145) that a printed copy of Young's paper on the Rosetta Stone had been put into Champollion's hands by de Sacy. In a very short time Champollion discovered where his predecessors had broken down, and having already written *De l'Écriture Hiératique des Anciens Égyptiens,* Grenoble, 1821, on September 17th, in the following year, he read his *Mémoire* on the hieroglyphs and exhibited his hieroglyphic Alphabet, with its Greek and demotic equivalents, before the Académie des Inscriptions. In the same year Champollion published his *Lettre à M. Dacier, relative à l'Alphabet des Hiéroglyphes phonétiques,* in which he fully described his system. In a series of *Mémoires* read at the Institut in April, May and June, 1823, he explained his system more fully, and these he afterwards published together, entitled *Précis du Système Hiéroglyphique des Anciens Égyptiens,* Paris, 2 vols., 1824. A second edition, revised and corrected, appeared in 1828. In June, 1824, Champollion arrived in Turin, where he devoted himself to the study of Egyptian papyri. Early in 1825 he arrived in Rome, and thence he went to Naples, where all the museums were opened for him. In 1826 he returned to Paris. In July, 1828, he set out on his long-planned voyage to Egypt, and returned in March, 1830, bringing with him a fine collection of antiquities and a number of copies of inscriptions which filled about two thousand pages. As soon as he returned to France he set to work to publish the rich results of his travels, but while occupied with this undertaking death overtook him on March 4th, 1832. An etched portrait of Champollion le Jeune will be found in *Les Deux Champollion, leur Vie et leurs Œuvres,* par Aimé Champollion-Figeac : Grenoble, 1887, p. 52. See also H. Hartleben,

Champollion, Sein Leben und sein Werk, Berlin, 1906. [With Introductions by Maspero and Meyer.] His most important works are:—

> *Rapport à son Excellence M. le Duc de Doudeauville, sur la Collection Égyptienne à Livourne,* Paris, 1826; *Lettres à M. le Duc de Blacas d'Aulps relatives au Musée royal Égyptien de Turin . . . (avec Notices chronologiques par Champollion-Figeac),* Paris, 1824–26; *Notice sur les papyrus hiératiques et les peintures du cercueil de Pétaménoph* (Extr. de *Voyage à Meroë* par Cailliaud de Nantes), Paris, 1827; *Notice descriptive des Monuments Égyptiens du Musée Charles X,* Paris, 1827; *Catalogue de la Collection Égyptienne du Louvre,* Paris, 1827; *Catalogue des Papyrus Égyptiens du Musée du Vatican,* Rome, 1826; *Monuments de l'Égypte et de la Nubie,* 4 Vols., fol., 440 planches, Paris, 1829–47; *Lettres écrites pendant son voyage en Égypte, en* 1828, 1829, Paris, 1829; 2me édition, Paris, 1833; collection complète. A German translation by E. F. von Gutschmid was published at Quedlinburg in 1835; *Grammaire Égyptienne, aux Principes généraux de l'Écriture sacrée Égyptienne appliqués à la représentation de la langue parlée; . . . Avec des prolégomènes et un portrait de l'éditeur, M. Champollion-Figeac,* Paris, 1836–41; *Dictionnaire Égyptien, en écriture hiéroglyphique, publié d'après les manuscrits autographes . . . par Champollion-Figeac,* Paris, 1841.

The results of Dr. Young's studies of the Rosetta Stone were first communicated to the Royal Society of Antiquaries in a letter from Sir W. E. Rouse Boughton, Bart.; the letter was read on May 19th, 1814, and was published the following year in *Archaeologia,* Vol. XVIII, pp. 59–72.[1] The letter was accompanied by a **translation of the demotic text** on the Rosetta Stone, which was subsequently reprinted anonymously in the *Museum Criticum* of Cambridge, Pt. VI, 1815, together with the correspondence which took place between Dr. Young and MM. Silvestre de Sacy and Åkerblad. In 1802 M. Åkerblad, the Swedish President at Rome, published his *Lettre sur l'Inscription Égyptienne de Rosette, adressée au citoyen Silvestre de Sacy,* in which he gave the results of his study of the demotic text of the Rosetta Stone; M. Silvestre de Sacy also had occupied himself in the same way (see his *Lettre au citoyen Chaptal, au sujet de l'Inscription Égyptienne du monument trouvé à Rosette,* Paris, 1802), but neither scholar had made any progress in the decipherment of the hieroglyphic text. In August, 1814, Dr. Young wrote to Silvestre de Sacy, asking him what Mr. Åkerblad had been doing, and saying, " I doubt whether the alphabet which Mr. Åkerblad

[1] *Letter to the Rev. S. Weston respecting some Egyptian Antiquities.* With 4 copper plates. London, 1814.

has given us can be of much further utility than in enabling us to decipher the proper names; and sometimes I have even suspected that the letters which he has identified resemble the syllabic sort of characters by which the Chinese express the sounds of foreign languages, and that in their usual acceptation they had different significations: but of this conjecture I cannot at present speak with any great confidence." . . .[1] To this M. de Sacy replied: . . . "Je ne vous dissimule pas, Monsieur, que malgré l'espèce d'approbation que j'ai donnée au système de M. Åkerblad, dans la réponse que je lui ai adressée, il m'est toujours resté des doutes très forts sur la validité de l'alphabet qu'il s'est fait. . . . Je dois vous ajouter que M. Åkerblad n'est pas le seul qui se flatte d'avoir lu le texte Égyptien de l'inscription de Rosette. M. Champollion, qui vient de publier deux volumes sur l'ancienne géographie de l'Égypte,[2] et qui s'est beaucoup occupé de la langue Copte, prétend avoir aussi lu cette inscription. Je mets assurément plus de confiance dans les lumières et la critique de M. Åkerblad que dans celles de M. Champollion, mais tant qu'ils n'auront publié quelque résultat de leur travail, il est juste de suspendre son jugement." (Leitch, Vol. III, p. 17.)

Writing to M. de Sacy in October of the same year, Young says: "I had read Mr. Åkerblad's essay but hastily in the course of the last winter, and I was not disposed to place much confidence in the little that I recollected of it; so that I was able to enter anew upon the investigation, without being materially influenced by what he had published; and though I do not profess to lay claim to perfect originality, or to deny the importance of Mr. Åkerblad's labours, I think myself authorised to consider my own translation as completely independent of his ingenious researches: a circumstance which adds much to the probability of our conjectures where they happen to agree. It is only since I received your obliging letter, that I have again read Mr. Åkerblad's work; and I have found that it agrees almost in every instance with the results of my own investigation respecting the sense attributed to the words which the author has examined. This conformity must be allowed to be more satisfactory than if I had followed, with perfect confidence, the path which Åkerblad has traced: I must, however, confess that it relates only to a few of the first steps of the investigation; and that the greatest and the most difficult part of the translation still remains unsupported by the authority of any external evidence of this kind." (Leitch, p. 18.)

[1] For these letters I am indebted to the third volume of the *Miscellaneous Works of the late Thomas Young*, M.D., F.R.S., etc., ed. John Leitch, London, 1855.

[2] *L'Égypte sous les Pharaons, ou recherches sur la Géographie, la Religion, la Langue, les Écritures, et l'Histoire de l'Égypte*, Paris, 1814.

Nearly three weeks after writing the above, Young sent another letter to M. de Sacy, together with a Coptic and a demotic alphabet, derived partly from Åkerblad, and partly from his own researches, and a list of eighty-six demotic words with the words corresponding to them in the Greek version. Of these words he says: "Three were observed by de Sacy, sixteen by Åkerblad, and the remainder by himself." In January, 1815, Åkerblad addressed a long letter to Young, together with which he sent a translation of some lines of the Rosetta Stone inscription, and some notes upon it. Regarding his own work he says: "During the ten years which have elapsed since my departure from Paris, I have devoted but a few moments, and those at long intervals, to the monument of Rosetta . . . For, in fact, I have always felt that the results of my researches on this monument are deficient in that sort of evidence which carries with it full conviction, and you, Sir, as well as M. de Sacy, appear to be of my opinion in this respect . . . I must however give you notice beforehand, that in most cases you will only receive a statement of my doubts and uncertainties, together with a few more plausible conjectures; and I shall be fully satisfied if these last shall appear to deserve your attention and approbation . . . **If again the inscriptions were engraved in a clear and distinct character like the Greek and Latin inscriptions** of a certain antiquity, it would be easy, by the assistance of the proper names of several Greek words which occur in it, some of which I have discovered since the publication of my letter to M. de Sacy, and of many Egyptian words, the sense of which is determined; **it would be easy, I say, to form a perfectly correct alphabet of these letters;** but here another difficulty occurs; the alphabetical characters which, without doubt, are of very high antiquity in Egypt, must have been in common use for many centuries before the date of the decree; in the course of this time, these letters, as has happened in all other countries, have acquired a very irregular and fanciful form, so as to constitute a kind of running hand." (Leitch, p. 33.) In August, 1815, Young replied to Åkerblad's letter and discussed the passages where his own translation differed from that of Åkerblad.

In July, 1815, de Sacy sent a letter to Young, which contains the following remarkable passages: "*Monsieur, outre la traduction Latine de l'inscription Égyptienne que vous m'avez communiquée, j'ai reçu postérieurement une autre traduction Anglaise, imprimée, que je n'ai pas en ce moment sous les yeux, l'ayant prêtée à M. Champollion sur la demande que son frère m'en a faite d'après une lettre qu'il m'a dit avoir reçue de vous. . . . Je pense, Monsieur, que vous êtes plus avancé aujourd'hui et que vous lisez une grande partie, du moins, du texte Égyptien. Si j'ai un conseil à vous donner, c'est de ne pas trop communiquer vos découvertes à M. Champollion. Il se pourrait faire qu'il prétendît ensuite à la priorité. Il cherche en plusieurs endroits de son ouvrage à faire croire qu'il a découvert beaucoup des mots de l'inscription Égyptienne de Rosette. J'ai bien peur que ce ne soit là que du charlatanisme; j'ajoute même que j'ai de fortes raisons de le penser. . . . Au surplus, je ne saurais me persuader que si M. Åkerblad, Et. Quatremère, ou Champollion avait fait des progrès réels dans la lecture du texte Égyptien, ils ne se fussent pas plus empressés de faire part au public de leur découverte. Ce serait une modestie bien rare, et dont aucun d'eux ne me paraît capable."* (Leitch, p. 51.)

In a letter to de Sacy, dated August 3rd, 1815, Young says: "You may, perhaps, think me too sanguine in my expectations of obtaining a knowledge of the hieroglyphical language in general from the inscription of Rosetta only; and I will confess to you that the difficulties are greater than a superficial view of the subject would induce us to suppose. The number of the radical characters is indeed limited, like that of the keys of the Chinese; but it appears that these characters are by no means universally independent of each other, a combination of two or three of them being often employed to form a single word, and perhaps even to represent a simple idea; and, indeed, this must necessarily happen where we have only about a thousand characters for the expression of a whole language. For the same reason it is impossible that all the characters can be pictures of the things which they represent: some, however, of the symbols on the stone of Rosetta have a manifest relation to the objects denoted by them. For instance, a Priest, a Shrine, a Statue, an Asp, a Mouth, and the Numerals, and a King is denoted by a sort of plant with an insect, which is said to have been a bee; while a much greater number of the characters have no perceptible connection with the ideas attached to them; although it is probable that a resemblance, either real or metaphorical, may have existed or have been imagined when they were first employed; thus a Libation was originally denoted by a hand holding a jar, with two streams of a liquid issuing from it, but in this inscription the representation has degenerated into a bird's foot. With respect to the epistolographic or enchorial character, it does not seem quite certain that it could be explained even if the hieroglyphics were perfectly understood, for many of the characters neither resemble the corresponding hieroglyphics, nor are capable of being satisfactorily resolved into an alphabet of any kind: in short, the two characters might be supposed to belong to different languages; for they do not seem to agree even in their manner of forming compound from simple terms." (Leitch, pp. 55, 56.)

Writing to de Sacy in the following year (May 5th, 1816) touching the question of the alphabetic nature of the inscription on the Rosetta Stone, Young says: "Si vous lisez la lettre de M. Åkerblad, vous conviendrez, je crois, qu'au moins il n'a pas été plus heureux que moi dans ses leçons Coptes de l'inscription. Mais le vrai est que la chose est impossible dans l'étendue que vous paraissez encore vouloir lui donner, car assurément l'inscription *enchoriale* n'est *alphabétique* que dans un sens très borné. . . . . . Je me suis borné dernièrement à l'étude des hiéroglyphes, ou plutôt à la collection d'inscriptions hiéroglyphiques. . . . . . Les caractères que j'ai découverts jettent déjà quelques lumières sur les antiquités de l'Égypte. J'ai reconnu, par exemple, le nom de Ptolémée dans diverses inscriptions à Philæ, à Esné et à Ombos, ce qui fixe à peu près la date des édifices où ce nom se trouve, et c'est même quelque chose que de pouvoir distinguer dans une inscription quelconque les caractères qui expriment les noms des personnages auxquels elle a rapport." (Leitch, p. 60.)

On November 10th, 1814, Champollion sent to the President of the Royal Society a copy of his *L'Égypte sous les Pharaons*, and in the letter which accompanied it said: "La base de mon travail est la lecture de l'inscription en caractères Égyptiens, qui est l'un des plus beaux ornemens du riche Musée Britannique; je veux parler du monument trouvé à Rosette. Les efforts que j'ai faits pour y réussir n'ont point été, s'il m'est permis de le dire, sans quelques succès; et les résultats que je crois avoir obtenus après une étude constante et suivie, m'en font espérer de plus grands encore." (Leitch, p. 63.) He asked also that a collation of the Rosetta Stone with the copy of it which he possessed might be made, and suggested that a cast of it should be presented to each of the principal libraries and to the most celebrated Academies of Europe. As Foreign Secretary of the Royal Society, Young replied saying that the needful collation should be made, and adding, "Je ne sais si par hasard M. de Sacy, avec qui vous êtes sans doute en correspondance, vous aura parlé d'un exemplaire que je lui ai adressé de ma traduction conjecturale avec l'explication des dernières lignes des caractères hiéroglyphiques. Je lui avais déjà envoyé la traduction de l'inscription Égyptienne au commencement du mois d'Octobre passé; l'interprétation des hiéroglyphiques ne m'est réussie qu'à la fin du même mois." (Leitch, p. 64.) In reply to this Champollion wrote, "M. Silvestre de Sacy, mon ancien professeur, ne m'a point donné connaissance de votre mémoire sur la partie Égyptienne et le texte hiéroglyphique de l'inscription de Rosette; c'est vous dire, Monsieur, avec quel empressement je recevrai l'exemplaire que vous avez la bonté de m'offrir." But it is clear from the facts given above and the extracts from letters of Young and de Sacy that Young had already done in October, 1814, what Champollion in November, 1814, also claimed to have done.

On August 2nd, 1816, Young addressed a letter[1] to the Archduke John of Austria, in which he reported further progress in his hieroglyphic studies, thus: "I have already ascertained, as I have

[1] This letter was printed in 1816, and circulated in London, Paris, and elsewhere; it did not appear in the *Museum Criticum* until 1821.

mentioned in one of my letters to M. de Sacy, that the enchorial inscription of Rosetta contained a number of individual characters resembling the corresponding hieroglyphics, and I was not disposed to place any great reliance on the alphabetical interpretation of any considerable part of the inscription. I have now fully demonstrated the hieroglyphical origin of the running hand,[1] in which the manuscripts on papyrus, found with the mummies . . . . . ." (Leitch, p. 74.)

The principal contents of Young's letters, however, incorporated with other matter, were made into a more extensive article, which was contributed to the *Encyclopædia Britannica,* Supplement, Vol. IV. He made drawings of the plates, which were engraved by Mr. Turrell, and, having procured separate copies, he sent them to some of his friends in the summer of 1818, with a cover on which was printed the title, "Hieroglyphical Vocabulary." These plates, however, were precisely the same that were afterwards contained in the fourth volume of the Supplement, as belonging to the article "Egypt." The characters explained in this vocabulary amounted to about two hundred; the number which had been immediately obtained from the stone of Rosetta having been somewhat more than doubled by means of a careful examination of other monuments. . . . . . The higher numerals were readily obtained by a comparison of some inscriptions in which they stood combined with units and with tens.[2] Young's article in the *Encyclopædia Britannica* obtained great celebrity in Europe, and was reprinted by Leitch in the third volume of the *Works of Dr. Young,* pp. 86–197; it contains eight sections:—

I. Introductory view of the latest publications relating to Egypt.
II. Pantheon.
III. Historiography.
IV. Calendar.
V. Customs and Ceremonies.
VI. Analysis of the Triple Inscription.
VII. Rudiments of a Hieroglyphical Vocabulary.
VIII. Various Monuments of the Egyptians.

This article is of very great importance in the history of the decipherment of the hieroglyphics, and had Young taken the trouble of having it printed as a separate publication there would have been less

[1] "Que ce second système (l'Hiératique) n'est qu'une simple modification du système Hiéroglyphique, et n'en diffère uniquement que par la forme des signes." Champollion, *De l'Écriture Hiératique des Anciens Égyptiens,* Grenoble, 1821. We should have expected some reference by Champollion to Young's discovery quoted above.

[2] Young, *An Account of some recent discoveries in Hieroglyphical Literature,* p. 17.

doubt in the minds of scholars as to the good work which he did, and the facts that were borrowed from it by Champollion would have been more easily identified.[1]

It has already been said (p. 142) that Champollion published at Paris in 1814 the first two parts of a work entitled *L'Égypte sous les Pharaons, ou recherches sur la Géographie, la Religion, la Langue, les Écritures et l'Histoire de l'Égypte avant l'Invasion de Cambyse*; these parts treated simply of the geography of Egypt. In a note to the Preface he tells us that the general plan of the work, together with the introduction of the geographical section and the general map of Egypt under the Pharaohs, was laid before the *Société des Sciences et des Arts de Grenoble*, September 1st, 1807, and that the printing began on September 1st, 1810. On p. 22 of his *Introduction*, referring to the Rosetta Stone, he says: " Ce monument intéressant est un décret des prêtres de l'Égypte, qui décerne de grands honneurs au jeune roi Ptolémée Epiphane. Ce décret est écrit en hiéroglyphes, en langue et en écriture alphabétique Égyptiennes, et en Grec." Now by the words " en langue et en écriture alphabétique Égyptiennes " we are clearly to understand that part of the Rosetta inscription which is written in demotic. Having referred to the studies of de Sacy and Åkerblad, and spoken of the words in demotic which the latter scholar had rightly compared with their equivalents in Coptic, " que nous y avons lus ensuite," Champollion adds in a foot-note, " Ce n'est pas ici le lieu de rendre compte du résultat de l'étude suivie que nous avons faite du texte Égyptien de l'Inscription de Rosette, et de l'alphabet que nous avons adopté. Nous nous occuperons de cet important sujet dans la suite de cet ouvrage. En attendant, nous prions le lecteur de regarder comme exacts les résultats que nous lui présentons ici." From this it is clear that as early as 1810 Champollion claimed to have made progress in the decipherment of the demotic text (texte Égyptien) of the Rosetta Stone, and it is now time to ask how much he was indebted to Åkerblad's letter for ideas and results. A comparison of Plate II at the end of Åkerblad's *Lettre sur l'Inscription Égyptienne de Rosette*, with Plate IV in Champollion's *Lettre à M. Dacier relative à l'Alphabet des Hiéroglyphes Phonétiques*, will show that *sixteen* of the characters of the alphabet printed by Åkerblad in 1802 were retained by Champollion in 1822; also, if Åkerblad's alphabet be compared with the " Supposed Enchorial Alphabet " printed at the foot of Plate IV accompanying Young's article " Egypt," printed in 1818 and

[1] Ich halte mich daher verpflichtet, alles auf unsern Gegenstand bezügliche dem Leser nachträglich genau mitzutheilen und zwar mit einer um so grössern Gewissenhaftigkeit, je höher durch dessen Kenntniss die Achtung gegen den trefflichen Forscher steigen wird, der besonders in der Erklärung der symbolischen Hieroglyphen so Manches zuerst aussprach, was man ohne den Artikel der Encyklopaedie gelesen zu haben, meistens als das Eigenthum Champollion's zu betrachten gewohnt ist. Schwartze, *Das Alte Aegypten*, p. 446.

published in 1819, it will be found that *fourteen* of the characters are identical in both alphabets. Thus it seems that a greater degree of credit is due to Åkerblad than has usually been awarded to him either by Young[1] or Champollion,[2] or, indeed, by writers on Egyptology generally.[3]

Having seen what foundations Young and Champollion had for their own works on the demotic text to rest on, we may return to the consideration of Young's hieroglyphic studies. On the four plates which appeared with his article "Egypt" he correctly identified the names of a few of the gods, Rā, Nut, Thoth, Osiris, Isis, and Nephthys, and he made out the meanings of several Egyptian ideographs. His identifications of kings' names were, however, most unfortunate. Thus of Ȧmenḥetep, he made Tithons; of Thi (a queen), Eoa; of Usertsen, Heron; of Psammetichus, Sesostris; of Nectanebus, Proteus; of Seti, Psammis; of Rameses II, Amasis; of Autocrator, Arsinoe, etc., etc. He correctly identified the names of Ptolemy and Berenice, although in each case he attributed wrong values to some of the hieroglyphic characters which formed these names. The hieroglyphic alphabet given by Young was as follows:—

206.[4]		ⲃⲓⲣ	true value	BA.
207.		ⲉ	"	R or L.
208.		ⲉⲛⲉ	"	TCH.
209.		ⲓ	"	I.

[1] Mr. Åkerblad was far from having completed his examination of the whole enchorial inscription, apparently from the want of some collateral encouragement or co-operation to induce him to continue so laborious an inquiry; and he had made little or no effort to understand the first inscription of the pillar which is professedly engraved in the sacred character, except the detached observation respecting the numerals at the end; he was even disposed to acquiesce in the correctness of Mr. Palin's interpretation, which proceeds on the supposition that parts of the first lines of the hieroglyphics are still remaining on the stone. Young, *An Account*, p. 10.

[2] "Feu Åkerblad essaya d'étendre ses lectures hors des noms propres grecs, et il échoua complètement." Champollion, *Précis*, 1 éd., p. 14.

[3] See Schwartze, *Das Alte Aegypten*, pp. 160, 162.

[4] No. 205, which is omitted here, is really two demotic characters the values of which are BA and R: to these Young gave the value BERE, and so far he was right, but he failed to see that what he considered to be *one* sign was, in reality, *two*. In Nos. 213 and 214 his consonants were right but his vowels were wrong. We are thus able to see that out of a total of fourteen signs he assigned correct values to six, partly correct values to three, and wholly wrong values to five. Champollion-Figeac, in his *Lettre au Directeur de la Revue Britannique au sujet des Recherches du Docteur Young sur les Hiéroglyphes Égyptiens*, p. 5, gives Young no credit whatever for the three partly correct values assigned to hieroglyphic characters by him.

210.		ⲕⲉ, ⲕⲏ	true value GEB.
211.		[illegible]	„ M.
212.		ⲛ	„ N.
213.		ⲟⲗⲉ	„ R or L.
214.		ⲟϣ, ⲟⲥ	„ S.
215.		ⲡ	„ P.
216.		ϥ	„ F.
217.		ⲧ	„ T.
218.		ⲱ	„ KHA.

In 1822 Champollion published his famous *Lettre à M. Dacier relative à l'Alphabet des Hiéroglyphes Phonétiques,* in which he stated his discovery of the Egyptian hieroglyphic alphabet in the following words: "Vous avez sans doute remarqué, Monsieur, dans mon Mémoire sur l'écriture démotique Égyptienne, que ces noms étrangers étaient exprimés phonétiquement au moyen de signes plutôt *syllabiques* qu'*alphabétiques.* La valeur de chaque caractère est reconnue et invariablement fixée par la comparaison de ces divers noms; et de tous ces rapprochements est résulté l'alphabet, ou plutôt le syllabaire *démotique* figuré sur ma planche I, colonne deuxième. L'emploi de ces caractères phonétiques une fois constaté dans l'écriture démotique, je devais naturellement en conclure que puisque les signes de cette écriture populaire étaient, ainsi que je l'ai exposé, empruntés de l'écriture *hiératique* ou sacerdotale, et puisque encore les signes de cette écriture *hiératique* ne sont, comme on l'a reconnu par mes divers mémoires, qu'une représentation abrégée, une véritable *tachygraphie* des *hiérographes,* cette troisième espèce d'écriture, *l'hiéroglyphique* pure, devait avoir aussi un certain nombre de ses signes doués de la faculté d'exprimer les sons; en un mot, qu'il existait également une série d'*hiéroglyphes phonétiques.* Pour s'assurer de la vérité de cet aperçu, pour reconnaître l'existence et discerner même la valeur de quelques-uns des signes de cette espèce, il aurait suffi d'avoir sous les yeux, écrits en *hiéroglyphes* purs, deux noms de rois grecs préalablement connus, et contenant plusieurs lettres employées à la fois dans l'un et dans l'autre, tels que *Ptolémée* et *Cléopâtre, Alexandre* et *Bérénice,* etc." (p. 5). Throughout this work there appears to be no mention whatever of Young's identification of *any* letters of the hieroglyphic alphabet, although on p. 2 Champollion says: "A l'égard de l'écriture *démotique* en particulier, il a suffi de la précieuse inscription de Rosette pour en reconnaître l'ensemble ; la critique est redevable d'abord aux lumières de votre illustre confrère, M. Silvestre de Sacy, et successivement à celles de feu Åkerblad et de M. le docteur Young, des premières notions exactes qu'on a tirées de ce monument, et c'est de cette même inscription que j'ai déduit la série des signes démotiques qui, prenant une valeur syllabico-alphabétique, exprimaient dans les textes *idéographiques* les noms propres des personnages étrangers à l'Égypte." That Champollion should not have known of Young's article " Egypt " is a thing not to be understood, especially as advance copies were sent to Paris and elsewhere as early as 1818. The whole matter is neatly summed up by Klaproth in his *Examen Critique des Travaux de feu M. Champollion.* He says :—For 10 years past people have been talking enthusiastically about the discovery of the " phonetic alphabet " made by the late M. Champollion, but very few people seem to have any clear idea either of what it really is, or of the results which it has been able to produce. Dr. Young, in England, is beyond contradiction the first author of this discovery. In 1818 he recognized the alphabetic value of the greater number of the signs which form the names of Ptolemy and Berenice, among which he has correctly determined the following seven, which correspond with the results obtained by Champollion. [Here follow the hieroglyphic characters for B, F, I, M, N, P, T.] The idea that the hieroglyphs could contain an alphabetic section never took root in his [Champollion's] mind.

Klaproth proceeds to quote a lengthy extract from Champollion's work, *De l'Écriture Hiératique,* Grenoble, 1821, wherein, after referring to the works of the Comte de Caylus, Barthélemy, Zoega, and M. de Humboldt, all of whom were agreed that the writing of the Egyptian MSS. was ALPHABETIC, that is to say, that it was composed of signs that were intended to recall the sounds of the spoken language, Champollion goes on to say :—A long study, and above all an attentive comparison of the hieroglyphic texts with those of the second kind, which are regarded as alphabetic, have led us to a contrary conclusion. As a result he then states the following :—

1. The writing of the Egyptian MSS. of the second kind (hieratic) is not alphabetic.
2. The second system is only a simple modification of the hieroglyphic system, and differs merely through the form of the signs.
3. This kind of writing is that called hieratic by the Greek writers, and must be considered as hieroglyphic tachygraphy.
4. Finally, the hieratic characters are **signs of things and not signs of sounds.**

Statement No. 4 proves beyond all doubt that when Champollion wrote the work in question he did not only **not believe in the alphabetic character** of any of the Egyptian signs, but also that he never suspected the possibility of such a thing. In the following year (1822) when he published his *Lettre à M. Dacier*, he gave in it an alphabet consisting of various characters discovered by himself, as well as those the value of which had been ascertained by Young, and showed that several of the signs which Young had believed to be syllabic were actually alphabetic! We are entitled to ask here, What was it that had caused Champollion to arrive at a conclusion diametrically opposed to that which he had asserted so confidently one year before? There is, in my opinion, only one answer possible to this question: Champollion altered his opinion because he had either read or had had read or explained to him the fact that Young had successfully identified the names of Ptolemy and Berenice in the hieroglyphic text on the Rosetta Stone and elsewhere. Champollion was swift to grasp the importance of this discovery and to employ the system inaugurated by Young to the decipherment of the hieroglyphic forms of Greek and Latin proper names other than those of Ptolemy and Berenice, and of titles like Autokrator.

It has been popularly supposed that it was Champollion who was the first to identify the name of **Cleopatra** on an obelisk at Philae, but it was not so, as we may see from Young's letter to M. Arago. The great astronomer asked Young why he did not publish " a simple statement of the dates of the several steps " which he had made in the recovery of the literature of the Egyptians. On July 4th, 1828, Young wrote to M. Arago as follows[1]:—" I told you the other day that I thought I had done quite as much as was necessary for asserting my claim, and that I had no reason to be over-anxious for establishing it any further and that the public at large was perfectly willing to concede it me. I thought M. Champollion had been unjust to me, but I freely forgave him, without requiring him to acknowledge his injustice; and on the other hand I was inclined to believe that he had also forgiven me, without my having made any concession to him. Now of the nine letters, which I insist that I had discovered, M. Champollion himself allows me five, and I maintain that a single one would have been sufficient for all that I wished to prove; the method by which that one was obtained being allowed to be correct, and to be capable of further application. The true foundation of the analysis of the Egyptian system, I insist, is the great fact of the original *identity of the enchorial with the sacred character, which I discovered and printed in* 1816,[2] and which M. Champollion probably rediscovered, and certainly republished in 1821 (1822?); *besides the reading of the name of Ptolemy, which I had completely ascertained*

[1] See Leitch, *Works of Dr. Young*, Vol. III, p. 464.
[2] The italics are mine.

and published in 1814, *and the name of Cleopatra, which Mr. Bankes had afterwards discovered by means of the information that I had sent him out to Egypt, and he asserts that he communicated indirectly to M. Champollion.* And whatever deficiencies there might have been in my original alphabet, supposing it to have contained but one letter correctly determined, they could and must have been gradually supplied by a continuous application of the same method to other monuments which have been progressively discovered and made public since the date of my first paper."

Young's assertion that the name of Cleopatra was identified by Mr. Bankes is supported by Henry Salt (see *Essay on Dr. Young's and M. Champollion's Phonetic System of Hieroglyphics*, London, 1826, p. 7), who declared that the discovery was made as far back as 1818! Mr. Bankes noticed that, as the Greek inscription upon the propylaeum at Diospolis Parva "furnishes the only example extant in all Egypt of the name of a queen Cleopatra preceding (instead of following) that of a king Ptolemy, so does the sculpture on the same building furnish the only example, where the female figure, offering, takes a precedence over that of the man; these therefore, it seemed more than probable, must be intended for Cleopatra and Ptolemy." Mr. Salt goes on to say that Mr. Bankes proceeded to confront the supposed name of Ptolemy, as furnished to him from the Rosetta Stone by Dr. Young, with the hieroglyphic designation over the male figure, and found an exact agreement. The next step was to examine whether the same two names could be found on the shaft of the obelisk which Mr. Bankes was removing from Philae, that being a known memorial of a Ptolemy and his two Cleopatras; and upon both being detected, not upon that only, but upon a little temple at Philae, where Mr. Bankes had discovered a dedicatory inscription in Greek of the same sovereign, the matter was brought to complete proof, and the result was communicated by Mr. Bankes both to Mr. Salt and Dr. Young, and noted by him also in pencil in the margin of many copies which he afterwards distributed. It was so noted, amongst others, in the margin of that sent to Paris to be presented to the French Institute by Monsieur Denon. To the plate of that obelisk M. Champollion refers for the discovery and proofs of this important name; but it will be obvious that, without other data, a mere collation of the Greek on the pedestal with the hieroglyphs on the shaft could not, in this instance, have led to such a result. Mr. Salt adds, "These facts are stated, not so much with a view of detracting from any credit assumed, on whatever grounds, by M. Champollion, as of proving that the chain of evidence which establishes this important name is much more full and complete than M. Champollion has been able to make it appear to his readers."

From the facts given above we are enabled to draw up the following statement as to the amount of work done in the decipherment of the Egyptian language by the early workers in this field.

Barthélemy[1] and **Zoega**[2] had come to the conclusion long before the labours of Åkerblad, Young, and Champollion, that the **cartouches contained proper names.** **Åkerblad** drew up an alphabet of the demotic characters, in which fourteen signs had correct values attributed to them. **Young** published a demotic alphabet in which the greater number of Åkerblad's results were absorbed ; he fixed the correct values to six hieroglyphic characters, and to three others partly correct values ; he identified the names of Ptolemy and Alexander, the numerals and several gods' names. **Champollion** published a demotic alphabet, the greater part of which he owed, without question, to Åkerblad, and a hieroglyphic alphabet, of which six characters had had correct values assigned to them by Young and the values of three others had been correctly stated so far as the consonants were concerned. By using the method of decipherment inaugurated by Young, Champollion was able to deduce the values of the remaining letters of the Egyptian alphabet. These facts are proved by the evidence collected in the preceding pages. No one with any knowledge of the subject would contend for one moment that the discoveries that Champollion made after he had once got his alphabet were not entirely his own, or that Young had any share in them, but that Young supplied the method and discovered the true values of several alphabetic characters—which Champollion himself adopted!—is incontrovertible. The credit that was Young's due has been strangely denied to him by a number of modern writers on Egyptology, but this is probably due to the fact that they have not made themselves acquainted with the literature dealing with the early history of Egyptian decipherment. Some who know the facts generally have confused Young's correct identification of several alphabetic signs with the incorrect translations that he made, and have condemned both, whilst others have totally ignored or misrepresented both. Most of the contemporaries of Young and Champollion, I mean men like Birch and Hincks and Brugsch, who did more than anyone else to establish Egyptology on a sound base and as a working system, thought highly of Young's labours, as the following extracts will show. Thus in Wilkinson's *The Egyptians*, pp. 195, 196, Birch says of his alphabet :—

> Amidst this mass of error and contradiction, the application of the phonetic principle by Young, in 1818, had all the merit of an original discovery . . . . . . and it was only by a comparison of the three kinds of writing that he traced

[1] Caylus, *Recueil d'Antiquités Égyptiennes, Étrusques*, etc., tom. V, p. 79.

[2] In *De Origine et Usu Obeliscorum*, p. 465. Conspiciuntur autem passim in Aegyptiis monumentis schemata quaedam ovata sive elliptica planae basi insidentia, quae emphatica ratione includunt certa notarum syntagmata, sive ad propria personarum nomina exprimenda, sive ad sacratiores formulas designandas.

the name of Ptolemy up in his own way, from the demotic into hieratic, into hieroglyphs.

But as regards Young's translations Birch honestly says :—

> His translations, however, are below criticism, being as unfounded as those of Kircher. How far even, in the decipherment, he proceeded correctly, may be doubted. . . . But even here [in interpretation] there is much too incorrect in principle to be of real use ; much of it is beneath criticism. —Birch, *Hieroglyphs*, p. 196.

And Hincks says :—

> In the first work of Champollion, his essay *De l'Écriture hiératique des Anciens Égyptiens*, published in 1821, he recognized the existence of only the first of these three ways of representing words, supposing that all the Egyptian characters represented ideas. When he discovered the erroneousness of this opinion, he used all possible efforts to suppress the work in which he had stated it. That work, however, contained a valuable discovery . . . . In the year after this publication, Champollion published his *Lettre à M. Dacier*, in which he announced the phonetic powers of certain hieroglyphics and applied them to the reading of Greek and Roman proper names. Had he been candid enough to admit that he was indebted to Dr. Young for the commencement of his discovery, and only to claim the merit of extending and improving the alphabet, he would probably have had his claims to the preceding and subsequent discoveries, which were certainly his own, more readily admitted by Englishmen than they have been. In 1819 Dr. Young had published his article "Egypt" in the Supplement to the *Encyclopædia Britannica* ; and it cannot be doubted that the analysis of the names "Ptolemaeus" and "Berenice," which it contained, reached Champollion in the interval between his publication in 1821 and 1822, and led him to alter his views. . . . . . The *Grammaire Égyptienne* ought to have been given to the public as his *sole* bequest in the department of Egyptian philology. It was published from a manuscript written in 1831, immediately before his last illness. Shortly before his decease, having carefully collected the sheets, he delivered them to his brother, with the remark, " Be careful of this ; I trust that it will be my visiting card to posterity." Even the warmest admirers of Champollion must admit that he left his system in a very imperfect state. Few, probably, will deny that he held many errors to the close of his life, both in what respects the reading of the characters, and in what respects the interpretation of the

texts.—Hincks, "On the Number, Names, and Powers of the Letters of the Hieroglyphic Alphabet," in *Trans. Royal Irish Acad.*, Vol. XXI, Section, POLITE LITERATURE, pp. 133, 134, Dublin, 1848.

In 1851 Brugsch, adopting the views which Lepsius[1] expressed in 1837, wrote :—

Saeculi enim hujus et initium usque quum cognitio hieroglyphorum, quibus veteres Aegyptii in sacra dialecto scribenda utebantur, densissimis tenebris scateret, ita quidem ut fere omnia, quae antea vel eruditissimi homines summo ingenii acumine explorasse sibi visi sunt, si hodie forte legimus risum vix tenere possimus : hoc lapide detecto postquam omnium animi ad spem enucleandi tandem istud monstruosum et perplexum per tot saecula quasi involucris involutorum genus signorum arrecti sunt, unus vir Champollio Francogallus exstitit, qui mira sagacitate incredibilique studio adjutus totam hieroglyphorum rationem nulla fere parte relicta luce clarius explanavit et exposuit.—Brugsch, *Inscriptio Rosettana*, Berlin, 1851, pp. 1, 2.

But in 1891, when he was the greatest Egyptologist in Europe, he wrote :—

Fast gleichzeitig mit dem alten Jomard . . . . hatte Dr. Young das Glück aus den hieroglyphischen Texten die Bezeichnungen für die Einer, Zehner, Hunderte, und Tausende richtig herauszuerkennen und überdies den hieroglyphischen Königsnamen—

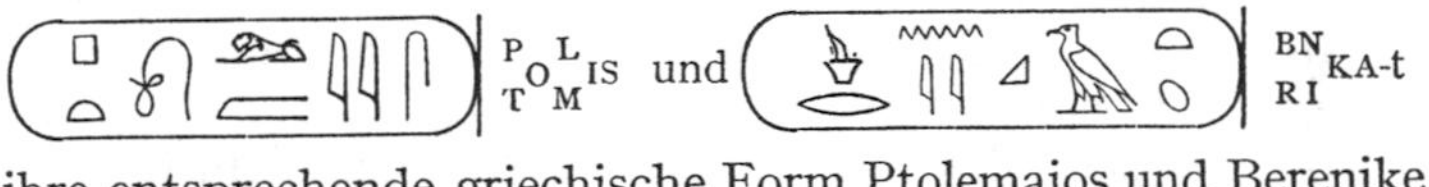

ihre entsprechende griechische Form Ptolemaios und Berenike gegenüberzustellen, eine Entdeckung, die ihm ALLEIN

[1] Ce fut en 1819, que le Dr. Young déclara le premier que les cartouches, ou encadrements elliptiques, dans le texte hiéroglyphique de l'inscription de Rosette, correspondaient aux noms propres grecs et particulièrement à celui de Ptolémée du texte grec, et aux groupes, du même nom, dans le texte intermédiaire en écriture égyptienne démotique ou vulgaire, groupes qui avaient été déjà reconnus et décomposés par MM. Silvestre de Sacy et Åkerblad. Il allait encore plus loin en supposant que chaque signe du cartouche représentait un son du nom de Ptolémée et en cherchant à les définir réellement un à un par une analyse très ingénieuse. . . . . . Plusieurs signes avaient été faussement interprétés et la preuve la plus évidente en était qu'il ne réussissait pas à lire d'autres noms que ceux de Ptolémée et de Bérénice. Il faut donc avouer que, malgré cette découverte, les opinions du Dr. Young, sur la nature du système hiéroglyphique, étaient encore essentiellement fausses et que cette découverte elle-même serait probablement restée infructueuse et à peine signalée comme découverte dans la science, si on avait suivi le chemin que son auteur lui-même avait proposé.—Lepsius, *Lettre à M. le Professeur F. Rosellini sur l'Alphabet Hiéroglyphique*, Rome, 1837, p. 11.

GEBÜHRT und die den Ausgangspunkt der späteren Entzifferungen bilden sollte . . . . . . Dr. Young's glückliche Zusammenstellungen der oben aufgeführten ägyptisch-hieroglyphischen Eigennamen mit ihren entsprechenden griechischen Vorbildern sollten ihm plötzlich die Augen öffnen und ihn [*i.e.*, Champollion] auf den rechten Pfad führen.—Brugsch, *Die Aegyptologie*, Leipzig, 1891, pp. 9, 11.

In his *Aegypten*, p. 14, Erman wrote :—

Ein solcher Ring mit Hieroglyphen 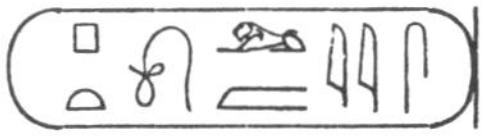

fand sich nun auch an den betreffenden Stellen der Inschrift von Rosette und er musste den Namen des Ptolemäus bilden. Es war der bekannte englische Naturforscher Thomas Young, der im Jahre 1819 diesen scharfsinnigen und völlig richtigen Schluss machte und wenigstens für einige Zeichen des Namens den Lautwert feststellte.

Unabhängig von Young kam gleichzeitig ein junger französischer Gelehrter, François Champollion, zu der gleichen Vermutung und ihm war es beschieden, sogleich ein völlig richtiges Resultat zu erhalten.

Another supporter of Young is Wiedemann, who says :—

Der erste, der es that und von dem richtigen Grundsatze ausging, dass die Königsnamen alphabetisch geschrieben sein müssten . . . . . war der berühmte englische Physiker Thomas Young (geboren 1773). Er erkannte in der häufigsten in dem Dekret von Rosette vorkommenden Gruppe den Namen Ptolemäus, er vermochte ein später zum grossen Teile bestätigtes hieroglyphisches Alphabet aufzustellen und sie über das System der ägyptischen Schrift vollkommen richtige Ansichten zu bilden. So haben wir denn in Young den eigentlichen Entzifferer der ägyptischen Schrift zu sehen, wenn es ihm auch nicht gelang, der Sprache selbst Herr zu werden.—Wiedemann, *Aegyptische Geschichte*, S. 29.

The opinion of Dümichen is just but grudging, for he says :—

Wenn wir die Frage so stellen : Wer hat zuerst einige hieroglyphische Zeichen in ihrem Lautwerthe richtig bestimmt ? oder besser gesagt, zufällig errathen, so müssen wir antworten : das war Th. Young ; den Schlüssel zur Entzifferung der Hieroglyphenschrift jedoch hat er nicht gefunden. François Champollion, geb. den 23. December 1790, gest. den 4. März 1832, er ist es, den die Wissenschaft der Aegyptologie in dankbarer Verehrung als ihren eigentlichen Begründer nennt . . . .—Dümichen, *Geschichte des alten Aegyptens*, Berlin, 1878, S. 304.

And Ebers held the same view :—

> Zwei grosse Männer, in England der auf vielen Gebieten des Wissens ausgezeichnete Thomas Young, in Frankreich François Champollion, begaben sich zu gleicher Zeit, aber unabhängig von einander, an die Arbeit. Beider Bemühungen lohnte schöner Erfolg. Champollion aber wird mit Recht vor seinem britischen Rivalen als Entzifferer der Hieroglyphen genannt werden müssen.—Ebers, *Aegypten in Bild und Wort*, Leipzig, 1879, Bd. II, S. 49.

French Egyptologists naturally supported Champollion, as will be seen from the extracts below. Chabas wrote :—

> Young, qui, le premier, fit l'application du principe phonétique à la lecture des hiéroglyphes. Cette idée fut, dans la réalité, le *fiat lux* de la science . . . . . Il avait bien reconnu dans les hiéroglyphes les noms de Ptolémée et de Bérénice, mais sans réussir à assigner à chacun des signes qui les composent leur véritable valeur ; . . . . . Quelques minces qu'ils soient, ces premiers résultats constitueraient en faveur du docteur Young un titre considérable, s'il ne les avait pas compromis lui-même en s'engageant dans une fausse voie, et en publiant des traductions tout aussi imaginaires que celles de ses devanciers. La solution du problème était réservée au génie de Champollion le jeune ; c'est un honneur que personne ne peut lui disputer.—Chabas, *L'Inscription de Rosette*, p. 5.

And Maspero wrote :—

> Un savant anglais du plus grand mérite, Th. Young, essaya de reconstituer l'alphabet des cartouches. De 1814 à 1818, il s'exerça sur les divers systèmes d'écriture égyptienne, et sépara mécaniquement les groupes différents dont se composaient le texte hiéroglyphique et le texte démotique de l'inscription de Rosette. Après avoir déterminé, d'une manière plus ou moins exacte, le sens de chacun d'eux, il en essaya la lecture. . . . . . . Ses idées étaient justes en partie, mais sa méthode imparfaite ; il entrevit la terre promise, mais sans pouvoir y entrer. Le véritable initiateur fut François Champollion. . . . . .—Maspero, *Histoire Ancienne*, Paris, 1886, pp. 729, 730.

It could hardly be expected that the system of decipherment proposed by Champollion would be accepted by those who had rival systems to put forth, hence we find old theories revived and new ideas brought to light side by side with Champollion's method of decipherment. Among those who attacked the new system were: Spolm, the misguided Seyffarth, Goulianoff and Klaproth. Spolm and Seyffarth divided hieroglyphs into euphonics, symphonics and aphonics, by which terms they seem to imply phonetics, enclitics and ideographics. Their hopelessly wrong theory was put forth with a great show of learning in *De Lingua et Literis veterum Ægyptiorum* at Leipzig, 1825–31. Goulianoff[1] did not accept Champollion's system entirely, and he wished to consider the phonetic hieroglyphs acrologic ; this also was the view taken by Klaproth in his *Lettre sur la découverte des hiéroglyphes acrologiques, adressée à M. de Goulianoff*, Paris, 1827, and also in his *Examen critique des travaux de feu M. Champollion sur les Hiéroglyphes*, Paris, 1832. To the first of these two works Champollion published a reply entitled *Analyse critique de la lettre sur la découverte des hiéroglyphes acrologiques par J. Klaproth* (Extr. du Bulletin de Férussac), Paris, 1827, in which he showed the utter worthlessness of the theory. In 1830, when the correctness of Champollion's system was not fully demonstrated, Janelli published at Naples his *Fundamenta Hermeneutica Hieroglyphicae*, in three volumes, in which the old symbolic theory of the hieroglyphs was re-asserted ! and there were many who hesitated not to follow the views of François Ricardi, the soundness of which may be estimated by the title of one of his works, " *Découverte des Hiéroglyphes domestiques phonétiques par lesquels, sans sortir de chez soi, on peut deviner l'histoire, la chronologie* (! !), *le culte de tous les peuples anciens et modernes, de la même manière, qu'on le fait en lisant les hiéroglyphes égyptiens selon la nouvelle méthode*," Turin, 1824.[1]

Champollion's system of decipherment and translation owes its acceptance chiefly to the famous *Lettre* which Lepsius addressed to Rosellini in 1837. In his discussion of the whole question of Egyptian decipherment Lepsius added to Champollion's system the cohesion and stability which it lacked, and stated clearly the facts which it would seem Champollion only partly realized. About this time **Samuel Birch,** who was then an Assistant in the Record Office, and Dr. **Edward Hincks** (1792–1866) in Ireland devoted themselves to a careful study of Champollion's system. To these men we owe the true explanation of the use of determinatives and phonetic complements, and the correct values of a large number of hieroglyphs. Hincks's paper in the *Transactions of the Royal Irish Academy* (Dublin, 1848, 8vo.), entitled " An attempt to ascertain the number, names, and powers of the letters of the Hieroglyphic Ancient Egyptian Alphabet," was so epoch-making that Dr. Brugsch declared that he was the first to use the correct system of decipherment.[2]

[1] See his *Essai sur les Hiéroglyphes d'Horapollon*, Paris, 1827.

[2] As regards Hincks's work on the demotic text on the Rosetta Stone Brugsch says, " Es liegt mir davon ein Abdruck vor unter dem Titel : 'The Enchorial Language of Egypt' (*Dublin Univ. Rev.* No. III, 1833, 8vo.). In dieser Abhandlung werden zum erstenmale diejenigen grammatischen Bestandtheile der Volksschrift, welche weniger leicht auf der Hand liegen und schwieriger aufzufinden sind, richtig bestimmt und aus bekannteren demotischen Texten nachgewiesen." *Zeitschrift der Deutsch. Morgen. Gesellschaft*, Bd. III, p. 263.

Birch and Hincks showed that they were able to translate Egyptian texts and to obtain valuable historical information from them, and this work was developed to a most remarkable degree by **Emmanuel de Rougé,** who produced translations of hieratic papyri and of many hieroglyphic stelae and other monuments. These three men were the real founders of Egyptology as we now know it, and their work formed the foundation on which **Chabas, Goodwin,** and **H. Brugsch** built with such conspicuous success.

Briefly, the way in which the greater part of the Egyptian alphabet was recovered is as follows :—It will be remembered that, on account of breakages, the only name found on the Rosetta Stone is that of Ptolemy. Shortly before Champollion published his letter to M. Dacier he had published an account of the obelisk[1] which Mr. Bankes brought from Philae, which was inscribed with the name of a Ptolemy, written with the same characters as that on the Rosetta Stone, and also contained within a **cartouche.** It was followed by a **second cartouche,** which Bankes and Young said was that of a queen. The obelisk was in a socket, bearing a Greek inscription containing a petition of the priests of Isis at Philae, addressed to Ptolemy, to Cleopatra his sister, and to Cleopatra his wife. Now, it was argued, if this obelisk and the hieroglyphic inscription which it bears commemorate the petition of the priests, who in the Greek speak of the dedication of a similar monument, it follows of necessity that the cartouche must contain the name of a Cleopatra. The names of Ptolemy and Cleopatra having, in the Greek, some letters that are alike, may be used for comparing the hieroglyphs which are used in each ; and if the characters which are similar in these two names express the same sound in each cartouche, their purely phonetic character is at once made clear. A previous comparison of these two names written in the demotic character shows that when they are written phonetically several characters, exactly alike, are used in each. The analogy of the demotic, hieratic, and hieroglyphic methods of writing in a general way leads us to expect the same coincidence and the same conformity in these same names, written hieroglyphically. The names Ptolemaios and Cleopatra written in hieroglyphs are as follows :—

No. 1, Ptolemy

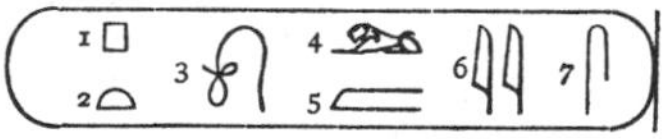

No. 2, Cleopatra

[1] "Observations sur l'Obélisque Égyptien de l'île de Philæ," in *Revue encyclopédique,* Mars, 1822.

Now in No. 2 cartouche, sign No. 1, which must represent K, is not found in cartouche No. 1. But we find as a variant, therefore both and = K, the first letter of the name of Kleopatra. Sign No. 2, a lion lying down, is identical with sign No. 4, in cartouche No. 1. This clearly is L. Sign No. 3, a reed, represents the short vowel E ; two of them are to be seen in character No. 6 in No. 1 cartouche, and considering their position their value must be AI in *αιος*. Sign No. 4 is identical with No. 3 in No. 1 cartouche, and must have the value O in each name. Sign No. 5 is identical with sign No. 1 of No. 1 cartouche, which, being the first letter of the name of Ptolemy, must be P. Sign No. 6 is not found in No. 1 cartouche, but it must be A, because it is the same sign as sign No. 9, which ends the name **ΚΛΕΟΠΑΤΡΑ**; sign No. 10 is No. 2 in Ptolemy; sign No. 11 is not a letter, but is a determinative that accompanies feminine proper names, *e.g.*, , Isis, and , Nephthys. Sign No. 7, an open stretched out hand, must be T. It does not occur in No. 1 cartouche, but we find from other cartouches that takes the place of , and the reverse. Sign No. 8 must be R ; it is not in No. 1 cartouche, and ought not to be there. In No. 1 cartouche sign No. 7 must be S, because it ends the name which in Greek ends with S. The remaining sign in cartouche No. 1 is , which must be M. Thus from these two cartouches we may collect twelve characters of the Egyptian alphabet, viz., A, AI, E, K, L, M, O, P, R, S, T, Ṭ. Now let us take another cartouche from the *Description de l'Égypte,* tom. III, pl. 38, No. 13, and try to make it out ; it reads :—

No. 3

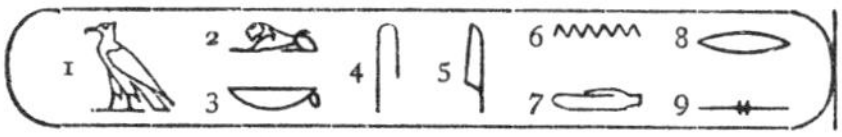

Now signs Nos. 1, 2, 4, 5, 7, and 8, we know from cartouches Nos. 1 and 2, and we may write down their values thus :—

ΑΛ . . ΣΕ . . ΤΡ.

The only Greek name which contains these letters in this order is Alexander, therefore let us assign to the signs , , and , the value of K, N and S respectively. We find on examination that the whole group corresponds, letter for letter, with the group which stands in the demotic text of a papyrus in the place of the Greek name **ΑΛΕΧΑΝΔΡΟΣ**. We have, then, gained three new phonetic signs—K, N, and S—and have determined the value of fifteen in all.

Again, let us take the cartouche of another lady :—

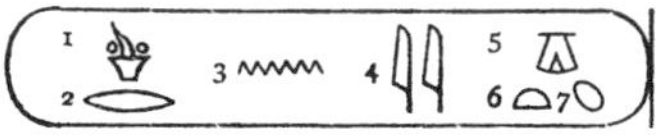

Now signs Nos. 2, 3, 4, 6, and 7 we know, and we may write them down thus :—

. RNAI . .

The only female name which contains these letters in this order is that of Berenice, and to and we may therefore assign the values B and K respectively. Thus we have gained two more signs.

If we take two other cartouches, viz. :—

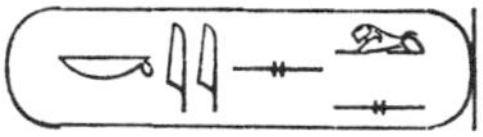 and 

we find that we are able to read the first at once KAISRS, which is clearly *Καισαρος*, or Caesar ; in the second the only sign we do not know is . Writing down the values we know we have A . TAKRTR, which is clearly *Αυτοκρατορ* ; thus the value of the second character must be U. In this manner the names of all the Ptolemies and the Roman Emperors were worked through, and eventually Champollion succeeded in making out the value of one hundred and eleven signs. At the foot of Plate I, in his *Lettre à Monsieur Dacier,* he writes his own name in hieroglyphs thus :—

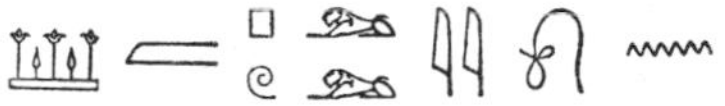

SHA- M -PU -LL - I - O - N .

The following are the letters of the Egyptian alphabet with their values as now accepted by Egyptologists :—

EGYPTIAN HIEROGLYPHIC ALPHABET

	A the Hebrew א		L
	Å a short a, e or i		H
	Ā the Hebrew ע		Ḥ
or	I or Y		KH, Gr. χ
or	U or W	or	S
	B		SH
	P		K
	F		Q
or	M		G
or	N	,	T
	R		TH
			Ṭ (D)
			TCH

COPTIC ALPHABET

ⲁ	A	ⲣ	R
ⲃ	B	ⲥ	S
ⲅ	G	ⲧ	T
ⲇ	D	ⲩ	U, Y
ⲉ	E	ⲫ	PH
ⲍ	Z	ⲭ	KH
ⲏ	Ê	ⲯ	PS
ⲑ	TH	ⲱ	Ô
ⲓ	I	ϣ =	SH
ⲕ	K	ϥ =	F
ⲗ	L	ϧ =	CH
ⲙ	M	ϩ =	Ḥ
ⲛ	N	ϫ =	DJ
ⲝ	X (KS)	ϭ =	TCH
ⲟ	O	ϯ =	TI (DI)
ⲡ	P		

THE EGYPTIAN LANGUAGE

Of the language which the Egyptian of the Palaeolithic and Neolithic Periods spoke nothing is known, but the decipherment of the Egyptian hieroglyphs has revealed many facts about the language which was in use among the Egyptians under dynastic rule. Benfey[1] tried to prove that the Egyptian language had sprung from a Semitic stock, and de Rougé[2] and Brugsch[3] accepted his arguments. Barthélemy, de Guignes, Giorgi, de Rossi and Kopp proclaimed unhesitatingly the identity of Coptic with Hebrew,[4] but Quatremère thought that Coptic was another tongue and had affinity with no other language.[5] Lepsius attempted to prove that the Indo-European, Semitic and Coptic families of languages were originally

[1] The whole of the facts which favour the theory that the Egyptian is allied to the Semitic languages are collected in his work *Ueber das Verhältniss der Aegyptischen Sprache zum Semitischen Sprachstamme*, Leipzig, 1844.

[2] *Mémoire sur l'inscription du tombeau d'Ahmès*, p. 195. " . . . . . . et presque toujours un fait curieux a été mis en évidence, à savoir, que la grammaire de la langue antique se rapproche bien plus décidément des caractères propres aux idiomes sémitiques."

[3] *Wörterbuch*, I. Vorrede, SS. 9–12. " Es steht mir nämlich fest, dass die altägyptische Sprache, d. h. die älteste Gestaltung derselben, im Semitischen wurzelt und dass wir von hieraus alle jene Erscheinungen zu erklären haben, welche sonst ohne jede Auflösung dastehen würden."

[4] Renan, *Histoire Générale des Langues Sémitiques*, p. 80.

[5] *Recherches*, p. 16.

identical,[1] and Schwartze[2] asserted that Coptic was analogous to the Semitic languages in its grammar, and to the Indo-European languages by its roots, but that it was more akin to the Semitic languages in its simple character and lack of logical structure. Bunsen and Paul de Lagarde thought that the Egyptian language represented a prehistoric layer of Semitism, and tried to show that the forms and the roots of the ancient Egyptian could be explained neither by Aryan nor Semitic singly, but by both of these families together, and that they formed in some way the transition from one to the other.[3] Stern believed that there was at one time a relationship between Egyptian and Semitic, which was proved by the pronouns and other words, but that a separation took place between Egyptian and its Asiatic relations at a very early period, and it followed its own course.[4] Prof. W. Wright held that "we have not a few structural affinities, which may perhaps be thought sufficient to justify those linguists who hold that Egyptian is a relic of the earliest age of Semitism, or of Semitic speech as it was before it passed into the peculiar form in which we may be said to know it historically."[5]

From the above it is clear that Lepsius, de Rougé and Brugsch believed in the affinity of Egyptian with the Semitic languages, and as they were Egyptologists their collective opinion is important. The general evidence on the subject was summed up by Erman in a valuable paper which he contributed to the *Zeitschrift d. Deutschen Morgen. Gesell.* (Bd. XLVI, pp. 93–129), and he added a list of Egyptian words with their Semitic equivalents, which strengthened his arguments considerably. Brockelmann, following Brugsch and Erman, would include Egyptian among the Semitic languages and, judging from the language of the Pyramid Texts, is more and more convinced of its similarity to the Semitic languages. But it must be pointed out that the Pyramid Texts were written under the Vth and VIth dynasties, and it has yet to be proved that in their original form they are not of Asiatic origin. Brockelmann also thinks that Egyptian separated itself from its Semitic sisters thousands of years ago, and that it developed itself more quickly than they for much the same kind of reasons that have made English go

[1] *Ueber den Ursprung und die Verwandtschaft der Zahlwörter in der Indo-Germanischen, Semitischen und Koptischen Sprache*, Berlin, 1836.

[2] *Das alte Aegypten*, pp. 976, 1033.

[3] Renan, *op. cit.*, p. 82.

[4] "Es besteht eine alte Verwandtschaft zwischen der aegyptischen, welche dem hamitischen Stamme angehört, und den semitischen Sprachen, wie sich unverkennbar noch in der pronominalbildung und in manchen gemeinsamen Wurzeln zeigt; doch scheint sich das aegyptische von den asiatischen Schwestern früh getrennt zu haben und seinen eigenen Weg gegangen zu sein. . . Die allgemeine Stammverwandtschaft der beiden Sprachen ist durch weitgehende Lautverschiebungen und Veränderungen verdeckt."

[5] *Comparative Grammar of the Semitic Languages*, p. 34.

far away from the other Germanic languages.[1] Whilst not venturing to criticize the opinions of the older Egyptologists, Wright thought that an examination of the Coptic alone readily suggests several considerations in support of the view that Egyptian is descended from the same stock as the Semitic languages. And as the most convincing of these considerations he mentions the "marvellous similarity, almost amounting to identity, of the personal pronouns, both separate and suffixed—a class of words which languages of radically different families are not apt to borrow from one another."[2] Renan, like Wright, was struck by the identity of the pronouns and the manner in which they are treated in the two groups of languages, and he regarded the identity that is apparent even in the details that seem to be secondary as a remarkable fact.[3]

The forms of the pronouns in hieroglyphs, Coptic and Hebrew, are as follows :—

	Egyptian			Coptic	Hebrew
Sing. 1.		*ȧnuk*	I	ⲁⲛⲟⲕ	אָנֹכִי
,, 2. m.		*entuk*	thou	ⲛ̀ⲑⲟⲕ	אַתָּה for אַנְתָּה أَنْتَ *anta*
,, 2. f.		*entut*	thou	ⲛ̀ⲑⲟ	אַתִּי for אַנְתִּי أَنْتِ *anti*
,, 3. m.		*entuf*	he	ⲛ̀ⲑⲟϥ	
,, 3. f.		*entus*	she	ⲛ̀ⲑⲟⲥ	
Plur. 1.		*enen*	we	ⲁⲛⲟⲛ	אָנוּ, אֲנַחְנוּ
,, 2.		*entuten*	you	ⲛ̀ⲑⲱⲧⲉⲛ	אַתֶּם for אַנְתֶּם أَنْتُمْ *antum*
,, 3.		*entu*	they	ⲛ̀ⲑⲱⲟⲩ	
,, 3.		*sen*		Assyr.  *shunu*	

The views of the German Egyptologists summarized above are not generally accepted, and the views held by those who think differently on the subject are set forth with skill and learning by Naville in his *L'Évolution de la Langue Égyptienne et les Langues*

[1] *Grundriss der vergleichenden Grammatik der Semitischen Sprachen*, Berlin, 1908, p. 3.
[2] *Comparative Grammar*, p. 33.
[3] Renan, *Hist. Générale*, p. 84 ff.

Sémitiques, Paris, 1920. To this work the reader is referred for the discussion of details which cannot be considered here. Many writers on the alleged affinity of Egyptian with the Semitic languages have tried to show that the Egyptians borrowed their words for numbers from the Semites, but from the examples quoted below it is tolerably certain that the Egyptians had their own set of words for numbers 1, 3, 4, 5 and 10. Thus we have for 1 UĀU, Copt. ⲟⲩⲁ; for 3 KHEMT, Copt. ϣⲟⲙⲛ̄ⲧ; for 4 FṬU, Copt. ϥⲧⲟⲟⲩ; for 5 ṬU, Copt. ϯⲟⲩ; for 10 MEṬ, Copt. ⲙⲏⲧ. These Egyptian words in no way resemble the Semitic אֶחָד, שָׁלוֹשׁ, אַרְבַּע, חָמֵשׁ, and עֶשֶׂר. The words for 6, SȦS or (Jéquier), Copt. ⲥⲟⲟⲩ; 7, SEFEKH, Copt. ⲥⲁϣϥ; 8, KHEMENU, Copt. ϣⲙⲟⲩⲛ; and 9, PSETCH, Copt. ⲯⲓⲧ, seem to be modifications of indigenous Egyptian words and to be connected with שֵׁשׁ, שֶׁבַע, שְׁמֹנֶה and תֵּשַׁע. That the Egyptian language contains Semitic words and forms of speech[1] there is no doubt whatever, but it seems to me that there is equally no doubt that the indigenous language of the Egyptians finds its true affinities in the Libyan languages of North Africa and in the Nuba languages of East Africa.[2] Throughout the Dynastic Period the influence of the Semitic languages on Egyptian must have been considerable, and it attained its maximum when the Egyptians began to occupy Western Asia. So far back as 1885 some authorities thought that Sumerian loan-words could be identified in the hieroglyphic inscriptions. In a paper now practically forgotten the late Dr. Strassmaier put forth the theory that a relationship existed between the Akkadian [*i.e.*, Sumerian] and Egyptian languages, and he printed a small list of Egyptian, Coptic and Sumerian words which he believed to be identical. See his paper "Akkadisch und Aegyptisch" in the *Album* presented to Dr. Leemans.[3]

[1] These are all ably described and set out with Sethe's characteristic clearness in his great work *Das Aegyptische Verbum*, 3 Vols., Leipzig, 1899–1902.

[2] See Reinisch, *Das persönliche Fürwort und die Verbalflexion in den Chamito-semitischen Sprachen*, Vienna, 1909; and *Die Sprachliche Stellung des Nuba*, Vienna, 1911.

[3] *Études Archéologiques, Linguistiques et Historiques*, dédiées à Dr. C. Leemans, Leide, 1885, pp. 105–107.

EGYPTIAN WRITING

The earliest known Egyptian writing consists of a series of **pictures** of objects, animate and inanimate, and the series of pictures that are found on the Neolithic antiquities discovered at Naḳâdah and other very early sites in Upper Egypt may be regarded as " inscriptions." As these cannot possibly be the earliest attempts to write made by the Egyptians, it may be assumed that the art of writing was known in Egypt from a very remote period. The origin of Egyptian writing has been much discussed,[1] but there is no reason why the pictographs in use among the Neolithic Egyptians should not have been invented by the indigenous peoples of the Nile Valley themselves. It seems that writing in all ancient countries started with pictographs, and that each nation developed its own writing in its own way. The dynastic Egyptians had three kinds of writing—Hieroglyphic, Hieratic and Demotic.

Hieroglyphic writing (Gr. ἱερογλυφικός) is called on the Rosetta Stone , " writing of the words of the god " ; the god alluded to is Tcheḥuti, , or Thoth, who was believed to have invented writing. Hieroglyphs were commonly employed for inscriptions upon temples, tombs, statues, coffins, and stelae, and the most important codices of the Theban and Saïte Recensions of the Book of the Dead are written throughout in them. The earliest hieroglyphic inscriptions known are those found upon the objects that were discovered at Abydos and Naḳâdah by de Morgan, Petrie and Amélineau. Hieroglyphic writing was used for ceremonial and monumental purposes until the IVth century A.D., but it is very doubtful if anyone living at that time could read or understand the inscriptions on the temples and tombs of the Dynastic Period. The number of hieroglyphs for which types have been made is about 2,860, including variants. These have been arranged in groups by modern Egyptologists, thus : Figures of Men, Figures of Women, Figures of Gods, Members of the Body, Figures of Animals, Figures of Birds, Trees, Plants, Flowers, etc., Water and Liquids, etc., either according to numbers or letters of the alphabet. But in respect of many hieroglyphs the grouping is purely arbitrary, for no one knows what objects many of them were intended to represent. The first fount of hieroglyphic type cast in England was designed by Mr. Joseph Bonomi and cast by Mr. Branston. The first book printed in these solid, handsome types was Birch's *Hieroglyphic Dictionary*, London, 1867, but the types were in existence several years earlier. The fount of hieroglyphic type in which the objects are drawn in outline was designed by Lepsius, who used it in printing the October–November number of the *Aegyptische*

[1] For a good summary of the views about it see Spiegelberg, *Die Schrift und Sprache der alten Aegypter*, Leipzig, 1907.

Zeitschrift in 1864. He says that he undertook the task of setting up a fount of hieroglyphic type soon after his return from his Mission in 1846, and that the fount was available for use in 1848.[1]

Hieratic (Gr. ἱερατικός) is the name given to the cursive writing that was used by the priests in copying literary compositions on papyrus, and by merchants and others for the purposes of everyday life. The oldest examples of its use in papyri date from the Vth dynasty, and the latest specimens of it are found in the funerary compositions of the "Book of Breathings," and "May my Name Flourish," and the abridged versions of the Book of the Dead of the Roman Period. The coffins of the XIIth dynasty were often covered with texts written in hieratic, and under the Priest-kings of the XXIst dynasty the whole Book of the Dead was written in hieratic. Hieratic codices began at the right-hand end of the papyrus, instead of at the left, as in the case of hieroglyphic codices. The finest codex of the class is that of Nesitanebtashru (the Greenfield Papyrus, B.M. 10554), the largest known;[2] the latest known complete codex is B.M. 10558, which is 59 feet long, and was written in the Roman Period. About this time all funerary works were written in hieratic or demotic, and the Vignettes and hieroglyphs were, seemingly, only used for purposes of ornament or to show respect for tradition. For those who wish to acquire a knowledge of the hieratic character the best method is to read over the hieroglyphic transcripts of hieratic texts published in such works as Erman's *Die Märchen des Papyrus Westcar*, 2 Vols., Berlin, 1890; Dévaud, *Les Maximes de Ptahhotep*, Fribourg, Texte, 1915; Vogelsang and Gardiner, *Die Klagen des Bauern*, Berlin, 1908; Grébaut, *Hymne à Ammon-Rā*, Paris, 1874, and those published by Budge in *Facsimiles of Hieratic Papyri*, First and Second Series, London, 1910, 1923. A very useful Sign-list for beginners was compiled by Levi, *Raccolta dei segni ieratici egizi nelle diverse epoche con i correspondenti geroglifici ed i loro differenti valori fonetici*, Turin, 1880. But for a comprehensive knowledge of the different forms of hieratic at different periods recourse must be had to that invaluable work of the lamented G. Möller, *Hieratische Paläographie*, Bände I–III, Leipzig, 1909–1912. The care displayed in this work and its accuracy are beyond all praise. The twenty-seven facsimiles reproduce specimen columns of texts during a period of about 3,000 years, namely, from the Vth dynasty to the Ist or IInd century A.D.

Demotic writing (Gr. δημοτικός) is a purely conventional modification of hieratic writing which was much used, especially for social and business purposes; it is said to have come into use about the time of the XXVIth dynasty,[3] and it lasted until the

[1] ". . . so dass sie bereits im Jahre 1848 zu ausgedehnter Verwendung kommen konnten." Vorwort to Theinhardt's *Liste*, Berlin, 1875.

[2] It is 123 feet long, 18½ inches wide, and contains 2,666 lines of text arranged in 172 columns.

[3] Spiegelberg says B.C. 800; see *Aeg. Zeit.*, Bd. XXXVII, p. 18 ff.

IIIrd century A.D. The early Egyptologists called it **Enchorial,** from the Gr. ἐγχώριος; on the Rosetta Stone it is called the "writing of books," . In the Roman Period copies of the Saïte Recension of the Book of the Dead were written wholly in demotic. Demotic texts are very difficult to read and need a careful and special study, but the help available for the student is now very considerable, and he can obtain much assistance from works like Möller, *Die Beiden Totenpapyrus*, Leipzig, 1913 (in this work the hieratic and demotic texts are side by side); Hess, *Roman von Stne Ha-m-us*, Leipzig, 1888; Hess, *Inschrift von Rosette*, Freiburg, 1902; Griffith, *Stories of the High Priests of Memphis*, Oxford, 1900; Spiegelberg, *Demotische Studien*, Leipzig, 1901–10; Spiegelberg, *Kanopus und Memphis* (*Rosettana*), Heidelberg, 1922, and the transcripts of demotic texts published by Révillout and Griffith.

The Egyptians who embraced Christianity, and are known as **Copts** (Arab قِبْط or اقْبَاط), did not, so far as we have any evidence, write copies of the Holy Scriptures in demotic, but made use of the letters of the Greek alphabet. But there were certain sounds in the Egyptian language for which the Greek alphabet did not contain letters, and in order to make Egyptian translations of the Old and New Testaments they invented six signs, based upon the demotic forms of ancient Egyptian hieroglyphs, and added them to the Greek alphabet. These six signs are:—

SH	ϣ	=		*sha*	F	ϥ	=	 (turned upright).
KH or CH	ϧ	=		*kha*	Ḥ	ϩ	=	 *ḥ*
DJ	ϫ	=		*dcha*	TCH	ϭ	=	 *k*

The Egyptian language written in Greek letters with these additions is called **Coptic,** قِبْطِى Ḳibṭiy, or قُبْطِي Ḳubṭiy. A good idea of the extent and scope of Coptic literature is best obtained from W. E. Crum, *Catalogue of Coptic MSS. in the British Museum*, London, 1905, and the list of published texts given by Mallon in his *Grammaire Copte*, Beyrouth, 1904. For descriptions and translations of Coptic letters, business documents and funerary texts see Hall, *Coptic and Greek Texts of the Christian Period*, London, 1905; Crum, *Coptic Ostraka*, London, 1909. The most useful Coptic grammars are those of Mallon and Stern. For beginners Parthey's *Vocabularium*, Berlin, 1844, is a most useful book; for advanced students Spiegelberg's *Koptisches Handwörterbuch*, Heidelberg, 1921, is invaluable. The New Testament in the dialects of Upper and Lower Egypt, edited and translated by the Rev. G. Horner, forms a most useful and instructive chrestomathy. (Published by the Oxford University Press, 1898 ff.)

EGYPTIAN WRITING MATERIALS

THE writing materials chiefly used by the ancient Egyptians consisted of papyrus, leather, palette, reeds, slices of calcareous stone, pieces of earthenware pots, ink and coloured ochres.

Papyrus[1] (in Egyptian *thuf,* or *thufi,* or *thef,* Heb. סוּף, Copt. ϫⲟⲟⲩϥ) was made from the *byblus hieraticus,* or *Cyperus papyrus,* which at one time grew all over the Delta and in the marsh lands near the Nile. The height of the plant was from 20 to 25 feet, and the largest diameter of its almost triangular stalk was from 3½ inches to 6 inches. All parts of the plant were used in much the same way as the date palm is used in Egypt and other countries in Africa. The large cabbage-like head was boiled and eaten, as it is in the Ṣadd region of the Sûdân to-day. The roots served as firewood, and the other parts were woven into mats and ropes and baskets and closely-fitting cases for mummies, and shallow floats or boats were made of the large stalks when tied together. The boat in which Isis set out to seek for Osiris was made of papyrus (Plutarch, *De Iside,* Squire's translation, p. 22), and the "ark of bulrushes" in which Moses was laid was probably made of the same material. When it was intended to make writing-paper from the plant the stalk was cut into sections and the layers were removed from them with a flat needle or spatula. These layers were cut into strips, which were laid side by side perpendicularly, and upon these another series of strips was laid horizontally. A thin solution of gum or some adhesive material was run in between the two layers of strips of papyrus, which were then pressed, or rolled, or beaten together and dried. By joining a number of such sheets of papyrus together a roll of almost any length could be made. The quality and texture of the papyrus or paper depended upon the size of the stalk and the age of the plant from which the strips were cut. The colour of the papyri that have come down to us varies from a rich brown to a silvery grey. The longest roll of papyrus in the world is the Great Harris Papyrus (B.M. 9900), which, including two blank sheets, one at each end, is 135 feet long by 16½ inches in width. This is a masterpiece of the papyrus-maker's art, and was specially made to record the benefactions of Rameses III to the priesthoods of Egypt and the historical summary of his reign. The next longest papyrus is the Book of the Dead that was written for Princess Nesitanebtashru of the XXIst dynasty, B.C. 1100–1000; it measures 123 feet in length by 18½ inches in width. It is made of three layers of papyrus and the sections are joined with great neatness; on it are written

[1] From the Greek πάπυρος; the derivation is uncertain.

172 columns of writing, chiefly hieratic, and the text contains 2,666 lines. Next to this in length are the Papyrus of Ani, 78 feet by 15 inches in width, the Papyrus of Nebseni, 77 feet by 13½ inches, the Papyrus of Nu, 65 feet by 13½ inches, and the Papyrus of Nekht, 46 feet 7 inches by 13½ inches. A good specimen of the papyri used for Government Reports is the Abbott Papyrus (B.M. 10221). The papyri used for ordinary literary compositions varied in length from 10 to 20 feet, and in width from 7 to 9 inches, and those inscribed with liturgical and magical compositions were a little wider. The papyri inscribed with bilingual contracts in demotic and Greek form a class by themselves and vary in width from 10 to 14 inches, and in length from 2 to 10 feet. The roll of papyrus, or book, was called *tchamā*, , Copt. ϫⲱⲙⲙⲉ, and was tied round with a piece of papyrus string, as we see in the hieroglyph . When it was necessary to seal it, a piece of mud was laid on the string and the impression on it was made by a ring, or a scarab which served as a seal, *tchebāt*, 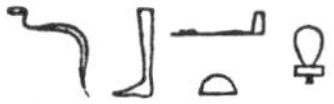. Specimens of mud sealings are tolerably common, but of special interest are the sealings of king Shabaka found at Ḳuyûnjiḳ (B.M. 5585), and the seals of Amasis II and Naifāarut (B.M. 5583, 5584). The Egyptian Christians wrote the Books of the Bible and their Patristic Literature upon papyrus, but instead of keeping to the use of the roll, like their non-Christian ancestors, they wrote their texts on small sheets of papyrus, which they bound up as books. Very fine examples of such books are Oriental 5000 and Oriental 5001. The former contains 156 folios measuring 11¾ inches by 8¼ inches, forming 20 quires, each of which is signed by a letter, and the latter contains 175 leaves measuring from 11 to 12¾ inches by 8½ to 9⅜ inches, forming 22 quires, each of which is signed by a letter. Both these books were probably written in the VIth century A.D.

Leather, or **skin,** was sometimes used as a writing material, but comparatively few examples of it have come down to us. Probably the best-known example is B.M. 10473, which is part of a **vellum roll** inscribed with Chapters from the Book of the Dead and the Vignette of the weighing of the heart of the deceased Nekht in the presence of Thoth. An ancient legal document connected with the temple of Heliopolis is said to have been written on leather, or skin.

As papyrus and leather must always have been costly articles in Egypt, scribes and their pupils were obliged to make use of other materials on which to write their drafts and school exercises, and "trial" copies of texts. For this purpose thin **slabs of soft white limestone** and pieces of broken **earthenware pots** were used; to these the name **ostraka** is commonly given. Good examples of the limestone slab are B.M. 5624, 5631 and 5632; the first is inscribed with a text relating to a grant of land about B.C. 1400; the second is inscribed with a copy of a legal document, and the third with five lines of a song. In some cases the scribe used a **wooden tablet,** covered with a thin layer of white lime or plaster, as his writing material. A good example is B.M. 5629, which contains a copy written in hieratic of the Lament of Khākheperȧ-Senbu, , a libationer of Heliopolis who flourished under the XIIth dynasty. This tablet, like B.M. 21633, was intended for use in schools. The Copts also wrote drafts of texts, letters, extracts from the Bible, etc., on slices of white limestone and on pieces of broken pots; for specimens see Table-Case A in the Coptic Room in the British Museum. From the IIIrd century B.C. to about A.D. 400 **ostraka** were extensively used by Government officials and others, who wrote on them receipts for taxes, lists of workmen and materials, invoices, letters, etc., in Greek and demotic characters. From the VIIth century onwards the Copts wrote many of their legal documents on leather, and little by little copies of the Scriptures came to be written on small sheets of well-prepared skin which were bound up in books like folios of papyrus.

The **palette** of the Egyptian scribe, called *gestȧ*, , or 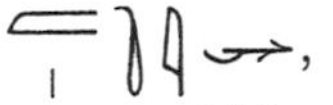, was a rectangular piece of wood, or ivory, or stone which varied in length from about 9 to 16 inches, and from 2 to 3 inches in width. At one end of it were two or more circular or oval hollows to hold ink; sometimes the circular hole was made in the form of the *shen* sign, Q, and the oval hollow in the form of a cartouche . A groove, sloping at one end, was cut lengthwise in the palette to hold the writing reeds. These were kept in their place either by a wooden or stone cover which fitted into the groove, or by a fixed covering like a small tunnel at one end of the groove. Sometimes a sliding cover entirely covered the reeds, much in the same way as the top of the modern pen-box in the East protects the pens. Sometimes loyal scribes caused a cartouche containing the name of the reigning king to be cut on one end of the palette, or the figure of Thoth. Some palettes have as many as a dozen hollows, and these probably belonged to scribes who painted the Vignettes on papyri. The inscriptions on palettes are usually in hieroglyphs, but B.M. 5524, made of ivory, is inscribed in hieratic, B.M. 5517, made of wood, is also inscribed in hieratic, and B.M. 12753, also made of wood, is inscribed in demotic. The palettes found in tombs are of two classes: (1) those that had been actually used by the deceased persons during their lifetime in the exercise of their profession, and (2) those that were votive offerings. Examples of the latter class are B.M. 52942 and B.M. 12778. The first of these is made of white alabaster and dates from the IVth or Vth dynasty; it has two circular hollows, which never had ink in them, and a groove with a sliding cover, also made of alabaster, length 11¾ inches. It was made for a superintendent of the priests called Senni, . The second is made of green stone and is 16 inches long. The positions of the hollows for ink are marked by lightly incised lines, and pieces of reeds are plastered into the groove. At one end, cut in outline, is a scene representing the deceased standing before Osiris with both hands raised in adoration; behind Osiris stand a goddess (Maāt, or Isis ?) and a dog-headed god, wearing the lunar horns and disk, , who is the representative of Thoth. The inscription, which is on both sides of the groove, reads: 1. 

"May Thoth, lord of the words of the gods, President of all the gods, grant exit from and entrance into Khert-Neter; let there not be repulse of soul to the Ka of the scribe of the . . . . . of the water of the temple of Menmaātrā (Seti I) in the House of Åmen, Åmenmes, speaker of the truth before Osiris, the lord of eternity. May Osiris, lord of Ta-Tchesert, give meat, and drink, and oxen, and geese, and linen garments, and incense, and bitumen oil, and every good and pure thing to the Ka of the . . . . . of the water in the House of Åmen-Rā, the king of the gods, Åmenmes, speaker of the truth before all the gods of Thebes." This palette was never used. The palette B.M. 5523, also made of green stone, is also probably to be regarded as a votive offering. It is a little less than 10 inches in length, and was made for the chief bowman, Meriti, , but was never used. The inscription reads 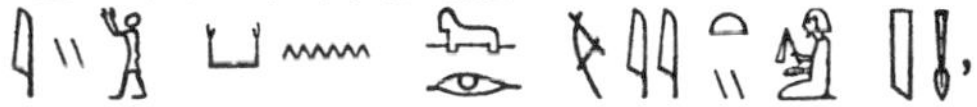, "Hail, Ka of Osiris, Meriti, the truth-speaker," and is clearly the address of the kinsman or friend who dedicated the palette to the deceased. By the side of hollows for the ink is a figure of the god Osiris with a green face;

he is in the form of a mummy, but wears a red collar. On Plate 5 of the Papyrus of Ani we see a palette being carried in the hand of a member of the funeral procession, but whether it was the great scribe's own palette or the offering of a friend is not clear. Of the palettes that were actually used by scribes the following are typical examples. B.M. 12784 is a thin strip of wood about 11¼ inches in length, with two hollows for ink and a groove running the whole length of it; a part of the sliding cover, which protected the reeds, of which four still remain, is wanting. The inscription reads , "Beneficent god, Lord of the Two Lands, Neb-peḥti-Rā," *i.e.*, Amāsis I, the first king of the XVIIIth dynasty, about B.C. 1600. The second example is made of wood, is 13 inches long, and has two circular and twelve oval hollows for ink or colours. At one end is a cartouche running the whole width of the palette containing the inscription

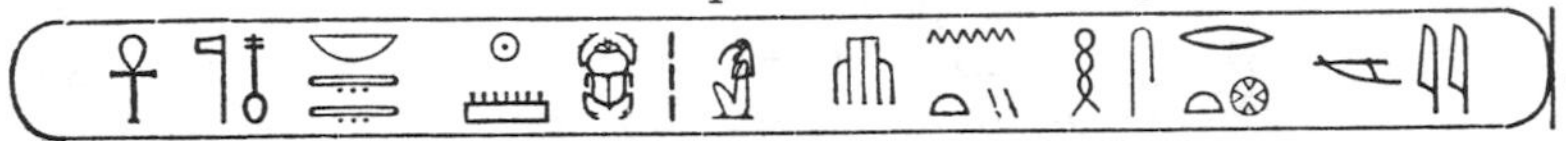.

"May live the beneficent god, the Lord of the Two Lands, Menkheperurā (Thothmes IV), beloved of Thoth, the Governor of Ḥeser." By the sides of the groove are the inscriptions :—

. 1. "May Thoth, the lord of the words of the gods, grant the knowledge of the writing which came forth from him, and penetration of the meaning of the words of the gods to the Ka of the Erpā, the great (?) Ḥa, at the head of the royal nobles (?), steward of the King's House, Rā-meri." 2. "May Åmen-Rā, Lord of the thrones of the Two Lands, the One God, living in (or by) Truth, grant the sweet wind that comes forth from his nostrils and great favours (or rewards, or praises) in the King's House to the Ka of the steward of the King's House, Rā-meri." Across the width of the palette is written , "scribe of the steward of the governor Nuna," and these words seem to imply that Nuna had the palette made to commemorate Rā-meri. In connection with the palette reference must be made to Chapter XCIV of the Book of the Dead, which contains a prayer wherein the deceased asks for an ink-pot and a palette to offer to Osiris. The palette was supposed

to contain a portion of the spirit or essence of Thoth, and an offering of ink-pot and palette propitiated Osiris, who also took the form of a palette on occasions. In the Chapter the deceased addresses Osiris as the "Aged God," and it is important to note that a figure of Osiris is attached to B.M. 5523. As already said, the face of the god is green, which is the colour given to the face of Osiris when it is intended to represent him as the "Old God," or the God of olden time, or the "Ancient of days."

Here, for convenience sake, may be mentioned a couple of objects that seem to have formed part of the equipment of a scribe or artist; they were found in Upper Egypt and were acquired by the Trustees in 1906 (B.M. 43047, 43072). Each object consists of two parts: (1) a flat piece of wood of the shape here shown—in the

case of the larger object it is 12¾ inches long—and (2) a parchment sheath 7¼ inches long, into which the wood slides. The front of the parchment sheath is raised and forms a flat projection with five holes, and attached to this, by leather thongs, is a circular cup with two raised bands, one at the top and one at the bottom. It is suggested that the five holes in the parchment case held reeds or pens, and that the cup attached to it was filled with water or varnish. The flat board may have been used for mixing colours upon, or it may have served merely as a rest for the wrist of the scribe or artist, always of course supposing that this instrument was used by a "writer" or painter. On the back of the parchment sheath is a design, stamped in black ink, consisting of annules, triangles, dots, flowering trees or plants, etc. The general appearance of this ornamentation suggests that the object is of Coptic origin, and that it is not the work of ancient Egyptians.

The ink-pot, *pus*, or *pes*, was usually made of glazed Egyptian porcelain, and varied in height from 1½ inches to 3 inches. The ink, or liquid colour, was probably contained in a pad of vegetable fibre or linen, which served the purpose of the little piece of sponge that is seen in the modern pen-cases of Orientals.

The **writing reed**, *ăr*, or perhaps *gash*, Copt. ⲕⲁϣ, was about 10 inches long, and the end used in writing was bruised and not cut; writing reeds were of various thicknesses. In late times a much thicker reed, which closely resembled that used by the Arabs and other Oriental peoples to-day, was employed, and when this was the case the end was cut like a quill or steel pen.

The black **ink** that the Egyptians used is commonly supposed to have been made of lamp-black, mixed with water and a little gum. But such an ink could be easily washed off the papyrus or tablet, for there was nothing in it to make it "bite" into the papyrus, or skin, or wood on which it was used. The Syrians and Arabs used to boil shavings of the root of the *arṭā* ارطا tree in wine,

A portion of the hieratic text of the Story of the Eloquent Peasant Khu-en-Ånpu. Copied under the XIIth dynasty. B.M. No. 10274.

Draft of a deed, written in the hieratic character on a slice of calcareous stone, concerning certain tombs which had been built on some land granted in the reign of Åmenḥetep III. The draft is dated in the reign of Ḥeremḥeb. XVIIIth dynasty. B.M. No. 5624.

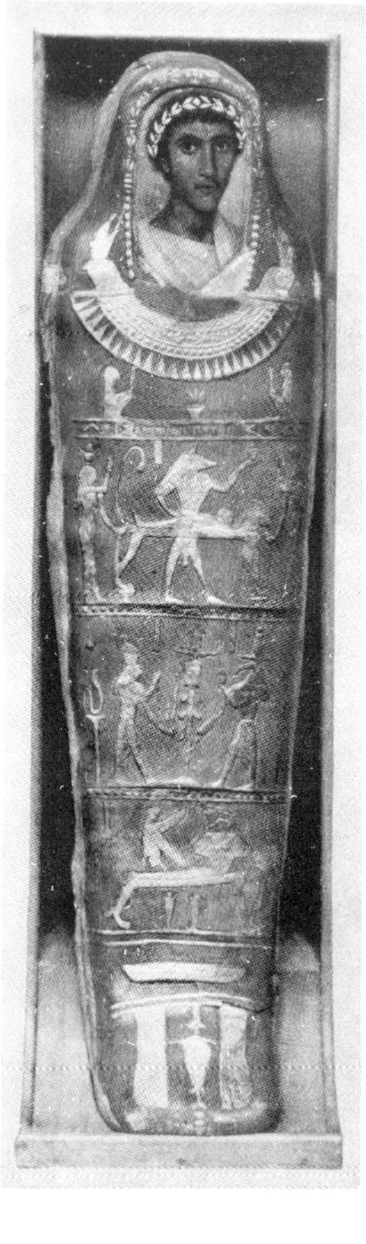

Mummy of Artemidorus, with a Greek inscription. About A.D. 300. B.M. No. 21810.

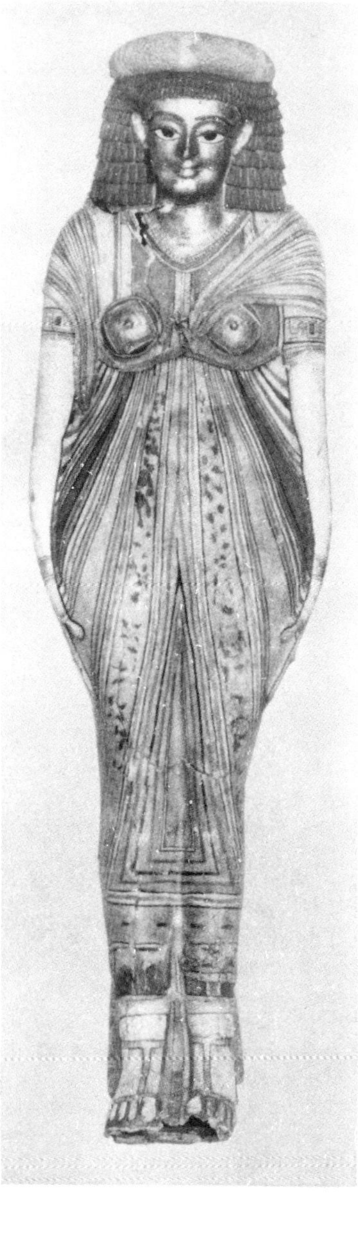

Painted and gilded cartonnage case for the wife of a Roman official in Egypt. About A.D. 200–300. B.M. No. 29585.

and having strained the liquor they added to it a little copperas[1] and gum, and so obtained an ink that was hard to erase from leather or parchment. And even if the colouring matter were rubbed off a skin, it was, and still is, possible to read what was written by means of the outlines of the letters which had been bitten into the skin by the acid in the ink. Another kind of indelible ink was made from wine, in which galls had been steeped, and gum-water,[2] with the addition of a little copperas. The scribe who gives the first recipe says that it was used for the manufacture of the ink employed in writing " by the Egyptian Fathers who lived in the desert of Scete." It is hardly likely that the Fathers invented this kind of ink, and it is far more probable that they copied a recipe that had been known to the scribes of ancient Egypt from the early dynastic period. In literary papyri the only inks used are black and red, the latter being made, probably, from red ochre. The Egyptians seem to have had no special name for black ink, for 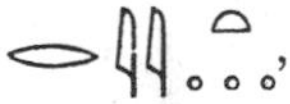, *rit,* is used for any kind of writing fluid. Blue and green colours were probably made from preparations of copper. The coloured ochres—white, yellow, brown, etc.—were carefully rubbed down on a small rectangular **slab** of granite, basalt, or marble with a hard stone **muller** before being mixed with gum and water. A good example of such a slab and muller is B.M. 5547, which was made for Queen Tui, , a wife of Rameses II. The scribe, or artist, who painted the brightly coloured vignettes in such papyri as those of Ani, Hunefer and Nekht, must have kept a stock of small lumps of prepared ochres similar to those that we see in the bronze bowl, B.M. 5556. Under the XVIIIth dynasty, when riches poured into Egypt from the Sûdân and Western Asia, bronze figures of the gods were plated with gold; *ushabtiu* figures were decorated with gold (B.M. 22742, 24390), but the precious metal was not used in illuminating the Vignettes of the Book of the Dead, however brightly coloured they may have been. The only example known to me of the use of gold in a papyrus is found in the copy of the Book of the Dead that was written for Ȧnhai, a singing woman and priestess of Ȧmen-Rā (B.M. 10472). Here, in the Vignette of the Sunrise, we see the god Rā-Ḥerȧakhuti, or Rā-Horus of the Two Horizons, in the form of a hawk, wearing the solar disk encircled by a serpent on his head. The disk of the sun is gilded, and the surface of the papyrus at this place seems to have been painted yellow before the gold leaf was laid over it.

[1] Sulphate of iron (?).
[2] See the recipes in the Syriac MS. Add. 14632, foll. 2 and 17 (Wright, *Catalogue of Syriac MSS.*, p. 581).

A LIST OF THE COMMONEST HIEROGLYPHS

1. Figures of Men

Sign	Value
	ḥāi
	ȧn
	kes
	tut
	ḥu
	ur, ser
	ȧau, semsu
	nekht
	nini
	khus
	qeṭ
	qes
	ȧti
	kharṭ, nu
	khefti
	mshā
	ȧ
	urṭ
	hen
	ṭua
	ȧmen
	ȧmen, ḥap
	uāb
	sath
	fa, atep, kat
	ḥeḥ
	menu, sau
	sheps
	kher

2. Figures of Women

à	
àri	
beq	
mes	
pāpā	
menā	
renn	

3. Gods and Goddesses

Åsår	Osiris
Ptḥ	Ptaḥ
Tatanen (god)	
Ptaḥ-tanen (god)	
Ånḥer	Onouris
Menu	Min
Åmsu (?)	
Åmen	Ammon
Åāḥ	Moon-god
Khensu	Khens
Shu (god)	
Rā (god)	
Set (god)	
Ånpu	Anubis
Tcheḥuti	Thoth
Khnemu	Khnoumis
Ḥāp	Nile-god
Kheperå (god)	
Bes (god)	
Ås-t	Isis
Nebtḥet	Nephthys
Nut (goddess)	
Sesheta (goddess)	
Maāt (goddess)	
Ānqet (goddess)	
Bast (goddess)	
Sekhmit (goddess)	
Un (Hare-goddess)	

4. Members of the Body

tep
tchatcha
ḥer
shen
usher

sher (?)
år
ān
rem
khabes
tå
åt
utcha
utchati
år
khent
fenṭ
r, ra
sep
tef
meṭu
åat
pestch
shāṭ
sekhen
n

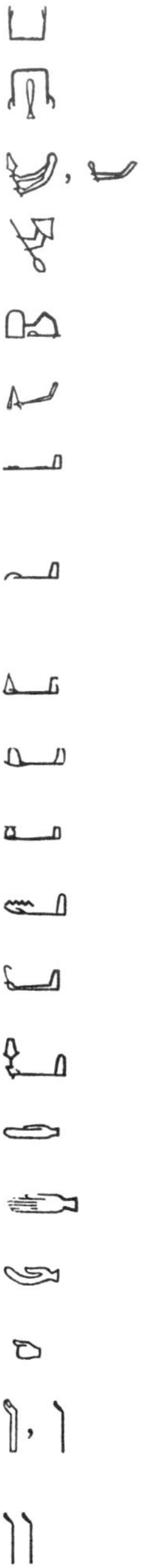

ka
ḥemka
tcheser
khen
āḥa
khu
ā
meḥ
remen
ṭa
m
ḥenk
åa
nekht
kherp
ṭ
shep
kep
am
tchebā
metr
āqa

tha

baḥ

ka

met

ḥem

åu

ān

uār

geḥs

teha

gerg

q

unem

b

ḥā

5. Animals

sesem

åḥ

beḥes

åb

åu

ba

sāḥ

khen

āa

mau

l, r

neb

kherefui

måu

sab

Ånpu (Anubis)

khekh

un

ab

khab

rer

ser

Set

penu

6. Members of Animals

åḥ

khent

- fenṭ
- shefit
- shesa
- peḥt
- peḥti
- ḥa
- at
- up
- ȧau
- up renpit (festival)
- āb
- beḥ / ḥu
- mestcher / ȧṭen
- peḥ
- khepesh
- uhem
- kap
- sab
- sti
- ȧuā

7. Birds

- a
- ma
- ti
- neḥ
- Ḥer Horus / bȧk
- Ḥer-Rā Horus-Rā
- Ḥer nub (?)
- Ȧment
- Khert neter
- Ḥer sma taui
- Ḥer-ȧakhuti
- sep
- ākhem
- mt / ner
- mut
- neb-ti
- m

	m[a], m[i]	
	mer	
	met	
	mer	
	mbaḥ	
	Tcheḥuti	Thoth
	gem	
	ḥam	
	ba	
	baiu	
	àakh	
	benu	
	bāḥ	
	ṭesher	
	usha	
	tchefa	
	tchefa	
	sa	
	apṭ	
	Gebb	
	rekh-ti	
	ḥetem	
	seṭa	
	āq	
	pa	
	khen	
	qema	
	then	
	tcheb	
	ur	
	netches	
	rekh	
	u	
	tha	
	sesh	
	senṭ	
	ba	

8. Members of Birds

	apṭ	
	ner	
	peq	

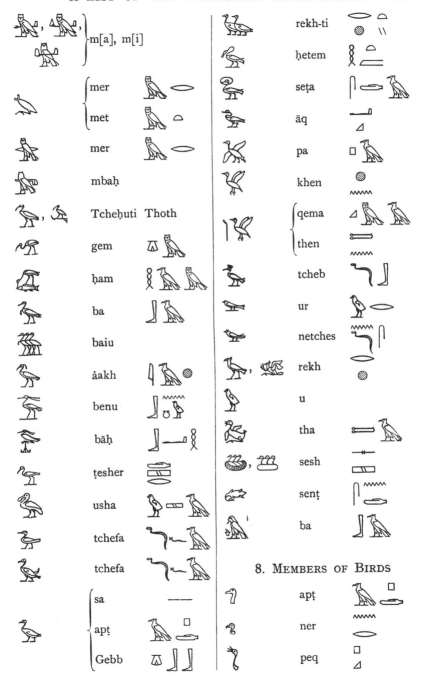

maā

rekh

ṭenḥ

shu
maāt

remen

sha

sa

9. Reptiles

shet

āsh

aṭ

àti

sag

Sebek (god)

kem

Ḥeqt (goddess)

ḥfen

ārā

àter

fenṭ

Āpep

tch

metch . . . .

f

per

āq

10. Fish

àn
rem

āntch mer (?) . . . .

bes

sepa

nār

kha

bes

khepṭ

11. Insects

bàt

Nesu bàt (royal title)

kheper

āff

senḥem

Serqit (goddess)

12. Trees and Plants

åam

bener

khet

renpt

ter

sepṭ

nekhb

nen

nesu / s[u]ten / su

res

shemā

res

å, e, i (short)

åi

sekh

āab

sha / akh

ḥen

ḥa

meḥ

uatch

taui

neḥem

uṭen

un / unem

untchu . . . . . .

kha

shen

ḥetch

utch

khesf

mes

beṭ

åt

shenu

benr

netchm

13. Heaven, Earth and Water

p-[et]

ḥer

gerḥ

åaṭ

thḥen

qer

rā

hru

sesu

Rā, the Sun-god

khu (?)

uben

ḥenmemt

Septt

sept

khā

pesṭ

shesp

åāḥ

åbṭ

sba

ṭua

Ṭua-t

ta

tch[et]

Taui, Egypt S. and N.

khas

Ḥa (god)

tchu, ṭu

åakh

sepa

ḥesp

åṭeb

ua

ḥer

- ges
- åm
- åner
- n
- mu
- mer
- sh
- shem
- Åmen (god)
- åu
- sen
- åakhuti
- båa (?)

14. Buildings

- n[ut]
- per
- pert er Kheru . . . . . .
- per ḥetch . . . . . .
- h
- mer
- nem
- ḥ[et]
- ḥ[et] neter
- ḥ[et] āat
- Nebt-ḥet (Nephthys)
- Ḥet-Ḥer (Hathor)
- āḥā
- usekh
- åneb
- taiti
- qenb
- ḥap
- tekhen
- utch
- khaker
- seḥ
- ārq
- ḥeb seṭ (a festival)
- ḥeb
- āa
- s
- seb
- mes

	thes	
	khem	
	Menu	
	Menu	„ (Min)
	qeṭ	
	p	

15. Ships

	uȧa	
	penā	
	uḥā	
	khenti	
	thau	
	āḥā	
	ḥem	
	kheru	
	ḥap	
	shesp	
	Ḥenu Boat	

16. Furniture

	s[et]	[ ] Isis
	ush	
	stcher	
	s	
	khemenu	
	. . . .	
	the fraction $\frac{2}{3}$	
	srer	
	ḥetep	
	uṭḥu	
	kher	
	qres	
	ȧa	
	tcheba	
	ȧn, ȧun	
	ḥen	
	ȧs	
	Shesmu	
	metcher	
	metcheṭ	
	menkh	
	ursh	

un ḥer

seri

khaib

utchā

uthes

maā

ȧa

17. Temple Furniture

khau

neter

khert neter (Underworld)

ṭeṭ

sma

sen

ȧab

ȧm

Seshait

18. Apparel

meḥ

k (Ptolemaïc)

khepersh

ḥetch

n

sekhemti

shuti

atef

usekh

ȧḥ, āḥ

Satchit (goddess)

shentch

ḥbs

nes

theb

shen

ṭemtch

tet

ānkh

tchas (?)

menȧ

kap

ā

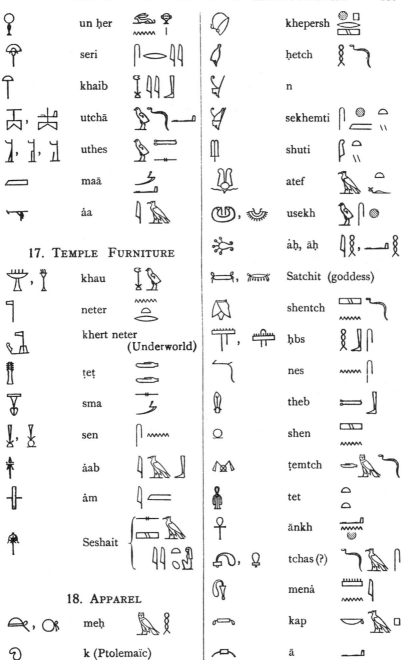

āper

sekhem
kherp
āba

m

ȧmen

khu

Abtch (Abydos)

ḥeqa

āu

uas
tchām

Uast (Thebes)

usr

. . . .

khu

Baba (god)

serekh

19. Arms and Armour

āam

āq (?)

res

skhent

setcheb

meṭḥ

tepi

khepesh

seshem

qeṭ

ṭem

nemmȧt

petch

set

petch

shesr

sun

sa

āa

kh

urrit

20. Tools and Implements

m (Ptolemaïc)

khenr

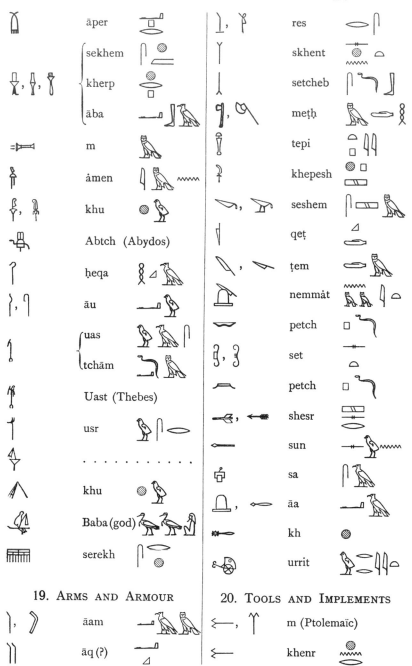

tȧt

setep

nu

ḥu

ma

maā

mer

ḥeb

shenā

tem

bȧa

ḥeqa

t

smen

tcha

menkh

ḥem

uba

mer

ab

netch

uā

Nit (Net) Neith

shems

qes

saḥ

ḥap

nub . . . . . .

ḥetch

tchām

sekht

21. Cords, Ropes, Etc.

u

stha

ȧmakh

au

shes

uga

shen

geb

ārf

ārq

ārq

meḥ

sheṭ

āntch

shenṭ

ua

ruṭ

sa

ḥ

ḥā, ḥer

sek

uaḥ

uṭen

pekhar
ṭebn

ȧth

ut

22. Vessels

Bastit (goddess)
merḥ

ḥes

qebḥ

ḥem

khent

khnem

ārt

ḥeqt
uba

ȧrp

nu

ȧn

ȧb

āb, uāb

mer
mȧ

āb

ta

khet
neser

ba

tcher

g

neb

k

kat

ḥeriḥeb

ȧt

ȧtr

ḥemt

ta

23. Offerings

ta

Nekhen (city)

ta

paut

pestch

sep

kh

ṭa

24. Writing and Musical Instruments

sesh

metchat

gau

bent

seshesh

nefer

Nefer-Tem (god)

sȧa

men

ȧba

25. Line Characters

sign of dual

sign of plural

sheben
nesb (?)

metch

metcht

ḥerit

ṭen

ki tchet . . . . . .

t

qen

ren

sen

seqer

ȧpt

nem

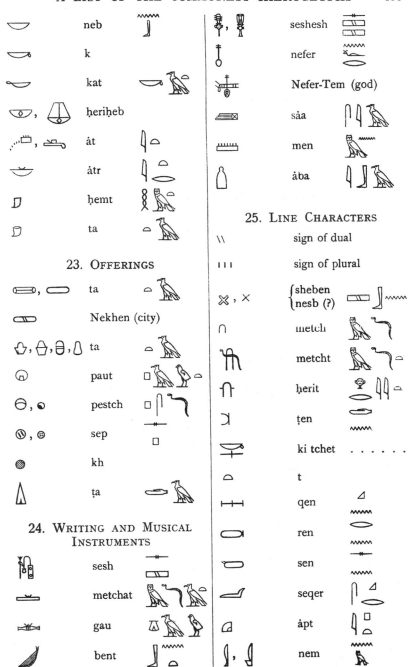

A LIST OF THE COMMONEST DETERMINATIVES

1. Men

	to call, exclamation
	pray, adore, praise
	exalted, rejoice
	disaster, overthrow
	turn back or away
	to run
	dance
	bend, to bow
	dwarf, pygmy
	skip
	make a pact
	form, image, mummy
	great, aged
	royal statue, image
	king
	old age
	beat, strike, strong

	to offer
	to sow
	pour out libation
	bear, carry
	build
	build
	evil, enemy
	support
	stab, pierce
	run
	pour out libation
	child, youth
	to sit, to set
	to offer
	to plough
	make music, joy
	bear, carry
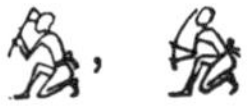	enemy, death
	captive, foreign enemy, criminal

 man

 eat, drink, speak, think

 rest, inactive

 praise

 pray

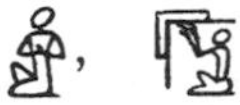 to hide, hidden

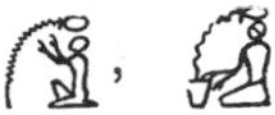 pour out libation

 multitude

 write

 blessed dead

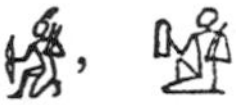 soldier

 god

 king

 shepherd

 dead, ancestor

 defeat, overthrow

 swim

2. Women

 woman

 lady

 dead woman

 pregnant woman

 to bring forth, childbirth

 to suckle

 to dandle

3. Gods and Goddesses

 Osiris

 Ptaḥ

 Ptaḥ-tanen

 Menu

 Ȧmen

 Shu

 Khensu

 Rā

 Ḥer (Horus)

 Ȧnpu (Anubis)

 Khnemu

 Ḥāpi (Nile)

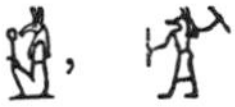 Set

 Tcheḥuti (Thoth)

 Bes

	woman, goddess
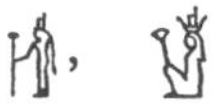	Åset (Isis)
	Nebt-ḥet (Nephthys)
	Ḥet-Ḥer (Hathor)
	Nut
	Maāt
	Sekhmit
	Bastit
	Sesheta
	Serqit

4. Members of the Body

	head
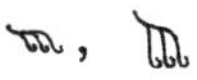	hair, temples, bald, what is lacking
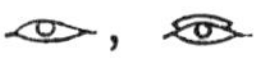	to see
	eye paint
	to weep
	beauty
	eye of Horus
	to die
	to see
	eyebrows
	nose, joy, breath
	jaws
	to cut, destroy
	to nurse
	embrace
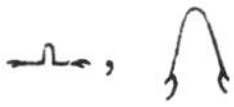	negation, not to have
	to give, strength
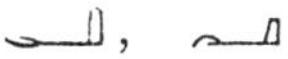	actions of the arm
	give, offer
	to wash
	strength
	hand
	grasp, seize
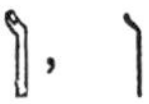	10,000
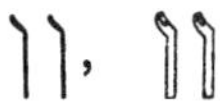	middle, the right
	to take, seize
	male, masculine

	testicles
	woman
	female (of a cow)
	walk, stand, enter
	return
	to walk, march
	to invade
	to eat
	flesh

5. Animals

	horse
	bull
	cow
	calf
	thirst
	ram
	goat
	cow calving, birth
	wrath, anger
	lion
	image
	Anubis and Upuatu
	evil

6. Parts of Animals

	bull, ox
	nose, breath
	nose, breath
	neck, to swallow
	horn
	tooth, tusk
	ear, to hear
	haunch, thigh
	bone
	beast, animal
	goad, tail, end
	heir, kinship

7. Birds

	hawk of Horus
	god, divine
	sacred bird
	vulture
	goddess Mut
	fatten, food
	to destroy, birds in general and a few insects

 to fly

 little, mean, bad

 nest, nestlings

8. Parts of Birds

 to fly, wing

 truth

 goddess, queen, female

9. Reptiles

 crocodile, anger

 gather together

 frog, goddess Ḥeqit

 goddess, divine woman

 worm

 evil, wickedness

10. Fish

 fish

11. Insects

 king of Lower Egypt

 the god Kheper

 winged solar disk

 grasshopper

 goddess Serqit

12. Plants and Trees

 tree

 wood

 time

 goddess Nekhbit

 plant

 papyrus swamp, the North

 Upper Egypt

 bud

 flower

 growing grain

 grain

 wine

 to grow

13. Heaven, Earth and Water

 sky, heaven

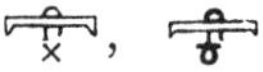 night, darkness

 rain, dew, storm

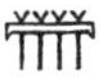 thunderstorm, hurricane

 sun, day, time

 Sun-god

 to shine, light, coruscate

winged disk

moon, night

star, god

land, earth, country

Upper and Lower Egypt

desert

nome

land

land

land, boundary

to be remote

stone, mineral

grain

water, sea, lake

canal, water-channel

sea, lake, water

island

pool, basin of water

14. Buildings

town, city

house, shed, building

goddess Nephthys

goddess Hathor

wall

destroy, overthrow

fort

door

pyramid

obelisk

stele, tablet, boundary stone

room, hall

stairway, to ascend

to open

the god Menu

15. Ships and Boats

boat, to sail

overturn

sail upstream

air, wind, breath

to steer

paddle

16. Furniture

chair of state

litter

to lie, to sleep

funerary chest, sarcophagus

clothing

to raise up, support

 shade

 scales, to weigh

17. Temple Furniture

 altar

 god

 Osiris pillar, backbone

 goddess Sesheta

18. Apparel

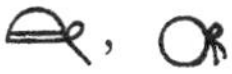 crown

 white crown

 red crown

 red and white crowns

 apron, waist-garment

 clothing

 uterus of Isis

 seal

 tassel, tuft

19. Arms and Armour

 alien, stranger

 support, pillar

 axe, hatchet

 anchoring post, to land

 to cut

 bow

 chariot

 block of execution

20. Tools and Implements

 to smite, fight

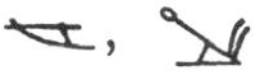 to plough, plough

 metal, mineral

 to shave, razor

 bone

21. Cords and Ropes

 cord, string, rope

 to fasten

 cord, string

 bag, packet, purse

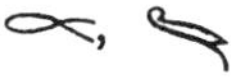 to tie, to untie

 name

 something with a strong smell, dead body, to count up

 smell, odour

22. Vessels

 unguent, ointment

 cool, cool water

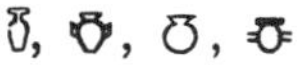 pot, vase, liquid

 milk

	wine
	heart
	stone pot
	pot, vase
	flame, fire, heat
	festival
	metal

23. Offerings

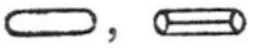	bread, cake
	bread

24. Writing and Musical Instruments

	abstract ideas
	. . . .

25. Line Characters

	to compute, reckon up
	furniture
	what is terrifying
	to divide, share
	circle
	. . . .

THE MUMMY

Mummy is the term that is generally applied to the body of a human being, animal, bird, fish, or reptile, which has been preserved by artificial means, and it has been commonly but wrongly used to describe human bodies that have been merely dried by the sun. The word is neither a corruption of the ancient Egyptian word for a preserved body, nor of the more modern Coptic form of the hieroglyphic name. The word "mummy" is found in Byzantine Greek (*μουμία, μώμιον*), and in Latin, and indeed in almost all European languages. It appears in Latin about A.D. 1000. See Wiedemann, *Herodots Zweites Buch*, Leipzig, 1890, p. 349. It is derived from the Arabic مُومِيَا, "bitumen," a word that in its original Persian form meant "wax." The Persian and Arabic word for mummy is مُومِيَّة, which means a body preserved "by wax or bitumen." The Syriac-speaking people called the substance used in making mummies "Mûmyâ," ܡܘܡܝܐ, the Greeks *πιττάσφαλτος*, and the Persians call a drug used in medicine موميائى. The celebrated Arabic physician Ibn Bêtâr (died A.H. 646), quoting Dioscorides,[1] who lived in the first century of our era, says that *Mumia* is found in the country called Apollonia, and that it flows

[1] *Materia Medica* (ed. Kühn, in *Medicorum Graecorum Opera*, tom. XXV, Leipzig, 1829, p. 101).

down with water from the "lightning mountains," and being thrown by the water on the sides of the water-courses, becomes hard and thick, and that it has a smell like that of pitch. Having further quoted the article by Dioscorides on Pittasphaltus, he adds, "What I say on this subject is as follows: The name *mûmîa* موميای is given to the drug of which mention has just been made, and to that which is called 'Bitumen of Judæa,' القفر اليهودى, and to the *mûmîa* of the tombs الموميای القبورى, which is found in great quantities in Egypt, and which is nothing else than a mixture which the Byzantine Greeks used formerly for embalming their dead, in order that the dead bodies might remain in the state in which they were buried, and experience neither decay nor change. Bitumen of Judæa is the substance which is obtained from the Asphaltites Lake, بحيرة يهودا." 'Abd al-Laṭîf[1] mentions that he saw *mûmîa*, or bitumen, which had been taken out of the skulls and stomachs of mummies sold in the towns, and he adds, "I bought three heads filled with it for half an Egyptian dirham," ولقد اشتريت ثلثة اروس مملوة منه بنصف درهم مصرى, and says that it varies very little from mineral pitch, for which it can be substituted if one takes the trouble to procure it.

About three or four hundred years ago Egyptian mummy formed one of the ordinary drugs in apothecaries' shops. The trade in mummy was carried on chiefly by Jews, and as early as the XIIth century a physician called Al-Magar was in the habit of prescribing mummy to his patients. It was said to be good for bruises and wounds. After a time, for various reasons, the supply of genuine mummies ran short, and the Jews were obliged to manufacture them. They procured the bodies of all the criminals that were executed in gaols, and of people who had died in hospitals, Christians and others. They filled the bodies with bitumen and stuffed the limbs with the same substance; this done, they bound them up tightly and exposed them to the heat of the sun. By this means they made them look like old mummies. In the year 1564 a physician called Guy de la Fontaine made an attempt to see the stock of the mummies of the chief merchant in mummies at Alexandria, and he discovered that they were made from the bodies of slaves and others who had died of the most loathsome diseases. The traffic in mummies as a drug was stopped in a curious manner. A Jew at Damietta who traded in mummies had a Christian slave who was treated with great harshness by him because he would not consent to become a Jew. Finally, when the ill-treatment became so severe that he could bear it no longer, the slave went to the Pasha and informed him what his

[1] See 'Abd al-Laṭîf, *Relation de l'Égypte* (tr. by De Sacy, Paris, 1810, p. 273), and *Abdollatiphi Historiae Aegypti Compendium* (ed. White, Oxford, 1810, p. 150).

master's business was. The Jew was speedily thrown into prison, and only obtained his liberty by payment of 300 pieces of gold. Every Jewish trader in mummy was seized by the local governor of the place where he lived, and money was extorted from him. The trade in mummy, being hampered by this arbitrary tax, soon languished, and finally died out entirely.[1]

The common word for treating a body with medicaments and bandaging it up in mummy form is *uta*, , and an embalmer was called *utu*, . Other words were *setekh*, , or *seṭekh*, 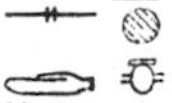, and *qes*,  or ; the former means literally "to embalm," and the latter "to wrap up in bandages." But *qes* may be a shortened form of *qeres*, 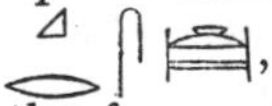, which generally means the mummy and coffin and all the funerary equipment. The word ⲕⲁⲥⲉ seems to mean "he who buries," or undertaker. The Coptic forms of 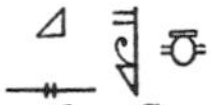 are ⲕⲉⲥ, ⲕⲏⲥ, ⲕⲱⲥ, ⲕⲱⲱⲥ, ⲕⲱⲱⲥⲉ, and they were used by the Copts to translate the Greek *ἐνταφιασμός, ταφή, ἐνταφιάζειν, θάπτειν*, etc.; the word ⲙⲓⲟ̀ⲗⲱⲡ, "mummy," is also given by Kircher, *Lingua Aegyptiaca Restituta*, Rome, 1643, p. 183, at the foot. The mummifier was called ⲣⲉϥⲕⲱⲥ; compare ⲟⲩⲟϩ ⲁⲩⲕⲱⲥ ⲙ̀ⲙ ⲡⲓⲥⲣⲁⲏⲗ ⲛ̀ϫⲉ ⲛⲓⲣⲉϥⲕⲱ̀ⲥ[2] = *καὶ ἐνεταφίασαν οἱ ἐνταφιασταὶ τὸν Ἰσραήλ*.[3]

The knowledge of the way in which the ancient Egyptians mummified their dead is obtained from the works of Greek historians, and from the examination of mummies that has been made by surgeons and anatomists during the last 150 years. According to Herodotus (II, 85), "When in a family a man of any consideration dies, all the females of that family besmear their heads and faces with mud, and then leaving the body in the house, they wander about the city, and beat themselves, having their clothes girt up, and exposing their breasts, and all their relations accompany them. On their part the men beat themselves, being girt up, in like manner. When they have done this, they carry out the body to be embalmed. There are persons who are appointed for this very purpose; they, when the dead body is brought to them, show to the bearers wooden models of corpses, made exactly like by painting. And they show that which they say is the most expensive manner of embalming, the name of which I do not think it right to mention on such an occasion; they then show the second, which is inferior and less expensive; and then the third, which is the cheapest. Having explained them all, they learn from them in what way they wish

[1] Pettigrew on *Mummies*, p. 4.
[2] Lagarde, *Der Pentateuch Koptisch*, Gen. 1, 2.
[3] Lagarde, *Librorum Vet. Test. Canon*, Gen. 1, 2, p. 51.

the body to be prepared ; then the relations, when they have agreed on the price, depart ; but the embalmers remaining in the workshops thus proceed to embalm. In the most expensive manner, first they draw out the brains through the nostrils with an iron hook, taking part of it out in this manner, the rest by the infusion of drugs. Then with a sharp Ethiopian stone they make an incision in the side, and take out all the bowels ; and having cleansed the abdomen and rinsed it with palm-wine, they next sprinkle it with pounded perfumes. Then having filled the belly with pure myrrh pounded, and cassia, and other perfumes, frankincense excepted, they sew it up again ; and when they have done this, they steep it in natron, leaving it under for 70 days ; for a longer time than this it is not lawful to steep it. At the expiration of the 70 days they wash the corpse, and wrap the whole body in bandages of flaxen cloth, smearing it with gum, which the Egyptians commonly use instead of glue. After this the relations, having taken the body back again, make a wooden case in the shape of a man, and having made it, they enclose the body ; and thus, having fastened it up, they store it in a sepulchral chamber,[1] setting it upright against the wall. In this manner they prepare the bodies that are embalmed in the most expensive way.

" Those who, avoiding great expense, desire the middle way, they prepare in the following manner. When they have charged their syringes with oil made from cedar, they fill the abdomen of the corpse without making any incision or taking out the bowels, but inject it at the fundament ; and having prevented the injection from escaping, they steep the body in natron for the prescribed number of days, and on the last day they let out from the abdomen the oil of cedar which they had before injected, and it has such power that it brings away the intestines and vitals in a state of dissolution ; the natron

[1] Compare *ταριχεύει δὲ ὁ Αἰγύπτιος· οὗτος μέν γε—λέγω δ' ἰδών—ξηράνας τὸν νεκρὸν ξύνδειπνον καὶ ξυμπότην ἐποιήσατο.* Lucian, *De Luctu*, § 21 (ed. Dindorf, Paris, 1867, p. 569).

Αἰγύπτιοι δὲ τὰ ἔντερα ἐξελόντες ταριχεύουσιν αὐτούς, καὶ σὺν ἑαυτοῖς ὑπὲρ γῆς ἔχουσιν. Sextus Empiricus, *Pyrrhoniarum Institutionum*, lib. III, cap. 24 (ed. J. A. Fabricius, Leipzig, 1718, p. 184).

Mortuos limo obliti plangunt : nec cremare aut fodere fas putant : verum arte medicatos intra penetralia collocant. Pomponius Mela, lib. I, cap. 9 (ed. Gronov., Leyden, 1782, p. 62).

Aegyptia tellus
Claudit odorato post funus stantia saxo
Corpora, et a mensis exsanguem haud separat umbram.

Silius Italicus, *Punicorum* lib. XIII, ll. 474–476
(ed. H. Occioni, Turin, 1889).

Balsama succo unguentaque mira feruntur
Tempus in aeternum sacrum servantia corpus.

Corippi, *De laudibus Justini*, lib. III, ll. 22–25
(ed. Antwerp, 1581, p. 4).

dissolves the flesh, and nothing of the body remains but the skin and the bones. When they have done this they return the body without any further operation.

"The third method of embalming is this, which is used only for the poorer sort: having thoroughly rinsed the abdomen in syrmæa, they steep it with natron for the 70 days, and then deliver it to be carried away."[1]

According to Genesis l, 3, the embalming of Jacob occupied 40 days, but the period of mourning was 70 days. From Egyptian documents it is known that the length of the period from the death of a man to his burial varied; in one case the embalming occupied 16 days, the bandaging 35 days, and the burial 70 days, *i.e.*, 121 days in all. In a second case the embalming occupied 66 days, preparations for burial 4 days, and the burial 26 days; in all 96 days. Elsewhere we are told that the embalming lasts 70 or 80 days, and the burial ten months.[2]

The account given by Diodorus (I, 91) agrees with that of Herodotus in many particulars, but some additional details are given. According to it, if any man died, all his relatives and friends threw dust or mud on their heads, and went round about through the town uttering cries of grief as long as the body remained unburied; during the interval between the death and the burial, they abstained from the use of baths and wine, they partook of no choice foods, and they put not on fine apparel. The methods of embalming were three in number; the most expensive, the less expensive, and the poorest of all. The first method cost one talent of silver, about £250; the second twenty minae, about £60; and the third cost very little indeed. The people who practise the art of embalming belong to a class of men in whose families this profession is hereditary, and they set down in writing a statement of the various methods of embalming practised by them and the cost of each, and ask the relatives of the dead man to decide upon the method to be adopted. When this question has been settled, the embalmers take the body into their charge, and they hand it to those who are fully acquainted with the process of embalming. The first of these, called the "scribe" (γραμματεύς), makes a mark on the left side of the body, which is laid upon the ground, to indicate where the incision is to be made. Next, a man, called the "ripper up" (παρασχιστής), with an Ethiopian stone (λίθον Αἰθιοπικόν) makes a cut in the side lengthwise of the size indicated by the scribe. Having done this, he flees away in all haste, pursued by his assistants, who hurl after him pieces of stone and call down curses, that vengeance may come upon him for this crime; for the Egyptians hold in abomination anyone who wounds or commits an act of violence upon the human body. The embalmers

[1] Cary's translation, pp. 126, 127.
[2] For the authorities see Wiedemann, *Herodots Zweites Buch*, p. 358.

(ταριχευταί) are held in high honour, and are treated with much consideration, because they are friends of the priests, and are allowed to enter the sanctuary as if they were ceremonially pure. Having assembled around the body, one of them puts his hand into it through the cut that has been made, and draws out everything that he finds inside, with the exception of the heart and reins (lungs ?) ; others clean the intestines, and wash them with palm-wine and balsams. Finally, having treated the body first with oil of cedar and other materials of this nature, and then with myrrh, cinnamon, and other sweet-smelling drugs and spices suitable for embalming purposes, they bring it into such a state of completeness that the eyelashes and eyebrows remain uninjured, and its form is so little changed that it is easy to recognize the features. The greater number of the Egyptians who keep the bodies of their ancestors in magnificent chambers, enjoy the sight of those who have been dead for several generations, and they feel great satisfaction in seeing the features and form of these bodies, and look upon them, to a certain extent, as contemporaries.

With reference to the fleeing away of the paraschistes it is difficult to understand what Diodorus had in his mind. A little further on he says that the embalmers were great friends of the priests, and as this was certainly the case, the man who performed the operation probably merely fulfilled a religious obligation in fleeing away, and had very little to fear. In some particulars Diodorus appears to have been misinformed, and in any case the knowledge he possessed of mummies could hardly have been at first hand. He lived too late (about B.C. 40) to know what the well-made Theban mummies were like, and his experience therefore would only have familiarized him with the Egypto-Roman mummies, in which the limbs were bandaged separately, and the contour of their faces, somewhat blunted, was to be seen through the thin and tightly drawn bandages which covered the face. A good example of a mummy made about this date is that of the lady Mut-em-Mennu, which is preserved in the British Museum, No. 6704 ; in this mummy the features of the face can be clearly distinguished underneath the bandages.

A curious idea about the fate of the viscera taken from the body obtained among certain Greek writers. Plutarch[1] says, in two places, that when the Egyptians have taken them out of the body of the dead man they show them to the sun as the cause of the faults which he had committed, and then throw them into the river, while the body,

[1] Οἱ τὸν νεκρὸν ἀνατέμνοντες ἔδειξαν τῷ ἡλίῳ, εἶτ' αὐτὰ μὲν εἰς τὸν ποταμὸν κατέβαλον, τοῦ δὲ ἄλλου σώματος ἤδη καθαροῦ γεγονότος ἐπιμέλονται. Plutarch, *VII. Sap. Conv.*, XVI., ed. Didot, p. 188. *Cf.* also Ἐπεὶ καλῶς εἶχεν, ὥσπερ Αἰγύπτιοι τῶν νεκρῶν τὴν κοιλίαν ἐξελόντες καὶ πρὸς τὸν ἥλιον ἀνασχίζοντες ἐκβάλλουσιν, ὡς αἰτίαν ἁπάντων ὧν ὁ ἄνθρωπος ἥμαρτεν. Plutarch, *De Carnium Esu, Oratio Posterior*, ed. Didot, p. 1219.

having been cleansed, is embalmed. Porphyry[1] gives the same account at greater length, and adds that the viscera were placed in a box; he also gives the formula which the embalmers used when showing them to the sun, and says that it was translated by Ekphantos[2] into Greek out of his own language, which was presumably Egyptian. The address to the sun and the other gods who are supposed to bestow life upon man, the petition to them to grant an abode to the deceased with the everlasting gods, and the confession by the deceased that he had worshipped, with reverence, the gods of his fathers, from his youth up, that he had honoured his parents, that he had neither killed nor injured any man, all these have a sound about them of having been written by someone who had a knowledge of the "Negative Confession" in the 125th Chapter of the Book of the Dead. On the other hand it is difficult to imagine any Greek acquainted with the manners and customs of the Egyptians making the statement that they threw the viscera into the river, for, when they were not placed in jars separate from the body, they were mummified and placed between the legs or arms, and bandaged up with the body, and the future welfare of the body in the nether-world depended entirely upon its having every member complete.

The evidence of Pettigrew and later surgeons shows that the accounts given by Herodotus and Diodorus are generally correct, for mummies both with and without ventral incisions are found, and some are preserved by means of balsams and gums, and others by bitumen and natron. The skulls of mummies, which exist by hundreds in caves and pits at Thebes, contain absolutely nothing, a fact which proves that the embalmers were able not only to remove the brain, but also to take out the membranes without injuring or breaking the bridge of the nose in any way. Skulls of mummies are found, at times, to be filled with bitumen, linen rags, or resin. The bodies that have been filled with resin or some such substance are of a greenish colour, and the skin has the appearance of being tanned. Such mummies, when unrolled, perish rapidly

[1] Ἐκεῖνο μέντοι οὐ παραπεμπτέον, ὅτι τοὺς ἀποθανόντας τῶν εὖ γεγονότων ὅταν ταριχεύωσιν, ἰδίᾳ τὴν κοιλίαν ἐξελόντες καὶ εἰς κιβωτὸν ἐνθέντες μετὰ τῶν ἄλλων, ὧν διαπράττονται ὑπὲρ τοῦ νεκροῦ, καὶ τὴν κιβωτὸν κρατοῦντες πρὸς τὸν ἥλιον μαρτύρονται, ἑνὸς τῶν ὑπὲρ τοῦ νεκροῦ ποιουμένου λόγον τῶν ταριχευτῶν. Ἔστι δὲ καὶ ὁ λόγος, ὃν ἡρμήνευσεν Ἔκφαντος[2] ἐκ τῆς πατρίου διαλέκτου, τοιοῦτος. Ὦ δέσποτα ἥλιε, καὶ θεοὶ πάντες οἱ τὴν ζωὴν τοῖς ἀνθρώποις δόντες, προσδέξασθέ με καὶ παράδοτε τοῖς ἀϊδίοις θεοῖς σύνοικον. Ἐγὼ γὰρ τοὺς θεούς, οὓς οἱ γονεῖς μοι παρέδειξαν, εὐσεβῶν διετέλουν ὅσον χρόνον ἐν τῷ ἐκείνῳ αἰῶνι τὸν βίον εἶχον, τούς τε τὸ σῶμά μου γεννήσαντας ἐτίμων ἀεί· τῶν τε ἄλλων ἀνθρώπων[3] οὔτε ἀπέκτεινα, οὔτε παρακαταθήκην ἀπεστέρησα, οὔτε ἄλλο οὐδὲν ἀνήκεστον διεπραξάμην. Εἰ δέ τι ἄρα κατὰ τὸν ἐμαυτοῦ βίον ἥμαρτον ἢ φαγὼν ἢ πιὼν ὧν μὴ θεμιτὸν ἦν, οὐ δι' ἐμαυτὸν ἥμαρτον, ἀλλὰ διὰ ταῦτα (δείξας τὴν κιβωτόν, ἐν ᾗ ἡ γαστὴρ ἦν). Porphyry, *De Abstinentia*, lib. IV, 10, ed. Didot, p. 75.

[2] Wilkinson reads "Euphantos" (*Ancient Egyptians*, III, 479).

[3] Wiedemann (*Herodots Zweites Buch*, p. 354) adds οὐδένα in brackets.

and break easily. Usually, however, the resin and aromatic-gum process is favourable to the preservation of the teeth and hair. Bodies from which the viscera have been removed and which have been preserved by being filled with bitumen are quite black and hard. The features are preserved intact, but the body is heavy and unfair to look upon. The bitumen penetrates the bones so completely that it is sometimes difficult to distinguish which is bone and which is bitumen. The arms, legs, hands and feet of such mummies break with a sound like the cracking of chemical glass tubing; they burn very freely, and give out great heat. Speaking generally, they will last for ever. When a body has been preserved by natron, that is, a mixture of carbonate, sulphate, and muriate of soda, the skin is found to be hard and to hang loosely from the bones, in much the same way as it hangs from the skeletons of the dead monks preserved in the crypt beneath the Capuchin convent at Floriana, in Malta. The hair of such mummies usually falls off when touched.

The Egyptians also preserved their dead in honey. ʻAbd al-Laṭîf relates that an Egyptian worthy of belief told him that once when he and several others were occupied in exploring the graves and seeking for treasure near the Pyramids they came across a sealed jar, and having opened it and found that it contained honey, they began to eat it. Someone in the party remarked that a hair in the honey turned round one of the fingers of the man who was dipping his bread in it, and as they drew it out the body of a small child appeared with all its limbs complete and in a good state of preservation; it was well dressed, and had upon it numerous ornaments.[1] The body of Alexander the Great was also preserved in "white honey which had not been melted."

The bodies of the poor were preserved by two very cheap methods; one method consisted of soaking in salt and hot bitumen, and the other in salt only. In the first process every cavity was filled with bitumen, and the hair disappeared; clearly it is to the bodies that were preserved in this way that the name "mummy" or bitumen was first applied. The salted and dried body is easily distinguishable. The skin is like paper, the features and hair have disappeared, and the bones are very white and brittle.

The general descriptions of the modes of mummification by classical writers quoted above naturally have not, at any time, satisfied expert surgeons and anatomists, but to speak of them as "dragomans' tales" is incorrect. The first Englishman who attempted to deal with mummies from the anatomical point of view was Thomas Greenhill[2] (born 1681, died 1741 (?)), who wrote

[1] ʻAbd al-Laṭîf, tr. De Sacy, p. 199.

[2] His mother, Elizabeth, was famous towards the close of the XVIIth century for having given birth to thirty-nine children, all of whom, with the exception of one, were born singly and baptized.

a work entitled Νεκροκεδία. This book " on the art of embalming, wherein is shown the right (*sic*) of Burial, the funeral ceremonies, especially that of preserving Bodies after the Egyptian method, and the several ways of preserving dead bodies in most nations of the world," was published in London in 1705 when Greenhill was 24 years of age! It was said to show great promise, but I cannot see that he did much to increase our knowledge about mummies. The trade in " mummy " as a drug flourished in the XVIIIth century, and among others who discussed it and wrote about it was the notorious Dr. J. Hill (born 1711, died 1775). Dr. Johnson's article " Mummy," in his *Dictionary*, was based upon the account of the so-called drug which Hill published in his *Materia Medica*, London, 1751, 4to. The surgeon who really did what Greenhill professed to do was Dr. T. J. Pettigrew (born 1791, died 1865), who published *A History of Egyptian Mummies and an account of the worship and embalming of the sacred animals of the Egyptians*, etc., with 11 plates, London, 1834. In this work he gave an account of his personal examination of several mummies, and, *inter alia*, a remarkable chapter on the Physical History of the Egyptians, the first attempt to discuss the subject ever made, I believe, by a competent authority. See also his " Account " of a mummy brought from Egypt by Mr. Gosset (in *Archaeologia*, Vol. XXVII); his " Account " of the unrolling of two others (in *Archaeologia*, Vol. XXXIV); and his " Observation on the mode of Embalming among the Egyptians " (in the *Jnl. of the Brit. Arch. Association*, Vol. XIV, 1849). Another student of the physical history of the Egyptians was Mr. G. R. Gliddon, who wrote the *Indigenous Races of the Earth* in 1857, a sort of supplement to his *Types of Mankind*, which he had produced in collaboration with Mr. J. C. Nott in 1854. His works, *Early History of Egypt* (1857), *Ancient Egypt* (New York, 1847, 8vo.), and his *Otia Aegyptiaca* (London, 1847) contain a great deal of useful information and show that he was a clear thinker. Following on the lines of Pettigrew, in recent years Dr. Elliot Smith has examined and described from the anatomical point of view a large number of Egyptian mummies, including those of the kings, queens and priests from Dêr al-Baḥarî, and the results of his investigations will be found in his " History of Mummification in Egypt " in *Proc. Royal Phil. Soc. of Glasgow*, 1910; *Journal of the Manchester Egyptian Society*, 1912; *Journal of Egyptian Archaeology*, Vol. I, p. 189 ff.; and in his *Catalogue of the Royal Mummies in the Cairo Museum*, Cairo, 1912. A list of all the important works on the mummification of the Egyptians will be found in Pagel-Sudhoff, *Einführung in die Geschichte der Medizin*, 2nd edition, Berlin, 1915, p. 33.

Whether the pre-dynastic Egyptians used any special means for preserving their dead cannot be said with certainty, but it seems as if they were content to remove the viscera and dry the body and then commit it to the grave. That mummification was practised in Egypt under the Old Kingdom is certain, and the mummy of the woman which Mr. Quibell found at Ṣaḳḳârah is declared to belong to the IInd dynasty. The body lay on its left side and was in the contracted, pre-natal position of which many examples exist in pre-dynastic graves. Each leg was wrapped, not bandaged, in a sheet of linen, and on the abdomen a sort of linen cushion was found.[1] The body of this woman was wrapped in linen as, probably, many other bodies had been wrapped for generations past, and we are not assuming a great deal in believing that mummification was practised under the Ist dynasty. A mummy found near the Pyramid of Mêdûm, and now in the Royal College of Surgeons in London, is thought to have been made "as early as the Vth dynasty, or possibly even earlier than this,"[2] but many mummies have been found that must have been made earlier than the Vth dynasty. When digging out the layers of tombs in the hill opposite the modern town of Aswân in 1886–87 we found several small, low chambers, each with a shallow pit in it containing a body wrapped in sheets of coarse linen. The chamber above the pit was usually about 18 inches in height, and was only large enough to hold a body in the pre-natal position; the depth of the pit varied from 2 to 4 feet, and the little chamber above it was filled with pieces of stone which were placed there to prevent the jackals from dragging out the body. Mr. Garstang, in his valuable book on the funerary customs of the Egyptians,[3] tells us that he found similar tombs at Bani Ḥasan, and bodies that had been treated in the same way. These tombs, with their small chambers and shallow pits, were the forerunners of the maṣṭabah tombs of the Vth and VIth dynasties, and the bodies in them were undoubtedly those of Egyptians who lived under the early dynasties of the Old Kingdom. In 1886 Maspero believed that the oldest mummy in the world was that of Sekeremsaf, the son of Pepi I (VIth dynasty) and elder brother of Pepi II, which was found at Ṣaḳḳârah in 1881, and is at Gîzah.[4] The lower jaw is wanting, and one of the legs has been dislocated in transport; the features are well preserved, and on the right side of the head is the lock of hair emblematic of youth. Maspero, and others following him, did not believe that the remains of the mummified body of a man which Howard Vysc found in the Pyramid of Menkaurā were those of the king who built the pyramid, but whether they are or not matters little, for the graves at Aswân and Bani Ḥasan and other places prove that the Egyptians mummified their dead under the IVth dynasty.

[1] See Quibell, *Excavations at Saqqara*, Cairo, 1908, pp. 13–18.
[2] Elliot Smith in *Jnl. Eg. Arch.*, Vol. I, p. 192.
[3] *Funeral Customs*, London, 1907.
[4] See Maspero, *Guide du Visiteur au Musée de Boulaq*, 1883, p. 47.

Under the Xth or XIth dynasty the embalmers were able to remove the fleshy portions of the body, leaving nothing but skin and bones. On one occasion when I was visiting a village to the north of Asyûṭ the natives brought in a considerable number of rectangular painted wooden coffins which they had found in some tombs in the hills, and which were made under the Xth or XIth dynasty. Each coffin contained a mummy that was wrapped in a single large sheet of brownish yellow linen, and it appeared to be a solid thing. I wished to acquire two of the coffins, viz., those of Ḥeni and Khati, but not the mummies, and I made arrangements to have the mummies taken back to the tombs from which they had come. Two natives went to lift each mummy out of its coffin, one taking the head and the other the feet, but when they began to lift them each mummy quite suddenly collapsed in the middle, and we heard the bones falling in a heap together inside the linen covering, which was laced up the back. When we cut the lacing we found the skull, and ribs, and bones of the arms and feet piled up in a heap among a lot of dust and small pieces of dried skin of a yellowish colour. The pieces of skin crumbled in the hand even when touched with the utmost gentleness. The natives gave me both mummies as *baḳshîsh*, and I packed each in a box and brought them to the Museum. Sir William Flower examined the bones and dust, and was much interested in an indentation in one of the skulls. He had the bones articulated at the Natural History Museum, and the skeletons are now exhibited with their coffins in the British Museum at Bloomsbury. The natives broke up all the other mummies of the "find," and from some of them they obtained wire gold rings, each with a scarab as a bezel. The rings were always on the little finger of the left hand. The coffins in which mummies of this period are found often contain baskets, tools, bows and arrows, etc. The mummies of the XIIth dynasty are dark-coloured, and the skin is brittle and dry; they are wrapped rather than bandaged in sheets of linen. Scarabs and amulets are frequently found with them.

The mummies of the XVIIIth dynasty found at Memphis closely resemble those of the Xth–XIIth dynasties in Upper Egypt. The breast cavity often contains the green basalt heart-scarab and various kinds of amulets, and sometimes the amulets ☥, 𓊽 and 𓎬 are attached to the neck under the chin. During this period the art of mummification attained its highest pitch of perfection, and the royal mummies[1] are masterpieces of the embalmer's craft. But the luxury of costly mummification fell to the lot of royal personages and the highest officials only; the ordinary citizen of limited means had to be content with the services of cheap embalmers, cheap methods, and cheap materials. The high priests of Åmen-Rā who

[1] For anatomical descriptions of the mummies from Dêr al-Baḥarî see Elliot Smith's *Catalogue*, Cairo, 1912, and *Egyptian Mummies*, London, 1924.

usurped the duties of the Pharaohs and became the Priest-kings of Upper Egypt, and the ladies of their families, were mummified, but the mummies of this period show many marks of inferiority. It is to the credit of the priest-kings that they repaired the royal mummies which the tomb-robbers had wrecked, but their agents who did the work lacked the skill of the great embalmers of the XVIIIth dynasty. The princesses of the families of the priest-kings and rich women of high rank attached great importance to mummification, but bitumen, pure and simple, played a large part in the preservation of their bodies, for the high priests were unable to provide the costly spices and medicaments which came from Western Asia and Nubia. The mummy of the lady Ḥentmeḥit, whose splendid coffins are in the British Museum (B.M. 48001), was discovered by the natives in 1887–88, and when I saw it in her inner coffin it was wrapped from head to foot in large sheets of papyrus inscribed with religious texts written in a bold hand in hieratic. When these were removed the mummy was an oblong black shapeless mass, which was stuck to the bottom of the coffin, and to get it out it had to be broken in pieces. Under the later dynasties of the New Kingdom a very large number of bodies were turned into mummies by being dipped, bandages and all, into bitumen, and they are quite black and very heavy. It was this class of mummy which the natives of Western Thebes broke with hatchets and used as fuel. The mummies of the early centuries of the Christian Era are poorly made and badly bandaged and, as may be seen from the mummies of members of the family of Cornelius Pollios, Archon of Thebes in the time of Hadrian (B.M. 6706, 6707), they are shapeless bundles. Scenes are painted on the wrappings athwart and along the body in which the deceased is represented adoring ill-shaped Egyptian deities; the hieroglyphic inscriptions are faulty copies of old religious formulae, and the name of the deceased is given in Greek as well as in Egyptian letters.

A remarkable example of a very late Graeco-Roman mummy, probably of the IVth century A.D., is the mummy of Artemidorus (B.M. 21810). The body is enveloped in a number of wrappings, and the whole is covered with a thin layer of plaster painted a pinkish-red colour. Over the face is inserted a portrait of the deceased, with a golden laurel crown on his head; on the breast, in gold, is a collar, each side of which terminates in the head of a hawk. The scenes painted in gold on the body are: (1) Anubis, Isis, and Nephthys at the bier of the deceased; (2) Thoth, Horus, uraei, etc., referring probably to the scene of the weighing of the heart; (3) The soul revisiting the body, which is attempting to rise up from a bier, beneath which are two jars; beneath this scene is a winged disk. Above these scenes in a band is inscribed, in Greek, "O Artemidorus, farewell," **ΑΡΤΕΜΙΔΩΡΗ, ЄΥΨΥΧΙ**; and above the band is a vase, , on each side of which is a figure of Maāt, . The bodies of children of this period have traces of gilding upon them (B.M. 30362–30364). And mummies of children have the hair curled and gilded, and hold bunches of flowers in their hands, which are crossed over their breasts.

In the early centuries of our era, mummies of wealthy people were wrapped in royal cloth made wholly of silk.[1] When Pisentios, Bishop of Coptos, and his disciple John took up their abode in a tomb in the "mountain of Tchêmi" (ⲡⲓⲧⲱⲟⲩ ⲛ̀ ϭⲏⲙⲓ = , the necropolis of Thebes) they found it filled with a number of mummies, the names of which were written on a parchment roll which lay close by them. The two monks took the mummies and piled them up one upon the other; the outer coffins were very large, and the coffins in which the bodies were laid were much decorated. The first mummy near the door was of great size, and his fingers and his toes were bandaged separately (ⲡⲉϥⲧⲏⲃ ⲛ̀ ϫⲓϫ ⲡⲉⲙ ⲡⲉϥϭⲁⲗⲁⲩϫ ⲕⲏⲥ ⲛ̀ ⲟⲩⲁⲓ ⲟⲩⲁⲓ); the clothes in which he was wrapped were made entirely of the silk of kings (ϩⲟⲗⲟⲥⲏⲣⲓⲕⲟⲛ[2] ⲛ̀ⲧⲉ ⲛⲓⲟⲩⲣⲱⲟⲩ).[3] The monk who wrote this description of mummies, and coffins, and silk, evidently described what he had actually seen. The huge outer coffins to which he refers belong to a very late period, as do also the highly decorated inner coffins; the fingers and toes being bandaged separately also points to a late Roman period. His testimony that silk was used for wrapping mummies is corroborated by the fact that between 1887 and 1890 a number of mummies wrapped in cloths covered with silk[4] were

[1] Silk, Heb. מֶשִׁי (Ezek. xvi, 10, 13), LXX, τρίχαπτον, σηρικός (Rev. xvii, 12), Syr. ܫܝܪܐ, was common in Greece and Rome at the end of the IInd century of our era. According to Aelius Lampridius (cap. 26), Heliogabalus was the first Roman who wore cloth made wholly of silk, *holoserica veste*, and an idea of the value of silk in the early days of its adoption in Europe is gained from the fact that Aurelian denied his wife a shawl of purple silk because a pound of silk cost one pound weight in gold (Flavius Vopiscus, *Vit. Aur.*, cap. 45). The custom of women wearing silk was railed at by Clement of Alexandria, Tertullian, Cyprian, Bishop of Carthage, Ambrose, Chrysostom and others; yet Basil, about A.D. 370, illustrated the doctrine of the resurrection from the change of the chrysalis into a butterfly. The custom in Italy of wrapping dead bodies in silk is probably not earlier than the end of the IIIrd century, and in Egypt we may place it about one hundred years later. On the use of silk by the ancients see Yates, *Textrinum Antiquorum*, pp. 161–249, and for the collected statements of ancient authors on the subject see G. D. Hoffman, *Observationes circa Bombyces, Sericum, et Moros, ex antiquitatum, historiarum, juriumque penu depromptae;* Tübingen, 4to., 1757.

[2] Greek ὁλοσηρικός.

[3] For the complete text see Amélineau, *Étude sur le Christianisme en Égypte*, p. 143.

[4] For excellent coloured representations of Byzantine mummies see Plates A and B in *Mémoires de la Mission Archéologique Française au Caire*, tom. III, Paris, 1890.

found. In the British Museum is a fine specimen (No. 17173), in which two men on horseback, four dogs, flowers, etc., are woven in green and yellow on a reddish ground. The whole is inside a circular border ornamented with flowers. This piece of silk is sewn on a piece of fine yellow silk, which is in turn sewn on a piece of ordinary mummy cloth to strengthen it.

Mummies of the Roman Period were identified by small **wooden labels,** of an average size of 5 inches by 2 inches, pierced at one end, and tied to the necks of the dead. (See page 224.) Unfortunately they are very easy to forge, for the natives use old wood from Egyptian coffins, and are able to imitate the inscriptions very closely, and many imitations are sold to tourists annually.

The Egyptian Christians appear to have adopted the system of mummifying, and to have mixed up parts of the old Egyptian mythology with their newly adopted Christianity. Already in the IIIrd century of our era the art of mummifying had greatly decayed, and although it was employed by wealthy people, both Christian and pagan, for two or three centuries longer, it cannot be said to have been generally in use at a period later than the IVth century. I believe that this fact was due to the growth of Christianity in Egypt. The Egyptian embalmed his dead because he believed that the perfect soul would return to its body after death, and that it would commune with it once more ; he therefore took pains to preserve the body from all the destroying influences of the grave. The Christian believed that Christ would give him back his body changed and incorruptible, and that it was therefore unnecessary for him to preserve it with spices and medicaments. The idea of embalming the body and keeping it in the house with the living seems to have been repugnant to many famous Christians in Egypt, and Antony the Great admonished his two faithful disciples not to allow his body to be taken into Egypt, but to bury it under the ground in a place known to none but themselves, lest it should be laid up in some dwelling and adored as a sacred relic. He disapproved of this custom, and had always entreated those who were in the habit of keeping the body above ground to give it up ; and, concerning his own body, he said, "At the resurrection of the dead I shall receive it from the Saviour incorruptible."[1]

The pre-Christian Egyptians protected their dead by drawing figures of ☥ *ānkh,* "life," upon the wrappings of their mummies,

[1] *μὴ ἀφεῖτέ τινας τὸ σῶμά μου λαβεῖν εἰς Αἴγυπτον, μήπως ἐν τοῖς οἴκοις ἀπόθωνται· τούτου γὰρ χάριν εἰσῆλθον εἰς τὸ ὄρος, καὶ ἦλθον ὧδε. Οἴδατε δὲ καὶ πῶς ἀεὶ ἐνέτρεπον τοὺς τοῦτο ποιοῦντας, καὶ παρήγγελλον παύσασθαι τῆς τοιαύτης συνηθείας. Θάψατε οὖν τὸ ἡμέτερον ὑμεῖς, καὶ ὑπὸ γῆν κρύψατε· καὶ ἔστω τὸ παρ' ἐμοῦ ῥῆμα φυλαττόμενον παρ' ὑμῖν, ὥστε μηδένα γινώσκειν τὸν τόπον, πλὴν ὑμῶν μόνων. Ἐγὼ γὰρ ἐν τῇ ἀναστάσει τῶν νεκρῶν ἀπολήψομαι παρὰ τοῦ Σωτῆρος ἄφθαρτον αὐτό.*—See Life of Antony by Athanasius. (Migne, *Patrologia,* Ser. Graec., tom. 26, col. 972.)

and painting it on the coffins and cartonnages. For this sign the Christian Egyptians substituted the Cross pure and simple. A remarkable proof of this is afforded by a portion of a mummy wrapping, on which the Cross is painted, which Sir H. Rider Haggard obtained near Asyût and presented to the British Museum in 1923 (B.M. 55056).

MUMMY CLOTH

THE bandages with which the bodies of men and animals are wrapped were, until comparatively lately, believed to be made of *cotton*. In 1646 Greaves stated in his *Pyramidographia* that the "ribbands, by what I observed, were of *linen*, which was the habit also of the Egyptian priests," and he adds, "of these ribbands I have seen some so strong and perfect as if they had been made but yesterday." Rouelle, in the *Mémoires de l'Académie R. des Sciences* for 1750, asserted that every piece of mummy cloth that he had seen was made of *cotton*, and Forster[1] and Solander, Larcher[2] and Maty, Blumenbach[3] and others accepted this opinion. Jomard thought that both cotton and linen were used for bandages of mummies;[4] Granville, in the *Philosophical Transactions* for 1825, p. 274, also embraced this view. The question was finally settled by Mr. Thomson, who after a 12 years' study of the subject proved in the *Philosophical Magazine* (IIIrd Series, Vol. V, No. 29, Nov., 1834) that the bandages were invariably made of linen. He obtained for his researches about four hundred specimens of mummy cloth, and employed Mr. Bauer of Kew to examine them with his microscopes. "The ultimate fibre of cotton is a transparent tube without joints, flattened so that its inward surfaces are in contact along its axis, and also twisted spirally round its axis: that of flax is a transparent tube jointed like a cane, and not flattened nor spirally twisted."[5] The coarse linen of the Egyptians was made of thick flax, and was used for making towels, awnings and sail-cloth;[6] the fine linen, Ὀθόνη, is thought by some to be the equivalent of the אֵטוּן מִצְרָיִם of Proverbs vii, 16. The Greek Σινδών = Heb. סָדִין, was used to denote any linen cloth, and sometimes cotton cloth; but the *σινδόνος βυσσίνης* with which mummies, according to Herodotus (II, 86), were bandaged, is certainly linen. The Egyptian word usually translated by "byssus" is  *shens*, Coptic ϣⲉⲛⲥ; ordinary words for linen are  *māk*,

[1] *De Bysso Antiquorum*, London, 1776, pp. 70, 71.
[2] *Hérodote*, Paris, 1802, p. 357.
[3] *Beiträge*, Göttingen, 1811, pt. 2, p. 73.
[4] *Description de l'Égypte; Mémoires sur les Hypogées*, p. 35.
[5] See Yates, *Textrinum Antiquorum*, London, 1843, p. 262, where the whole subject is carefully discussed.
[6] Comp. שֵׁשׁ בְּרִקְמָה מִמִּצְרַיִם, Ezekiel xxvii, 7.

 *mennui*,  *nu*, Coptic ⲛⲁⲧ = ὀθονίων βυσσίνων (Rosetta Stone, l. 17). One piece of linen of very fine texture obtained at Thebes had 152 threads in the warp, and 71 in the woof, to each inch, and a second piece described by Wilkinson (*Ancient Egyptians*, III, 165) had 540 threads in the warp, and 110 in the woof.[1] One of the cities in Egypt most famous for its linen industry was  Åpu, the Panopolis of the Greeks,[2] the ϧⲙⲓⲙ or ϣⲙⲓⲛ of the Copts, and Akhmîm of the Arabs; but as Egypt exported great quantities of this material, and also used immense quantities for bandages of mummies, it is certain that other cities also possessed large linen manufactories. The city of Tanis was the centre of the linen trade in Lower Egypt. Pelusium also had its linen manufactories, and the name of one special linen cloth that was woven there was that of the city itself, and has survived in the French word "blouse" (*i.e.*, Pelouse, or Pelusium).[3]

The length and breadth of mummy bandages vary from about 3 feet by $2\frac{1}{2}$ inches, to 13 feet by $4\frac{1}{2}$ inches; some are made with fringe at both ends, like a scarf, and some have carefully made selvedges. Mummies of the IInd and IIIrd dynasties are wrapped in sheets of linen about 4 feet square. The pads that are laid between the limbs are made of pieces of linen from about 18 inches to 2 feet square. Under the XVIIIth dynasty linen sheets 9 feet to 12 feet square have been found. The saffron-coloured pieces of linen with which mummies are finally covered measure about 8 feet by 4 feet; the dye was obtained from the *carthamus tinctoria.* Usually two or three different kinds of linen are used in bandaging mummies. Mummy cloths are with very few exceptions quite plain, and it is only in the Greek times that the fine outer linen covering is decorated with figures of gods, etc., in gaudy colours. Several square pieces of linen in the museums of Europe are ornamented with blue stripes, and it is pretty certain that the threads that form them were dyed with indigo before they were woven into the piece. As far back as the time of Thothmes III it was customary to inscribe texts in the hieratic and hieroglyphic characters upon mummy cloths, and at that period large Vignettes accompany the Chapters

[1] See also an interesting letter by De Fleury to M. Devéria on "Les Étoffes Égyptiennes" in *Rev. Arch.*, tom. XXI, Paris, 1870, pp. 217–221.

[2] Πανῶν πόλις, λινουργῶν καὶ λιθουργῶν κατοικία παλαιά, Strabo, XVII, l. 42. In the map published by Yates (*Textrinum Antiquorum*, p. 250) to show the divisions of the ancient world in which sheep's-wool, goat's-hair, hemp, cotton, silk, beaver's wool, camel's-wool, camel's-hair and linen are found, the only other districts where linen was made besides Egypt are Colchis, Cinyps, and a district near the mouth of the Rhine.

[3] Lumbroso, *Recherches sur l'Économie Politique de l'Égypte*, p. 108. This is on all fours with "muslin" from Môsul, "damask" from Damascus, "dimity" from Damietta, and "calico" from Calicut.

from the Book of the Dead; after the XXVIth dynasty hieratic only appears to have been used for this purpose, and the bandages, which are rarely more than 4 inches wide, are frequently so coarse that the text is almost illegible. Badly drawn Vignettes, in outline, usually stand at the top of each column of writing. It is worthy of note that Egyptian ladies marked their linen with indelible ink; see the fringed winding-sheet of Tcheḥuti-sat (B.M. 37105).

The cultivation of flax was a very important industry in Egypt, for the dead as well as the living had to be clothed, and there are many representations of its culture and treatment on the monuments.[1] Examples of the "**combs**" with which the flax to be made into cloth was heckled, and of the **spindles** and **whorls** which the weavers used are to be seen in the British Museum (B.M. 18182, 41563). On some of the spindles portions of the linen threads still remain (B.M. 6119, 6477, etc.).

The marvellous skill that the Egyptians displayed in making linen did not die out with the fall of the native sovereigns of Egypt, and the Copts, or native Christians of that country, have carried on the industry with splendid success until the present day. Although they ceased to mummify their dead—for, in my opinion, the hope of the resurrection of the body given by Christianity practically killed the art of embalming—they continued to dress them in garments that are remarkable for the beauty of the designs and needlework with which they are decorated. A great "find" of fine examples of this work was made at Akhmîm, the ancient Panopolis, in 1886–87. The graves at Akhmîm are about 5 feet deep, and are not indicated by any mound. The bodies appear to have been buried with natron sprinkled over them, for many of their garments are covered with crystals of this substance; and they appear also to have been buried with their best clothes on. The head was provided with a band or cap, and was sometimes supported on a pillow. The body wore a tunic, and the feet had stockings, sandals or shoes upon them; the head, breast, arms, and fingers were decorated with ornaments. The condition in life of the deceased was indicated by inscriptions on rectangular wooden tesserae or by his tools, which were buried with him. The body was entirely covered with linen and laid upon a board, and thus dressed was then deposited in the earth. The chief ornaments found in the tombs at Akhmîm are: hair-pins and combs made of wood or bone; ear-rings of several shapes and forms made of glass; silver and bronze filigree work, gold with little gold balls, and iron with pendent agates; necklaces made of amber, coloured glass, and blue and green glazed faïence beads; torques, or neck-rings, made of bronze; bracelets, open and closed, made of bronze, iron, glass and horn; finger-rings of bronze; and bronze belt buckles made in the form of a

[1] See Newberry, *Beni Ḥasan*, Vol. I, pl. 29; Vol. II, pll. 4 and 13; Klebs, *Reliefs*, p. 53 f.

Christian cross. A large number of ivory crosses are also found; the cross which is found so often on these objects was not used merely as an ornament, but as a special symbol and emblem of Christianity.[1] The most ancient and the greater number of the tombs that contained these belong to the IInd or IIIrd century after Christ, and the most recent to the VIIIth or IXth century;[2] they are taken from bodies of Christians and heathen which were buried with or without coffins, and in private or common burial-places. The Museum of Gobelins possesses a piece of cloth, the threads of the woof of which are made of pure silk, and this is said by M. Gerspach,[3] the Director of the National Manufactory at Gobelins, to belong to a period subsequent to the VIIIth century, because silk does not appear in Egyptian tapestries until that century. It may then be considered that the Coptic linen work found at Akhmîm covers a period of eight centuries, viz., II–IX. M. Gerspach adds:—

> "Il est fort probable que les Coptes ont continué, pendant plusieurs siècles encore, une fabrication dans laquelle ils excellaient; ils ont vraisemblablement travaillé à ces milliers de pièces représentant les grands hommes de l'Islam, montrant des villes, des paysages et des animaux que possédait le calif Mostansser-Billah et qui furent brûlées au Caire en 1062 avec les immenses richesses accumulées dans le Dépôt des étendards" (p. 2).

Of the character, style, design, and antiquity of Coptic linen work he says:—

> "Le style est plus ou moins pur, mais il dénote constamment une grande liberté de composition et de facture; il est exempt de minuties et de subtilités, même lorsque nous ne comprenons pas très bien la pensée de l'artiste. Quand il ne se rattache pas à la décoration romaine ou à l'art oriental, il est original, il a un caractère propre, une saveur particulière, qu'il soit fin comme nos dentelles ou épais et obtus comme les ornements des races inférieures; il constitue alors, dans une manifestation intime et populaire, un genre spécial qu'on nommera peut-être bientôt le style copte. À première vue, en effet, on retrouve l'antiquité dans les pièces les plus

[1] I owe these details to Forrer, *Die Gräber und Textilfunde von Achmim—Panopolis*, Strassburg, 1891, pp. 12, 13. This book contains 16 plates, on which are photographed, in colours, 250 pictures of the textile fabrics and the other most interesting objects found at Akhmîm.

[2] According to Forrer (p. 26), the foundation of the cemetery at Akhmîm may be dated in the Ist or IInd century after Christ, and the decay of the art of the best kind is to be sought at the end of the VIIth or in the course of the VIIIth century after Christ.

[3] *Les Tapisseries Coptes*, Paris, 1890, p. 2. This most interesting work contains 153 reproductions in one or more colours of the most important designs found on Akhmîm linen.

simples, qui sont aussi les plus anciennes ; en général, ces morceaux sont d'une seule couleur, pourpre ou brune, avec des filets clairs en lin écru. Le dessin est sommaire, net, sobre, bien combiné, harmonieux, d'une grande franchise plastique, dans le style qu'adoptera ultérieurement l'art héraldique ; naturellement, dans la figure il est plus faible que dans l'ornement, car le tapissier, avec sa broche, ne trace pas aussi facilement que le céramiste avec son pinceau ; nous devons excuser les tapissiers coptes, leurs successeurs de tous les temps et de tous les pays ayant comme eux fait plus ou moins de fautes de dessin . . . . . Les tapisseries polychromes[1] sont généralement postérieures à cette première série, mais il importe de faire remarquer que certains modèles primitifs n'ont pas été abandonnés et qu'on les retrouve dans les tissus modernes du bas Danube et de l'Orient . . . . . Jusqu'ici[2] le dessin est clair et lisible ; maintenant nous arrivons à une suite inférieure ; les lignes se compliquent et les formes deviennent épaisses ; . . . . . l'ornement est encore dans un bon esprit, mais les figures sont faibles . . . . . Avec les siècles suivants, nous tombons dans une décadence relative, moins profonde que celle de la mosaïque au IXe siècle ; le corps humain est contourné, strapassé ; les têtes sont bestiales ; les animaux sont difformes et fantastiques, pourvus de sortes de tentacules ; ils se transforment en ornements ; la flore n'est même plus ornemanisée ni conventionnelle ; certains motifs sont incompréhensibles ; l'ornement, mieux tenu, présente toujours des combinaisons intéressantes ; . . . . même dans leurs fautes, les Coptes continuent à prouver qu'ils sont décorateurs."

THE MUMMY-GRID AND MUMMY-BOARD

IN many of the rectangular wooden coffins that have been found in the mountains that lie behind the modern town of Asyûṭ, in Upper Egypt, and in those that extend to the north and south of it, the mummies were raised a few inches from the bottom of the coffins by means of **wooden grids**, which had been painted white or yellow. Most of these grids were broken up and thrown away by the natives, who, because no one would buy them, regarded them as useless, but one was secured and it is now preserved in the British Museum (No. 46639). The reason for placing the grid in the coffin is unknown to me.

The so-called "**mummy-board**" is a flat wooden covering which was of the same shape and size as the mummy on which it was laid,

[1] Of the IVth century.
[2] Vth century.

and which seems to have been introduced into funerary paraphernalia by the priests and priestesses of Ȧmen-Rā at Thebes. This covering is slightly rounded so that it may lie firmly on the mummy, and on the end which rests on the face of the mummy a human face is carved, which was intended to be a portrait of the deceased. In some cases the face was carved in high relief on a separate piece of wood, which was pegged to the board, and in others the face is carved on the board itself in much lower relief. This board is covered with figures of the gods and mythological scenes painted in bright colours, which are rendered more conspicuous by a coat of varnish. The back of the board was often painted a mauve or purple colour, and on it in yellow outlines were painted figures of the boat of the sun, the mummy lying on its back with grain plants growing up from it, and other funerary scenes. A fine typical example of this class of object is B.M. 22542. This is decorated with an elaborate pectoral, figures of the gods, sacred symbols of Osiris and Isis, and at the foot, between crowned uraei, is a cartouche containing the prenomen and nomen of Ȧmenḥetep I, , Tcheserkarā Ȧmenḥetep, one of the earliest kings of the XVIIIth dynasty and a great benefactor of the priesthood of Ȧmen at Thebes. This board was presented to the British Museum in 1889 by Mr. A. F. Wheeler, and has been the subject of many paragraphs in the newspapers. On the back of another example (B.M. 15659) is a memorandum roughly written in hieroglyphs, showing that the board and the mummy to which it belonged were repaired by the inspectors of mummies and tombs, probably under the rule of the Priest-kings of the XXIst dynasty.[1] Another instructive example of the mummy-board is that which was made for Ḥentmeḥit (B.M. 48001), a priestess and singing woman in the temple of Ȧmen-Rā at Thebes. The face and head-dress were carved with elaborate care, and the middle and lower parts of the board are decorated with hollow-work panels containing figures of the gods. Their background is a layer of linen, dyed pink or purple, and as the board was heavily gilded before being covered with a layer of purple varnish, the effect, when it was first made, must have been very striking. With the end of the rule of the Priest-kings the mummy-board disappeared from coffins, but we seem to meet with survivals of it in B.M. 35464, 36502. These are long flat boards of the shape of a mummy, but neither has a face either cut or painted upon it; they resemble somewhat in form the head-stones that are seen in old Arab and Turkish cemeteries. On No. 36502 figures of the deceased on his bier and the four Canopic jars are painted. Beneath these are figures of seven gods, *i.e.*, the Seven Spirits of Chapter XVII of the Book of

[1] It is dated in the third year of a king whose name is not given; see *Guide to the First, Second and Third Egyptian Rooms*, p. 50.

the Dead, and extracts from the SHAI EN SENSENU, or "Book of Breathings," written in hieroglyphs. On the reverse is a scene in which are depicted the light of Rā, lord of heaven, falling on the body of the deceased (Chapter CLIV), and figures of the Seventy-Five Forms of Rā. In No. 35464 the scenes are painted on one side only of the board, and the text of thirty-nine lines is written in demotic. For the sake of convenience I have called these **memorial boards.**

THE CARTONNAGE MUMMY-CASE

THE object of the mummy-board is not clear, unless we assume that it was intended to take the place of a complete second inner coffin, and so save expense. But it may also have been devised with the view of hiding the mummy-bandages, and of beautifying the mummy. Another way of beautifying the mummy was to place it in a **cartonnage case** with a moulded face. This case was made of layers of linen with plaster run in between them, and when the mummy had been placed inside it the edges of the sheet of plastered linen, which formed the case, were sewn together down the back. The case was then treated as a coffin, so far as decoration was concerned. The face was painted flesh-colour, rosettes, lotus flowers, etc., were painted on the head-dress; below the pectoral are the usual scenes with gods and goddesses, Utchats, etc., and the inscriptions contain the usual prayers for offerings. The mummy in a brightly painted cartonnage case is often found with an inner and an outer coffin, a fact which suggests that the cartonnage case, like the mummy-board, was intended to hide the mummy from sight. Cartonnage cases seem to have been kept in stock by the undertaker, for on some of them the prayers and inscriptions are painted all complete, but spaces are left blank for the insertion of the names of those who were to occupy them (see B.M. 6687). Another form of cartonnage case was made, not of plaster and linen, but papyrus. In such cases the papyrus was moulded into form on the actual body of the deceased, and the exact shape of the features and other physical characteristics are reproduced in detail. When, like the two fine examples in the British Museum (29585, 29586), such cartonnages are painted with representations of the dress and jewellery usually worn by the deceased woman, the effect is lifelike. In the Ptolemaïc and Roman Periods cartonnage cases that covered the whole of the mummy became rare, and many Egyptians were content to provide the dead with cartonnage head-cases having gilded faces and pectorals with a hawk's head near each shoulder. Attached to the pectoral was a strip of cartonnage on which the name of the deceased and a prayer for offerings were painted; some mummies are provided with cartonnage feet-cases. Interesting examples of the painted cartonnage pectoral of the Roman Period are those of Sheret-Menthu, inscribed with a prayer to Rā-Ḥeraakhuti-Khepera (B.M. 6966),

Uaḥȧbrā, an official of the temple of Osiris Bakhat (B.M. 6969), and that of Afu, inscribed with an address to Temu and Kheperȧ (B.M. 54146). Cartonnage pectorals were kept in stock by the undertaker, and spaces were left in which to add, after they had been bought, the names of the persons for whom they were intended (B.M. 6967 and 34262). The cartonnage case B.M. 20744 is of special interest. It contains the mummy of a very young woman, which is kept in position by a block of wood fixed by pegs to the cartonnage under the feet ; the case is laced up the back and has not been opened. The wooden arms attached to a cartonnage case, as in this instance, are probably unique. The face is gilded and the case is inscribed with the name of the deceased, and is decorated with the characteristic scenes of the XXth or XXIst dynasty ; but these have at some time all been washed over with a layer of bitumen, probably with the view of making the identification of the mummy impossible.

BEADWORK ON MUMMIES

UNDER the XXVIth dynasty, or later, when the Egyptians were unable to provide their dead with mummy-boards or cartonnage cases, they frequently covered their mummies with sheets of beadwork. The beads were of the bugle variety, were made of blue or green glazed Egyptian porcelain, and varied in length from half an inch to one inch. They were arranged in diamond pattern, and frequently a small flat, round bead made of the same material, though not always of the same colour, was threaded where the ends of the bugle-beads met. This blue beadwork covering typified the blue sky of night, and in late times faïence figures of Nut the Sky-goddess were attached to it. The usual ornaments found sewn to it are (1) a flat faïence scarab, with outstretched wings, or a small light green scarab without base, and (2) figures of the Four Sons of Horus in faïence or beadwork.

SHROUDS

HOWEVER well and carefully made the mummy, the desire to ornament it or cover it with some decorative material seems to have been prevalent in the minds of the Egyptians under the New Kingdom. The shrouds of Ȧmenḥetep III and Saptaḥ and other kings were inscribed all over with religious texts, and the mummy of Ḥentmeḥit, a priestess of Ȧmen, was wrapped in one large sheet of papyrus inscribed in hieratic with Chapters from the Theban Book of the Dead. In the late Ptolemaïc and Roman times, when mummy-boards and cartonnage cases and beadwork coverings were not to be got, shrouds were painted with figures of gods and representations of bugle-beadwork. A typical example of such a shroud is that of the lady Seusertsetes,  (B.M. 17177).

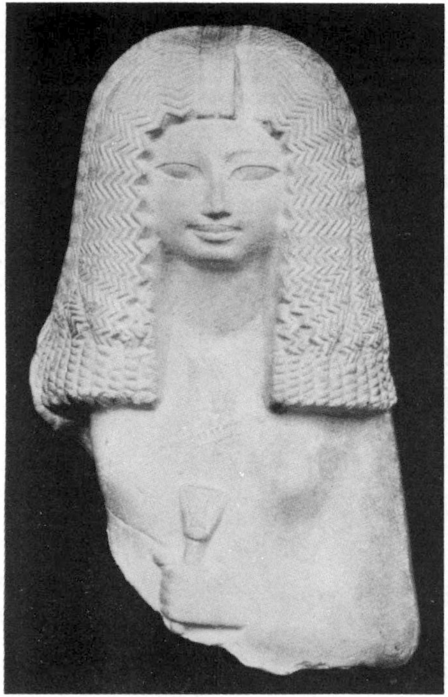

Cast of the upper part of a figure of a priestess who flourished under the XVIIIth dynasty. From the original in the possession of R. Mond, Esq.

An Egyptian handmaiden. XVIIIth dynasty. B.M. No. 32743.

A temple maiden holding a cat. B.M. No. 32733.

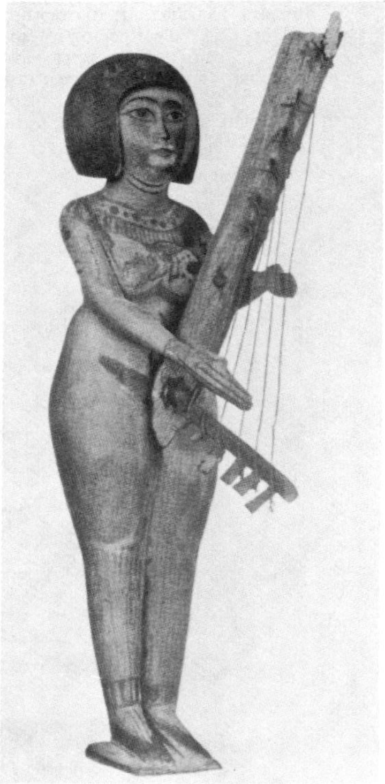

Figure of a musician playing a six-stringed harp. B.M. No. 48658.

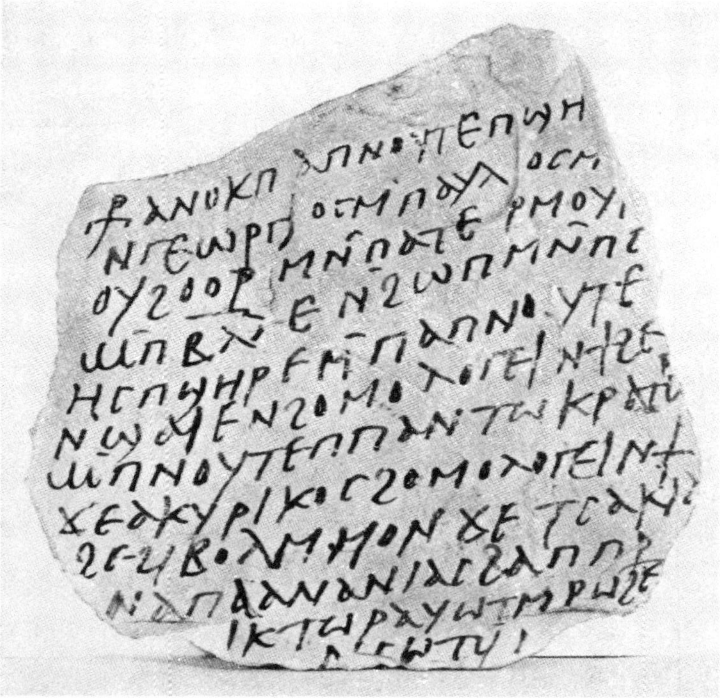

Coptic letter from Papnoute to Apa Victor concerning his property.
B.M. No. 20004.

1

2

3

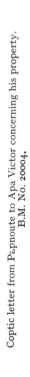

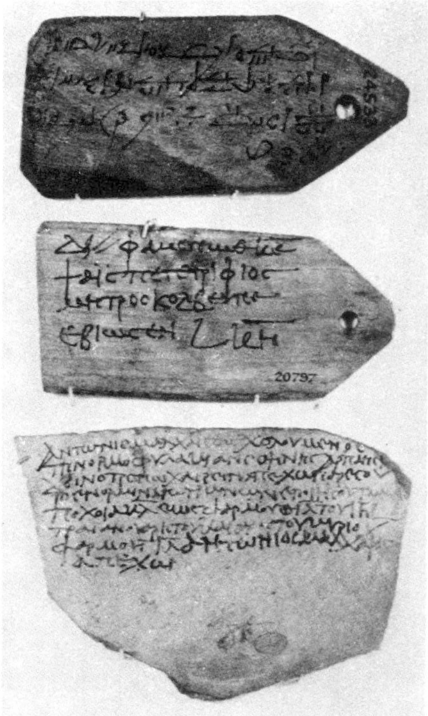

1 Wooden mummy label for Bêsis inscribed in Demotic. B.M. No. 24533.

2 Wooden mummy label for Psaïs, inscribed in Greek. B.M. No. 20797.

3 Receipt in Greek for dock dues paid by Harpaesis to Antonios Malcaio in the reign of Trajan. B.M. No. 5970.

On a later example we have a full-face figure of Osiris within the shrine of "living uraei," the weighing of the heart and the Judgment Scene, and the deceased sowing and reaping, and drawing water by means of the *shâdûf* (Arab. شَادُوف)[1] from a well (B.M. 30092).

MODELS OF PERSONAL ATTENDANTS AND SLAVES IN THE TOMB

It has been the custom of many peoples in primitive times to kill a number of slaves and others when a king died, and to bury their bodies with him in his tomb, their idea being that the spirits of the murdered people would accompany the spirit of their dead king and minister to him in Dead Land. When an Egyptian governor died in Nubia as many as 1,000 oxen were slain for the funeral feast, and when his body had been placed in the chamber provided for it, the sacrificial victims, who were all local Nubians, were laid outside on the floor of the corridor; whether they were drugged or not before they were strangled cannot be said, but it is probable that they were. The corridor was then filled in with earth, stones, etc., much in the same way as the pits in which African kings were buried in the Sûdân during the last century. In the tombs of Dafûfah and Karmân the members of the Harvard-Boston Expedition (1913–15) found in one royal grave the remains of from 200 to 300 men, women and children (see the *Bulletin*, Boston, December, 1915, p. 71). The evidence available shows that the chiefs of the pre-dynastic Egyptians, and probably some of the kings of the Archaic Period, were surrounded in their graves by the bodies of many murdered subjects, slaves and others, and the contents of several tombs of the dynastic Egyptians show that funeral murders were common even under the New Kingdom.[2] The walls of maṣṭabahs and other early tombs are covered with scenes in which slaves are seen ploughing and sowing and reaping, and performing works of all kinds for their lords, and their presence is usually explained by saying that they were painted or cut on the walls to gratify the pride of the owner of the tomb. But I think that these pictures or reliefs were painted and cut on the walls because it was believed that the deceased by means of words of power could endow all these *simulacra* with life and motion, and make them provide for his wants and minister to him in the Other World. Without a suitable retinue of slaves and workmen and women the spirit of a dead nobleman would command no respect among the inhabitants of Åmenti, and would starve.

[1] The water-raising machine is well described by Lane, *Modern Egyptians*, Vol. II, p. 30.

[2] I have summarized the facts in my *Osiris and the Egyptian Resurrection*, Vol. I, p. 197 ff.

Under the XIIth dynasty the kinsmen of the dead were not content to entrust the well-being of their beloved ones to paintings and sculptures on the walls of the tombs alone, so they placed in the tombs groups of painted wooden figures of slaves, male and female, butchers, bakers, handicraftsmen and others. Some groups are engaged in killing the sacrificial bull and dismembering him, others are grinding grain and making the flour into cakes and loaves, others are baking the bread-cakes, others are bringing offerings and preparing beer, and others are ploughing and working at their trades. The utterance of the necessary words of power would set all these figures in motion and turn the wooden models of oxen and loaves, etc., into food for the KAU of the dead. Models of granaries[1] provided with several bins, each filled with a special kind of grain, were also placed in the tombs at this period, and models of pleasure boats and war boats. Feasting, boating and fighting were, apparently, supposed to be the most congenial pursuits of the denizens of the Other World. The largest and most representative collection of such models was found by Garstang in the XIIth dynasty tombs at Bani Ḥasan and is well described in his work.[2]

MUMMY LABELS OR TICKETS

THE **mummy label** is a thin strip of hard or soft wood which varies in length from 3 to 6 inches, and in breadth from 2 to 4 inches, and is pierced at one end with a hole large enough to permit the passage of the thick papyrus string by which it was attached to the mummy. Usually the label is rectangular, but many examples of it have the ends either rounded or in the form of a truncated pyramid. All are inscribed, some in Greek, some in demotic (*i.e.*, Egyptian), and some in both languages, the Greek being on one side and the demotic on the other. The greater number of these objects actually served as labels and nothing else, for they were tied to mummies that were being transported from one part of Egypt to another, and served for purposes of identification only. Mummies must have been despatched to specially sacred sites, such as Abydos, in all periods of Egyptian history, but curiously enough no labels of the Dynastic Period appear to be known. Those that are now to be seen in the great collections in Cairo, London and Berlin, all belong to the first four centuries of the Christian Era, and they seem to owe their existence to some regulation or law introduced into the administration of Egypt by the Romans. But, if such a law existed, it must have concerned one part of Upper Egypt only, for all the labels now known were found in the district that lies between Sûhâḳ and Gîrgâ, and chiefly in and about the town of Akhmîm (Panopolis). Some of the labels now in the British Museum were found attached

[1] For a model of a granary of the VIth dynasty see B.M. 21804.
[2] *Funeral Customs*, London, 1907.

to mummies that had been heaped up in the rock-hewn tombs behind Akhmîm, but the greater number were found in a box with several small rolls of papyrus inscribed in demotic. There were no mummies in the tomb in which they were found, and it is possible that they represent the transactions of some Mummy Transport Agency, and were preserved by the successive agents for reference. The labels and the inscriptions on them have little historical interest, for the Greek inscriptions only record the names, ages, and dates of the deaths of a number of artisans, merchants and officials of quite humble station in life. The demotic inscriptions often contain prayers, either that the deceased persons may receive funerary offerings, or that their souls may appear before Osiris-Seker and be numbered among the souls of those who are his followers. Such inscriptions suggest that the mummies to which the labels had been attached had been despatched to Abydos and buried there. But philologically the labels are of great importance, especially those which are bilingual, for they supply a mass of information about the Graecized forms of Egyptian names, the pronunciation of the language, etc. The collection of mummy labels made by Dr. Forrer is described and translated by Spiegelberg, *Aegyptische und Griechische Eigennamen aus Mumienetiketten der Römischen Kaiserzeit*, Leipzig, 1901. The Berlin Collection is published by Krebs, " Griechischc Mumicnetikette aus Aegypten " in *Aeg. Zeit.*, Bd. XXXII, 1904, p. 37 ; and a comprehensive selection of the collection in the British Museum has been published and translated, with notes and explanatory introduction by H. R. Hall, in *Proc. Soc. Bibl. Arch.*, Vol. XXVII, 1905, pp. 13–20, 48–56, 83–91, 115–122, 159–165. Descriptions of other important collections will be found in Revillout, " Planchettes bilingues trouvées à Sohag," in *Rev. Ég.*, tom. VI, pp. 43–45, 100–101 ; tom. VII, 29–38 ; Wessely, *Holztäfelchen der Sammlung der Papyrus Erzherzog Rainer*, Bd. V, 11 (1892) ; and Le Blant, " Tablai Égyptiennes," *Rev. Arch.*, New Series, tom. XVIII, 1875.

THE BOOK OF THE DEAD

In modern Egyptological works the writers, when they speak of the " Book of the Dead," are referring in reality to one Recension of one only of the Books of the Dead that were known to the Egyptians, and that one is the Theban Recension of the great collection of religious and magical texts which the Egyptians called " Chapters of Coming Forth by (or in) the Day," , and which was compiled under the XVIIIth dynasty. The oldest collection of Egyptian religious texts known is found inscribed on the walls of the chambers and corridors of the pyramids of Unȧs, Tetȧ, Pepi I, Merenrā and Pepi II, kings of the Vth and VIth dynasties at Ṣaḳḳârah. The texts are all hieroglyphic, and many of the sections, or paragraphs, were copied from a very much older collection of texts of a similar character, which were divided into Chapters. Unfortunately, none of the Chapters of this older collection has come down to us, and therefore it is useless to speculate as to its origin and age and authorship. But it is fair to assume that the Chapters that were repeated on the walls of the pyramids of the kings named above represented substantially the beliefs of the Egyptians of the Vth and VIth dynasties concerning the dead, and continuity of religious thought in the higher classes of Egyptians at least. The collection of texts in the royal pyramids is now commonly known as the **Pyramid Texts.** They were discovered more or less by accident. Until the time of Mariette's Directorship of the Service of Antiquities of Egypt it was generally assumed, though why it is hard to say, that pyramids never contained inscriptions. Determining to test this theory, Mariette ordered the pyramids of Ṣaḳḳârah to be opened, and the discovery of the Pyramid Texts was the result. It is one of the ironies of fate that this great excavator of the Serapeum and of the finest temples in Egypt died without knowing the contents and importance of the texts that he had brought to light. After Mariette's death the excavation of the pyramids was continued by Maspero, with the generous financial help of Mr. J. M. Cook, of Messrs. Thos. Cook and Sons. Maspero directed E. Brugsch Bey to make paper " squeezes " of the inscriptions in the pyramids, a work that was attended with dire results as far as the green paste inlay of the hieroglyphs was concerned; when these were ready he began to publish the texts in the *Recueil des Travaux,* with translations of them in French. The text of Unȧs appeared in tom. III, pp. 177–224 and tom. IV, pp. 41–78; that of Tetȧ in tom. V, pp. 1–60, and the texts of Pepi I, Merenrā and Pepi II in tom. VII, pp. 145–176, tom. VIII, pp. 87–110, tom. IX, pp. 177–190, tom. X, pp. 1–28, tom. XI, pp. 1–30, tom. XII, pp. 53–95, 136–195 and tom. XIV. These sections were reprinted by him and appeared in a single volume entitled *Les Inscriptions des Pyramides de Saqqarah,* Paris, 1894. The translations made by Maspero showed that he possessed an unrivalled knowledge of the Egyptian language, and his faculty of divining the meanings of *hapax legomena* and the general significance of the darkest passages in the texts was almost uncanny; they represent one of the greatest triumphs of Egyptian decipherment. Some ten years later the paper squeezes in the Berlin Museum were carefully examined by K. Sethe, who prepared an edition of the Pyramid Texts, which appeared under the title *Die altägyptischen Pyramidentexte nach der Papierabdrucken und Photographien des Berliner Museums,* 2 vols., 1908–10, Leipzig 4to. Supplementary volumes (III and IV) containing indexes, epigraphical notes, etc., were published by him in 1922; his long-promised translation[1] has not, it seems, appeared.

[1] A French translation has been attempted by Louis Speleers, *Les Textes des Pyramides Égyptiennes,* Vol. I, Brussels, 1923.

The second great collection of religious and magical texts was compiled under the Middle Kingdom, and many Chapters of it are found written in cursive hieroglyphs, or a kind of hieratic, on the rectangular wooden **coffins of the XIth and XIIth dynasties.** A considerable number of these are versions, more or less complete, of Chapters of the Pyramid Texts, but side by side with these are many Chapters that were composed at a later period. These represent beliefs and ideas of a religious character that were unknown to the Egyptians under the Vth and VIth dynasties, and they prove that a very considerable development of religious thought had taken place in the minds of the people since the Pyramid Texts were compiled. The Pyramid Texts were intended to benefit not the dead Egyptians in general, but their kings only; none of the maṣṭabah tombs contains copies of any of their Chapters, and no relatives of any Erpā or Ḥa or Smer, however important, imagined for one moment that their departed kinsman could or would share in the Ṭuat the greatness and glory of the kings of Egypt, or that the Pyramid Texts could be made to apply to him. On the other hand, the **Texts of the Middle Kingdom** might be used to benefit any and every dead person whose kinsfolk could afford to have them cut upon the walls of his tomb or written upon his coffin. In the oldest copies of the Pyramid Texts Rā is represented as paramount in heaven, but in the latest Osiris is the lord of heaven, and king and judge of the dead, and in this character he appears in the Texts of the Middle Kingdom. The spirits and souls of dead kings in heaven were now obliged to share their domain with the spirits and souls of such nobles and officials of high rank as succeeded in satisfying Osiris and his Tchatchau, or Assessors, in the Judgment when hearts were weighed in the Balance of Truth. No edition of the Texts of the Middle Kingdom has appeared as yet, but a good idea of their contents may be gathered from the following works: Lepsius, *Aelteste Texte des Todtenbuchs*, Berlin, 1867, 4to.; Birch, *Coffin of Amamu*, London, 1886; and the copy of Wilkinson's transcript from a coffin of the Middle Kingdom (which has disappeared), published by Budge in *Hieratic Papyri in the British Museum*, First Series, Plates XXXIX–XLVIII, London, 1910. And a long series of hieroglyphic transcripts from the texts of the magnificent painted wooden sarcophagi and coffins from Al-Barshah in Upper Egypt, now preserved in the Museum in Cairo, was published by Lacau in Maspero's *Recueil des Travaux* (*Textes Religieux*), tomm. XXVI–XXXIII. Transcripts of another group of Chapters from the tomb of Ḥerḥetep in Cairo were published by Maspero in *Mémoires de la Mission Archéologique*, tom. I, pp. 136–144.

We have seen that the first and oldest collection of religious and magical texts, *i.e.*, the Pyramid Texts, which were written for the exclusive use and benefit of dead kings, was inscribed upon the walls of the chambers and corridors in hieroglyphs; and that the second collection of such texts, which were written for the benefit of nobles and officials of high rank, was written on rectangular coffins in cursive hieroglyphs or hieratic; and we may now add that the third collection of such texts was written upon rolls of papyrus, first of all in hieroglyphs, and at a later period in hieratic also. The home of this third collection was Thebes, and it is therefore known as the **Theban Recension** of the Book of the Dead, or the "Chapters of Coming Forth by Day." The total number of the Chapters that are now known is about 190. A few of them are derived directly from the Pyramid Texts, several of them are versions of Chapters found among the Texts of the Middle Kingdom, and the remaining Chapters are of Theban origin, and illustrate the great development that had taken place in the minds of the Egyptians concerning religious matters and eschatology in general. The whole work was believed to have been composed by Thoth, the personification of the mind of the Creator, the keeper of the words of the gods, and the inventor of writing. The Theban Recension, or the Book of the Dead, as it is now called, has been described as a collection of spells, but the description is misleading and inadequate. It does contain a large number of *ḥekau*, , or mighty words of power, which were written to enable the deceased to supply himself with everything he needed in the Ṭuat, or Other World, and to journey successfully to the realm of Osiris, and to overcome every enemy that might attempt to kill or injure him or to impede his progress. Besides these it contained a number of spells that would enable him to take the form of certain animals, birds and reptiles, and even of some of the gods, whenever it was necessary for him to do so. But all these spells and formulas were the products of beliefs held in bygone ages, and were only retained as the result of the innate ultra-conservatism of the Egyptians. No text that was thought to be of the least use for preserving their bodies or souls was ever abandoned entirely. The Book of the Dead proves beyond all doubt that from the time of the Middle Kingdom the Egyptians believed in the Last Judgment, and that the future of a man's soul in the Other World depended upon the manner of life that he had led upon earth. The soul of the sinner was annihilated, and the soul of the righteous man entered into everlasting life. The Assessors of Osiris, who were incorruptible and strictly just and impartial, weighed the hearts of men in the Great Balance, and the final decision of Osiris was in accordance with the finding of Thoth, the personification of truth and eternal justice. So important was this weighing of the heart that a picture of the Judgment Scene was attached to the great rolls of papyrus upon which the Book of the Dead was written, and this and the texts that accompany it form the chief characteristic of the Theban Recension of the great papyri written under

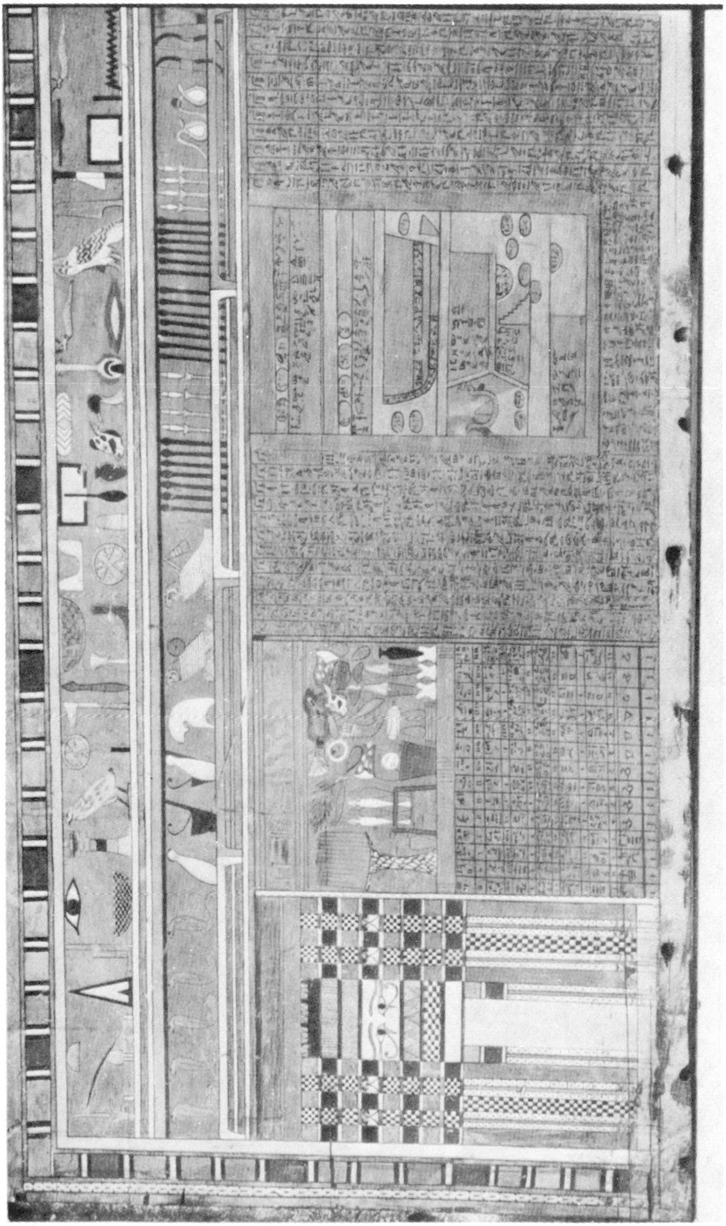

Chapters of the earliest Recension of the Book of the Dead with Vignettes showing the Islands of the Blest (later the Elysian Fields), and the "false door" of the tomb, and the table of offerings. XIIth dynasty. From a coffin found at Al-Barshah in Upper Egypt. B.M. No. 30840.

The Weighing of the Heart of Ani, the scribe, in the Great Scales in the Judgment Hall of Osiris. From the Papyrus of Ani. B.M. No. 10470.

1 Horus, the son of Isis, introducing the scribe Ani, who has been declared to be a "speaker of the truth" by Thoth, into the presence of Osiris.
2 The scribe Ani kneeling before Osiris. From the Papyrus of Ani. B.M. No. 10470.

The Funeral Procession of the Scribe Ani. From his Papyrus in the British Museum.

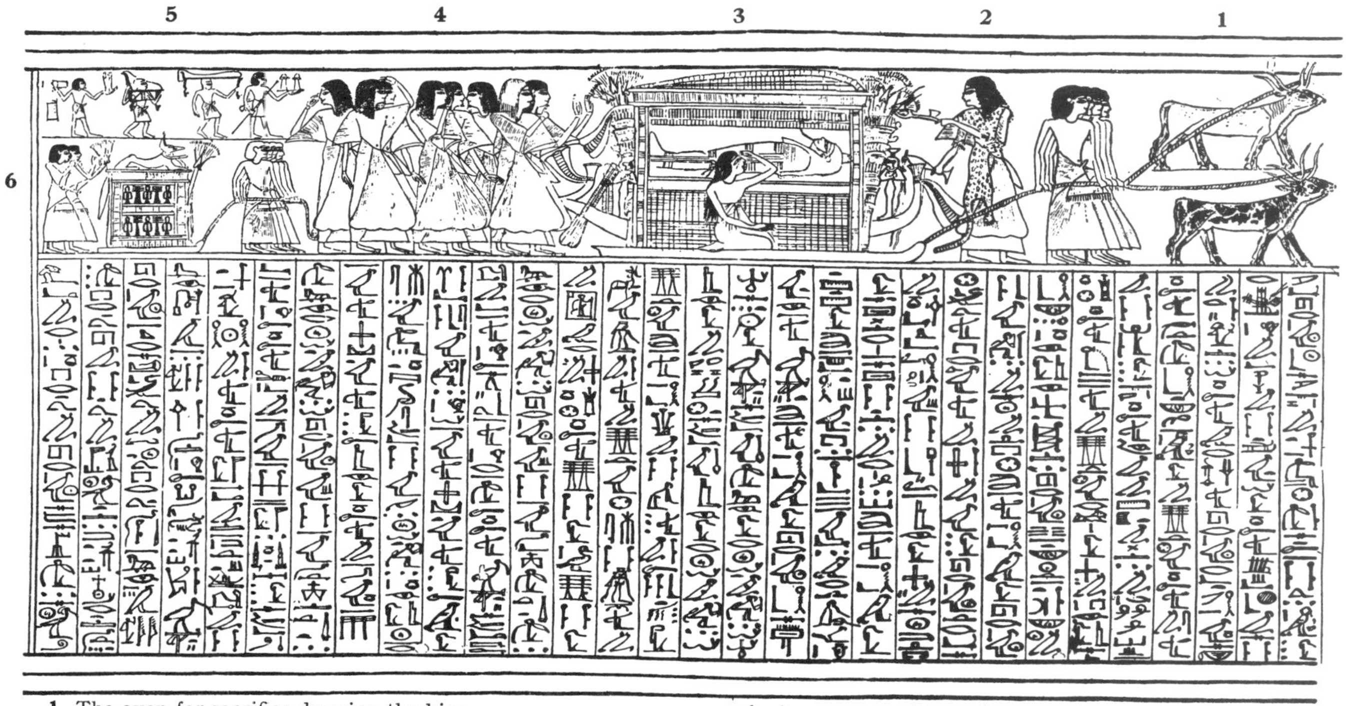

1. The oxen for sacrifice drawing the bier.

2. A priest holding a censer of burning incense, and sprinkling the bier with natron water.

3. The bier. By the side of it sits Ani's wife Tutu.

4. A company of friends, one of whom is addressing the mummy.

5. Servants carrying vases of unguents, a couch, a chair, palette, etc.

6. The coffer containing the "Canopic" Jars.

THE FUNERAL PROCESSION OF THE SCRIBE ANI—*continued.*

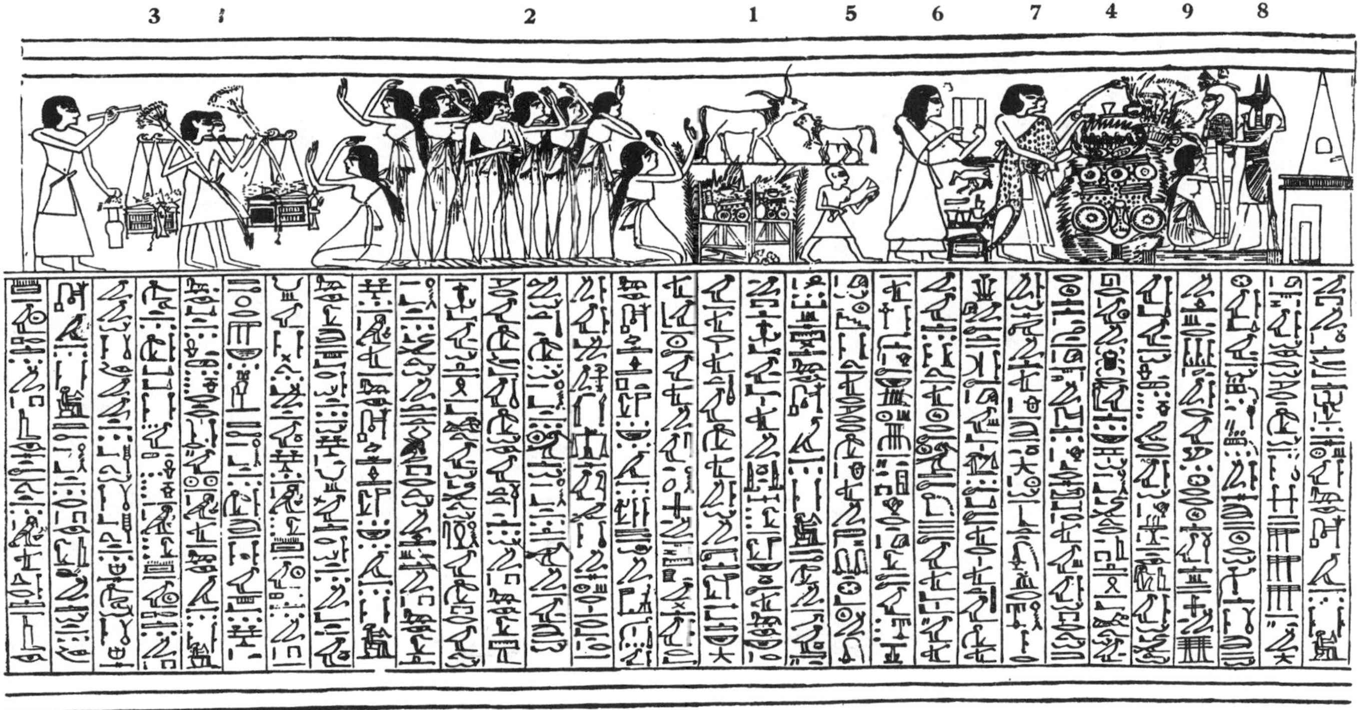

1. Cow and calf for sacrifice and a heap of offerings.
2. The group of wailing women.
3. Servants carrying vegetables, fruit and flowers to the tomb.
4. The ceremony of "Opening the Mouth" at the door of the tomb.
5. An assistant priest carrying a haunch of beef.
6. A priest reciting the text of the Book of Opening the Mouth.
7. Two priests, one holding the implement Urt-ḥekau, and the other sprinkling natron water.
8. Anubis receiving the mummy of Ani.
9. Ani's wife Tutu kneeling at the feet of the mummy.

the New Kingdom. Another striking characteristic of the work is the section of Chapter CXXV which is known as the Negative Confession. This enshrines the moral and religious code of Osiris, and makes quite plain the high standard of morality and the exalted character of the personal religion of which Osiris demanded proof before applicants were admitted into his kingdom. In our limited space here it is impossible to describe even briefly the general contents of the Theban Recension of the Book of the Dead, and the reader is referred for a summary of them to the Monograph, *The Book of the Dead,* with 25 illustrations, which the Trustees of the British Museum published in 1820.

The Egyptian text of the Theban Recension is derived from copies of the Book of the Dead which were written on papyri for scribes and high officials under the XVIIIth and XIXth dynasties. No two papyri contain the same Chapters or the same number of Chapters ; in no two papyri is the order of the Chapters the same, and it is tolerably certain that a person selected the Chapters for his papyrus for himself. And in no two codices is the treatment of the Vignettes exactly the same. In 1874, under the auspices of the Second International Congress of Orientalists, a Committee was formed to discuss the possibility of publishing the text of the Theban Recension, and its members, Birch, Lepsius, Chabas and Naville, made arrangements for carrying out the work. Naville undertook to prepare the edition, and his Committee thankfully accepted the services of this distinguished scholar. At the instance of Lepsius the Berlin Academy voted a sum of 3,000 marks for preliminary expenses, and the Prussian Government voted 4,800 thalers for its publication. Twelve years later Naville, having meanwhile examined all the papyri in all the great libraries and museums in Europe, published in two volumes, folio, *Das Aegyptische Todtenbuch der XVIII bis XX Dynastie,* Berlin, 1886. The first volume contains the hieroglyphic texts, which were beautifully drawn by Madame Naville ; and the second contains the variant readings. In a small quarto volume, published a few months later, Naville gave a history of the Theban Recension, and discussed its importance, and described its palaeography and the papyri that he had used, and gave a list in hieroglyphs of the Chapters. This work is, and always will be, invaluable for the study of the Book of the Dead.

With the view of providing material for the great work the Trustees of the British Museum published a complete photographic reproduction of the *Papyrus of Nebseni* (B.M. 9900), London, 1876, fol., and a coloured lithographic reproduction of texts on the coffin of Amamu (XIth or XIIth dynasty), entitled *Egyptian Texts of the Earliest Period,* London, 1886 (Translations by Birch). Other editions of single papyri, published in France and Holland, were : Guieyesse, *Le Papyrus Funéraire de Soutimes,* Paris, 1877 ; Devéria, *Le Papyrus de Neb-qed,* Paris, 1872 ; Mariette, *Papyrus of Ȧmenḥetep,*

Paris, 1876; Leemans, *Papyrus of Qenna*, Leyden, 1882. In 1888 the British Museum acquired the Papyrus of Ani, which contained Chapters that were in no other papyrus of the Theban Recension and a comprehensive series of Vignettes, which for completeness, accuracy, and beauty of colour is, to this day, unique. This papyrus was written in the latter part of the XVIIIth dynasty, and is of exceptional importance. A facsimile edition of the papyrus was prepared for the Trustees by Mr. W. Griggs, but the text was faulty, for the films of some of the negatives perished in places. The edition was sold out and a second, which was more accurate in every way, was prepared by Mr. F. C. Compton Price,[1] and as this was soon sold out Mr. P. Lee-Warner obtained permission from the Trustees to issue a facsimile of the papyrus in a smaller size, together with a transcript of the text printed in hieroglyphic type and a translation and introduction.[2]

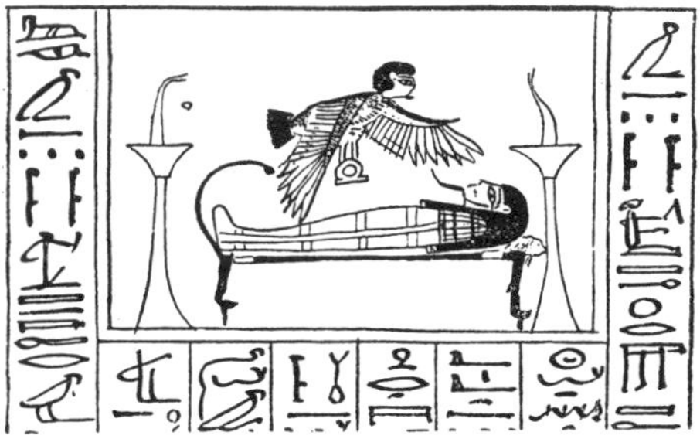

The mummy of the scribe Ani on its bier in his tomb being visited by his soul in the form of a human-headed hawk.

In 1890 the British Museum acquired the Papyrus of Nu, , the steward of the keeper of the king's seal, the son of Ȧmenḥetep and the lady Senseneb, who flourished in the early part of the XVIIIth dynasty. This papyrus contains 131 Chapters of the Theban Recension, including two versions each of Chapters XXXB, LXIV, CXXXVI and CLIII; it is as old as the papyrus of Nebseni, if not older, and is therefore the first authority for the text of the Theban Recension. As it contained a large number of Chapters that were wanting in the later papyri I prepared an edition of the unmutilated Chapters,[3] adding to them the Chapters that were

[1] Soon after its publication the Trustees instructed me to prepare an edition of the Egyptian text with interlinear transliteration and translation, a running translation and introduction, etc. This appeared in a 4to. volume in 1895.

[2] Budge, *The Book of the Dead, Papyrus of Ani*, Medici Society, 2 vols., London, 1913.

[3] A complete transcript of the hieroglyphic text was published by me in *The Papyri of Hunefer, Ȧnhai*, etc., London, 1899, fol.

extant in the other great Theban papyri, and published it with an English translation and Egyptian Vocabulary, under the title *The Chapters of Coming Forth by Day*, 3 vols., London, 1897. This edition ran out of print quickly, and two editions of the translation, each in three volumes, were issued in 1901 and 1909 respectively; and a revised and enlarged edition of the Egyptian text was issued in three volumes in 1910 and a revised edition of the Vocabulary in the following year. A translation of portions of the Theban Recension was published by Renouf in the *Proceedings of the Society of Biblical Archaeology*, Vols. XII–XIX.[1]

Under the XIXth, XXth and XXIst dynasties many fine copies of the Theban Recension were written in hieratic, and those which were made for the wives and daughters of the high priests of Åmen-Rā are of special interest. Among such may be mentioned the Papyrus of Queen Netchemet,[2] the Papyrus of Nesi-Khensu,[3] and the Papyrus of Nesitanebtashru.[4] The hieratic papyrus published by de Rougé belongs to a somewhat later date.[5]

Under the XXVIth and following dynasties many copies of the Book of the Dead were made, and these contain what is commonly known as the **Saïte Recension.** Under the XXVIth dynasty it was usually written in hieroglyphs, but in the Ptolemaïc and Roman Periods the texts were commonly written in hieratic. One of the finest copies known to belong to the Roman Period, written in hieratic, is B.M. 10558; the Vignettes in it are drawn in black outline and are remarkable for their delicacy and accuracy.

Curiously enough the Book of the Dead became known to scholars first of all through the latest Recension of it—that is to say, the Saïte. The earliest publications of parts or whole copies of it were made by J. Marc Cadet, *Copie figurée d'un rouleau de papyrus, trouvé à Thèbes, dans un tombeau des Rois*, Strassburg, 1805; Fontana, *Copie figurée d'un rouleau de papyrus trouvé en Égypte, publiée par Fontana et expliquée par Joseph de Hammer*, Vienna, 1822; Senkowski, *Exemplum Papyri Aegyptiacae quam in peregrinatione sua repertum Universitati Cracovienski dono dedit*, Petropoli, 1826;[6] Young, *Hieroglyphics*, London, 1823, fol., Plates I–VI; Hawkins, *Papyri in the Hieroglyphic and Hieratic Character from the Collection of the Earl of Belmore*, 23 plates, London, 1843, fol.;[7]

[1] These were reprinted in his *Life Work*, edited by W. H. Rylands, Maspero and E. Naville, 1st Series, Vols. I–IV, Paris, 1904.

[2] Published in facsimile, with translation by Budge, *Papyrus of Hunefer*, London, 1899.

[3] Published by Naville, *Papyrus Funéraires de la XXIe Dynastie*, Paris, 1912.

[4] *I.e.*, the Greenfield Papyrus. Published by Budge, *The Funerary Papyrus of Princess Nesitanebtashru, daughter of Painetchem II*, London, 1912, 4to.

[5] *Rituel Funéraire des Anciens Égyptiens*, Paris, 1861, fol.

[6] This book was published at the expense of the Academy of St. Petersburg and never came into the market.

[7] The descriptions, etc., were the work of Birch, but Hawkins was his official superior, and as such signed the Preface.

Rosellini, *Breve notizia intorno un frammento de Papiro funebre egizio esistente nel ducale museo di Parma*, Parma, 1839, 8vo.; "Description de l'Égypte," ed. Jomard, *Antiquités*, tom. II, pl. 64 ff. The most important publication, however, was that of Lepsius, who in 1842 reproduced the complete text of a papyrus at Turin, which contained 165 Chapters, under the title of *Das Todtenbuch der Aegypter*. Champollion called the Book of the Dead the "Rituel Funéraire," and this misleading title was adopted by de Rougé who, in his *Études sur le Rituel Funéraire des Anciens Égyptiens*,[1] brought forward his reasons for so doing, and considered that all he said "justifie suffisamment, suivant nous, le titre choisi par Champollion." Now, the famous "Grammaire" proves that Champollion had examined every part of the work which he called a "Rituel," and the many short passages which he translated show that he recognized the nature of its contents and rightly appreciated its great value from a religious point of view. But he analysed no complete Chapter of it, and he translated no paragraph of any length, and the assertions that have been made to the effect that he was the first translator of the Book of the Dead are incorrect statements based upon insufficient information on the subject. Now the Saïte Recension is no funerary Ritual, a fact which was pointed out by Lepsius as far back as 1842,[2] but it is almost as wrong to call it "Book of the Dead" as funerary Ritual, and it is unsatisfactory and misleading. For the texts in it do not form a connected whole; they represent several grades of religious thought which were evolved during a period of from three to four thousand years, and they tell us nothing about the lives of the dead with whom they were buried. Moreover, the Egyptians possessed many works of a funerary character that are, in exactly the same way as the Theban and Saïte Recensions, "Books of the Dead," *e.g.*, the "Book of the Two Ways," the "Book Åmmi Ṭuat," the "Book of Gates," the "Book of Breathings," the "Book of Traversing Eternity," etc. The title "Book of the Dead" is only a translation of Kitâb al-Mayyitûn, which was the Arabic name given by the natives in Egypt to the roll of inscribed papyrus that the tomb robbers found in almost every fine tomb in Thebes. Champollion, after his return from Egypt, called such a roll "Livre des Morts," Lepsius called his reproduction

[1] In *Revue Archéologique*, N.S., tom. I, 1860, pp. 69–100, 234–249, 337–365.

[2] Dieser Codex ist kein Ritualbuch, wofür es Champollion's Bezeichnung "Rituel Funéraire" zu erklären scheint; es enthält keine Vorschriften für den Todtenkultus, keine Hymnen oder Gebete, welche von den Priestern etwa bei der Beerdigung gesprochen worden wären: sondern der Verstorbene ist selbst die handelnde Person darin, und der Text betrifft nur ihn und seine Begegnisse auf der langen Wanderung nach dem irdischen Tode. Es wird entweder erzählt und beschrieben, wohin er kommt, was er thut, was er hört und sieht, oder es sind die Gebete und Anreden, die er selbst zu den verschiedenen Göttern, zu welchen er gelangt, spricht. Lepsius, *Vorwort* (*Todtenbuch*), p. 3.

of the Turin Papyrus "Das Todtenbuch," and their example was followed by Brugsch, Devéria, Ebers, Erman, Golénischeff, Lauth, Lieblein, Maspero, Naville, Pleyte, and others. Birch, in deference to the views of Bunsen, used the title "Funereal Ritual," but, like Goodwin and Renouf, always spoke of the "Book of the Dead" when referring to the  "Chapters of Coming Forth by Day." Chabas spoke of the work as "Le Pire-em-hrou" (Oriental Congress, *Compte Rendu,* tom. I, Paris, 1876, p. 37 ff.), and Devéria boldly translated the title as "Livre de sortir du jour" (*Catalogue,* Paris, 1874, pp. 48–129). A facsimile of the text of the Saïte Recension as published by Lepsius was republished by C. H. S. Davis and, under the title of the "Egyptian Book of the Dead," appeared at New York in 1892. And Lieblein published an *Index de tous les Mots contenus dans le Livre des Morts,* Paris, 1875, that is to say, a Vocabulary to the Saïte Recension. Only two **translations of the Saïte Recension** have appeared, viz., that by Birch entitled the "Funereal Ritual" in Bunsen's *Egypt's Place in Universal History,* Vol. V, pp. 123–333, London, 1867, and that by Pierret, *Le Livre des Morts des Anciens Égyptiens. Traduction complète d'après le papyrus de Turin et les MSS. du Louvre,* Paris, 1882. Translations of a number of Chapters, which probably belong both to the Theban and Saïte Recensions, were published by Pleyte in his *Chapitres Supplémentaires du Livre des Morts,* Leyden, 1881, 3 vols.

The most remarkable funerary papyrus of the Graeco-Roman Period is that of Kerasher, or Gersher, a coloured facsimile of which is published in my *Facsimiles of the Papyri of Hunefer, Ȧnhai, Kerasher,* London, 1899, fol. The Vignettes are painted in gaudy colours, and one of them represents the Judgment Scene in the Hall of Osiris; the text is written in hieratic and contains the SHAI EN SINSIN, or "Book of Breathings." About the time when this was written it became customary to bury with a mummy a small roll of papyrus inscribed in hieratic with a series of short extracts from the Saïte Recension, including the Negative Confession of Chapter CXXV. The little roll was formed of a sheet of papyrus of from 6 to 12 inches square, and the text on it was supposed to contain all that was necessary to effect the acquittal of the deceased in the Hall of Osiris and to ensure his resurrection. Other short and popular funerary works at this time were the "Book of Traversing Eternity," the "Book of Breathings," and the "Book May my Name Flourish," the last-named being based upon a well-known passage in the Pyramid Texts.[1]

[1] English translations of all these will be found in my *Chapters of Coming Forth by Day,* 1 vol., London, 1923; see also Birch, "On some Egyptian Rituals of the Roman Period" in *Proc. Soc. Bibl. Arch.,* Vol. VII, p. 49.

Reproductions of the Book of the Dead **written in demotic** have been published by Revillout, E., *Rituel Funéraire de Psamuth*, Paris, 1880, and by Lexa, F., *Das Demotische Totenbuch der Pariser Nationalbibliothek*, Leipzig, 1910. Here, too, must be mentioned the two papyri that were acquired at Thebes by Mr. A. H. Rhind in 1861, and were published in facsimile by him two years later. The texts in them are of a funerary character and are based on the Book of the Dead; they are written in hieratic and demotic. A translation of the hieratic text was published by Birch in Mr. Rhind's *Facsimile* in 1863, and as a result of Birch's remarks on the decipherment of demotic Brugsch republished the papyri in a work entitled *Henry Rhind's Zwei Bilingue Papyri, Hieratisch und Demotisch, übersetzt und herausgegeben*, Leipzig, 1865, 4to. The description "Bilingue" is likely to mislead, and therefore it may be pointed out that the texts are not written in two languages; the language is one, namely, Egyptian, but the forms of writing are two, namely, hieratic and demotic. A new edition of these Rhind papyri was published some ten years ago by Moeller, *Die Beiden Totenpapyrus Rhind*, Leipzig, 1913, 4to. The man for whom they were written was Mentsaf, , the son of Menkarā, 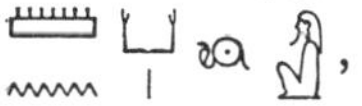, and Tasheritpament, 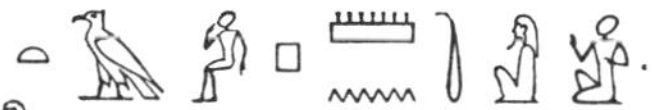. His wife was called Tȧnit, 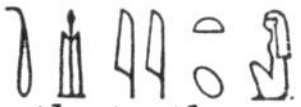. This is a most useful book, and all must lament that the activities of Moeller were brought to an end by his death during the Great War.

ANOINTING TABLETS

DURING the recital of the Book of Opening the Mouth over the figure of the deceased or his mummy in the tomb, vessels containing the Seven Holy Oils were brought into the Ṭuat Chamber, and the ceremony of anointing took place according to the directions given by the Rubrics. In the case of a king the oils were presented in alabaster flasks or bottles, but for a man of lesser rank only a few drops of each of the seven oils were poured into seven circular hollows which were cut in a rectangular slab of alabaster measuring about 5½ inches by 2½ inches. The names of the oils are: (1) Seth-ḥeb, (2) Ḥeknu, (3) Sefth, (4) Nem, (5) Tuaut, (6) Ḥa-āsh, (7) Tet-ent-Theḥenu. These are the forms of the names as given on the slab of the Kher-ḥeb priest Ȧṭenȧ, . The British Museum Collection contains three fine examples of such slabs, which are here shown.

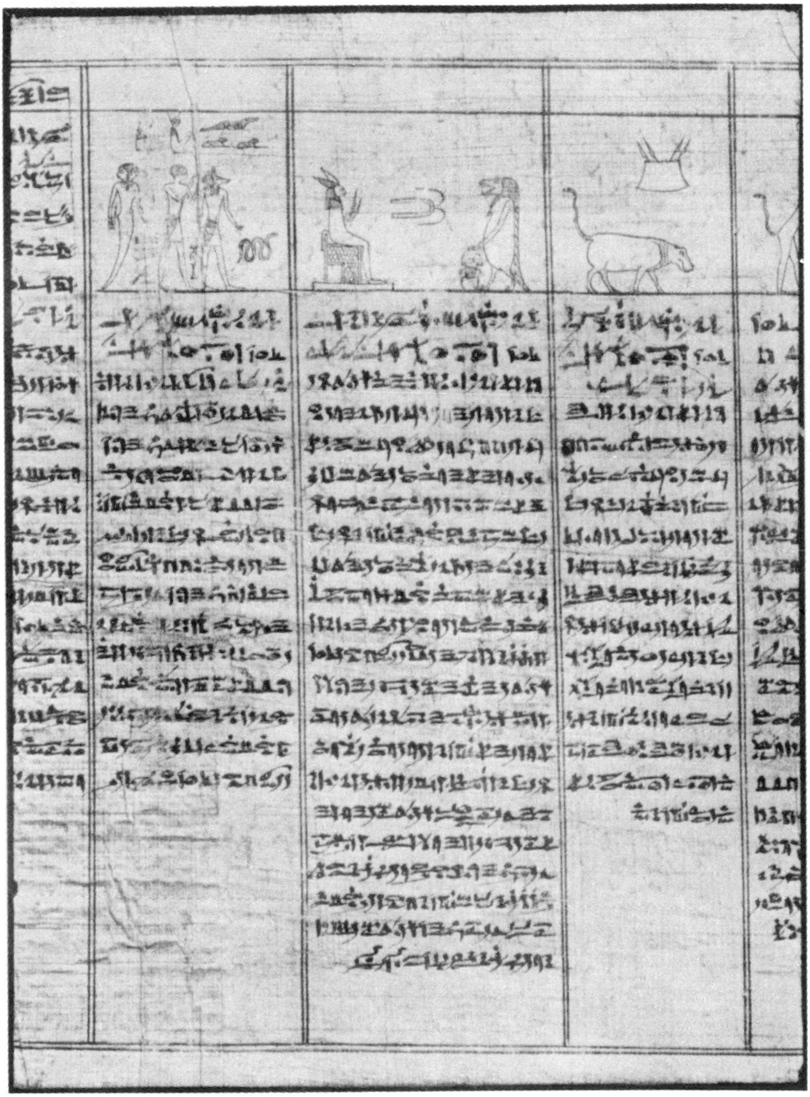

Vignettes and texts in hieratic copied from the Saïte Recension of the Book of the Dead in the early part of the Roman Period; all the Vignettes are in black outline and are beautifully drawn. B.M. No. 10558.

Painted wooden sepulchral chest in the form of a pylon, with figures of the amulets of Ỉsis and Osiris. XXVIth dynasty or later. B.M. No. 43433.

Rectangular painted limestone shrine, with pyramidal roof, of Ȧni, a gardener of Ȧmen. On each side, in relief, is a figure of the deceased holding a tablet inscribed with a hymn to Rā. XVIIIth dynasty. B.M. No. 561.

No. 6123.—*With hollows below the names.*

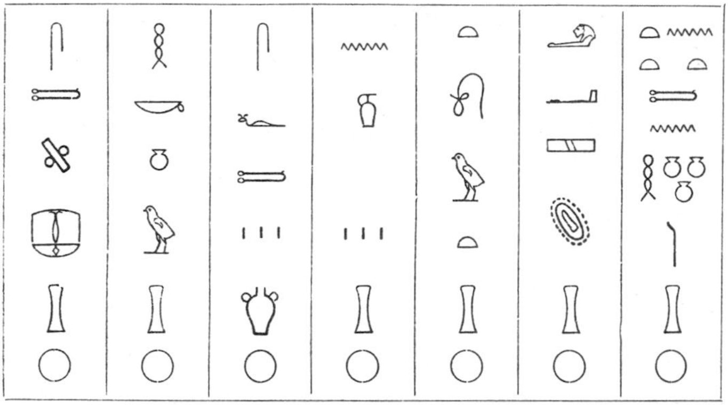

No. 6122.—*With hollows above the names.*[1]

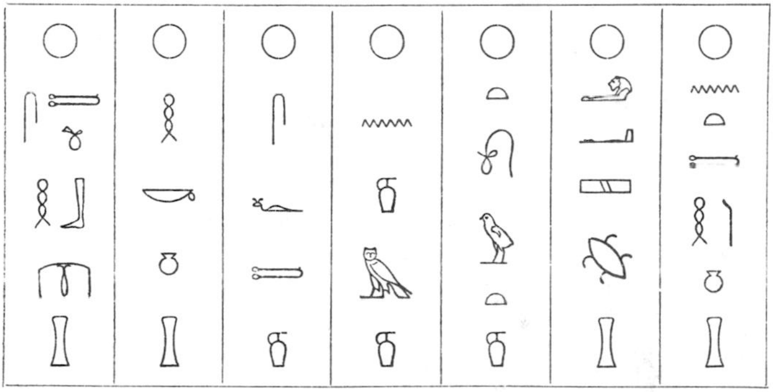

No. 29421.—*Without hollows for the oils.*

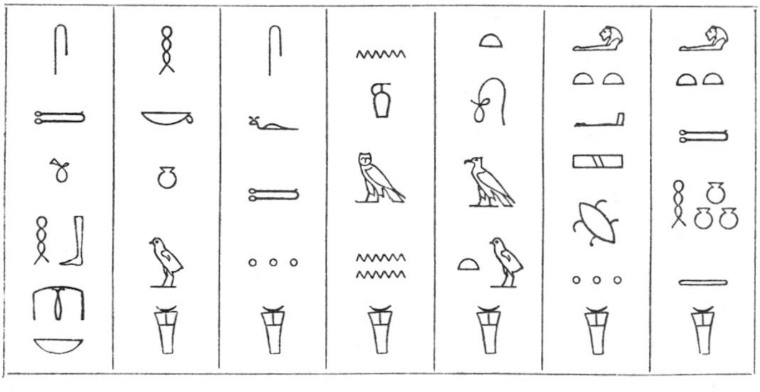

[1] On the back of this slab, cut in outline, are the two signs  which refer to the magical protection given by the oils.

THE VASES OF THE FOUR SONS OF HORUS, OR "CANOPIC" JARS

Canopic jars is the name given to the series of four jars in which the principal internal organs of a deceased person were placed. They were thus named by the early Egyptologists, who believed that in them they saw some confirmation of the legend handed down by some ancient writers that Canopus, the pilot of Menelaus, who is said to have been buried at Canopus, in Egypt, was worshipped there under the form of a jar with small feet, a thin neck, a swollen body, and a round back. Each jar was dedicated to one of the four sons of Horus, who originally represented the four cardinal points, and each jar was provided with a cover which was made in the shape of the head of the deity to whom it was dedicated. The names and characteristic heads of each are: (1) **Mestȧ** or **Ȧmset,** , , man-headed. (2) **Ḥāpi,** , dog-headed. (3) **Ṭuamutef,** , jackal-headed. (4) **Qebḥsenuf,** 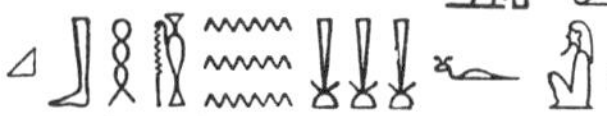, hawk-headed. Mestȧ represented the south, Hāpi the north, Ṭuamutef the east, and Qebḥsenuf the west. These four gods are, in some texts, said to be the children of Horus, and in others the children of Osiris. Each jar was hollowed out and received one of the larger organs after it had been steeped in bitumen and wrapped up in bandages; the covers of the jars were then fastened on by plaster. Mr. Pettigrew examined the contents of one set of vases, and he found that the vase dedicated to Mestȧ contained the stomach and large intestines; that dedicated to Ḥāpi, the small intestines; that dedicated to Ṭuamutef, the lungs and heart; and that dedicated to Qebḥsenuf, the liver and gall-bladder.

The oldest Canopic jars date from the XIth or XIIth dynasty, and are made of wood or stone. Under the XVIIIth dynasty many handsome sets are known in fine alabaster, aragonite, calcareous stone, and blue or green glazed porcelain. The jars of the XXVIth dynasty are poorly made, and in the Graeco-Roman Period the covers generally lack the characteristic heads of the four gods. Many sets in earthenware have the same diameter throughout, and the gods are painted on them in outline. Wooden jars are often painted in gaudy colours. Several **wooden models** of Canopic jars are known, and their existence may be due either to the poverty of the friends of the deceased persons or to the dishonesty of the funeral furnisher. But models were buried with the dead under the XVIIIth dynasty, a fact proved by the set of blue glass models (B.M. 51074–51077) which came from the Valley of the Tombs of the Queens at Thebes. When the viscera were left in the body, **figures of the four sons of Horus,** made of wax, gold, silver, or porcelain, were laid over the organs that they were supposed to protect. For examples in **white and red wax,** see B.M. 15563, 15564, 15573, 15578, 8889–91 and 54850. The inscriptions on stone Canopic jars were engraved, and on wood and porcelain jars they were written or painted. In papyri of the XVIIIth and XIXth dynasties, the Vignettes of the 17th Chapter of the Book of the Dead show that Canopic jars were placed in a sepulchral chest, upon the sides of which were painted figures of the four gods, in the form of men, but each having its characteristic head. Out of the cover there rises the sun with the head and arms of a man, and in each hand he holds ☥ *ānkh*, "life" (*Papyrus of Ani*, pl. 8). On papyri and coffins of a later period the jars are shown arranged in a row under the bier. In the 151st Chapter of the Book of the Dead the four gods are shown standing in the mummy chamber, one at each corner; the inscriptions which refer to them read :—

I. 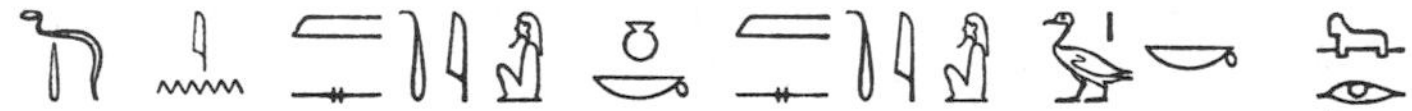

metch àn Mestà nuk Mestà sa - k Àsàr
Says Mestà, "I am Mestà son thy, O Osiris.

i - à un - à em sau - k serut - nà per - k
Come have I that may be I in protection thy. Make to flourish I house thy,

men sep sen utu en Ptaḥ mà utu en Rā tchesef
firm, firm, has commanded Ptaḥ, as commanded Rā himself."

II. 

metch àn Ḥāpi nuk Ḥāpi sa - k Àsàr
Says Ḥāpi, "I am Ḥāpi son thy, O Osiris.

i - nà un - à em sau - k thes - k tep
Come have I that may be I in protection thy. Tie up [I] for thee head

āt - k ḥui nek khefti k kher - k
and limbs thy, smiting down for thee enemies thy beneath thee.

erṭa - nà nek tep tchetta
Give I to thee head [thy] for ever."

III. 

metch ȧn Ṭuamutef nuk sa - k Ḥer meriu - k

Says Ṭuamutef, "I am son thy Horus loving thee.

i - nȧ netch tef Ȧsȧr em ṭa ȧri nek

Come have I to avenge father [*my*] *Osiris, not allowing to be done to thee*

nek - f ṭa - ȧ su kher reṭui - k tchetta sep sen

destruction his. Place I it under feet thy for ever and ever."

IV. 

metch ȧn Qebḥsenuf nuk sa - k Ȧsȧr i - nȧ

Says Qebḥsenuf, "I am son thy Osiris. Come have I

un - ȧ em sau - k ṭemṭ - ȧ qesu - k

that may be I in protection thy. Gather together I bones thy,

saq - ȧ āt - k ȧn - nȧ nek ȧb - k ṭa - ȧ

collect I limbs thy, bring I for thee heart thy, place I

nek su ḥer ȧset - f em khat - k seruṭ - nȧ per - k

for thee it upon seat its in body thy, make flourish I house thy."

The inscriptions on the outsides of the jars, which are sometimes accompanied by inscribed figures of the four gods, vary considerably; some consist of a few words only, but others occupy several lines. These inscriptions show that each of the four gods was under the protection of a goddess; thus Isis guarded Mestȧ, Nephthys guarded Ḥāpi, Neith guarded Ṭuamutef, and Selkit or Serqit guarded Qebḥsenuf. The following are examples of the formulae inscribed on these jars:—[1]

[1] These inscriptions are taken from the set of Canopic jars exhibited in the British Museum, Nos. 886 to 889; they were made for the commander of soldiers 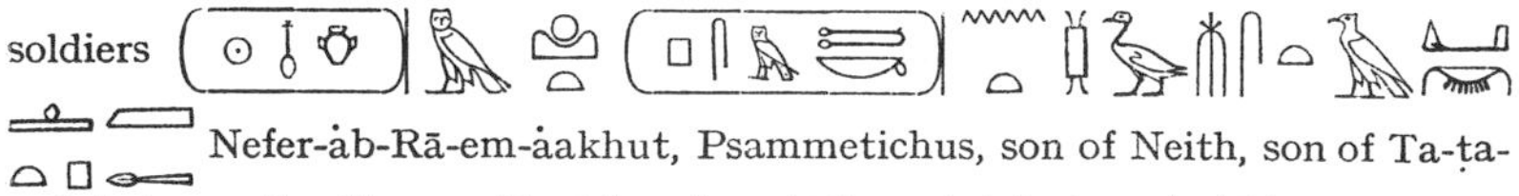 Nefer-ȧb-Rā-em-ȧakhut, Psammetichus, son of Neith, son of Ta-ṭa-nub-ḥetep. See Sharpe, *Egyptian Inscriptions*, 1st Series, pl. 114.

I. ÅMSET.

metch ån Åset sam - å tchat setep - å
Says Isis, "Conquer I the foe, make I

sa ḥer Åmseth enti åm - å sa Åsår
protection over Åmseth who is in me. The protection of Osiris [is]

sa Åmseth Åsår[1] Åmseth
the protection of Åmseth, [for] Osiris [is] Åmseth."

II. ḤĀPI.

metch ån Nebt-ḥet ḥap - å sesheta åri - å bessa
Says Nephthys, "Hide I the secret thing, make I protection

ḥer Ḥāpi enti åm - å sa Åsår sa
over Ḥāpi who is in me. The protection of Osiris [is] the protection of

Ḥāpi Åsår pu Ḥāpi
Ḥāpi, [for] Osiris [is] Ḥāpi."

III. ṬUAMUTEF.

metch ån Net seṭua - å
Says Neith, "Make pass the morning I

semasher - å hru neb ḥer åri maket en
make pass the night I of day every in making the protection of

Ṭuamutef enti åm - å sa Åsår
Ṭuamutef which is in me. The protection of Osiris

sa Ṭuamutef Åsår pu Ṭuamutef
[is] the protection of Ṭuamutef, [for] Osiris [is] Ṭuamutef."

[1] Here follow the name and titles of the deceased.

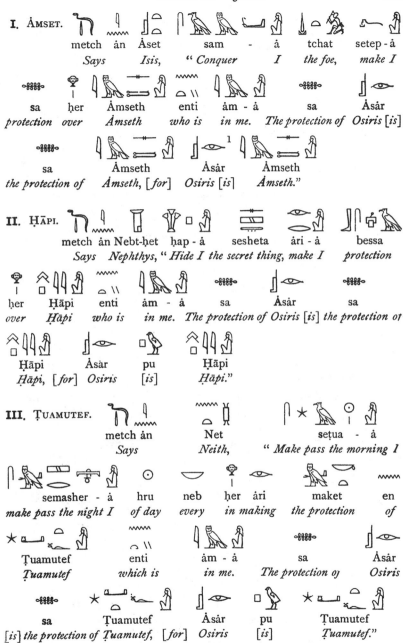

IV. Qebhsenuf.

metch ȧn Serqit seqeṭet
Says Serqit, ...

sa - ȧ hru neb ȧri maket en Qebḥsenu-f
"protection my day every in making protection of Qebḥsenu-f

entet ȧm - ȧ sa Ȧsȧr sa Qebḥsenu-f
which is in me. The protection of Osiris [is] the protection of Qebḥsenu-f,

Ȧsȧr pu Qebḥsenu-f
[for] Osiris [is] Qebḥsenu-f."

Frequently the first parts of these inscriptions read *qenȧ em āāui-ȧ ḥer enti ȧm-ȧ,* "I embrace with my two arms that which is in me;" the variants for being *sekhen* and *ȧnq;* frequently also they only contain the names and titles of the deceased preceded by the words *ȧmakhi kher,* "watchfully devoted to," which are followed by the names of the four gods. Often the same formula is repeated on all four jars.

In the Saïte and Ptolemaïc Periods the character of the inscriptions on Canopic jars changes greatly. Thus in the set that was made for Tche-Bast-ȧuf-ānkh, , the son of Ḥer and the lady Ānkhet (B.M. 22374 ff.), the inscription on the jar of Ȧmseth begins, "Thy bread is to thee. Thy beer is to thee. Thou livest upon that on which Rā lives. [Ȧmseth] protects the Osiris [here follow titles and genealogy] in every place to which he may journey." The inscription on the jar of Ḥāpi opens with the words, "Ḥāpi says:—Thy bread is to thee by the favour of the Kau (?). Thy beer is to thee by the favour of the god Ubunu, . Thy meat shall not be separated from thee. Ḥāpi protects the Osiris in the Khent-Ȧqer of Osiris, the Prince dwelling in Ta-she (the Fayyûm) of Osiris, the Soul of the Ṭuat of Un-Nefer," . The inscription on the jar of

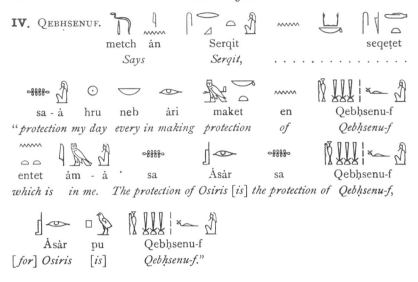

Ṭuamutef reads :—" Ṭuamutef gives thee thy bread in the Hall of the House of Rā . . . . . The Osiris shall be with his Ka for ever. Thy heart (mind ?) is to thee in the House of the Heart[s]. Thy breast is to thee in the House of the Breast[s]. Thou livest like Rā among them. Thy food is with that of the gods of heaven, thy portion is among them. Thy body is everlastingness, [thou] art complete (?) for ever." The opening words of this passage are taken from the first part of Chapter XXVI of the Book of the Dead. The inscription on the jar of Qebḥsenuf begins :—" Qebḥsenuf gives thee purification (or, washing). Thou appearest before thy son, thou appearest before Horus, appearing from Ȧtem, appearing from . . . . . Thou shalt act by day and by night as the overseer of the gods who are helpless. Qebḥsenuf endows the Osiris with a spirit before the gods who are the judges of eternity." Thus from first to last in this set of jars the object of the inscriptions is to procure funerary offerings for the deceased, and the protecting goddesses are not mentioned.

CHESTS FOR CANOPIC JARS 

THE Canopic jars that were made for the viscera of men of high rank were usually placed in rectangular chests, the interior of which was divided into four equal spaces by wooden partitions, and these chests were placed in the tomb with the mummy. It is probable that, when the ceremony that took place in the tomb in accordance with Chapters CXXXVII and CLI of the Book of the Dead was performed, the jars were removed from the chest and each placed in its duly appointed corner of the mummy chamber. In the Vignettes of the papyri and in pictures on coffins the four jars are frequently depicted as standing in a row under the mummy as it lies on its bier. But many sets of jars have been found in sealed chests, and it is tolerably clear that in most cases the jars remained in the chests after they were carried to the tomb. The chests are from about 18 inches to 24 inches square, and are made of the wood of the sycamore-fig tree ; see the chests of Sen and Guatep (XIIth dynasty) in the British Museum (30722, 30838). The alabaster jars of the latter have wooden heads. At a later period the Canopic chest was made in the form of a pylon and mounted on runners, so that it might be drawn to the tomb in the funeral procession. On the chest of Nebi,  (B.M. 35808), the sons of Horus and the four allied goddesses are painted in white outline on a black ground. On one end are Neith and Serqit, and on the other Isis and Nephthys, and on one side are Mestȧ and Ḥāpi, and on the other Ṭuamutef and Qebḥsenuf. On the outside of the cover is a figure of the goddess Nut. Sometimes, as in the case of the chest of Ḥentmeḥit (B.M. 51813), the box is painted black and is without inscriptions. The priestesses of Åmen-Rā of the XXIst dynasty revived many of the funeral customs of the XIth and XIIth dynasties, and it seems that more Canopic chests were made during the rule of the Priest-kings than at any other period of Egyptian History.

An interesting class of sepulchral boxes comes from Akhmîm, the ancient Panopolis, which deserves special mention. The largest of them in the British Museum (18210) is 3½ feet long and 3 feet high. Each side tapers slightly towards the top, and is in the shape of a pylon. The hollow cornice is ornamented with yellow, black, and red lines upon a white ground. Beneath it are two rows of ornaments: the first is formed by , and the second by  repeated several times. Beneath each line is a row of five-rayed stars ★★★★★. The front of the box is ornamented with  and uraei wearing disks  and a winged disk . Behind is a hawk upon a pedestal, before which is an altar with offerings. On the right-hand side is Thoth, with both hands raised, pouring out a libation; and on the left is a hawk-headed deity with both hands raised, also pouring out a libation. On the back of the box is a hawk, with extended wings, and sceptres . On the right-hand side of the box is a figure of the deceased, kneeling, having his left hand raised, and above him are two cartouches . Behind him are three jackal-headed deities, each having his left arm raised, while his right hand is clenched and laid upon his stomach. On the left-hand side of the box the deceased is represented in the same attitude, and behind him are three hawk-headed deities. These six gods form the Vignettes of the CXIIth and CXIIIth Chapters of the Book of the Dead; the hawk-headed were called Horus, Mestȧ, and Ḥāpi, and the jackal-headed Horus, Ṭuamutef and Qebḥsenuf; they are figured in Lanzone, *Dizionario*, Tav. XXVI. In two sides of the box are two pairs of rectangular openings about 6 inches from each end;[1] the use of these is unknown to me.

THE HEAD-REST OR PILLOW

THE Egyptians, in common with many other peoples, both ancient and modern, in all parts of Africa, were in the habit of using a head-rest or pillow during sleep, and in all essentials it has remained unchanged in shape and form. At a very early period the head-rest that a man had used during his lifetime was buried with him in his

[1] For the description of a similar box see my article in *Proc. Soc. Bib. Arch.*, 1886, pp. 120–122.

grave or tomb, where it was actually placed under his neck. But the significance of the head-rest, *i.e.*, the lifting up of the head of the deceased, caused men to deposit it with the dead even after their bodies had been mummified and the head-rest was useless. When the Egyptians realized that the large head-rest was unnecessary for the mummy, they made small models of it in haematite and other substances, and placed them with the dead as protective amulets (see AMULETS). And the editors of the Theban Recension of the Book of the Dead included in it a word of power (Chapter CLXVI) that would "lift up the head of the deceased in the horizon," and the picture of a head-rest formed the Vignette. The head-rest , *urs*, was usually made in three pieces, viz., the curved neck-piece on which the neck rested, the column or support, and the base; it varied in height from 6 to 10 inches, and was made in many materials—wood, ivory, granite, alabaster, calcareous stone, earthenware, etc. The column may be round or square, and the base is oblong. A few typical examples may be described. The head-rest of Guatep (XIIth dynasty) is of ivory and is about 6½ inches in height. The neck-piece rests on a rectangular plaque, which in turn rests on two supports, each made in the form of the Tet of Isis, ; these take the place of the ordinary column, and are fastened into the ivory base, which has bevelled edges (B.M. 30727). Many fine examples of the head-rest are made of alabaster, and one of the oldest is that which was made for Ȧṭenȧ, the Smer uāt and Kher-ḥeb priest of Abydos under the VIth dynasty, 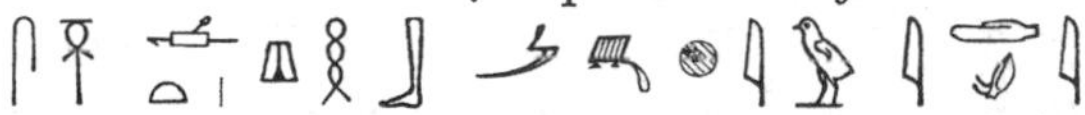 (B.M. 2523). The neck-piece rests on a rectangular plaque, and the fluted column, which is slightly concave, and increases in diameter towards the bottom, rests on a thick rectangular base. In the example B.M. 51806 the column and base, which has rounded corners, are made of a single piece of hard wood, to which the neck-piece is fastened by a rectangular slot and a peg with an ivory head. The column is fluted, and on each of two flutings is a lotus flower, , above which is a head of Bes, both flower and head being in relief. On each end of the base is a figure of Bes in high relief. The god wears a large feather on his head, and his thighs are girt about with a leopard skin. One figure holds a serpent in each hand, and the other the Utchat, , in one hand and the  in the other. On another example (B.M. 2529*a*) are cut a number of lion-headed gods, the signs 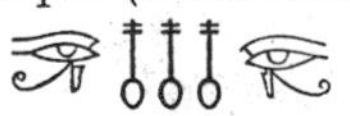 on the front, a figure of Bes, , on the back, and the ape of Thoth holding the Utchat, , on each side. Sometimes heads of Bes are cut on the ends of the neck-piece, and legs like those of a folding stool take the place of the column and base; in the case of B.M. 18156 the ends of the legs are cut in the forms of necks and heads of geese. The neck-piece is sometimes supported by two columns (B.M. 17102), and sometimes by six thin rods (B.M. 17102), and even by twenty-one (B.M. 18155). The head-rest has sometimes the form of an animal, *e.g.*, B.M. 20753, which is in the form of a stag, the horns being curved downwards to form the neck-piece. On another example (B.M. 35804) the neck-piece is decorated with lotus flowers and the Utchat cut in outline and coloured, , the Utchat being in the centre where the back of the neck of the deceased would rest; on the upper side, at each end, there are also lotus flowers. On the lower side of the base are 19 lines of hieroglyphs, written in black ink, which show that this head-rest was made for the married woman Aāua, , the daughter of Ḥer, a priest of Menthu, and the lady Nes-Mut, . Then follows the text of the LVth Chapter of the Book of the Dead: "I am the Jackal of jackals. I am Shu, drawing in air in the presence of the god Åakhu to the uttermost limits of heaven, to the uttermost limits of earth, to the uttermost limits of the flight of the Nebeḥ bird, . May there be given unto me the air (or, breath) of these Ḥunnutiu [gods], . The mouth of Osiris shall be opened, he shall see with his eyes." Following this Chapter come versions of Chapters LXI and LXII, and it is clear that these words of power, coupled with the use of the head-rest, were believed to secure for the deceased air and water and everlasting life in the "horizon of heaven." The head-rest B.M. 26256 is an example of a very rare type. The neck-piece is inlaid with an ivory plaque decorated with a linear design of lotus buds and flowers, surrounded by eight ivory rosettes; at each end is inlaid a lotus flower. The column is square, and each side is inlaid with an ivory panel. On each of the two larger panels is cut in outline the figure of a man seated on a framework stool, who in one hand holds a lotus flower, and in the other a spear (?) made in the form of a flower with buds. On one of the smaller panels is cut in outline the figure of a man holding a lotus flower with an abnormally long stalk. On each flower a bird, , is perched. On the other smaller panels is cut in outline the figure of a man holding one spear (?) upright with the crook of his arm, and another spear, round which his left leg is crooked, in his right hand. The base is inlaid with two ivory panels, one on each end; these have the form of truncated pyramids, and on each is cut in outline a lion. This head-rest belongs to a very late period, and the engravings on the ivory suggest Coptic workmanship. The object seems too small to have been actually used as a head-rest for the dead, and it is possible that it was only placed in the grave or tomb as the result of custom. In the Saïte and Ptolemaïc Periods the head-rest was carelessly made, and was both undecorated and uninscribed; often it was merely a rough block of wood with slightly concave sides and a slight projection in the place of a base. In the Roman Period head-rests were often made of terra-cotta; a typical example is B.M. 49332. This example is solid, and the column is nearly as thick as the neck-piece and base are long; it appears to have been glazed or burnished.

PECTORALS IN PORCELAIN AND STEATITE

THE custom of inserting a scarab of green stone in the breast of a man in place of his heart does not seem to be older than the XVIIIth dynasty, although the text which is often found inscribed upon it was believed to have been discovered by Prince Ḥerṭaṭaf in the reign of Menkaurā (Mycerinus), a king of the IVth dynasty. Under the XIXth and XXth dynasties the green stone scarab was frequently placed, not inside the body, but between the bandages of the breast, and later still it was enclosed in a rough framework and laid outside the bandages on the breast of a mummy. Out of the scarab and its frame grew the **pectoral,** several examples of which are usually found in all great collections of Egyptian antiquities. Porcelain and glazed steatite pectorals vary in size from 5½ inches by 4¼ inches to 3½ inches by 3 inches. They are all made in the form of a funerary edifice, with a heavy cornice, , and the predominant colour of the glaze is blue or bluish green. In some pectorals, *e.g.*, B.M. 7865, a blue-glazed porcelain scarab is inserted, and as a boat is painted below it, , it is clearly intended to represent the beetle-headed god Kheperȧ. A figure of Isis, , and the ṭeṭ, , and the one Utchat, , are seen on the left, and a figure of Nephthys, , and the tet, , and the other Utchat, , on the right. On the base of the scarab, in a lighter colour, is a version of Chapter XXXB of the Book of the Dead. The pectoral was made for the "lady of the house, Ḥent-taui." On another example, belonging probably to the same period as the aforementioned, a model of the heart takes the place of the scarab, and it has above it a woman's face in red porcelain. The heart is placed in a boat, with Isis standing in the stern and Nephthys in the bows. On the reverse, in brown on a white ground, are  and  (B.M. 29369). Another example, in blue porcelain, likewise has the model of a human-headed heart inserted, and as there is a kneeling figure of a man with his hands raised in adoration of the heart, it would seem that it was supposed to have absorbed the qualities of the god Kheperȧ. On the reverse of this pectoral a man-headed heart is drawn with  and  on each side of it (B.M. 14654). On other and smaller pectorals the decoration and designs are simpler. Thus we have on the obverse the jackal of Anubis, , and on the reverse  (B.M. 29370); or the deceased, a priestess, kneeling in adoration before Anubis, above whom is the  (B.M. 14653); or the deceased kneeling in adoration before Osiris on the obverse, and a figure of Anubis on the reverse (B.M. 7849); or figures of four gods on the obverse, and the deceased, the scribe Pa-meḥt, , kneeling in adoration before Anubis *couchant* and a winged disk on the reverse (B.M. 7847). The pectorals in steatite are of unusual interest because the figures are often in relief. Thus on B.M. 7852 the deceased Sebek-ḥetep (?) is kneeling in adoration, with both hands raised, before Anubis, who is lying on the top of his building and holding the sceptre  between his fore paws. Round his neck is an object resembling a pair of tongs, , and above his back is the whip . On the reverse are the signs  cut in outline. On B.M. 14626 the deceased stands in adoration before Anubis, who is lying on the top of a four-pillared shrine, with the utchat above him, all the figures being in relief. On the reverse, which has no cornice, is a scene representing Isis and Nephthys seated in the solar boat with the  between them; the figures and the boat are in relief. Above the figures is the solar disk with outspread wings, and below them is a row of lotus flowers and buds in relief. A similar decoration is found on B.M. 7850, where the flowers are in outline, like the figures on the obverse and reverse. The porcelain pectorals of the XXVIth dynasty are of little interest, for the work is poor, and the texts, where they occur, are full of inaccuracies, having been copied by men ignorant of what they were writing.

Wooden case for the head of a mummy. XXIInd–XXVIth dynasty. B.M. No. 17264.

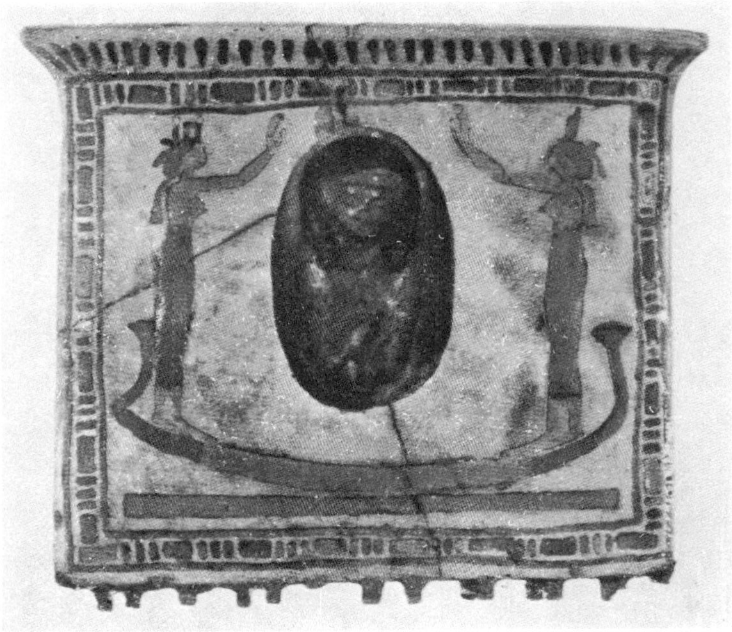

Porcelain pectoral with a human-headed heart-scarab inlaid. XXIst dynasty. B.M. No. 29369.

Ushabti figure of Pa-mer-åḥau. XVIIIth dynasty. B.M. No. 5512.

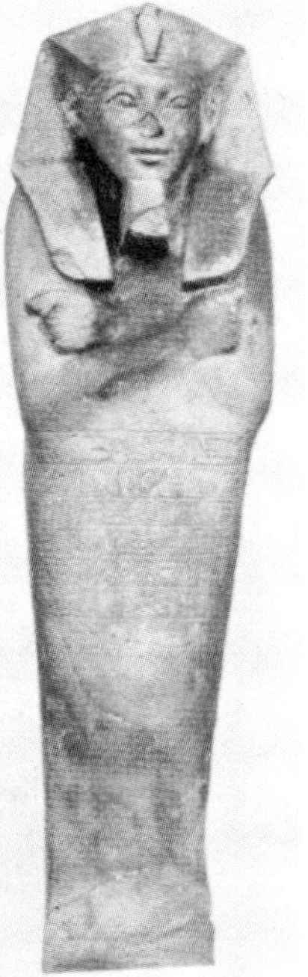

Ushabti figure of King Åāḥmes I. B.M. No. 32191.

Blue glazed porcelain ushabti and coffin of Åmen-mes-en-Uast. XVIIIth dynasty. B.M. No. 53892.

SHAUABTIU OR USHABTIU FIGURES

Shauabti, , is the name that was given under the XVIIIth and following dynasties to the figure of the deceased[1] which was placed in the tomb in order to perform certain agricultural labours for the deceased. Various explanations have been given of the name, some connecting it with the verb "to answer," and translating it by "answerer" (respondent), and others holding it to mean a figure made of *shauabti* wood.[2] But as the figure itself must be the Osirian equivalent of the man (or woman), who was murdered at the burial of a chief in primitive times, and sent to the Other World to work for his master, it is far more likely that the name "shauabti" represents the word for the funerary victim in some early African tongue. Be this as it may, there is no doubt what the figure was intended to do for the person whom it represented, *i.e.*, when it happened that the deceased in the Other World was called upon to perform any work that was obligatory, that is to say, digging the furrows, and irrigating the cultivated plots, and carrying the sand of the East to the West, it was the duty of the figure to cry out "Here am I." Moreover, the figure was not to hearken to anyone except the person whom it represented, as we see from the inscription first noticed by Erman and quoted by Borchardt,[3] which ends, "Obey the person who made thee: obey not his enemies," 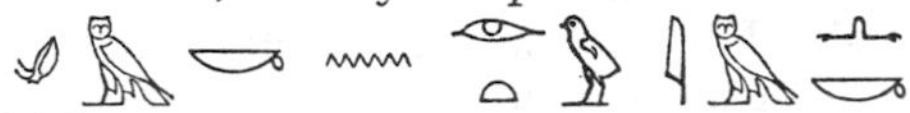
.

The Shauabti figure of the New Kingdom seems to be the equivalent of the personal servant of the deceased, of whom many examples are found in the tombs of the Old and Middle Kingdoms. But as no one servant could perform all the work which had to be done in and about the house of a great official or man of high rank, and as a nobleman's household consisted of many servants, it was considered necessary to place more than one Shauabti in the tomb of a king, or nobleman, so that all his needs in the Other World might be satisfied. Many officials (*e.g.*, Åmenḥetep and Ānkhef-en Khensu)[4]

[1] This appears to be certain from the text on the figure made for User, son of Qahaṭu, in the Berlin Museum (No. 10814), the inscription on which begins 
. See Borchardt, *Aeg. Zeit.*, Bd. XXXII (1894), p. 117.

[2] When the figure is made of stone or bronze or faïence this argument must fail, unless we assume that the Egyptians overlooked the incorrect use of the word.

[3] *Aeg. Zeit.*, Bd. XXXII (1894), p. 117.

[4] Brit. Mus. 35289, 35290.

had large boxes full of Shauabtiu buried with them, and they provided themselves each with 365 Shauabtiu—one for every day in the year. Seti I seems to have had a supply of figures sufficient for two years, for Belzoni found over 700 in his tomb at Thebes. It is a moot point whether many of these were not votive offerings made by kinsfolk and friends, for there is evidence that, in some cases at least, the *ḥeka*, or word of power, which is inscribed upon them, was recited by one or more of the kinsfolk of the deceased.

Shauabtiu figures are made of plain or zoned alabaster, granite, basalt, crystalline sandstone, porphyry and diorite limestone, wood, mud, glazed faïence, etc. The Shauabti, later Shabti, was sometimes laid on the mummy itself, as we see from the mummy of Katebet in the British Museum, and sometimes it was laid in or by the coffin. In tombs which contained a large number of figures, probably votive, they have been found lying scattered about on the floor. The Shauabti figure is found in tombs of all periods, from the VIth dynasty to the Roman Period, but it is almost certain that the religious views as to its use and importance that prevailed under the VIth dynasty were greatly modified when the cult of Osiris became predominant under the XIIth dynasty. Many of the oldest figures are uninscribed and their hands are invisible. Under the XIIth dynasty the name and titles of the person for whom the figure was made are written or cut upon it, and the arms are crossed at the wrist, and the palms of the hands lie flat on the breast. Under the XVIIIth dynasty the hands are treated differently, and a *ḥeka*, which forms Chapter VI of the Theban Recension of the Book of the Dead, is cut upon the figure. Thus in the limestone Shabti of Āāḥmes I, the first king of the dynasty (B.M. 32191), the arms are crossed at the wrists, and each hand is clenched, as if grasping an amulet. The hieroglyphic text reads :—

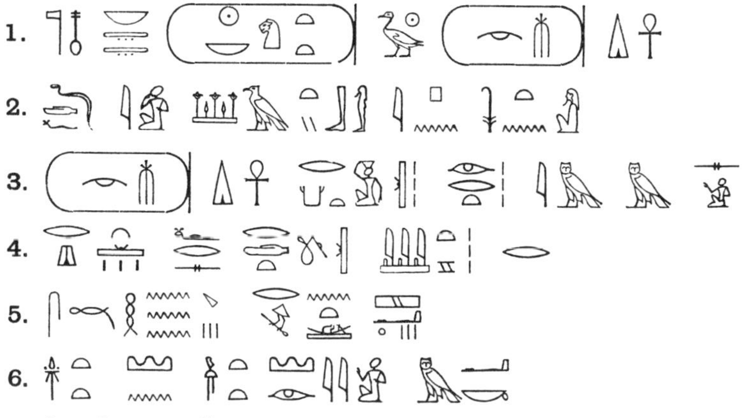

(Height, 11½ ins.)

In the Shabti figure of Ȧmenḥetep II (B.M. 35365) the arms are crossed as before, but in each hand the king grasps the symbol of "life," ☥. The text reads : 1. 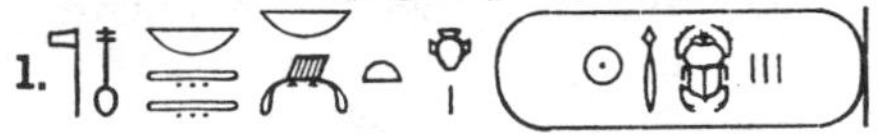

In the handsome Shabti of Parmer-ȧḥu (B.M. 8703), of about the same period, the figure has the form of a mummy and no hands are visible. The text contains some interesting variants, and reads :—

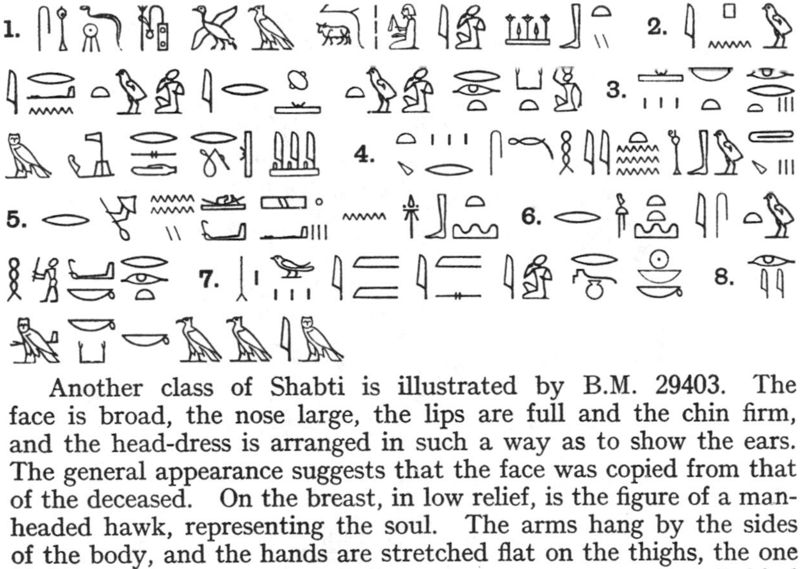

Another class of Shabti is illustrated by B.M. 29403. The face is broad, the nose large, the lips are full and the chin firm, and the head-dress is arranged in such a way as to show the ears. The general appearance suggests that the face was copied from that of the deceased. On the breast, in low relief, is the figure of a man-headed hawk, representing the soul. The arms hang by the sides of the body, and the hands are stretched flat on the thighs, the one resting on the ṭeṭ , and the other on the tet, . Behind the left shoulder two hoes, , are cut in outline, and behind the right shoulder a ropework basket (?) is cut in outline. The usual text fills seven lines, and begins, ; then follows a blank space for the name of the deceased, which was not filled in, and after it . This figure probably belongs to the XVIIIth dynasty, but it is possible that it may be older.

The inscriptions on the fragments of the Shabti figures made for Åmenḥetep III show that a text other than the VIth Chapter of the Book of the Dead was preferred by him. Thus on B.M. 8690 the inscription reads :— 1. 

. The beginnings of these lines were probably on the upper portion of the figure, which is wanting. It is a curious fact that the upper parts of the three or four Shabtiu in the British Museum that were made for Åmenḥetep III are wanting.

The text of the VIth Chapter of the Book of the Dead that is found on the beautiful blue-glazed faïence Shabti of Seti I (B.M. 22818) well represents the version current under the XIXth dynasty. The king is shown wearing the usual royal head-dress, with a uraeus over the forehead, and a deep collar or breastplate, and wide bracelets on the wrists. The arms are folded over the breast ; in the left hand he holds a hoe, , and in the right hand a hoe and the cord of a basket (?) 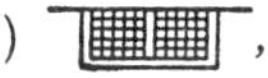, which hangs over his left shoulder. The text reads :— 1. 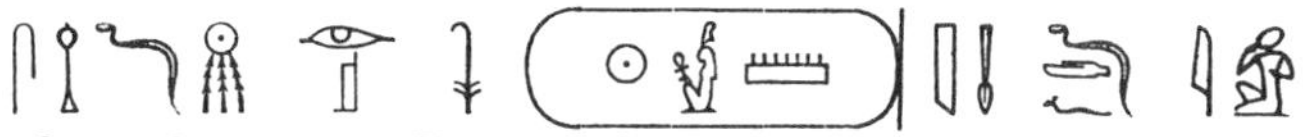

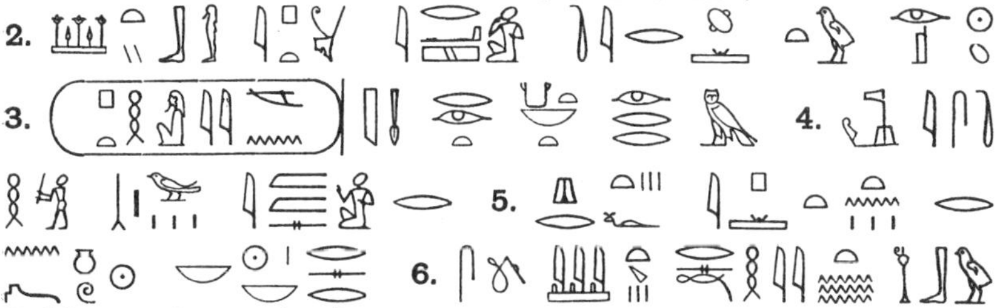

7. [the rest is wanting.]

The huge hard sandstone Shabti (B.M. 55485) of the Nubian king Taharq (the Tirhâḳâh of the Bible) supplies us with the version of the VIṭh Chapter that was accepted at Napata in the VIIIth century before Christ. This Shabti is 1 foot $8\frac{1}{2}$ inches in height. The king wears a short thick head-dress, with a uraeus over his forehead, and the ears rest upon the lower part of the head-dress. The face is evidently a portrait, but the beard is unusually long. The hands rest upon the breast, and one grasps a hoe, , and the other the string of a bag or basket, which hangs behind the shoulders. The text reads: 1. 

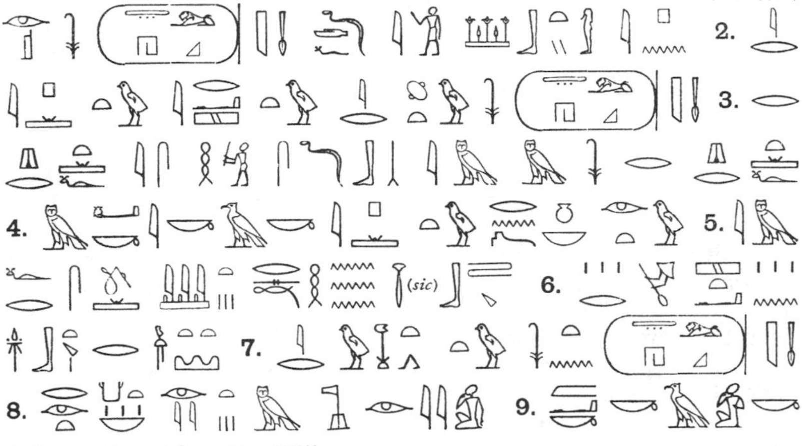

. The variants are of interest, and not the least remarkable are the last two words, "I am thou," in which the figure makes itself identical with the deceased.

Under the XVIIIth and XIXth dynasties the Ushabtiu figures that were buried with persons of importance were made chiefly of stone—white, grey, green or black—and when limestone was used the inscriptions were usually coloured red or blue. But a large number of Ushabtiu were made of wood and Egyptian porcelain, or faïence—green, or brown, or red—and a few of bronze (*e.g.*, B.M. 32692, which bears the name of the royal scribe Ȧni, . The position of the hands varies, and sometimes the figure is represented as wearing the costume of everyday life. A very interesting variety of figure is offered by the small class in which the face and hands are coloured red and the inscriptions are written in brown paint upon a white or yellowish-white background. A good example is B.M. 53974. The deceased Tcheḥuti-mes, , wears a heavy wig which falls back, showing the ears, and on his breast hangs a heart amulet, , and he holds a hoe, , in each hand. Behind his right shoulder hangs the basket (?) 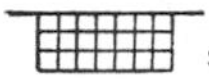, and behind his left is a circle . In B.M. 30004 there is a sort of counterpoise, , on each side of the basket (?). Ushabtiu made of wood for women sometimes wear gilded pectorals and bracelets (B.M. 22743), and figures of stone also were sometimes gilded in parts. Thus B.M. 24390 has a gilded face, and there are traces of gold on the main swathings ; it was made for Ȧuȧ, , a libationer of Ȧmen, , and it is interesting to note that the inscription begins with the words *Nesu ṭa ḥetep*, . Already in the Old Kingdom the Shabti was sometimes inscribed with a prayer for sepulchral offerings[1] instead of Chapter VI of the Book of the Dead, but it is possible that such figures were votive offerings made by kinsfolk or friends of the deceased. The priests, or those who supplied Ushabtiu figures, kept a number in stock with spaces left blank in the text for the addition of the name of the purchaser ; compare B.M. 36434. Under the Priest-kings of the XXIst dynasty the makers of Ushabtiu succeeded in covering their figures with a most beautiful blue glaze ; some of the finest examples of these bear the names of Princess Nesi-Khensu, Queen Ḥenttaui, Queen Maātkarā, Panetchem and Pānkhi. The last two were priests of Ȧmen-Rā, king of the gods of Thebes. Under the XXVIth dynasty Ushabtiu hold the hoe and basket and mattock (?) in their hands, which rest on the breast, and stand on a square pedestal and have a rectangular plinth down the back ; many of them were cast in moulds, and are easily recognized by their light bluish-green colour. The Ushabtiu of the Ptolemaïc and Roman Periods are coarse and badly made, and the inscriptions are garbled, or are wholly wanting.

USHABTIU IN SMALL SARCOPHAGI AND COFFINS

In most of the great collections of Egyptian antiquities there are seen a number of wooden Ushabtiu lying in models of sarcophagi or coffins ; sometimes both figure and coffin bear inscriptions, and sometimes the coffin alone is inscribed. In some cases the figure is swathed in linen, like a mummy, and in others it is bare and lies upon pads or wads of linen. The earliest examples belong to the XIIth dynasty, and the latest to the XXth or XXIst. Among the examples in the British Museum the following are of special interest. The wooden model coffin B.M. 16007 contains two wooden Ushabtiu wrapped in a strip of linen on which is inscribed the name " Tcheḥuti-mes,"  (Thothmes). On each figure is written a copy of the version of the VIth Chapter of the Book of the Dead which probably dates from the XIIth dynasty, and it is quite clear that the two figures were expected to dig the furrows, irrigate the fields and carry sand for the deceased if called upon. But on

[1] *E.g.*, B.M. 32556, .

the cover of the coffin, written in very cursive characters, is an inscription, beginning with the words , in which Osiris is entreated to give to the Ka of the deceased Thothmes "sepulchral meals, and every good and pure thing whereon the gods live," . The inscription ends with the statement,  , "Behold, it is his sister Åntef who makes his name to live."

On the model wooden sarcophagus B.M. 21707 there is written in cursive characters a copy of the version of the VIth Chapter that was current early in the XVIIIth dynasty, and at the end of it is the statement, "Behold, it is his brother Tetåres (?) , who makes his name to live." And the little wooden figure B.M. 15765 was made and dedicated to Åpu-sa-Khensu, , by his brother Åpu-Nefer, . There is no reason to doubt the view expressed by Birch so far back as 1864,[1] that the Shabti does represent the deceased, and that the figure was supposed, under the influence of the *ḥeka*, or word of power, to perform for him in the Other World whatever work had to be done there, and, in fact, to serve as his personal servant.[2] But when the lady Åntef dedicated two figures of her brother Thothmes, it is clear that she intended each of them to benefit her brother in some way, and to do work for him; or perhaps she meant one to work for Thothmes and one for his Ka. And when over 700 Ushabtiu were buried with Seti I it is perfectly certain that the current opinion of the day was that every one of them would do work for the king in the Other World and form a member of his personal retinue. But the existence of the models described above may be explained in another way. Thothmes, the brother of the lady Åntef, may have been drowned, or his body may have been devoured by wild beasts, and so there was nothing of him to bury. She therefore had the model sarcophagus and the figures made, and inscribed, and buried, trusting that the words of power would be as efficacious as if the body of her brother had been there. I am informed that in the Semliki Valley and other parts of Africa, when a body has been wholly destroyed and there is nothing to bury, the kinsfolk take a piece of wood and lay it on a mud bier, and heap earth over it, and perform over it the funeral ceremonies that are usually performed over a grave with a dead body in it.

[1] *Aeg. Zeit.*, Bd. II, p. 89.

[2] See Borchardt, "Die Dienerstatuen" (in *Aeg. Zeit.*, Bd. XXXV, 1897, p. 119).

And here it is convenient to mention the unique blue-glazed porcelain Shabti figure (height, 9 inches) with coffin of Åmen-mes (length, 11⅜ inches) which forms one of the most striking objects in the collection of glazed Egyptian porcelain in the British Museum (53892). The deceased wears a wig and collar with a pectoral plaque inscribed with the name of Åmen-Rā, . A short cloak covers his shoulders and upper arms, and his arms hang by his sides, the extended hands resting upon his thighs. On each wrist is a wide bracelet. The deceased was a "king's scribe and overseer of the treasury of Åmen," 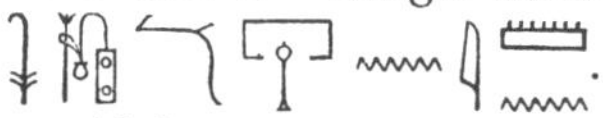. The porcelain coffin is of the usual anthropoid form common to the period, and a curious feature of the cover is that the beard is gilded. The figures of the gods and the inscriptions are in black outline. The hands are crossed over the breast, the right grasping  and the left . On the breast is a seated figure of Nut, with outstretched wings. Down the front is the inscription, "Osiris, fan-bearer on the right hand of the king, king's scribe, overseer of the Great House, overseer of the treasury of the sanctuary of Åmen, Åmen-mes of Thebes," 
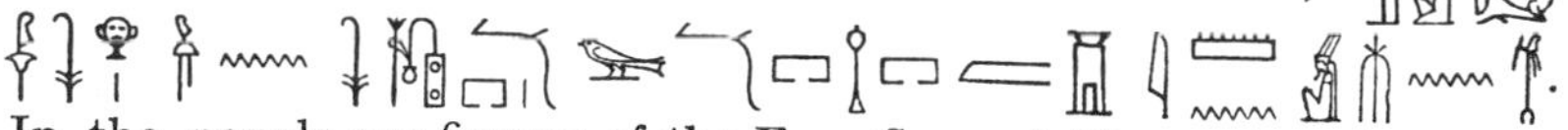.
In the panels are figures of the Four Sons of Horus, two figures of Thoth opening the doors of two of the Four Winds (see Chapter LXI of the Book of the Dead), and Isis and Nephthys. The inscriptions mention Geb, Ånpu, Ṭuamutef, Sep, Ḥāpi, etc. On the outside of the body of the coffin are painted in black outline figures of Nephthys (at head), Isis (at foot), the Utchats, Mestȧ, Ḥer-netcḥ-tef, Qebḥsenuf, Anubis, and two figures of Thoth, each opening the door of one of the Four Winds. The text of Chapter VI of the Book of the Dead, which we should expect to find on the figure, is wanting. There is reason to believe that the coffin and figure were not found in a tomb, but on the ground under a large heap of sand near the entrance to the Valley of the Tombs of the Queens. They were probably votive offerings.

OBJECTS FOR THE TOILET IN THE OTHER WORLD

In all periods the Egyptians have suffered severely from disease of the eyes, and there seems never to have been a time when they did not apply unguents and medicaments to them to minimize the effects of the heat and glare of the day and of the bitter cold of the night. They used many kinds of salves and ointments of a soothing nature, but these were not sufficient to preserve the eyes from

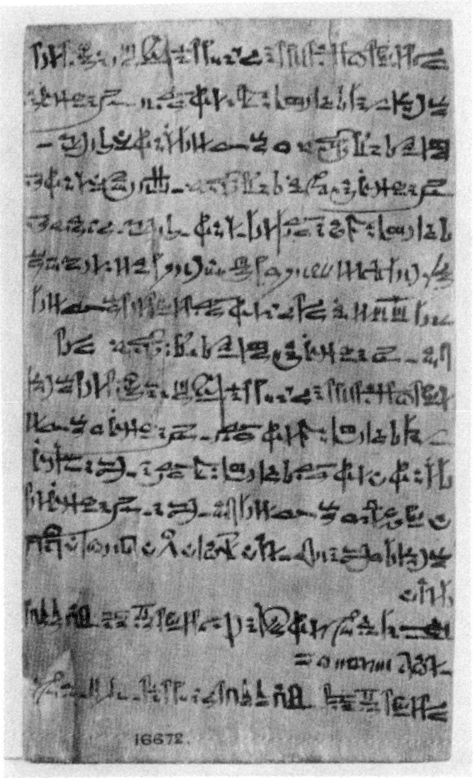

Wooden tablet inscribed in hieratic with a magical text on behalf of princess Nesi-Khensu. XXIst dynasty. B.M. No. 16672.

Painted and gilded plaster head-case for the mummy of a woman, with models of her two feet. IIIrd century A.D. B.M. No. 29477.

Stone figure of a human-headed hawk, with pendent breasts, symbol of the Ba, or human soul. From Nubia. Meroïtic Period. B.M. No. 53965.

rheum and inflammation, and at a very early period the use of mineral compounds became common, both among men and women. The mineral powder in commonest use was , *mesṭem-t*,[1] the ⲥⲧⲏⲙ of the Copts, and the στίμμι of the Greeks, or stibium. This seems to have been a black powder, the sesquisulphuret of antimony, but oxide of copper, , *uatch*, sulphide of lead, and many other substances were used. I brought home several specimens of the powder which was used in the Sûdân in 1905–6, and an expert chemist informed me that the substance was black oxide of manganese. *Mesṭem-t* was used in the countries to the East of Egypt, and in a painting on a wall in the tomb of Khnemu-ḥetep at Bani-Ḥasan we see a company of the Nomads (Āamu) bringing a present of it to this nomarch in the reign of Usertsen II. And it will be remembered that Jezebel "set her eyes in stibium" (וַתָּשֶׂם בַּפּוּךְ עֵינֶיהָ, II Kings ix, 30), and that the daughter of Zion was told that her lovers would seek her life, even though "she rent asunder her eyes with stibium" (Jeremiah iv, 30), an allusion to the wide-open appearance which stibium gives to women's eyes in the East.

The **stibium-pot** or tube (or more commonly the **koḥl-pot,** from the Arabic كحل) is one of the commonest toilet necessaries found in the tombs, and the varieties known are many. The simplest form consisted of a hollow tube of alabaster, steatite, ivory, wood or glass, from 2 to 6 inches high. A good example in ivory is B.M. 6179; the bone tube with circular bands grooved on the outside is still filled with the black paste (B.M. 6184). Another interesting example in bone or ivory is in the form of the god Bes (B.M. 2571). The god wears a decorated tunic and deep anklets, and stands on a cluster of lotus flowers. Sometimes a piece of a reed 7½ inches long was used for a tube, and the example B.M. 51068 is inscribed  (?), which seems to suggest that the powder in the tube will make the user to attain to the greatest beauties of the god Set, who is here drawn with emblems of life, , on each side of him. The inscription is written within notched palm branches, indicating length of years, and below the hieroglyphs is the sign . In short, it was claimed that the powder in the tube would give everlasting youth and beauty. Sometimes the single tube is in the form of a woman wearing a heavy pigtail (B.M. 2570), and when made of steatite or alabaster it is sometimes

[1] Var. . The Egyptians seem to have had a special preparation, ⲥⲧⲏⲙ ⲛ̄ⲕⲃ̄ⲧ.

supported by a dog-headed ape (B.M. 26355, 37190). The green-glazed steatite example B.M. 21895 is being embraced by the arms and legs of a dog-headed ape. The single glass koḥl-tube is well represented by B.M. 2589, which is in the form of a column with a lotus capital. Porcelain single tubes are often inscribed, *e.g.*, B.M. 27376, which is glazed green and has written upon it in black ink , "Beneficent god, Lord of the Two Lands, Lord of Crowns, Nebkheperurā (Tutānkhȧmen), giver of life for ever." Another example gives the prenomen of Tutānkhȧmen and the name of his wife Ānkhnesȧmen,  (B.M. 2573). Of the double tube there are several varieties. Sometimes they are uninscribed and are made of wood (B.M. 2598). An example in obsidian (B.M. 2599) has on it a figure of Bes in relief; an example in steatite has a flat back support on which are cut in outline figures of Osiris, Isis and Nephthys (B.M. 30052); and an example in wood (B.M. 37202) is inscribed with the prenomen of Ȧmenḥetep III and Queen Tî, . In ivory we have the beautiful example B.M. 22839. The two tubes are in the form of columns, between which is a triangular shaft, with a notched collar in which the koḥl needle is to rest when not in use. Each tube had a little rectangular cover which worked on a pivot, but one of these is wanting. The double tubes held, presumably, two kinds of eye-powder, one medicinal and one that was applied to the eyelids as an ornament. Koḥl-pots with three tubes are not common, and the example B.M. 2612 is of unusual interest. It is made of terra-cotta and is in the form of the triple crown with plumes, , and the front of each crown is decorated with a different linear design. The koḥl-stick, by which the powder was applied to the eyes, is made of wood, and its head is in the form of the hawk of Horus. This triple tube was probably made during the Ptolemaïc Period, when the triple crown was in common use. Of koḥl-pots with four tubes several examples are known, and the example in wood which was made for the scribe Ȧāḥmes (B.M. 27196) gives us an idea of when the contents of the tubes were used. On the back of the plinth is an inscription which contains a prayer that Ȧmen-Rā will give all kinds of good and pure things to the Ka of Ȧāḥmes, Scribe and Clerk of the Works, 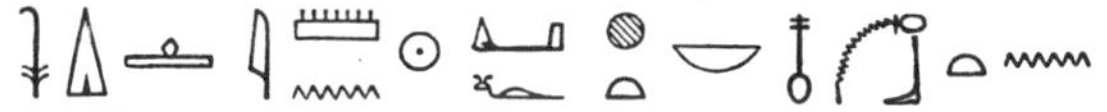
. On the outside of the tube to the

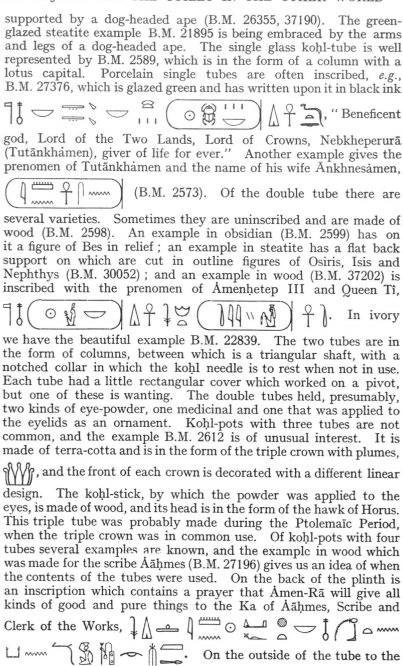

left of the plinth is inscribed: , "Fine eye-paint [for use] every day." On the front of the next tube we have , the meaning of which is that the contents of that tube are to be used from the first month of the season of AKHAT to the fourth month of the same (*i.e.*, from the end of July to the end of November). On the front of the next tube we have , which directs that the contents of that tube were to be used from the end of November to the end of March, *i.e.*, during the whole of the season of PERT. The inscription on the fourth tube reads: 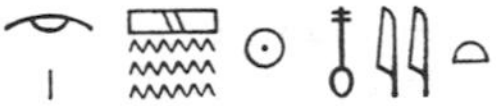 , and directs that the contents of that tube were to be used from the end of March to the end of July, *i.e.*, during the whole of the season of SHEMU. Thus we see that the Egyptians found it necessary to use different medicines for the eyes at different seasons of the year, in addition to the medicine that had to be used daily. In the space between the four tubes there is a fifth hole or tube, which probably contained the common medium for applying the medicines to the eyes. The koḥl-stick stood in a small metal holder fastened between the two front tubes. In the example B.M. 2606, which is made of green-glazed steatite, the koḥl-stick was provided with a small hollow between the four tubes. On the outside of the first tube is the name of the scribe Mes, , and on the outsides of the other three are  "life,"  "happiness," and  "stability," respectively. In a third example (B.M. 18176) the wooden block containing the four tubes is sunk into a pretty little four-legged stand, inlaid with ivory. Another interesting example of the four-tubed koḥl-pot was formerly in the collection of Lord Grenfell. It was made for the scribe Åtef, , and was inscribed with a prayer to Åmen-Rā for a "beautiful (or good) life, favour and love for the Ka of the follower of his lord, the scribe Åtef,"
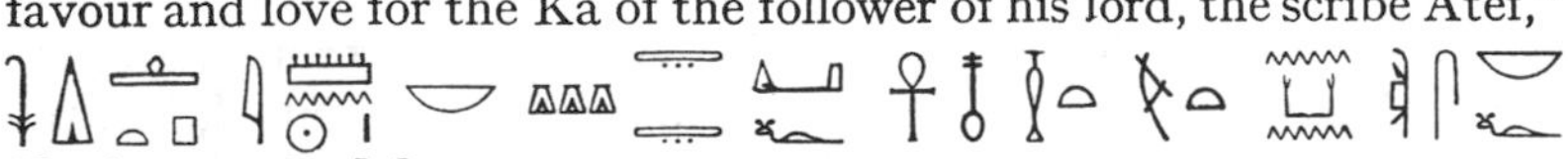
. One tube contained powder for daily use, , the second powder that "opened the eyes," 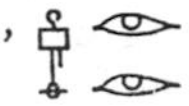, the third powder that cleansed (?) the eyes, , and the fourth powder that removed rheum from them, .

The example in blue-glazed porcelain (B.M. 2611) suggests that at one period five different kinds of eye-paint were in use, for it has five distinct tubes. Some Egyptians carried their koḥl-tubes about with them, as we see from B.M. 12539, which is a leather bag, about 7 inches long, containing parts of three koḥl-tubes and a stick.

The koḥl for daily use was often kept in a small vase or pot made of alabaster, haematite and other hard stones, porcelain, glass, etc. Examples of the rarer kinds of pots are the greenish-blue opaque glass pot and cover decorated with gold rims (B.M. 24391); the haematite pot, with a thick band of gold round the top (B.M. 32151); the purplish-grey marble pot with handles in the form of heads of uraei (B.M. 12753); the pot, made of the same material as the preceding, with handles in the form of dog-headed apes (B.M. 20759); and the almost spherical pot, which has its neck and cover encircled with gold (B.M. 32150). Koḥl-pots in alabaster are very common, and every large collection of Egyptian antiquities contains several examples; the greater number of them appear not to have been used, and must be regarded as votive offerings.

The **koḥl-stick** with which the stibium was applied to the eyelids was made of wood, bronze, haematite, glass, etc., and the end that was dipped in the powder was pear-shaped and larger than the other. This thick end was moistened with water or scented unguent and then drawn along the eyelid, under the eye , or over the eye . When not in use the stick rested either in its special cavity, or in a metal ring attached to the pot or tube.

The **mirror** (in Egyptian  *ānkh-t*, or 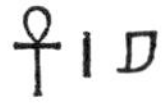,  *un-ḥer*,  *maa-ḥer*,  *ir*[1] (or *il*), Copt. ⲉⲓⲁⲗ) was usually made of sheets of copper or very highly refined bronze. Some mirrors are perfectly circular, others are oval, others pear-shaped, and others have shapes irregular and abnormal. The pear-shaped bronze mirror B.M. 37176, 10 inches long, has a wooden handle in the form of the god Bes. The massive oval bronze mirror B.M. 2732 is mounted in a wooden handle, which resembles the standard , on which the gods are represented as standing. At the top of the handle, close to the bronze, a figure of the Utchat, , is cut on each side; these were inlaid, but the inlay has fallen out. The massive oval mirror B.M. 38150 is fixed by a peg into a solid bronze handle, which has the shape of a lotus column decorated on each side with the head of Hathor in relief, with the face of a woman and the ears of a cow. Another heavy oval mirror is pegged into a solid bronze lotus-shaped handle, and has a

[1] Var. , Spiegelberg, *Kopt. Handwörterbuch*, p. 24.

figure of the hawk of Horus, , on each side of it (B.M. 32583). A smaller mirror of similar shape, and with a similar handle, rests between two pairs of uraei, one pair on each side (B.M. 20756). In B.M. 20773 the handle is made in the shape of a woman with outspread arms and hands touching the sides of the calix of a lotus. Of special interest is B.M. 29428. The handle of this weighty example terminates in a head of Hathor on each side. The goddess's face is that of a woman with ears showing prominently against the heavy folds of her wig. From the top of her head springs a pair of horns, , and between them rests the disk of copper that forms the mirror proper, . The handle of the little mirror B.M. 2733 is made of wood, and is in the form of one of the steering-poles of Horus, . One of the oldest examples of the bronze mirror is B.M. 2736. It is set in a handle of green-glazed steatite, in the form of a lotus column, and is inscribed with the name of Menthu-em-ḥat, the son of Ḥeqȧb, . It probably dates from the XIIth dynasty. As an example of the inscribed mirror of a late period may be mentioned B.M. 51067. The mirror itself, which is oval and somewhat pear-shaped, is set between a pair of horns, which project from a double-headed hawk of Horus; the handle is of ivory. On the front of the mirror is cut in outline a representation of the shrine of Mut, the lady of heaven. Above the cornice of the shrine is a row of uraei wearing disks, , and beneath it are three winged disks, ; on each side of the door is a lotus column with uraei, and on each side of the shrine is an Utchat, . The goddess, wearing the crowns of the South and the North, is seated within the shrine, and before her stands the deceased lady, , Tuṭȧ (?), the daughter of Ḥer and Ȧāḥerṭas, offering a mirror (?). Below this shrine are two lines of hieroglyphs, the general meaning of which seems to be, "The follower of Mut, the Eye of Rā, the Lord of heaven, the Mistress of the gods, made[1] this mirror. May she grant life, strength, health, a long life, and a great old age with happiness, to Tuṭȧ," etc. The text reads: **1.** 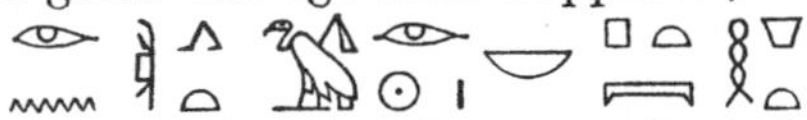  **2.**  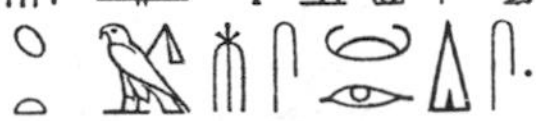. **Mirror cases** were made of bronze and wood, and the names of their owners were sometimes inscribed on the bronze cases, which were usually circular. Sometimes the

[1] *I.e.*, she dedicated this mirror to the shrine of Mut as a votive offering.

wooden cases were made in the form of the solar disk resting on the horizon, or in the form of ♀ (B.M. 51063). Examples of **Coptic mirrors** and mirror cases will be found in the Coptic Room in the British Museum (51062–51065).

Tweezers.—Pairs of tweezers, for removing hairs from the face or other parts of the body, were usually made of bronze, the ends being, at times, in the form of human hands; they vary in length from 2 to 6 inches. Impurities or irregularities in the surface of the skin were removed by a **strigil,** or scraper, but ancient Egyptian examples of the instrument are rare. The iron strigil (B.M. 18181) probably belongs to the Roman Period. **Pumice stone** also was used for removing excrescences from the skin, and for polishing it. Many examples of **hair-pins,** and many varieties, are known. They are usually made of wood, bone, ivory, bronze, etc., and vary in length and thickness. The heads are often made of gold, or are decorated with bands of metal, and frequently are in the forms of birds or animals. The greater number of the hair-pins now known belong to a comparatively modern period. The **tooth-comb** was generally made of wood or bone or ivory, and many examples are known. The back of a comb with a single row of teeth is often carved with serrated edges, and its sides are decorated with ornamental devices of various kinds. Double combs, *i.e.*, combs with two rows of teeth, have the teeth of one row thicker and longer than the other. The large combs that were used for purely decorative purposes and those that were votive offerings terminate in figures of animals in hollow-work. In 1920 a great number of wooden **Coptic combs** were brought to light in Egypt, and a selection of them is in the British Museum. They vary in length from 7 to 9 inches, and most of them are 3 inches wide; at one end the teeth are fine, and at the other they are coarse. The surface between the rows of teeth in some is ornamented with rows of annules, some large and some small, and in others with designs in fretwork. In one example we have figures of three men and two birds (B.M. 54475), in a second the figure of a horse (?) eating leaves from a tree (B.M. 54478), and in a third the figure of a bird which is probably intended to be a peacock (B.M. 54477). In the last two examples the figures are cut in a sort of sunk panel.

The **toilet-box.** It is pretty certain that in all periods toilet-boxes were placed in the tombs of both men and women of high rank or of official position; these, of course, varied in size according to their contents. The larger boxes were made of wood, either plain or inlaid with designs in porcelain, ebony, ivory, etc., and the smaller ones, which in shape much resemble the modern jewel-case, were made of ivory, ebony and acacia wood. What were the exact contents of such boxes is not known, unfortunately, and the only toilet-box that has come down to us with its contents complete is that of , Tutu, the wife of Ani the scribe (B.M. 24708).

When found the cover was in its place on the box, and was fastened to it by a papyrus cord which was twisted round the knob in front of the box and sealed with a clay seal. The natives who found the box broke the seal and opened the box because they believed that there were gold objects, necklaces, etc., inside it, but they were disappointed. The inside of the box is divided into four compartments by wooden divisions, which are ornamented with red wood and ebony, and these contain (1) a terra-cotta vase, filled with an unguent, or some substance that took the place of soap, for rubbing over the body; (2) two alabaster vases containing unguents, which were probably scented; (3) a large piece of pumice stone to be used in rubbing the skin smooth; (4) a double stibium tube bound with leather and provided with two koḥl-sticks, or "needles," as the Arabs call them, one made of wood and the other of ivory—one tube probably contained a powder that was to be smeared under and over the eyes during the Inundation, when the glare is well-nigh insupportable, and the other a medicinal (mineral ?) powder to be used during the season when the air is filled with sand and dust; (5) an ivory comb, with carved back; (6) a bronze "shell" on which the unguents were to be rubbed down and mixed; (7) a pair of gazelle-skin sandals, with turned-up toes—the outer skin has been stained pink; (8) three little cushions made of papyrus stained red. These last may have been used for resting the elbows upon.

It has usually been assumed that the Egyptians had no soap, but in the later period of their history they must have had some good equivalent, for the word , *antchir*, is found in demotic papyri, and the same word occurs in Coptic under the form ⲁⲛϫⲓⲣ, which is generally translated[1] by "soap."

Scented oils, pastes, pomades; **lip-salve and ḥinnâ.** The Egyptians of all classes were greatly addicted to the use of oils and unguents, because the anointing of the body with almost any kind of grease or fat promotes a refreshing feeling of well-being, especially in hot climates. Oil or unguent for anointing the body was almost as necessary for the Egyptians as food, and the myriads of unguent flasks, bottles, jars and vases that have been found in the tombs show they believed that the dead were as much in need of unguents as the living. The so-called "cone" which we see on the heads of the guests, male and female, at a feast, was a contrivance for holding scented unguent, which, being slowly melted by the heat of the head, ran down over the hair and dripped on to the shoulders, and so gradually made its way over all the upper part of the body. Many tribes in the Eastern Sûdân at the present day place small receptacles containing grease on their heads, and let it melt and run over their shoulders and bodies, in much the same way as the Egyptians did.

[1] See Spiegelberg, *Kopt. Handwörterbuch*, p. 7.

In 1887, at Wâdi Halfah, when large tins of soft soap were served out for the use of one of the " Black " battalions, the soldiers went down to the river to bathe and, having well lathered themselves, each put a lump of soap on the top of his head, and then sat down in the shallow water in the sun and sang songs. What the unguents were perfumed with is not known, but it is probable that any and every strong-smelling vegetable oil or essence known to the Egyptians was used by them. And no doubt many of the oils and essences possessed medicinal and curative properties; each of the **Seven Holy Oils** mentioned on p. 239 must have been a specific for some ailment. Whether the Egyptians knew how to prepare **scents,** using spirit for the purpose, is not known, but it is probable that they did not. Evidence supplied by mummies and by drawings proves that the Egyptian lady reddened her lips with some substance, but no sample of **red lip-salve** seems to have been found in the tombs. It is equally certain that she stained the nails of her fingers and toes with *ḥinnâ* حِنَّا (*Lawsonia inermis*), but how the tincture was made is not known. The unguent that was placed in jars in the tombs has now the appearance of a brown thick viscous substance, and specimens of it which are still liquid can be seen in the alabaster vases B.M. 4501, 21981 and 4500; in the last-mentioned it has percolated through the pot, which is now stuck tightly to the mount. A specimen of the substance, but quite dry and hard, is preserved in B.M. 4654, and the alabaster bottle B.M. 36384 also contains an unguent.

BEADS AND NECKLACES, RINGS, BRACELETS, ETC., FOR USE IN THE OTHER WORLD

THE enormous numbers of beads of almost every kind found in the tombs of all periods prove that they were highly prized as ornaments by the Egyptians. They occur in many shapes—round, oval, rectangular, both square and oblong, celt-shaped, tube-shaped, etc.—and they were made of diorite, jasper, mother-of-emerald, lapis-lazuli, crystal, amethyst, sardonyx, onyx, carnelian, agate of various kinds, sard, garnet, haematite, porcelain, glass, gold, silver, and even of clay and straw. Strung as necklaces they were worn by the living and the dead. And when figures of the gods and sacred animals, and amulets, and pendants of certain shapes, which were made of certain materials, were interspersed among them, such collections, or necklaces, were supposed to bring protection and well-being to their wearers. Every stone was believed to possess a certain magical power or influence which it never failed to make operative when it was addressed in the proper manner, or when it was cut into a certain form, or had divine words of power cut upon it. In primitive times, before men found out how to perforate them, beads were pressed in rows into bands or collars of mud laid upon the breast, and from this arrangement the necklace developed. Under the Ancient and Middle Kingdoms beads were generally made of crystal, carnelian, amethyst and agate of various kinds, but the arts of the lapidary and jeweller culminated under the XIIth dynasty. The necklaces and bead-work ornaments in general of this period remain unsurpassed in fineness of work, beauty of design, and good taste. An examination of the plates in de Morgan's *Fouilles à Dahchour*, Vienna, 1903, and Vernier's *Catalogue*, Cairo, 1908, will afford abundant proof of this statement. Under the XVIIIth dynasty the pendants and other additions to the beads were made of gold, and in some cases (B.M. 14693) all the beads and the attachments by which they were fastened round the neck were made of gold. Another example of a necklace of gold beads is B.M. 3075; the centre pendant is in the form of a heart. Necklaces made of carnelian beads with gold pendants were popular at this period. In one example (B.M. 3081) the pendants are in the form of crocodiles and leaves, the centre pendant being inlaid with lapis-lazuli. In another (B.M. 14694) the carnelian beads are cut into facets and the pendants are in the form of 𓄤, meaning "good luck"; and in a third (B.M. 30355) the gold pendants are in the forms of a lotus and a hawk (the central one). In another necklace the beads are made of chalcedony and lapis-lazuli; each is in the form of a celt and has a flat band of gold round the thickest part (B.M. 24772). In B.M. 3077 gold shells are ranged at intervals among the beads, and the gold pendants are in the form of the lock of hair—which is symbolic of youth—and fish. From the centre pendant, a lotus flower inlaid with green and red stones, hangs a sub-pendant in gold 𓁨, *ḥeḥ*, signifying a "hundred thousand years." In many necklaces the pendant 𓄤, *nefer*, is very common, but it is often mixed with beads of a much later period (B.M. 18172); this is due to modern stringing. In some of the best necklaces both beads and pendants are made of the same material. In B.M. 3097 the beads are made of dark carnelian and the pendants of light carnelian, the latter having the forms of the foot and leg 𓂾, the hand 𓂧, the face 𓁷, the *utchat* 𓂀, the bee (or hornet) 𓆤, the fish 𓆛, and the *nefer* 𓄤. In the Graeco-Roman Period necklaces made of glass beads with gilded insides were very popular, and of these B.M. 35119 is a good example. In the same period the ends of long oval beads were often set in little caps of gold, and a central bar with a pendant and gold bosses set with stones hanging from it is often seen (B.M. 24772). Necklaces made of porcelain beads glazed in various colours were very common in all periods, but to give anything like an adequate description of them a volume would be necessary. In the late Roman Period glass and gold were the materials chiefly used for beads.

Rings were made of gold, silver, bronze, carnelian, agate of various kinds, green and blue-glazed porcelain, etc. Interesting examples[1] in **gold** are: Massive gold ring with bezel in the form of a cylinder of blue glass set in a gold mount (B.M. 2922). Gold ring with the signs  repeated several times on the outside in gold wire after the manner of the modern West African "Zodiac" rings; the  is inlaid with lapis-lazuli (B.M. 54533). Massive gold ring inscribed with the prenomen of Åmenḥetep IV,  (B.M. 37644). Gold ring with blue glass scarab in a gold frame set as a bezel; the inscription reads: "Maātkarā (Ḥatshepsut), flesh and bone of Åmen-Rā" 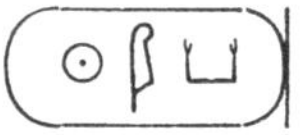  (B.M. 2933). Thick hollow gold split ring with the cartouche  in wire-work in a rectangular cavity (B.M. 54459). Gold ring with rectangular bezel with a human-headed hawk inlaid (B.M. 20871). Gold ring with rectangular bezel in lapis-lazuli inscribed with the figure of a man-headed lion, wearing the crown  and trampling upon a prostrate foe. On the obverse and reverse are the names and titles of Thothmes III, 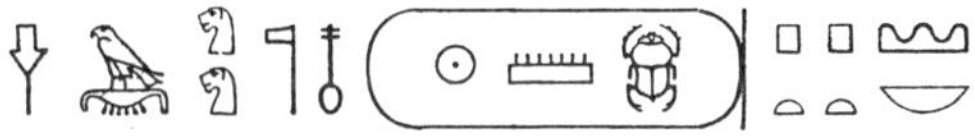 (B.M. 4349). Gold ring with rectangular bezel on which are cut figures of two gods adoring the cartouche of Åmenḥetep II 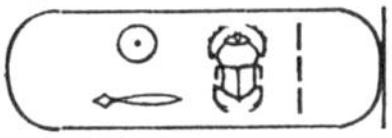, and between them the sign  (B.M. 54549). Massive gold ring inscribed with the name of the "son of Rā, Ptolemy, living for ever, beloved of Ptaḥ,"  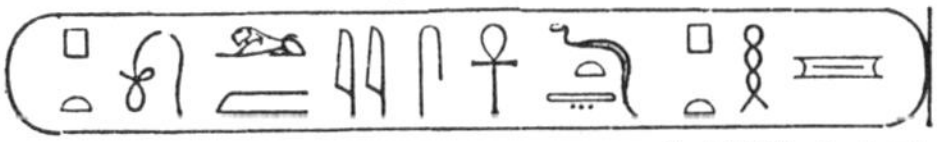 (B.M. 36468). Gold ring with stamp inscribed 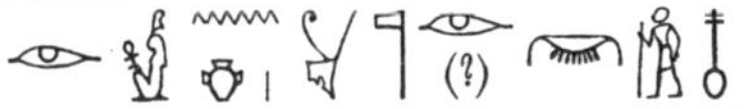 (B.M. 51088). Gold ring of the Ptolemaïc Period with figures of Isis (?), Osiris (?) and Sarapis (B.M. 2965). In **silver** may be noted the ring with large, circular bezel stamp of a priest and libationer with two

[1] See Section III, Signet-rings and stamps, in Hall, *Catalogue of Egyptian Scarabs*, p. 273 ff.

cartouches, Shashanq and Psemthek, 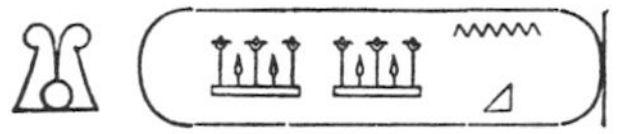
 (B.M. 24777). Examples in **sard** and **carnelian** are: A large ring inscribed  (B.M. 17772); a ring with a figure of Isis cut on the bezel (B.M. 29036); a small ring with  cut on the bezel (B.M. 54604); others inscribed with the figure of a fish (B.M. 5460), and with the title "Mut lady of heaven and the Two Lands," . The bezel of the **chalcedony** ring (B.M. 54605) is inscribed with a flower. Under the XVIIIth dynasty a large number of pretty blue and green **glazed porcelain** rings were produced, and those with hollow-work bezels are specially interesting. Sometimes the figure represented is Thoueris (B.M. 54556), sometimes Osiris with figures of Isis and Nephthys in a boat (B.M. 54594), but usually the subject chosen is floral in character (B.M. 3071). There are many varieties of porcelain rings with solid bezels, and on these we have floral devices (B.M. 54575), or a raised ornament (B.M. 54576), or the *utchat*  (B.M. 54574), or stamped inscriptions (B.M. 24179) relating to the cult of Åmen-Rā, or to the Disk  (B.M. 27386). Many rings, in addition to the common decoration of lotus buds, have on them the figure of a cat with several kittens (B.M. 17842, 54645), or an ichneumon (B.M. 21931), or a hawk (B.M. 24762), or an aegis of Bast (B.M. 3064, 3063, 29032), or of a goddess wearing the double crown  (B.M. 54644). Among the glazed porcelain rings are several examples that have attached to them an elongated stamp-seal, which when the ring was worn must have covered the upper parts of three or four fingers. One of these, a fine example in a rich blue-coloured glaze, was evidently worn on New Year's Day, for the inscription reads, "May every year begin (or open) happily,"  (read  (?))  (B.M. 36459). Another class records the names and titles of "Åmen-Rā, Governor of the Company of the gods, great god, lord of heaven, giver of life and happiness,"  (B.M. 29220). And yet another class records the name and titles of the goddess "Mut, the lady of heaven, Mistress of the gods, Lady of Asher," , var.  (B.M. 36458, 28467). The ring in hard **green stone** (B.M. 54340) has a bezel in the form of a cartouche inscribed with the following

signs : ; it is the work of the Saïte or of a later period.

The ancient Egyptians, like their modern successors, and Africans generally, wore **armlets, bracelets** and **anklets** made of gold or silver, sometimes inlaid with turquoise, garnets, carnelians and other coloured stones, and lapis-lazuli and the paste made from it, and ivory. Some of the bracelets made under the XVIIIth dynasty were very heavy, *e.g.*, those of Queen Ḥatshepsut, each of which weighed more than half a pound avoirdupois. Men as well as women wore beautiful bracelets, as we see from the monuments. A handsome product of the goldsmith's art is the pair of gold bracelets, inlaid with lapis-lazuli and lapis-lazuli paste (B.M. 14594, 14595). The centres are decorated with figures of Harpokrates sitting on a lotus flower between two uraei wearing disks. Inside is cut an inscription in hieroglyphs stating that these bracelets were made for the "princess Patareshnes, the daughter of the chief of all the bowmen Nemareth, whose mother was the daughter of the great chief of the Libyan desert," 
. Nemareth was the descendant in the fifth generation of Buiu-uaua, a Libyan prince, and the father of Shashanq (Shishak of I Kings xiv, 25), King of Egypt about B.C. 966.

THE CYLINDRICAL SEAL OR SEAL-CYLINDER

THE cylindrical seal was in use in Egypt before dynastic civilization began, and there is good reason for believing that it is of indigenous origin ; but when it first made its appearance cannot be said. It was thought at one time that the Egyptians borrowed it from the Babylonians, but the discovery of cylindrical seals made of wood and ivory in pre-dynastic graves makes this view untenable. The Egyptians and the Babylonians may have borrowed it from the same source, but there is no evidence to show that either nation borrowed it from the other. The oldest seal-cylinders are made of wood or ivory, but steatite was soon found to be more durable, and the greater number of those that were made after the VIth dynasty were of glazed or unglazed steatite. A few are known of copper, and a few are made of a blue paste composition. They vary in length from half or three-quarters of an inch to nearly four inches in length, and in their diameter, which is usually uniform throughout, from a quarter of an inch to nearly one inch. They are usually pierced like bugle-beads, for they were carried on a string or wire, and when unpierced a small hollow was made at each of the flat ends to catch the ends of a clip which served as a holder. When the seal-cylinder was first used by pre-dynastic sealers it was rolled over moist mud by the flat of the hand, but their successors found that they obtained a better and more even impression if they inserted a metal rod in the cylinder and held that tightly at each end when they rolled the cylinder over the mud placed to receive the impression. Some of the seal-cylinders of the VIth dynasty resemble sections of copper tubes, and it is possible that they had cores that fitted into some kind of frame. A picture of the seal-cylinder being rolled over the mud is preserved in the hieroglyph 𓍶, *shen*, the circle representing the end of the cylinder, and the line the mud. The Egyptians of the Old Kingdom seem to have thought that this sign represented a signet ring, as have some modern Egyptologists, and later it was regarded and treated as the bezel of a ring.[1] The seal-cylinder was sometimes kept in a box, but it was more commonly attached by the rod inside it, or by its frame, when it had one, to a string or necklace and worn by the owner. The seal with its string or necklace is represented by the hieroglyphs 𓋨 and 𓋩; the phonetic value of the former is *khetem*, 𓐍𓏏𓅓𓋨, and the word means both the seal and the impression, but the value of the latter seems to be unknown. The finest and handsomest seal-cylinders were made under the VIth, XIIth and XIIIth dynasties. The use of them decayed under the New Kingdom, but it was revived under the XXVIth dynasty. Reproductions of all the important seal-cylinders will be found in Hall, *Catalogue*, p. 261 ff., and Newberry, *Scarabs*, pll. II–VIII.

THE SCARAB

SCARAB (also Scarabe and Scarabee)[2] is the name given by Egyptologists to the model of a certain beetle, of which myriads of examples of various sizes and of various materials have been found in mummies, and coffins, and tombs, and in the ruins of temples and other buildings in Egypt. They have also been found in other countries, the inhabitants of which from a remote period had trading and other relations with the Egyptians. The name is derived from the Latin *scarabaeus* or *scarabeus*, a beetle of the genus *Lamellicorn*; the Greek name of this beetle is *κάραβος*, and the forms *σκαράβειος* and *σκάραβος* are said to be of doubtful authenticity. The particular beetle of which the Egyptians made so many myriads of models belongs to the family called by naturalists *Scarabaeidae* (Coprophagi, or dung-feeders) of which *Scarabaeus sacer* is the type. What views the primitive

[1] Hall, *Catalogue of Egyptian Scarabs*, p. x.

[2] For plurals compare "Battening like scarabs in the dung of peace," Massinger, *Duke of Milan*, III, 1; and "You are scarabees that batten in her dung," Beaumont and Fletcher, *Elder Brother*, IV, 1; and "I scorn all earthly dung-bred scarabies," Drayton, *Idea*, XXXI.

Egyptians held concerning this beetle we do not know, and judging by the descriptions of it which we find in the works of certain Greek writers, the Greeks cannot have had any real knowledge of this beetle's ways and habits. Aelian, who calls it *κάνθαρος*, says that it had no female, *ἄθηλυ ζῶόν ἐστι* (*De Nat. Animal.* X, XV, ed. Didot, p. 172), and Porphyry says that all the beetles were males *κάνθαρος γὰρ πᾶς ἄῤῥην* (*De Abstinentia*, IV, 9, ed. Didot, p. 74). According to Horapollo, the Egyptians, when they wished to write the expression "only-begotten," drew the picture of a beetle *Μονογενές . . . . . . κάνθαρον ζωγραφοῦσι*, for the creature is self-produced, being unconceived by a female, *μονογενὲς μὲν ὅτι αὐτογενές ἐστι τὸ ζῶον, ὑπὸ θηλείας μὴ κυοφορούμενον*. The beetle also represented "generation," "father," "world" and "man," and Horapollo goes on to say that when the male is desirous of procreating, he takes some ox dung and shapes it into a spherical form like the world. He next rolls it from east to west, looking himself towards the east. Having dug a hole, he buries the ball in it for twenty-eight days; on the twenty-ninth day he opens the ball and throws it into the water, and from it the scarabaei come forth. The idea of *generation* arises from its supposed acts. The scarabaeus denotes a *father* because it is engendered by a father only, and *world* because in its generation it is fashioned in the form of the world, and *man* because there is no female race among them. There are three species of scarabaei. The first has the form of a cat and has thirty toes, which correspond to the thirty days of the month. The second has two horns and is in the form of a bull, and was associated with the moon, and the third has only one horn, and, like the ibis, was associated with Mercury.[1] The scarabaeus, as an "only begotten" creature, seems to have attracted the notice of Christian writers, and one of them likens it to Christ as the Only begotten of His Father.[2]

On the whole, modern naturalists, until comparatively lately, seem to have been inclined to accept many of the statements about the *scarabaeus sacer* made by ancient writers. Latreille, in the Appendix to Cailliaud's *Voyage à Méroé*, Paris, 1823–27, identified the *scarabaeus sacer* with the species that he named *Ateuchus Aegyptiorum* or *ἡλιοκάνθαρος*.[3] Mr. J. O. Westwood

[1] *Horapollinis Niloi Hieroglyphica*, ed. Leemans, Amsterdam, 1835, p. 11.

[2] See the exposition of St. Luke's Gospel by Ambrose, Bishop of Milan (*Opera*, Paris edition, 1686, tom. I, col. 1528, No. 113), "Vermis in cruce: scarabeus in cruce: et bonus vermis qui haesit in ligno bonus scarabeus qui clamavit è ligno. Quid clamavit? *Domine, ne statuas illis hoc peccatum.* Clamavit latroni: *Hodie mecum eris in paradiso.* Clamavit quasi scarabeus: *Deus, Deus meus, quare me dereliquisti?* Et bonus scarabeus qui lutum corporis nostri ante informe ac pigrum virtutum versabat vestigiis: bonus scarabeus, qui de stercore erigit pauperem."

[3] Tom. II, p. 311. "Cet insecte est d'un vert parfois éclatant; son corselet est nuancé d'une teinte cuivreuse à reflet métallique." Compare Aelian, *De Nat. Animal.* IV, 49; Aristotle, *Hist. Animal.* IV, 7; Pliny, *Nat. Hist.*, XI, 20 ff. and XXIX, 6.

said[1] that the species were usually black, but that among them were some that were adorned with the richest metallic colours. Having described the peculiarity of the structure and situation of the hind legs, he points out that this peculiar formation was most serviceable to its possessors in rolling the balls of excrementitious matter in which they enclose their eggs; whence these insects were named by the first naturalists "Pilulariae." These balls are at first irregular and soft, but by degrees, and during the process of rolling along, become rounded and harder; they are propelled by means of the hind legs. These balls are from $1\frac{1}{2}$ inches to 2 inches in diameter, and in rolling them along the beetles stand almost upon their heads, with them turned from the balls. These manœuvres have for their object the burying of the balls in holes, which the insects have previously dug for their reception; and it is upon the dung thus deposited that the larvae, when hatched, feed. It does not appear that these beetles have the instinct to distinguish their own balls, as they will seize upon those belonging to another, in case they have lost their own; and, indeed, it is said that several of them occasionally assist in rolling the same ball. The males as well as the females assist in rolling the pellets. They fly during the hottest part of the day.

With this evidence from an expert naturalist before him the Egyptologist, in dealing with the scarab, was obliged to say that the dung-feeding beetle which it represented collected a ball of excrementitious matter, and that, having rolled it into a pit which it had prepared to receive it, the beetle laid eggs in the ball, which the larvae fed upon when they were hatched out. And this the Egyptologist continued to say until J. Henri Fabre published his monograph on the "Sacred Beetle,"[2] when he learned that the habits and customs of the *scarabaeus sacer* had been wrongly described both by ancient and modern writers. A brief summary of M. Fabre's account of this beetle may well be given here. The sacred beetle, the biggest and most famous of our dung-beetles, is black, and his long legs move with awkward jerks, as though driven onward by some internal mechanism. When he comes to feed, his little red antennae unfurl their fan—a sign of anxious greed. The edge of his broad flat head, or shield, is notched with six angular teeth arranged in a semi-circle. This is used as a digging-tool, and also as a rake for scraping together the matter which suits him best when he is selecting the material for the maternal ball. When he is collecting for his own needs he is less careful, and he scrapes stuff together with his notched shield more or less at random. The forelegs play a great part in the work. They are flat, bow-shaped, supplied with powerful

[1] *An Introduction to the Modern Classification of Insects*, London, 1839, Vol. I, p. 204 ff.

[2] See *Souvenirs Entomologiques*, Vols. I and V, and the English translation by A. Teixeira de Mattos, *The Sacred Beetle and others*, London, 1919.

nervures and armed on the outside with five strong teeth. When he wishes to remove an obstacle or clear a space he flings his toothed legs to right and left with an energetic sweep. The legs then collect the stuff which is raked together by the shield and push it under the insect's belly, between the four hinder legs. These legs are long and slender, especially the last pair, slightly bowed and finished with a very sharp claw. They serve as compasses, and are capable of embracing a globular body in their curved branches and of verifying and correcting its shape. Their function is, in fact, to fashion the ball. They heap the material under the body of the insect and impart to it their own curve and give it a preliminary outline. The roughly shaped mass is turned from time to time, and turns round under the beetle's belly until it is rolled into a perfect ball. The ball varies in size from that of a walnut or small apple to that of a man's fist.

Having made the ball of food which he intends to eat, he clasps it with his two long hind legs, the terminal claws of which, planted in the mass, serve as pivots. He obtains a purchase with the middle pair of legs, and using his toothed fore-arms as levers, he moves backwards, with his body bent, his head down and his hind-quarters in the air. The rear legs move backwards and forwards continually and, the claws shifting to change the axis of rotation, they keep the load balanced and push it along by alternate thrusts to right and to left. Sometimes the beetle will try to roll his food-ball up a slope, and in doing so will make a false step, when the ball will slip out of his grip and roll down to the place whence it started. But nothing daunts the beetle, and he will try and try, ten and even twenty times, to roll it up the slope before he abandons the slope and chooses another path. Sometimes two beetles will be seen pushing the same ball ; but this does not represent a partnership between the sexes, nor community of family, nor community of labour, but an attempt at robbery. The beetle that comes to help intends to steal his neighbour's ball. M. Fabre tells us that he has seen one beetle come and knock down the beetle which was rolling along his ball and seize the ball by leaping upon it. The owner of the ball could do nothing but turn his ball round and round, which caused the robber to fall off on the ground. The robber and the robbed then began to fight each other, and on several occasions the latter was defeated and his ball carried off by the robber in triumph. Sometimes a second robber came and robbed the robber. Fabre's conclusion is that theft is a general practice among the scarabaei. The hole which the beetle prepares for his food-ball is a shallow cavity about the size of the fist : it is dug in soft earth, usually in sand, and communicates with the outside by a short passage just wide enough to admit the ball. When the ball is in the cavity, the beetle goes in and stops up the entrance and then devotes all his energies to devouring the ball. When the ball is eaten, the beetle comes out from the cavity and looks about him until he can find another patch of dung from which to make another ball. The beetle feasts in this way from May to June, and then buries himself in the cool earth until the first autumn rains come, when he leaves his refuge and comes out and makes preparations for reproducing his species. M. Fabre has proved once and for all that the balls which beetles roll along are balls of food, and that they never contain the eggs of the beetle. How was it, then, that ancient writers were led to believe that they did? This question is answered by M. Fabre, who tells us that the female beetle fashions the food for the larva into a pear-shaped mass, and that in this the insect deposits her *egg*, not eggs. This "pear" is found in a space underground which the beetle excavates, and it is reached by means of a shaft about 4 inches deep and a horizontal gallery. This crypt acts as an incubator, for the rays of the sun strike the ground only a few inches above the "pear." In shape and size this "pear" resembles the little Midsummer's Day pears which delight the children of Southern Europe; the largest is about $1\frac{3}{4}$ inches in length and the smallest $1\frac{3}{8}$ inches. The surface is even and is glazed with a thin layer of red earth, and the outer layer soon becomes as hard as wood. The mother beetle does not place her egg in the large round part of the pear, where we should expect to find it, but in the narrow part of the pear, in the neck, right at the end. In this neck is a niche with polished and shiny walls, and this is the hatching chamber of the egg. The egg is 10 millimetres long and 5 millimetres wide in the widest part. It is white in colour, and only the rear end, which adheres to the top of the niche, touches the walls of the niche. The larva, or grub, appears from 6 to 12 days after the egg is laid, and it begins to feed upon the floor of its niche, *i.e.*, the "pear" at the bottom of the neck. It has a fine white skin with pale slate-coloured reflections proceeding from the digestive organs. It is bent into the form of a broken arch or hook, and at the bend the third, fourth, and fifth segments of the abdomen swell into an enormous hump, and the creature looks as if it were carrying a knapsack. Its head is small, slightly convex, bright red in colour and studded with a few pale bristles. In due course the grub sheds its skin and becomes a nymph, and M. Fabre says: "There are very few inhabitants of the insect world that can compare for sober beauty with the delicate creature which, with wing-cases recumbent in front of it like a wide pleated scarf and forelegs folded under its head like those of the adult beetle when counterfeiting death, calls to mind a mummy kept by its linen bandages in the approved hieratic attitude. Semi-transparent and honey-yellow, it looks as though it were carved from a block of amber. Imagine it hardened in this state, mineralized, rendered incorruptible; it would make a splendid topaz gem."[1]

[1] *Sacred Beetle*, translation, p. 98.

An examination of the nymph showed M. Fabre that the fore-limbs lack the tarsi which the remaining legs possess, and that the toothed limb ends bluntly, without any trace of a terminal appendage. In the others the tarsus is easily distinguishable. The sacred beetle is born maimed; his mutilation dates from the beginning. Further observation showed M. Fabre that the nymph occupied 28 days, as Horapollo said, in assuming his final shape as a beetle. Horapollo said that the creature obtained its release from its hard shell through the action of its mother, who threw it into water, whereby the shell became dissolved; but in this he was wrong. It is true that the shell was drenched with water, but the water that drenched it was the rain, which soaked through the earth into the hollow in which the "pear" was hidden, and dissolved it. The young and perfect beetle made its way along the horizontal passage, and up through the shaft to the surface of the ground, where it at once began to collect food for itself and to fashion a dung ball after the manner of its forbears. With the above facts before us we can see now why Horapollo and other ancient writers made so many mistakes in describing the *scarabaeus sacer*. They mistook the ball of food for the "pear," of which they knew nothing, and therefore could not deduce the existence of the mother-beetle. Horapollo somehow knew that the beetle deposited only one egg in the ball (*i.e.*, "pear") and therefore called that egg the "only-begotten"; but as a matter of fact the scarabaeus deposits a single egg in each of several balls (*i.e.*, "pears") in a season. The existence of the larva was wholly unknown to Horapollo, Aelian and Porphyry, and none of them realized that when two or more beetles were seen rolling along the food-ball each beetle was watching his opportunity to steal the ball for himself.

The reverence shown by the Egyptians to the scarab as an emblem of incarnation of the Creator of the universe was not shared by neighbouring nations. Thus Physiologus, after describing how scarabs roll up their eggs in balls of dung, and how they push them backwards and how the young, having come to life, feed upon the dung in which they are hatched, goes on to say that we may learn of a certainty that scarabs are heretics who are polluted by the filth of heresies; that these balls, which are formed of filth and nastiness, and which they roll backwards and not forwards, are the evil thoughts of their heresies, which are formed of wickedness and sin, and which they roll against mankind, until they become children of error, and by being participators in the filth of their heresies they become other beings like unto them (Land, *Anecdota Syriaca*, tom. IV, p. 77, cap. 56). And the ignorance of the habits and manner of life of the scarabaeus, which is displayed by certain Syrian writers of repute upon natural history, is astounding; here is a specimen: "The scarabaeus receives conception through its mouth, and when it comes to bring forth, it gives birth to its young through its ears. It has the habit of stealing, and wherever it finds small things, and things of gold and silver, it takes them and hides them in its hole. And if it finds pulse in the house, it takes it and mixes it up with other things, and [it mixes] chick-peas with beans, and beans with lentils, and rice with millet and wheat, and everything which it finds it mixes together in the place where it hides itself. Thus it does the work of the cooks who mix such things together to make to stumble those who buy pulse at the shops. And if any man takes notice of it and smites it, it takes vengeance upon his clothing. If having collected pieces of money and taken them forth to the race-course to play with them, they be taken away from it, it wanders about, and turns hither and thither, and if it finds them not it straightway kills itself."[1]

And Bar-Hebraeus, commenting in ܐܘܨܪ ܐܪ̈ܙܐ, on Psalm lxxviii, 45, and referring to the words ܫܕܪ ܒܗܘܢ ܚܠܛܐ ܘܐܟܠ ܐܢܘܢ (Heb. יְשַׁלַּח בָּהֶם עָרֹב, he sent among them the gad-fly, LXX, Ἐξαπέστειλεν εἰς αὐτοὺς κυνόμυιαν), "he sent against them crowds of insects and they devoured them," includes the scarab (ܚܶܢܦܽܘܣܳܐ, plur. ܚܶܢ̈ܦܽܘܣܶܐ; ܚܶܢܦܽܘܣܬܳܐ, plur. ܚܶܢܦܽܘ̈ܣܝܳܬܳܐ) among noxious creatures like dog-flies, scorpions, ants, etc., ܚܠܛܐ . ܗ̄ . ܕܒܘ̈ܒܐ ܘܩܡ̈ܠܐ ܘܥܩܪ̈ܒܐ ܘܚܡ̈ܪܥܐ ܘܫܘܫܡ̈ܢܝܬܐ ܘܩܘܠܡܐ ܘܙܘܪ̈ܙܘܪܝܬܐ ܘܪ̈ܚܫܐ ܘܫ̈ܪܨܐ . ܘܗܢܐ ܕܚ̈ܡܝܢ ܠܐܠ̈ܦܐ ❖

The texts afford abundant proof that from the earliest times the *scarabaeus sacer* was associated in the minds of the Egyptians with the Sun-god, by whatever name he was called. It is clear that this association had a religious significance, and the name of the insect in Egyptian, KHEPRERÀ, , or , suggests what that significance was. The root of this name is *kheper*, , or 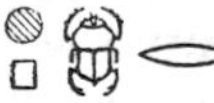, or , meaning "to come into existence, to become, to take birth, to spring into being," and the god of which this beetle was an incarnation was called KHEPERÀ, , or , *i.e.*, "the god who came into being" [of and by himself]. This god is often depicted with a beetle on his head, or with a beetle, with or without outstretched wings, instead of a head. He came into being in primeval time when nothing but himself existed, and was self-produced and self-existent. By an effort of his will he created the sun, and heaven, and earth, and the gods, and men, and every animate creature, and everything inanimate. The

[1] Ahrens, *Das Buch der Naturgegenstände*, text, p. 41, translation, p. 62.

creation of this universe began, it was thought, when the ball of the sun appeared above the horizon, and in one way or another all life sprang from and depended upon that ball. Primitive man in the Nile Valley marvelled at the sight of the solar ball mounting up in the sky and then rolling across it to the place where it rolled down below the horizon and disappeared. By some reasoning, to us inexplicable, he associated it with the balls of dung which he saw the dung-beetles rolling along the ground in the spring and summer. He knew that young beetles appeared on the earth, and he assumed that they came out of the balls which the full-grown beetles made, for he knew nothing about the grub and the larva of the beetle. Life came out of the ball of the beetle, and life came out of the solar ball in the sky, which was also rolled along, therefore the roller of the solar ball must be a beetle, and from first to last a god who had the form of a beetle was declared by the Egyptians to be the creator of the universe. Kheperȧ was a very ancient form of the Sun-god, whose cult at an early period extended from one end of the Nile Valley to the other, and it may well be the oldest of all the solar cults in Egypt. The use of the scarab as a religious amulet does not begin with the introduction of the worship of Rā into Egypt, as some have supposed, for the cult of the scarab is indigenous, being probably of Sûdânî origin, whilst that of the man-god Rā was brought from the East, and did not become predominant in Egypt until the IVth or Vth dynasty.

The Egyptian wore the scarab amulet at first with the idea of equipping himself with the power of the great Sky-beetle, and as a protection against evil, visible and invisible; and it gave him life and health and strength daily. Soon, however, he connected in his mind the daily course of the sun with the period of his own life, and the sunset with the death of his mortal body. But the sun derived power from the great Sky-beetle to rise again daily, and the Egyptian argued, "Why should not the beetle which I wear, if placed on my dead body, give it power to rise again?" In this way the ideas of **resurrection** and **renewed life** became associated with the beetle, and men began to attach scarabs to the dead, and to bury them in the tombs, with the view of preventing the death of the deceased from being eternal.

The Egyptians selected two kinds of beetles as originals for the copies or models of them which they made, namely, the *scarabaeus sacer* and the *Goliathus Atlas*. The former is the type of the thousands of scarabs that exist in our great collections, and the latter is that which is copied in the heart scarabs. A specimen of the *Goliathus* caught by Dr. Junker was 10 cm. (4 in.) long and 4½ cm. (nearly 2 in.) wide. The wing-cases were brown, the thorax was black with white bands, and the sides of the abdomen and the legs were of a dark olive-green colour.[1] Sir Harry Johnston says that the *Ceratorrhina* goliath was much used in native medicine and

[1] *Travels in Africa*, Vol. II, p. 450.

sorcery.[1] It appears early in August in large numbers, and disappears when the rains cease ; it makes a ball as large as an apple.[2]

Livingstone, knowing nothing about the " pears " in which the mother-beetle deposits her eggs, says that whilst the larvae are growing they feed upon the balls of dung.[3] He thought that the natives connected this beetle with ancestor worship because he saw a large beetle hung up before a figure in a spirit-house of a burnt and deserted village.[4] The modern Sûdânî women eat beetles and say that they make them prolific, and the ancient Egyptians used the shell of a beetle mixed with oil, etc., as a medicine to assist a woman in labour to give birth to her child.[5]

Scarab amulets were made of almost every kind of material—wood, hard stone, steatite, ivory, glazed faïence or Egyptian porcelain, iron, etc. ; they vary in length from half an inch to about two inches. The earliest scarabs made were used as amulets and nothing else, but when the Egyptians began to make them is not known. Many scarabs of undoubtedly ancient workmanship have been found bearing on their bases the name of Khufu (Kheops), Khāfrā (Khephren), Menkaurā (Mycerinus), kings of the IVth dynasty and builders of pyramids, and of Unȧs, a king of the Vth or VIth dynasty. This fact has led many to assume that these scarabs were made under the Old Kingdom, but all the known facts go to show that all the scarabs bearing these names were made at a much later period. There is nothing surprising in this. The names of the great kings were regarded and used as " words of power " under the New Kingdom, and probably earlier, and the scarab-makers of the Saïte Period might well consider the names of the builders of the three great pyramids at Gîzah as eminently suitable for talismanic inscriptions. But why the name of Unȧs should have been considered to be a " word of power " is hard to understand.[6] A few scarabs are known which seem

[1] George Grenfell, in Bentley, *Pioneering on the Congo*, Vol. II, p. 944 ; and see Vol. I, p. 405.

[2] Baker, *Albert Nyanza*, p. 240.

[3] *Travels*, p. 24.

[4] *Last Journals*, Vol. II, p. 27.

[5] *Ebers Papyrus*, Plate XCIV.

[6] Hall suggests (*Catalogue*, p. xii) that , Unȧs, was confused with 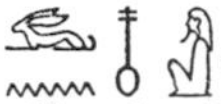, Un-nefer, a title of Osiris, but another explanation may be offered. When the Rev. J. Loftie was making his collection of scarabs (afterwards purchased by the British Museum) he lived for some winters at Gîzah and Cairo, with the view of collecting scarabs of every king of Egypt, including Menȧ or Menes ! He employed several natives, both at Gîzah and Ṣaḳḳârah, and to assist them he wrote the cartouches of the kings he wanted on slips of paper, which they carried about with them whilst searching. The scarabs which he failed to find one winter were often forthcoming the next, and as the names of the kings of the Old Kingdom are comparatively simple and easy to copy, it is probable that the expert forgers of " anticas " who then lived in Gîzah village helped him out of his difficulties. For years scarabs bearing the names of the three great pyramid builders were very common at Gîzah.

to belong to the period immediately following the VIth dynasty, but the use of the scarab **did not become general** until the **XIth and XIIth** dynasties. At this period names of kings were inscribed on the bases of scarabs as "words of power," and the scarab was supposed to carry in itself both the life-giving power of Kheperȧ and the power of the king whose name was cut upon it. The best scarabs of this period are beautifully made, and the actual form of the *scarabaeus sacer* is copied with marvellous accuracy. Officials and men of high rank had their names cut upon their scarabs, which were then **used as seals,** and such scarabs were buried with their owners, presumably with the idea that in addition to their value to them as amulets, they would be useful to them in transacting business in the Other World. When the scarab was used merely as a seal by its owner it was carried on a string or wire attached to a ring of some kind, and not worn. Frequently it was mounted as the bezel in a ring of gold or silver-gold, which was worn on the finger like an ordinary ring. Under the XIIth dynasty a great development in the arts of the jeweller and the lapidary took place, at any rate in the north of Egypt, and the ornaments of the period, with their minute and accurate inlays of carnelian, mother-of-emerald, lapis-lazuli, etc., are very remarkable examples of skill, good taste and judgment; they were never equalled by the best handicraftsman of the XVIIIth dynasty at Thebes. Side by side with the scarab, the use of **scaraboids** and **cowroids** became common; both varieties were inscribed on their bases, the backs of the former being usually quite plain. But neither scaraboids nor cowroids were regarded as amulets, and they possessed no religious significance.

Under the XIIth dynasty the principal home of the jeweller and lapidary was Memphis, where no doubt the beautiful jewellery found at Dahshûr was made. A fine example of the gold-mounted scarabs of the period is exhibited in the British Museum (30711). As Memphis declined and Thebes grew in importance, the scarabs made by Theban craftsmen began to improve in workmanship, and they soon equalled those of Memphis in accuracy of form and beauty. The scarabs which the officials used as seals bore their owners' names and titles on their bases, but a great many scarabs were made in glazed faïence, and as the material of which they were made rendered them too fragile to be used as seals, it is clear that they were used as religious amulets only. The scarabs bearing the name of Thothmes III are remarkable for their number and treatment, and they proclaim the great importance that was attached to his name as a *ḥeka* ("word of power"). Under the XIXth dynasty a space was left between the body of the scarab and the base, which was attached to it by the legs only. The scarab-makers of the XXVIth dynasty copied the style and treatment of the scarabs of the XIIth, XVIIIth and XIXth dynasties, and their work is unrivalled for its delicacy and "cleanness." Their workmanship in hard stone, mother-of-emerald, green and black basalt, yellow jasper, etc., is remarkably fine ; it is perhaps best exhibited in the scaraboids, cowroids, and plaques of the period. With the close of the XXVIth dynasty the use of the scarab as a seal declined, but a form of it was in demand for funerary purposes, that is to say, for attachment to the outer wrappings of mummies and glazed-faïence beadwork. The commonest form of it was made of glazed faïence, light green in colour, and beneath the body there is a small ring by which it could be sewn to beadwork. Scarabs of this class are uninscribed and have no bases. How long this class of scarab continued to be made cannot be said. The actual evidence supplied by scarabs shows that they were used from the VIth to the XXVIth dynasties, *i.e.*, for a period of between two and three thousand years. If we accept the traditions recorded in the Papyrus of Nu we must lengthen this period and add to it the years of the reigns of the kings from Semti to Pepi II.

The Rubrics in the Book of the Dead show that the Egyptians considered it necessary to write certain *ḥekau*, or " words of power," on certain kinds of stone, and this fact suggests that they attributed magical properties to such stones. Thus the heart-scarab was to be made of a certain kind of green stone (basalt ?), the Tet of carnelian, the Uatch amulet of mother-of-emerald, and so on. The stone most used for scarabs was steatite, which is usually light grey in colour, but as the *scarabaeus sacer* in Egypt was usually black, the craftsman covered the natural colour of the stone with some kind of dark wash or pigment, and later with green or blue glaze. Under the XIIth dynasty many scarabs were made of amethyst, but as the cutting of inscriptions upon them was very difficult work, their bases were covered with thin plates of gold, on which the names of the owners were cut or stamped. The jewellery of the XIIth dynasty found by de Morgan at Dahshûr includes scarabs made of carnelian, sard, obsidian, haematite, various kinds of agate, lapis-lazuli, and the choice of material by the scarab-maker at that time seems to have been untrammelled by any religious regulations. Gold was used but rarely.[1] Scarabs in ivory are not common, though Wilkinson found a batch of about thirty in an XVIIIth dynasty tomb at Western Thebes. Although models of the *scarabaeus sacer* existed in millions in Egypt, few large-size models, or **colossal scarabs,** such as would be deposited in temples, are now known. The largest example is in the British Museum (Central Saloon 965). It is made of green granite, is uninscribed, and is 5 feet long and 3 feet high, and weighs about 43 cwt. It was brought from Constantinople by Lord Elgin, but where it stood originally is not known. Another colossal scarab, which was made

[1] The two hollow-work gold scarabs, with the prenomen of Thothmes III stamped upon their bases, in the British Museum (29159, 29160) are modern imitations ; they were made by a goldsmith at Luxor.

in the reign of Åmenḥetep III, was found by Legrain at Karnak; it stands on a high pedestal at the west end of the sacred lake of the temple of Åmen.

In the space here available it is wholly impossible even to summarize the various inscriptions and designs that are found cut on the bases of scarabs, but a brief general description of their more important characteristics may be attempted. **Royal Scarabs** of the Old and Middle Kingdoms. The principal feature of these is, of course, the royal name. Sometimes one of the king's names only is given, *e.g.*, 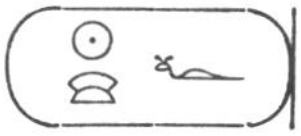 Khāfrā (Khephren), 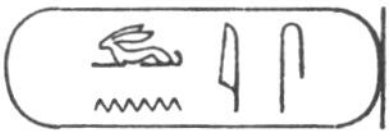 Unȧs, 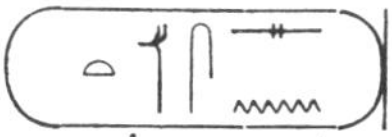 Usertsen (Senusert), and sometimes the royal name in a cartouche stands with spirals or linear ornaments on each side of it. The cartouche may be preceded by , "beneficent god," or plumes  or 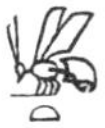, King of the North, or , King of the South and North, or , Horus, or , son of Rā, and on some the uraei of sovereignty, each wearing a crown, appear. In the field are often seen the signs , "life," , "stability," , "gold," , the two Utchats, , the plant of the North (lotus ?); occasionally the frame of the Horus name  takes the place of the cartouche. The **scarabs of officials** give the names and titles of their owners, often at some length, and many of them are ornamented with spirals or linear designs, a form of decoration which is said to be of foreign origin. The titles are often important as throwing light upon the history of Egypt, religion and administration. Many scarabs have nothing but linear designs[1] inscribed on their bases, and the most intricate of these contain *motifs* which have survived in Coptic and Arabic decorative patterns found on walls and house furniture and in manuscripts. The scarabs of the **Hyksos Period** are very important, both historically and artistically. They form a very large class, and from most of them, through the operation of the salts in the Delta mud, the glaze and colour have entirely disappeared. Outwardly they are not as attractive in appearance as the scarabs of Upper Egypt. The Hyksos scarabs have preserved for us the names of many Hyksos kings of which no other memorials exist, and from them the list of the kings of the XVth and XVIth dynasties has received many authentic additions. The names of

[1] These are best studied from the photographic reproductions given in Hall's *Catalogue*, when originals are not available.

princelings and kinglets are sometimes given between parallel lines thus, 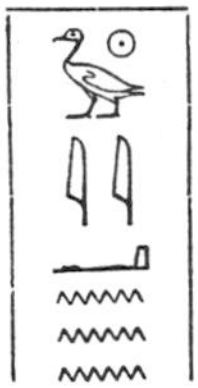 " son of Rā Iāmu," but more often without lines. The names of really great Hyksos kings are given in cartouches, *e.g.*, , Khian, , Āa-userrā, 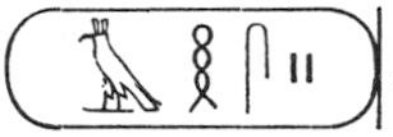, Neḥsi, the " Black." The scarab-makers of the Hyksos Period copied the decorations of the scarabs of the XIIth dynasty, and thus we find on their scarabs the Utchats, the winged disk , the lotus cluster, the spirals, the hawk wearing the crown of the North , etc. The entire bases of many of their scarabs are filled with hunting scenes, figures of lions, crocodiles, small animals of the desert, the ass (?), the Hathor-headed standard, the gryphon, the winged uraeus, the fish and , and the whole base of one is occupied by a beetle, .[1] An interesting feature on some of them is the human figure shown full face, one being surrounded with annules.[2] It seems fairly certain that the Hyksos associated no religious beliefs with the scarab, and that they only used it as a seal or wore it for an ornament.

The designs on the scarabs of the XVIIIth and XIXth dynasties have much in common with those on the scarabs of the XIIth dynasty, and the scarab-makers of the period initiated little. Scarabs bearing the prenomen or nomen of Thothmes III and his titles were made in myriads, and the popularity of his name as a " word of power " was very great. His cartouche was decorated with uraei and other emblems of his might and power, and borders of spirals and annules often appear. Under the XVIIIth dynasty, especially in the reigns of Thothmes III and Åmenḥetep III, a custom grew up of inscribing texts commemorative of great or important events on the bases of scarabs, which were made of steatite and were as large as the Goliath beetles of the Sûdân. Thus Thothmes III caused a scarab to be made and inscribed with a record of his erection of the obelisks at Karnak;[3] Åmenḥetep III commemorated his marriages and hunting exploits by issues of scarabs; and Åmenḥetep IV had specially large scarabs made in honour of Åten—the solar disk.[4] The inscriptions fill the bases of these scarabs, and they are without ornament.

A very large number of scarabs bear no names on their bases, which are entirely filled with representations of flowers, designs that

[1] Newberry, *Scarabs*, plate XXV, No. 27.
[2] *Ibid.*, plate XXV, Nos. 4, 5, 6.
[3] Preserved in Berlin; see the official *Verzeichniss*, p. 417, No. 3530.
[4] See the unique specimen B.M. 51084; Hall, *Catalogue*, p. 303, and Budge, *Tutānkhāmen*, p. 104.

are floral in character, spirals, annules, hieroglyphs of amulets, figures of men, animals, trees, fish, reptiles, etc. Many more have figures of gods and goddesses cut on their bases, *e.g.*, Åmen, Åmen-Rā, Mentu, the War-god of Thebes, Rā, Rā Ḥer-Åakhuti, Khnem, Horus, Ptaḥ, Thoth, Shu, Maāt, Isis, Hathor, Bes and other Sûdânî gods, and Set (comparatively rarely). Another large class is inscribed with short legends containing statements of devotion to or trust in some deity, and good wishes, *e.g.*, Khensu in Thebes is protector, ; Åmen is protector, ; Åmen is the guide to the seat of the heart (*i.e.*, happiness), ; the favour of Åmen of Thebes is protection, ; unite thyself to peace, ; Ptaḥ of the Beautiful Face is the lord of the rewards of men, ; Ho, everyone, Ptaḥ of Memphis is the giver of strength,  ; Åmen-Rā is the guide of happiness, ; Åmen, be not afraid, 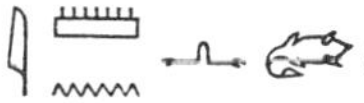; Ptaḥ is the guide to happiness, ; I am true of heart, ; the peace of Åmen-Rā, the self-produced, , etc. Some scarabs were given as gifts with good wishes, thus: thousands of good things [to you], ; every good thing [be thine], ; a happy year! ; a happy new year from the high priest of Åmen, Peṭa-Åst, ; may thy house be abundant in food with strength to thee,  . There is no doubt that scarabs, both inscribed and uninscribed, were given to the gods as votive offerings, and that those on which the power of Åmen and Ptaḥ is proclaimed were carried back to their homes by the faithful who had visited the great sanctuaries of these gods at Thebes and Memphis. Scarabs were never used as **currency**, as was once thought.

Scarabs inscribed with certain kings' names were made and worn for centuries after the death of the kings whose names they bear. Thus the scarabs found at **Naucratis** cannot be older than the VIIth century B.C., but many of them bear the prenomens of Thothmes III, Seti I and Rameses II. Material, workmanship and design all point to the XXVIth dynasty as the period when they were made. Some appear to be the work of Egyptian craftsmen, but the greater number must have been made by the Greek settlers at Naucratis. Scarabs have also been found at Ialysos and Kamiros in Rhodes, and at Tharros in Sardinia. At Ialysos porcelain and steatite scarabs are rare, and this is true also of Kamiros as far as concerns the tombs. But a well on the Acropolis was found to contain many specimens mixed with objects that appear to be of about the same date as the early tombs. In those tombs at Kamiros, where black and red-ware vases were obtained, as at the spot called Fikellura, no scarabs were found. The scarabs seem to be distinctly associated with pottery made under Oriental or more particularly Assyrian influence. The scarabs disappeared when the purely Greek style of black and red vase decoration came into force. The scarabs of Tharros are indisputably of Phoenician origin, but whether they were produced by the Phoenicians proper or by their later descendants, the Carthaginians, whose influence began to prevail in Sardinia as early as about B.C. 500, is somewhat uncertain.[1]

The **Phoenicians** borrowed the use of the scarab from Egypt, and as their country was overrun by Shalmaneser III, King of Assyria B.C. 859–824, and by many of his successors, it is only natural that the scarab inscribed with devices to suit the Assyrian market should find its way to Nineveh and Babylon, the Phoenician adopting in return the cone, the form of gem commonly used by the Assyrians for seals. A good example of the Phoenicio-Assyrian scarab is No. 1029, exhibited in the long Table Case in the Second Semitic Room of the British Museum. It is made of green jasper, and measures 1¾ inches in length. On the base is inscribed a man who stands adoring a seated deity; above is a seven-rayed star, and between them is ☥ *ānkh*, "life." Beneath is inscribed in Phoenician characters, להודו ספרא, "Belonging to Hôdô the Scribe." For other examples see the specimens exhibited in the same case. As an example of the adoption of the chalcedony cone by the Phoenicians, see No. 1022, on which are cut the figure of a man standing before a fire altar and the name Palzîr-shemesh in Phoenician characters. The scarab in relief,[2] with outstretched wings inlaid with blue, red and gold, carved upon an ivory panel found at Abu Ḥabbah, about five hours' ride to the south-west of Baghdad, together with a number of miscellaneous ivory objects, is a proof of the knowledge of the scarab in Mesopotamia. That the panel was not carved by an Egyptian workman is very evident.[3] Scaraboids in

[1] Murray, A. S., "Introduction" to A. H. Smith's *Catalogue of Engraved Gems in the British Museum*, London, 1888, p. 13.

[2] See Table-Case I (Babylonian Room).

[3] The two rectangular weights (?) found at Nimrûd by Sir A. H. Layard (*Nineveh and Babylon*, London, 1867, p. 64) have each, on one face, the figure of a scarab inlaid in gold in outline; the work is excellent, and is a fine example of Phoenician handicraft. Exhibited in the Assyrian Room, Table Case C, Nos. 14 and 15.

agate and crystal, etc., are a small but very interesting class; at times the device is purely Egyptian, and the inscriptions in Phoenician letters are the only additions by the Phoenicians. B.M. Nos. 1024 and 1036 are tolerably good examples of them. The former is inscribed on the base with three hawks with outspread wings, and two of them have disks on their heads; these, of course, represent the hawk of Horus. The Phoenician inscription gives the name Eliâm. The latter is inscribed with a beetle in a square frame, and on the right and left is an uraeus ; each end of the perpendicular sides of the frame terminates in *ānkh*, and above and below it is a figure of Rā, or Horus, hawk-headed, holding a sceptre . The name, inscribed in Phoenician characters, is "Mersekem." In 1891, while carrying on excavations at Dêr, a place about three and a half hours to the south-west of Baghdad, I obtained a steatite scarab inscribed with an uraeus , *ānkh* , and an illegible sign, together with an oval green transparent Gnostic gem inscribed with the lion-headed serpent **XNOYBIC**. Both objects were probably brought from Lower Egypt.[1]

Dr. Birch describes in *Nineveh and Babylon* (London, 1853, pp. 281, 282) a series of eleven scarabs[2] which Sir Henry Layard dug up at 'Arâbân, a mound situated on the western bank of the Khâbûr, about two and a half days' journey north of Dêr on the Euphrates, and about 10 miles east of the 'Abd al-'Azîz hills. With one exception they are all made of steatite, glazed yellow or green or blue. Two of them are inscribed with the prenomen of Thothmes III; one bears the prenomen of Amenophis III, with the titles "beautiful god, lord of two lands, crowned in every land"; one is inscribed *men Kheperà àt Àmen*, "established of Kheperà, emanation of Àmen"; two are inscribed and , and belong to the same period; one is inscribed with a hawk-headed lion and a hawk; one bears the legend, "beautiful lord, lord of two lands," *i.e.*, the North and South; one is inscribed with a human-headed beetle, with outstretched wings, in the field are uraei and of beautiful workmanship; and one is inscribed with and an uraeus having on its head. The scarab in haematite is inscribed with the figure of a king seated on a throne, and a man standing before him in adoration; between them is .

[1] The numbers are G. 475 and 24314.

[2] Another scarab from 'Arâbân was presented to the British Museum by Mrs. Garratt in 1917. It was given by Layard to Miss de Salis, and on its base is cut a figure of Anubis or Set.

With the exception of this last scarab, it is pretty certain that all belong to the period of the XVIIIth dynasty, for they have all the appearance of such antiquity, and they possess all the delicacy of workmanship found upon scarabs of this time. The design on the haematite scarab appears to be a copy from an Egyptian scarab executed by a foreign workman, but it may be that the hardness of the material made the task of engraving so difficult that the character of the design was altered in consequence. The presence of these scarabs at 'Arâbân is not difficult to account for. Thothmes I, one of the early kings of the XVIIIth dynasty, carried his victorious arms into Mesopotamia, and set up a tablet to mark the boundary of the Egyptian territory at a place called Nî, on the Euphrates, and the authority of the Egyptians in that land was so great that when Thothmes III arrived there several years after he found the tablet still standing. The kings who immediately succeeded Thothmes III marched into this land, and that their followers should take up quarters on the fertile banks of the Khâbûr, and leave behind them scarabs and other relics, is not to be wondered at. The antiquities found at 'Arâbân are of a very miscellaneous character, and, among other things, include an Assyrian colossus inscribed "Palace of Meshezib-Marduk the king" (B.C. 700), and a Chinese glass bottle inscribed with a verse of the Chinese poet KEĬN-TAU, A.D. 827–831; it is possible that the scarabs described above may have been brought there at a period subsequent to the XVIIIth dynasty, but, in any case, they themselves belong to this period.

Etruscan scarabs. Gems engraved in the form of beetles or scarabs had their origin in Egypt. Thence the scarab found its way into Greece and Etruria, partly through the commerce of the Phoenicians, and partly under the influence of Greek residents in Egypt during the VIth century B.C., or nearly so. The Greeks cared little for the scarab, but the Etruscans admired them greatly, and their lapidaries made them in large numbers for their fellow-countrymen. The Etruscans owed the subjects which they engraved on their scarabs to the Greeks, and these are taken from the legends of Greek heroes, and very rarely from myths of the gods. The figures are represented in profile and constantly engaged in action; and the workmanship is laboriously minute. The beginning of scarab-engraving in Etruria was assigned by Murray to the end of the VIth century and the beginning of the Vth century B.C. The inscriptions are in Etruscan, but the Greek names inscribed on scarabs have been modified in the spelling to suit Etruscan habits, and not seldom they are wrongly applied. Inscriptions are more frequent in the later period of engraving than in the earlier. The elaborate gold mounts, and the absence of mountings specially adapted for sealing, suggest that the Etruscans did not generally use their scarabs as seals. Necklaces of scarabs have been found, and the well-known taste of the Etruscans for jewellery worn on the person suggests that they wore their scarabs mounted on bracelets, like the Greek scaraboids, or set as bezels in their finger rings. On the sources of the designs on Etruscan scarabs see Murray's "Introduction," pp. 22, 23, and for details of the scarabs from Ialysos, Kamiros, Tharros and Etruria see Mr. A. H. Smith's description in his *Catalogue of Engraved Gems*, London, 1888.

The **Gnostics** inscribed the scarab on the gems worn by them, and partly adopted the views concerning it held by the Egyptians. On an oval slab of green granite, in the British Museum, is inscribed a scarab encircled by a serpent having his tail in his mouth. The same design is found on another oval, but the beetle has a human head and arms; above the head are rays, and above that the legend ЄΙΛΑΜΨ; to the right is a star, to the left are a star and crescent, and beneath the hind legs three stars.

The first published classification of scarabs was made by the late Dr. Birch in his *Catalogue of the Collection of Egyptian Antiquities at Alnwick Castle* (printed by the Duke of Northumberland for private circulation, London, 1880), pp. 103–167, 236–242, in which he described 565 scarabs. The arrangement he followed was: (1) Names of gods and emblems; (2) historical inscriptions, names of kings and historical representations; (3) names of officers. Catalogues of public collections of scarabs have been published by myself[1] and by Newberry,[2] and catalogues of private collections by Loftie,[3] Petrie,[4] Frazer,[5] Ward[6] and myself.[7] And a miscellaneous collection of seal-cylinders has been published by Newberry,[8] with descriptions and a "scientific" introduction. But for a comprehensive treatment of scarabs as a whole the student must rely solely upon the *Catalogue of Egyptian Scarabs, etc., in the British Museum*, the first volume of which has been published by the Trustees of that Institution. This volume, the work of Dr. H. R. Hall, deals with Royal Scarabs (*i.e.*, scarabs with royal names on them). In it, after a description of the proper use of the scarab as a religious amulet, the scarab is treated as a **seal**, and its correct place assigned to it in the series of objects which the Egyptians used as seals, viz., **cylinder-seals, button-seals** (imported from abroad), **scaraboids, cowries** and **plaques**. The volume contains full descriptions of 2,891 scarabs, seal-cylinders, seal-amulets, etc., and is illustrated by 1,518 full-sized photographic reproductions and line drawings,

[1] Budge, *Catalogue of Egyptian Antiquities in the Fitzwilliam Museum, Cambridge*, pp. 87 ff.; and *Catalogue of the Egyptian Antiquities in the Harrow School Museum*, p. 14 ff.

[2] *Scarab-shaped Seals in the Cairo Museum*, London, 1907.

[3] *Essay on Scarabs*, London (no date).

[4] *Historical Scarabs*, London, 1889.

[5] *Catalogue of Scarabs*, London, 1900.

[6] *The Sacred Beetle*, London, 1902.

[7] *Hilton Price Collection*, p. 17 ff.; and *Lady Meux Collection*, p. 185 ff.

[8] *Scarabs*, London, 1908.

which are distributed throughout the book. The inscriptions are often reproduced, with translations, in hieroglyphic type. Here, for the first time, the student has a mass of material for study not found elsewhere, and the photographic reproductions are infinitely superior to and more accurate than the published hand-made copies of the designs and inscriptions on the bases of scarabs. In many instances the hand-copies give a totally false impression of the appearance of the scarab, and when, as in many cases, the copyist has not been able to read the inscription, his copies have destroyed the chance of anyone else doing so without consulting the originals.

THE SCARAB OF THE HEART

FROM first to last in the Dynastic Period the Egyptians attached great importance to the preservation of the heart of a man, and the help of the priest and the magician was invoked to prevent any evil befalling it. It was taken from the body and mummified, and placed in one of the so-called "Canopic" jars, and a scarab, usually made of a greenish or black stone, was inserted in the body to take its place; hence the name "heart scarab." On this scarab was cut, in hieroglyphs, a prayer which the deceased was to recite when his heart was weighed in the Hall of the Two Maāti goddesses in the presence of Osiris, and which was held to possess very special importance. The Theban Recension of the Book of the Dead contains several spells that were written with the view of giving a heart to the deceased and of effecting its preservation, viz., Chapter XXVI—the Chapter of giving a heart, , to the Osiris (*i.e.*, the deceased). Chapters XXVII and XXVIII—the Chapters of not letting the heart (or, breast ) of a man be carried away from him in the Khert-neter (the underworld). Chapter XXIX—the Chapter of not letting the heart, , of a man be plucked away from him in the Khert-neter (a variant of this Chapter in the Papyrus of Ani speaks of a heart of *seher-t* stone, ). Chapter XXX—the Chapter of not letting the heart, , of a man be driven away from him in the Khert-neter. Chapter XXVI is also known as "Chapter of the heart of lapis-lazuli" (); Chapter XXVII as "Chapter of the heart of *neshem-t* stone," ; Chapter XXIXB as "Chapter of the heart of *seher-t* stone," . Chapter XXX exists in two versions, A and B, and the latter is known as "Chapter of the heart of green basalt" (or, green jasper). Of all the Chapters the most important was Chapter XXXB, which is found in all the great Codices of the Book of the Dead that were written early in the XVIIIth dynasty. But the Chapter belongs to a much earlier period, for it was known and copied upon coffins that were made under the XIth and XIIth dynasties,[1] and the Rubrics of the LXIVth Chapter of the Book of the Dead show that ancient Egyptian traditions assigned it alternatively to the Ist and IVth dynasties. The Papyrus of Nu mentions both traditions. According to the first (see sheet 13) the Chapter was found inscribed on a foundation-stone in the shrine of Ḥennu during the reign of Ḥesepti, *i.e.*, Semti, , a king of the Ist dynasty. And according to the second "it was found in Khemenu (Hermopolis) upon a slab of alabaster (?) of the South, and was cut in real lapis-lazuli under the feet of the god [Thoth] in the time of His Majesty, the King of the South and North Menkaurā, by prince Ḥerṭaṭaf,"

Several papyri ascribe the "finding" of the Chapter to the reign of Menkaurā (Mycerinus), and make Hermopolis, the city of the Eight Gods of the Cycle of Thoth, its place of origin. The text of it, as given in the Papyrus of Nu, reads :—

My heart of my mother, twice; {my heart / or breast} of my being.

Stand not up against me at my testifying. Tender no evidence

against me at my testifying. Contradict me not

[1] See *Aeg. Zeitschrift*, 1866, p. 55 (Goodwin, "On a Text of the Book of the Dead belonging to the Old Kingdom").

before the Assessors. Make not thy failing (?) for me

in the presence of the Guardian of the Scales. Thou art my Ka dweller in

my body, Khnemu making strong my members. Come forth

thou to happiness, transport us thereto. Make not to stink

my name to the Divine Lords who make men and women.

Be there standing up. Make fair for us. Make fair hearing

joy [-tidings] at the weighing of words. Speak not lies

against me near God the Great. Assuredly be thou lifted up

living.

The Rubrics to this Chapter read:—A. Then make a beetle

of ȧnmeḥf stone fashioned [and] plated with gold, place [it] in-

side the heart of a man. [It will] perform for him the Opening of the Mouth.

Anoint with myrrh. B. Recite [this Chapter] over a beetle of

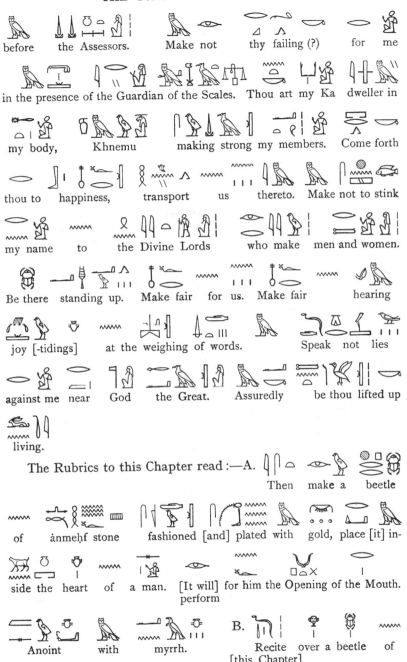

meḥf stone, encased in silver-gold, its suspending ring

[being of] silver. Place [it] on the åakhu (*i.e.*, deceased) at his neck.

Some copies of the Chapter prefix to it the words  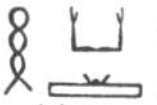, meaning that it is to be recited as a *ḥeka, i.e.*, as a magical utterance. The word occurs in Coptic under the form ϩⲓⲕ, which is by general consent translated "magic,"[1] but this meaning does not explain the word fully. The Pyramid Texts show that *ḥeka*, 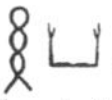, is in the first instance a property of the gods and something that is inherent in their nature. It was transmitted to the dead who succeeded in reaching the abode of the gods, but, as we see from Chapter XXIV of the Book of the Dead, the *ḥeka* which the gods had given to them could be stolen from them. Without *ḥeka* the dead could not live in heaven with the gods. Each day Rā used *ḥeka* to render impotent the schemes and wiles of the monster Āpep, and similarly the beatified dead used the *ḥeka* which Rā gave them to defeat the fiends and devils who attacked them. And as *ḥeka* rendered powerless every hostile being, so it destroyed the sicknesses and diseases that were caused by devils, and its power destroyed the effect of poisons. In the text in the pyramid of Unȧs the king is said to have eaten all the gods, and by so doing to have gained possession of their *ḥeka* and *sȧa, i.e.*, knowledge.[2] In a remarkable passage in the Teaching of Khati[3] the king says that God created *ḥeka* for the benefit of men : "He made for them *ḥeka* to put to flight [untoward] happenings and [evil] visions by night and by day."[4] Thus it is clear that men could obtain possession of *ḥeka*, and that by means of it they acquired supernatural powers. Now, in one of the Rubrics to Chapter XXXB, the Chapter is said to have been "found" in Khemenu, or Hermopolis, the city of Thoth, and this god was, of course, the author of this *ḥeka*. But Thoth was the heart or mind of Rā, therefore the source of this *ḥeka* is Rā himself. When the deceased recited it he would be in the Hall of Judgment, looking

[1] For examples see Spiegelberg, *Kopt. Handwörterbuch*, p. 229.

[2] , "Their *ḥeka* is in his belly"; , "He has swallowed the knowledge of every god" (lines 519, 520).

[3] Golénischeff, *Les Papyrus Hiératiques, Nos.* 1115*A et* 1116*B*, St. Petersburg, 1913, lines 136, 137.

[4] And see Gardiner's translation in the *Jnl. of Egyptian Archaeology*, Vol. I, Part I, p. 34.

on when his heart was placed in the Great Scales to be weighed, and his soul was standing by his side. Apparently he had no fear about the evidence that his soul might give, but the *ḥeka* that is put into his mouth proves that he was not sure that the testimony of his heart would be wholly in his favour. He was afraid that his heart might be hostile to him and gainsay him before the Assessors, and that it might in some way fail him when he who belonged to the Scales was dealing with it. " He of the Scales " in the earliest times was the Ape of Thoth, and later was Anubis, who acted under the direction of the Ape. As a kind of excuse for addressing his heart, the deceased says, " Thou art my KA (*i.e.*, my mental and spiritual nature), [and] Khnem, the strengthener and maintainer of my members " (*i.e.*, body). In other words, he throws the responsibility for all his mental and physical doings upon his heart, and then goes on to tell it not to make his name to stink before the Shenit, or nobles of the kingdom of Osiris, and not to tell lies about him, or to utter calumnies before the Great God, the Lord of Åmentt. Now, Chapter XXXB has hitherto been translated as a prayer, and the deceased has been thereby represented as a humble suppliant who is entreating his heart to be kind and gracious to him, as if there was a possibility that it might be cruel and hostile to him, and thereby destroy his chance of entering the kingdom of Osiris. But as Chapter XXXB is a *ḥeka* of divine origin, *i.e.*, a " word of power," it seems to me that the deceased is not making supplication to his heart, but commanding it concerning the things that it must and must not do, and that in translating it we should use the imperative instead of the precative.

Of the green basalt heart scarab there are many varieties, and each typical variety has its own peculiar characteristics. The form most approved of by the Egyptians consisted of a scarab of fine hard basalt or green crystalline stone, set in a gold frame, with a loop at the top by which it was suspended from a wire or chain hanging round the neck. The folds of the wings of the beetle were indicated either by lines of gold painted on the back, or by pieces of gold inlaid therein. One of the oldest specimens of the heart scarab is B.M. 7876. This scarab is made of very hard green stone, polished, and where the head of the beetle should be is a human face, which suggests that the individuality of the deceased was supposed to be merged in that of the Beetle-god. The scarab is set in a plinth of gold on the base of which are stamped extracts from Chapters XXXB and LXIV of the Book of the Dead. On the edge of the plinth is cut the cartouche of **Sebekemsaf** 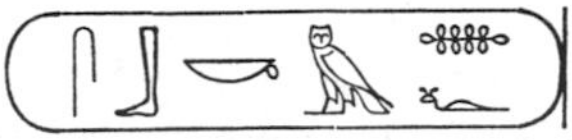, a king of the XIVth dynasty, about B.C. 2300. The text of Chapter XXXB has some interesting variants, but contains only a shortened form of the prayer which was to be recited as *ḥekau* 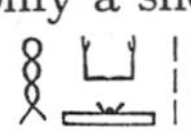, *i.e.*, a magical formula of divine origin. The deceased says: "My heart of my mother, my heart of my mother. My heart of [my] becomings (transformations ?). Let no one stand up against me bearing testimony against me, let no one thrust himself against me to repulse me among the Tchatchau (*i.e.*, the Two and Forty Assessors)." The text reads:—

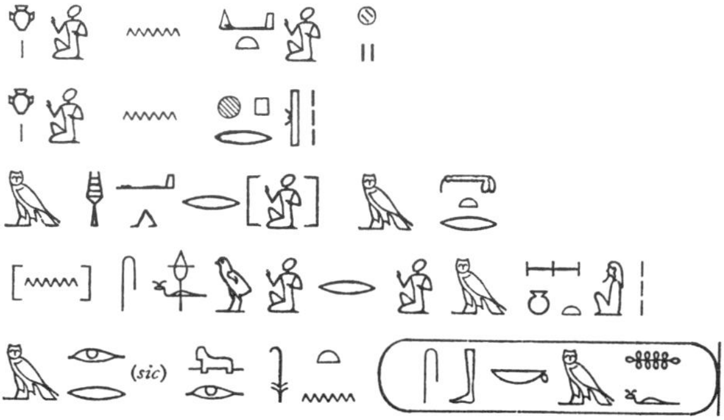

Sometimes the scarab is joined to a heart that is pierced for suspension, and the heart itself is inscribed with the signs , *i.e.*, "life," and the symbols of Osiris and Isis. On the wings of the scarab is cut the prayer, "Mayest thou go forth over the sky in threefold peace (or, offerings). Mayest thou sail hither and thither according to the dictates of thy heart. May the ferryman (or, ferry-boat) transport thee so that thou mayest look upon the lord of the gods. May he give thee thine eyes to see and thine ears [to hear]" 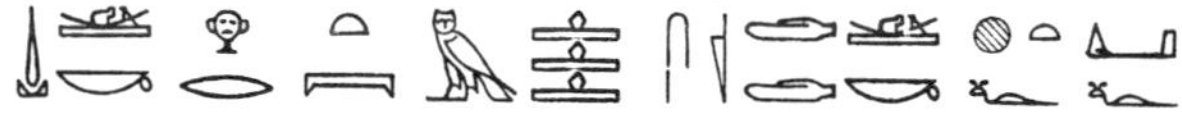  . This scarab was made for the lady Âui 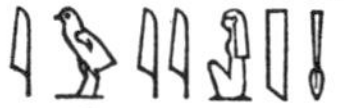 (B.M. 7925). The oldest heart scarabs contain nothing but the text of Chapter XXXB and the name of the deceased, *e.g.*, B.M. 7923, which was made for the steward . Others have the text with a space for the name left blank (B.M. 7877). This was a "trade" scarab purchased in the *bazâr* and not specially made for the deceased. Though the Rubric of Chapter XXXB orders that the heart scarab be set in a gold frame, very few examples in our museums have this setting; this is accounted for by the fact that the natives who found the scarabs stripped off the gold and melted it. A fine example in which the setting is preserved, and also the gold wire by which it was suspended from the neck, is B.M. 24401; it was made for the royal scribe Rensenb . Some heart scarabs have no inscription on the base, which is filled with figures of the gods. Thus on B.M. 7930 is a figure of Osiris Khenti Åmenti, "Lord of the Holy Land," , with Isis on one side and Nephthys on the other. A space of two lines is left blank for an inscription. Others have this scene cut on the base, and figures of Rā and Osiris, and the moon and Utchats on the back, (B.M. 15500, 15507, 35402). On B.M. 7931 we have a figure of the deceased standing with his hands raised in adoration before Osiris. On the back of some heart scarabs the Benu Bird of Heliopolis takes the place of Rā. Thus on B.M. 7883 are cut the Boat of Rā , a figure of Osiris with , and the Benu with ; and on B.M. 7878 we have the Benu Bird and the inscription "The Divine Heart of Rā," . This last-named scarab was made for Ani, , and on its base is a shortened form of Chapter XXXB. A few examples are known in which a human head takes the place of the head of the beetle, *e.g.*, B.M. 7999. The text of the Heart Chapter is usually cut across the base of the scarab in horizontal lines, but in one instance the lines are cut perpendicularly (B.M. 33868). On this scarab the names of the father and mother of the deceased are recorded, which is unusual. B.M. 7917 shows that the heart scarab was sometimes made of material other than green basalt. This example is in white limestone, and was made for a SEM priest, who was also the high-priest (Ur-kherp-ḥem) of Ptaḥ . It is surprising to find that the relatives of such a high ecclesiastical official should have disregarded the direction of the Rubric of Chapter XXXB. The use of the heart scarab continued down to the Graeco-Roman Period, as we see from B.M. 7966. This example is made of a hard crystalline green stone, with an uninscribed polished base. On the back of it are cut four figures; the first is probably the deceased, the second is Anubis, who carries a palm branch, the third carries a sistrum, and the fourth holds a long staff in the right hand and a cornucopia in the left. This model is a very accurate representation of the *scarabaeus sacer*.

Examples of the heart scarab in glazed porcelain with parts of Chapter XXXB written on the base are not very common, but several good specimens are known, viz., the cobalt-coloured scarabs B.M. 34289, 7868 and 7869. The last-named was made for a

libationer of Åmen called Rā-mes 
. The wooden heart scarab B.M. 24752 is of interest, for the inscription on the base is of an unusual character. It reads: "The king gives an offering. May Osiris give sepulchral meals, oxen, geese, and things of all kinds pure and good to the Osiris, the lady of the house, the singing woman of Åmen, Ruru-Uas." 

.

In some cases a heart of green stone or glazed porcelain was made to serve as the heart scarab. Thus the green-stone heart which was made for Pa-ser  (B.M. 29439) is set in a gold frame, with gold bands across the back to represent the folding of the beetle's wings, and on the base of it is cut the greater part of Chapter XXXB. Another good example is the hard crystalline green-stone heart B.M. 15619, which was made for the royal scribe, Nekht-Åmen, scribe of the divine offerings of all the gods, 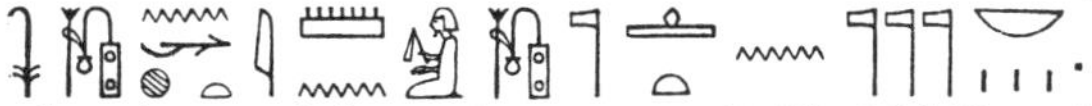. Good examples in glazed porcelain and stone are B.M. 29440 and 8805. The former is a heart coloured cobalt on one side and green on the other. The upper part is shaped to represent a woman's wig, and in the hollow, in red porcelain, is a woman's face. Below the face, in yellow colour, is the Benu Bird, *i.e.*, the soul of Rā. On the base, written in black on a green ground, are the opening words of Chapter XXXB. The latter (B.M. 8805) is made of stone, the upper part of which, when complete, was in the form of the head of a woman wearing a wig and necklace. Below the face was inlaid in blue and red porcelain the figure of a man-headed hawk, , *i.e.*, the BA, or soul of the deceased. A portion of this interesting object, unfortunately, is wanting.

In the late period the base of the heart scarab was flattened out, and ultimately became a pylon-shaped pectoral, as in B.M. 7858. On the base the shape of the beetle is outlined with  above it, and  (the horizon) below it. In the three lines of hieroglyphs enclosing the oval we have the name of the deceased, the scribe Piaai, , and the prayer, "May thy soul rest in Khert-neter, O scribe of the divine books. May thy soul appear as a living being." 

. The "lord of the two lands," , mentioned in the top line was probably one of the late Pharaohs. A still later example is B.M. 24767. Here on the one side, cut in relief, we have the beetle in a boat with Isis on one side and Nephthys on the other. Above is the Ṭeṭ, and below, in relief, are two jackals, probably intended for Anubis and Up-uatu. On the flat side, or base, is cut a part of Chapter XXXB, and the last line says that this "Chapter of the heart," , was written for Ḥer-Nekht, an overseer of the peasants (or, corvée ?) 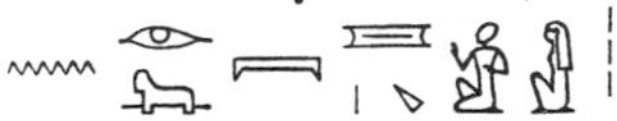 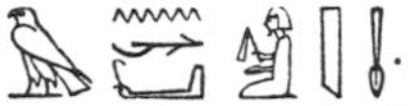. There are a few mistakes in the text, but the general sense is clear. A tradition was current among the old men of Luxor and Ḳûrnah in 1886–90, that, in the first half of the XIXth century, when so many heart scarabs were found in the tombs, the bases of many of them were covered with plates of gold, on which lines of hieroglyphs were cut or stamped. In such cases the base of the scarab itself was uninscribed. I have been shown many heart scarabs with gold coverings having lines of hieroglyphs stamped on them, but there is reason to believe that the plates of gold were made by a Coptic goldsmith at Luxor, and that the inscriptions were stamped upon them by a friend and partner of his who lived at Karnak. An example of this kind of work was presented to the British Museum by Mr. Somers Clarke, F.S.A., and is exhibited in the Fourth Egyptian Room (26978). The native at Karnak possessed great skill in the making of "anticas," and the scarabs that he made deceived sometimes both the ordinary tourist and the archaeologist. His models were genuine XVIIIth dynasty scarabs, which he had obtained from Wilkinson, and he obtained the steatite from the hills whence his ancestors obtained theirs 3,000 years before. In glazing his scarabs he used the blue and green glaze which he chipped off from fragments of glazed pottery and melted in a rude furnace; but his glazing was uneven, and no one was more conscious of its defect than he was. Through the good offices of a well-known English collector he obtained from England a small portable furnace, with crucibles, etc., and his glazing improved wonderfully. His friends among the dragomans in Luxor told him when scarabs bearing the cartouches of Thothmes III or Rameses II were in demand, and he took care to provide a supply. Through a friend he obtained from an amiable English professor a list of the cartouches of all the kings of the XVIIIth and XIXth dynasties, and then he made it easy for a collector to complete his series of scarabs of these kings without delay. Finding that heart scarabs were in demand he set to work and made several, but his ignorance of the correct forms of the hieroglyphs caused him, when cutting the Chapter of the Heart, to make mistakes that were recognizable as such by beginners in the study

of Egyptian Archaeology, and he abandoned that class of work. He then made a series of large steatite scarabs, on the bases of which he cut the figures of all the kings of the XVIIIth and XIXth dynasties, and their prenomens in cartouches, and sometimes their titles—" Beautiful god," " Lord of the Two Lands," etc. He mounted each scarab in a gold setting, and covered the base with gold leaf, and then fastened it to a chain made of gold of a low quality or to a bronze collar. Some of them he sold very successfully to collectors, but before he could dispose of them all he died, and his family asked me to come and see the " anticas " which he had left behind and help them to dispose of them. On examining the collection I found several heart scarabs of the kind described above, and duplicates of two scarabs which had been bought by the British Museum and by the Fitzwilliam Museum, Cambridge, some years before. Maspero was with me when I examined the collection, and he thought the objects such good examples of native forgeries that he purchased them *en bloc* on behalf of the Egyptian Government, and took them with him on his *dahabiyyah* when he returned to Cairo. The specimen purchased by the British Museum may be thus described. Green-glazed steatite scarab, measuring 3 inches by $1\frac{15}{16}$ inches by $1\frac{1}{8}$ inches, set in a metal frame $\frac{3}{16}$ inch wide, with a band across the back and another down the body over the place where the wings meet when folded. On the gilded base is cut the figure of a king wearing the crown , a collar or necklace, and a loincloth, with projecting linen attachment. The king is kneeling, and holds in his right hand the whip , and in the left an offering  (*sic*), or perhaps a censer. In front of him is a sitting lion, and behind him is a hawk, with the solar disk on his head. In the field are the prenomen of Thothmes III, 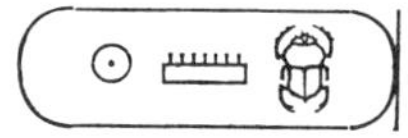, and the sign  (part of the title  (?)), and some garbled hieroglyphs. The scarab has on it pieces of linen, which are intended to suggest that it was taken out from among the bandages of the mummy of Thothmes III. It was fastened by a loop in the setting to a piece of gold chain about 10 inches long, which was in turn fastened to a large hoop of perfectly genuine bronze. The number of this forgery is 18190.

HISTORICAL SCARABS

THE principal Historical Scarabs belong to the reigns of Ȧmenḥetep III and his son Ȧmenḥetep IV, and all of them were made and issued to commemorate events in their reigns which these kings considered to be of great importance. The beetle that was taken as the model for them was not the *scarabaeus sacer*, but the *Goliathus*, large specimens of which attain a length of nearly 5 inches. As a preface to these scarabs mention must be made of the large scarabs which some think were issued by Åmenḥetep III to commemorate his marriage with Tî. The fine specimen in the British Museum (Hall, *Catalogue*, No. 1724) is made of green-glazed steatite and is 3¼ inches in length. The text reads :—

3. 1. 2.

Brit. Mus. 4004.

1. *Neter nefer neb àri khet Neb-Maāt-*
God beneficent, lord maker of things, Neb-Maāt-

Rā, Åmen-Rā meri 2. *sa Rā meri-f*
Rā, of Åmen-Rā beloved, son of Rā whom he loves,

Åmenḥetep ḥeq Uast [ānkh] mà Rā hru
Åmenḥetep, governor of Thebes, living like Rā day

neb 3. *Ḥemt nesu ur-t Tî,*
every. Woman of the King, great lady, Tî,

ānkh-t.
the living one.

The size and beauty of the scarab suggest that it had some special significance, but, as is the case with the scarab that records the names of the father and mother of Tî, no regnal year of the king is mentioned, and it is therefore impossible to say when it was issued.

I.—The Wild-Cattle Hunt by Åmenḥetep III in the IInd year of his reign.—The scarab from which the text is taken was formerly in the MacGregor Collection at Tamworth, and is now in the British Museum (No. 55585). Photographs of it have been published by Fraser (*Catalogue*, frontispiece) and Budge (*Tutānkhåmen*, pl. VI), and a drawing by Newberry (*Scarabs*, pl. XXXII) ; translations have been made by Fraser and Newberry. The text reads :—

[In] Year two under the Majesty of Horus the living one, bull mighty

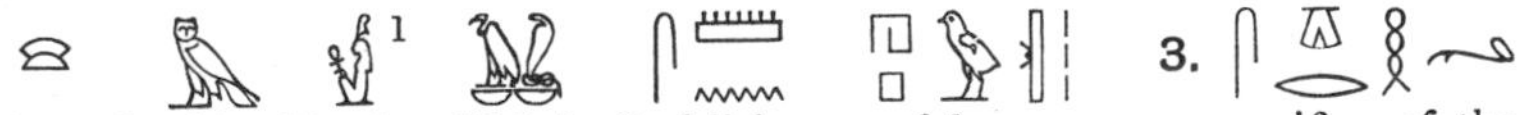

diademed with Truth,[1] Nebti Stablisher of laws, pacifier of the

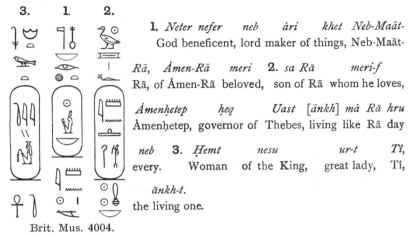

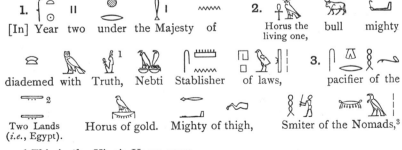

Two Lands (*i.e.*, Egypt).[2] Horus of gold. Mighty of thigh, Smiter of the Nomads,[3]

[1] This is the King's Horus-name.
[2] This is the King's name as the chosen one of Nekhebit of Nekhen and Uatchit of Per-Uatchit.
[3] This is the King's name as the Horus of gold.

King of the South and the North. Lord of the Two Lands. Nebmaāt-Rā[1] 4. Son of Rā. Åmenḥetep, Governor of Thebes,[2]

Giver of life. King's woman, great lady, Tî, living one like Rā.

A marvellous thing 5. happened through His Majesty. One came to say

to His Majesty: There are wild cattle upon the plain (*i.e.*, desert) 6. of the

district of Shetep. Set out by boat His Majesty sailing down stream

in the King's barge Khā-em-maāt 7. at the time of evening.

Receiving a way prosperous [he] arrived in peace at the district of

Shetep 8. at the time of daybreak. Mounted His Majesty upon

a horse, his bowmen all following him. 9. [Were] directed

the captains, [and] the officers of company of bowmen all of it,

likewise the young folk 10. of the locality to keep watch

over the wild cattle. Moreover commanded His Majesty

[1] This is the King's name as the Reed and the Bee, *i.e.*, King of the South and the North (Nesu båt).

[2] This is the King's name as the son of Rā.

to cause to be 11. drawn these wild cattle into

an enclosure with a ditch (?). Commanded 12. His Majesty

to [count] these wild cattle in their entirety. The list of them—

wild cattle 170. The list of [those which] 13. brought in His Majesty

by hunting (*i.e.*, slaughter) on this day— wild cattle 56. Waited

His Majesty four days 14. inactive, giving fire[1] to

his horses. Mounted His Majesty upon a horse. 15. List[2] of these

cattle [which] he brought in from the hunt. Wild cattle 20 16. [+ 20. Total]

wild cattle 96.

II.—SCARAB GIVING THE NAMES OF THE FATHER AND MOTHER OF QUEEN Tî and the southern and northern boundaries of Åmen-ḥetep's kingdom. The text printed below is taken from B.M. 4095. Many translations of it have been published: see Hall, *Catalogue*, p. 170. The first four lines give the five titles and names of Åmen-ḥetep as in No. 1.

1. 

2. 

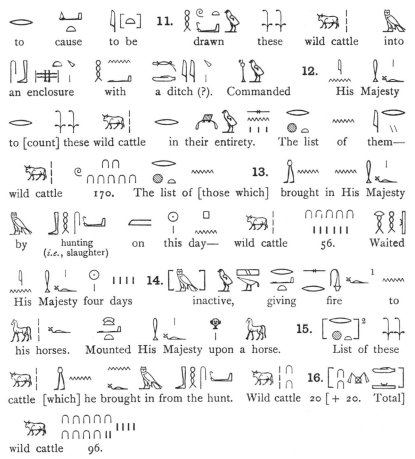

[1] *I.e.*, to allow them to recover their dash and fire.
[2] The beginnings of the last two lines are mutilated.

3. 

4. 

5. 

King's woman, great lady Tî, living one. Name of her father

Iuȧa. Name of her mother Thuȧa, wife

of the king mighty. His boundary southern

[reaches] to Karei.[1] {[His] northern boundary reaches} to

Naharn.[2]

III.—The lion-hunts of Ȧmenḥetep III during the first ten years of his reign.—Many examples of this scarab are known, and many translations of the inscription have been made. The following text is from B.M. 4096:—

1. 

2. 

3. 

4. 

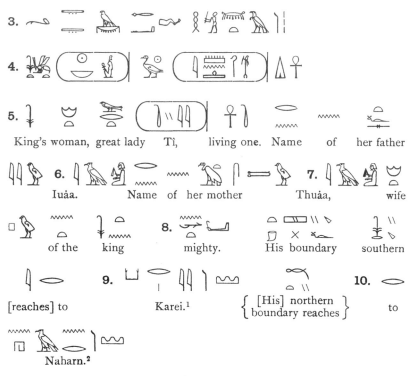

[1] The capital of this district in later times was Napata, the modern Marawi, at the foot of the Fourth Cataract.

[2] Northern Mesopotamia בֵּית נַהֲרַיִם, ܒܝܬ ܢܗܪܝܢ.

5. 

List of the lions

6. 

brought in His Majesty by his own shooting, beginning

7. 

with year I up to year X. Lions fierce 102.

IV.—The arrival in Egypt of Gilukhipa, the Mitanian bride of Åmenḥetep III, in the tenth year of his reign.—The inscription on this scarab was first published by Brugsch in *Aeg. Zeit.*, Bd. XVIII (1880), p. 82, from an example in the possession of Madame Hoffmann; for the inscription on the example in the Berlin Museum see Newberry, *Scarabs*, pl. XXXII, and for the mutilated example B.M. 49707 see Hall, *Catalogue*, p. 171. A transcript of Brugsch's text, with my English translation, was published by me in the *Mummy*, Cambridge, 1893, p. 243.

1. 

2. 

3. 

4. 

5. 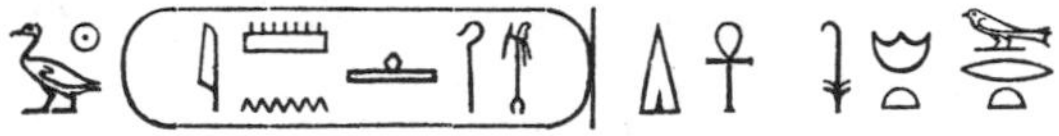

6. 

7. 

Marvellous thing! the bringing

8. 

for His Majesty, life, strength, health, of the daughter of the prince
[be to him!]

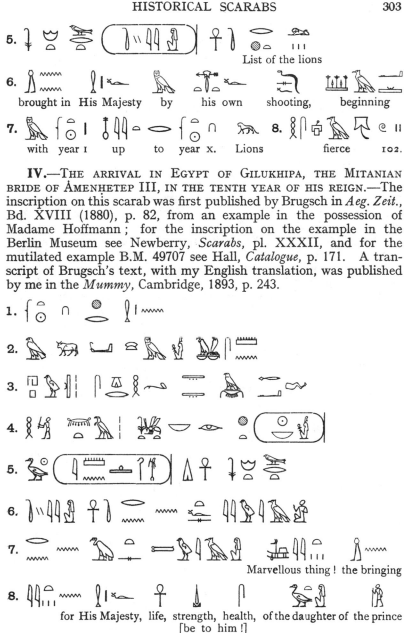

of Neherna,

9. 

Satârna, Kilgipa[1]

10. 

[and] the chief women of the ladies (ḥarîm),

11. 

womenfolk 317.

V.—THE CONSTRUCTION OF A LAKE IN WESTERN THEBES FOR QUEEN TÎ BY ÅMENḤETEP III IN THE ELEVENTH YEAR OF HIS REIGN.—The inscription on the base of the scarab recording the execution of this work was first published by Rosellini (*Monumenti Storici*, tav. XLIV, No. 2), who obtained it from an example in the Vatican. It was partly translated by him, and its contents were discussed by Dr. Hincks, to whom Egyptology owes much, in his paper "On the Age of the Eighteenth Dynasty of Manetho" (*Transactions of the Royal Irish Academy*, Vol. XXI, Dublin, 1848, p. 7). A transliteration of another example preserved at Alnwick Castle was printed, together with an English translation, by Dr. Birch in his *Catalogue* of the Duke of Northumberland's Collection (London, 1880, p. 127), and a reprint of the translation was given by him in *Records of the Past*, Old Series, Vol. XII, p. 41. Another copy of the text was printed by Stern in *Aeg. Zeit.*, 1887, p. 87, note 2, and this, corrected, was given by me in the *Mummy*, Cambridge, 1893, p. 244. The text reads :—

1. 

Year XI, month III of Akhat,[2] day I under [the Majesty of] 2. Horus,

the bull mighty, diademed with Truth, Nebti. 3. Establisher of laws,

pacifier of the Two Lands, Golden Horus, Mighty of thigh, 4. smiter of the Nomads

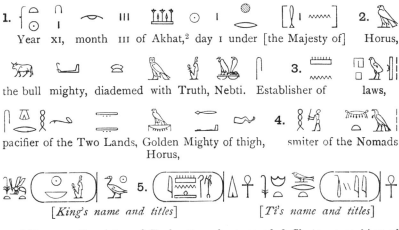

[*King's name and titles*] 5. [*Tî's name and titles*]

[1] She was the sister of Tushratta, who succeeded Shutarna as king of Mitani.

[2] The season Akhat = July 19th–November 15th.

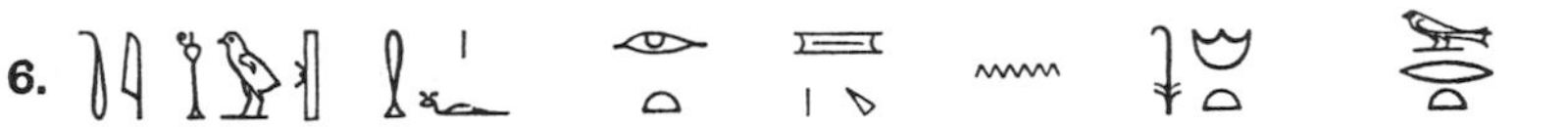

Commanded His Majesty the making a lake for the king's woman, great lady,

Tî living one, in her estate of Tchārukha.

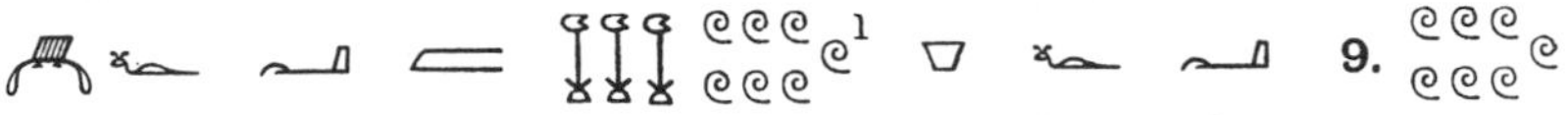

Its length cubits 3,700,[1] its width cubits 700.

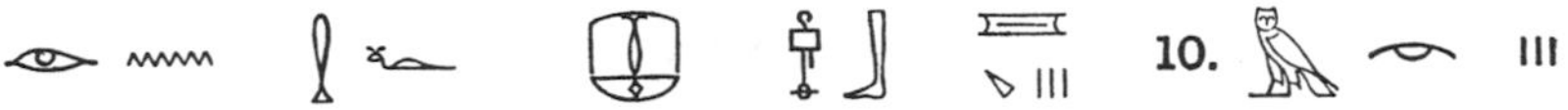

Made His Majesty the festival opening of the lake in month III

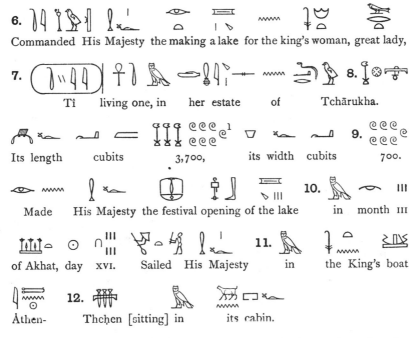

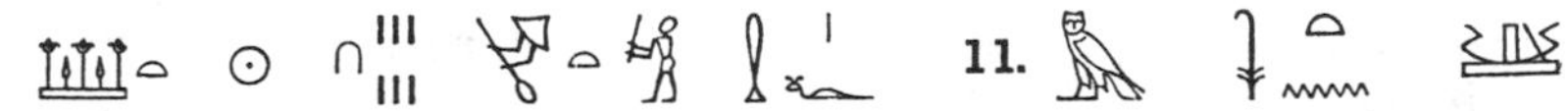

of Akhat, day XVI. Sailed His Majesty in the King's boat

Åthen- Thehen [sitting] in its cabin.

This scarab is of special interest because it shows that already, in the eleventh year of his reign, he publicly acknowledged the cult of Åten. The lake which he dug on the estate that he settled on Tî was, reckoning the cubit at 18 inches, 1,850 yards long and 350 yards wide. It was not in the Eastern Delta, as was formerly supposed, but in Western Thebes, and it is probably represented now by Birkat Habû. The name of the boat or barge in which the king sailed over the lake means "The Disk Sparkles," and it was probably given to it with the intent of letting the people know that the cult of Åten or Åthen was in the ascendant.

VI.—A large steatite scarab found at Sadêngah in the Egyptian Sûdân shows that Åmenḥetep IV followed the example of his father in "issuing" specially large scarabs to commemorate events of importance. This scarab, which is now in the British Museum[2] (No. 51084), has seven lines of text cut on the base, and the prenomen of the king is cut on one side of the scarab, and his nomen on the other. The last three lines contain the names and titles of the king and his queen Nefertiti, and the first four form an address by the king to a "beneficent god" who is the "great one of

[1] *Not* 3,600. The figures are clear on the Alnwick scarab; see Newberry, *Scarabs*, Pl. XXXIII.

[2] See Hall, *Catalogue*, No. 2868, p. 302; Budge, *Tutānkhåmen*, p. 104.

roarings," , whose name is great and holy, and who is present in the Seṭ Festival like Tathunen, . After a break is mentioned "Åten in heaven, stablished of face, the gracious one in Ȧnu (Heliopolis)." The breaks in the text make it impossible to grasp the exact meaning of the inscription as a whole, but it is possible that it represents an attempt to identify some local thunder-god with Åten. The mention of Tathunen is interesting, for he was one of the old non-solar gods of Egypt.

AMULETS

THE Egyptians, in common with almost every other nation of antiquity, attached to their mummified dead, and wore on their persons when living, a number of objects which they believed would secure for them protection from fiends and devils, and enable them to escape from the sicknesses and diseases that they produced in their bodies, and from accidents and calamities of all kinds. To such objects they gave the name of *m'ket,* 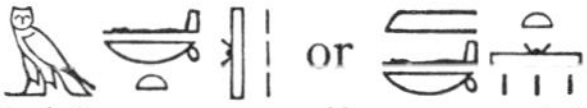, "protective things,"[1] from *māk,* , or *mek,* , "to protect." These objects were believed to have the power to protect a man, either because the substances of which they were made contained special properties that were beneficial to those who wore them on their bodies, or because they were thought to be the abodes of benevolent spirits. In the earliest times these "protectors" were probably portions of the bodies of ancestors—a toe or finger joint, a piece of skin, or even a dried eye-ball—objects that are used to this day as fetishes in many parts of the Sûdân. Later, objects connected with the various cults and regarded as holy were chosen as "protectors," but in process of time men forgot what their special attributes were, and the greater number of them became mere amulets, which were worn on the body as ornaments or decorations of dress. The word "amulet" is derived from the Arabic *ḥimâlah,* حَمَالَة, the name of the cord or chain on which the case of an amulet hangs, and also of the amulet itself. Egyptian amulets are of two classes, the inscribed and the uninscribed, the former being the more powerful. The inscriptions on the most important amulets are *ḥekau,* 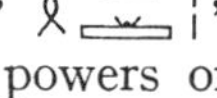, *i.e.,* magical utterances which conferred extraordinary powers on the spirits of the dead,

[1] Another favourite word is , *i.e.,* "strengtheners."

and were composed by Thoth, the lord of the words of the god, . The principal Egyptian amulets were :—

I.—The Ṭeṭ, . This object was formerly said to represent a mason's table, and a Nilometer, and the primitive roof tree, the horizontal bars representing its branches on the north, south, east and west. But it has nothing whatever to do with any of these things. The text of Chapter CLV of the Book of the Dead associates it with the backbone, *peṣṭ*, , and vertebrae, *thesu*, , of Osiris, and it is clear that is a conventional representation of a part of his spinal column. The oldest form of this part was , which represents the *sacrum*, and, when the Egyptians forgot what it represented, they lengthened the hieroglyph and straightened the projections and made the sign .[1] The meaning of the word *Ṭeṭ* is "firmness," "stability," and the "setting upright of the Ṭeṭ" was a very important ceremony in the cult of Osiris. The Rubric of Chapter CLV directs that the Ṭeṭ shall be made of gold, but as a matter of fact very few examples of the amulet in gold are known ; when made of wood, or wax, or bitumen they were often gilded. Several examples are known in hard stones, *e.g.*, lapis-lazuli (B.M. 20623), carnelian (B.M. 8272), and lapis-lazuli, carnelian, and mother-of-emerald inlaid (B.M. 20636). Many varieties of the Ṭeṭ are found in glazed porcelain, and in some of them the top is surmounted by the Atef crown of Osiris (B.M. 739). The Chapter of the Ṭeṭ reads :—

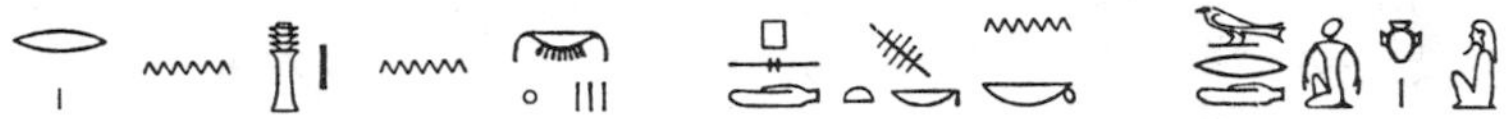

Chapter of the Ṭeṭ of gold. Thy backbone is to thee, Urṭ-àb,[2]

thy vertebrae are to thee, Urṭ-àb. I set myself on thy side.

I give thee seed under thee. Verily I have brought to thee

a Ṭeṭ of gold, rejoice thou in it. RUBRIC. Recite

[1] See Budge, *Osiris and the Egyptian Resurrection*, Vol. II, p. 280.
[2] He whose heart is at rest.

over a Ṭeṭ of gold fashioned on a core of sycamore wood dipped in juice of ānkhåmu plants. Place on the deceased at his neck the day of the union with the earth. If be placed for him strengthener this at his neck he will be a spirit honoured dwelling in Khert Neter on the day of the beginning of the year, like those who are followers of Osiris regularly, millions of times.

II.—The **Tet,** . This amulet has been commonly called the "Tie" or "Buckle," but the earliest writers about it were wholly uncertain as to what object it represented.[1] The text that is often found engraved upon it is Chapter CLVI of the Book of the Dead, and this indicates that it was supposed to bring to the wearer the virtue of the blood of Isis, and her words of power, and her magical spells and works. The object represented by is no ornament of the goddess but is a part of her body,[2] and there is little room for doubt that the hieroglyph is intended to be a picture of her genital organs.[3] On coffins and statues we often see one hand of the figure holding and the other , thus indicating that the deceased regarded amulets made in the form of the sacrum of Osiris and the uterus of Isis as mighty protectors in the Other

[1] See Birch, *Aeg. Zeit.*, 1871, p. 13, and Maspero, *Mémoire sur Quelques Papyrus du Louvre*, p. 8.

[2] See my *Osiris and the Egyptian Resurrection*, Vol. I, p. 276, Vol. II, p. 280.

[3] , t-t, is probably an old form of , *ati-t*, vulva, which exists in Coptic under the forms ⲱⲧⲉ, ⲟϯ and ⲁⲧⲉ; compare also ⲧⲟⲧⲉ.

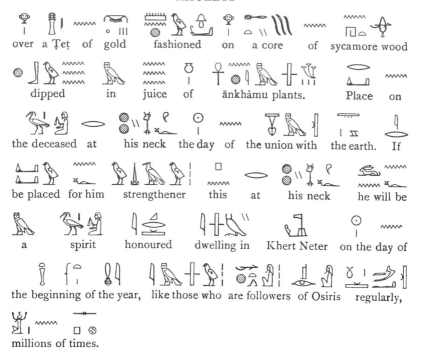

World. The Tet was most commonly made of red jasper, carnelian, porphyry, red glass, red faïence and sycamore wood; sometimes it was made entirely of gold, and sometimes when made of stone or faïence it was set in a gold frame or was gilded. Typical examples in red stone are B.M. 20619 and 20641; the former (in a gold wire frame) was made for Rāmes, , and the latter for the lady Maȧ, . Instances of the use of stones that were not red are B.M. 20646 and 20621. The former is of mottled stone and was made for a *Sem* priest of Ptaḥ, called Ȧriri (?) , who was also high priest of Memphis, ; and the latter, made of black schist, was made for Meri, a controller of sepulchral offerings, . The text inscribed on the Tet reads:—

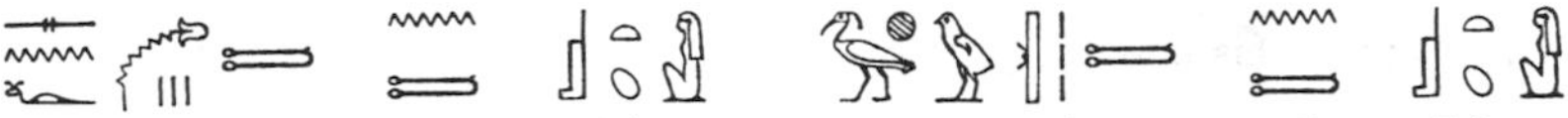

The blood of Isis, the magic of Isis,

the words of power of Isis, [are] strengtheners protecting

great one this destroying the doer of things abominable to him.

RUBRIC. 

Recite over a Tet of carnelian red jasper (?) dipped

in juice of ānkhȧmu flowers, fashioned of the core

of the sycamore. Place [it] on spirit (*i.e.* the deceased) this at

his neck [on] the day of union with the earth. If be done

for him this will the magical spells of Isis protect his limbs.

Will rejoice Horus, the son of Isis, in him [when] he sees

him. Not shall be hidden the way from him. His [one] hand is to

heaven, his [other] hand is to earth regularly. Do not thou

allow to see it person any. Verily there is

none above his powers (?).

In the Saïte Recension of the Book of the Dead the Rubric adds: "If this writing be known [by the deceased] he shall be among the followers of Osiris Un-Nefer, whose word is truth. The gates of Khert-neter shall be opened to him. A plot of ground, with wheat and barley, shall be given to him in Sekhet-Åanru (*i.e.*, the Field of Reeds). His name shall be like the names of the gods who are there, that is to say, the Followers of Horus who reap [the grain] there."

III.—The **Head-rest** or **Pillow**, , *Urs.*[1] As an amulet the head-rest is usually made of haematite, and is uninscribed; it is a model of the large head-rests made of wood, alabaster and stone, which were placed under the necks of mummified bodies to "lift up" their heads. The *ḥeka*, or text, inscribed on the head-rest amulet is a version, more or less complete, of Chapter CLXVI of the Book of the Dead, which is found in all the great Codices of the XVIIIth dynasty. The text on B.M. 20647 reads:—

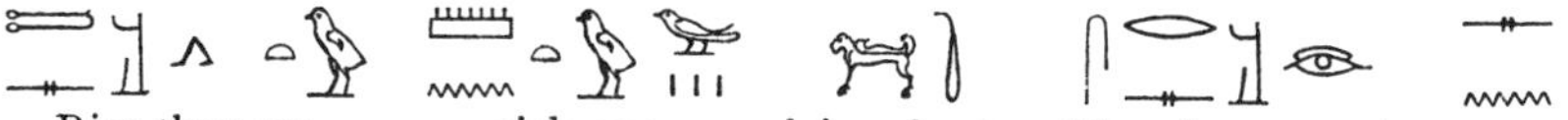

Rise thou up, sick one, lying dead. They keep watch over

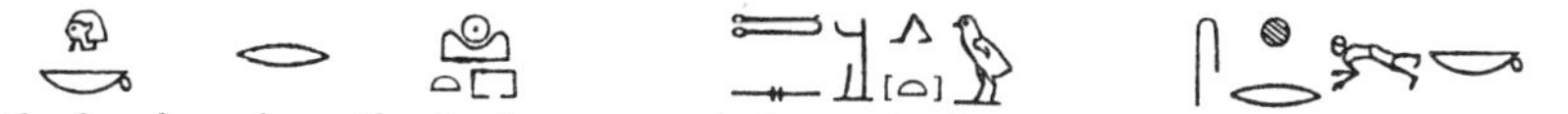

thy head in the horizon, being raised up. Thou overthrowest

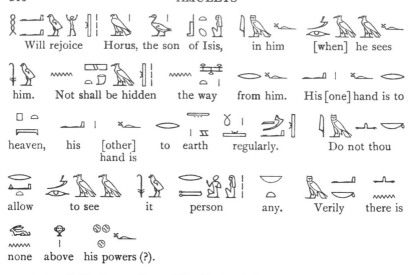

thine enemies. Thou triumphest over those who work against thee.

[1] See Birch in *Aeg. Zeit.*, 1868, pp. 32–54.

Has commanded to be done for thee [this] Horus, avenger of his father

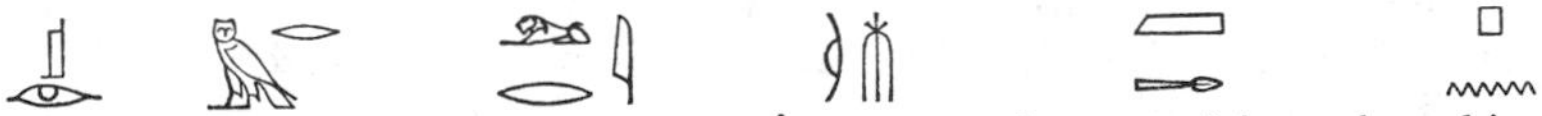

Osiris, governor of the store, Åāḥmes, whose word is truth, this.

Thou cuttest off the heads of thine enemies. Not shall they

carry off from thee ever thy skull. Verily slaughter

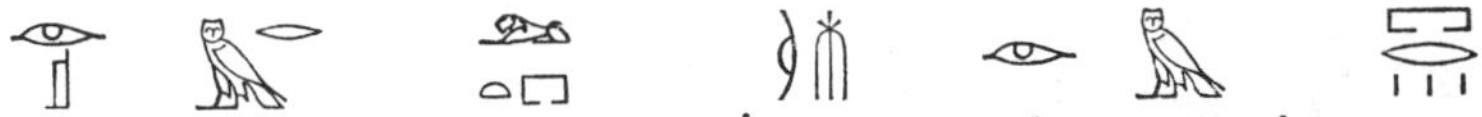

Osiris, governor of the store, Åāḥmes, makes at the appearances

of the heads of his enemies. Not shall they carry off his head

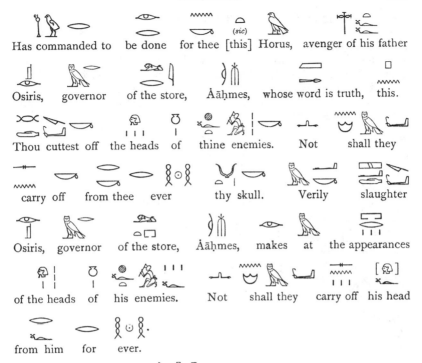

from him for ever.

IV.—The **Heart,** , *åb.* The importance that the Egyptians attached to the heart is proved by the Chapters of the Book of the Dead (XXVI–XXXB) that deal with the heart. To them it was the source of all life and thought, and it seems to have been the seat of the BA, , or heart-soul, and perhaps also of the KA, , or natural disposition of a man. When taken from the body that was to be mummified it was embalmed separately and placed with the lungs in a jar (Canopic vase) which was under the special protection of Ṭuamutef, one of the Four Sons of Horus. At a comparatively early period the model of a heart, made of a special kind of stone, was inserted in the mummy in place of the heart, or was laid upon the breast. Sometimes the upper part of it was made in the form of a human head, and hands were crossed over it (B.M. 15598), and sometimes a figure of a man-headed hawk, typifying the soul, was inlaid on one side of it (B.M. 8005). An interesting example of the heart amulet is described by Birch in his *Catalogue of the Egyptian Antiquities in Alnwick Castle,* p. 224. On one side are cut the signs , *Net* (Neith) and , the Benu bird, and the legend , *Nuk ba Khepera,* " I am the soul of

Kheperȧ," and on the other is the ordinary Heart-Chapter (XXXB). So the heart, after death, or a model of it, could become the abode of the soul of Kheperȧ (who was also incarnate in the *scarabaeus sacer*), and therefore could, and, in the opinion of the Egyptians, *did* live again. Amulets of the heart are made of many kinds of hard stone—carnelian, red jasper, red faïence, and coloured paste. The Chapters of the Book of the Dead which relate to the heart are XXVI–XXXB. In the Papyrus of Ani (pl. 33) there are Vignettes of the four principal amulets, viz., the , the , the , and the , and the text which is given beneath the Vignette of the Heart reads :—

Chapter of a heart of carnelian (?). I am the Benu bird, the soul of

Rā, the guide of the gods to the Ṭuat. [When] come forth souls

upon earth to perform the wishes of their KAS, shall come forth

the soul of Osiris Ani to perform the wish of his KA.

V.—The **Vulture,** , *nerȧu-t.* The vulture amulet is not common, and few examples of it are known ; it seems to have come into general use under the XXVIth dynasty. The text of which it forms the Vignette in the Saïte Recension of the Book of the Dead is not found in Codices of the Theban Recension. The amulet was supposed to bring to the deceased the protection of " Mother " Isis. It was placed on the neck of the mummy on the day of the funeral. The text reads :—

Chapter of a vulture of gold placed on the neck of the glorified one.

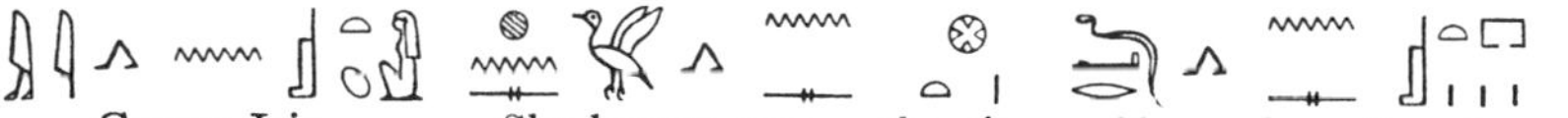

Comes Isis. She hovers over the city. She seeks the places

hidden of Horus at his appearance from the papyrus swamps,

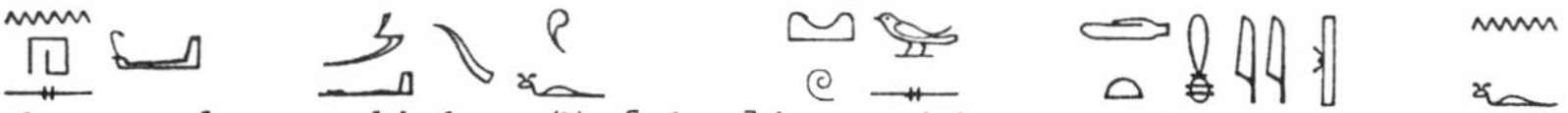

she roused up his horn (?) [when] it was sick. He joined himself to the side of the divine bark. Was decreed for him the rule of the world.

He wages a war great, he makes to be remembered [his]

deeds. He sends forth his fear. He creates awe of himself.

His mother, the great lady, she makes protection for him, hastening (?)

[her] steps for Horus. RUBRIC. Recite over a vulture

of gold inscribed chapter this upon it. Place [it] at the neck of

glorified one this [on] the day of union with the earth (*i.e.*, funeral).

VI.—The **Collar,** , *usekh.* This amulet also came into common use about the time of the XXVIth dynasty, but examples of it are rare, especially in gold (see B.M. 16980). In the Graeco-Roman Period little difference was made between the pectoral and the collar, as may be seen from the examples made of cartonnage in the British Museum. Each has two heads of Horus, one by each shoulder, a fact that suggests that the collar and pectoral were supposed to carry with them the protection of Horus of the Two Horizons, Ḥer-àakhuti. A collar forms the Vignette of Chapter CLVIII of the Saïte Recension of the Book of the Dead, the text of which reads :—

Chapter of the collar of gold placed on the neck of the glorified one.

My father, my brother, my mother Isis, unfetter me, make me to see.

I am one among the unfettered ones [who] see Geb.

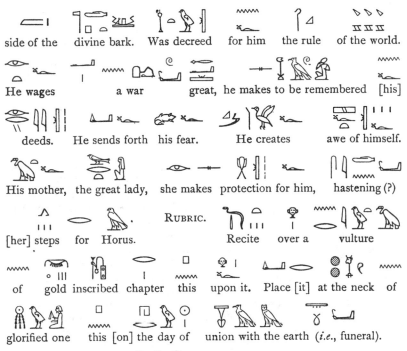

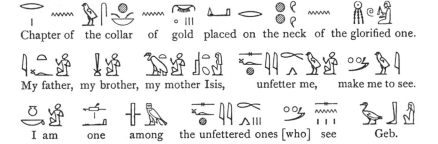

RUBRIC. 

Recite over a collar of gold inscribed chapter this

upon it. Place [it] on the neck of glorified one this the day of

union with the earth.

VII.—The **Papyrus Column Sceptre,** , *Uatch.* The name of this amulet is derived from or , to be green, verdure, freshness, etc., and it was supposed to bestow the strength and vigour of youth upon its wearer. It is usually made of mother-of-emerald, and two forms of it are known; in the one the amulet is in the form of a miniature papyrus column in the round (B.M. 8201), and in the other the column is cut in relief upon a flat tablet with a rounded top. Both forms were worn as pendants (B.M. 8212, 13328). A picture of the amulet without a tablet under it forms the Vignette of Chapter CLIX of the Saïte Recension of the Book of the Dead, which is a comparatively modern composition. In the Vignette of Chapter CLX we see Thoth in the form of an ibis-headed man giving a rectangular plaque to the deceased scribe Nebseni. Thoth is called the "great god," and before him are the words, "the giving of an Uatch of *neshmet*" .

The text reads :— 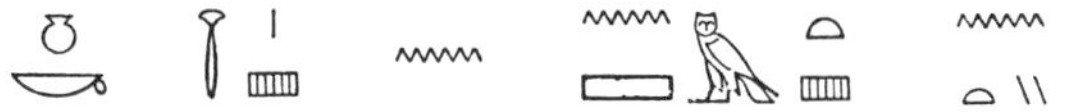

I am the Uatch of mother-of-emerald, which

is deadly in its operation, which the hand of Thoth adores it.

Its abomination is slaughter. It is strong, I am strong.

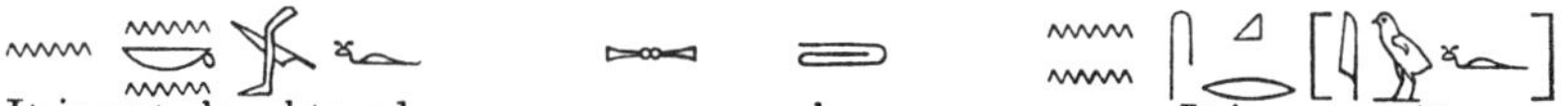

It is not slaughtered, conversely (*i.e.*, I am not slaughtered). It is not smitten,

I am not smitten. The words of Thoth are thy protection. Come

in peace, great one of Heliopolis, great one, dweller in Pe.

Advances Shu to him, he finds him in

Shenemu in his name of Neshmet,

making his seat in the stronghold of the god, the great one.

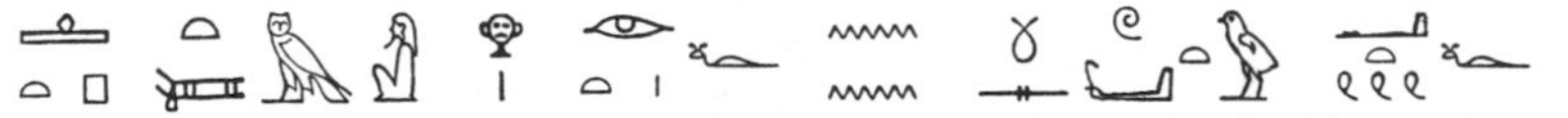

Rests Tem upon his Eye, not fettered are his members.

According to the Rubric to Chapter CLIX of the Saïte Recension the Uatch amulet was to be laid upon the neck of the deceased.

VIII. The **Life** amulet ☥, or ☥, or ☥, *ānkh*. This amulet is found in almost every material which the Egyptians used for making amulets, and was worn by the living to maintain and prolong life, and laid with the dead to renew their life and effect their resurrection. What object is represented by ☥ is not known. About its meaning there is no doubt, fortunately, for ancient authorities, both Greek and Coptic, say that *ānkh* (Copt. ⲱⲛϩ, ⲱⲛϧ) means "life." The gods possessed ☥, and always carried it with them, and without it they would not have been gods. They could bestow this quality, or essence, or attribute, upon the souls of the righteous, who attained the power and status of the gods forthwith. In later times ☥ stood for more than mere "life"; it meant the life that could not die—immortality.[1] An interesting proof of this is afforded by B.M. 84412. This is a large *ānkh* amulet, 9¼ inches long, made of bluish-green Egyptian porcelain. Within the loop of the ☥ are 𓊽, "stability," and 𓋹, "well-being," and on top of the 𓊽, in low relief, is the sign for "one hundred thousand millions of years" 𓁨. It is possible that ☥ was

[1] As in Coptic ϭⲓⲛⲱⲛϩ = Gr. ἀθανασια (see Spiegelberg, *Kopt. Handwörterbuch*, p. 181).

used by the pre-dynastic Egyptians as an amulet, and though their dynastic successors do not seem to have known exactly what it represented, from the fact that they associate it with 𓊽 and 𓎬, it would appear that they associated it with the human body. Many Egyptologists have suggested identifications for ☥, but none is satisfactory, and the fact is that no one knows what this sign represents.[1] The Egyptian Christians, or Copts, adopted both the sign ☥ and its meaning in connection with the Cross of Christ, and it is seen frequently on gravestones (see the stele of Plēïnos in the Coptic Room of the British Museum). During some excavations made by the late Colonel G. T. Plunkett, R.E., and myself in 1887, near the Monastery of St. Simeon at Aswân, we found the remains of an episcopal staff with a silver head. This head was formed of ☥, 𓊽, 𓎬 and 𓈌, joined together thus [glyph], and the fusions seem to represent the bishop's attempt to merge the symbols of the three great Egyptian amulets into the great Symbol of Christianity. The loop of the ☥ stands for the solar disk ☉, and 𓈌 for the horizon, but it was Christ, and not Rā, Whose rising with healing in His wings was indicated by the solar disk on the horizon 𓈍. Thus the object represented the "Life" of Christ, Isis and Osiris, and the bishop who affixed it to his pastoral staff no doubt used it, as did the ascetics in other parts of Egypt, to drive away devils and evil spirits, and to cure diseases.

IX.—The **Utchat**, 𓅱𓍑𓄿𓂀, or "Symbolic Eye." This amulet was made of faïence, glazed in various colours, wood, granite, haematite, carnelian, lapis-lazuli, gold, silver, copper and many other materials. Its name is derived from *utcha*, 𓅱𓍑𓄿𓏛, "to be in good health," "sound and comfortable in mind and body." The reason why this amulet was so popular is obvious. The source of all health and happiness was the right Eye of Horus the Elder, and later the right Eye of Rā, which was able to protect both the living and the dead. The two Utchats, one facing to the right and the other to the left, represented the two eyes of Horus, *i.e.*, the sun and the moon, or, as late texts seem to indicate, the southern and northern halves of the sun's daily course. The twin Utchats, 𓂀𓂀, appear on coffins as early as the VIth dynasty, and indicate

[1] See Jéquier, "Les Talismans ☥ et 𓍶," in *Bull. de l'Institut Français*, Cairo, 1913, p. 123.

that the dead were under the protection of the Eyes of the Sun and Moon. On sepulchral boxes we often find them with a triple between, . The Utchat amulet is made both as a solid plaque and in hollow-work, and when made of carnelian the eyebrow is carefully marked (B.M. 15624, 29041). Sometimes a uraeus wearing a solar disk is attached, (B.M. 29040), and sometimes it is provided with a wing and the leg and claw of a bird (hawk ?) (B.M. 29222). The examples in faïence are interesting, some having a head of Hathor stamped on them (B.M. 7357), others a figure of Bes (B.M. 21547). In some two pairs of Utchats are united, (B.M. 7386). Occasionally the Utchat is quite round, and is outlined on one side, and on the convex side about 50 small eyes are shown in relief (B.M. 30035). Egyptian tradition told the story of how the Eye of Rā had suffered injury and eclipse through a mighty storm which had been stirred up by Set, or Āpepi, and also of how the Eye of the Moon had been swallowed up by the same monster, but in each case the Eye was "brought back," *i.e.*, restored to its original state, by Thoth. The Book of the Dead (Chapter LXVII) provides a *ḥeka*, or spell, which the deceased can use to prevent himself from suffering through a similar calamity. It reads :—

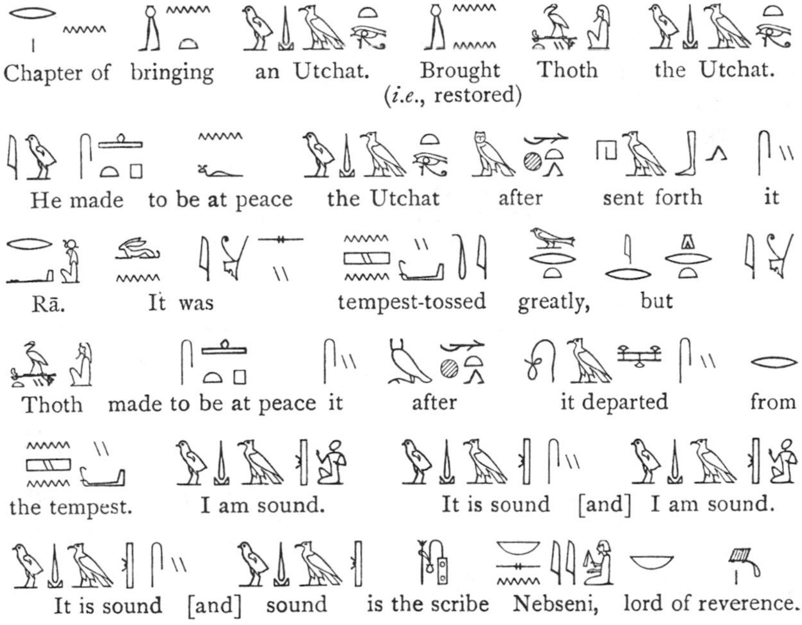
Chapter of bringing an Utchat. Brought (*i.e.*, restored) Thoth the Utchat.
He made to be at peace the Utchat after sent forth it
Rā. It was tempest-tossed greatly, but
Thoth made to be at peace it after it departed from
the tempest. I am sound. It is sound [and] I am sound.
It is sound [and] sound is the scribe Nebseni, lord of reverence.

The Egyptians celebrated a great festival in honour of the "Filling of the Utchat" on the last day of the sixth month of their year, on which day the Sun-god Rā was believed to obtain his maximum strength. The Vignette of Chapter CXL in the Saïte Recension shows us the deceased adoring Anubis, and a god sitting with the Utchat on his head, , with Rā, , behind him. The Chapter is ordered to be recited over two Utchat amulets. The first amulet was to be made of lapis-lazuli or *mag* stone, , either plated with or set in gold, and offerings were to be made to it. The second amulet was to be made of *khenem* stone, , and laid on some part of the body of the deceased, and when the Chapter had been recited over these, the deceased would become one of the gods, and would be able to take his seat in the boat of the Sun-god. During the recital of the Chapter at the moment when the Utchat was full, fires were to be kindled on twelve altars—four in honour of Rā-Tem, four for the Utchat, and four for the Two Companies of the Gods who sang, "Hail to thee, Rā, overthrower of Ăpep! Hail to thee, Rā, self-produced, who camest into being as Kheperȧ! Hail to thee, Rā, destroyer of thine enemies! Hail to thee, Rā, who hast broken the skulls of the impotent rebels, the Mesu Beṭshu" . The day of the filling of the Utchat was the longest day of the Egyptian year.

X.—The **Cow,** , **Ahat.** An ancient tradition held that in primitive times, when the Sun-god Rā was about to set for the first time, he felt that when he had lost the vital heat which had been in him in the daytime he would become an inert, dead mass. His mother, the Sky-goddess, appealed to a mighty god by his secret names, and Rā was at once surrounded by flames of fire, which prevented his death. In the Saïte Period, or earlier, the editor of the Book of the Dead included a Chapter (CLXII) containing a series of *ḥekau*, or words of power, which were to be recited on behalf of the deceased with the intention of preserving the vital heat in his body for ever. The Chapter is entitled "Chapter of making to become heat (or, fire) under the head of the Ȧakhu," . The god addressed in the *ḥeka* is Par, or Pal , and his secret names are , HAQAHAGAḤERḤER, , ȦULȦUȦAQERSAȦNQLEBATI, , KHALSERȦU, and

KHALSATÅ, 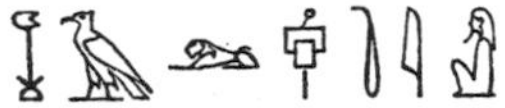. The Rubric orders the Chapter to be recited over a figure of a cow in fine gold, which is to be placed on the neck of the deceased. The Vignette shows the cow wearing a disk and plumes between her horns, and she has a *menȧt* suspended from her neck. Besides this a figure of the cow was to be written on a piece of new papyrus and placed under the head of the deceased, who would then retain the vital heat which he possessed during his life. When the image of the goddess was placed in position on the body the following prayer was to be said: " O Åmen, O Åmen who art in heaven, turn thy face upon the dead body of thy son, and make him sound and strong in Khert-Neter." The amulets of the Cow, which have been found under the heads of mummies, are circular in form, and are made up of a series of layers of linen gummed together; they are slightly concave in shape, and therefore fit the back of the mummy's head. The linen is covered with a thin layer of plaster, upon which are drawn in black outline: (1) a four-headed Ram-god adored by six dog-headed apes; (2) the cow Ahat, the Four Sons of Horus, an Utchat goddess, and a serpent adoring a man-headed Hawk-god; (3) a god with two heads facing in opposite directions, the boat of Ḥer-Sepṭ, the Boat of Kheperȧ, and a boat containing the soul of the deceased. All these scenes are enclosed in a circle that is intended to represent the pupil of the Eye of Rā, and outside it extracts in hieroglyphs from Chapter CLXII are given. See the examples in the British Museum—No. 37330, which was made for Tcheḥer (Teôs), the son of Utchat-Shu, No. 35875, which was made for Ḥer , and No. 37909, which was made for Ta-kharṭ-Khensu, .

XI.—The **Frog,** 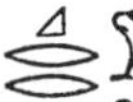, *qerer.* The frog was an incarnation of the goddess Ḥeqit, 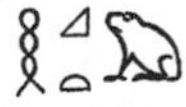, who played a very important and prominent part in Egyptian mythology. She is mentioned in the Pyramid text of Pepi I,[1] and she was present when Ruṭ-Ṭeṭ, the wife of the priest of Rā, gave birth to the three boys[2] who afterwards became kings of Egypt under the names of Userkaf, Saḥurā and Kakaȧ. She presided over conception and birth, and was present when Osiris was united to Isis after his death. Her cult flourished at Abydos under the XIXth dynasty and later. On the bas-reliefs there she is seen assisting Anubis to reconstitute the body of Osiris, and she is present when the soul of Osiris is rejoining

1  l. 570.

2 *Westcar Papyrus*, ed. Erman, Plate 9.

its body. And it was assumed that she was present at the birth of every king and every person of royal rank. The four great primeval gods, Nen, Ḥeḥ, Kek and Nāu, are depicted in the form of a frog. The frog amulet appears in two forms, one being about 5 inches long and the other about half an inch long. The former, the *matla-mĕtlo* (*Pyxicephalus adspersus*), appears from out of the sands of the desert as soon as the rains begin to fall, and the natives associate with it the idea of new life and fertility. The latter, the small tree-frog, appears suddenly in myriads as soon as the Nile begins to rise in the Sûdân, and the women of many tribes in Africa eat them, as they do the *scarabaeus sacer*, to make themselves fertile.[1] Models of this little tree-frog were made in large numbers in steatite, faïence, hard stone, and gold, and were worn as pendants on necklaces, pectorals, etc. (for specimens see B.M. 14609, 14758, 29050). According to King (*The Gnostics*, London, 1864, p. 139) the frog was not an uncommon device for a heathen's signet, and it was often adopted by early converts. It came into the list of emblems of the resurrection of the body on account of the complete change of nature it goes through in the second stage of its existence, *i.e.*, from a fish to a quadruped. And Plutarch says (*De E. Delphico*, X) that the frogs and the snakes on the basis of the bronze palm-tree which the Corinthians dedicated to Phoebus typified the spring. The Copts also regarded the frog as a type of the resurrection, and on a Christian lamp described by Lanzone (*Dizionario*, p. 853) there is a raised figure of a frog surrounded by the legend, Ἐγώ εἰμι Ἀνάστασις, " I am the resurrection." In the catacombs of Alexandria the frog is often seen associated with the Cross,[2] each being intended to typify resurrection. From Egypt the cult of the frog passed westwards, and even at the present day glazed earthenware models of the giant frog may be seen in many houses in Morocco and the neighbouring countries.

An interesting example of the association of the frog with the symbol of virility is afforded by a bronze handle of a knife or dagger which was formerly in the well-known Collection of Dr. Fouquet in Cairo. This handle is 2½ inches in length, and is formed by the figure of a pygmy who is standing on the top of a lotus flower and holding a cluster of lotus flowers. He is furnished with a large phallus, which is out of all proportion to his size, and on the end of it is perched a frog. The little green tree-frogs which swarm when the Nile is beginning to rise in the Sûdân have already been mentioned, and the frog and the pygmy together recall the Sûdânî belief in the frog as a symbol of fertility and fecundity. When the Fouquet Collection was sold in Paris in 1923 the bronze handle described above was purchased for the British Museum, where it is now preserved in the Greek and Roman Department.

[1] Johnston, *George Grenfell*, Vol. II, pp. 613, 615.
[2] Birch, *Ancient Pottery*, Vol. I, p. 52.

XII.—The **Nefer,** [hieroglyphs] (or perhaps [hieroglyphs]). The fundamental idea attached to this amulet is not very clear, but from the fact that this same word is used to express young man, and maiden, and young horse and well-favoured cow, we may assume that it was supposed to bring to its wearers the strength, gladness and happiness of youth. The word also means good, and what is good, pretty or beautiful, and perhaps also perfect and perfection. Neter nefer, [hieroglyphs], is the well-doing or beautiful god. The amulet was made of glazed faïence, carnelian, etc., and large numbers were made to string on necklaces and pectorals. Originally it represented the human heart with an attachment, but in the XXVIth dynasty popular ideas associated it with a musical instrument, and it was commonly held to typify joy and gladness.

XIII.—The **Ba,** or Soul amulet, [hieroglyph], a man-headed hawk. This amulet was made of gold and inlaid with semi-precious stones, *e.g.*, lapis-lazuli and carnelian, and was laid on the breast of the mummy with the object of enabling the soul of the deceased to visit its body in the tomb. Sometimes the amulet takes the form shown in the hieroglyph above, and sometimes the wings are outspread; a good, characteristic example is B.M. 57323. In the Vignette to Chapter LXXXIX of the Book of the Dead the soul is seen hovering over the mummy, which is lying on its bier, and in the text the deceased is made to say, "Grant that my soul may come to me from wheresoever it may be . . . . . Let me have possession of my Ba (soul) and of my Åakhu (spirit). Let me not lie down as a dead being in Ånu (Heliopolis), the place wherein souls are joined unto their bodies in thousands (?). Let my soul appear before the gods, and grant that it may journey, O ye gods who tow along the Boat of the Lord of Millions of Years, in the eastern sky with you and follow on to the place where it was yesterday. And let it have peace, peace in Åmentt. May it look upon its natural body, may it rest upon its *sāḥu* (spirit-body), and may its body neither perish nor suffer corruption for ever!"

XIV.—The **Sma,** [hieroglyph] or [hieroglyphs]. This amulet represents the lungs, [hieroglyphs], *sma,* and it was believed to impart to the wearer of it the power to breathe freely, and to prolong the existence of the breath of life in the body. It is usually made of dark-coloured stone, and varies in length from three-quarters of an inch to an inch and three-eighths; the examples in the British Museum (8291 and 24082) are uninscribed.

XV.—The **Sun on the horizon,** [hieroglyph]. This amulet was made of red jasper, red paste or red glass, carnelian, and other stones of a reddish colour (B.M. 8297, 8299, 8300). It symbolized the strength of Horus the rising sun, and was believed to afford to the wearer heat and protection in life, and renewed life, or resurrection after death.

XVI, XVII, XVIII.—**Crown** amulets. These were: The Red Crown of the North (Lower Egypt), , **Ṭeshert**; the White Crown of the South (Upper Egypt), , **Ḥetchet**; the Two Crowns of the South and North, , **Sekhemti**.

XIX.—The **Two Feathers**, or , *Shuti* , . This amulet represents the two plumes which some of the gods wear, *e.g.*, Ȧmen and Osiris. The straight plumes, , are those of Ȧmen, and indicate the power of generation, virility, and the plumes with curved tops are the feathers worn in the Atef Crown, , by Ptaḥ-Seker-Osiris, the triune god of the Egyptian Resurrection. From first to last the feather symbolized air and light. The Shuti amulet was made in stone, sometimes dark, sometimes light (B.M. 8143, 20618), and also in solid gold, but the natives melt down the latter as soon as they find one.

XX.—The **Shen,** , originally represented the end of a cylindrical seal being rolled over the moist mud which is to take the impression of the seal, but at a very early date it was associated with the idea of a **ring** with an attachment which bore an inscription and was used as a seal. The word *shen*, , , means "to encircle," and *shenu*, or , means "circle." The determinative is sometimes or , and sometimes , and it is possible that the **cartouche amulet,** , is only a modification of this sign. In any case the Shen represents the all-embracing power of the sun, and probably also eternity.

XXI.—The **Cartouche,** . This amulet is made of lapis-lazuli (B.M. 13469) and dark stone, and sometimes a pair of plumes, , are attached to it (B.M. 8166, 8168). The hieroglyph is used as a determinative for *ren*, , the word for name, and it is possible that the idea underlying the use of this amulet was the preservation of the name of the deceased in perpetuity, or as long as the solar disk continued to revolve in the sky.

XXII.—The **Serpent's head,** , *Ārār-t*. This amulet is made of red jasper, red paste, carnelian and other reddish stones. It represented Isis as the great serpent-goddess, and was placed inside the wrappings of mummies and attached to their necks to prevent their being devoured by worms in the tombs. It was also worn by the living as a protection against snake bite. The *ḥekau*, or words of power, which are found engraved on the amulet, are taken from two Chapters of the Book of the Dead (XXXIV and XXXV) which were intended to prevent the deceased from being devoured by worms or serpents in the Other World. In Chapter XXXIV he says, "I am flame emanating from the brow of the god of Eternity . . . . . I am the Maftet," *i.e.*, the divine Lynx,

One example (B.M. 23301) contains an address to the Great God in Khert-Neter, , another gives the name of the deceased,  (?), who held the office of 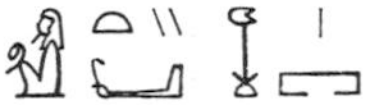 (B.M. 3125), and a third is inscribed with a text beginning  (B.M. 14898).

XXIII.—The **Menȧt**, 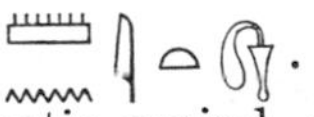. This amulet was in use in Egypt in the early dynastic period, and was probably invented by the pre-dynastic Egyptians. It was worn by gods, goddesses, kings, priests, and others, and it often forms the pendant of a necklace, being made of lapis-lazuli, dark stone or glazed faïence, and, when attached to large statues, of bronze. The primitive idea associated with this amulet was physical well-being, in the male virility and in the female fecundity, and it was buried with the dead with the idea of renewing their sexual instincts and powers in the Other World. In Lower Egypt the Menȧt was a prominent attribute of Ptaḥ of Memphis, and in Upper Egypt of Hathor, whether as a fine cow or beautiful woman. Two characteristic examples are B.M. 8172, 8173, but one of the finest examples known is B.M. 41515. It is 6¾ inches long by 2⅜ inches. The upper part consists of an aegis of Hathor set between two papyrus columns, the one surmounted by the Uraeus of the South, and the other by the uraeus of the North. The goddess wears a plaited head-dress, and a heavy curl falls by each side of her face. Above her head is a small shrine , in which is a serpent, upright, wearing a disk and horns 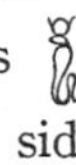. The aegis rests upon another shrine, which is flanked on each side by a lotus pillar surmounted by a head of Hathor. Within the shrine are figures of two goddesses in the form of women, the one wearing  and the other a sistrum (?). On the reverse of the *menȧt* this shrine is provided with two doors and two bolts. On one door is cut in outline the figure of a goddess with horns (?), and on the other the figure of a woman kneeling, with a lotus in her hand and a bird on her head. The doors and bolts show that the shrine has a funerary character. Below, within a circle, in sunk relief, is a figure of the cow of Hathor, with a solar disk in red stone inlaid between her horns. An altar, with offerings upon it, stands before her, and luxuriant plants form a background for her. The two goddesses symbolized by this *menȧt* were Nebtḥetep, , and Ḥetḥer, lady of heaven, ; compare B.M. 20760 and 300, and and , in Lanzone, *Dizionario*, tav. XVI, 3rd register.

XXIV.—The **Fly.** A few examples are known of an amulet made in the form of a fly, , but the head, instead of being that of the insect, is that of a man or woman. This amulet is made of green stone or green-glazed faïence; typical examples are B.M. 3134, 3135. The common Egyptian word for a fly is , *āff*, but it is possible that at one period the Egyptians represented the soul as a human-headed fly, just as they depicted it as a human-headed hawk, and if this be so the name of the amulet would probably be "Ba."

XXV.—The **Ladder,** , *maqet*, Copt. ⲙⲟⲩⲕⲓ. In many tombs of the Old and Middle Kingdoms models of a ladder, , made of steatite and wood have been found, and some time elapsed after the finding of them before it was realized that they were amulets. These models are symbols of the Ladder by which, according to a very ancient legend, Osiris ascended into heaven. In primitive times the Egyptians thought that in some places the floor of heaven touched the mountains, and that the spirit-bodies of the dead stepped from the tops of the mountains on to the crystal (or alabaster ?) floor of heaven. But in some parts there was a considerable space between the earth and this floor, and then the spirit-bodies needed a ladder. The legend stated that Osiris wished to enter heaven, but that on account of his want of strength he was unable to spring up to it, and that he would never have reached heaven at all had not Rā provided him with a ladder. According to one form of the legend Osiris was helped to ascend the ladder by Rā and Horus, who stood one on each side of it, and according to another the two helpers of Osiris were Horus the Aged and Set. To make the ladder perform its functions it was necessary for the deceased to recite the *ḥeka*, or word of power, which was specially composed for this purpose. In the text as given in the Pyramid of

Bronze Menåt of Hathor from the tomb of Åmenḥetep III. XVIIIth dynasty. B.M. No. 20760.

Bronze aegis of Shu and Tefnut from the tomb of Åmenḥetep III. B.M. No. 388.

The four mud bricks, with their amulets upon them, from the walls of the tomb of Ḥent-meḥit, a singing woman of Åmen-Rā. XXIst dynasty. B.M. Nos. 41544–41547.

Group of Gnostic gems in the British Museum engraved with scenes illustrating the cult of the rising sun, Khnoubis, Abrasax, Sophia as a nude woman, and the birth and Crucifixion of Christ.

Pepi (line 192 f.) the dead king is made to say, "Homage to thee, O divine Ladder! Homage to thee, O Ladder of Set! Stand thou upright, O divine Ladder! Stand thou upright, O Ladder of Set! Stand thou upright, O Ladder of Horus, whereby Osiris appeared in heaven when he worked magic on Rā . . . . . Pepi is thy son, Pepi is Horus. Thou hast given birth to Pepi even as thou didst give birth to the Lord of the Ladder. Give Pepi the Ladder of Horus, give him the Ladder of Set, whereby he shall appear in heaven when he has worked magic on Rā . . . . . Pepi rises like the uraeus on the forehead of Set. Every god and every spirit stretches out his hand to Pepi on the Ladder. Pepi has collected his bones, and gathered together his flesh, and he has gone quickly into heaven by means of the two fingers of the god, the Lord of the Ladder,"

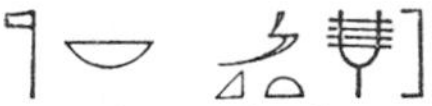 (line 196). In another place we read, "Homage to thee, O thou Ladder! . . . . . Give thy hand to this Pepi. This Pepi seats himself between the two great gods. This Pepi is at the head of the thrones. His hand grasps Sekhet-Ḥetep. He sits among the stars that are in the sky" (lines 472, 473). In the Papyrus of Ani (pl. XXII) a Vignette of the Ladder is given, and in Chapter CXLIX (Åat XI) the deceased says, "I set up a Ladder among the gods, and I am a divine being among them." In the Papyrus of Nu we read, "The Osiris Nu, whose word is truth, appears upon your Ladder which Rā has made for him, and Horus and Suti grasp him by the hand,"  (Chapter CLIIIA, l. 34).

XXVI.—The **Two Fingers,** , *tchebāui*. This amulet has been found in coffins and among the swathings of mummies, and it is usually made of a thin slab of dark green or black stone, or obsidian, or haematite, which is rounded at one end and shaped to represent the index and medius fingers at the other; it varies in length from 3 inches to 3¾ inches, and is sometimes gilded (B.M. 8361, 8362, 8366). This amulet was believed to secure for the deceased the assistance of the two fingers of Horus, who would help him to ascend the Ladder by which Osiris mounted to heaven.

XXVII.—Amulets in mother-of-emerald. This stone was believed to possess magical properties, and amulets made of it were supposed to transmit health and strength to the wearers. Examples are the small plaque in the British Museum (8231), 1¼ inches long, with perforated projection for suspension, which is inscribed with a garbled version of some words from Chapter XXXB, and a portion of a papyrus sceptre, which has been reworked (20602).

XXVIII.—The **Head of Hathor**. Under the XVIIIth dynasty the cult of the goddess Hathor, either in the form of a fat and well-favoured cow or a lovely woman, became prominent, and votive offerings to her shrines were very numerous. These consisted of scarabs, and plaques on which figures of her head were cut, and small gold models of the head of the goddess set upon a standard.[1] These last were usually mounted upon bases made of alabaster or still more precious stone, and as the head on the standard had two faces, each base had steps at its front and back . Gold amulets of the head of the goddess on a standard were worn on necklaces, and B.M. 26977 is a good example of them; it is 1⅜ inches in height; the face of the goddess is triangular, and the ears are large and resemble those of a cow.

This amulet gave to the wearer the protection of Hathor, to whom women prayed for offspring. The cult of Hathor as a cow-goddess probably originated in the great cattle-breeding districts in the Sûdân, and the flint amulet, B.M. 32124, which seems to represent a cow's head, suggests that the cult of the cow existed in the Neolithic Period.

XXIX.—The **Kef-pesesh,** , or **Peseshkef,** , which had the shape , was used in the ceremony of "Opening the Mouth" (see Index). The oldest known example of this instrument as an amulet is B.M. 37279, which is 2¼ inches long, and is 1¾ inches in its widest part. Another example is B.M. 30848, which is made of a reddish carnelian, and is mounted in a gold setting fashioned in the form of the head of a woman wearing a heavy wig. The jawbones of the deceased were made incapable of work by mummification, but when they were touched by the Peseshkef their former power returned to them.

XXX.—The amulets **Neterui** (?) . These amulets are usually made of haematite, or some other kind of hard, dark stone. Under the Old Kingdom, and probably much earlier, the Egyptians gave these instruments the forms of axe-heads attached to handles,[2] as above, but under the XXVIth dynasty they appear in the forms  (B.M. 8330, 8331). The instruments represented by both forms were used in the ceremony of Opening the Mouth, and they completed the work begun by the Peseshkef. The Sem priest said to the deceased in this ceremony, "Osiris Unȧs, thy mouth is opened for thee," and the Rubric indicates that whilst these words were being said by him he presented to the face of the deceased two

[1] This standard may represent the windpipe.
[2] See the text of the Pyramid of Unȧs, l. 27.

instruments made of "iron (?) of the South," , and "iron (?) of the North," , respectively. The two gods represented by are Horus and Set, whilst the two represent two different kinds of metal. These amulets were placed among the wrappings of the mummy near the head, and they were supposed to open the mouth of the deceased and obtain for him the protection of Horus and Set.

XXXI.—The **Steps,** . With this amulet is associated the idea of resurrection, and it is also symbolic of the steps that Shu used to stand upon when he lifted up the Sky-goddess Nut from the embrace of the Earth-god Geb, and of the throne of Osiris. In the fourth section of the Vignette of Chapter X of the Book of the Dead three sets of steps are depicted. And in the Papyrus of Anhai (pl. 8) we see the mummy of the deceased lying on the top of the steps, ,[1] and two figures of Khnem standing, one at its head and the other at its feet. Above, in the blue vault of heaven, are the Eight White Spheres. The amulet of the Steps is usually made of glazed faïence—green, blue or white.

Neolithic amulets. The Neolithic Egyptians appear to have worn models of animals and reptiles made of flint as amulets, and a few examples of these have come down to us. Thus we have the **crocodile** (B.M. 32117), 2 7/16 inches in length, and the **hippopotamus** (B.M. 43066), 3 inches in length. The latter object has a perforated projection on its back, and it is quite clear that it was worn as a pendant. The flint objects and (B.M. 32097, 54429) are also probably amulets.

In every Egyptian collection of importance a large number of **rings,** having a gap in each, will be found; they are made of gold, red jasper, obsidian, red-glazed faïence, shell, stone and glass. Some of those made of gold have a small ring at each end for a wire to pass through (?), and they may thus have been used as ear-rings or pendants for necklaces; on the other hand, they may have been used as amulets. Some have thought that they may have served in some way as buttons.

GNOSTIC AMULETS

THE Egyptians in all periods of their history believed firmly in the magical powers possessed by certain stones, especially when *ḥekau*, or words of power, names of gods, and figures of supernatural beings, when in human or animal forms, were inscribed upon them. Amulets, in some form or other, were absolute necessaries of life to them, and

[1] These steps were in Khemenu (Hermopolis).

when they lost faith in the native varieties that were within their reach, they adopted those that they believed would give them the protection of foreign gods. The Egyptians who embraced Christianity were in this respect no different from their pre-Christian ancestors, but their amulets represented more complex beliefs than the old Egyptian amulets did, and the greater number of these were drawn from the Indian, Persian, Syrian, and Hebrew religions. Some authorities think that Gnosticism is older than Christianity, and some forms of it undoubtedly were in existence many centuries before the Christian Era. The word is derived from the Greek γνῶσις, " knowledge," but the knowledge was of a special and superior kind, transcendental and celestial in character. The Egyptian Kherḥeb, , or priest who performed the sacramental ceremonies in the chapels of the Pyramids of Gîzah in the IVth dynasty, claimed to possess this transcendental knowledge in precisely the same way as did the priest of any Gnostic sect in the Ist or IInd century A.D. In most respects Gnostic amulets only reproduce ancient Egyptian ideas, with additions. The soul of the Egyptian made its way to heaven by the use of spells, prayers, the knowledge of names of power, and the use of symbolic amulets, and the soul of the Gnostic relied on precisely the same things to help his soul into heaven. But his priest helped him materially by simplifying the intricate system of magical figures and symbols and texts, and condensing their powers into a single word, or name, or figure, or symbol. Provided with a magical stone on which any one of these was cut, the Gnostic believed that all heaven was open to his soul when it left his body, and that no devil or demon could resist his will and pleasure. To this belief the Gnostic amulet wholly owes its existence. According to Gnostic teaching Christ Himself was obliged to use words of power to enable Him to descend into hell and to return to the earth, and the Gnostic endeavoured to provide himself with similar means of overcoming the Powers of darkness. This is no place to attempt to summarize the various Gnostic beliefs that are represented on the amulets, or to describe in detail every Gnostic inscription or figure, but the notes given below will indicate their general character. To those who wish to follow up the study of these most interesting but puzzling amulets, the books recommended are : (1) The *Pistis Sophia*, a work probably of the IInd century A.D., the Coptic text edited by Schwartze. There is a German translation by C. Schmidt (*Koptisch-gnostische Schriften*, Bd. I, 1905), and a good English translation by the Rev. G. Horner is now available. (2) The Coptic texts of the two " Books of Ieû," edited with a German translation by C. Schmidt, Leipzig, 1892. (3) Hilgenfeld, *Ketzergeschichte des Urchristentums*, Leipzig, 1884. (4) Lipsius, *Der Gnosticismus*, Leipzig, 1860. (5) Mansel, *The Gnostic Heresies*, London, 1875. (6) Liechtenhahn, *Die Offenbarung im Gnosticismus*, Göttingen, 1901. (7) Staehlin, *Die Gnostischen*

Quellen. Hippolyte, Leipzig, 1890. (8) The list of Gnostic works by Harnack in his *Geschichte*, Parts I and II. (9) E. de Faye, *Introduction*, Paris, 1903. (10) Matter, *Histoire Critique du Gnosticisme*, 2 vols. and plates, Paris, 1828. (11) C. W. King, *The Gnostics and their Remains*, London, 1864. (12) Bellermann, *Drei Programmen über die Abraxas-Gemmen*, Berlin, 1820. There are good articles on "Gnosticism" in Ersch and Gruber's *Encyclopädie* (by Lipsius); in Hastings, *Encyclopaedia of Religions*, Vol. VI, p. 231 ff.; and in the *Encyclopaedia Brit.*, XIth edition, Vol. XII, p. 152 ff.

Gnostic amulets are made of various kinds of green stone and green plasma, green basalt, greenish-grey granite, sard, carnelian, chalcedony, haematite, and, rarely, crystal. They are usually flat and oval in shape, and from half an inch to 3 inches in length; the greater number of them have a bevelled edge, and it seems that they were mounted as bezels in rings, or set in metal frames and worn as pendants. Green stone seems to have been preferred, just as green basalt was the correct material of which to make heart-scarabs. According to Galen, "Some indeed assert that a virtue of this kind is inherent in certain stones, such as is in reality possessed by the Green Jasper, which benefits the chest and mouth, if tied upon them. Some indeed set the stone in a ring, and engrave upon it a serpent with his head crowned with rays. . . . . Of this material I have had ample experience, having made a necklace of such stones, and hung it round the patient's neck, descending low enough for the stones to touch the mouth of the stomach, and they proved to be of no less benefit than if they had been engraved in the manner laid down by King Nechepsos" (*De Simp. Med.*, Book IX; King, *The Gnostics*, p. 74).

Almost all the Gnostic amulets now available for study were found in Egypt, and chiefly in Lower Egypt and the Fayyûm. The designs on the oldest of them, which are pre-Christian, were inspired by the reliefs on monuments like the Metternich-Stele. On one we have the scarab , the hawk of Horus and Rā , the star ★, the crescent moon , and the winged, bird-bodied man holding "life," , in each hand and standing upon a crocodile and two scorpions (B.M. G. 35). This design is given a Gnostic meaning by the words cut on the reverse, **ΙΑΩ ΑΒΡΑΜΑ ΜΑΡΙ**. On another we have a beetle, , within an oval formed by a snake with its tail in its mouth. The beetle is the self-existent one, Kheperà in Egyptian, and the serpent is the protector of the Sun-god and his visible emblem, the sun. The legend on the reverse is one of the well-known Gnostic legends (B.M. G. 455). On a third, a flat, heart-shaped pendant, we have on the obverse the well-known figures of Horus and Rā, each hawk-headed, and seated on a throne and holding a sceptre 𓌀 and ☥. Between them is a winged serpent with a disk on its head, and ☥ suspended from its body. On the reverse is cut the inscription here given, which is thus rendered by C. W. King: "One Bait, one Athôr, one their power, Akôri.[1] Hail, Father of the World! Hail, triformed god!" The Egyptian triad referred to is probably Kheperȧ-Shu-Tefnut, but the Gnostics identified these purely Egyptian figures with triune gods of their own, and the Christians among them with the Christian Trinity (B.M. G. 1). A portion of the scene in which the deceased is represented reaping in the Elysian Fields seems to be reproduced on B.M. G. 46 and 227. On these haematite ovals the bowed figure of an aged man is seen reaping, and on the reverse of 46 is the word CΧΙѠΝ, which may be connected with the Egyptian *sekh*, 𓋴𓐍𓌳, to reap. Another purely Egyptian figure is seen on B.M. G. 69, that is, Harpokrates rising up out of a lotus. Twelve rays emerge from his head, and he holds in his left hand a whip, to the top of which a crescent moon is attached. By the flower is a lizard. On the reverse is a legend in which the well-known ΑΒΛΑΝ ΑΘΑΝ, "thou art our father," surrounded by a serpent with its tail in its mouth, occurs (B.M. G. 69). Another example shows us Harpokrates in a boat, with two serpent attendants and two adorers (B.M. G. 68). In Harpokrates the Egyptians, Gnostic Christians, Gnostics and followers of Mithras saw the supreme God of heaven and earth. Below the boat is the name ΑΒΡΑCΑΞ, "Abrasax," which will be mentioned again later on. The haematite plaque B.M. G. 139 shows an extraordinary mixture of beliefs. A naked woman is standing below a crown which is held over her head by two winged angels; on each of her hands rests a bird; before her stands a Cupid holding a looking-glass, and behind her is a jug, emblematic of purification; the inscription reads ΦΑCΙC ΑΡΙѠΡΙΦ, "the manifestation of Ariôriph." On the reverse is Harpokrates seated on a flower with four buds, which springs from a lamp with two burners formed of two phalli united at the bases. Around him are the seven planets, and triads of beetles, hawks, ibises, crocodiles, goats, and uraei, symbolic of Kheperȧ, Thoth, Horus, Sebek, and other Egyptian gods. Above these are the great names ΙΑѠ, Iaô, and ΑΒΡΑCΑΞ, Abrasax. From an Egyptian point of view the naked woman is Hathor, but to the Gnostics SOPHIA, and to the Ophites ACHAMOTH. In the Revelation of Marcus it is said that the Supreme Quaternion came down from heaven

ЄΙC ΒΑΙΤ
ЄΙC ΑΘѠΡ ΜΙ
Α ΤѠΝ ΒΙΑ ЄΙC
ΔЄ ΑΚѠΡΙ ΧΑΙΡЄ
ΠΑΤЄΡ ΚΟCΜΟΥ ΧΑ
ΙΡЄ ΤΡΙΜΟΡΦЄ ΘЄΟC

[1] ΑΚѠΡΙ, not ΑΧѠΡΙ, as King prints it.

in the form of a naked woman, and that she was revealed to Marcus as TRUTH. She opened her mouth and uttered a Word, which became a Name, which we know as Christ Jesus.[1]

Several Gnostic amulets were believed to be talismans of great power through the names of the Hebrew Archangels that were written upon them, and through magical signs that were not of Hebrew origin. Thus on B.M. G. 110 we have the signs **NJ ✱ NJ** ▽ (?) surrounded by a serpent, and outside these are the names **ΓΑΒΡΙΗΛ, ΦΝΙΗΛ, ΡΑΓΑΥΗΛ, ΟΥΡΙΗΛ, ΡΑΦΑΗΛ, CΟΥΡΙΗΛ, ΜΙΧΑΗΛ.** On the reverse are the great name **ΙΑω** and the legend, which to me is incomprehensible. An example inscribed with the names of Hebrew Archangels, **ΙΑω**, and what is apparently a prayer to them, is afforded by B.M. G. 201, where we have **ΜΕΙΧΑΗΛ ΓΑΒΡΙΗΛ ΡΑΦΑΗΛ CЄCЄΝΤЄ ΚΙΒΑΡΑΝΓΗ ΝΙΑω.** This amulet is made of chalcedony.

ΟΥΑΗΙ ΘΥΗΘ
ΥΑΗ ΗΙΗΛΑΨЄΙΗ
Α ΒΙΒΙ ΟΥΒΙΒΙΟ
ΥCΦΗCΦΗΚΟ
ΥΘΧΖΘΚΗΦΑΘ
ΚΘ

Abraxas Amulets.—These are Gnostic amulets on which is cut one form or another of the god Abraxas or Abrasax, who was especially esteemed by the Basilidans, a Christian philosophic sect which was founded by Basilides in the last half of the Ist or first half of the IInd century. He was an Egyptian who was born at Alexandria, and who professed to be a pupil of Glaucias, a disciple of St. Peter. The figure which he invented for his god consisted of the body of a man with the head of a cock, two arms, one hand holding a shield and the other a whip, and two legs, which were in the form of serpents. This figure represented a Pantheos with Five Emanations; the cock's head represents Phronesis, the serpent-legs Nous and Logos, and the arms Sophia and Dynamis. The shield symbolizes Wisdom, and the whip Power. The sum of the numerical values of the letters of his name = 365 (**Α** = 1, **Β** = 2, **Ρ** = 100, **Α** = 1, **C** = 200, **Α** = 1, **Ξ** = 60, total 365), and he was said to be the lord of the 365 Heavens, and of the angels and Aeons thereof. The Aeons were arranged in pairs by Valentinus, and were fifteen in number, each containing a male and a female.[2] A knowledge of the names of the Aeons enabled its possessor to do what Christ (Whom the Basilidans call **ΚΑΥΛΑCΑΥ**) did—triumph over all powers, both celestial and terrestrial. The meaning of the name Abrasax has been discussed by King and others, but no satisfactory derivation for it seems to have been found. According to Leemans (Papyrus III, 210–213) the Egyptian form

[1] King, *The Gnostics*, p. 39, and Plate V, No. 1.

[2] We have the same idea in the companies of gods of Heliopolis and Hermopolis, and in the Babylonian story of the Creation.

of the name is , but the name Abrasax can hardly be of Egyptian origin. A good example of the cock-headed Abraxas is given on B.M. G. 54, where he is seen holding a shield inscribed with the name of ΙΑΩ; on the reverse is the legend ΑΒΩ ΧΩΝ ΙΩΧ, surrounded by a serpent. More elaborate figures of Abraxas, or Abrasax, are given by Matter (Pll. V and VI). In one he is called ΓΙΓΑΝΤΟΡΗΚΤΑ, or "breaker of giants" (No. 1); in another he stands above the material world, he is called ΚΕΝΕ, and around him are the names of ΙΑΩ, or Mithras, ΑΔΩΝΑΙ, the Hebrew God, אדני, and Michael the Archangel. The letters ΚΦΛ = Kurios, Phôtos and Logos, respectively, and his shield called ΕΛΠ(ΙS) indicates "hope" (No. 3). On another amulet he is seen surrounded by the Seven Spirits of Ialdabaoth in the form of the Seven Stars of Michael-Ophiomorphos (No. 5), and on others he is identified with Ananaël, an ass-headed god (No. 6). Other forms of Abrasax in the character of ΙΑΩ are well shown on B.M. G. 11, 14 and 18, and all are modifications of the Egyptian four-winged pantheistic figure. A form of this four-winged figure with the head of the jackal Anubis is well shown on B.M. G. 119; in the field are a beetle , a crescent, and a star. Compare also the examples given by Matter (Pl. II, C).

Khnoubis amulets, or Agathodaemon Talismans. This god's name is spelt ΧΝΟΥΜΙC, ΧΝΟΥΦΙC, ΧΝΟΥΒΙC; he is represented in the form of a huge serpent having the head of a lion, from which proceed seven or twelve rays. When the rays are seven in number, on the end of each stands one of the seven vowels, ΑΕΗΙΟΥΩ, and each vowel symbolizes one of the seven heavens. On almost every Khnoubis amulet the name of the god is cut on some part of it, and on the back of the amulet is the triple **S** on a bar 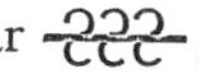, the exact signification of which is unknown. The Seven Vowels, arranged or grouped in various combinations, are found on many Gnostic amulets. Thus on the obverse of B.M. G. 33 we see the lion-headed Khnoubis, this time with a man's body, and an ass-headed god,[1] holding up a standard of unique form, in exactly the same way as on scarabs we see the obelisk of Åmen being held up by priests; on the reverse the Seven Vowels are cut thus:—

ΑΕΕΗ
ΗΗΙΙΙΙΟΟ
ΟΟΟΥΥΥΥ
ΥΥΩΩΩ
ΩΩΩΩΩ

The slaughter of the dragon by an angel or god on a horse is often represented on Gnostic amulets. On B.M. G. 88 and 149 the horseman is called Solomon, CΑΛΟΜΩΝ; on the reverse is cut CΦΡΑΓΙC ΘΕΟΥ, "seal of God." On the bronze pendant B.M. G. 498 we have the same scene on the

[1] The engraver may have intended the head to be that of a jackal (Anubis), but the head actually engraved is that of an ass.

obverse, and on the reverse the names ΙΑΩ, ϹΑΒΑΩ[Θ], ΜΙΧΑΗΛ, ΓΑΒΡΙΗΛ, ΟΥΡΙΗΛ. Below these names are a star, ✱, and the Mithraïc Lion. On B.M. G. 323 the obverse has a similar scene, but on the reverse are a bird, a serpent, and an unidentifiable object. **Christian Gnostic amulets** are rare, but on B.M. G. 231 the Crucifixion seems to be depicted; the inscription on the reverse throws no light on the scene. A remarkable scene is represented on B.M. G. 469. A woman is standing beside a tree, and is giving birth to a child from her left side, whilst a figure in front of her is presenting to her face ☥, the symbol of "life"; on the other side of the tree is an animal. On the reverse is a large ☥, and round it runs the inscription ЄΙϹ ΘΕΟϹ Ν ΟΥΡΑΝΩ. This amulet is made of a dark reddish stone, and was given to the British Museum by Sir H. Rider Haggard. The scene calls to mind the birth of Horus among the papyrus swamps of the Delta, when Åmen-Rā presented ☥ to Isis and Thoth 𓎿, or magical protection.[1] On the other hand it may refer to the birth of the Buddha in the Lumbini Garden, when the child was brought forth from his mother's left side. But no animal was present at the birth of Horus or the Buddha, while both an ox and an ass were in the stable when Christ was born. The inscription "One God of heaven" seems to connect the amulet with Christian rather than with non-Christian or Buddhistic legends. Two names from the Old Testament, which was all but ignored by the Gnostics generally, are sometimes found on Gnostic amulets, namely Solomon and Moses. On one amulet published by Matter (Pl. X, No. 1) are the three names ΙΑΩ, ϹΟΛΟΜΟΝ and ϹΑΒΑΩ, and on another are the names ΙΑΩ, ϹΑΒΑΩ and ΜΟΥϹΗ, with a serpent. Some amulets are inscribed with bearded, mummy-like figures which are symbolic both of Osiris and our Lord, and these are accompanied by Gnostic inscriptions and emblems (B.M. G. 25). An amulet published by Matter (Pl. II, B, No. 6) shows us the Cross, ✚, and the legend ΟΣΙΡΙΣ, Osiris, and King (Pl. VI, No. 4) publishes an amulet on which the Cross has a human head; the reverse of the latter is inscribed with eight vowels, thus ΑΙΟΥ / ΗΕΩΙ.

In the designs on the amulets of the IIIrd century A.D. the Mithraïc influence is very strong. On the obverse of B.M. G. 434 we have a six-armed man with a torch in each of four hands, and a serpent in each of the other two; on the reverse is a figure of ΙΑΩ in the form of an ape with a tail. Babylonian influence is shown in the palms and in the dress of the goddess who is represented on B.M. G. 8. The lion of Mithras and two stars appear on B.M. G. 156,

[1] See Budge, *Gods of the Egyptians*, Vol. II, plate facing p. 208.

with an inscription in the so-called "enigmatic" writing used by magicians in Egypt in the late period. The Egyptian mythical animals, the Ākhekh, , and the Sefer, , and the Sag, , find their descendants in the animals cut on B.M. G. 86 and 459. But the origin of the crocodile with a serpent's head and neck, and a tail ending in a bird's head, on B.M. G. 552 is not clear. On the obverse of B.M. G. 25, a large oval green stone plaque, Osiris in mummy form, bearded and wearing a five-pointed crown, is seen ascending into heaven with the help of four beings, two of whom have wings, who stand on a three-zoned planisphere. On the reverse he is seen standing amid eight stars or heavens. The four figures who raise Osiris are the four sons of Horus in Gnostic forms, and the planisphere represents the earth. The inscription is composed chiefly of vowels :—

YOIYHIYHIYHIXI
IHYTIOXωXYO
HYIOIYΔHTX(?)IX

Below the angels on one side is **IYO** and on the other **Iה(?)I** The large letters appear to be forms taken from some Semitic alphabet ; compare the drawing in King, Pl. VI, No. 1, but the original of this drawing must have been a modern, or rather a mediaeval copy, for it has on it the astrologer's pentagon, commonly called "Solomon's Seal."

From what has been said above it is clear that Egypt was the earliest home of the amulets now called "Gnostic," and that the Indians, Persians, Hebrews, Greeks, and the Gnostic sects added nothing of fundamental importance to the religious magic of the Egyptians. The chief object of the Egyptians, as well as of all these peoples with religions alien to that of the Egyptians, was to attain to a happy resurrection, and to a new and immortal life, and to gain absolute freedom to travel at will through all heaven. But not all Gnostic amulets were made with such a high purpose, for some were merely intended to protect their wearers from attacks by diseases of various kinds. This is certain from an amulet in the Cabinet de Sainte-Geneviève published by Matter (Pl. II, C, No. 4). On the obverse is a figure of the lion-headed serpent Khnoubis, facing a hawk-headed mummy ; behind him is a draped woman wearing on her head the emblem of Isis, . Below these, resting on a stand, is the so-called "vase of sins," to which four serpents are attached. In the field are the Seven Vowels **AEHIOYω**. The whole scene is surrounded by a serpent with its tail in its mouth. "Vase of sins" is the name that Matter gave to the pot or vase seen on the Gnostic amulets, because he thought that it represented the jar or vessel in which the embalmers placed the viscera of the deceased. This jar, he thought, was held up to the gods, who were assured by the priest that it contained the sources of all the sins committed by the deceased during his lifetime, and therefore the sole portion of him deserving of future punishment. Now the object on the amulets is not a vase at all, but a representation of the uterus of the goddess Isis, or of one of her many forms, and the legend on the reverse of the amulet proves this; it reads: **ΤΑССΟΝ ΤΗΝ ΜΗΤΡΑΝ ΤΗС ΔΕΙΝΑ ΕΙС ΤΟΝ ΙΔΙΑΝ ΤΟΠΟΝ Ω ΤΟΝ ΚΥΚΛΟΝ ΤΟΥ ΗΛΕΙΟΥ.** "Place the womb of Such-and-such a one in its proper place, O circle of the sun." Thus the amulet was intended to protect the woman who wore it from "a frequent complaint in ancient times, owing to the abuse of the hot bath" (King, *op. cit.*, p. 153). Round the edge of the obverse is an inscription, which was probably added by one of the owners of the amulet; it reads: **СΤΡΑΠΙΝΝΑΠΟ ΚΑΙΝΕΙΑΛΛΥΧΝΟΥ ΩΡΩΖΟΕΡΟΝΧΩ.** Other amulets on which the "vase" of Isis is represented are B.M. G. 238 and 479. On the latter the Khnoubis figure is called **ΙΑΩ** or **ΙΑΩΙ**, and on the reverse, below the bird and altar and double SS, are the two names **ΟΡΩΡΙΟΥΘ** and **ΙΑΩ**. The serpent that surrounds the scene on each of these gems suggests that they were used by the Ophites, perhaps exclusively. The black stone oval (B.M. G. 486) on which is cut a beetle with the bearded head of a god is probably another Ophite amulet; in this example eleven rays proceed from the head, and round them is written **ЄΙΛΑΜΨ**, the **СЄΜЄС** being omitted. As an example of the mixture of Indian and Egyptian gods B.M. G. 251 may be noted, for it also is an Ophite amulet. On the obverse stands a deity with three faces and three pairs of arms and hands. On her right side is a figure of Harpokrates, and on her left is the lion-headed serpent Khnoubis; on the reverse is the snake coiled into a circle, within which are the seven stars of the Seven Planets or of the Seven Heavens.

In the space available here it is not possible even to summarize the inscriptions that are found on Gnostic amulets, and that up to the present have defied all attempts to translate them. But enough is now known about them to justify the statement that some of them contain garbled forms of the names of the Thirty Aeons and their rulers mixed up with the Seven Vowels arranged in mystic order, and some of them magical names such as are found in the two Books of Ieû, and others series of letters, each letter of which is the first of a word in some Oriental language. Gnostic amulets were copied largely in the Middle Ages, and the names of gods, Aeons, and Archangels became greatly corrupted, and formulae also, for there seems to be little doubt that Abracadabra, the great word of power used by wizards, is derived from **ΑΒΛΑΝΑΘΑΝΑΛΒΑ**, as King and others have stated.

How the bodies of the slaves, male and female, throughout the country, and those of the destitute (and the maimed, the halt, the blind, and the half-witted, who must have existed in the great towns like Memphis, Heliopolis, Hânês, Abydos, Thebes, etc.) were disposed of is not known for a certainty. But judging from the well-known customs of the peoples of Africa before the coming of Islâm, we may assume that the destitute dead were carried out into the desert, or to the slopes of the hills, and left there for the hyenas and desert wolves, and jackals, to dispose of. In regions where the hills came down to the river-bank they were probably thrown into the Nile and became the food of the crocodiles. The bodies of the poorer members of the fallâḥ, or peasant, class, also must have been treated in much the same way. In fact, large numbers of people were never " buried " at all in our sense of the word, for all the land on each side of the Nile was required for agricultural purposes and any and every part of it was far too valuable to turn into a cemetery. The body of the ordinary citizen was either dried in the sun, or washed with a solution of natron, and then placed in a hollow in the sand on the edge of the desert, or thrust into a cave in the skirts of the hills. In either case the wild beasts must have dragged the dead from their resting-places and devoured them. Sometimes the body was wrapped loosely in a coarse linen cloth and buried in a hole dug in the sand, with his stick to support his steps, and his sandals to protect his feet during his long journey to the Other World. Nobles and men of high rank and authority in the community, and wealthy civilians, were really " buried," *i.e.*, they were laid in graves or caves in the hills which were carefully guarded, and under the early dynasties their bodies were wrapped in skins, or placed in baskets, or in earthenware chests, or in rudely made boxes. It is probable that the deceased, when carried to his grave, was accompanied by his kinsfolk and friends, whose number depended upon his social importance and wealth, and who, as they went, intoned praises of him, whilst the women of his house bewailed their loss with shrill cries. Whether any ceremonies, religious or magical, were performed at the grave of the ordinary citizen is not known, but under the earliest dynasties, at least, only kings and royal personages, and priestly and civil officials, and hereditary landowners, could afford to have tombs and to have adequate funerary rites and ceremonies performed when they were deposited in them.

The funeral of a great official must have been a very elaborate affair, especially under the XVIIIth dynasty, when Egypt was filled with the gold of the Sûdân and the tribute of Western Asia, and it is impossible for us to realize to the full the magnificence of the funerary equipment and the pomp that attended the burial of the mummy of a really great king and conqueror like Thothmes III. Treating of the burial of a king in Egypt, Diodorus says (I, 72), that when a king died all the inhabitants of the country wept and rent their garments ; the temples were closed, and the people abstained from sacrifices and celebrated no festival for a period of seventy-two days. Crowds of men and women, about two or three hundred in number, went round about the streets with mud on their heads, and with their garments knotted like girdles below the breasts (*σινδόνας ὑποκάτω τῶν μαστῶν*), singing dirges twice daily in praise of the dead. They denied themselves wheat, they ate no animal food, and they abstained from wine and dainty fare. No one dared to make use of baths, or unguents, or to recline upon couches, or even to partake of the pleasures of love. The seventy-two days were passed in grief and mourning as for the death of a beloved child. Meanwhile, the funeral paraphernalia was made ready, and on the last day of mourning the body, placed in a coffin, was laid at the entrance to the tomb, and according to law, judgment was passed upon the acts of the king during his life. Every one had the power to make an accusation against the king. The priests pronounced a funeral oration over the body, and declared the noble works of the king, and if the opinion of the assembled multitude agreed with that of the priests, and the king had led a blameless life, they testified their approval openly ; if, on the other hand, the life of the king had been a bad one, they expressed their disapprobation by loud murmurs. Through the opposition of the people many kings have been deprived of meet and proper burial, and kings are accustomed to exercise justice, not only because they fear the disapprobation of their subjects, but also because they fear that after death their bodies may be maltreated, and their memory cursed for ever.

It is very doubtful if the above description of the mourning is not somewhat exaggerated, and there appears to be no authority in Egyptian inscriptions for the statement that many kings were deprived of their meet and proper burial because of the disapproval of their past lives shown by the people. This account by Diodorus is more valuable for the indication of the great and solemn respect that was shown to dead kings, as sons of the god Rā and as lords of the land of Egypt, than for its strict accuracy of detail. The customs observed at the burial of kings would be respectfully imitated at the funerals of the nobles and officials of his court, and the account, by the same writer, of what happened after the mummy of an Egyptian gentleman was prepared for burial, may next be mentioned.

According to Diodorus (I, 92), when the body is ready to be buried, the relatives give notice to the judges and the friends of the deceased, and inform them that the funeral will take place on a certain day, and that the body will pass over the lake ; and straightway the judges, forty in number,[1] come and seat themselves in a semi-circle above the lake. Then the men who have been commissioned to

[1] Is it possible that Diodorus has confused the forty judges at the lake with the forty-two judges or assessors of the Book of the Dead, before each of whom the deceased was supposed to declare that he had not committed a certain sin ?

prepare a boat called βᾶρις,[1] bring it to the lake, and they set it afloat under the charge of a pilot called Charon. And they pretend that Orpheus, travelling in Egypt in ancient times, was present at a ceremony of this kind, and that he drew his fable of the infernal regions partly from his remembrance of this ceremony,[2] and partly from his imagination. Before the coffin containing the dead man was placed in the boat on the lake, every person had the right to bring accusations against him. If any accuser succeeded in showing that the deceased had led a bad life, the judges made a decree which deprived the body of legal burial; if, on the other hand, the accusation was found to be unjust, the person who brought it was compelled to pay heavy damages. If no one stood forth to bring an accusation, or if an accusation seemed calumnious, the relatives of the deceased ceased to mourn and began to praise the dead man and his virtues, and to entreat the gods of the infernal regions to admit him into the place reserved for good men. The Egyptians never praised the birth of a man, as did the Greeks, for they believed that all men are equally noble. The people being gathered together, add their cries of joy, and utter wishes that the deceased may enjoy everlasting life in the underworld in the company of the blessed. Those who have private burial places lay the bodies of their dead in the places set apart for them ; but those who have not, build a new chamber in their house, and set the body in it fixed upright against the wall. Those who are deprived of burial, either because they lie under the ban of an accusation, or because they have not paid their debts, are merely laid in their own houses. It happens sometimes that the younger members of a family, having become richer, pay the debts of their ancestors, secure the removal of the condemnatory sentence upon them, and give them most sumptuous funerals. The great honours that are paid to the dead by the Egyptians form the most solemn ceremonies. As a guarantee for a debt, it is a customary thing to deposit the bodies of dead parents, and the greatest disgrace and privation from burial wait upon those who redeem not such sacred pledges.

In this account also there are many details given for which proof is still wanting from the Egyptian monuments.

An attempt may now be made to describe briefly what happened after death to the body of a man of high rank who departed this life at Thebes towards the end of the XVIIIth or beginning of the XIXth dynasty—that is to say, about B.C. 1450. The facts are all known, and it is only necessary to focus them on the person of one man. We must imagine, then, that we are living on the east bank of

[1] In Egyptian :  *barei.*

[2] Thus Orpheus brought back from his travels in Egypt the ceremonies, and the greater part of the mystic rites celebrated in memory of the courses of Ceres, and the whole of the myth of hell. The difference between the feasts of Bacchus and of those of Osiris exists only in name, and the same may be said of the mysteries of Isis and those of Ceres. Diodorus, I, 96.

the Nile, near the temple of Åmen-Rā, in the Northern Åpt at Thebes, in the XVth century before Christ. One morning at dawn, even before the officials who conduct the dawn services in the temples are astir, we are awakened by loud cries of grief and lamentation, and on making inquiries are told that Ani, the great scribe of the offerings of the gods in the temple of Åmen-Rā, is dead. As he was the receiver of the revenues of the gods of Abydos, as well as of Åmen-Rā of Thebes, his death naturally causes great excitement in the temples and the immediate neighbourhood. His forefathers for generations have been temple-officers of the highest rank, and it is certain that his funeral will be a great event, and that numbers of the hereditary aristocracy and government officials will assist at the ceremony. He leaves no wife to mourn for him, for she is already dead, and is now lying in a chamber of a rock-hewn tomb, not yet finished, however, nine miles away across the river, awaiting the coming of her husband. She was called Tutu, and belonged to one of the oldest and most honourable families in Thebes, and was a member of the famous college of singers of Åmen-Rā, and also of the choir of ladies, each one of whom rattled a sistrum or beat a tambourine in the temple of that god. The hewing of this tomb was begun under Ani's directions many years before his death, and the work had gone on year by year for several years; Ani spared neither trouble nor expense. Ani was probably an old man when he died. He was a learned man, and knew the religious literature of Egypt well; he himself wrote a fine, bold hand, and was, it seems, no mean artist with his pencil. He was a tried servant of the king, and loved him well, but he loved his god Åmen more, and was very jealous for his honour and for the glory of his worship in the temple of the Northern Åpt. All his ancestors had been in the service of the god and he, or his father, had seen the disastrous consequences of the reign of Åmenḥetep IV, who tried to overthrow the supremacy of Åmen-Rā, the King of the Gods. It was even said that the oldest of them had seen Åmen—who, until the expulsion of the Hyksos by the kings of Thebes, had occupied the position of a mere local deity—suddenly become the national god of Egypt. Whether Ani believed in his innermost heart any or all of the official religion is another matter. His official position brought him into contact with the temporal rather than the spiritual affairs of the Egyptian religion, and whatever doubts he may have had in matters of belief, or concerning the efficacy of the magic of his day, he professed to be a devout follower of Osiris, and died in the hope of resurrection through him.

For some days past it had been seen that Ani's death was to be expected, and many of his colleagues in the temple had come to visit him from time to time, one bringing a charm, another a decoction of herbs, etc., and a few had taken it in turns to stay in his room for some hours at a time. One night his illness took a decidedly serious turn, and early in the morning, a short time before daybreak, when, as the Orientals say, the dawn may be smelled, Ani died. The news of his death spreads rapidly through the quarter, for all the women of his house rush frantically through the streets, beating their breasts, and from time to time clutching at their hair, which is sprinkled with the thick dust of the streets, and uttering wailing cries of grief. In the house, parties of mourning women shriek out their grief, and the rest of the household add their tears and sobs. The steward of the house has sent to the *Kher-ḥeb*, or priest who superintends and arranges the funerals of the wealthy and great, and informed him of Ani's death, and as quickly as possible this official, together with his assistants, makes his way to Ani's house. Having arrived there he takes Ani's body into his charge, and proceeds to discuss with Ani's son the method by which the body shall be preserved, and the style of the funeral. While his assistants are taking away the body to the embalming house, he sends quickly to the western bank of the Nile and summons the chief mason of the necropolis to his presence. When he arrives the *Kher-ḥeb* instructs him to go to Ani's tomb with a body of men and to finish hewing whatever chambers and pillars remain in a half-completed state, and to paint upon the plastered walls certain scenes representing recent events in Ani's life, for which he supplies him with details and notes. The *Kher-ḥeb* knows that for many years past Ani, and one or two of his friends among the scribes, had been writing and illuminating with Vignettes a fine copy of the Book of the Dead; he remembers that this work remains unfinished, and he therefore sets a skilful scribe to finish it in the style in which Ani would probably have finished it. Parties of professional mourners are next organized, and these go round about the city at stated times, singing in chorus—probably accompanied by reed pipes—funeral dirges, the subjects of which are the shortness of life and the certainty that all must die, and the instability of all human affairs. These dirges were sung twice daily, and Ani's friends and colleagues, during the days of mourning, thought it to be their duty to abstain from wine and every kind of luxury, and they wore the simplest and plainest garments, and went quite unadorned.

Meanwhile it was decided that Ani's funeral should be one of the best that money could buy, and as while he was alive he was thought to be in constant communion with the gods, his relatives ordered that his body should be mummified in the best possible way, so that his soul, , *ba*, and his spirit, , *ȧakhu*, whensoever they returned to visit his body in the tomb, might find his , *ka*, or "double,"[1] there waiting, and all three might enter into com-

[1] I have used the word "double" to translate  simply because it is convenient to do so, but I doubt if that or any other single word known to us represents the ideas which the primitive Egyptians attached to . The rendering of *ka* has presented difficulties to every Egyptologist, as we may

munion with the body and enjoy reunion with it. No opportunity must be given to these four essential parts of the man to drift away one from the other, and to prevent this the perishable body, 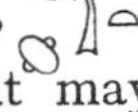, *kha-t*, must be preserved in such a way that each limb of it may be identified with a god, and the whole of it with Osiris. Moreover, the tomb must be made a fit and proper dwelling-place for the *ka*, which will never leave it as long as the body to which it belongs lies in its tomb. The furniture of the tomb must be of the best, and every material, and the workmanship thereof, must also be of the best.

The *Kher-ḥeb* next goes to the embalming chamber and orders his assistants to begin their operations upon Ani's body, over which assistants are preparing to recite protective formulas. The body is first washed and then laid upon the ground, and one of the assistants traces with ink on the left side, over the groin, a line, some few inches long, to indicate where the incision is to be made ; another assistant takes a knife, probably made of flint, and makes a cut in the body the same length as the line drawn in ink by his companion. The Greeks called the man who ripped up the body lengthwise a παρασχιστής. Whether this man was then driven away with sticks and stones thrown after him, as Diodorus states, or not, is a point upon which the inscriptions give us no information. The intestines and the heart and the lungs, the liver and gall-bladder and the stomach, were then carefully taken out and washed in palm wine and stuffed with sweet-smelling spices, gums, etc. They were next smeared all over with an unguent, and then carefully bandaged with strips of linen many yards long, on which were inscribed the names of the four sons of Horus[1]

see by the variety of meanings that have been suggested, *e.g.*, person, personality, self, individual, genius, spirit, emblem, type, being, principle, image, semblance, statue, εἴδωλον, simulacrum, idol, double, ghost, etc. The number and variety of these renderings seem to me to prove that no modern man knows, or can ever know, exactly what the primitive African meant when he invented the word *ka*. The *general* meaning of the word was first pointed out by Birch, in his *Mémoire sur une Patère*, Paris, 1858, p. 59 ff., and supplementary evidence as to its general correctness was supplied by Maspero in 1878 at the Congress at Lyons, by Renouf in *Trans. Soc. Bibl. Arch.*, Vol. VI, p. 494 ff., and by Brugsch, Dümichen, Bergmann, Wiedemann and others. For the divergent and contradictory modern views on the subject see Moret, "Le Ka des Égyptiens, est-il un ancien totem ?" (in *Revue des Religions*, 1913) ; Steindorff, "Der Ka und die Grabstatuen" (in *Aeg. Zeit.*, Bd. XLVIII, pp. 152–159) ; von Bissing in the *Sitzungsberichte* of the Bavarian Academy, 1911, Abth. V ; Breasted, *Development*, p. 52 ff. ; Maspero in *Memnon*, tom. VI, p. 125 ff., and in *Revue Critique*, 1912, No. 43 ; Moret, *Mystères Égyptiens*, p. 199 ; and Sottas in *Sphinx*, tom. XVII, p. 33.

[1] Compare 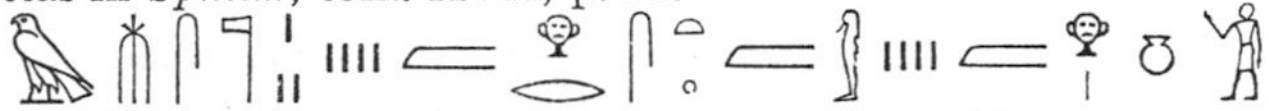 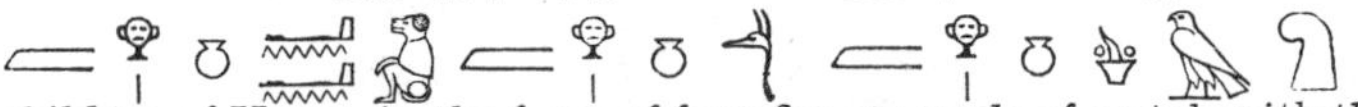 "the four children of Horus, in the form of four figures made of metal, with the face of a man, with the face of an ape, with the face of a jackal, and with the face of a hawk."

who symbolized the four cardinal points and of the four goddesses who took the viscera under their special protection. While this was being done a set of four alabaster jars was brought from the *Kher-ḥeb's* establishment, and in each of these one of the four packets of embalmed viscera was placed. Each jar was inscribed with a formula, and all that was wanted to make it the property of Ani was to inscribe his name upon it in the blank spaces left for the purpose. Each jar had a cover made in the form of the head of the son of Horus to whom it was dedicated. The jar of Mestȧ, , had the head of a man, and in it was placed the stomach ; it was under the protection of Isis. The jar of Ḥāpi, , had the head of an ape, and in it were placed the smaller intestines ; it was under the protection of Nephthys. The jar of Ṭuamutef, , had the head of a jackal, and in it was placed the heart ; it was under the protection of Neith. The jar of Qebḥsenuf, , had the head of a hawk, and in it were placed the liver and large intestines ; it was under the protection of Serqit. The inscriptions on the jars state that the part of the deceased in it is identified with the son of Horus to whom the jar is dedicated, and that the goddess under whose charge it is protects it. The covers of the jars are fastened on by running in liquid plaster, and they are finally set in the four divisions of a coffer on a sledge with a vaulted cover and a projecting rectangular upright at each corner. It was of the greatest importance to have the internal organs[1] preserved intact, for without them a man could not hope to live again.

The brain is next removed through the nostrils by means of an iron rod curved at one end, and is put aside to be dried and buried with the body ; at every step in these processes religious and magical sentences are recited. The body thus deprived of its more perishable parts is taken and laid to soak in a tank of liquid natron for a period of seventy days.[2] At the end of this time it is taken out and carefully washed and dried, and it is seen that it is of a greenish-grey colour ; the skin clings to the bones, for the flesh beneath it has shrunk somewhat, but the hair of the body is well preserved, the nails of the hands and feet still adhere to the skin, and the face, though now drawn and very thin, has changed but little. Longitudinal slits are next made in the fingers and toes and the fleshy

[1] In mummies of the best period the internal organs are sometimes found in packets beneath the bandages.

[2] Compare , "Thy seventy days are fulfilled in the Chamber of Embalmment," Gardiner, text in Garis Davies, *Amenemhēt*, p. 56.

parts of the arms, thighs and legs, which are then stuffed with a mixture of sweet spices and natron and sewn up again. The cavity in the skull is now filled up with a mixture of spices, powdered plaster and natron, and the nostrils, through which it was inserted, are plugged up with small linen pledgets dipped in an astringent liquid; white stone eyes, with pupils of black obsidian, are also inserted in the eye-sockets. Large quantities of gums, spices, natron, etc., are pounded and well mixed together, and with them the breast and stomach are carefully packed through the slit in the side. While certain formulae are being recited, a gold plate inscribed with the *Utchat*, , or eye of Horus, is laid upon the slit to indicate that this god watches over this body as he did over that of his father Osiris. The nails of the hands are stained with *ḥinnâ* (Arab. حنّاء), and on the little finger of the left hand is placed Ani's gold ring, in the bezel of which is mounted a glazed steatite scarab inscribed on the base with his name and titles. The ring gave to the deceased the protection and strength of the Sun-god. No one was buried without one or more rings, and if the relatives of the deceased were not able to buy them in gold or silver, they made use of faïence rings, glazed in various colours, and even of small strings of beads, or linen, or straw, which they tied on the fingers in lieu of rings. The legs are then brought closely together, and the arms are laid on the body with one wrist crossed over the other. The *Kher-ḥeb* next provides a large and handsome scarab made of green basalt which is set in a frame of gold. Over the back of it is a horizontal band of the same metal, at right-angles to which, on the side of the tail of the beetle, runs another band which joins the frame; at the head of the scarab is a gold loop, through which is now threaded a thick gold wire sufficiently long to go round Ani's neck. This scarab was part of the stock-in-trade of the *Kher-ḥeb*, and all that was necessary to make it Ani's property was to inscribe his name and titles upon it in the blank line left for the purpose at the head of the flat base. This done the scarab was covered with a thin gold plate and laid upon Ani's breast at the neck.[1] The inscription upon it is Chapter XXXB of the Book of the Dead, and contains a prayer, addressed by Ani to his heart, that there might not be brought against him adverse evidence when it was weighed in the Balance in the Judgment Hall of Osiris, that his name might not be "made to stink," *i.e.*, vilified, before the POWERS who examined and judged the dead. The prayer ends with a petition that no false evidence may be borne against him in the presence of the god.

And now the bandaging begins. The body is first of all smeared all over with unguents. Pieces of linen are then torn into strips

[1] According to some Rubrics of Chapter XXXB the scarab was to be placed "within the heart" of a person, where it would "open the mouth,"

about 3 inches wide, and one edge of each strip is gummed. On one end of each of these the name of Ani has been written in hieratic characters to facilitate the identification of the mummy during the process of bandaging. The embalmers having bandaged the fingers, hands, and arms, and toes separately, begin to bandage the body from the feet upwards. The bandages cling tightly to the body, and the gummed edge enables each fold of the bandage to obtain firm hold ; the little irregularities are corrected by small pledgets of linen placed between the folds and gummed in position. These linen bandages are also held in position by means of narrower strips of linen wound round the body at intervals of 6 and 8 inches, and tied in a double knot. On these fine linen bandages passages from the Book of the Dead, and formulae which were intended to give power to the dead, are written. One end of a very thick bandage of eighteen to twenty-five folds of linen is laid under the shoulders, and the other is brought over the head and face, and rests on the upper part of the chest ; this is held in position by a bandage wound round the neck and tied in a double knot at the back of the neck. The same plan is adopted with respect to the feet, but before the bandage which secures all is tied, thick pads of linen are laid on the top of the feet to prevent any injury happening to them when the mummy is made to stand upright.[1] The bandaged arms having been pressed closely into the sides, and the fore-arms and hands having been laid upon the stomach, the bandaging goes on again, while formulae are recited by the *Kher-ḥeb*. Each bandage had a special name,[2] each

[1] Referring to the embalming of the feet, the following extract is of interest. "After these things perform the embalming operations on his right and left arms, and then the . . . . and the children of Horus, and the children of Chent-āat, shall carry out the embalming operations on the two legs of the deceased. Rub the feet, legs, and thighs of the deceased with black stone (?) oil, and then rub them a second time with the finest oil. Wrap the toes in a piece of cloth, draw two jackals upon two pieces of linen with colours mixed with water perfumed with *ānti*, and each jackal shall have his face turned towards the other ; the jackal on the one bandage is Anubis, lord of Ḥert ; the jackal on the other is Horus, lord of Ḥebennu. Put Anubis on the right leg, and Horus on the left leg, and wrap them up in fine linen. To complete the embalming of the legs, take six measures of *ānchamu* flowers, natron and resin, and mix with water of ebony gum, and put three measures on the right leg and three measures on the left. Then put some fresh (?) *senb* flowers made into twelve bundles (?) on the left leg, and twelve bands of linen, and anoint with the finest oil." Maspero, "Le Rituel de l'Embaumement," pp. 43, 44, in "Mémoire sur Quelques Papyrus du Louvre" (extrait des *Notices et Extraits des Manuscrits*, tom. XXIV, 1re partie, Paris, 1875).

[2] *E.g.*, one of the bandages of the nostrils was called , *nehi*, and the other 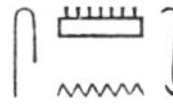, *smen ;* a head bandage , *ḥeḥti-su*, the two bandages of the cheek , *ānkhti-su*, the two bandages of the top of the head , *meḥ utchati*.

bandage gave power to the deceased, and was inscribed with words and figures of gods, which also gave him power, and the adjustment of each in its proper position required both care and judgment. More folds of linen are laid on the body perpendicularly,[1] and more bandages are wound round the body horizontally, until, little by little, it loses its shape beneath them. When a length of about three hundred cubits has been used in folds and bandages, a coarse piece of linen is laid on the body and is sewn up at the back. Over this again a saffron-coloured linen sheet is laid, and this, having been deftly sewn over the head, down the back, and under the feet, is finally held in position by a perpendicular bandage of brownish-coloured linen, passing from the head to the feet and under them up the back to the head, and by four horizontal bandages of the same-coloured linen, one round the shoulders, one round the middle of the body, one round the knees, and one round the ankles. Thus the mummy is complete.

During the seventy days that have been spent in embalming and bandaging Ani's body the coffin-makers have not been idle, and they have made ready a covering of wood to be laid on the mummy, and two beautiful coffins. The covering, in the form of a mummy, is slightly vaulted, and has a human face, bearded, on it; it is handsomely painted outside with collar, figures of Nut, Anubis, and Up-uatu, the full names and titles of Ani in perpendicular lines of inscription, the cartouches of the king in whose time he lived, and scenes in which Ani is adoring the gods. On the inside of the cover, on the purple ground, are painted in a light yellow colour pictures of the horizon, the spirits of the East, in the form of apes, adoring Rā, the lion gods of the morning and evening with a disk on their united

[1] While the head was being bandaged the following petition was recited by one of the embalmers :—" O most august goddess, O lady of the west, O mistress of the east, come and enter into the two ears of the deceased ! O doubly powerful, eternally young, and very mighty lady of the west, and mistress of the east, may breathing take place in the head of the deceased in the nether-world ! Grant that he may see with his eyes, that he may hear with his two ears, that he may breathe through his nose, that he may utter sounds from his mouth, and articulate with his tongue in the nether-world ! Receive his voice in the hall of truth and justice, and his triumph in the hall of Geb in the presence of the great god, lord of the west. O Osiris (*i.e.*, the deceased), the thick oil that cometh upon thee furnisheth thy mouth with life, and thine eye looketh into the lower heaven, as Rā looketh upon the upper heaven. It giveth thee thy two ears to hear that which thou wishest, just as Shu in Ḥebīt (?) heard that which he wished to hear. It giveth thee thy nose to smell a beautiful perfume like Geb. It giveth to thee thy mouth well furnished by its passage (into the throat), like the mouth of Thoth, when he weigheth Maāt. It giveth thee Maāt (Law) in Ḥebīt. O worshipper in Ḥetbenben, the cries of thy mouth are in Siut, Osiris of Siut cometh to thee, thy mouth is the mouth of Up-uatu in the mountain of the west." (See Maspero, " Le Rituel de l'Embaumement," p. 27, in "Mémoire sur Quelques Papyrus du Louvre" (extrait des *Notices et Extraits des Manuscrits*, tom. XXIV, 1re partie, Paris, 1875).

backs, etc., etc.[1] The inner coffin is equally handsome, and carpenter and artist have expended their best labour upon it ; before Ani was embalmed he was measured for it and, due allowance having been made for the bandages, it fits the mummy exactly. It is in the form of a mummy, and the sycamore planks of which it is made are about 2 inches thick ; the bottom is in one piece, as is also each of the sides ; the rounded head-piece is cut out of a solid piece of wood, and the foot-piece is also separate ; all these parts are pegged together with wooden pegs about 2 inches long. On the cover is pegged a solid face, carved out of hard wood, which was intended to be a portrait of Ani ; bronze eyelids and obsidian eyes are fixed in it, and a carved wooden beard is fastened to the chin. Solid wooden hands are fastened to the breast, the one holding the amulet of the blood of Isis, 𓎬, and the other the amulet of the backbone of Osiris, 𓊽. The whole coffin, inside and out, is next covered with a thin layer of plaster on which scenes and inscriptions are painted in red, light and dark green, white and other colours. Both coffin and cover are then varnished a light yellowish-red colour. At the head is Nephthys, and at the foot is Isis, each making speeches to Ani and telling him that she is protecting him. On the cover outside is Nut, and between two series of scenes, in which Ani is represented worshipping the gods, are two perpendicular lines of inscriptions recording his name and titles ; at the foot of these are figures of Anubis and Up-uatu. The sides of the coffin are ornamented with figures of gods in shrines, the scene of the weighing of the heart, Ani drinking water from the hands of the goddess Nut or Hathor, standing in a tree, Shu lifting up Nut from the embraces of Geb, etc. Inside the coffin are painted figures of a number of gods and genii with instructions referring to them, and the goddesses Nut and Hathor ; the first covers Ani with her wings, and the second, as mistress of the nether-world, receives Ani into her arms. Around the edge of the coffin near the cover, from head to foot, run two lines of inscription, one on each side, which repeat at considerable length the name and titles of Ani. The outer edge of the coffin, and the inner edge of the cover, are "rabbeted" out, the one to fit into the other, and on each side, at regular intervals, four rectangular slots about $1\frac{1}{2}$ inches by 2 inches by $\frac{3}{8}$ inch are cut ; to fasten the coffin hermetically, tightly fitting wooden dowels, 4 inches long, are pressed into the slots in the coffin, and pegs driven from the outside of the coffin through them keep them firmly in position. Ani's body having been placed in this coffin, the cover is laid upon it, the ends of the dowels fit into the slots in the sides, and coffin and cover are firmly joined together ; wooden pegs are driven through the cover and dowels, the "rabbets" fit tightly, the little space between the coffin and cover is "stopped"

[1] A fine example of such a covering is that of Nesi-pa-ur-shefi, preserved at Cambridge.

with liquid plaster, and thus the coffin is sealed. Any injury that may have happened to the plaster or paintings during the process of sealing is repaired, and the whole coffin is once more varnished. This coffin is, in its turn, placed inside an outer coffin, which is painted, both inside and outside, with scenes similar to those on the inner coffin; the drawing is, however, more free, and the details are fewer. The outer coffin being sealed in the same way as that inside it, Ani is now ready to be carried to his everlasting home in the Theban hills.

On a day fixed by the relatives and friends, all the various articles of funerary furniture which have been prepared are brought to Ani's house, where also the mummy in its coffins now lies awaiting the funeral; the *Kher-ḥeb* sees that the things necessary for a great man's funeral are provided, and arranges for the procession to start on the first auspicious day. This day having arrived, the *Kher-ḥeb's* assistants come and, gathering together the servants and those who are to carry burdens, see that each has his load ready and that each knows his place in the procession. When all is ready the funeral train sets out from Ani's house, while the female servants wail and lament their master, and the professional mourners beat their breasts, feign to pull out their hair by handfuls, and vie with each other in shrieking the loudest and most often. They have not a great distance to go to reach the river, but the difficulties of passing through the narrow streets increase almost at every step, for the populace of Thebes loved the sight of a grand funeral as much as that of any European country to-day. After some few hours the procession reaches the river, and there a scene of indescribable confusion happens; every bearer of a burden is anxious to deposit it in one of the boats which lie waiting in a row by the quay; the animals that draw the sledge, on which Ani's bier is laid, kick out wildly and struggle while being pushed into the boat, people rush hither and thither, and the noise of men giving orders, and the shouts and cries of the spectators, are distracting. At length, however, the procession is embarked and the boats push off to drop with the current across the Nile to a place a little north of the Temple of Thothmes III, opposite Asâsîf. After an hour spent in disembarking, the procession reforms itself in the order in which it will march to the tomb, and we see for the first time what a splendid funeral has been provided. We may describe the procession as it is actually represented in the Papyrus of Ani. One man carries Ani's palette and box of instruments which he used for writing and drawing, another carries his staff and perfume pots (?), another his bed, another his chair, others bring the *ushabtiu* figures in a box with a vaulted cover and made like a tomb; and behind them, drawn by two men, is a coffer surmounted by a jackal, on a sledge decorated with lotus flowers, in which stand the four jars which contain Ani's viscera. Next follow the men bearing everything which Ani made use of during his life, as, for example, the palette which he carried in order to keep accounts and to make lists of all the precious things that were brought to his lord as gifts and tribute. Next comes the funerary canopy under which is laid the mummy of Ani, placed in a boat which is mounted on a sledge drawn by four oxen; at the head of the chest is a figure of Nephthys, and at the foot a figure of Isis. The boat is supplied with oars; at the head stands a white-robed *Sem* priest wearing a panther skin; he holds a bronze censer, , filled with burning incense in the left hand, and with the right he sprinkles natron water on the ground from a vase . In the Vignette of the Funeral Procession in the Papyrus of Ani his wife Tutu is seen kneeling by the boat and tearing her hair in grief. Behind the boat follow a number of white-robed men, one of whom has his head powdered. Next follow more funerary offerings and flowers carried in boxes suspended from the ends of poles which the men who carry them balance on their shoulders. In front of these walk a number of women with breasts uncovered and dishevelled hair, who in their wailing lamentations lament the dead and praise his virtues. Among these would probably be the female servants of Ani's house.

Meanwhile the procession has moved on and has entered one of the rocky defiles to the north of Dêr al-Baḥarî, whence, winding along through the Valley of the Tombs of the Kings, they march on to a remote place beyond the Western valley. The progress of the train is slow, for the ground is rough and rocky, and frequent halts have to be made; on the right hand and on the left, kings and nobles are buried in splendid tombs, and almost every hill which they climb hides the mummy of some distinguished Egyptian. A few miles further on, in the side of a hill, a rectangular opening is seen, and when the procession arrives at the foot of it, a number of workmen, attendants, tomb-guardians and others are seen assembled there. The mummy in its coffins is lifted off the funerary sledge and carried up the hill to the rectangular opening, which proves to be the mouth of Ani's tomb; there it is set upright, and before it the attendants pile up tables with sepulchral offerings and flowers, and animals for sacrifice are also brought there. The wailing women and the distant relatives of Ani here take farewell of him, and when they have descended the hill the coffin is let down the slanting passage by ropes into the chamber, where it is hoped that Ani's friends will bring sepulchral offerings to his *ka* at the appointed seasons. This chamber is rectangular and has two rows of square pillars in it. From it there leads a passage about 6 feet wide by 7 feet high, and passing through this we see to the right and left a series of chambers upon the walls of which are painted in vivid colours the pictures of Ani and his wife Tutu making offerings to the gods, and inscriptions recording his prayers and their answers. The walls of some rooms are occupied entirely with scenes drawn from the daily events of his life. As he was a scribe, and therefore no mean artist, we are probably right in assuming that he superintended the painting of many of them himself. Some of the rooms have their walls unornamented, and it would seem that these were used for the living-rooms of the priests who visited or lived in the tombs for the purpose of carrying out the various sepulchral rites at their appointed times. We pass through or by seventeen chambers, and then arrive at a flight of steps which leads down to the chamber in which the mummy and coffin are to be placed. Hewn in the wall just above the top of the flight of steps is a square niche, in which, seated on one seat, are two stone figures of Ani and his wife; he has an open roll of papyrus on his knees and holds a palette in his hand, and she has lotus flowers in both hands, which rest on her knees. The plinth of the statues is inscribed with the names and titles of Ani and Tutu. Beneath, let into the wall, is a stone stele, the surface of which is divided into two parts; the upper part contains a representation of Ani adoring the sun-god Rā, and the lower contains about thirty lines of inscription in which Ani prays that Rā, Osiris and Anubis will cause all kinds of sepulchral foods to be supplied for his *ka*, or genius; that they will grant his coming forth from and going into the nether-world whenever he pleases; that his soul may alight on the trees which he has planted; that he may drink cool water from the depths of the Nile when he pleases, etc.

The mummy in its coffin has been brought down the steps, and is now carried into a large chamber on the left, where its final resting-place is to be. As we pass into this room we see that a part of it is already occupied by a coffin and the funerary furniture belonging to it. When we come nearer we find that it is the coffin of Tutu, Ani's wife. Close by her is a table of alabaster covered with shapely vessels of the same substance, filled with wine, oil, and other unguents; each of these fragile objects is inscribed with her name. On the table are spoons made of ivory of the most beautiful workmanship. They are shaped in the form of a woman. The body is stained a deep creamy colour, the colour of the skin of the Egyptian lady, who guarded herself from the rays of the sun; the hair is black, and we see that it is movable; when we lift it off we see the name of "Tutu, the sistrum bearer," engraved beneath. On a second stand, made of wood, we find the articles for her toilet—mirror, *koḥl* pot in obsidian, fan, etc.—and close by is the sistrum which she carried in the temple of Åmen-Rā upon earth, and which was buried with her, so that she might be able to praise that god with music in his mansions in the sky. Chairs and her couch are there too, and stands covered with dried flowers and various offerings. Removing the lid of the coffin we see her mummy lying as it was laid a few years before. On her breasts are strings of dried flowers with the bloom still on them, and by her side is a roll of papyrus containing a copy of the service which she used to sing in the temple of Åmen in the

Åpts when on earth. Her amethyst necklace and other ornaments are small, but very beautiful. Just over her feet is a blue-glazed steatite *ushabti* figure.

While we have been examining Tutu's funerary furniture, the servants of the *Kher-ḥeb* have brought down the coffin, which is placed on a bier along the east wall, and the chairs and couch and boxes and funerary offerings, and arranged them about the chamber. In a square niche in the wall, just over the head of the coffin, Ani's writing palette and reeds are placed, and by their side is laid a large roll of papyrus nearly 90 feet long, inscribed in hieroglyphs during his lifetime and under his direction with the oldest and most important Chapters of the Theban Recension of the Book of the Dead; the Vignettes, which refer to the Chapters, are beautifully painted, and in some as many as thirteen colours are used; and in every work connected with Ani's tomb there is a simple majesty that was characteristic of the ancient Egyptian gentleman. At each of the four corners or sides of the bier is placed one of the so-called Canopic jars, and at the foot are laid a few stone *ushabtiu* figures, whose duty it was to perform for the deceased such labours as filling the furrows with water, ploughing the fields and carrying the sand, if he were called upon to do these. When everything has been brought into this chamber, and the tables of offerings have been arranged, a priest, wearing a panther skin and accompanied by another who burns incense in a bronze censer, approaches the mummy and performs the ceremony of "opening the mouth," , *un re*, while a priest in white robes reads from a roll of papyrus or leather. The act of embalming has taken away from the dead man all control over his limbs and the various portions of his body, and before these can be of any use to him in the Other World a mouth must be given to him, and it must be opened so that his *ka* may be able to speak. The XXIst and XXIInd Chapters of the Book of the Dead refer to the giving of a mouth to the deceased, and the Vignette of the XXIInd Chapter represents a priest, called the "guardian of the scale," , *àri mākhet*, giving the deceased his mouth. In the Vignette to the XXIIIrd Chapter a priest is seen performing the operation of opening the mouth, 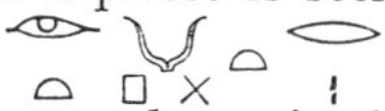 *àrit upt re*, with the instrument , and the deceased says in the text, "Ptaḥ[1] has opened my mouth with that instrument of iron with which he opened the mouth of the gods."[2] Whilst these sacred ceremonies are being performed

[1] Some copies read Shu.

[2] 

the crowd of friends at the door of the tomb is being entertained by singers and dancers and acrobats. When the mouth of the deceased had been opened, his *ka* gained control of his speech, intelligence and limbs, and was able to hold intercourse with the gods, and to go in and out of his tomb whenever he pleased. When the formulae are finished and all rites performed, Ani's near relatives and friends withdraw from the mummy chamber and make their way up the stairs, through the long passage and into the first chamber, where they find that animals have been slaughtered, and that many of the assistants and those who accompanied the funeral are eating and drinking of the funerary offerings. When the last person has left the mummy chamber, masons bring along slabs of stone and lime which they have ready and wall it up; the joints between the stones are so fine that the blade of a modern penknife can with difficulty be inserted to the depth of half an inch. We have seen Ani's body embalmed, we have watched all the stages of the manufacture of his coffin, we have seen the body dressed and laid in it, we have accompanied him to the tomb, we have gone through it and seen how it is arranged and decorated, and we have assisted at the funeral ceremonies; in his beautiful tomb, then, let us leave him to enjoy his long rest in the company of his wife. Ani did not cause such a large and beautiful tomb to be hewn for him merely to gratify his pride; with him, as with all educated Egyptians, it was the outcome of the belief that his soul would revivify his body, and was the result of a firm assurance in his mind of the truth of the doctrine of immortality, which is the foundation of the Egyptian religion, and which was as deeply rooted in them as the hills are in the earth.

THE CEREMONY OF THE FOUR BLAZING FLAMES

WE obtain our knowledge of this ceremony from the Papyrus of Nebseni and the Papyrus of Nu, both of which were written under the reigns of the early kings of the XVIIIth dynasty. As its object was to bring the vital heat of Rā into the body of the deceased in the mummy-chamber and to make him live and move about in all the mansions of Osiris at pleasure, it is probably of Heliopolitan origin, though the Rubric says the Chapter was found at Hermopolis. The Papyrus of Nebseni gives only a very short section of the text which was recited during the performance of the ceremony, and omits all the supplementary Chapters and Rubrics which are supplied by the Papyrus of Nu only. The ceremony was performed in the mummy-chamber with great secrecy. No one was to be present except the father or son of him who performed it, and such assistants as were absolutely necessary to carry it out. The objects required were four earthenware bowls or dishes, which were brought into the mummy-chamber and sprinkled with incense; when this was done the bowls were filled with the milk of a white cow, which was to be used in quenching the flames when the recital of the text was finished. The substance to be burnt was *ȧṭmȧ* cloth, , which was smeared with Libyan unguent, . As soon as the flames were kindled in the four bowls each bowl was given into the hands of a man who had the name of one of the Four Sons of Horus inscribed on his upper arm. These four men represented the four gods who sat upon the four pillars which supported Horus, both as god and as sky, and were called Mestȧ or Ȧmset, Ḥāpi, Ṭuamutef and Qebḥsenuf. Judging by the Vignette to Chapter CLI of the Book of the Dead in the Papyrus of Mut-ḥetep, each man took his place in one corner of the chamber, which was called "Ṭuat," , and was a type of the underworld, and kept the flame from the oiled cloth burning whilst the text, now known as Chapter CXXXVIIA, was recited. This text may be summarized thus:—

Fire comes to thy *ka*, O Osiris Khenti Ȧmenti,
Fire comes to thy *ka*, O Osiris Nu the steward.
Fire comes to thy *ka*, O Osiris.
The Two Sisters of Rā (Isis and Nephthys) come likewise.
The Fire rises in Ȧbṭu (Abydos), it comes to the Eye of Horus.
The Eye of Horus is on thy brow, O Osiris, and protects thee,
The Eye of Horus is on thy brow, O Nu, and protects thee.
Thine enemies have fallen, O Osiris,
Thine enemies have fallen, O Osiris Nu.
These four flames enter into thy *ka*, O Osiris,
These four flames enter into thy *ka*, O Osiris Nu.
Hail, Sons of Horus, ye protected Osiris, your Divine Father,
Protect ye now the Osiris Nu.
Ye destroyed the enemies of Osiris, who lives with the gods;
He smote Suti (or Set) and light dawned on the earth.
Horus avenged his father Osiris, and joined him to his *ka*.
Destroy ye the enemies of the Osiris Nu.
Make him to live with the gods, and destroy his Enemy,
And make him to join himself to his *ka*.
The Eye of Horus has avenged thee, O Osiris Nu.
O Osiris Khenti Ȧmenti, grant light and fire to the soul that dwells in Ḥensu (Herakleopolis).
O Sons of Horus, give ye power to the living soul of the Osiris Nu within his flame.[1]

[1] The soul in Ḥensu and the soul of the deceased are represented in the Vignette to Chapter CLI in the Papyrus of Mut-ḥetep.

The recital of these words was believed to effect the union of Nu and his *ka* with Osiris and his *ka*, and this being done, all the spirits and gods in the underworld would identify him with Osiris and pay to him honour as to the god. Another effect of the recital of this Chapter was to bring the spirits of Isis and Nephthys into the Ṭuat Chamber to guard the mummy of the deceased, the former kneeling at his feet and the latter by his head. But other precautions had to be taken to safeguard the mummy, for bodiless spirits of evil might force their way through the walls of the chamber and attack it and destroy it. To prevent this a powerful amulet was placed in each of the four walls, and a set of these amulets preserved in the British Museum shows us exactly what they were like. The Rubric to Chapter CXXXVIIA in the Papyrus of Nu directs how each is to be made and where it is to be placed, and thus our knowledge of these amulets and their use is tolerably complete. The amulets are four in number :—

(1) A blue-glazed faïence (, *tchehen-t*) Ṭeṭ $2\frac{1}{8}$ inches high, set in a rectangular brick of Nile mud, measuring $4\frac{1}{8}$ inches by $4\frac{1}{8}$ inches, and inscribed with four lines of hieratic text (B.M. 41547). This, with the face of the Ṭeṭ turned towards the east, was to be placed in a cavity in the west wall, and the cavity was to be walled up with earth mixed with cedar juice. It repulsed all enemies coming from the east.

(2) A mud figure of Anubis couchant on his pedestal, , set upon a nearly rectangular brick of Nile mud measuring 6 inches by 4 inches, and inscribed with four lines of hieratic text (B.M. 41545). The Rubric orders that the mud of which Anubis is made shall be mixed with incense. This brick, with the face of Anubis turned towards the west wall, was to be placed in a cavity in the east wall, and the cavity was to be walled up. It repulsed all enemies coming from the south (west ?).

(3) A piece of a reed, $7\frac{5}{8}$ inches in length, set up in a brick of Nile mud measuring $6\frac{1}{2}$ inches by $4\frac{3}{8}$ inches, inscribed with five lines of hieratic text (B.M. 41544). The Rubric directs that the reed *unām*, , shall be smeared with bitumen, or pitch, and set light to, and that the brick shall then be placed in a cavity in the south wall, with the front of it facing the north. The cavity was then walled up, and this amulet repulsed all enemies coming from the north.

(4) A wooden figure of a woman wearing a heavy wig, and having her hands clenched and lying on her breasts, set in a brick of Nile mud measuring $6\frac{1}{8}$ inches by $4\frac{1}{8}$ inches, inscribed with five lines of hieratic text (B.M. 41546). The Rubric directs that the figure is to be seven finger [breadths] in height, and that it is to be made of

åmm wood, ⟨hieroglyphs⟩. On this figure the ceremony of "opening the mouth" was to be performed, and then it was to be placed in a cavity in the north wall, with the face of the figure towards the south. The cavity was then walled up, and this figure repulsed all enemies coming from the south. This ceremony was to be performed by a man who was washed clean, and was ceremonially pure, and who had neither eaten meat or fish, or had intercourse with women [recently].

The hieratic texts on the four bricks may be transcribed thus :—

I. 1. ⟨hieroglyphs⟩

⟨hieroglyphs⟩ 2. ⟨hieroglyphs⟩

3. ⟨hieroglyphs⟩ 4. ⟨hieroglyphs⟩

⟨hieroglyphs⟩ (?), "O thou who comest quickly, I repulse thy steps . . . . . I repulse behind the Ṭet of Rā on the day of fighting against slaughter. I am protecting the Osiris Ḥent-meḥit, the truth-speaker."

II. 1. ⟨hieroglyphs⟩ 2. ⟨hieroglyphs⟩

⟨hieroglyphs⟩ 3. ⟨hieroglyphs⟩

⟨hieroglyphs⟩ 4. ⟨hieroglyphs⟩

⟨hieroglyphs⟩, "Keep watch, Osiris Ḥent-meḥit. He who is on his Hill (*i.e.*, Anubis) watches thy moment. Assuredly I have overthrown the Aṭu Crocodile fiend. I am protecting the Osiris Ḥent-meḥit."

III. 1. ⟨hieroglyphs⟩ 2. ⟨hieroglyphs⟩

⟨hieroglyphs⟩ 3. ⟨hieroglyphs⟩

⟨hieroglyphs⟩ 4. ⟨hieroglyphs⟩

⟨hieroglyphs⟩ 5. ⟨hieroglyphs⟩, "I defend thee from slaughter—blocking the way of the hidden one. I repulse them setting flame in the regions of the dead. I obstruct their ways. I am protecting the Osiris Ḥent-meḥit."

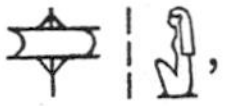, " [I] have come to build thee up ; I will not allow thee to be overthrown (?). I have come to hurl missiles ; I will not let missiles be hurled at thee. I am protecting the Osiris Ḥent-meḥit."

FIGURES OF EGYPTIAN GODS

THE gold, silver, bronze, wooden and faïence **figures of gods** in Egyptian collections may be reckoned by thousands, and they vary in size from ½ inch to 15 inches or more. Bronze statues were usually cast in moulds in one or more pieces, the core being made of sand or earth. When cast in pieces the limbs were soldered together and the edges smoothed with a file or scraper. The core is frequently found inside the statue, where it was left by the workmen to strengthen the casting. Figures of gods in gold are comparatively few, the gods most often represented in this metal being Åmen-Rā, Rā, Khensu, and Nefer-Åtmu ; figures of these gods were also made of silver and plated with gold, and a figure of the god Set, made of bronze plated with gold, is also known (B.M. 18191). Bronze figures of gods were sometimes inlaid with gold, and the eyes were made of gold or silver with obsidian pupils. Glazed faïence figures of gods are very common, and certain gods were made of this substance, which up to the present have rarely been met with in bronze. They were usually cast from moulds, and follow fairly closely the design and patterns of the bronze figures ; they do not occur much earlier than the XXVth or XXVIth dynasty, and although wretched copies of them were made for hundreds of years after, they do not appear to have continued in use among all classes of people in Egypt. It may be mentioned in passing that the natives of Egypt at the present day make use of the old moulds, found chiefly in Upper Egypt, to cast figures of the gods in gold and silver, which they sell to the traveller as genuine antiquities.

Figures of the gods of Egypt are found among the ruins of houses and in temples and tombs. According to M. Mariette[1] those found among the ruins of towns are of two kinds : (1) Those that were placed in a niche, cut in the form of a shrine, and that represented the divinity to the service of which the inhabitants of the house were attached, and before which, on certain days, offerings

[1] *Catalogue Général des Monuments d'Abydos*, p. 1.

were laid ; (2) those that were placed in cavities of the walls of the inner chambers of the house, and that were supposed to be able by magical influence to protect the inhabitants of the house from spells and the results of incantations, and from other malignant influences. The use of this latter class of statuettes, or small figures, is as old as the XVIIIth dynasty, at least. The figures of gods found in temples are very numerous and are votive. The Egyptians seem to have believed that the gods inhabited statues or figures, made in their honour, and on this account they often made them very beautiful, so that they might form worthy habitations for them. On certain days prayers were said before them, and offerings were made to them. As figures of many different gods are found in the same temple, it follows that a worshipper wishing to place a figure of a god in a temple was not bound to offer one of the god to whom the temple was dedicated ; supposing the temple to be one of Ptaḥ, he could offer a figure of Rā, or Khnemu, or of any god he pleased. Figures of gods were supposed to answer questions, for it will be remembered that when Khensu was asked if he would go to the land of Bekhten to cure a daughter of the prince of that land of her sickness, he inclined his head in assent. When he arrived in that land, he held a conversation with the demon that possessed the maiden, and when the demon agreed to come out from her, provided that a feast were made in his honour, the god, through his priest, assented. Figures of gods other than Osiris, Isis, and Nephthys are not commonly found in tombs ; it is true that many examples in faïence are found in the wrappings of mummies, but in these cases they were simply used as amulets like the Tet of Isis, the Ṭeṭ of Osiris, the pillow, and many others. Figures of gods made of every sort of material were also buried in the sand around temples and tombs with the view of guarding them from every evil influence. The following is a list of the most important of the gods and goddesses of whom figures were made in bronze and glazed faïence :—

Tmu, , or **Åtmu,** , the "Closer" of the day or night, usually represents the sun at sunset. He wears the crowns of Upper and Lower Egypt ; in the right hand he holds , and in the left . **Nefer-Åtmu,** the son of Ptaḥ and Sekhmit or Bast, represents the power of the heat of the rising sun. Figures of this god were made in gold, silver, bronze, and faïence. In metal, he stands upright, wearing lotus flowers and plumes on his head ; in his left hand he holds , and in his right . Sometimes each shoulder is inlaid in gold with an *Utchat* (B.M. 22921). In faïence he has the same head-dress, but stands on a lion ; in faïence, too, he is often accompanied by his mother Sekhmit or Bast (B.M. 250*b*, 260*a*).

Åtmu.

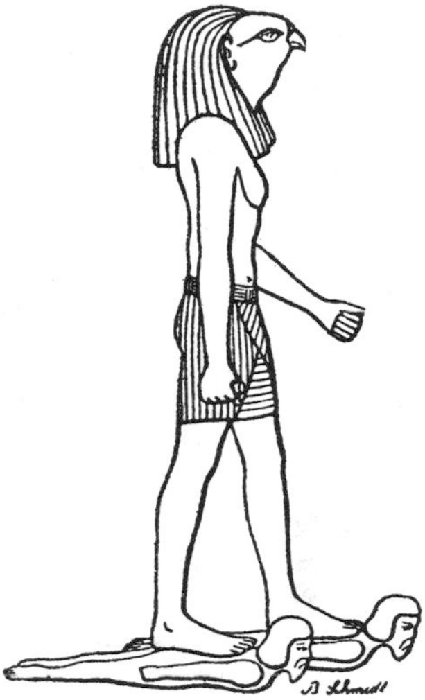

Ḥer (Horus).

Rā.

Menu.

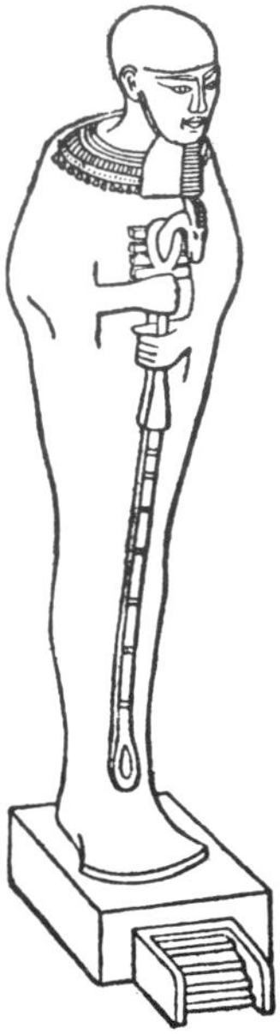

Ptaḥ.

I-em-ḥetep (Imouthis).

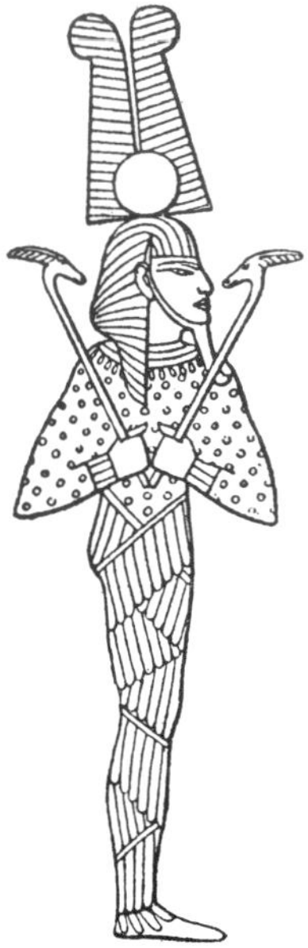

Ptaḥ-Tatenen.

Tcheḥuti (Thoth).

Set.

Ḥer-pa-khart̤, *i.e.*, Horus the Child, , represents the morning sun. During the night he was supposed to be engaged in fighting Āpep, the serpent, who, at the head of a large army of fiends, personifications of mist, darkness, and cloud, tried to overthrow him. The battle was renewed daily, but the Sun-god always conquered, and appeared day after day in the sky. Bronze and faïence figures of this god represent him hawk-headed and wearing disk and uraeus.

Horus, , the morning sun, son of Isis and Osiris, is usually called "the avenger of his father," in reference to his defeat of Set. Figures in bronze and in faïence represent him hawk-headed and wearing the crowns of Upper and Lower Egypt. This god was distinguished in name only from Ḥer-ur, the elder brother of Osiris.

Rā, 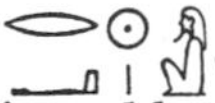, the Sun-god, was also the creator of gods and men; his emblem was the sun's disk, and he represents the sun at noonday. His worship was very ancient, and the Heliopolitan theologians said that he was the offspring of Nut, or the sky. He assumed the forms of several other gods, and is at times represented by the lion, cat, and hawk. In papyri and on bas-reliefs he has the head of a hawk, and wears a disk, in front of which is a uraeus .

Menthu-Rā, , in bronze figures is hawk-headed, and wears the disk, in front of which are two uraei, and plumes; at times figures have two hawks' heads on a single body. Menthu was the old War-god of Hermonthis.

Menu or **Min,** 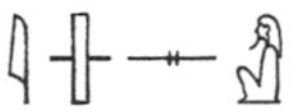, , formerly read **Khem** and **Åmsu,** represented "generation" or the productive power in Nature: figures of him, , in bronze and faïence, are tolerably numerous.

Khnemu, , the "Moulder," the Χνούμις, Χνοῦβις, Χνοῦβι, Κνήφ or Κνοῦφις of the Greeks, is one of the oldest gods of Egypt, and was especially worshipped in Nubia, at Philae, where he is represented making man out of clay on a potter's wheel, and at Elephantine. Like Åmen-Rā he is said to be the father of the gods,[1] and with this god and Ptaḥ and Kheperȧ he shared the

[1] Father of the fathers of the gods and goddesses, the lord who evolveth from himself, maker of heaven, earth, the underworld, water, and mountains

.

name of "creator of men." Khnemu put together the scattered limbs of the dead body of Osiris, and it was he who created the beautiful woman who became the wife of Bata in the Tale of the Two Brothers. In bronze and faïence, figures of this god represent him with the head of a ram, and wearing plumes, ; these figures are tolerably common.

Ptaḥ, , the "Opener," perhaps the oldest of all the gods of Egypt, was honoured with a temple and worshipped at Memphis from the time of the Ist dynasty. He is said to be the father of the gods, who came forth from his eye, and of men, who came forth from his mouth. He is represented in the form of a mummy, and he holds a sceptre composed of , *usr,* "strength," , *ānkh,* "life," and , *ṭeṭ,* "stability." At the back of his neck he wears the *menȧt* . With reference to his connexion with the resurrection and the netherworld he is called **Ptaḥ-Seker-Åsȧr**, and is represented as a little squat boy, with bent legs, and his hands on his hips. Sometimes he has his feet on the head of a crocodile; on the right side stands Isis, on the left Nephthys; at his back is a human-headed hawk, emblematic of the soul; on each shoulder is a hawk, and on his head is a beetle, the emblem of Kheperȧ, the self-begotten god. In faïence figures of this god are very common, but in bronze they are rare.

Iemḥetep, , the Imouthis of the Greeks, was the first-born son of Ptaḥ and Nut. He is represented both standing and seated, holding a sceptre, , in the right hand, and in the left; at times he holds on his knees an open roll, upon which is inscribed his name. The bronze figures of this god are usually of very fine workmanship, often having the inscriptions inlaid in gold; in faïence, figures of this god are very rare.

Thoth, in Egyptian **Tcheḥuti** (Teḥuti), , the "Measurer," was the scribe of the gods, the measurer of time and inventor of writing and numbers. In the Judgment Hall of Osiris he stands by the side of the balance, holding a palette and reed ready to record the result of the weighing of the heart, as announced by the dog-headed ape who sits on the middle of the beam of the scales. In bronze figures he is represented with the head of an ibis, but he has upon it sometimes horns and plumes. In faïence figures he has also the head of an ibis, and occasionally he holds an *Utchat,* , between his hands in front of him (B.M. 490*a*).

Set or **Sut** or **Setesh,** 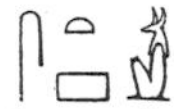, Gr. Σήθ, was one of the sons of Geb and Nut, and was brother of Osiris, and husband of Nephthys. His worship dates from the Vth dynasty, and he continued to be a most popular god in Egypt until the XIXth dynasty ; kings delighted to call themselves " beloved of Set," and to be compared to him for valour when the records of their battles were written down. He probably represented the destructive power of the sun's heat. Between the XXIInd and XXVth dynasties a violent reaction set in against this god ; his statues and figures were smashed, his effigy was hammered out from the bas-reliefs and stelae in which it appeared, and from being a beneficent god, and a companion of Åmen and his brother-gods, he became the personification of all evil, and the opponent of all good. His persistent hatred of Osiris is mentioned below. Set, under the form of **Sutekh,** was chosen by the Hyksos for their god. Bronze figures of Set are very rare indeed. The British Museum possesses two examples, Nos. 18191 and 22897 ; each represents the god standing upright, in each he has the characteristic animal's head, which is, probably, that of the camel, and wears the crowns of Upper and Lower Egypt,  ; each figure was originally gilded, and each has a hole drilled in a projecting piece of metal, from which it was suspended and worn. When I acquired the larger figure it was bent double, evidently by a violent blow, given probably when the reaction against this god's worship set in. Faïence figures of Set I have never seen.

Osiris, in Egyptian *Åsår,* , the great god and king of the underworld, the judge of the dead, was the son of Geb and Nut, and husband of Isis ; he was murdered by his brother Set, who was in turn slain by Horus, the son of Osiris and the " avenger of his father." According to Plutarch (*De Iside et Osiride,* xii–xx) Osiris was the wise and good king of Egypt, who spent his life in civilizing his subjects and in improving their condition. Having brought them out of degradation and savagery, he set out to do the like for the other nations of the world. Upon his return his brother Set, together with seventy-two other people, and the queen of Ethiopia, made a conspiracy against him. They invited him into a banqueting room, and by an artful device made Osiris get into a box which Set had previously caused to be made to fit him. As soon as Osiris had lain down in it, the conspirators nailed the cover on it and, having poured molten lead over it, they carried it by river to the sea, the waves of which washed it up at Byblos. As soon as Isis heard of what had happened, she set out to search for her husband's body, and eventually found it ; but having carried it off to another place, it was accidentally discovered by Set, who forthwith broke open the chest and tore the body into fourteen pieces, which he scattered up and down the country. Isis then set out to search for the pieces of her husband's body, and she found all but one; wherever she found a piece she buried it, and built a temple over it. He was the type of all mummies, and the deceased is made like unto him, and named after him, and identified with him. Bronze figures of this god represent him as a mummified figure wearing the crown ; in his right hand he holds the whip , and in the left the crook . Figures of this god in faïence are not very common. In the large bronze figures, about 2 feet in height, he wears the White Crown. One of the largest known painted stone figures of the god is preserved in the British Museum (Northern Eg. Gallery).

Isis, in Egyptian *Åset*, , was a daughter of Geb and Nut; she married her brother Osiris. Bronze figures represent her (1) standing and wearing upon her head, and (2) seated, suckling her child Horus, who is sitting on her knees, at her left breast, and wearing disk and horns upon her head. Faïence figures of both kinds are common. Isis usually stands at the foot of the bier of Osiris.

Nephthys, in Egyptian *Nebt-ḥet*, , was also a daughter of Geb and Nut; she married her brother Set. Bronze figures, which are not common, represent her standing draped in a long tunic, and wearing on her head; in faïence, figures of this goddess are very numerous, and follow the style and design of those in bronze. A number of rectangular faïence **pendants** have been found in which **Isis, Nephthys and Harpokrates** (Horus) stand side by side.

Anubis, in Egyptian *Ånpu*, , was, according to some legends, the son of Nephthys and Osiris, who mistook that goddess for Isis; elsewhere he is said to be the son of Rā. He is always represented as having the head of a jackal, and he is one of the chief gods of the dead and the nether-world. He presided over the embalming of the mummy, he led the mummy into the presence of Osiris, and watched over the ceremony of weighing the heart, and he is often represented standing by the bier with one hand laid on the mummy. The belief that this god acted in this capacity survived for some centuries after Christ, and a remarkable proof of this fact is given by a light-green, glazed faïence plaque in the British Museum (22874). On the obverse, Anubis, jackal-headed, in relief, stands by the side of a bier in the shape of a lion, also in relief; on the reverse, in relief, are two lines of inscription in Coptic which read, ⲁⲥⲓⲏⲥ ⲉⲧⲱⲛⲕ, "May she hasten to arise." At each end is a pierced

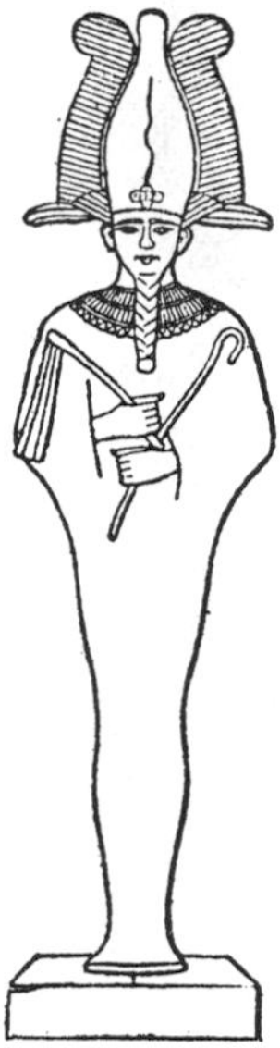

Åsår (Osiris).

Åset (Isis).

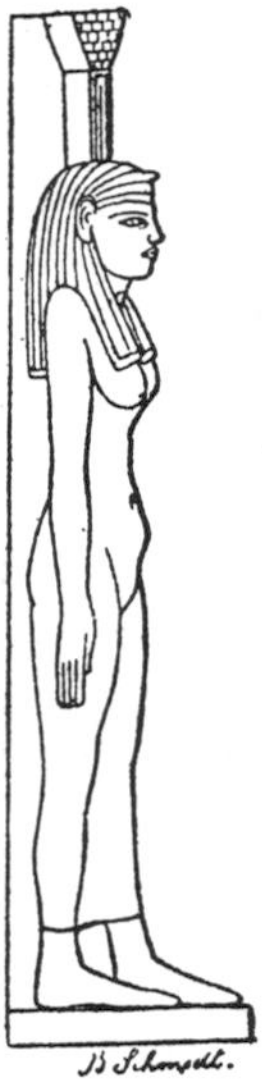

Nebt-Ḥet (Nephthys).

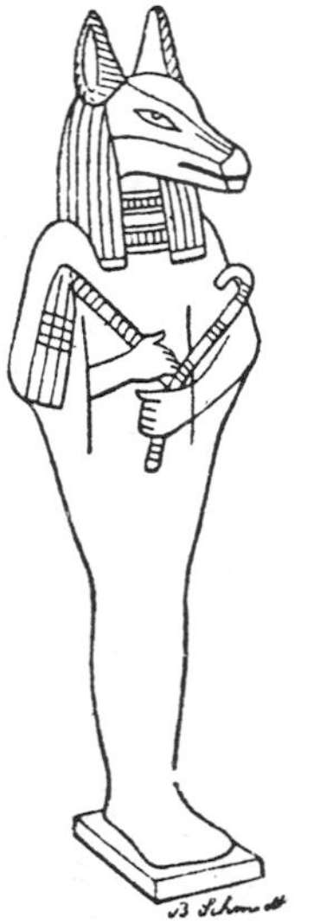

Ånpu (Anubis)

Ḥāpi, the god of the Nile.

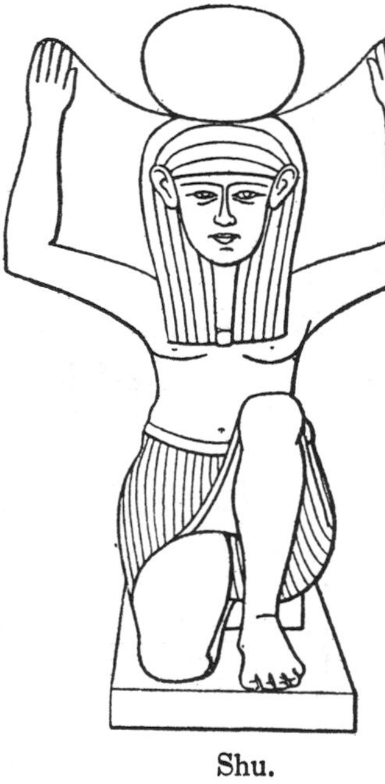

Shu.

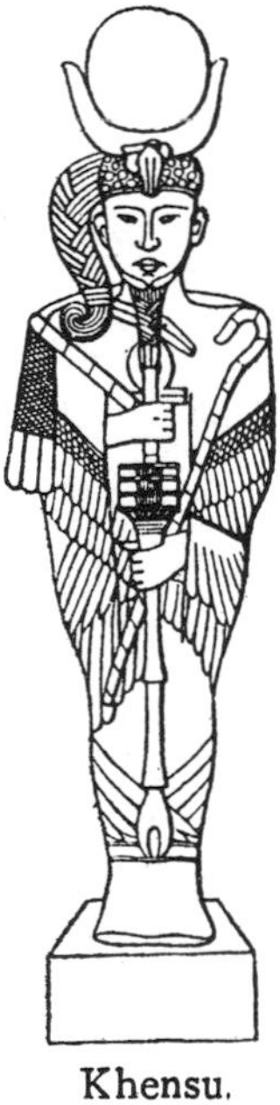

Khensu.

Khensu Nefer-Ḥetep.

Åmen-Rā.

Khnemu.

The Apis Bull.

projection whereby the plaque was fastened to the mummy. The plaque is an interesting example of the survival of ancient Egyptian ideas among the Egyptians after they had embraced Christianity. A counterpart of Anubis who is also represented as a jackal is **Up-uatu,** , "the opener of the ways." Bronze and faïence figures of this god represent him standing and having the head of a jackal.

Shu, , and **Tefnut,** , were emanations of Temu or Kheperȧ; Shu typified light, heat and air, and Tefnut moisture. In papyri and on coffins Shu is represented in the form of a man, standing with both arms raised, lifting up Nut, or the sky, from the embrace of Geb, the earth. In bronze and faïence figures he is in the form of a man kneeling on his right knee and supporting on his shoulders the sun's disk and the horizon with his upraised arms. There is in the British Museum (11057) a fine example of an aegis in bronze with the heads of **Shu** and **Tefnut,** , his sister, upon it. Shu is bearded and wears two pairs of plumes upon his head; Tefnut has the head of a lion and wears a disk and uraeus; B.M. 389 is an example of these gods in faïence. Standing figures of Shu, in faïence, have sometimes on the head.

Ḥāpi, (the old form of the name appears to be Ḥepr,), the god of the Nile, is depicted as a man, sitting or standing, holding a table or altar on which are vases for libations, , and lotus flowers and fruits, and with a clump of lotus flowers upon his head. He is also represented standing upright, with a table of offerings of plants, fruits and flowers before him (B.M. 11069). On his head he wears , and in front is an *Utchat,* .

Khensu, , was, under the New Kingdom, associated with Ȧmen-Rā and Mut in the Theban triad, and was god of the moon. In bronze figures he is human-headed, and wears a crescent and disk; in faïence figures he is made like a mummy, and holds sceptres of different shapes in his hands. **Khensu Nefer-ḥetep** was worshipped with great honour at Thebes, and he is said to have played a very prominent part in the Story of the Possessed Princess of Bekhten. **Khensu-pa-kharṭ,** , has all the attributes of Harpokrates, and figures of him in bronze are not common. A very fine specimen is B.M. 11045.

Åmen-Rā, , and Mut and Khensu formed the great triad of Thebes; the word *Åmen* means "hidden." Under the New Kingdom Åmen usurped the attributes of all the other great gods. Before the expulsion of the Hyksos by Seqenen-Rā his position was that of the local god of Thebes; subsequently he became the national god of Egypt. He was said to be the maker of things above and of things below, and to have more forms than any other god. He made the gods, and stretched out the heavens, and founded the earth; he was lord of eternity and maker of everlastingness. The Egyptians affirmed of him that he was ONE, the ONLY ONE. In bronze figures he stands upon a plinth, he holds the sceptre  in his left hand, and on his head he wears the disk and feathers ; at times he holds a scimitar (B.M. 28, 29). He is also represented seated on a throne, and the throne was sometimes placed inside a shrine, the top of which was ornamented with uraei, winged disk, etc., and the sides and back with hollow-work figures of Isis, Nephthys, and Osiris (B.M. 11013). On the pedestals he is called "Åmen-Rā, lord of the thrones of the world, the president of the Apts (*i.e.*, Karnak), lord of heaven, prince of Thebes," . He is, at times, one of a triad consisting of Åmen, Menu, and Rā (B.M. 18681). The faïence figures of this god are similar to those in bronze , and he appears together with the other members of his triad, Mut and Khensu.

Apis or **Ḥāpi,** 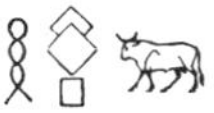, "the second life of Ptaḥ," and the incarnation of Osiris, was the name given to the **sacred bull of Memphis**, where the worship of this god was most ancient, having been introduced from Heliopolis by Kakau, a king of the IInd dynasty. He was the "living emblem" of **Ptaḥ-Seker-Åsår,** the triune god of the Egyptian resurrection. He is variously called "the son of Ptaḥ," "the son of Tmu," "the son of Osiris," and "the son of Seker." In bronze Ḥāpi is sometimes represented in the form of a man with a bull's head, between the horns of which are a disk and a uraeus wearing a disk. Usually, however, he is in the form of a bull having a disk and a uraeus between the horns; on the back, above the shoulders, is engraved a vulture with outstretched wings, and on the back, over the hind quarters, is a winged scarab. The bull usually stands on a rectangular pedestal, on the sides of which are inscribed the name and titles of the person who had him made; on the same pedestal is frequently a figure of this person kneeling in adoration before him. Figures of Apis in bronze are commoner than those in faïence. According to Herodotus

(II, 27–29) Apis was the calf of a cow incapable of conceiving another offspring; "and the Egyptians say, that lightning descends upon the cow from heaven, and that from thence it brings forth Apis. This calf, which is called Apis, has the following marks: it is black, and has a square spot of white on the forehead; and on the back the figure of an eagle; and in the tail double hairs; and on the tongue a beetle." But there is a mistake in this description, for on the forehead of the Apis Bull B.M. 37448 the blaze is *triangular*, not four-sided, as Herodotus (III, 28) says, *ἐπὶ τῷ μετώπῳ λευκὸν τετράγωνον.*

When Apis was dead he was called Åsår Ḥāpi, 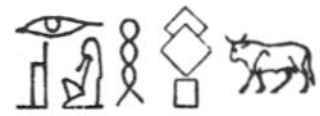, or **Serapis** by the Greeks, and he is represented on coffins in the form of a bull with disk and uraeus on his head; on his back is the mummy of the deceased, above which the soul, in the form of a hawk, is seen hovering. The place where the Apis bulls that lived at Memphis were buried was called the **Serapeum**, and Mariette discovered at Ṣaḳḳârah their tombs, dating from the time of Åmenḥetep III down to that of the Roman Empire. Above each tomb of an Apis bull was built a chapel, and it was the series of chapels that formed the Serapeum properly so called.

The **Mnevis** bull, 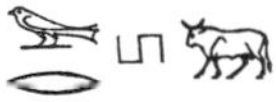, was worshipped at Heliopolis, and is thought by some to represent the same symbolism, and to be identical in form with Apis; he is called the "renewing of the life of Rā."

Mestȧ, Ḥāpi, Ṭuamutef and Qebḥsenuf, the four children of Horus, are common in glazed faïence, but rare in hard stone, gold, silver, bronze and wax.

Sati, , **Ānqit,** 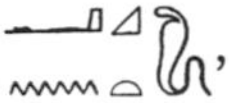, and Khnemu formed the triad of Elephantine, and Sati seems to resemble Nephthys in some of her attributes. She usually stands upright, holding  in her right hand, and  in her left. The British Museum possesses one example (110) in bronze, in which she is represented seated. On her head she wears the crown of Upper Egypt, in the front of which is a uraeus; a pair of horns follows the contour of the White Crown, and above them is a star. No. 11143 is a fine bronze figure of a woman, standing upright upon a pedestal; her right arm hangs by her side, but her left arm is bent, and her hand, holding an object, is laid upon her breast. She has the same head-dress as No. 110, and seems to be the same goddess. The British Museum possesses one example also in faïence (13664) in which the goddess stands upright.

Sebek, , represented the destroying power of the sun, and his worship is as old as the VIth dynasty. In bronze (B.M. 22924) he stands upright, and has the head of a crocodile surmounted by horns, disk, plumes and uraei, which have disks and horns .

Ȧnḥer, , "the leader of the celestial regions," which Shu supports, is usually represented wearing plumes , and holding a dart ; he is at times called , *neb māb,* "lord of the dart." This god is represented in relief, standing upright and wearing plumes; in his right hand he holds and in his left the sceptre ; see the glazed faïence pendant B.M. 11335. His sceptre is usually composed of , , and arranged perpendicularly one above the other. He is sometimes called *Ȧn-ḥer Shu sa Rā,* " Ȧn-ḥer Shu, the son of Rā."

Bes, , a god whose worship in Egypt dates from a very remote period, seems to have possessed a double character. He is represented as a grotesque person with horns and eyes on a level with the top of his head, his tongue hangs out, and he has bandy legs. He wears a crown of feathers on his head, and a leopard's skin thrown round his body. As a warrior, or the god of war, he is armed with a shield and sword, and sometimes he has a bow ; he was also the god of music and the dance, and in this character he is represented as a tailed creature, half man, half animal, playing a harp, or striking cymbals together and dancing. It is thought that he symbolized the destructive power of Nature, and in this capacity he is identified in the Book of the Dead with Set ; as the god of joy and pleasure figures of him are carved upon the *koḥl* jars, and other articles used by Egyptian ladies in their toilet. The worship of this god seems to have been introduced into Egypt from , *Neter ta, i.e.,* the land which was situated by the eastern bank of the Nile, supposed by the Egyptians to be the original home of the gods. Figures of this god in bronze and faïence are very common, and they represent him as described above. Some figures of him in faïence are 14 inches high, and are sometimes in relief and sometimes " in the round." A large mould used for making flat figures of the god was presented to the British Museum (20883) by the late F. G. Hilton Price, F.S.A., who obtained it from Bubastis. The beautiful figure in the round in blue-glazed faïence (B.M. 28112) is about 14 inches high. A remarkable example of the use of the head and face of this god is furnished by a bronze bell in the British Museum (6374). The plumes on his head form the handle, and the head, hollowed out, forms the bell.

The Mnevis Bull.

Kheperȧ.

Mestȧ.

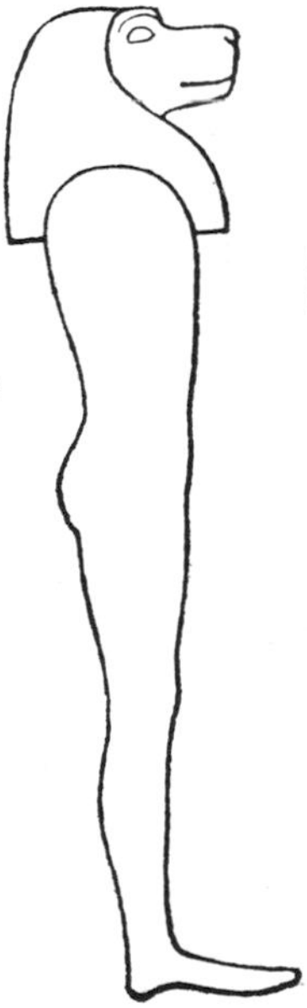

Ḥāpi.

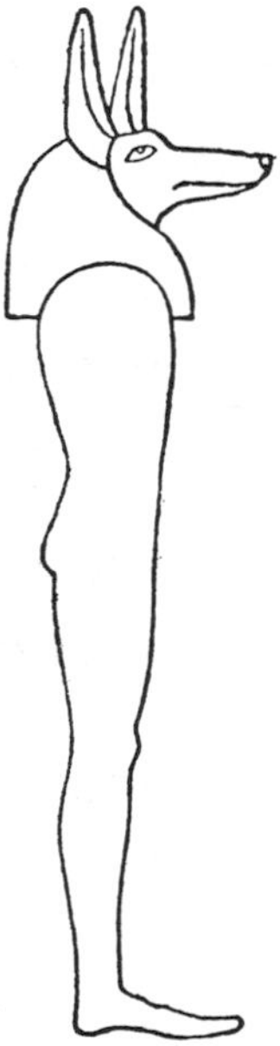

Ṭuamutef.

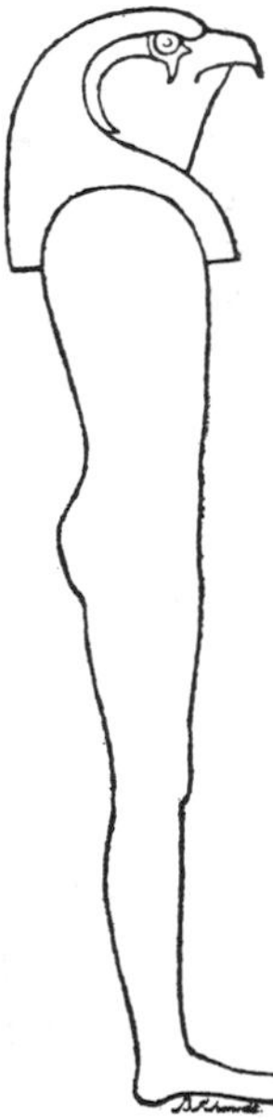

Qebḥsenuf.

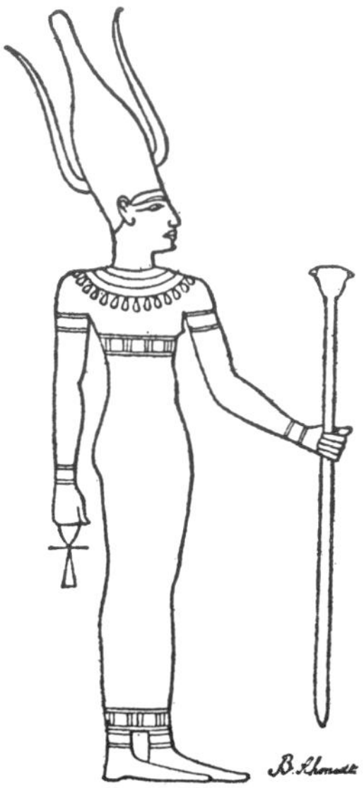

Sati.

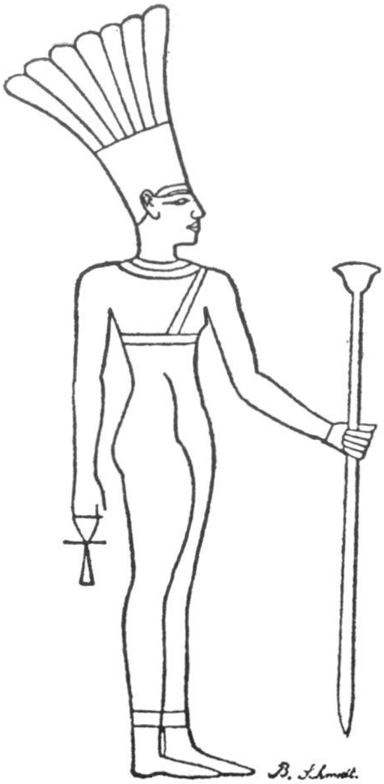

Ānqit.

Sebek.

Ånḥer.

Bronze and faïence statues of this god, to which have been added the distinguishing characteristics of many other gods, also exist. B.M. 17169 is a bronze ithyphallic bird with two pairs of outstretched wings and the legs of a man, from the knees of which spring serpents, the arms of a man, and the head of Bes. Above the wings is a second pair of outstretched arms, with clenched fists, and on each side of his head, in relief, are the heads of a ram, a dog-headed ape, a crocodile, and a hawk (?). Above the head are two pairs of horns, two pairs of uraei and two pairs of plumes, between which is a disk. In this figure are united the attributes of Åmen-Rā, Menu, Horus, Khnemu, Sebek, and other gods. No. 1205, a bronze cast from a genuine bronze, makes this polytheistic figure stand upon crocodiles; the whole group is enclosed within a serpent having his tail in his mouth. A very interesting example of a similar kind of figure in faïence is described by Lanzone in his *Dizionario*, p. 211, tav. LXXX, and compare B.M. 11821. It need hardly be said that such figures belong to a very late period, and they are found imitated on gems inscribed for the Gnostics; see B.M. G. 10, 11, 12, 151, 205, etc. On the Metternich Stele Bes is represented in much the same way as in the bronze figures, but in the pair of outstretched arms and hands he holds sceptres of 𓋹, 𓊽, , knives, , etc., and in those which hang by his side he holds and 𓋹; he has on his head in addition eight knives and the figure , "myriads of years." He stands on an oval in which are a lion, two serpents, a jackal, crocodile, scorpion, hippopotamus and tortoise. This scene is repeated very accurately on a Gnostic lapis-lazuli plaque in the British Museum (12), on the back of which is an address to **ΙΑΩ ΣΑΒΑΩΘ** = יָה צְבָאוֹת with whom this polytheistic deity was identified. Figures of the god Bes are common on gems and seals other than Egyptian, and on a small Babylonian cylinder that was in the possession of the late Sir Charles Nicholson he is represented in the form in which he ordinarily occurs . On a red carnelian cylinder in the British Museum (Reg. No. 49/6-23/10) he is engraved, full face, wearing plumes, and holding a lotus flower in each hand; on each side of him is a male bearded figure, with upraised hands and arms, supporting a winged disk. This seal was inscribed for Arsaces, and belongs to the Persian Period.

Sekhmit, , also written , was the wife of Ptaḥ, and was, in this capacity, the mother of Nefer Åtmu and I-em-ḥetep; she was the second person of the triad of Memphis. She represented the violent heat of the sun and its destroying power, and in this capacity destroyed the souls of the wicked in the underworld. In bronze and faïence figures she has the head of a lion, upon which she wears the disk and uraeus, and she holds in her right hand and in her left; she is sometimes seated with her hands laid upon her knees.

Bast, , represented the heat of the sun in its softened form as the producer of vegetation. She has often the head of a lion, but, properly speaking, the **head of a cat** is her distinguishing characteristic; in her right hand she holds a sistrum, on her left arm she carries a basket, and in her left hand she holds an aegis. She was chiefly worshipped at Bubastis, Pa-Bast, where a magnificent temple was built in her honour. Bronze figures of this goddess are tolerably numerous, and she is represented, both sitting and standing, wearing the disk and uraeus on her head. In faïence, standing figures hold a sceptre (B.M. 236), or (B.M. 233), or an aegis (B.M. 11297); when seated she often holds a sistrum (B.M. 272); a fine large example of the goddess seated is B.M. 277. Such figures are sometimes inscribed with the prayer, "may she grant all life and power, all health, and joy of heart," , or, "I am Bast, the lady of life," .

Menḥit, , represented the power of light or heat, or both; in faïence she is represented as an upright woman, walking, having a lion's head, upon which she wears a disk and uraeus; in her right hand is , and in her left .

Mut, , the World-mother, was the wife of Åmen, and the second member of the Theban triad; she is called the "lady of Åsher," , the name given to a district to the south of the great temple of Åmen-Rā at Karnak, where her temple was situated. She symbolized Nature, the mother of all things. In bronze and faïence figures she is represented as a woman, seated or standing, wearing a head-dress in the form of a vulture, surmounted by the crowns of Upper and Lower Egypt; she holds in her right hand, and in her left.

Net, , or Neith, the "Weaver" or "Shooter," also a Mother-goddess, was a counterpart of the goddess Mut, and was also identified with Hathor; she wears the crown of Lower Egypt on her head, and she is often represented armed with bow and arrows. In bronze and faïence figures of this goddess are tolerably common.

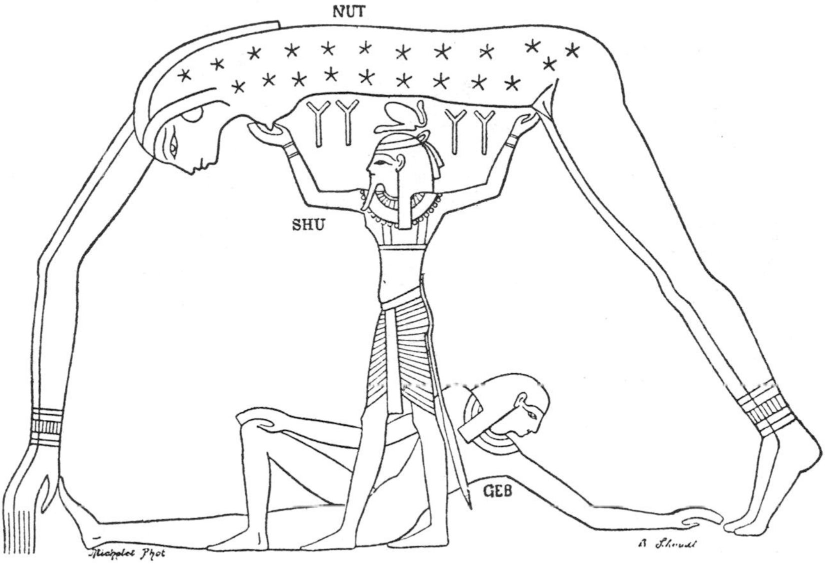

The god Shu lifting up Nut from Geb.

On the head of the god is , meaning magical power and strength (*Ḥeka*). The four signs represent the Four Pillars which stood, one at each of the Four Cardinal Points, and supported the heavens.

Bes.

Bast.

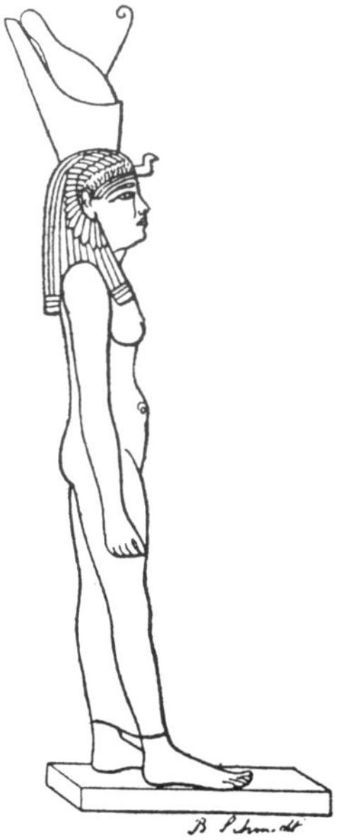

Mut.

Maāt.

Ḥet-Ḥert (Hathor).

Nefer-Åtmu.

Maāt, , the "daughter of Rā and mistress of the gods," symbolized Law, and she is always represented with , *maāt,* emblematic of Law, upon her head ; in papyri two Maāti are shown together, each wearing , but sometimes this feather alone takes the place of the head. These are the Maāti goddesses of Upper and Lower Egypt. In figures of bronze, lapis-lazuli, and faïence Maāt is represented sitting down.

Hathor, in Egyptian , or , **Ḥet-Ḥert,** the "house of Horus," is identified with Nut, the sky, or place in which she brought forth and suckled Horus ; she was the wife of Ȧtmu, a form of Rā. She is represented as a woman, cow-headed, with horns and a disk between them, and shares with Isis and Mut many of their attributes.[1] She is often represented as a cow coming forth from the mountain of the west. The worship of Hathor is exceedingly ancient, and she was supposed to be the goddess of beauty, love, and joy, and the benefactress of the world. The forms[2] in which she is depicted on the monuments are as numerous as the aspects from which she could be regarded. Full-length figures of this goddess in bronze and faïence are comparatively few, but plaques and pendants of faïence upon which her head is inscribed or painted are common.

For a fine example in bronze of Hathor, cow-headed, wearing horns, disk, uraeus and plumes, see B.M. 22925. In two interesting bronze hollow-work *menàts* Hathor is represented in profile ; B.M. 20760 shows the goddess wearing a uraeus on her forehead, and four uraei on her head ; she has the usual head-dress of women falling over her shoulders. Beneath is a Hathor-headed sistrum, with pendent uraei, resting on . Beneath in an oval is the cow of Hathor, wearing , standing in a boat. Above, on each side, is a uraeus. One wears the crown of Upper Egypt, , and the other wears the crown of Lower Egypt. This beautiful object was found at Dêr al-Baḥarî, and is inscribed with the prenomen of Ȧmenḥetep III 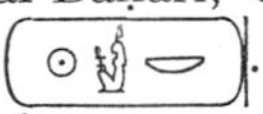. B.M. 300 represents the goddess with a vulture head-dress, wearing . Below, in relief, are a figure of the goddess and a floral ornament ; it is inscribed , "Hathor, lady of heaven."

Nu, , was the god of the sky and the husband of Nut.

[1] A list of the gods with whom she is identified is given in Lanzone, *Dizionario,* pp. 863, 864.

[2] On a pendant (B.M. 302) she is represented at full length, in relief.

Nut, , the sky, the wife of Geb, and mother of Osiris, Isis, Set, Nephthys, Anubis, Shu, and Tefnut, was represented by a woman having a vase of water  on her head, and holding  in her right hand and  in her left. She was painted on the outside of coffins, and was supposed to protect with her wings the deceased within. Figures of this goddess in bronze or faïence are unknown to me.

Geb, , was the husband of Nut, the sky, and father of Osiris, Isis, and the other gods of that cycle ; figures of this god in bronze or faïence are unknown to me.

Serqit, , daughter of Rā, wife of Horus, and identified with Sesheta and Isis, symbolized the scorching heat of the sun. A bronze figure in the Louvre (see Pierret, *Panthéon Égyptien*, p. 17 ; Lanzone, *Dizionario*, tav. CCCLXII) gives her the body of a scorpion, and the head of a woman wearing disk and horns, by which she is identified with Isis. There is a similar figure in the British Museum (11629) on the base of which are the words , " Isis, Giver of Life " ; a small bronze scorpion, B.M. 18667, also gives her the head and arms of a woman with disk and horns. The figures of this goddess, other than bronze, are usually made of lapis-lazuli.

Maȧḥes, 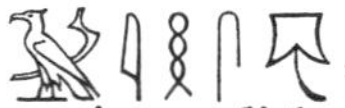, is sometimes represented as a man, lion-headed, wearing a disk and uraeus ; a few figures of this god in faience are known.[1]

Seker, 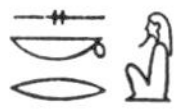, or Socharis, a form of the night-sun, is represented as a man, hawk-headed, holding ,  and  in his hands.

There are among the Egyptian gods in the British Museum two examples (1419 and 22930) of a **polytheistic figure** of considerable interest. They have hawks' ithyphallic[2] bodies, human legs and feet, each of which stands on a crocodile, and human hands and arms ; the front of the head is in the form of a jackal's head, surmounted by plumes and disk, and the back is in the form of a ram's head, surmounted by a disk and uraeus. In the right hand is a whip , and in the left an object which I cannot identify. Each group

[1] See Lanzone, *Dizionario*, p. 272.

[2] In B.M. 22930 the hawk's body is more distinct, and has a head, surmounted by a disk, and the feathers of the tail rest upon a hippopotamus.

Maåḥes.

Seker.

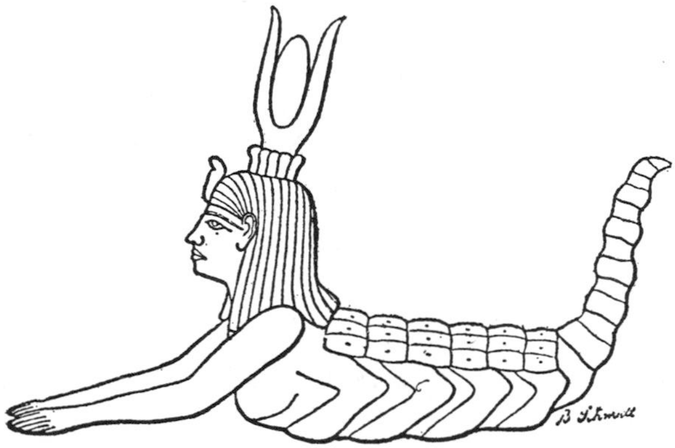

Serqit.

Geb.

Nut.

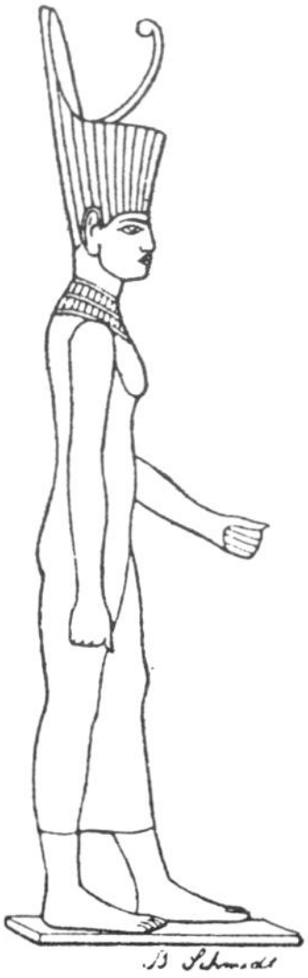

Net (Neith).

Ta-urt (Thoueris).

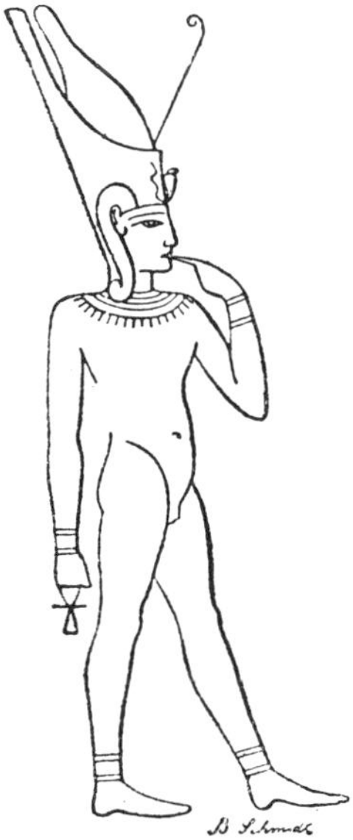

Ḥer-pa-kharṭ (Harpokrates).

Sesheta.

stands on a pedestal with a circle formed by a serpent having his tail in his mouth. These figures have much in common with those described under the name Bes, and may be variant forms of this god.

Another figure of interest is B.M. 24385, which represents a seated woman, with the head of a sheep, surmounted by disk, uraeus, and horns; behind this head-dress is the tail of a scorpion. The right hand is laid underneath her left breast, which she touches with her finger and thumb, and the left rests upon her knee. The Museum of the Louvre possesses a similar figure with the addition of a naked child whom she holds upon her knees, and whom she is about to suckle. Lanzone (*Dizionario*, p. 841; for the figure see tav. CCCXI) thinks that the sheep and scorpion-headed goddess represents Isis, and the child, Horus.

Ta-urt, , or Thoueris, was the wife of Set, and she is usually represented in bronze and faïence with the head and body of a hippopotamus, the hind quarters of a lion, and the tail of a crocodile. On her head she wears a modius which is sometimes surmounted by a disk, horns, and plumes, .

Sefekh-Ȧabu, or **Sesheta**, is a form of the goddess Hathor that was worshipped in Hermopolis, and was also adored in Memphis from the earliest dynasties.

Neḥeb-ka, 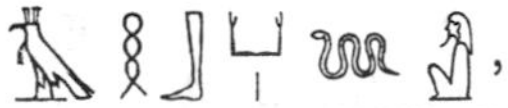, is a god mentioned in the Book of the Dead (Chapter XVII, 61; Chapter XXX, 3, etc.), and pictures of him are found upon coffins. In bronze figures he has the body of a man and the head of a serpent; in wood he has the body of an animal and the head of a serpent, and holds  in his paws (B.M. 11779), in faïence he has an animal's body and a serpent's head, and either holds  outstretched in his paws (B.M. 11795), or raises them to his mouth (B.M. 1197). He sometimes wears plumes and horns.

GRAECIZED FIGURES OF EGYPTIAN GODS

In many large collections of Egyptian Antiquities that include objects of the Ptolemaïc and Roman Periods will be found a numerous group of red terra-cotta figures of Egyptian gods and goddesses to whom the Greeks, and possibly the Romans also, paid adoration. The gods chosen by them were not the old solar gods of Heliopolis and Memphis, but Osiris and the members of his family—Isis, Nephthys, Horus, Anubis—and, curiously enough, the old Sûdânî god Bes. The group of such figures in the British Museum

(VIth Egyptian Room) contains examples of all the known forms of importance, and an examination of them reveals the following facts: **Isis** has several forms, and the large number of figures shows that this goddess was a great favourite. (1) She is seen on plaques in the form of a large, handsome woman seated on a throne offering her right breast to Horus, who is lying across her knees. She has on her head the horns, disk and plumes of Hathor, but her body is arrayed in a voluminous Greek garment which reaches down to her ankles. (2) In the old mythology Isis was associated with Sepṭ, or Sôthis, the rise of which heralded the Inundation, and she travelled over the heavens in a boat. This made her a goddess of navigation, and we see her in the form of a Juno-like woman wearing her characteristic head-dress and Greek attire, and holding in her right hand a rudder, as the great protectress of ships and of all who go down to the sea in ships. (3) She was identified with Hathor, and so appears in the form of a nude woman, wearing the disk, plumes and horns of that goddess on her head, a necklace and pendant, armlets and sandals. (4) Isis also appears on plaques and pectorals in the form of a serpent, with the disk and horns, , on her head. A jug near her indicates her character as mother of abundance and prosperity, and the sistrum, , placed in her dress, her connection with and patronage of music and dancing. On a plaque at Berlin (8164) we see her with the disk and horns on her head in a shrine surmounted by the "living uraei," side by side with Osiris, also in serpent form and wearing the crowns of the South and North, . (5) As the goddess of the star Sepṭ, *i.e.*, Sôthis or Sirius, the Dog-star, she rides upon a dog, who has a star on his head between his ears.

Osiris appears on stelae of the Ptolemaïc and Roman Periods in his usual form as a mummy wearing the Atef Crown, , and holding and , and in this form he is associated with Isis, the woman-goddess. But the form of Osiris that is most common in terra-cotta figures is **Osiris Apis,** , Åsår-Ḥāp, or **Serapis.** The original form of Åsår-Ḥāp was that of a bull, but in the terra-cotta figures he is represented as a man with masses of curly hair and a thick beard; in his hair he wears the horns of the ram, sacred to Åmen, and on his head is the modius. In these figures there is no trace of the Apis Bull or of the mummy-form of Osiris. The Greeks brought to Egypt the image of the god of the dead at Sinope, and called it Åsår-Ḥāp, which was the name at that time of the god of the dead of the Egyptians. The people in general preferred the form of the handsome bearded man to that of a mummy, and so the terra-cotta figures of the god of Sinope multiplied

PLATE XXVIII

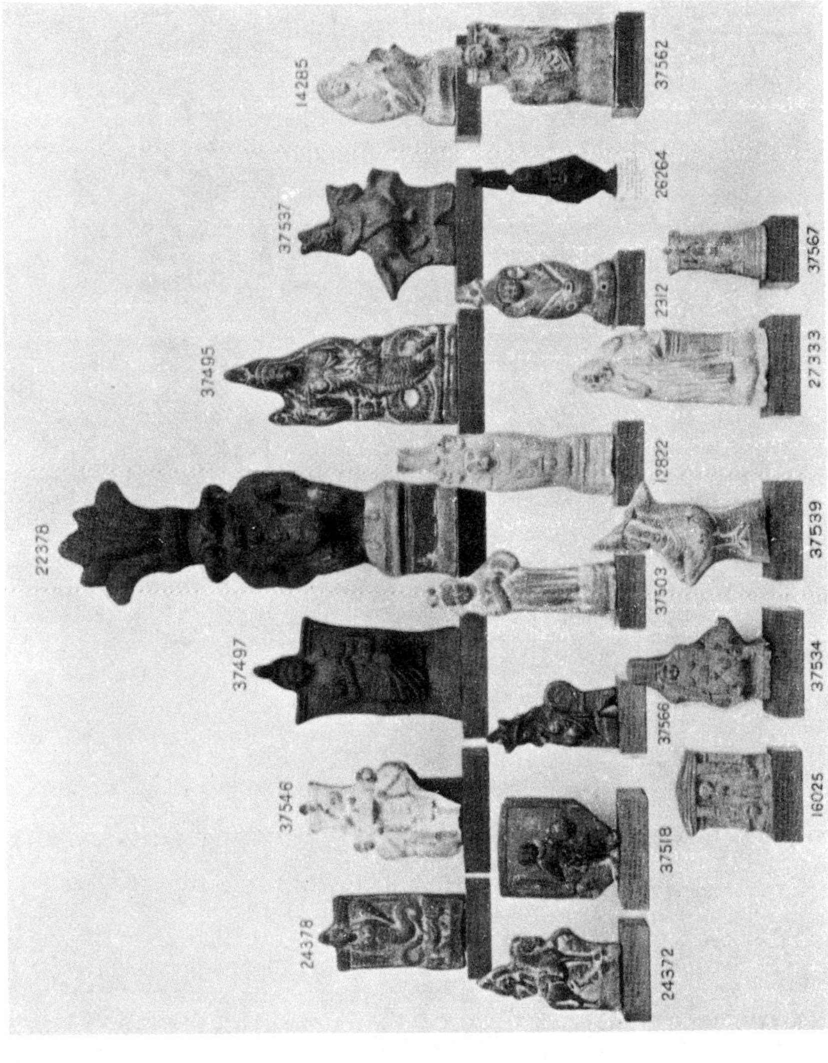

A group of figures of Graecized Egyptian gods, Isis, Osiris, Harpokrates, Serapis, etc. in the British Museum. Ptolemaïc and Roman Periods.

Wooden Ptaḥ-Seker-Åsår figure with sarcophagus and four hawks. XXVIth dynasty. B.M. No. 18162.

Hollow figure of Osiris which contained the Papyrus of Ånhai. XXIst dynasty. B.M No. 20863.

Mummied cat. B.M. No. 37348.

Ḥāpi Mestå Ṭuamutef Qebḥsenuf

A set of "Canopic" jars in aragonite.

in Egypt. But terra-cotta figures of Osiris in the form of a mummy are known, and there are two such in the British Museum (2312, 26264) in which he is seen wearing the Atef Crown.[1] Sometimes Serapis is associated with an eagle (or vulture ?), on which he seems to be riding, but I know of no incident in the life of Osiris that can be referred to by such figures.

The most popular member of the family of Osiris was , " Horus the Child," Ḥerpkhraṭ or **Harpokrates,** ʽΑρποκράτης, and he appears in many forms : (1) As a babe lying on the lap of Isis. (2) As an old man, in which character he seems to have been confused with Horus the Aged. (3) As a babe seated upon a lotus flower. This clearly identifies him with the young Sun-god, who in the Vignette of Chapter LXXXIB of the Theban Book of the Dead is seen rising out of a lotus flower.[2] (4) As a young Egyptian prince, the heir of Osiris, wearing the Crowns of the South and North, . (5) As a young, virile god, ithyphallic, like Menu, the god of procreation, and like the ithyphallic Osiris on his bier. (6) As a successor of Åmen, riding a ram, sacred to Åmen, or a goose, a bird also sacred to Åmen. (7) As a military knight riding a horse. On his head he wears the crowns of the South and the North, and he holds a long spear in his right hand, ready to transfix a foe ; this is often represented on Gnostic amulets (King, *Gnostic Gems,* Pl. VI, No. 7). In this form he represents Ḥerur, who slew Set, and Ra, who speared Āpep, and Osiris, who slew Set, or Typhon. This form of Harpokrates was adopted by the Copts for Saint George and other military knights. (8) As a god, wearing the triple crown, and seated on a plinth which is being carried by two priests ; in the crook of his left arm is a torch or a horn of abundance. He symbolized the rising Nile, and was regarded as the giver of life and strength and of all food and wealth and prosperity. (9) As a draped youth with his hand in a pot—probably of phallic significance. (10) As a naked man, clasping with his left hand the legs of a naked girl who is sitting on his left shoulder (Berlin, 9181).

Figures of the other members of the family of Osiris—Nephthys and Anubis—are rare, and we may pass on to those of **Bes,** which are comparatively numerous. In one character he appealed to the popular imagination as the god of mirth and jollity, and of singing and dancing, and his plumes and general appearance proclaim his Sûdânî origin. But this god of pleasure was also renowned as a fighter, and in the terra-cotta figures he is brandishing a sword in his right hand and grasping a shield in his left. For his history generally see the description of him in the section on figures of the

[1] There is also a compact well-made bronze figure of him which dates from the Ptolemaïc Period (B.M. 26264).

[2] Thus is he seen on Gnostic amulets, where he is called **CEMC EIΛAM**, the " everlasting sun." King, *Gnostic Gems,* p. 35.

gods. Egyptianized forms of purely Greek and Roman gods are to be found in all large collections of such figures, and figures of Helios were represented with the attributes of Rā and Horus; Artemis and Aphrodite were made to resemble Hathor, and Neith, and Isis and Mersegert; Priapus was treated as a form of Menu, Hercules and Mars as forms of Horus and perhaps Bes, and so on. It seems that figures of any and every god who struck the popular imagination, no matter whence he came or what his origin was, were made and circulated by the merchants and dealers in such wares. The people kept them in their houses as protectors, and placed them in the graves with their dead as amulets in exactly the same way as the older Egyptians had done with their figures of gods in bronze, wood and faïence.[1]

WOODEN FIGURES OF ÅSÅR AND PTAḤ-SEKER-ÅSÅR

UNDER the XVIIIth dynasty the Egyptians placed the great papyrus rolls inscribed with the Chapters of the Theban Recension of the Book of the Dead either in the coffins with the mummies of those for whom they were written, or in niches cut in the walls of their tombs. Early in the XIXth dynasty they adopted a new plan, and placed the roll inside a wooden figure of the god Osiris, which was placed by the side of the coffin in the tomb. One of the oldest examples of such figures is B.M. 9861. The god is in the form of a mummy and is painted white, but his beard and head-dress are greenish-black. He wears the White Crown, with plumes, and above his head is painted the solar disk; his arms are bent at the elbows; his hands rest on his breast, and in one he holds a bronze model of a flail or whip with three thongs,[2] inlaid with carnelian. The figure, including its rectangular pedestal, is $30\frac{1}{2}$ inches in height. Down the front is a line of hieroglyphs which read: "NESU ṬA ḤETEP Osiris Khenti-Åmentt, Ånpu, dweller in the Chamber of Embalmment, lord of the Holy Land, may they grant entrance into and exit from Khert Neter to the Osiris **Hu-Nefer** the truth-speaker for ever," 
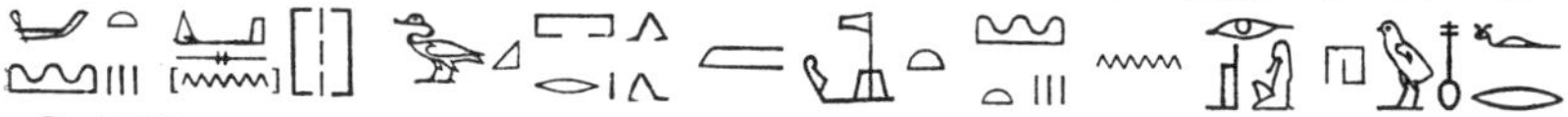
. The figure is hollow, and the roll of papyrus was pushed

[1] Figures in the British Museum which illustrate the above remarks are: Harpokrates on goose (37539), on horse (24372), enthroned (37546), with jar (37566), draped (37503), on lion throne (37567), as warrior (37518), with Serapis (37562); Serapis and eagle (14285); Osiris (2312, 26264); Isis with Harpokrates (37497), as woman-serpent (37495, 12822); Bes on lions (16025), Bes, 17 inches high (22378); Baubo on pig (37534).

[2] The  which the other hand held is missing.

up into it through a hole in the pedestal. From its neck hangs a *menȧt* on which is inscribed "Osiris, lord of eternity," . The splendidly coloured papyrus which was found in it is now in the British Museum (9901).

Another typical painted Osiris figure is B.M. 20868. The god is in the form of a mummy, and his hands, which hold the  and , rest on his breast. He wears the White Crown, with plumes, and a collar, and his cloak or shoulder-cape is decorated with large black spots and surrounded by a circle of small white spots. The body, from the waist downwards, is covered with scale (?) work, or perhaps feather-work. The face and hands are painted green, which suggests old age in the god; the *menȧt* hanging behind from the neck is uninscribed. The pedestal is in the form of , *maāt*, and through a hole in it a roll of papyrus was pushed up into the hollow figure of the god. This papyrus was the copy of the Book of the Dead which was written for Ånhai, , a priestess of Åmen-Rā about B.C. 1000, and is now in the British Museum (10472). But not every Egyptian official could afford to have a large roll of papyrus in its case placed in his tomb, and the custom grew up of making the figure of the god solid and placing a small roll of papyrus in a rectangular cavity sunk in the pedestal. The god was now called **Åsår-Seker,** 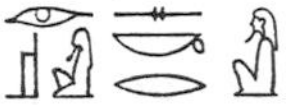, *i.e.*, "Osiris, the coffined one," and he was given the Atef Crown . The inscriptions on the figure also were of a different character. Thus on B.M. 23046 the inscription down the front contains a prayer that Osiris will give sepulchral offerings to the deceased Peṭa-Mut, priest of Åmen-Rā, king of the gods, and scribe of the That of Mentu, lord of Thebes,  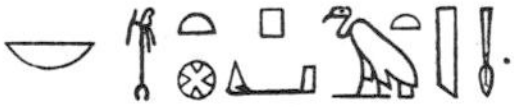. On each side of the figure are painted two of the Four Sons of Horus. The figures made at Åpu (Panopolis) are differently fashioned and ornamented. They are not hollow in their entire length, and only a small cavity is made in the breast of the figure to hold the papyrus, the entrance to it being at the back of the neck. In the example B.M. 16784 the figure wears the Atef Crown, the face is gilded, and the whole front of the body is covered with a large hawk-headed pectoral painted in bright colours. Above the lower part of the abdomen is a figure of the goddess Nut, with widely extended arms, and she holds a feather, , symbolic of air, in each hand. Down the back of the figure runs a line of hieroglyphs giving the name of the deceased, Åni, the son of

Åni and Meḥttath, which is followed by a prayer to Osiris and Seker-Osiris dwelling in Åpu for funerary offerings. The body of the figure is painted the deep red colour that is a characteristic of all funerary objects from Åpu (Akhmîm). In the Saïte and Graeco-Roman Periods the Seker-Osiris figures were much smaller, and no attempt was made to place the papyrus inside them. When the papyrus to be placed under the protection of the god was a hieratic copy of the Book of the Dead it was inserted in a long cavity made in the side of the pedestal (B.M. 9870), and when it was a very small roll the cavity was made in the pedestal just in front of the feet of the figure. Under the XXVIth dynasty we find that not only papyri were inserted in the pedestal, but sometimes portions of the body of the persons for whom the figures were made. In such cases the portion of the body was mummified and wrapped in bandages and laid in a rectangular cavity cut in the fore-part of the pedestal. On this a cover made in the form of a sarcophagus was fitted, and upon this was set the figure of a hawk, , Horus-Sepṭ. Frequently each angle-post was surmounted by a hawk. The object of placing a part of the body of the deceased in the pedestal is clear. It was believed and hoped that the mortal part of the man would be changed, and that the deceased would become the very bone and flesh of the god; the presence of Seker-Osiris was sufficient to effect this. And when Ptaḥ is associated with Seker-Osiris, it was believed that the resurrection of the deceased would follow as a matter of course, and that he and the triune god of the resurrection would share and share alike. Under the influence of this belief the character of the inscriptions changed, and in one (B.M. 9742) we read, " Homage to thee, O flesh and bone proceeding from this god, Efflux proceeding from Tem,"  . And on the pedestal of this figure, after the now common opening words , " the King gives an offering," comes a long prayer that Ptaḥ-Seker will give to the deceased Pekhet, , or Pakhet, , the son of Ḥer, , funerary offerings and truth-speaking before all the gods. And Osiris is to protect him and enable him to live again in the Ṭuaṭ, and to go forth from it [at pleasure].

The pedestals of some of the figures are supposed to represent the lake of cool water in which the deceased will bathe and enjoy himself. On the top of one pedestal a rectangular lake or tank is painted (B.M. 36424) with lotus flowers and buds growing in it. And the long inscription begins, " Thou art cleansed, Osiris, the cool water that comes forth from Elephantine bathes thee," 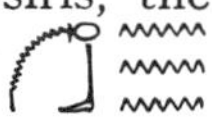

 "Thy soul lives, thy seed germinates, thou renewest thy youth as governor of the Living Ones,"  . The name of the deceased appears to have been Tchau, , the son of Ḥer-âru, , and both father and son were engaged in the linen trade at Panopolis (?).

FIGURES OF ANIMALS, BIRDS AND REPTILES, SACRED TO THE GODS

THE **figures of animals** found in the temples, tombs and ruined houses of Egypt may, like those of the gods, be divided into three classes :—(1) Votive ; (2) those worn as amulets either by the living or dead ; (3) those that stood in houses. They are made of hard stone, bronze, steatite, basalt, faïence, wood, wood gilded, lapis-lazuli, wax, plaster, and many other materials. Those in bronze, stone, and wood were usually made for temples, and to stand in tombs ; those in faïence, lapis-lazuli, and other semi-precious stones were placed on the bead-work or under the folds of the wrappings of mummies, or were worn suspended to necklaces by the living ; those placed in the walls of houses, but which have not sufficient distinguishing characteristics to give many details, were usually made of faïence cast in moulds. A comprehensive collection containing many examples of all three kinds will be found exhibited in the British Museum (Fifth Egyptian Room). The animals, birds and reptiles of which figures are most commonly found are :—

1. **Ape,** dog-headed, , wearing disk and crescent, sacred to Thoth and Khensu. Figures in bronze, stone, wood and faïence, in which he is represented sitting, sometimes on a pedestal with steps, or standing, are common ; sometimes he holds  (B.M. 1442), and sometimes a goat (B.M. 11910).

2. **Hippopotamus,** , *Ta-urt,* Thoueris, standing on the hind-quarters of a lion, and holding the tail of a crocodile ; figures in bronze and faïence are common. The most beautiful example of this composite animal in green basalt is preserved in the Museum at Gîzah, a cast of which is exhibited in the Egyptian Gallery of the British Museum (1075). See also the fine example in red and yellow agglomerate (B.M. 35700).

3. **Cow,** sacred to Hathor, with disk between her horns, .

4. **Lion,** , couchant or standing, sacred to Horus. Examples are very common in faïence. Frequently the body of the lion has a lion's head at each end of it, and sometimes there is a lion's head at one end and a bull's head at the other ; on the back, between the two heads, is the disk of the sun , the whole representing the sun on the horizon, . The two heads, facing in opposite directions, are supposed to represent the south and north, *i.e.*, the sun's course daily. An example in which each lion's head has two faces, one looking towards the south and the other towards the north, is figured in Lanzone, *Dizionario*, tav. CVI.

5. **Sphinx,** , couchant or sitting on his haunches, sacred to Harmakhis. Figures in bronze and faïence are tolerably common. The Sphinx at Gîzah is the symbol of Ḥer-em-åakhu-t, , or Horus on the Horizon.

Sphinx.

6. **Bull,** , sacred to Apis, having disk and uraeus between his horns, and the figures of a vulture with outspread wings, and a winged scarab on his back, and a triangular blaze on his forehead. Figures in bronze and stone are more common than in faïence.

7. **Ram,** , sacred to Khnemu or Åmen-Rā ; figures in bronze and faïence are tolerably common.

8. **Cat,** , sacred to Bast, lady of Bubastis. Large votive figures of the cat were made of bronze and wood, the eyes being inlaid with obsidian and gold ; B.M. 22927 has the eyes, and a large number of the hairs of the body, inlaid with gold. The smaller figures worn for ornament by the votaries of Bast are made of bronze, stone, rock-crystal, lapis-lazuli, faïence, etc. ; in the smaller figures the cat is represented with one, two, or more kittens, and the top of the sceptre is often ornamented with a cat.

9. **Jackal,** , sacred to Ånpu (Anubis), or to Up-uatu. In bronze figures, which are numerous, he stands on a pedestal which fitted on to the top of a sceptre or staff; faïence figures are not very common. A large number of wooden models from the top of sepulchral boxes are known.

10. **Hare,** , sacred to Osiris Unnefer; figures in faïence are common.

11. **Sow,** , sacred to Set (?), was the abomination of Horus, , according to Chapter CXII of the Book of the Dead; figures of this animal in faïence are fairly common. B.M. 11897 has a head at each end of its body.

12. **Hippopotamus,** , sacred to Set, or Typhon; many large and beautiful examples of this animal in glazed faïence and steatite exist in public and private collections.

13. **Stag,** . Figures in which the animal is represented with its legs tied together ready for sacrifice are known in bronze, *e.g.*, B.M. 1696.

14. **Hedgehog,** a few examples of which, in bronze and faïence, are known.

15. **Shrew-mouse,** sacred to Horus (?), examples of which are more common in bronze than in faïence.

16. **Ichneumon.** Examples in bronze, in which the animal wears disk and horns and plumes, are known, but figures in faïence are rare.

17. **Crocodile,** , sacred to Sebek; examples in bronze and faïence are fairly common.

18. **Vulture,** , sacred to Mut; figures of this bird in bronze and faïence are few.

19. **Hawk,** , sacred to Horus; votive figures are made of bronze, stone, and wood, and the hawk wears either the crown of Upper or Lower Egypt, or both crowns united. In smaller figures, worn for ornament, it wears a disk (B.M. 1889) or  (B.M. 1850), or plumes (B.M. 1859); it is often man-headed, when it represents the soul , and sometimes two hawks are on one pedestal, and each has the head of a man. A form of Horus, worshipped in Arabia under the name of **Sepṭ,** , is often found in hard stone and wood; figures made of the latter material are generally found on the small chests which cover the portions of human bodies placed

in the pedestals of Ptaḥ-Seker-Åsår figures. When complete they have plumes on their heads.

20. **Ibis,** , sacred to Thoth; figures in bronze and faïence are not rare.

21. **Frog**; figures in bronze and faïence are common.

22. **Fish,** . The five kinds of fish of which figures in bronze and faïence are known are the Oxyrhynchus, Phagrus, Latus, Silurus, and the Lepidotus; of these the Oxyrhynchus, Silurus, and Lepidotus are the commonest. The Oxyrhynchus fish (B.M. 1953) has on its back horns, disk, and uraeus; fish were sacred to Hathor, Isis, Mut, and other goddesses.

23. **Scorpion,** , sacred to Serqit. Figures in bronze have often a woman's head on which are horns and disk, and, if mounted, the sides of the base have inscriptions upon them which show that the scorpion was regarded as Isis–Serqit. Faïence figures of this reptile are tolerably numerous.

24. **Uraeus,** , or serpent, sacred to or emblem of **Meḥen,** , or **Mersegert,** ; figures in bronze and faïence are not rare.

25. **Scarab,** , emblem of the god Khepera. The largest scarab known is preserved in the British Museum (Southern Egyptian Gallery, 74), and is made of green granite; it was probably a votive offering in some temple, and was brought from Constantinople, whither it was taken after the Roman occupation of Egypt. The scarabs worn for ornament round the neck, and in finger-rings, were made of gold, silver, every kind of valuable stone known to the Egyptians, and faïence. B.M. 11630 is an interesting example of a horned scarab; B.M. 2043, in faïence, has the head of a hawk, and B.M. 12040 has the head of a bull.

26. The **camel,** , *gemla* (?), Copt. ϫⲁⲙⲁⲩⲗⲓ, was known to the pre-dynastic Egyptians, and earthenware figures of the animal were found at Naḳâdah.

27. The **ostrich,** , *nu,* was well known to the Egyptians of all periods, and the eggs of the bird, , were buried with the dead. An ostrich egg-shell, perforated at one end, was found in a pre-dynastic grave at Khizâm (B.M. 36377). Figures of the bird are unknown.

28. The **bear,** , *ruabu,* was known and hunted by the pre-dynastic Egyptians, but no figures of the animal have been found.

VESSELS IN EARTHENWARE, STONE, GLASS, ETC., FOR OFFERINGS TO THE DEAD

THE pre-dynastic Egyptians made offerings of various kinds of food to their dead, such offerings being packed in **earthenware** vessels, which were placed near the dead in their graves. The use of the **potter's wheel** was unknown, and all such vessels were shaped by the hand or foot of the potter. They vary greatly in shape and size, and though in form and substance and colour many appear to be duplicates, it will be found by the use of the measure and callipers that very few are exactly identical. The oldest pottery vases are usually red and black, the red colour being derived from a salt of iron; sometimes vases all red and all black are found, but they are relatively few. All three kinds were burnished. In the Archaic Period unburnished, buff-coloured pottery came into fashion, and these vases are decorated with designs, drawn in red outline, representing primitive African farm settlements with ostriches grazing near them, boats, some with sails, figures of animals and human beings, palm-trees, etc. To this period belong probably the vases that have wavy handles or are decorated with a rope border. A fine collection, containing many good examples of all the kinds of earthenware vessels mentioned above, will be found in the British Museum (Sixth Egyptian Room). For descriptions and illustrations of pre-dynastic and early dynastic pottery vases in other collections see de Morgan, *Recherches*, Paris, 1896, and *Premières Civilisations*, Paris, 1909; Reisner, *Early Dynastic Cemeteries*, Leipzig, 1908, Pt. I, pl. 51ff.; Quibell, *Archaic Objects* (Cairo Catalogue), 2 vols., Cairo, 1904–5; von Bissing, *Tongefässe*, Cairo, 1913; Petrie, *Naqada*, London, 1896, etc., *Royal Tombs, Abydos*, Parts I–III; Naville, *Cemeteries of Abydos*, and other works published by the Egypt Exploration Fund.

Little by little during the Archaic Period stones of various kinds were used in making sepulchral vessels, and many beautifully shaped bowls, dishes, saucers, vases and pots were made in **granite, diorite, basalt** of various colours, **porphyry,** etc. A large number of bowls, with lugs and flat rims, made of red and yellow breccia, were obtained from Al-'Amrah, near Abydos, and typical examples of these are B.M. 35699, 53886, 36331 and 43061. The boring and polishing of these vessels prove that under dynasties I–III the worker in stones had already acquired wonderful skill. Characteristic specimens of the sepulchral vessels of this period are to be seen in the British Museum. But working in granite and diorite was no easy matter, even for the skilled workman, and vases made in these and other hard stones must have been expensive luxuries; and it was probably these considerations that led to the introduction of **alabaster** and **aragonite** and to their extended use. From the IVth dynasty onwards countless vases, bowls, saucers, pots, jars, jugs,   were made in these materials ; in the Graeco-Roman Period marble took the place of alabaster. Sepulchral pots from Nubia, of native workmanship, are usually made of sandstone. The beautiful shapes of alabaster vessels for perfumes, oils, etc., are well illustrated by the British Museum Collection. Alabaster vases were often inscribed on the covers or sides with the names of the persons for whom they were made, and when the names are those of kings and other royal personages they serve to date the object. One of the Persian kings of Egypt had his names engraved on alabaster vases in Egyptian and cuneiform characters (B.M. 91456). Some of the large aragonite, or "zoned alabaster," vases appear to have been used as measures for liquids, *e.g.*, B.M. 4839, a handsome example with two handles and a cover, and bearing a statement as to its capacity, which reads , "eight *hen*[1] and three-quarters." Sepulchral vases were also made of glazed **steatite,** *e.g.*, B.M. 4762, a black-and-green vase inscribed with the prenomen and nomen of Thothmes I , Ākheperkarā Tcheḥutimes, diademed like Rā. Among the sepulchral vases of Thothmes III were some made of solid **gold,** with the king's prenomen engraved on their sides, and under the XVIIIth dynasty it was customary to make bowls, vases and libation pots of *tchām*,  or , a kind of whitish gold, which probably contained silver. Large numbers of vases were made of **bronze** ; libation buckets were also made of bronze. These are ornamented with figures in relief representing the deceased adoring the gods, or with designs cut in outline representing the adoration of the dead and the worship of Osiris. The ladles belonging to these have handles with ends in the shape of the heads of geese, and, in some respects, resemble old English toddy ladles. These buckets and ladles belong to the XXVIth dynasty and Ptolemaïc Period (B.M. 36319). Many of the stone vases found in tombs are only **models,** and were never intended to contain offerings, and many models were made of **wood.** These were painted to resemble variegated glass, and sometimes they were covered all over with plaster gilded (B.M. 30454, 30455, 35276, 32598 and 9528), with an inscription beginning 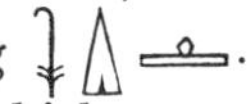. Gilded models are represented by B.M. 35273, 35274, which were made for Rameses II and are inscribed with the names of two kinds of eye-

[1] Compare Hebrew *hîn*, הִין. The Hebrew *hîn* = 6·06 litres, the Egyptian *hen* = 0·456 litre.

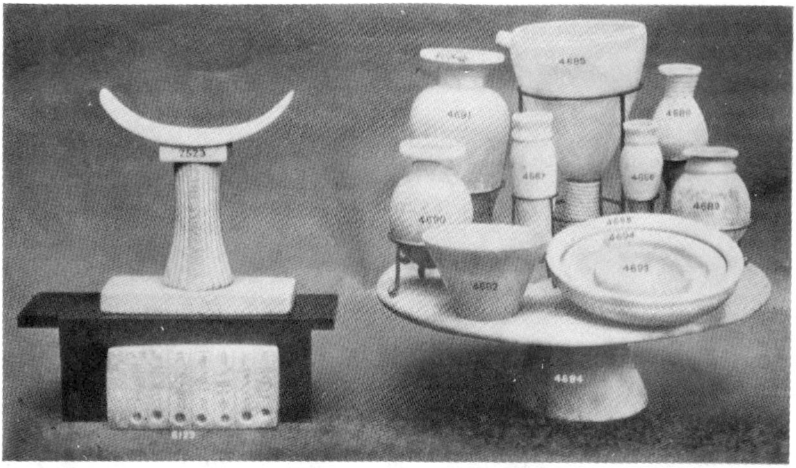

Alabaster pillow, unguent slab, and set of vessels on their stand which were made for Åṭenȧ, Kher-ḥeb of Abydos. VIth dynasty. B.M.

A group of bottles, bowls, vases, jugs, etc. made of hard stone of various kinds, breccia, etc. of the early dynastic period. B.M.

A group of burnished red ware flasks, bottles, etc. in the British Museum. XVIIIth dynasty.

A group of alabaster vases, bowls, etc. XVIIIth and following dynasties. B.M.

paint,  and . Sepulchral vases, bottles, jugs and flasks for unguents were made also of **opaque glass,** or glass paste, which was composed of flint, lime, soda, alkali, manganese and copper. This paste was known under the Old and Middle Kingdoms and small vessels, beads, amulets, etc., were made of it. But transparent glass in our sense of the word was unknown to the Egyptians until after the XXVIth dynasty. Mr. Chauncey Murch of Luxor acquired a hollow cylindrical seal-shaped object, 2⅝ inches long and 1 inch in diameter, which is formed of an outside tube of semi-transparent material lined with two layers of paste, coloured blue and white respectively. This remarkable object was found in the pyramid of Pepi II and is inscribed with the prenomen of this king, 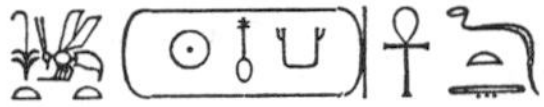, "King of the South and North, Neferkarā, the ever-living." By the side of the cartouche is a line of hieroglyphs which reads, , "the *smer*, superintendent of the servant[s] of the god, *neb Ḥer* (?)." Soon after this object was found it was submitted to certain experts in Cairo who declared that the outside semi-transparent material was glass, and therefore that the Egyptians were able to make transparent glass under the VIth dynasty. On my suggestion Mr. Murch sent the tube to London by me, wishing it to be deposited for examination in the British Museum (where, by the way, it still is). A careful examination of it has been made, and I am convinced that the semi-transparent substance is crystal, and that its peculiar glassy appearance is due to the reflection of the blue paste behind it. Were the paste removed the tube would be seen to resemble the crystal of which the figure of the goddess Taurt (B.M. 24395) is made, and that was found in the same place as the tube. The internal flaws that are seen in ancient crystal objects and amethyst scarabs appear both in the tube and in the figure of the goddess.

Under the New Kingdom the use of opaque glass of various colours became very general, and large quantities of it were cut up into plaques and roundels for inlaying in metal and in coffins and other wooden objects. Fine examples of variegated opaque glass vases are B.M. 36344 (with two handles), B.M. 4743 (with four handles); the glass alabastra (B.M. 4745 and 30762), and the handsome fish (B.M. 55193), which was found at Tall al-'Amârnah by Mr. Hayter. The glass jug (B.M. 47620), inscribed with the prenomen of Thothmes III, 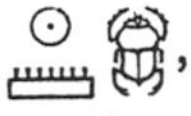, probably came from the tomb of this king, and the large handsome, two-handled vase (B.M. 36343), and the blue-glass bowl (B.M. 36342), certainly did. The light-blue glass *koḥl* pot (B.M. 24391) belonged to Ḥatshepsut's funerary equipment, as also did the fine deep-blue glass set of

"Canopic" jars (B.M. 51074–51077). Other interesting objects in opaque glass are a deep-blue scarab from the beadwork of a mummy (B.M. 22872), a cobalt-blue head-dress of Bes, which was inlaid in a statue of the god (B.M. 29674), and two two-handled white glass vases, with decorated rims (B.M. 29210, 54431). A pretty little vase, ▽, of mottled black-and-white glass (B.M. 17043) which formed part of the funerary equipment of Princess Nesi-Khensu, fell to pieces in consequence of the salt which it had by some means absorbed. It may be mentioned in passing that much of this opaque glass paste is porous.

Sepulchral vases made of the ordinary "potters' clay" or of the so-called Egyptian porcelain were often **glazed,** and under the New Kingdom the art of glazing steatite and earthenware was carried almost to perfection, as may be seen in the lavender-coloured glazed bowl bearing the name and titles of Rameses II (B.M. 4796) and the beautiful little blue vases made for Princess Nesi-Khensu (B.M. 13152, 17402). It is clear from the different shades of colour in the vases and other objects that were made for the same person that the potter mixed the ingredients for his flux by rule of thumb, and that he was never sure what colour his vessels or figures would be when they came out of the furnace.

In tombs of the XIIIth–XVIIth dynasties various kinds of vessels, bottles, jugs, etc., made of **black ware** are found, and they are usually assigned to the Hyksos period. In tombs of the XVIIIth dynasty flasks and bottles made of **red polished ware** are found. Some of the flasks have spouts and necks in the form of human heads (B.M. 29934, 29935), some have the forms of dwarfs, of a seated man, a woman playing a guitar (B.M. 5114), women carrying their babes under their arms (B.M. 24652, 54694), and a wine-skin inscribed with the name of Sanni (B.M. 5117). A selection of typical examples is exhibited in the British Museum; they were probably of Syrian origin. Another interesting class of sepulchral vessels are the **false-necked vases** that are commonly called **Bügelkannen** or "pseudamphorae." These vases are of the well-known Mycenaean type, and were imported into Egypt from Greece. According to Spiegelberg (*Geschichte der Aegyptischen Kunst*, p. 57) the Egyptians made copies of this class of vase in their native-glazed faïence. Under the XXVIth dynasty flat, circular, convex vases or bottles made of glazed faïence came into common use as votive offerings. The neck is in the form of a lotus flower, with an ape at each side, and where the body of the vase joins the neck it is ornamented with a pattern formed of rows of papyrus flowers and pendants. On the upper part of the flat edge which goes round the vase a new year's wish is inscribed thus: 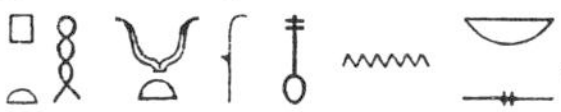, "May Ptaḥ open a happy year for its owner"; or 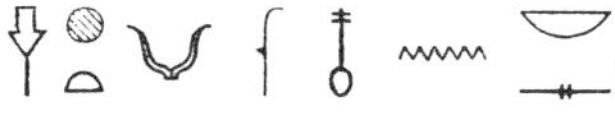, "May

Sekhmit open a happy year for its owner"; or "May Isis open a happy year for its owner"; or "May Åmen-Rā open a happy year for its owner" (B.M. 4767, 4768, 24651). The **Meroïtic** sepulchral vases are of fragile make, have graceful shapes and forms, and are frequently painted with simple but pretty designs.

FUNERARY TERRA-COTTA CONES

THIS name was given by the early Egyptologists to the terra-cotta conical objects that were at one time found in large numbers in and about the tombs at 'Asasîf and Ḳûrnah in Western Thebes. It is doubtful if any have been found elsewhere in Egypt. The oldest of them date from the XIIth dynasty, and they were in general use under the XVIIIth and XIXth dynasties; none has been found that can be later than the XXVIth dynasty. They vary in length from 6 to 10 inches, and in diameter, at the larger end, from 2 to 4 inches. The base or face of the cone usually bears upon it an inscription, in hieroglyphs stamped in relief, containing the name and titles (if any) of the person in whose tomb it was found; these inscriptions appear to have been made with a stamp with the characters incuse. The end of the cone bearing the inscription is sometimes coloured red and sometimes white. The style and character of the inscriptions are illustrated by the following examples:

1. Cone of Userḥat, overseer of the cattle of Åmen, (B.M. 9659). 2. Cone of the ERPĀ ḤA-Ā, Menthu-em-ḥat, fourth priest of Åmen, Scribe of the sanctuary of the temple of Åmen, inspector of the priests in the buildings of the King's House, (B.M. 35681). 3. Cone of Ruru, a superintendent of the Matchaiu (Police of Thebes) (B.M. 35650). 4. Cone of Nefer-renpit, (B.M. 9700). 5. Cone of the Overseer of the House of Khensu, (B.M. 9641). 6. Cone of Åmenemḥat, scribe and accountant of the . . . . of the South and North,

(B.M. 9640). 7. Cone of a second priest of Menkheperrā called Ȧmenemka,  (B.M. 35660). 8. Cone of Nefer-ḥeb-f, a priest of Ȧmenḥetep II, and his sister, the lady of the house, Tauai,   (B.M. 9687). 9. Cone of Meri, chancellor of the god, high priest of Ȧmen, Director of the priests of the South and the North, overseer of the estates of Ȧmen, keeper of the granary of Ȧmen, sealer-in-chief (?) in the king's house (life, strength, health to it !), and inspector of the cattle of Ȧmen.

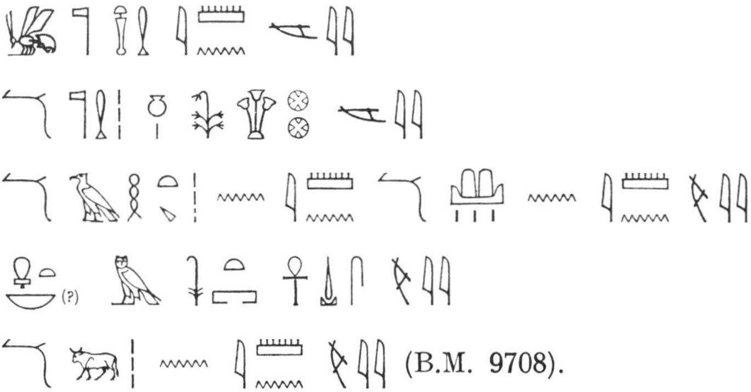

(B.M. 9708).

As to the use of these cones opinion is divided. The simplest explanation is that they are models of the pyramidal loaves of bread, , or of a pyramidal-shaped offering of some kind which we see worshippers presenting to the various gods. If they were models of loaves of bread they were placed in the tomb with the view of supplying bread to the *ka* of the deceased person. Birch thought that they were used to mark the site and extent of tombs, or were worked as ornaments into the building of the tomb. Hodges, Tyler, Cull and others attributed to them a phallic signification. And others, having seen bricks with pyramidal sides (*e.g.*, B.M. 35697) with one repetition of the inscription, or more, upon them, have said that the cones were seals. But an examination of the shape of any such brick shows that the object of impressing the name and titles of the deceased upon it several times[1] was to make it to represent several cones. This is proved by the pyramid shape of the sides of the brick, and the cones were assuredly not seals.

[1] B.M. 35468 has four stamps or impressions upon it.

THE EGYPTIAN GRAVE AND TOMB

Of the Palaeolithic and early Neolithic graves in Egypt nothing is known ; the earliest graves in the Nile Valley consist of shallow hollows dug in the sandy or stony soil which lies between the River Nile and the mountains on each side of the river. These hollows have no fixed shape, but they are usually oval or circular. The graves in late Neolithic cemeteries lie very close together and often overlap, and sometimes one part of a body lies in one grave and the other part in another. The body was often wrapped in a reed mat, and sometimes in the hide of an animal, probably a bull or gazelle ; the men buried in hides were chiefs. The body was laid upon its left side, the head usually faced the south, and the knees were bent up on a level with the top of the breast, and the hands were placed before the face—the usual pre-natal position. Round the body were placed vessels made of coarse earthenware filled with offerings of food, and with these are often found flint weapons and implements. The food offerings were intended for the use of the deceased on his journey to the Other World, and the flint weapons were given to him to enable him to defend himself against the attacks of enemies and to kill beasts when he went hunting. No attempt to mummify the dead was made at this period. Later the body was placed in a very rough box or basket, and sometimes an earthenware cover was placed over the grave to prevent the body being dragged out of its grave by animals, or broken up when new graves were being dug close by. Sometimes the body was dismembered, and its limbs were buried in the sand or mud, until such time as all the flesh had been eaten off the bones ; this done the bones were collected and brought to a grave and finally buried. This custom persists in some parts of the Sûdân to this day. When the body was laid in its final position the grave was filled in with earth or sand and stones; whether its place was marked by any kind of monument cannot be said. The Land of the Dead was believed to be situated in the west, and therefore isolated graves and cemeteries, and rock-hewn tombs, are usually found on the western bank of the Nile. The best and fullest material for the study of the graves of the Neolithic and Archaic Periods will be found in de Morgan, *Recherches,* Paris, 1896–7 ; *Les Premières Civilisations,* Paris, 1909 ; Reisner, *Early Dynastic Cemeteries,* Parts I and II, Leipzig, 1908 ; *Archaeological Survey of Nubia,* Vols. I–IV, Cairo, 1910 ; Petrie, *Naqada,* London, 1896 ; Quibell, *Archaic Objects,* 2 vols., Cairo, 1904–5. For the literature on the subject generally see the list of Baillet, *Recueil de Travaux,* tom. XXII, p. 180 ff., and for a summary see Wiedemann, *Umschau,* Bd. I, pp. 561 ff., 590 ff.

Under the IIIrd dynasty, and perhaps even under the IInd dynasty, chiefs and men of importance were buried in graves that were cut in the rock. Long before this time men of importance must have been buried in clefts in the rocks and in small natural caves, but now attempts were made to place the dead in pits more or less deep, which were sunk in the skirts of the hills and mountains. Both at Aswân and at Bani-Ḥasan[1] the tomb consisted of a small square chamber which was hewn in the rock, and a shallow pit was dug in the floor of it to hold the body. Sometimes a recess was cut in the pit for the body, and this was clearly the prototype of the mummy chamber which is always found, in one form or another, in the great tombs of the later dynasties. At Aswân we found the remains of the wooden coffins in which the bodies were buried, but at Bani-Ḥasan the coffins discovered by Dr. Garstang were made of earthenware, and were usually oval in form. From these early dynastic tombs it is clear that the tomb of any important man must contain: 1. A chamber, which gives access to a pit, and in which

Entrance to a Maṣṭabah at Ṣaḳḳârah.

offerings to the dead can be placed. 2. A shallow pit or shaft. 3. A recess to hold the body. All these requisites are found in the **Maṣṭabah,** which may now be briefly described. "Maṣṭabah" is the name that the Arabs gave to the low, long stone building which marks the site of a tomb at Ṣaḳḳârah, because its length, in proportion to its height, is great, and as it reminded them of the long, low seat, or *dîwân*, which was familiar to them, they called it maṣṭabah, *i.e.*, "bench." The maṣṭabah is a heavy, massive building of rectangular shape, the four sides of which are four walls symmetrically inclined towards their common centre. The exterior surfaces are not flat, for the face of each course of masonry, formed of stones laid vertically, is a little behind the one beneath it, and if these recesses were a little deeper, the external appearance of each

[1] See Garstang, *Funeral Customs*, London, 1907, p. 26.

side of the building would resemble a flight of steps. The stones that form the maṣṭabahs are of a moderate size, and, with the exception of those used for the ceiling and architrave, have an average height of 18 or 20 inches. The width and length of the maṣṭabah

Three Maṣṭabahs at Gîzah.

vary; the largest measures about 170 feet long by 86 feet wide, and the smallest about 26 feet long by 20 feet wide; they vary in height from 13 to 30 feet. The ground at Ṣaḳḳârah is formed of calcareous rock covered to the depth of a few feet with sand; the foundations of the maṣṭabahs are always on the solid rock. The plan of the

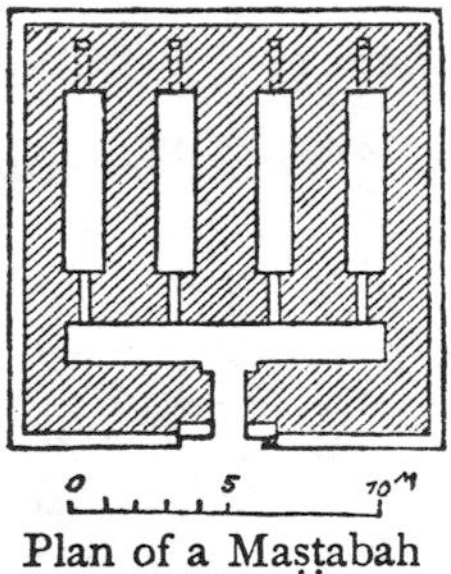

Plan of a Maṣṭabah with four sardâbs.

Transverse section at the bottom of a sardâb.

maṣṭabah is a rectangle, and the greater axis of the rectangle is, without exception, in the direction from north to south. Moreover, at the pyramids of Gîzah, where the maṣṭabahs are arranged symmetrically, the plan of their arrangement is like a chess-board, the squares of which are uniformly elongated towards the north. Maṣṭabahs are **oriented astronomically** towards the true north, and in the cases where they are a few degrees out this difference must be attributed not to design but to negligence. It has been asserted that maṣṭabahs are only unfinished pyramids, but properly considered, it is evident that they form a class of buildings by themselves, and that they have nothing in common with the pyramid, save in respect of being oriented towards the north, this orientation being the result, not of a studied imitation of the pyramid, but of a religious intention, which at this early period influenced the construction of all tombs, whatever their external form. The maṣṭabahs at Ṣaḳḳârah are built of stone and brick; the stone employed is of two kinds, the one being very hard, and of a bluish-grey colour, and the other being comparatively soft, and of a yellowish colour. The bricks also are of two kinds, the one yellowish and the other black; both sorts were sun-dried only. The bricks of a yellowish colour seem to have been used entirely during the earliest dynasties, and the black ones only appear with the second half of the IVth dynasty. However carefully the outside of the maṣṭabah was built, the inside is composed of sand, pieces of stone thrown in without design or arrangement, rubble, rubbish, etc., and but for the outside walls holding all together many of them must have perished long since. The eastern face of the maṣṭabah is the most important, for, four times out of five, the entrance is in it; it is sometimes, but very rarely, plain. Some yards from the north-east corner is, at times, a very high, narrow opening, at the bottom of which the masonry of the maṣṭabah itself assumes the form of long vertical grooves, which distinguish the stelae of this epoch; a stele, with or without inscription, sometimes takes the place of this opening. At a distance of some feet from the south-east corner is generally another opening, but larger, deeper and more carefully made; at the bottom of this is sometimes a fine inscribed calcareous stone stele, and sometimes a small architectural façade, in the centre of which is a doorway. When the eastern face has the opening at the south-east corner which has just been described, the maṣṭabah has no interior chamber, for this opening takes its place. When the maṣṭabah has the façade in the place of the opening, there is a chamber within. When the entrance to the maṣṭabah is made on

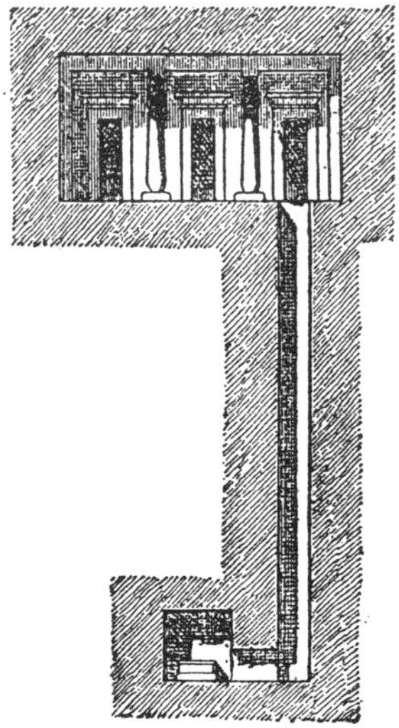

The upper chamber, the pit, and the sarcophagus chamber of a Maṣṭabah.

the north side, the façade is brought back to the end of a kind of vestibule, and at the front of this vestibule are set up two monolithic columns, without abacus and without base, which support the architrave, which supports the ceiling. The entrance to the maṣṭabah is sometimes made from the south, but never from the west; the top of the maṣṭabah is quite flat.

The interior of the complete maṣṭabah consists of three parts—the **chamber,** the **sardâb,** and the **pit.** Having entered the upper **Chamber** by the doorway in the side, it is found to be either without any ornamentation whatever, or to be covered with sculptures. Near the bottom of the chamber usually facing the east is

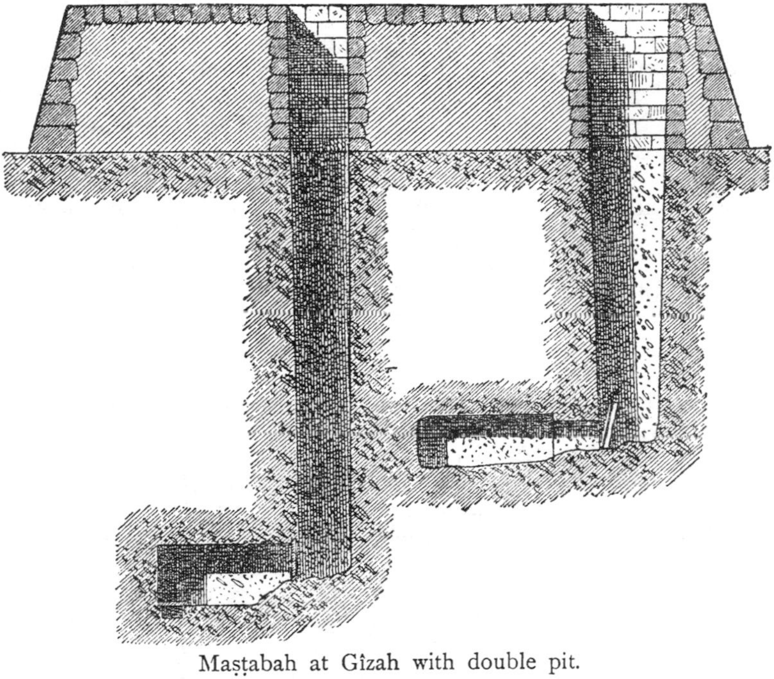

Maṣṭabah at Gîzah with double pit.

a **stele,** which, whether the walls are inscribed or not, is always inscribed. At the foot of the stele, on the bare ground, is often a **table of offerings** made of granite, alabaster, or calcareous stone; **two obelisks,** or two supports for offerings, are often found at each side of this table. Besides these things the chamber has no furniture, and it rarely has a door. Not far from the chamber, oftener to the south than to the north, and oftener to the north than to the west, is a lofty but narrow nook hidden in the thickness of the masonry, and built with large stones; this nook is called the **Sardâb.**[1] Sometimes

[1] A *sardâb,* سرداب, strictly speaking, is a lofty, vaulted, subterranean chamber, with a large opening in the north side to admit air in the hot weather.

the sardâb has no communication whatever with the other parts of the maṣṭabah, but sometimes a rectangular passage, so narrow that the hand can only be inserted with difficulty, leads from the sardâb into the chamber; in the sardâb statues of the deceased were placed, and the narrow passage served to conduct to them the smoke of incense or perfume. In primitive times the offerings in the tomb were supposed to be absorbed by an immaterial personality of the deceased which was called the KA 𓂓. But later a figure of the deceased was placed in the tomb, and in this the KA was believed to dwell; for this reason the figure in the sardâb is called the "Ka figure," or the "Ka statue." The interior of the sardâb is never inscribed, and nothing but statues, inscribed with the names and titles of the persons whom they represented, have ever been found in it. Statues were at times placed in the court in front of the maṣṭabah. The **pit,** square or rectangular in form, but never round, leads to the chamber where the mummy was laid; it is situated in the middle of the greater axis of the maṣṭabah nearer to the north than the south, and varies in depth from 40 to 80 feet. The top part of the pit, where it passes through the platform on which the maṣṭabah stands, is built of fine large stones. There was neither ladder nor stairway leading to the chamber at the bottom of the pit, hence the coffin and the mummy, when once there, were inaccessible. At the bottom of the pit, on the south side, is an opening into a passage from four to five feet high; this passage leads obliquely to the south-east, in the same direction as the upper chamber, and soon increases in size in all directions, and thus becomes the **sarcophagus chamber.** This chamber is exactly under the upper chamber, and the relatives of the deceased when standing there would have the deceased beneath their feet. In one corner of the lower chamber stood the rectangular sarcophagus made of fine calcareous stone, rose granite or black basalt; the top of the cover was rounded. The chamber contained no statues, *ushabtiu* figures, amulets, Canopic jars, nor any of the numerous things which formed the furniture of the tomb in later times; in the sarcophagus were, at times, a head-rest, 𓊫, or a few vases, but little else. When the body had been placed in the sarcophagus, and the cover of the sarcophagus had been cemented down on it, the entrance to the passage at the bottom of the pit was walled up, the pit itself was filled with stones, earth and sand, and the deceased was thus preserved from all ordinary chances of disturbance.

The tombs of the maṣṭabah class stop suddenly at the end of the VIth dynasty; of tombs belonging to one of the first three dynasties, M. Mariette[1] found 4 at Ṣaḳḳârah; of the IVth dynasty 43; of

[1] A full description of the great necropolis of the Old Kingdom at Ṣaḳḳârah will be found in *Les Mastaba de l'Ancien Empire,* by Mariette and Maspero, Paris, 1882, Part I. Full descriptions of the maṣṭabahs, with plans and copies of the texts, will be found in Parts II–VI. See also the descriptive articles by Mariette in *Revue Archéologique,* Série 2me, tom. XIX, p. 8 ff.

Winnowing Wheat. From a Vth dynasty Tomb at Ṣaḳḳârah.

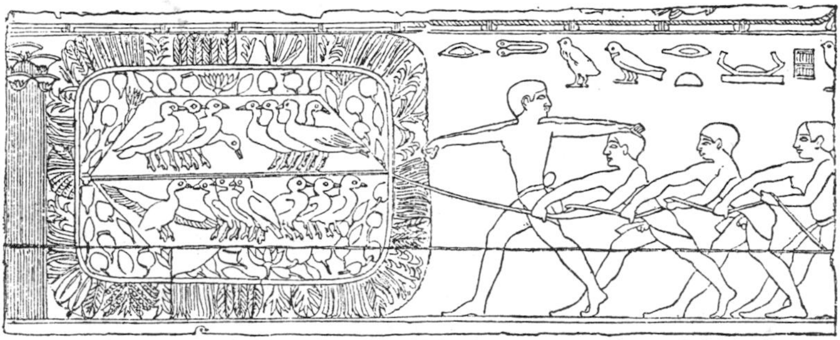

Netting Wild Fowl. From a Vth dynasty Tomb at Ṣaḳḳârah.

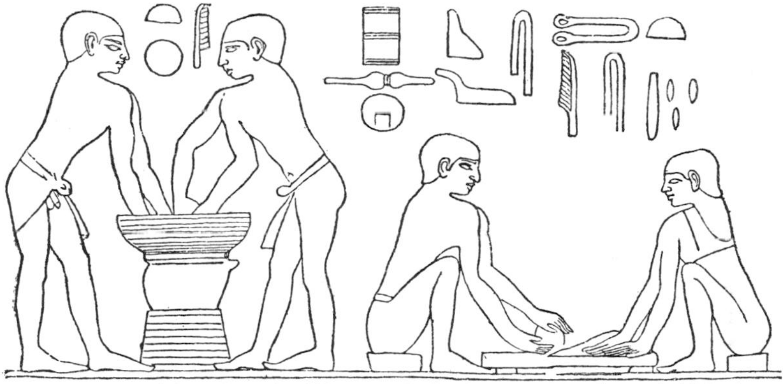

Bakers making Bread. From a Vth dynasty Tomb at Ṣaḳḳârah.

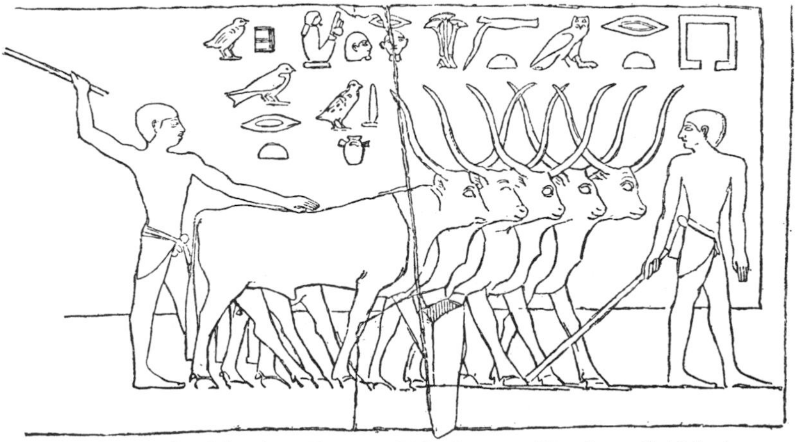

Cattle on the March. From a Vth dynasty Tomb at Ṣaḳḳârah.

the Vth dynasty 61; and of the VIth dynasty 25. The maṣṭabahs of the **first three dynasties** have but one upper chamber, which is built of brick, the stelae are very deeply cut, the hieroglyphs and the figures are in relief, and display more vigour than at any other time; the inscriptions are terse, and the use of phonetic signs less common than in later times. These tombs can hardly be said to be oriented at all, for they are, at times, as much as twelve degrees west of the true north. In the second half of the **IVth dynasty,** maṣṭabahs have a size and extent hitherto unknown; they are either built entirely of black brick or of stone. Their orientation becomes exact, the figures and hieroglyphs are well executed, the formulae become fixed, and the statues in the sardâbs, which are very numerous, unite the vigour of those of the first half of the IVth with the delicacy of those of the Vth dynasty. The famous wooden statue of the Shêkh al-Balad belongs to this time. In the **Vth dynasty,** maṣṭabahs are not so large, and they are always built of stone; inside there are more chambers than one; they are approached by long passages, and the statues are not so characteristic as those of the latter half of the IVth dynasty. The maṣṭabahs of the **VIth dynasty** show a decided decadence, and lose their fine proportions; the figures are in light relief, the formulae become longer, and the chambers are built of brick and covered with thin sculptured slabs of stone.

The walls of the upper chambers of maṣṭabahs are frequently covered with scenes which, according to M. Mariette, are without any representation of divinities and religious emblems, the names of deities and characters employed in the course of writing naturally excepted. The inscription which asks the god Anubis to grant a happy burial to the deceased, after a long and happy old age, to make his way easy for him on the roads in the underworld, and to grant the bringing to the tomb of a perpetual supply of funerary gifts, is inscribed in bold hieroglyphs over the entrances to the tombs and upon the most conspicuous places on the stelae in the upper chambers. The scenes depicted on the walls of the maṣṭabahs are divided by Mariette into three classes: (1) Biographical; (2) Sepulchral; and (3) Scenes representing funerary gifts. **Biographical scenes** are found in tombs of all periods. The deceased is represented hunting or fishing, taking part in pleasure excursions by water, and listening to music played before him accompanied by the dancing of women; he is also represented as overseer of a number of building operations in which many workmen are employed. It is tolerably certain that these scenes are not fictitious, and that they were painted while the person who hoped to occupy the tomb was still alive, and could direct the labours of the artist. The prayer that the deceased might enter his tomb after a long and prosperous life has a significance which it could not possess if the tomb were made after his death. The sepulchral scenes refer to the passage of the mummy in a boat to Åmenti. **Sepulchral scenes** represent the deceased, having colossal proportions compared with the other figures, sitting or standing with a round table before him, upon which fruits, flowers, vegetables, ducks, haunches of beef, etc., etc., are placed. These offerings are sometimes carried in before the deceased on the head or hands of servants and others, who often lead beasts appointed for slaughter; they were brought into the tomb in an appointed order, and an endowment to ensure their presentation in the tomb on the specified festivals and seasons was specially provided. The scenes in the tombs that represent agricultural labours, the making of wine, etc., etc., all have reference to the bringing of funerary gifts; and it is certain that estates,  *nut ent per tchetta*, "estates of the house of everlasting" (*i.e.*, the tomb), were set apart to supply palm branches, fruit, etc., for the table of the dead. The act of bringing these gifts to the tomb at the appointed seasons was probably connected with some religious ceremony, which seems to have consisted in pouring out libations and offering incense, bandages, etc., by the  *kher ḥeb*, or priest. The Egyptian called the tomb  *per tchetta*, "the everlasting house," and he believed that the KA  or "individuality" of the deceased resided there as long as the mummy of his perishable body,  *kha*, was there. The KA might go in and out of the mummy chamber and refresh itself with meat and drink whensoever it pleased; the  *ba*, or *soul*, and the  *àakhu*, or spirit, or spirit-soul, visited the mummy to which they belonged, and enjoyed reunion with its body, and its KA, and its ÅB (heart), and its SEKHEM (vital power), and its KHAIBIT (shadow), and its REN (name).

THE PYRAMID TOMB

ONE of the oldest Egyptian monuments is the famous **Step-Pyramid of Ṣakkârah,** which is now known to be the tomb of **Tcheser,** a king of the IIIrd dynasty. Because of its steps, or terraces, the Arabs call it "Al-Haram al-Madarragah." This pyramid has six steps, which are in height about 38 feet, 36 feet, 34½ feet, 32 feet, 31 feet and 29½ feet respectively; the width of each is from 6 to 7 feet. The lengths of the sides at the base are: north and south 352 feet, east and west 396 feet, and the actual height is about 197 feet. The pyramid is oblong in shape, and its sides do not exactly face the cardinal points. The arrangement of the chambers inside the pyramid is quite peculiar to itself, and the green and black glazed tiles (now in the British Museum, 2437 ff.), which were inlaid in the walls of the chambers, show that the art of funerary decoration had reached a high standard in Tcheser's day. It is difficult to understand why this king decided to cover the small underground chamber that was to hold his body with a mighty building having steps, or stages, which seems to have been the first of its kind known in Egypt. And it is equally difficult not to think that this style of building was suggested to him either by something that he had heard of the funerary monuments in Asia, or by some person of Asiatic origin who possessed sufficient influence with the king to make him reject the brick or stone maṣṭabah as a tomb, and introduce a new form of royal tomb into Ëgypt. There is no doubt that this pyramid was a tomb, and it is very probable, as Mr. W. Simpson suggested in 1893,[1] that the step-pyramids were in Egypt what the pagodas were in China, the stupas in India, and the ziggurats, with their four or seven stages, in Babylonia and Assyria. The steps of the Ṣaḳḳârah Pyramid may well be compared with the steps, or stages, of the Birs-i-Nimrûd and of the ziggurat of Bel at Babylon. Attached to the ziggurat there was a building called "gigunu," which may be compared to the tomb-chamber or to the funerary temple that was attached to each pyramid in Egypt, and both ziggurat and pyramid were connected with a dead king or god. If we compare the general arrangement of the buildings round the ziggurats with that of the buildings grouped round the Sun-temples[2] excavated by von Bissing, and with that of the temples, etc., attached to the great pyramids of the IVth dynasty, an extraordinary general similarity is evident. But whether the ziggurat of Bel at Babylon was or was not the tomb of Bel, as classical writers thought (Aelian, *Varia Historia,* XIII, 3), is a matter for excavators to decide; meanwhile reference may be made to the discussion printed by Prof. Langdon in his *Babylonian Epic of Creation,* Oxford, 1923, p. 35 f. It may be noted in passing that the form of the ziggurat was due to a religious conception concerning the formation both of heaven and of hell; and the type persists in later monuments, *e.g.,* the Black Obelisk in the British Museum. There were three, or four, or seven heavens and seven hells, which decreased in size, the former ascending and the latter descending.

Of pyramid tombs that have no steps, or terraces, the finest and most awe-inspiring are the three great Pyramids of Gîzah, which were built by Khufu, Khāfrā and Menkaurā respectively. These colossal monuments have been admired and wondered at for several thousands of years and have formed the subjects of countless speculations and theories. The building of them has been attributed to the Hebrew Patriarchs, and to genii, and many Muslim writers

[1] *Trans. Soc. Bibl. Arch.,* Vol. IX, p. 307 ff.
[2] See Borchardt, *Das Re-Heiligtum,* Berlin, 1905.

believed that they were the granaries in which Joseph stored up grain for use during the years of famine which he had foretold. According to some distinguished thinkers the arrangement of the chambers, the lengths and angles of the inclination of the corridors, etc., represented mysteries the knowledge of which was of the highest importance to the human race, and every measurement had its esoteric meaning and symbolism. The present writer is convinced that the Great Pyramid was built not to serve as an astronomical instrument or as a standard of measurements for the world, but as **a tomb** and as **nothing but a tomb.** Pyramids stand in cemeteries, and the tombs of the officials of the kings who built them are clustered about them. The pyramid-tomb is to all intents and purposes a maṣṭabah of which the greater part is above ground; it consists of the chamber, or chapel, in which funerary gifts were offered, the corridor, or passage, and the sarcophagus chamber. The actual pyramid contained the corridor and the sarcophagus chamber, and although the chamber, sometimes called temple or chapel, in which the funerary gifts were offered, was a building separate from the pyramid, it nevertheless formed an integral part of the pyramid plan.

The Pyramids of Gîzah. The names of the ancient writers who have described the Pyramids are given by Pliny (*N.H.* XXXVI, 12, 17); in modern times they have been examined by Shaw (1721), Norden (1737), Pococke (1743), Fourmont (1755), Niebuhr (1761), Davison (1763), Bruce (1768), Volney (1783), Browne (1793), Denon and Jomard of Napoleon's Mission (1799), Hamilton (1801), Caviglia, the excavator of the Sphinx, and Belzoni (1817), Wilkinson (1831), Perring and Vyse (1837), Lepsius (1842–5), Petrie (1881) and others. The plan that was followed in building a pyramid was first scientifically enunciated by Lepsius, who thought that before the actual building of a pyramid was begun a suitable rocky site was chosen and cleared, a mass of rock if possible being left in the middle of the area to form the core of the building. The chambers and galleries leading to them were next planned and excavated. Around the core a truncated pyramid building was made, the angles of which were filled up with blocks of stone. Layer after layer of stone was then built round the work, which grew larger and larger until it was finished. Lepsius thought that when a king ascended the throne he built for himself a small but complete tomb-pyramid, and that a fresh coating of stone was built round it every year that he reigned; that when he died the sides of the pyramid were like long flights of steps, which his successor filled up with right-angled triangular blocks of stone; and that the door of the pyramid was walled up after the body of its builder had been laid in it, and thus it became a finished tomb. The explanation of Lepsius may not be correct in all details, but at least it answers satisfactorily more objections than do the views of other theorists on this matter. It has been pointed out that near the core of the pyramid the work is more carefully executed than near the exterior—that is to say, as the time for the king's death approached the work was more hurriedly performed. During the investigations made by Lepsius in and around the pyramid area he found the remains of about seventy-five pyramids, and noticed that they were always built in groups.

The pyramids of Gîzah were plundered early in dynastic times, and the tomb robbers did great damage in the search for treasure. They were opened by the Persians during the Vth and IVth centuries before Christ, and it is probable that they were also entered by the Romans. The Khalîfah Mâmûn (A.D. 813–833) entered the Great Pyramid, and found that others had been there before him. The treasure which is said to have been discovered there by him is probably fictitious. Once opened, it must have been evident to everyone what splendid quarries the pyramids formed, and very few hundred years after the conquest of Egypt by the Arabs they were laid under contribution for stone to build mosques, etc., in Cairo. At the end of the XIIth century Malik al-Kâmil made a mad attempt to destroy the pyramid built by Mycerinus; but after months of toil he only succeeded in stripping off the covering from one of the sides. It is said that Muḥammad 'Ali was advised to undertake the senseless task of destroying them all.

The Great Pyramid. This, the largest of the three pyramids at Gîzah, was built by Khufu 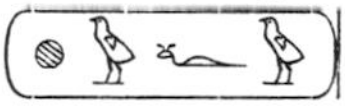, or Cheops, the second king of the IVth dynasty, who called it 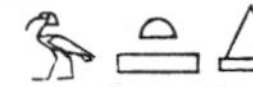 "Åakhut," *i.e.*, "(horizon of) splendour." His name was found written in red ink upon the blocks of stone inside it. All four sides measure in greatest length from 750 to 755 feet each, but the length of each was originally about 20 feet more; its height now is 451 feet, but it is said to have been originally about 481 feet. The stone used in the construction of this pyramid was brought from Ṭura and Muḳaṭṭam, and the contents amount to 82,549,000 cubic feet. The area covered by the pyramid is about 12 acres. The flat space at the top of the pyramid is about 30 feet square, and the view from it is very fine.

The entrance (A) to this pyramid is, as with all pyramids, on the north side, and is about 43 feet above the ground. The passage A B C is 320 feet long, 3¼ feet high, and 4 feet wide; at B is a granite door, round which the path at D has been made. The passage D E is 125 feet long, and the large hall E F is 155 feet long and 28 feet high; the passage E G leads to the pointed-roofed Queen's Chamber H, which measures about 17 by 19 by 20 feet. The roofing-in of this chamber is a beautiful piece of mason's work. From the large hall E F there leads a passage 22 feet long, the ante-chamber in which was originally closed by four granite doors, remains of which are still visible, into the King's Chamber, J, which is lined with granite, and measures about 35 by 17 by 19 feet. The five hollow chambers K, L, M, N, O were built above the King's Chamber to lighten the pressure of the superincumbent mass. In chamber O the name Khufu was found written. The air shafts P and Q measure 234 feet by 8 inches by 6 inches, and 174 feet by 8 inches by 6 inches respectively. A shaft from E to R leads down to the subterranean chamber S, which measures 46 by 27 by $10\frac{1}{2}$ feet. The floor of the King's Chamber, J, is about 140 feet from the level of the base of the pyramid, and the chamber is a little to the south-east of the line drawn from T to U. Inside the chamber lies the empty, coverless, broken, red granite sarcophagus of Cheops, measuring $7\frac{1}{2}$ by $3\frac{1}{4}$ by $3\frac{1}{3}$ feet. The account of the building of this pyramid given by Herodotus (II, 124–126) is as follows: " Now, they told me, that to

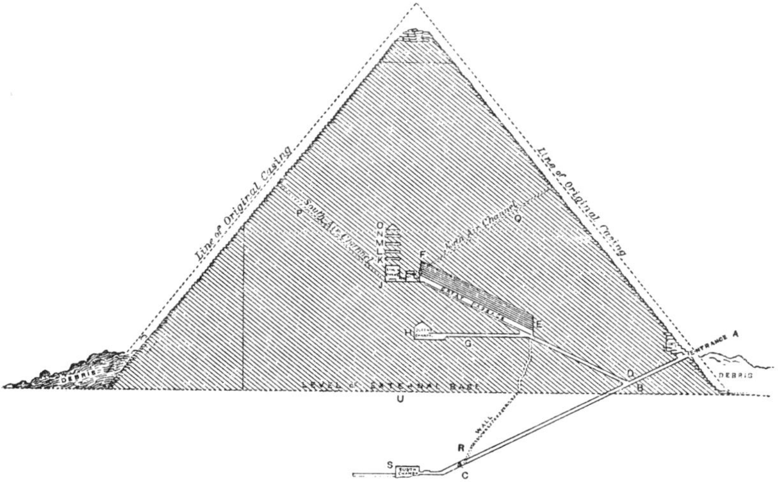

Section of the Pyramid of Cheops at Gîzah. From Vyse, *Pyramids of Gîzeh*, Vol. I, p. 2.

the reign of Rhampsinitus there was a perfect distribution of justice, and that all Egypt was in a high state of prosperity; but that after him Cheops, coming to reign over them, plunged into every kind of wickedness. For that, having shut up all the temples, he first of all forbade them to offer sacrifice, and afterwards he ordered all the Egyptians to work for himself; some, accordingly, were appointed to draw stones from the quarries in the Arabian mountain down to the Nile, others he ordered to receive the stones when transported in vessels across the river, and to drag them to the mountain called the Libyan. And they worked to the number of 100,000 men at a time, each party during three months. The time during which the people were thus harassed by toil, lasted ten years on the road which they constructed, along which they drew the stones, a work, in my

The Pyramid of Khufu (Cheôps) at Gîzah and the Sphinx.

The "Step Pyramid" built by Tcheser, a king of the IIIrd dynasty at Ṣaḳḳârah.

Gilded wooden anthropoid coffin of Ȧn-Ȧntef, a king of Egypt. XI–XIVth dynasty. B.M. No. 6652.

Outer coffin of Ḥent-meḥit, a singing woman of Ȧmen-Rā. XXIst dynasty. B.M. No. 51101.

opinion, not much less than the pyramid: for its length is five stades (3,021 feet), and its width 10 orgyae (60 feet), and its height, where it is the highest, 8 orgyae (48 feet); and it is of polished stone, with figures carved on it: on this road then ten years were expended, and in forming the subterraneous apartments on the hill, on which the pyramids stand, which he had made as a burial vault for himself, in an island, formed by draining a canal from the Nile. Twenty years were spent in erecting the pyramid itself: of this, which is square, each face is 8 plethra (820 feet), and the height is the same; it is composed of polished stones, and jointed with the greatest exactness; none of the stones are less than 30 feet. This pyramid was built thus; in the form of steps, which some call crossae, others bomides. When they had first built it in this manner, they raised the remaining stones by machines made of short pieces of wood: having lifted them from the ground to the first range of steps, when the stone arrived there, it was put on another machine that stood ready on the first range; and from this it was drawn to the second range on another machine; for the machines were equal in number to the ranges of steps; or they removed the machine, which was only one, and portable, to each range in succession, whenever they wished to raise the stone higher; for I should relate it in both ways, as it is related. The highest parts of it, therefore, were first finished, and afterwards they completed the parts next following; but last of all they finished the parts on the ground, and that were lowest. On the pyramid is shown an inscription, in Egyptian characters, how much was expended in radishes, onions and garlic, for the workmen; which the interpreter,[1] as I well remember, reading the inscription,[2] told me amounted to 1,600 talents of silver. And if this be really the case, how much more was probably expended in iron tools, in bread, and in clothes for the labourers, since they occupied in building the works the time which I mentioned, and no short time besides, as I think, in cutting and drawing the stones, and in forming the subterraneous excavation. [It is related] that Cheops reached such a degree of infamy, that being in want of money, he prostituted his own daughter in a brothel, and ordered her to extort, they did not say how much; but she exacted a certain sum of money, privately, as much as her father ordered her;

[1] Herodotus was deceived by his interpreter, who clearly made up a translation of an inscription which he did not understand. William of Baldensel, who lived in the XIVth century, tells us that the outer coating of the two largest pyramids was covered with a great number of inscriptions arranged in lines. (Wiedemann, *Aeg. Geschichte*, p. 179.) If the outsides were actually inscribed, the texts must have been purely religious, like those inscribed inside the pyramids of Pepi, Tetȧ, and Unȧs.

[2] " . . . . . their surfaces exhibit all kinds of inscriptions written in the characters of ancient nations which no longer exist. No one knows what this writing is or what it signifies." Mas'ûdi (ed. Barbier de Meynard), tom. II, p. 404.

and contrived to leave a monument of herself, and asked every one that came in to her to give her a stone towards the edifice she designed: of these stones they said the pyramid was built that stands in the middle of the three, before the great pyramid, each side of which is a plethron and a half in length." (Cary's translation.)

The second pyramid at Gîzah was built by Khā-f-Rā, 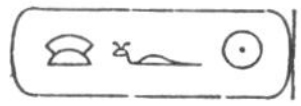, or Chephren, the third king of the IVth dynasty, who called it 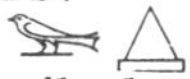, *ur, i.e.*, the "Great." His name has not been found inscribed upon any part of it, but the fragment of a marble sphere inscribed with the name of Khā-f-Rā, which was found near the temple, close by this pyramid, confirms the statements of Herodotus and Diodorus Siculus, that Chephren built it. A statue of this king, now in the Gîzah Museum, was found in the granite temple close by. This pyramid appears to be larger than the Great Pyramid because it stands upon a higher level of stone foundation; it was cased with stone originally and polished, but the greater part of the outer casing has disappeared. An ascent of this pyramid can only be made with difficulty. It was first explored in 1816 by Belzoni (born 1778, died 1823), the discoverer of the tomb of Seti I and of the temple of Rameses II at Abu Simbel. In the north side of the pyramid are two openings, one at the base and one about 50 feet above it. The upper opening leads into a corridor 105 feet long, which descends into a chamber $46\frac{1}{2}$ by $16\frac{1}{3}$ by $22\frac{1}{2}$ feet, which held the granite sarcophagus in which Chephren was buried. The lower opening leads into a corridor about 100 feet long, which, first descending and then ascending, ends in the chamber mentioned above, which is usually called **Belzoni's Chamber.** The actual height is about 448 feet, and the length of each side at the base about 692 feet. The rock upon which the pyramid stands has been scarped on the north and west sides to make the foundation level. The history of the building of the pyramid is thus narrated by Herodotus (II, 127): "The Egyptians say that this Cheops reigned 50 years; and when he died, his brother Chephren succeeded to the kingdom; and he followed the same practices as the other, both in other respects, and in building a pyramid; which does not come up to the dimensions of his brother's, for I myself measured them; nor has it subterraneous chambers; nor does a channel from the Nile flow to it, as to the other; but this flows through an artificial aqueduct round an island within, in which they say the body of Cheops is laid. Having laid the first course of variegated Ethiopian stones, less in height than the other by 40 feet, he built it near the large pyramid. They both stand on the same hill, which is about 100 feet high. Chephren, they said, reigned 56 years. Thus 106 years are reckoned, during which the Egyptians suffered all kinds of calamities, and for this length of time the temples were closed and never opened.

From the hatred they bear them, the Egyptians are not very willing to mention their names; but call the pyramids after Philition, a shepherd, who at that time kept his cattle in those parts." (Cary's translation.)

The third pyramid at Gîzah was built by Men-kau-Rā, 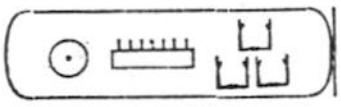, or Mycerinus, the fourth king of the IVth dynasty, who called it , *Ḥer*. Herodotus and other ancient authors tell us that Men-kau-Rā was buried in this pyramid, but Manetho states that Nitocris, a queen of the VIth dynasty, was the builder. There can be, however, but little doubt that it was built by Mycerinus, for the sarcophagus and the remains of the inscribed coffin of this king were found in one of its chambers by Howard Vyse in 1837. The basalt sarcophagus, which measured 8 by 3 by 2½ feet, was lost through the wreck of the ship in which it was sent to England, but a fragment of it is preserved in the British Museum (6646). The cover of the coffin which was found in it, and fragments of the coffin itself, and also the human remains, are in the British Museum. Some think that the coffin is a "restoration" of the XXVIth dynasty, and that the human remains are not those of the king. The formula on the coffin is one that is found upon coffins down to the latest period, and is an extract from the Pyramid Texts.

The pyramid of Men-kau-Rā, like that of Chephren, is built upon a rock with a sloping surface; the inequality of the surface in this case has been made level by building up courses of large blocks of stones. Around the lower part the remains of the old granite covering are visible to a depth of from 30 to 40 feet. It is unfortunate that this pyramid has been so much damaged; its injuries, however, enable the visitor to see exactly how it was built, and it may be concluded that the pyramids of Cheops and Chephren were built in the same manner. The length of each side at the base is about 354 feet, and its height is variously given as 204 and 210 feet. The entrance is on the north side, about 13 feet above the ground, and a descending corridor about 104 feet long, passing through an ante-chamber, having a series of three granite doors, leads into one chamber about 44 feet long. In this chamber is a shaft which leads down to the granite-lined chamber about 20 feet below, in which were found the sarcophagus and wooden coffin of Mycerinus, and the remains of a human body. It is thought that, in spite of the body of Mycerinus being buried in this pyramid, it was left unfinished at the death of this king, and that a succeeding ruler of Egypt finished the pyramid and made a second chamber to hold his or her body. At a short distance to the east of this pyramid are the ruins of a temple which was probably used in connection with the rites performed in honour of the dead king. In A.D. 1196 a deliberate and systematic attempt was made to destroy this pyramid by the command of the Muḥammadan ruler of Egypt. The account of the character of Mycerinus and of his pyramid as given by Herodotus (II, 129, 134) is as follows : " They said that after him, Mycerinus, son of Cheops, reigned over Egypt ; that the conduct of his father was displeasing to him ; and that he opened the temples, and permitted the people, who were worn down to the last extremity, to return to their employments, and to sacrifices ; and that he made the most just decisions of all their kings. On this account, of all the kings that ever reigned in Egypt, they praise him most, for he both judged well in other respects, and moreover, when any man complained of his decision, he used to make him some present out of his own treasury and pacify his anger. . . . . . This king also left a pyramid much less than that of his father, being on each side 20 feet short of three plethra ; it is quadrangular, and built half way up of Ethiopian stone. Some of the Grecians erroneously say that this pyramid is the work of the courtesan Rhodopis ; but they evidently appear to me ignorant who Rhodopis was ; for they would not else have attributed to her the building such a pyramid, on which, so to speak, numberless thousands of talents were expended; besides, Rhodopis flourished in the reign of Amasis, and not at this time ; for she was very many years later than those kings who left these pyramids." (Cary's translation.)

In one of the three small pyramids near that of Mycerinus the name of this king is painted on the ceiling.

The Pyramids of Abu Roâsh lie about 6 miles to the north of the Pyramids of Gîzah. Their original number is not known ; they appear to have been built under the IVth dynasty, for one of them, which now stands on an almost inaccessible hill, was the tomb of Ṭeṭfrā, . In ancient days they were approached by means of a causeway, which is still about a mile long.

The Pyramid of Rigaḥ, when excavated by Borchardt and Schäfer, was found to be a Sun-Temple, which was built by Userenrā (Enuserrā), a king of the Vth dynasty.

The Pyramids of Abuṣir, built by kings of the Vth dynasty, were originally fourteen in number, but owing to faulty workmanship only three of them are now standing. The most northerly pyramid was built by 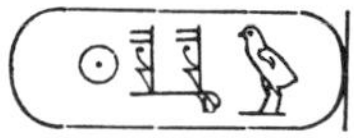, Saḥu-Rā, the second king of the Vth dynasty ; its actual height is about 120 feet, and the length of each side at the base about 220 feet. The blocks of stone in the sepulchral chamber are exceptionally large. Saḥu-Rā made war in the peninsula of Sinai, and he founded a town near Asnâ, and he built a temple to Sekhmit at Memphis.

The pyramid to the south of that of Saḥu-Rā was built by , Userenrā Ȧn. This king, like Saḥu-Rā, also made war in Sinai. The largest of these pyramids is now about 165 feet high and 330 feet square; the name of its builder is , Neferȧrikarā. Abuṣir is the Busiris of Pliny.

The Pyramid of Unȧs, , lies to the south-west of the Step Pyramid of Ṣaḳḳârah, and was reopened and cleared out in 1881 by M. Maspero, at the expense of Messrs. Thomas Cook and Son. Its original height was about 62 feet, and the length of each side at the base 220 feet. Owing to the broken blocks of sand which lie round about it, Vyse was unable to give exact measurements. Several attempts had been made to break into it, and one of the Arabs who took part in one of these attempts, "Aḥmad the Carpenter," seems to have left his name inside one of the chambers in red ink. It is probable that he is the same man who opened the Great Pyramid at Gîzah, A.D. 820. A black basalt sarcophagus, from which the cover had been dragged off, an arm, a shin bone, and some ribs and fragments of the skull from the mummy of Unȧs were found in the sarcophagus chamber. The walls of the two largest chambers and two of the corridors are inscribed with ritual texts and prayers of a very interesting character.[1] The fine granite column in the Northern Egyptian Vestibule in the British Museum was one of four which stood in the funerary chapel of this pyramid.

The Pyramid of Tetȧ, 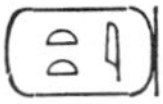, called in Egyptian Ṭeṭ-Ȧsut, , is one of the southern group of pyramids at Ṣaḳḳârah. The Arabs call it the "Prison Pyramid," because local tradition says that it is built near the ruins of the prison where Joseph the patriarch was confined. Its actual height is about 59 feet; the length of its sides at the base is 210 feet, and the platform at the top is about 50 feet. The arrangement of the chambers and passages and the plan of construction followed are almost identical with those of the pyramid of Unȧs. This pyramid was broken into in ancient days, and two of the walls of the sarcophagus chamber have literally been smashed to pieces by the hammer blows of those who expected to find treasure inside them. The inscriptions, painted in green upon the walls, have the same subject-matter as those inscribed upon the walls of the chambers of the pyramid of Unȧs.

[1] These and the inscriptions from the pyramids of Tetȧ, Pepi I, Pepi II, etc., were published by Maspero, with a French translation, in *Les Inscriptions des Pyramides de Saqqarah*, Paris, 1894, and without a translation by Sethe, *Die Altaegyptischen Pyramidentexte*, Leipzig, 1908 f. Another French translation has been begun by Speleers, L., *Les Textes des Pyramides*, Brussels, 1923.

The Pyramid of Pepi I, or , "Rāmeri, son of the Sun, Pepi," is one of the central group of pyramids at Ṣaḳḳârah, where it is called the Pyramid of Shêkh Abu Manṣûr; it was opened in 1880. Its actual height is about 40 feet, and the length of each side at the base is about 250 feet; the arrangements of the chambers, etc., inside is the same as in the pyramids of Unȧs and Tetȧ, but the ornamentation is slightly different. It is the worst preserved of these pyramids, and has suffered most at the hands of the spoilers, probably because, having been constructed with stones that had been taken from tombs ancient already in those days, instead of stones fresh from the quarry, it was more easily injured. The granite sarcophagus was broken to take out the mummy, fragments of which were found lying about on the ground; the cover, too, smashed in pieces, lay on the ground close by. A small rose-granite box, containing alabaster jars, was also found in the sarcophagus chamber. The inscriptions are, like those inscribed on the walls of the pyramids of Unȧs and Tetȧ, of a religious nature; some scholars see in them evidence that the pyramid was usurped by another Pepi, who lived at a much later period than the VIth dynasty. The pyramid of Pepi I, the second king of the VIth dynasty, who reigned, according to Manetho, 53 years, was called Men-Nefer, , and numerous priests were attached to its service.

The Pyramids of Dahshûr. These lie about 4 miles to the south of "Pharaoh's Maṣṭabah" (*Maṣṭabat al-Fir'aûn*), and consist of three stone and two brick pyramids. The larger of the **brick pyramids** was covered with stone slabs, and was, it seems, the tomb of Usertsen III (XIIth dynasty); the length of each side at the base is about 350 feet, and its height is about 150 feet. The smaller of the brick pyramids, which was probably built by Ȧmenemḥat III, is about 90 feet high, and the length of each side at the base is about 343 feet. Both these pyramids were excavated by J. de Morgan, who has described his work, and the discovery of the wonderful jewellery of the Princesses Sat-Hathor and Merit in the "Gallery of the Princesses" in *Fouilles à Dahchour*, 1894–1895, Vienna, 1903. The largest of the **stone pyramids** is about 326 feet high and the length of each side at the base is about 700 feet; some think that it was built by Seneferu, and if this be so it is the oldest true pyramid-tomb in Egypt. The second stone pyramid is about 321 feet high, and the length of each side at the base is about 620 feet; it is commonly called the **Blunted Pyramid,** because the lowest parts of its sides are built at one angle and the completing parts at another.

The Pyramid of Mêdûm.[1] This pyramid, with its three stages,

[1] This name seems to be derived from one of the old Egyptian names of the district, *i.e.*, "Methun-en-ka," , "Methun of the bulls," or "Mer-Tem," 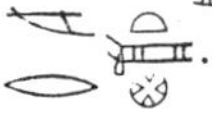.

which are about 70, 20 and 25 feet high respectively, is about 120 feet high, and is commonly known as the "Liar Pyramid" (*Al-Haram al-Kaddâb*). The building was never completed, and the name of the king who built it is unknown; because the maṣṭabah tombs of several of the kinsfolk of Seneferu lie near it, some have not hesitated to regard it as the tomb of that king. It was opened by Maspero in 1881, but the sarcophagus chamber was empty. This pyramid, like the Step-Pyramid of Ṣaḳḳârah, was probably built under Asiatic influences.

Some of the Princes of Thebes, both Menthuḥeteps and Ȧntefs, were buried in pyramid-tombs, but they were not like the pyramids of Ṣaḳḳârah and Gîzah. They were built for the most part of brick, and consisted of a rectangular substructure with sides sloping slightly inwards as they ascended, and a high roof in the shape of a pyramid. For their general shape see the Vignettes of the funeral processions in the Papyrus of Ani and the Papyrus of Hunefer. The Abbott Papyrus in the British Museum (10221) enumerates the pyramid-tombs of three Ȧntef kings, of Sebekemsaf, Seqenenrā Tauā, Seqenenrā Tauāā, Kames, Ȧāḥmes Sapȧri and Menthuḥetep Nebḥaprā.

The Pyramids in the Sûdân. The Nubian kings of the XXVIth dynasty built pyramid-tombs, and those of the great king Piānkhi, and his successors Shabaka, Shabataka and Tanutȧmen, have been found at Kurrû, which lies opposite Tanḳâsî, a few miles downstream from the foot of the Fourth Cataract. Near the pyramids of Kurrû were found a number of **graves of horses.** Each horse was buried standing upright with his head towards the south. Bones of horses were also found at Meroë in 1905.[1] The Nubian king Tirhâḳâh and his successors, for about 350 years, built their pyramid-tombs at Nûrî, about 5 miles from Napata (the modern Marawi), near the foot of the Fourth Cataract. For an account of the excavations carried out there by the Harvard-Boston Expedition see Reisner, *Harvard African Studies*, II, Cambridge, Mass., 1918; *Sûdân Notes and Records*, Vol. II, p. 238, and Vol. IV, p. 60. About B.C. 300 the capital of the Nubian Kingdom was removed to Meroë, the capital of the Island of Meroë, and there the kings and the Meroïtic Queens, each of whom bore the title of "Ḳundâḳâ," *i.e.*, "Chief," and probably also their pure negroid successors, built themselves pyramid-tombs until the period of the downfall of the Meroïtic power in the IVth century A.D. Thus pyramid-tombs were built for kings in the Sûdân for about 1,000 years.[2]

[1] Budge, *Egyptian Sûdân*, Vol. I, p. 344.
[2] For accounts of the American excavations see *Sudan Notes*, Vol. V, p. 173.

THEBAN TOMBS OF THE MIDDLE AND NEW KINGDOMS

EGYPTIAN tombs belonging to a period subsequent to the maṣṭabahs and pyramids usually have the three characteristic parts of these forms of tomb, viz., the chapel, the passage to the sarcophagus chamber, and the sarcophagus chamber itself excavated in the solid rock. Sometimes, however, the chapel, or chamber for offerings, in which the relatives of the deceased assembled from time to time, is above ground and separate from the sarcophagus chamber, as in the case of the pyramid. Tombs having the chapel separate are the oldest, and the best examples are found at Abydos.[1] On a brick base about 50 feet by 35 feet, and 4 or 5 feet high, rose a pyramid to a height of about 30 feet; theoretically such a tomb was supposed to consist of chapel, passage and pit, but at Abydos, owing to the friable nature of the rock, these do not exist, and the mummy was laid either in the ground between the foundations, or in the masonry itself, or in a chamber which projected from the building and formed a part of it, or in a chamber beneath. This class of tomb is common both at Thebes and Abydos. Tombs hewn entirely out of the solid rock were used at all periods, and the best examples of these are found in the mountains behind Asyûṭ,[2] at Bani-Ḥasan,[3] at Al-Barshah,[4] at Thebes,[5] and in some of the tombs at Aswân.[6] The tombs at all these places have preserved the chief characteristics of the maṣṭabahs at Ṣaḳḳârah, that is to say, they consist of a chamber and a shaft leading down to a corridor, which ends in the chamber containing the sarcophagus and the mummy.

The bold headland that rises up in the low range of hills that faces the whole of the island of Elephantine, just opposite to the modern town of Aswân, was found to be literally honeycombed with tombs, tier above tier, of various epochs. In ancient days there was down at the water's edge a massive stone quay, from which a broad, fine double **stairway,** cut in the living rock, ascended to a layer of firm rock about 150 feet higher. At Thebes and at Bani-Ḥasan, where such stairs must have existed, they have been destroyed, and only the traces remain to show that they ever existed. At

[1] Abydos étant surtout une nécropole du Moyen Empire, c'est la petite pyramide qui y domine. Des centaines de ces monuments, disposés sans ordre, hérissaient la nécropole et devaient lui donner un aspect pittoresque bien différent de l'aspect des nécropoles d'un autre temps. Mariette, *Abydos*, tom. II, Paris, 1880, p. 39.

[2] See Griffith, *The Inscriptions of Siut and Der Rifeh*, London, 1889.

[3] Garstang, *Burial Customs*, London, 1907.

[4] See Newberry, *Beni Hasan*, Pts. I–III; *El-Bersheh*, Pts. I and II (Eg. Exp. Fund Memoirs).

[5] Gardiner, *Tomb of Amenemhet*, London, 1915; *Tomb of Antefoker*, London, 1920; *Topographical Catalogue of Private Tombs at Thebes*, London, 1913.

[6] Budge, *Proc. Soc. Bibl. Arch.*, Vol. X, 1888, pp. 4–40.

Aswân it is quite different, for the whole of this remarkable stairway is intact. It begins at the bottom of the slope, well above the highest point reached by the waters of the Nile during the Inundation, and, following the outward curve of the hill, ends in a platform in front of the tombs of the VIth dynasty. Between each set of steps is a **smooth slope,** up which the coffins and sarcophagi were drawn to the tomb by the men who walked up the steps at each side. At the bottom of the stairs the steps are only a few inches deep, but towards the top they are more than a foot. On each side of the stairway is a wall which appears to be of later date than the stairs themselves, and about one-third of the way up there is a break in each wall, which appears to be a specially constructed opening leading to passages on the right and left respectively. The walls probably do not belong to the period of the uppermost tier of tombs, and appear to have been made during the rule of the Greeks or Romans. A narrow pathway leads from the stairway to the tombs of the XIIth dynasty, which are round the corner and face the north. The most interesting of these is that of , Sarenput, in the front of which is a large platform on which stood a handsome stone portico with square pillars. The scarped rock was ornamented with inscriptions, rows of cattle, etc., etc., and passing through the doorway a chamber, or chapel, having four rectangular pillars was reached. A passage, in the sides of which were niches having Osiris figures in them, leads to a beautifully painted shrine in which was a black granite seated figure of the deceased;[1] thus the sardâb and the stele of the maṣṭabah are side by side. On the right-hand side is a tunnel which, winding as it descends, leads to the sarcophagus chamber which was bricked up and was situated exactly under the shrine containing the figure of the deceased. Sarenput lived in the time of Usertsen I, and was " great governor in Ta-sti," , or viceroy of Nubia. The walls inside were covered with a layer of plaster upon which scenes and inscriptions were painted.[2]

During the XVIIIth dynasty tombs on the plan of the rock-hewn tombs of the XIIth dynasty were commonly built, but the

[1] The remains of this statue were presented to the British Museum by Sir Francis (the late Field-Marshal Lord) Grenfell, in 1887; it is exhibited in the Northern Vestibule (1010).

[2] For a full account of this tomb see my paper in *Proc. Soc. Bibl. Arch.*, November, 1887, p. 33 ff. A tomb of great importance was discovered at Aswân in 1892 by Signor E. Schiaparelli, who published the hieroglyphic text with a commentary in his valuable paper "Una Tomba Egiziana Inedita della VIa Dinastia," Roma, 1892 (in the *Memorie della Reale Accad. dei Lincei*, Pt. I, pp. 21–53, in Vol. I of the Fourth Series). A plan of the tomb and a copy of the text were published by de Morgan (*Catalogue*, tom. I, pp. 162–173). The best text yet published is that of Sethe (*Urkunden*, Bd. I, ss. 120–131).

inscriptions, which in ancient days were comparatively brief, now become very long, and the whole tomb is filled with beautifully painted scenes representing every art and trade, every agricultural labour, and every important event in the life of the deceased. The biography of the deceased is often given at great length. If a soldier, the military expeditions in which he took part are carefully enumerated, and the tribute brought to the king from the various countries is depicted with the most careful attention to the slightest detail of colour and form. The mummy chamber was made exactly

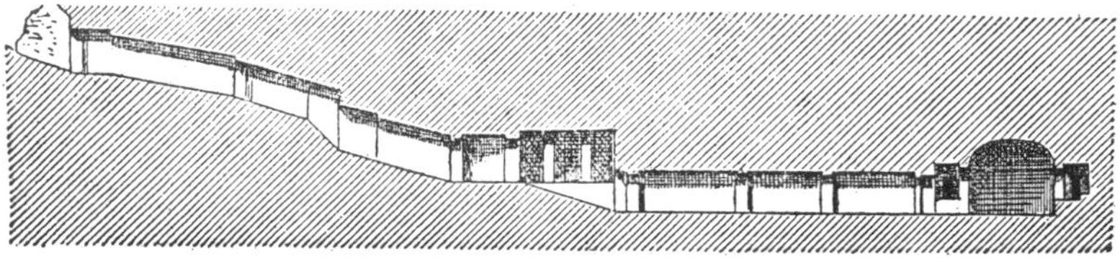

Section of the Tomb of Seti I in the Bibân al-Mulûk.

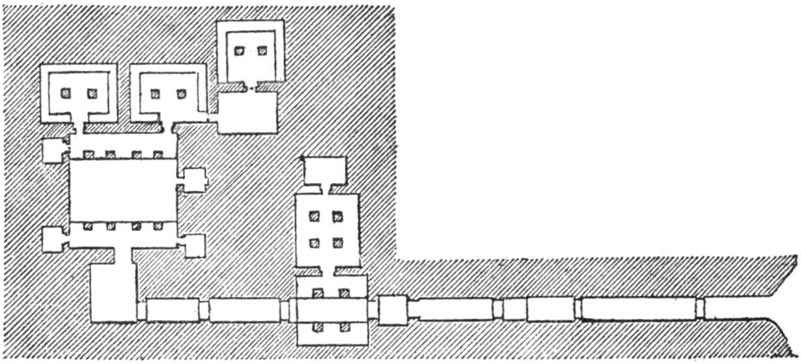

Plan of the Tomb of Seti II in the Bibân al-Mulûk.

under the chapel, but the position of the pit which led to it varied. Under the XVIIIth and XIXth dynasties the tombs of kings and private persons possessed a size and magnificence that they never attained either before or since. The finest specimens of these periods are the famous Tombs of the Kings which are hewn in the living rock in the eastern and western valleys at Thebes; those in the latter valley belong to the XVIIIth dynasty, and those in the former belong to the XIXth dynasty. The royal tombs here consist of long passages or corridors, usually three in number; these recede into the mountain, and the third corridor ends in a large chamber which opens into a fine hall containing the cavity in which the royal sarcophagus is placed. The walls are decorated with scenes and texts from the Book of Gates, the Book "Ȧmmi Ṭuat," the Litany of Rā, the Book of Rā during the Hours of the Night, and other mythological works. According to Strabo these tombs, which he calls *σύριγγες*, or "pipes," because of their length, were 40 in number, but now 43 or 44 are known. The finest tomb of the group is that of Seti I, and the beauty of the scenes painted on the walls can hardly be too highly praised. Under this king Egyptian funerary art seems to have been at its culminating point, for neither sculptor nor painter appears to have produced anything so fine after this date. The tomb is entered by means of two flights of steps, at the bottom of which is a passage terminating in a small chamber. Beyond this are two halls having four and two pillars respectively, and to the left are the passages and small chambers that lead to the large six-pillared hall and to the vaulted chamber in which stood the sarcophagus of Seti I. Here also is an inclined plane which descends into the mountain for a considerable distance; from the level of the ground to the bottom of this incline the depth is about 150 feet; the length of the tomb is nearly 500 feet. The designs on the walls were first sketched in outline in red, and the alterations by the master designer or artist were made in black; this tomb was never finished. Each chamber in this tomb has its peculiar ornamentation, and there is little doubt that each chamber had its peculiar furniture; it is thought that many articles of furniture, pieces of armour, weapons, etc., etc., were broken intentionally when they were placed in the tomb. For a full description of the tomb, and copies of the Vignettes and text, see Lefébure, *Les Hypogées Royaux de Thèbes*, Paris, 1886.

Under the XXVIth dynasty a great renaissance of Egyptian art took place, and artists and craftsmen devoted themselves to reproducing the fine work of the Old Kingdom. Their energies found ample scope in funerary work, and the scribes of the period covered the walls of the tombs of nobles like Peṭạ̄menȧp[1] with extracts from the Pyramid Texts and copies of ancient versions of the Book of Opening the Mouth and the Liturgy of Funerary Offerings.

It has already been said that relatively few of the labouring classes were "buried," and this is certainly true for the unofficial and poor Egyptian under the Old and Middle Empires. But under the New Kingdom it seems that a number of caves in the mountains to the west of Thebes and Aswân and other places were set apart as communal burying places, wherein the bodies of those who could not afford separate graves were laid. I have seen such caves at Thebes, in which the mass of decayed mummies was several feet deep, and in which dried bodies and skulls and bones were heaped up along the sides nearly to the roofs. The pit and passages of a forsaken tomb were often made to accommodate hundreds of bodies. At Aswân we found many pits full of mummies, and it was from

[1] See Dümichen, *Der Grabpalast des Patuamenap*, Leipzig, 1884.

these that I obtained the hundreds of skulls that I collected for the late Professor Macalister of Cambridge. The absence of valuable funerary furniture and ornaments rendered such bodies of no account to the professional tomb-robber, and the inaccessible situation of the places where they were laid made it unlikely that they would be thrown out to make room for others, or be disturbed by any except the cemetery jackals and the wolf of the desert.

In the early centuries of the Christian era the tombs in the mountains of Egypt formed dwelling-places for a number of monks and ascetics, and it would seem that the statues and other objects in them suffered at their hands. An instance of the use of a rock-hewn tomb by Pisentios, Bishop of Coptos, is made known to us by an Encomium on this saint by his disciple John.[1] The tomb in which Pisentios lived was rectangular in shape, and was 52 feet wide; it had six pillars and contained a large number of mummies. The coffins were very large and profusely decorated, and one of the mummies was clothed in silk, and his fingers and toes were mummified separately; the names of those buried there were written on a small parchment roll (ⲛ̄ ⲟⲩⲧⲟⲙⲁⲣⲓⲟⲛ ⲛ̄ ϫⲱⲙ ⲙ̄ ⲙⲉⲙⲃⲣⲁⲛⲟⲛ). Pisentios conversed with one of the mummies, who begged the saint to pray for his forgiveness; when Pisentios had promised him that Christ would have mercy upon him, the mummy lay down in his coffin again.

THE EGYPTIAN SARCOPHAGUS

It is difficult to make a hard-and-fast distinction between the massive stone receptacle of the mummy and coffin, or coffins, of the deceased, and the huge wooden outer coffin, which served the same purpose as the stone receptacle to which the name of "sarcophagus" is generally given. Both kinds of receptacle were made of stone and wood, and both kinds appear in two forms, namely, the rectangular and the anthropoid. In Egyptological literature generally, "sarcophagi" and "coffins" are spoken of as if, to all intents and purposes, they were the same things. There is much to be said in favour of this custom[2] when describing anthropoid sarcophagi and coffins of the New Kingdom, but when the sarcophagus is rectangular to me it represents the funerary chamber, and the coffin when it is anthropoid. The oldest Egyptian sarcophagi found at Gîzah are rectangular and are made of granite and limestone, and belong to the IVth dynasty; but examples of almost the same period are known in wood. The cover of the stone sarcophagus is either

[1] For the Coptic text and a French translation see Amélineau, *Étude sur le Christianisme en Égypte au Septième Siècle*, Paris, 1887.

[2] Lacau says, "La distinction courante mais vague entre 'les sarcophages' et 'les cercueils' ne m'a pas semblé utile à retenir . . . . Je me suis servi partout du mot sarcophage." (*Sarcophages*, tom. I, Cairo, 1904.)

flat, in fact a huge slab, or rounded, with raised ends. Running round the edge of the inside of the cover is a "rabbet," which is carefully chiselled to fit a hollow corresponding in the sarcophagus; when the cover was finally lowered into its place a layer of fine cement was run in between, and thus the sarcophagus was hermetically sealed. In addition, pegs of wood were driven into holes drilled sideways through the cover and the sarcophagus. The cover was lifted by means of one or more projections at each end. A fine example of the sarcophagus of the IVth dynasty is that of Khufuānkh, . Its sides are sculptured with a series of false doors and styles and floral ornaments, and there are two projections at each end of the cover. For a reproduction see *Le Musée Égyptien*, pl. XXI, and there is a complete cast in the British Museum (1111). The sarcophagus of Menkaurā (Mycerinus), found in his pyramid at Gîzah, was like a small building, and closely resembled that of Khufuānkh as far as decorative treatment is concerned (see the drawings in Vyse, *Pyramids*, Vol. II, London, 1840, facing p. 84). Under the XIIth dynasty sarcophagi were made of granite and hard crystalline limestone. Thus the sarcophagus of Usertsen (Senusert) II, which Mr. W. Fraser found in the king's pyramid at Al-Lâhûn, is made of red granite and measures 8 feet 11 inches by 4 feet 2 inches by 2 feet; and the sarcophagus of Ȧmenemḥat, which Petrie found in the Pyramid of Ḥawârah, is of hard crystalline limestone, and measures 8 feet 10 inches by 4 feet by 2 feet 7 inches. It has a sub-plinth and a rounded cover, and is ornamented with the false-door decorations and styles that are so characteristic of the sarcophagi of the IVth and Vth dynasties. In the tombs of private individuals who lived under the XIth and XIIth dynasties the place of the stone sarcophagus was taken by large and massive wooden rectangular coffins, the best examples of which are probably those from Al-Barshah in the Museum in Cairo[1] and in the British Museum[2], and those from Meïr.[3] The largest of these are nearly 8 feet long, and the covers are made of wood nearly 7 inches thick. The coffins of the same period from Bani-Ḥasan are smaller, but they are of the same type, and the decorations are of the same kind; Dr. Garstang has given a detailed description of the method followed in their construction.[4] The great kings of the XVIIIth dynasty were buried in stone sarcophagi closely resembling those of the XIIth dynasty. Thus the sarcophagus of Thothmes I is made of a solid block of red crystalline sandstone and is about 7 feet 4 inches in length,

[1] Described by Lacau in *Sarcophages antérieurs au Nouvel Empire* (No. 28083 ff.), Cairo, 1904.

[2] See British Museum *Guide*, pp. 42, 43 f.

[3] See Lacau, *op. cit.*, No. 28061 ff.

[4] *Burial Customs*, pp. 164, 165.

and that of Queen Ḥatshepsut measures 8 feet 2 inches by 2 feet 8 inches by 3 feet 1 inch.[1] Both are covered with figures of gods and hieroglyphic texts. The sarcophagus of Ȧmenḥetep IV was made of granite, but it was smashed by the natives, who offered the cartouches cut from it for sale to tourists about 1890. King Ai and Ḥeremḥeb[2] each had a granite sarcophagus with a cornice. Many of the sarcophagi from Memphis of this period are anthropoid in form; they are made of granite, their sides being sparingly decorated. The great Theban sarcophagi of the XIXth dynasty are also anthropoid in form, and are made of granite. A perpendicular line of inscription runs from the breast to the feet, and the surface of the cover on each side of it is divided, by three or four lines of inscription at right-angles to it, into sections on which are inscribed figures of gods. The inscriptions continue down the sides of the sarcophagus. The sarcophagus of Hunefer the scribe, who flourished early in the XIXth dynasty, is made of grey granite and measures 7 feet 4 inches by 4 feet by 2 feet 7 inches.[3]

Under the XXth dynasty granite was used freely in making anthropoid sarcophagi and coffins, but the cover was treated differently, and it took the form of a thick slab, on which a figure of the deceased was sculptured in relief. The figure is often bearded, and the hands project, as it were from bandages, and grasp the amuletic symbols of Osiris, 𓊽, and Isis, 𓎬. An unusual variation in the form of the sarcophagi of this period is afforded by that of Rameses III, for it is made in the form of a cartouche 𓍷, and on the cover is sculptured in relief a figure of the king in the character of Osiris, and holding the 𓋾 and 𓌅, the symbols of the god's sovereignty and power. The cover is preserved in the Fitzwilliam Museum, Cambridge, and the sarcophagus is in the Louvre. The latter is ornamented with figures of the gods, and Vignettes from the great funerary work that describes the passage of the Sun-god through the hours of the night. The texts are lengthy extracts from the Book "Ȧmmi Ṭuat."

Under the XXVIth dynasty most of the sarcophagi from Memphis and the Delta are rectangular in form, and are made of green and black basalt and variegated hard stone. A figure of the deceased in the character of a god or goddess is usually sculptured in relief on the outside of the cover, and on the inside a figure of the goddess Nut is usually found; inside, on the bottom of the sarcophagus, is a figure of Hathor-Ȧmenti. The best examples of this period are entirely covered with hieroglyphic inscriptions containing texts taken from works akin to the Pyramid Texts, a result due to the

[1] Davis, *Tomb of Ḥătshopsîtû*, p. 81.
[2] Davis, *Tomb of Ḥarmhabi*, p. 91.
[3] Budge, *Catalogue* (Fitzwilliam Museum), p. 4.

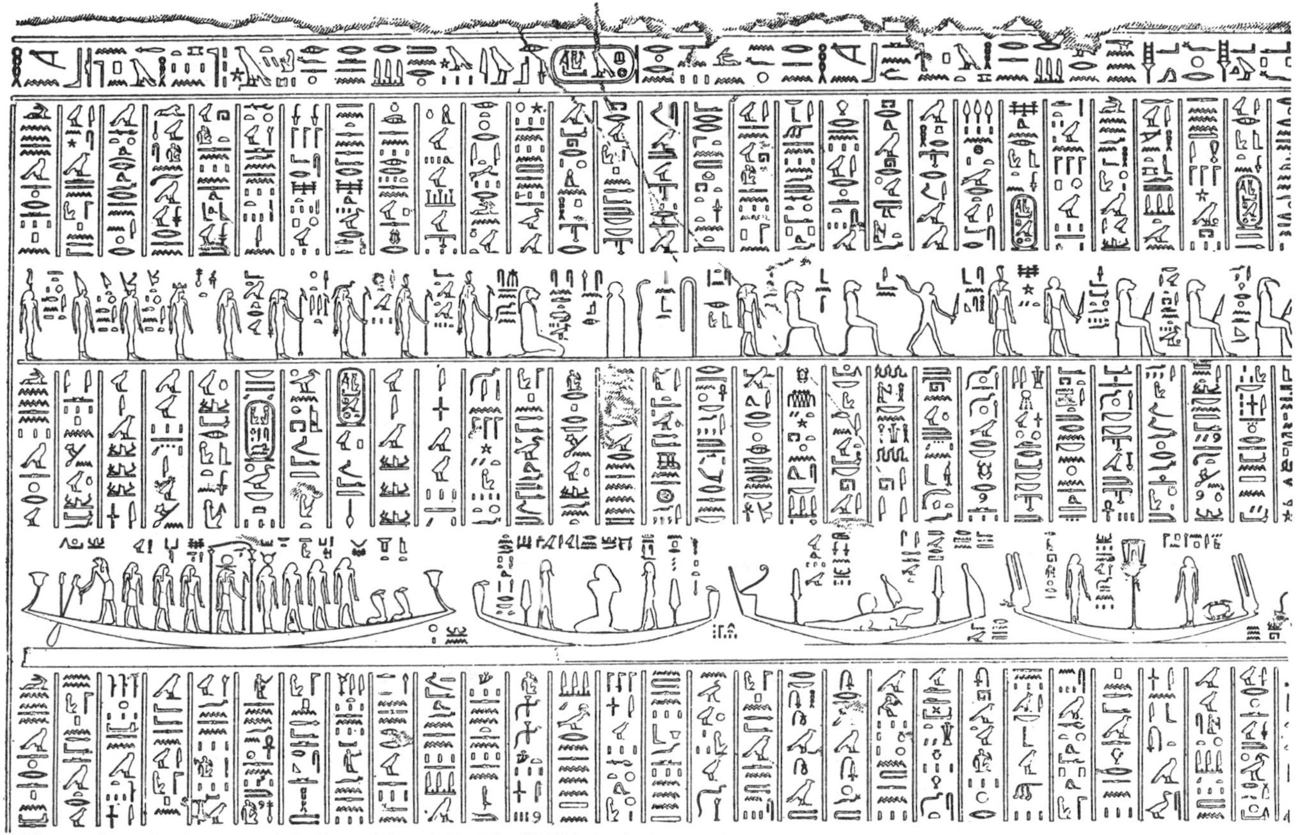

Vignettes illustrating the journey of the Sun-god through the Other World during the hours of the night; the texts describe the dwellers in the various sections of the Ṭuat, and give the addresses made to them by the god.
From the sarcophagus of Nekht-Ḥer-Ḥebit, King of Egypt, about B.C. 378. (Brit. Mus. No. 10.)

newly awakened interest in the funerary art and monuments and literature of the Old Kingdom. The hieroglyphs are well cut, and show very great attention to detail, but there is a meagreness about them which makes them easily recognizable as the product of a late period. One of the best known of this class is the sarcophagus of Ānkhnes-Neferȧbrā, daughter of Psammetichus II and Queen Tekhauath, 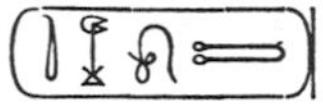 (B.M. 32). It was usurped by Ȧmen-ḥetep Pimenth, who added an inscription round the top edge. It measures 8 feet 6 inches by 3 feet 9½ inches by 3 feet 8 inches and weighs about 5 tons 15 cwt.[1] The sarcophagi which were made after the XXVIth dynasty are sometimes rectangular, having covers with human faces, and sometimes have rounded ends; good examples are the grey granite sarcophagi of Nesqeṭiu, , from "Campbell's Tomb" at Gîzah (B.M. 3), and Ḥapmen,  (B.M. 23). The anthropoid sarcophagi in basalt of this period are well represented by those of Uaḥȧbrā, , and Psemthek (B.M. 1047 and 1384), which, though smaller, closely resemble the huge sarcophagi of Tabnith and Eshmûnâzâr, king of Sidon in the first half of the IVth century B.C., which are described on page 431. At this period the sides and ends of sarcophagi are decorated with rows of figures of gods, each one of whom was supposed to protect a certain member of the body of the deceased. Under the XXXth dynasty and during the Ptolemaïc Period sarcophagi were very massive, and one of the finest examples of these is the sarcophagus of Nekhtḥerḥeb - meri - Ȧmen,  (the Nektanebês of the Greek writers), king of Egypt about B.C. 378 (B.M. 10). It is 10 feet 4 inches in length, 5 feet 4 inches in width, and 3 feet 11 inches high, and weighs nearly 7 tons. The cover is wanting. On the inside are figures of gods, at the head and foot are figures of Isis and Nephthys, and on the edge is a border of the amuletic symbols of Osiris and Isis, . The outside is covered with the Vignettes and texts[2] of the Ist, IInd, IIIrd, VIth, VIIth and IXth Sections of the Book "Ȧmmi Ṭuat," or Guide to the Other World, which the deceased was supposed to use. Another sarcophagus on which Vignettes and texts from the "Ȧmmi Ṭuat" and the "Book of the Gates" are also cut is that of Qemḥap (B.M. 1504).

[1] The complete text and translation are published in my *Sarcophagus of Ānkhnesrā-neferȧb*, London, 1885.

[2] See Budge, *Egyptian Heaven and Hell*, Vol. I, London, 1906; Vol. II contains the Book of Gates, and Vol. III a summary of the contents of each work, of which complete translations are given.

The sarcophagus is rectangular and the cover has the form of a truncated pyramid. Other fine, and in some ways more perfect, examples of this class of monument are the sarcophagi of Ānkhḥap, 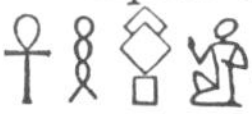, Tcheḥer, , Thaḥerpta (?), , in the Egyptian Museum.[1] The number of such sarcophagi found in the Museums of Cairo, Europe and America cannot possibly represent all that were made in the Ptolemaïc Period, and we may assume, as is the case with sarcophagi of the Old Kingdom, that many of them are still in the earth or in the tombs in the hills. Under Roman rule, in the case of men of high rank, the coffin seems to have been dispensed with, and a wooden sarcophagus took its place. This consisted of two parts: a long rectangular base-board, from 6 to 8 feet long and from 2 feet 6 inches to 3 feet in breadth, on which the badly made and much-bandaged mummy was laid, and a rectangular, vaulted cover, with angle-posts, from 1 foot 3 inches to 2 feet in height. Pictures of the old Egyptian gods of the dead are painted on the outside of the cover, and on its inside are often found the Twelve Signs of the Zodiac. The gods and scenes painted on such sarcophagi seem to have been chosen solely for their decorative characteristics.

THE EGYPTIAN COFFIN

THE desire to keep the bodies of the dead from touching the earth appears to be a fundamental characteristic of African peoples. The Neolithic Egyptians wrapped them in mats and skins and reed baskets, and at the present time many African peoples wrap up their dead in "trade cloth" and place them carefully in recesses made at one side of the bottom of the grave. The early dynastic Egyptians placed their dead in the contracted position and laid them sometimes in rough wooden boxes, and sometimes in round or oval earthenware boxes. In some cases the box or coffin was placed over the body or bones like an inverted basin. When the Egyptians began to bury their dead stretched out at full length and lying on their backs, the coffins were lengthened, and under the VIth dynasty both forms of coffin were used. The coffin is painted in monochrome, and brief inscriptions are painted in black on it, either a single line of text down the cover, or a single line round the top edges of all four sides. Of the coffins made under dynasties VII–X little is known.

Under the XIth dynasty the coffin was covered with texts written in cursive hieroglyphic characters, and it was evidently the forerunner of the coffins of kings and nobles of the XIIth dynasty. This is proved by Wilkinson's tracing made from a coffin now lost.

[1] Full descriptions, with text and plates, will be found in Maspero, *Sarcophages des Époques Persane et Ptolemaïque*, Cairo, 1908.

The coffin was made for Queen Khnem-nefer-ḥetchet, the wife of King Menthu-ḥetep, , and was inscribed with twenty-three Chapters of the Middle Kingdom Recension of the Book of the Dead.[1] It is probable that the coffin of Amamu[2] (B.M. 6654) belongs to this period.

At Al-Barshah and elsewhere in Upper Egypt under the XIIth dynasty coffins were made of thick planks of various kinds of wood and were rectangular in shape, and except in size they are practically duplicates of the massive wooden sarcophagi which were made at this period. There is an inscription on the outside of the cover of one line or more, which usually begins with  and contains a prayer by the deceased to Ȧnpu or Osiris, or both, for a liberal supply of funerary offerings, and a "happy burial," *i.e.*, a stately funeral, in a good and safe tomb, and the due performance of all the prescribed rites and ceremonies when his body is laid to rest. An inscription, also in one line or more, runs round the top edges of the two sides and two ends of the coffin, and at right-angles to this are six, eight, or twelve lines of hieroglyphic text in which the deceased declares himself to be the vassal of the Four Sons of Horus—Mestȧ, Ḥāpi, Ṭuamutef and Qebḥsenuf—and other gods. Usually these short perpendicular lines of text are six in number, three on each side, but the correct number is eight, four on each side, and they were intended to represent the four main bandages of the mummy. At one end of one side of the coffin the two Utchats, , are painted, and they were intended to secure for the deceased the strength and protection of the two eyes of Ḥer-ur, *i.e.*, the Sun and Moon, by day and by night for ever. Sometimes these Utchats rest upon the doorway of the tomb, with its folding-doors shut and bolted. The doorway is to all intents and purposes a copy of the "false door" seen in the maṣṭabah tombs of the IVth dynasty at Gîzah and Ṣaḳḳârah. In some instances a small rectangular door is actually cut in one side of the coffin, and it seems to have been specially made to provide a means of ingress and egress for the soul when it visited its body in the tomb. A good example of this door is afforded by the coffin of Menthu-ḥetep (B.M. 6655); here the door has a sliding panel. The inside of the cover is sometimes decorated with stars, but usually it is covered with texts written in hieratic. On the upper edges are painted representations of all the objects that were to be offered to the deceased according to the Liturgy of Funerary Offerings. On one side another "false door" and the Vignette of the Islands of the Blessed are painted in colours, and

[1] For a facsimile of Wilkinson's tracing see Budge, *Hieratic Papyri*, 1st Series, pll. XXXIX–XLVIII, London, 1910.

[2] For a facsimile see Birch, *Egyptian Texts of the Earliest Period*, London, 1886.

all the rest of the space on both sides is covered with hieratic texts. On the floor of the coffin are diagrams illustrating the various sections of the Kingdom of Osiris and the "Two Ways" thither, the one by land and the other by river. The texts on the sides contain extracts from the Pyramid Texts of the VIth dynasty, and Chapters from the great collection of religious texts that was compiled by the priests under the Middle Kingdom. But all coffins of the period of the XIth and XIIth dynasties were not so elaborately decorated, and many of them are made of thin planks of not very sound wood, which were merely washed over with a mixture of lime and yellow ochre.

Between the XIIth and the XVIIIth dynasties the shape of the coffin was changed, probably as a result of the growth of the cult of Osiris, and the **anthropoid coffin** came into use. One of the finest examples of this kind of coffin is undoubtedly that of king **Ȧn-Ȧntef** (B.M. 6652). The eyes and eyelids are inlaid after the manner of the statues of the Old Kingdom, and the face was intended to be a portrait. The body is covered with gilded feather-work—a form of ornamentation that seems to have originated at this period—and stars, and the inscriptions contain addresses to the deceased by Isis and Nephthys. Some assign this coffin to the XIth dynasty, but it probably belongs to a later period. A great many coffins in the various large National Collections belong to the period that lies between the XIIth and the XVIIIth dynasties, but it is quite impossible to assign anything like exact dates to them. The oldest of them have carved wooden faces, set in heavy wigs, and the fronts are decorated with figures of the goddess Nut under the form of a vulture, and with painted feather-work (B.M. 52050, 52051). The inscription down the front, in addition to a prayer for offerings, frequently includes the words from the Pyramid Texts, "Thy mother Nut spreads herself over thee in her name of Mystery of Heaven, she makes thee to live as a god, and to be without enemies."

The Egyptian text reads: 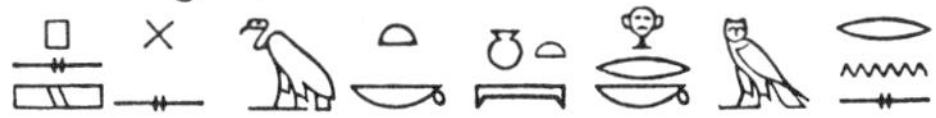

.

The finest and most beautiful painted coffins found in Egypt date from the XVIIIth dynasty,[1] and the nobles and priests of Ȧmen-Rā were provided with most luxurious funerary equipment. It was no uncommon thing for a great noble to be buried in three coffins, the outermost serving as a sarcophagus. The coffins are well shaped and well made, and both inside and outside are covered with Vignettes and long texts from the Theban Book of the Dead, and

[1] A good series of reproductions of fine coffins will be found in Gauthier, *Cercueils Anthropoïdes des Prêtres de Montou*, Cairo, 1913, and the *Guide* to the Egyptian Rooms I–III in the British Museum, London, 1924.

from the Book of Gates, the Book "Ȧmmi Ṭuat," and scenes from the work describing the passage of the dead Sun-god Ȧfu-Rā through the hours of the night. Numerous small scenes, in which the deceased is seen adoring Osiris and his company of gods of the dead, and various forms of the Sun-god, are painted on every available space. Vignettes and texts were painted in bright colours upon the layer of plaster with which the coffin was overlaid, and the whole coffin, both inside and outside, was given a thick coat of yellowish varnish. The passage of thirty-four centuries has diminished the brightness of the colours and made their general effect to be now harmonious and pleasing, but when such a coffin left the hands of the scribe and artist the effect of this medley of hard, uncompromising colours and disconnected subjects must have been somewhat crude and startling. Good typical examples of painted Theban coffins are those of Nesipaurshefit, a councillor and scribe, now in the Fitzwilliam Museum, Cambridge. The uniformity in the make of the coffins of the XVIIIth and XIXth dynasties that bear the names of priests and priestesses of Ȧmen-Rā, and the similarity of the scenes and texts painted on them, suggest that the priesthood of Ȧmen included among its members funerary artists, scribes and craftsmen. The coffins made early in the XVIIIth dynasty are the finest and best, and the coffins of some of the royal ladies now in the Cairo Museum, with their rich inlays of lapis-lazuli, opaque glass of various colours, carnelian, mother-of-emerald, etc., are of most interesting and beautiful workmanship. The troubles caused by the attitude of Ȧmenḥetep IV to Amen and the gods of the dead arrested the work of the undertaker for a time, and destroyed much of his skill, for the coffins of the XIXth dynasty lack the finish and delicacy of colouring of those of about B.C. 1500.

Under the XVIIIth and XIXth dynasties the use of stone for anthropoid coffins became general, and granite, basalt, alabaster and other hard stones were often employed. The kings of the XVIIIth dynasty had their large and massive sarcophagi made of granite and crystalline sandstone, but their coffins were usually of wood. Noblemen and high officials were sometimes permitted to have stone coffins, and Merimes, Viceroy of the Sûdân in the reign of Ȧmenḥetep III, provided himself with a black granite coffin, which is inscribed with the usual prayer for offerings and the speech of the goddess Nut (B.M. 1001).

The figures and inscriptions on stone coffins of this period are well cut, and the work is carefully executed throughout. The granite and basalt coffins of the XIXth dynasty exhibit much coarser work, and add nothing to our knowledge; it seems as if they were the equivalents of the sarcophagi of the earlier period. One important exception must be noted, namely, the alabaster coffin of Seti I which is now preserved in Sir John Soane's Museum in Lincoln's Inn Fields. This fine coffin is covered with hieroglyphic inscriptions,[1] filled in with blue paste, containing Chapters from the Theban Book of the Dead, and a version of the so-called Book of Gates, with Vignettes. It is 9 feet 4 inches in length, 3 feet 8 inches in width, and with its cover in position was about 5 feet in height.

The makers and decorators of wooden coffins of the XIXth and XXIst dynasties copied the work of the XVIIIth dynasty, but the influence of the priests of Åmen caused a modification in the character of the scenes painted upon them. The arrangement of these is different, and figures of the various forms of Åmen-Rā take the place of the old gods of Heliopolis, Memphis, Hermopolis and Abydos. The coffins of the priests and priestesses of Åmen form a class by themselves, as may be readily seen by examining the collections of them in Cairo and in the British Museum. The decorations are elaborate, but the work is not good, and the raised plaster figures of the gods, the beetle, the solar disk, and the amuletic symbols of Osiris and Isis, which are stuck on the covers, only add to their garishness. The dwindling of the power and material resources of the priest-kings of the XXIst dynasty is reflected in the poorness of work of many of the coffins. The beautiful coffins of Ḥentmeḥit (B.M. 48001 and 51101) and her mummy-board are remarkable exceptions; the free use of gold in the decoration of her coffins suggests that she was of royal blood.

The coffins of the period following the XXIst dynasty exhibit many varieties of decoration, but it happens sometimes that the wood is left in its natural colour and state. The faces are painted red, brown, green, flesh-coloured, and the eyes, made of obsidian, are inlaid between eyelids of the same material, or glass or bronze. Under the XXVIth dynasty, and later, coffins were often covered with hieroglyphic texts from the Saïte Recension of the Book of the Dead, and the Vignettes of the Weighing of the Heart, the Soul visiting its body in the tomb, and the sun shining upon the mummy as it lies on its bier, often appear on them. A rich man was sometimes buried in three wooden coffins at this period, and the outermost coffin in such cases was of massive but ugly construction. Some of them are 8 feet long and 3 feet broad, with sides 3 or 4 inches thick. The inscriptions are so badly and carelessly written that the scribe or artist cannot have understood what he was writing or painting. On the other hand, the handsome and well-shaped granite and basalt coffins which became fashionable at this period show that, although the art of mummifying was decaying and the national religion was changing, very successful attempts were made to reproduce fine examples of ancient work (see B.M. 1384, 1047, 17, 33, 39, 47, etc.). Soon after the XXVIth dynasty a great local manufactory of wooden coffins sprang up at Åpu (Panopolis),

[1] For texts and translations see Budge, *Egyptian Heaven and Hell*, Vol. II, London, 1906, and Budge, *An Account of the Sarcophagus of Seti I*, London, 1908.

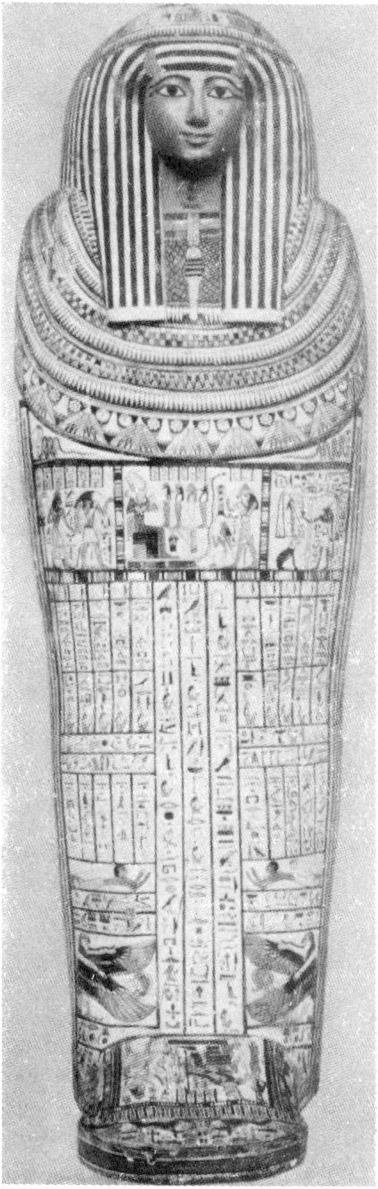

Painted wooden coffin of Pen-sen-sen-Ḥer, on which is painted the scene of the Last Judgment. XXVth dynasty. B.M. No. 24906.

Painted coffin from the Oasis of Khârgah. Roman Period. B.M. No. 52949.

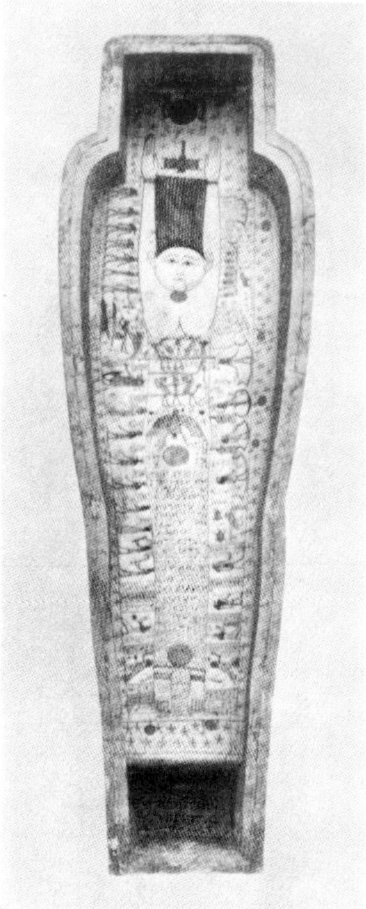

Inner coffin of Ḥer-netch-tef-f, a prophet of Åmen, ornamented with astronomical texts and Vignettes. Ptolemaïc Period. B.M. No. 6678.

Painted base-board of the sarcophagus of Soter, archon of Thebes. A.D. 110. B.M. No. 6705.

and a very considerable number of them were found there between 1884 and 1887. The faces are gilded, the head-dress is painted dark-blue or green, and the lower part of the body of the coffin, below the elaborate pectoral and figure of Nut and figure of the mummy with its Canopic jars, is covered with figures of the gods and short extracts from late funerary works like the Lamentations of Isis. In Lower Egypt, at this time, huge coffins, more than 8 feet in length and 4 feet in breadth, were made of green and black basalt, and the large, broad human faces on them have flat ears and noses and thick blubbery lips. They were in demand in Palestine, for Tabnith, king of Sidon about B.C. 380, was buried in one, and the body of the cover bears on it a long inscription cut in large hieroglyphs and containing a prayer for meat and drink and apparel and liberty of motion in the Other World. The Phoenician inscription giving the name of Tabnith is cut on the front of the foot of the coffin. His son Eshmûnâzâr was buried in a coffin of similar size and shape, but it has no hieroglyphic text upon it, and the front of the body of the coffin is covered with an inscription in Phoenician characters. The use of stone coffins was more common in Lower than in Upper Egypt, and this was because they did not perish from the action of moist earth as rapidly as wooden ones. In the Ptolemaïc Period the coffin was usually rectangular in form, and was made of thin planks of wood, which were decorated with figures of the gods of the dead who were favourites at that period, painted in bright colours. In the Roman Period the coffin was often dispensed with altogether. The body, more or less well bandaged, was laid upon a large flat rectangular board, which varied in size from 8 feet by 2 feet 6 inches to 6 feet by 1 foot 8 inches, and had a slot in it at each corner. A large rectangular wooden canopy, with angle-posts and a vaulted roof, was lifted over it, and when the ends of the angle-posts had been driven into the slots in the base-board, pegs were driven through the ends that projected through the slots, and canopy and board became fastened together. On the outside of the canopy were painted figures of the gods, and a favourite decoration of the inside was figures of the Twelve Signs of the Zodiac. This idea was derived from earlier coffins of the Egyptians (*e.g.*, B.M. 6678), on which we have figures of the gods of the constellations, the five planets, the Signs of the Zodiac, and the thirty-six (or, thirty-nine) Dekans. Sometimes we have a gilded figure of the Ba, or soul of the deceased, in the form of a hawk perched upon the ridge in the centre of the canopy. The base-board is lined with a large sheet of brown linen, on which a large figure of the goddess of Ȧmenti, or Nut, or Hathor is painted in the form of an Egypto-Greek woman with masses of jet-black hair. On coffins of this class the name of the deceased is written sometimes in hieroglyphs and Greek letters and sometimes in demotic and Greek letters. The great oases in the Western Desert probably passed under the rule of Egypt in the time of the Middle Kingdom, and there is little doubt that the Egyptian governors who ruled Khârgah were buried there with the same pomp and ceremony as they would have been in Egypt. Few funerary remains older than the time of Darius have been found in that oasis, but since the railway was taken thither by a great sugar company many things have been brought from it to Egypt. Among these is the finely painted coffin B.M. 52949. The variations in the scenes painted on the coffin suggest that it was made and decorated locally, and the hieroglyphic inscription down the back shows by the numerous mistakes in it that the artist was copying a religious formula which he could neither copy correctly nor understand. The coffin may be dated in the IIIrd or IVth century A.D.

Whilst the natives were digging down the limestone hills between Akhmîm and Sûhâḳ to burn and turn into lime suitable for mortar they found a considerable number of tombs. Each tomb contained generally one or two chambers, and in each chamber there were several mummies (all of the Roman Period), as often without as with coffins. The coffins were long rectangular boxes made of thin planks of wood, and the covers were formed by a single thin plank. They were painted a yellowish-white colour inside and out, and the names, which were carelessly scrawled at one end of the cover, were in cursive Greek letters. But these coffins were of great interest, because on one end of each of the large ones there was a life-size portrait plaster head of the deceased, and on the other a pair of plaster feet; sometimes a pair of plaster hands lay on the middle of the coffin. Sometimes the plaster head rested on the mummy, and the flat projection from the neck served as a sort of pectoral. The faces on all these heads were undoubtedly intended to be portraits, and a collection of fine specimens of them is exhibited in the British Museum (24780, 24781, etc.). All these burials seemed to me to date from the IIIrd century A.D. The coffins that some have attributed to the Vth and VIth centuries I have never seen.

THE ḤETEP, OR TABLET FOR SEPULCHRAL OFFERINGS

THE graves of the pre-dynastic Egyptians prove that the inhabitants of the Nile Valley were accustomed to make offerings of food and drink to their dead, and it is probable that their forefathers had done the same for scores of generations. Many of the modern peoples of the Sûdân, and not only those who inhabit that portion of it which is called Egyptian, also spread out offerings of fruit, grain, meat and beer, which they are convinced are of service to their dead kinsfolk. As long as the Egyptians buried their dead in shallow oval hollows in the sand, or in cavities lined with sun-dried bricks, the sepulchral offerings were laid in the graves with the bodies.

But when they began to mummify their dead, and to build sepulchres in stone over them, they adopted the custom of placing their funerary gifts at first upon reed mats and then upon slabs of stone which they laid on the ground as nearly as possible over the place where the mummy lay. In the maṣṭabah tombs the tablet for offerings was laid on the ground at the foot of the "false door," or of the inscribed stele that at a later period took its place in the so-called Ṭuat Chamber. The stone slab served as a table for the Ka of the deceased when it left its chamber to partake of the offerings provided for it, and the soul, as it alighted on the stele, or passed through the "false door" on its way to or from the mummy chamber, would be gratified by the sight of the gifts made to its former associate in the flesh. In primitive times the offerings were, as is the case to-day in many parts of Central Africa, laid upon leaves; later the reed mat took the place of the leaves, and at a still later period the stone slab superseded the mat. The tomb of a king was supplied with offerings of meat, milk, wine, beer, fruit, vegetables, unguents, etc., daily, and the priests whose duty it was to recite the liturgy of Funerary Offerings would take care that everything which the royal Ka needed was supplied. Nobles and priestly officials had to be satisfied with offerings made to their tombs on festival days only; but what was to happen to the Ka of the man whose kinsfolk were too poor to make any offerings in his tomb or at his grave? This

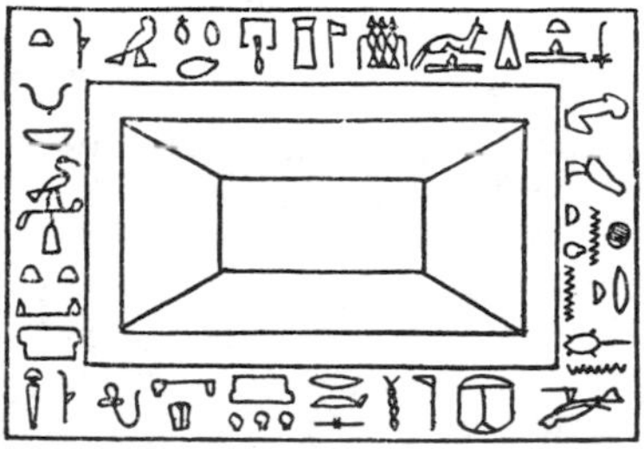

Rectangular stone vessel to receive libations made to Khart-en-Khennutu. Vth dynasty. Brit. Mus. No. 1176.

difficulty was appreciated at a very early period, and the priests devised a way out of it. Figures of the things offered—bread-cakes, geese, haunches of beef, fruits, etc.—were cut in outline or sculptured in relief on the tablet for offerings, and an inscription was cut upon the face or its edges, in which Anubis or Osiris was called upon to provide the Ka of the deceased with *per kheru*, , or *pert kheru*, , *i.e.*, "things that appear at the word." The deceased, himself an immaterial entity, uttered the necessary word of power, and offerings as immaterial as himself appeared from out of the sculptures on the tablet as soon as he had done so, and, so to speak, a shadow fed upon shadows. Certain kinds of offerings were laid upon circular tables, which appear in the inscriptions under the form of , , and . The alabaster table of Ȧṭenȧ, a *Kher ḥeb* who flourished at Abydos under the VIth dynasty, is seen with its unguent vessels upon it.

The tablet upon which food and drink offerings were laid, and which was placed at the doorway of the "false door," or wherever the sepulchral stele stood, is a rectangular slab made usually of limestone, basalt, granite, etc., with a projection on one side which

Stone Tablet for offerings made for Uashka. Vth or VIth dynasty.
Brit. Mus. No. 1156.

is often grooved and which was supposed to serve as a kind of spout. The Egyptians called it "Ḥetep," , or , and the things that were laid upon it "Ḥetepet," , or . The tablet varies in size from 6 inches to 3 feet in length, and from about 4 inches to 15 inches in width. In addition to the figures of the offerings, rectangular hollows, presumably to hold libations, were cut in the face of the tablet, and in the tablet of Uashka (B.M. 1156)[1] we see figures of the members of the family of the deceased bringing bread-cakes, vessels of unguents, etc. A figure of the tablet for offerings is outlined, and in the inscription the deceased asks Anubis for *pert kheru* daily and at every festival. The inscription begins with the words , which probably means that the king has contributed towards the materials for the funerary offerings. In later times this formula was inscribed on every sepulchral stele and tablet, but it can only have been added as a matter of form. A good example of a Ḥetep, or tablet for offerings, of the Old Kingdom is B.M. 1345,[2] which is inscribed with a text stating that it was dedicated to the official

[1] See *Hieroglyphic Texts*, Pt. I, pl. 23.
[2] *Ibid.*, pl. 5, No. 9.

Kanefer, , by his pious son. A very interesting model in bronze in the British Museum (5315) shows that the Ḥetep was sometimes mounted on a stand with four legs, and so became a veritable table. This Ḥetep is made of sheet bronze and is 12½ inches long, 5½ inches wide, and 7 inches high ; on one side and one end are projections in the form of the handle shown in . Arranged on it are bronze models of three flat saucers, one with a raised rim, eight small vases , one vessel shaped like a wine-glass , one libation vessel , one bottle , two vases with long spouts, two unguent pots , one jar with a painted base, and parts of two other vases. On the front edge the inscription  , "The *Pert Kheru* of the Smer uāt, the Kher ḥeb Åṭenå," is engraved twice. This stand and its models tell us what the *Pert Kheru*, for which every deceased person prayed, was like.

The reliefs of the offerings on the tablets vary in number according to the period. Under the New Kingdom the vessels used in the ceremonies connected with offerings were represented prominently on the Ḥetep, but little by little the number of the figures of the objects offered increased until, as we see in the case of Cairo 23013, they filled most of the surface-space. In this example the offerings are arranged in the order in which they were presented, and it is interesting to note that some of the cakes bear impressions of seals and have special names. This custom of stamping sacred bread has been perpetuated by the Copts in their sacramental cakes. On many Ḥeteps two rectangular hollows are cut for libations, and two libation vases are sculptured near them, and it is probable that one hollow and one vase were used for the wine or beer of Upper Egypt, and the other hollow and vase for the wine or beer of Lower Egypt. The inscription on a fine, large Ḥetep contains the name and titles of the deceased, and prayers, which are usually addressed to Anubis, Thoth, , and Osiris, for funerary offerings. In the Graeco-Roman Period the decoration of Ḥeteps was modified very considerably. The hollows, which were formerly rectangular, are now made in the form of a cartouche ; the offerings represented are few in number, and a very favourite scene, which is cut into or sculptured on the main surface, represents the deceased seated receiving on his hands the water of life from the goddess Nut or Hathor, who stands in a sycamore tree. Sometimes two trees, each with a goddess, are represented, and in these cases the deceased stands whilst he receives the celestial water from one, and sits whilst he receives it from the other.[1] The texts that accompany these figures are badly written and inaccurate versions of Chapters LIX and LXII of the Book of the Dead. In the Vignette of the former we see Nut in her tree pouring out water for the deceased, who kneels before her, and in the text he entreats her to give him air and water. In the text of Chapter LXII the deceased prays that access to the "mighty flood" may be granted to him by Osiris, and that Thoth-Ḥāpi, the Nile-god, will grant him power to drink at will. During the Graeco-Roman Period models of Ḥeteps were attached to statues, and even to mummies, apparently as amulets. Examples are B.M. 26813, which has a pierced projection so that it may be suspended, and measures 5⅛ inches by 4⅞ inches, and B.M. 53999; on the former four cakes are represented, and on the latter one only. An interesting Ḥetep of the Roman Period is B.M. 48509. Here we have two cartouche-shaped libation hollows, two libation vases, with lotus flowers and a modified form of the ☥, resting on a conical base, between them. Above, arranged in two groups, and in relief, are twenty stamped bread-cakes, and below the libation vases is a small frieze with a number of offerings in relief. These include a gazelle, with its legs tied together for sacrifice, a bull's head, , a joint of meat with the bone, , ten bread-cakes, stamped as before, vegetables, flowers, and a large two-handled water-pot, with its pointed end resting in a stand, and a stopper made in the form of ☥. A channel for the libations is marked on all four sides of these reliefs. The edges of the Ḥetep are decorated with a pattern of rosettes and lotus flowers.

Besides the Ḥetep tablet for the canonical offerings, the Egyptians also heaped up their miscellaneous gifts to the dead on a stand or kind of table, which was placed in the tomb. This rested either on a single central support, , or on four legs, , and was called "Khaut," , in Coptic ϩⲏⲟⲩⲉ or ϣⲏⲩⲉ, *i.e.*, altar. The table with a single support has survived in the small table which was found in the house of every well-to-do person in Cairo and Syria, and is called "Khuwân,"[2] خُوان, and the table with four legs in the altar which is seen in Coptic churches. The Egyptians also had another word for altar, , *khait*, but this appears to have been an altar that was specially set

[1] See Ahmed Bey Kamal, *Tables d'Offrandes* (in the Cairo Catalogue), Cairo, 1909, pl. XLI ff.

[2] *Khuwân* is a Persian word, and its literal meaning is a large tray with a foot; it is doubtful if it is connected with the Egyptian *Khaut*, as has been suggested.

apart for the burning of incense. Among the offerings that were laid upon the Ḥetep was **incense,** 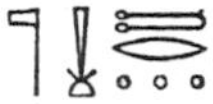, or , *senther* or *senter,* or , *sthi neter, i.e.,* "smell of the god," in Coptic ⲥⲟⲛⲧⲉ. Incense was burnt in the tomb, and water in which natron had been dissolved was sprinkled on the ground before the presentation of the offerings began; that this was done is proved by the Vignettes in the Papyrus of Ani and the Papyrus of Hunefer. The **censer** was usually made wholly of bronze, and consisted of a long handle made in the form of a pillar with a lotus capital, the lower end of which terminated in a head of Horus wearing a disk. From the capital of the pillar a flat shovel projected, and a small pot attached to the handle held the incense that was to be burnt. One of the names of the censer was "Hand of Horus," , and the British Museum possesses a fine example of this form of the instrument (B.M. 41606). It is 18¾ inches in length, and from the capital of the lotus pillar which forms the handle a hand projects , and on this rests the pot that contained the red-hot ashes on which the incense was sprinkled. The other end terminates in a head of the hawk of Horus wearing a disk and uraeus. On the handle is a kneeling figure of a man with his hands resting upon a receptacle for incense in the form of a cartouche.

In every set of vessels that are represented on the Ḥeteps there is a large one that resembles the **lustration vase,** , but it has no spout. Two good examples of this vase are B.M. 25567 and 25566. The former is 12¾ inches in height, and is inscribed with the name and titles of Princess "Nesitanebtȧshru, the great chief lady of the ladies of the high [priest of] Ȧmen-Rā, king of the gods,"

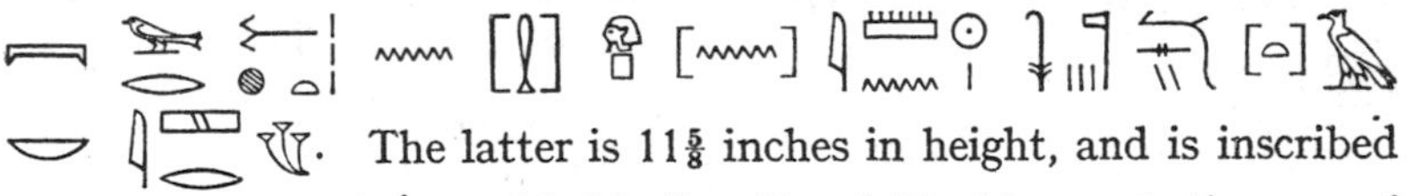. The latter is 11⅝ inches in height, and is inscribed with the name of Ȧstemkhebit I, wife of Menkheperrā, the son of Painetchem I, and with a prayer to Isis for a Ḥetep and libations. The inscription is on the flat rim and opens with the usual words, 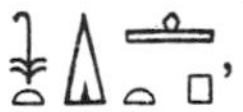, and continues,  . This is followed by 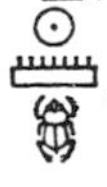, the name of her husband.

Another important adjunct to the ordinary equipment of the Ḥetep was the **libation bucket,** of which few, if any, ancient examples are known. There are several fine ones in the British

Museum, and the following is a description of the typical example 38212. This bucket is pear-shaped, and is made of bronze; it is about 16 inches in height, and its massive solid copper handle is securely attached to it by means of the two lugs on the rim. The sides are ornamented with two scenes, in which all the figures and texts are cut in outline: **1.** The deceased Ḥer adoring Osiris, who is standing with a table of offerings before him, and saying, "I grant unto thee from myself all strength," . Behind Osiris stands Ḥernetchteff presenting "life," , and saying, "I give to thee victory over thy enemies," . Next come figures of Isis and Nephthys, the latter saying, "I give thee from myself every kind of pleasant, pure and sweet thing" and the former, "I give thee from myself offerings of rich food in abundance." **2.** The deceased standing upright and offering incense and a libation of natron water to his father and his mother, who are seated on chairs of state, with an altar heaped with offerings before them. He says to his father, "This thy water is given to thee, thy water is to thee before Horus in this thy name of Qebḥ,"

a formula that is well known from the Pyramid Texts. A single line of text runs round the bucket under these scenes and reads,

Thus the father of Ḥer was called Peṭa-ȧmen-neb-nest-taui, and his mother, who was a sistrum-bearer of Ȧmen-Rā, Ȧriru (?). From two lines of text which run round the upper end of the bucket we learn that he was a priest of Sebek and other gods, and also of King Nekhtḥerḥeb , and a scribe of the offerings of various gods.

SEPULCHRAL STELAE AND TABLETS

THE sepulchral stele of the Old Kingdom is a development of the **false door,** which is a striking feature of the maṣṭabah tomb. The false door was a large stone slab built into the wall immediately

False door of Uashka.
Vth or VIth dynasty. Brit. Mus. No. 1156.

above the pit or shaft that led downwards to the mummy chamber, and on it, in well-defined spaces, were cut the name and titles of the deceased. On the flat surface on each side of the space that represented the door we find frequently figures of the deceased and his wife and their children, sculptured in low relief. On the surface above the door is usually sculptured a scene in which the deceased and his wife are represented as seated one on each side of a table loaded with funerary offerings, . The inscriptions that accompany these figures read, "incense 1,000, eye-paint 1,000, stibium 1,000, *ḥatt* oil 1,000, wine 1,000, *nebes* fruit 1,000, *nebset* cakes 1,000, oxen 1,000, geese 1,000, suits of apparel 1,000," etc. And we are to understand that the deceased prays that all these things may be supplied to him in abundance whenever he (or she) requires them. Frequently figures of the offerings required, loaves of bread, , skins of wine, , haunches of beef, , bundles of incense, , geese, , etc., are sculptured round about the table of offerings. The deceased may or may not be accompanied by his wife or "sister," but if the latter is not seated at the table with him she is often seen sculptured on the slab by the side of the door. On the larger false doors both sides of the sunk part representing the door itself are fitted with figures of the sons and daughters of the deceased, who are presenting offerings of fruit, flowers, meat, geese, vessels of drink, and linen garments (B.M. 1156). In many maṣṭabah tombs the architrave above the false door is filled with a long list of the titles of the deceased, and the text of a prayer in which he prays for a happy burial after a fine old age and a supply of offerings at all the great festivals throughout the year. No details of the personal life of the deceased are ever given, nor any historical information except the names of the kings,[1] and no mention is made of his age or of the date of his death. On some of the largest false doors the actual door space is filled with a selection, more or less complete, of names of offerings chosen from the great list of canonical offerings, which were ordered to be made when the Liturgy of Funerary Offerings was recited in the tomb (B.M. 658, 718, 1429, 1480). During the recital of this work about one hundred and fifty objects were presented by the Kher ḥeb, who said or sang the formula appropriate to each offering and, as the Egyptians believed,[2] so brought about the transmutation of its substance.

The sepulchral stone stelae of the XIth, XIIth and XIIIth dynasties may, for practical purposes, be divided into two classes, viz., those that are **rectangular,** and those that have **rounded tops.** The former have usually a palm-leaf cornice, which is more or less elaborately sculptured, and a raised border. In the sunk portion the surface is divided by lines into sections which are filled with incised scenes representing the wife and sons and daughters of the deceased worshipping him and presenting offerings to him. The offerings on the table are elaborately sculptured, and the name of every member of the family is given. Sometimes the rectangular

[1] The false door of Ptaḥshepses in the British Museum is of special interest, for he gives the names of several kings whom he served.

[2] This Liturgy, with Vignettes, is given in my *Liturgy of Funerary Offerings*, London, 1909.

stele is sculptured on a stele with a rounded top, as, for example, in B.M. 1312, which was set up to the memory of Mer by his wife Renseneb, . Under the Middle Kingdom the greater number of funerary stelae have rounded tops, which are

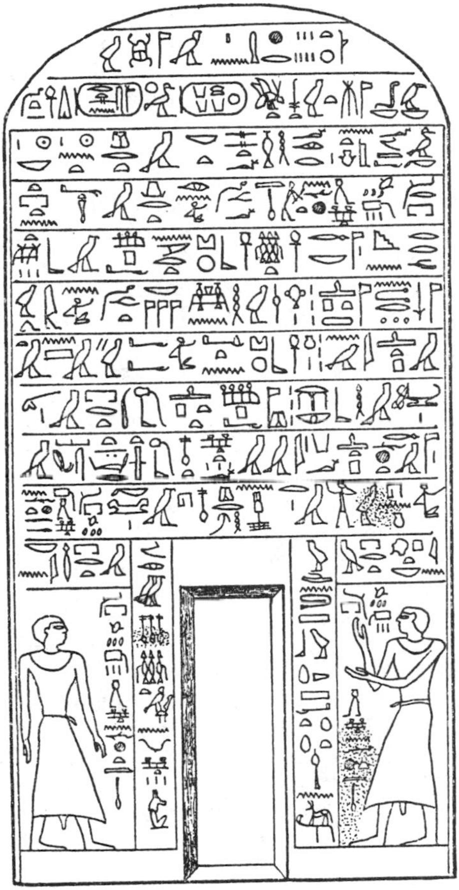

Limestone sepulchral stele of Nekht-Anḥer dated in the 7th year of the reign of Khākaurā Usertsen (Sen Usrit ?) III. XIIth dynasty. Brit. Mus. No. 575.

ornamented with a cartouche containing the name and titles of the king under whom the deceased served (B.M. 575), or the Winged Disk, Beḥuṭ, Lord of heaven (B.M. 574), or the Winged Disk, with uraei, , and the king's name (B.M. 583), or the Utchats and the symbol of eternity, 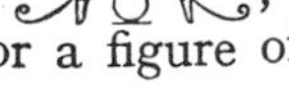, and the Jackals of the South and North (B.M. 940), or a figure of Osiris Khenti Åmenti (B.M. 222).

In some cases a rectangular cavity is cut in the lower half of the stele, which shows that the stele had its origin in the "false door" of the maṣṭabah tomb, and this was intended to serve as a means of egress and ingress when the soul went to visit the body in the tomb. A cavity of this kind is cut in the stele of Nekht-Ȧnḥer, which has a rounded top (B.M. 575), and in the stele of Sa-Hathor, which is rectangular and has a cornice (B.M. 569); in the latter a squatting figure of Sa-Hathor is seated in the cavity, or doorway. The inscriptions on the sepulchral stelae of the Middle Kingdom differ greatly from those of the Old Kingdom, and they often contain historical information of the greatest importance. They begin with the usual formula , "the king gives an offering," and this is followed by a prayer to one or more gods of the dead, usually Osiris and Anubis, for funerary offerings for the Ka of the deceased. Frequently the text goes on to enumerate the offices held by the deceased, and sometimes a brief account is given of the work that he did in his life. Thus the official Sa-Hathor, who served Ȧmenemḥat II, tells us on his sepulchral stele in the British Museum (No. 569) that he directed the work of making the sixteen statues of the king that were set up near the royal pyramid, and also that he was sent on the king's business to the Land of the Turquoise, *i.e.*, Sinai, and to Nubia, from which he brought back the Sûdânî tribute to the king. Another official, Khentiemsemti, who was a highly trusted adviser of his king, tells us that he visited Abu (Elephantine) and worshipped Khnem, the great god of the First Cataract (B.M. 574); and we owe to the sepulchral stele of Ikhernefert, which was set up at Abydos and is now in Berlin (No. 1204), a most valuable description of the great festival ceremonies that were celebrated at Abydos in connection with the resurrection of Osiris. Still more remarkable is the sepulchral stele of Ȧntef, the son of Sent, who describes his mental qualities and characteristics, and explains to us the system that he followed in dealing with his superiors, equals and inferiors in the daily course of his official work (B.M. 581). The sepulchral stelae of the XIIth dynasty contain a great mass of information on many points, and well repay careful study. The collection in the British Museum is particularly interesting, and good copies of them are easily accessible.[1]

Under the New Kingdom the position of the sepulchral stele in the tomb varied, and it was placed either in the mummy chamber, at the head or foot of the coffin, or in the corridor leading to it. And the decoration, colouring, arrangement of Vignettes and inscriptions, are different from those of the Old and Middle Kingdoms. In the older periods the deceased is seen surrounded by his family and the chief persons of his household, but now figures of Osiris and the other

[1] See Hall, H. R., *Hieroglyphic Texts from Egyptian Stelae, etc.*, Pts. II–VI, London, 1912–22.

Sepulchral stele of Ṭeḥuti (Tcheḥuti), a royal kinsman, overseer of the king's throne, and Ka-priest of the king. XIIth dynasty. Brit. Mus. No. 805.

gods of the dead take their places, and in many cases the "family" character of the stele has disappeared. The inscriptions are longer and often contain tolerably full biographies of the deceased persons, and sometimes they cover not only the stele, but the walls of the

Painted limestone sepulchral stele of Sebek-ḥetep, a scribe of the wine cellar, and his sister Tchauf, priestess of Hathor. XVIIIth dynasty. Brit. Mus. No. 1368.

chamber in which it is placed. These biographies frequently contain information that is not met with elsewhere, or they supply supplementary details of great value in piecing together the history of a reign. The sepulchral stelae of the XVIIIth dynasty are large and handsome, and the figures and Vignettes are full of life and spirit. The stone stelae of the later dynasties are not of very great interest except in matters of decoration and general arrangement. Under the XXVIth dynasty the stelae are larger in size, and the inscriptions, which are often copies of texts of the Old Kingdom, are cleanly cut in small hieroglyphic characters. After this period the decoration of the stele deteriorated, the inscriptions are badly cut and contain many mistakes, and it is quite clear that the placing of a stele in the tomb had at that time become a mere matter of form. On stelae of the Ptolemaïc Period the inscriptions are often in demotic or Greek instead of hieroglyphs, and the upper halves are decorated with long rows of figures of gods, sometimes cut in high relief, who have the attributes and wear the costumes of Greek gods.

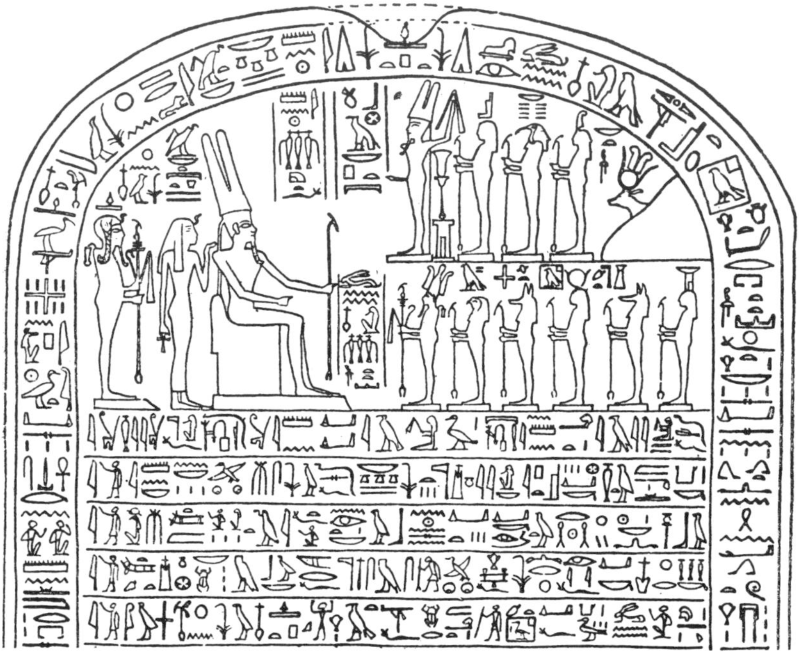

Granite sepulchral stele of Ṭaṭaȧ, an overseer of the scribes of Ȧmen, on which are cut figures of Ȧmen, Mut, Khensu, etc. XIXth dynasty. From Dêr al-Baḥarî. Brit. Mus. No. 706.

Many Egyptians were too poor to have elaborately inscribed stone stelae set up in their tombs, and had to be contented with **wooden sepulchral stelae.** A few of those known are as old as the XVIIIth dynasty, but the remainder belong to the later dynasties and to the Ptolemaïc Period. Almost all of them have rounded tops; they vary in length from 6 inches to 2 feet 3 inches, and in width from 4 inches to nearly 2 feet. Sometimes the stele stands upon two pedestals having steps on each side. The inscriptions and scenes upon them are usually painted in white, green, red, yellow, or black upon a light- or dark-brown ground. On the back there are sometimes painted figures of the rising sun, , and the symbols of the eastern, , and western horizons, . A typical example is the stele of Uaḥȧbrā (B.M. 8464). Here we have three registers containing: (1) The winged solar disk of Beḥuṭ, , with pendent uraei of Nekhebit and Uatchit, and the jackals Ȧnpu of the embalmment chamber and Ȧnpu of the Hall. (2) The boat of the Sun-god of night Ȧfu, , seated on a throne under a

Limestone sepulchral stele of Th-Imḥetep, a priestess of Memphis who died in the 10th year of the reign of Cleopatra. Brit. Mus. No. 147.

fold of the body of the great serpent Meḥen; on each of the raised ends of the boat is a solar disk. With the god in the boat are the beetle of Kheperȧ, , Thoth, lord of the words of the gods, , Maāt, Isis, Ḥu, Sȧa, the herald, , *uhem*, and the steersman. In front of the boat the deceased stands and "praises the god," . (3) Here the deceased is offering incense, , and praising Osiris Khenti Ȧmenti, behind whom stand Horus, Isis, Nephthys, Thoth, Ȧnpu, Upuatu, and the four sons of Horus, who are seated. Below these registers is the prayer to certain gods for funerary offerings which is characteristic of this class of stele under the XXVIth dynasty and later. It reads: "May **Rā** of the Two Horizons, great god, lord of heaven, of variegated colours, who comes forth from the horizon, and **Ȧtem,** lord of the lands of Ȧnu, and the gods who live in Ȧnu, and **Osiris Khenti Ȧmentt,** great god, lord of Ȧbtt (Abydos), and **Osiris, lord of Restt,** and **Isis,** great lady among the goddesses (?), and **Nephthys,** sister of the god, and **Ȧnpu,** dweller in the embalmment chamber, lord of Tatchesertt, and **Upuatu,** lord of the roads, and **Hathor,** mistress of Ȧmentt, and the gods in Khert-neter, give funerary offerings, beer, oxen, geese, wine, milk, unguents, cool water, oil, linen garments, and tables heaped with rich foods and containing every kind of beautiful and pure thing. . . . [to the Ka of] Osiris the soul of the god (?), Uaḥȧbrā, begotten by . . . . . the truth-speaker and brought forth by the lady of the house . . . . .,[1] the truth-speaker."

The painted wooden stele (B.M. 8468) is one of the finest examples known,[2] and is interesting because the inscription painted upon it contains a hymn to the Sun-god instead of the ordinary prayer. In the upper register are the winged disk with the beetle of Kheperȧ, , Nekhebit and Uatchit, each holding the symbol of eternity, , and the two jackals. In the middle register the deceased Nesui, , who is declared to be a "truth-speaker before the gods of the Ṭuat," is adoring "The Company of the great gods who dwell [in Ȧnu]." His soul, in the form of a human-headed hawk, who is accompanied by his shadow , stands in the bows of the boat adoring Rā-Ḥer-ȧakhuti, and the other gods and goddesses, Osiris, Kheperȧ, Shu, Tefnut and Geb. In the lower register Nesui is seen adoring Osiris and his sisters Isis and Nephthys, Horus, son of Isis, Hathor, mistress of the Ṭuat, Ȧnpu and Upuatu. Of each of the last two named it is said, "He gives all his protections," . The gods in the lower register are described as the "company of the great gods who are in Ȧmentt," , and the deceased prays that "they will give [him] their protection," 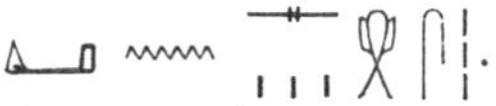. Below the registers are five lines of inscription containing extracts from hymns to Rā and to Horus of the Two

[1] Blank spaces are left for the names of his father and mother.

[2] It was purchased by the Trustees in 1841 from the collection of Signor Anastasi.

Wooden stele of Nesui. Painted with scenes representing the deceased and his soul, with its shadow, adoring Rā and his gods, and Osiris and his gods. The supports of the stele are in the form of the mythological stairway to heaven. On the top of it is the figure of Nesui's soul in the form of a man-headed hawk, which suggests that the stele formed the resting-place of the soul when it visited the tomb. XXIInd dynasty. B.M. No. 8468.

Sepulchral stele of Plêïnôs, a "reader," sculptured with Alpha and Omega, the Christian Cross and Egyptian ānkhs. VIIIth or IXth century A.D. B.M. No. 679.

Sepulchral stele of John, a monk, who died on the 5th day of Phamenoth in the 14th year of an Indiction. VIIIth or IXth century A.D. B.M. No. 665.

Horizons which are found in Chapter XV of the Theban Recension of the Book of the Dead. The text reads :—

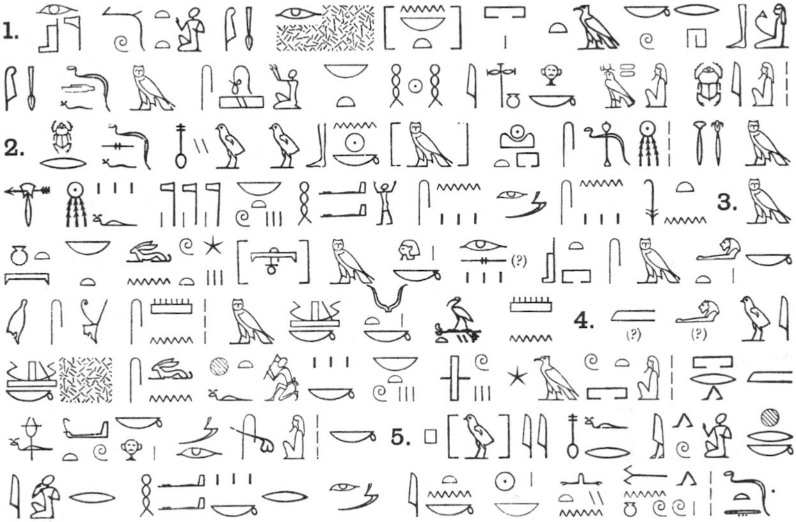

(**1**) "The Osiris Nesui, the truth-speaker, born of the lady of the house, Takureheb, the truth-speaker, says in paying adoration to the Lord of Eternity :—Hail (or homage) to thee, Rā-Ḥer-ȧakhuti-Kheperȧ (**2**) the self-created god, twice beautiful in thy rising in the horizon. [He] illumines the Two Lands (*i.e.*, Egypt) with his beams. All the gods rejoice [when] they see the King (**3**) in the heavens. The Mistress of the Hour (*i.e.*, the guiding goddess) is upon thy head, she makes her place before thee. The White Crown and the Red Crown are stablished in thy boat.[1] Thoth is stablished (**4**) in the front of thy boat. All thine enemies have been destroyed. The gods who dwell in the Ṭuat come forth with bowings to meet thee and to see thy (**5**) beautiful form. Let me come before thee with (?) those who exult in thee to see thy Disk every day, never suffering any repulse whatsoever."

It is important to note that the soul of the deceased, in the form of a painted wooden man-headed hawk, with a gilded face, is perched on the top of the stele of Nesui. There seems to be little doubt that the stele was regarded as the place on which the soul alighted when it went to the tomb to visit the body that it had formerly occupied, and, as the stele represented a door, that the soul passed through it at will. In fact, the stele appears to have formed the resting-place of the soul whenever it was pleased to remain on the earth to hold converse with the Ka of which, in some respects, it must have been

[1] Read "on thy brow" ;  must be a mistake for , but the scribe did not erase his mistake.

thought by the Egyptians to be a counterpart. The two pedestals of this stele, each with six steps, suggest that the stele itself was regarded as the throne of the soul.

Men of high rank and wealthy Egyptians arranged for large sepulchral tablets to be placed in their tombs as a matter of course, but humbler folk had to content themselves with small stelae, which are often badly made and poorly painted and inscribed with texts containing many mistakes. The greater number of these smaller stelae were provided not by those whose names they bear, but by their kinsfolk and friends, who were anxious that their dead relatives should not want for funerary offerings of food and drink and apparel. Such stelae represent the deceased adoring and praying to Osiris, who is seated and who holds the whip and crook. The inscription is always short, and reads, "May he (*i.e.*, Osiris) give offerings and divine food in abundance," , as on the stele of Paṭaȧmen, , the overseer of the workmen of the temple of Ȧmen, 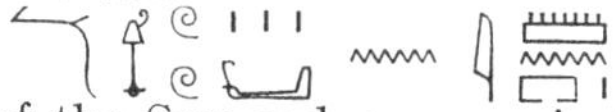 (B.M. 8484). In a few cases some form of the Sun-god appears instead of Osiris, and in one instance we have Ptaḥ, the Lord of Maāt (B.M. 8497). The blue-glazed porcelain plaque which was made for Ȧmenemȧpt, , "a scribe and overseer of the offerings of the Lord of the Two Lands" (B.M. 6133), is a very fine example of the votive stele of the XXth or XXIst dynasty.

FOUNDATION DEPOSITS

AMONG the ceremonies that were performed when the foundation was laid of a temple, or pyramid, or fortress, was the deposit, in a secure and secret part of it, of a series of pieces of each material that was used in the construction of the building. And the founder's name was usually cut or stamped on each piece. The deposit that Rameses II placed in the foundation of one of his buildings at Thebes included models of his bricks, of which a specimen has come down to us, viz., one in green-glazed faïence. The brick measures 14¼ inches by 7¼ inches by 2⅝ inches, and on the obverse and reverse are the king's prenomen and nomen in cartouches surmounted by disk and plumes, . On the edges are painted in black the king's Horus-, Nebti- and Rā-names and some of his titles, *e.g.*, Meri-Maāt, Meri-neteru, etc. (B.M. 49234). Examples of slabs of stone are B.M. 29951 and 29952. A foundation deposit from a temple built by Psammetichus I at Tall Dafannah (Daphnae, Tahpanhes) in the Eastern Delta included a rectangular faïence plaque inscribed , a mud brick, rectangular plaques of gold, silver, copper, lead, carnelian, jasper, lapis-lazuli, each inscribed either with the king's prenomen or nomen, and several fragments of lead and copper ore. The faïence plaque is $2\frac{3}{4}$ inches long, and the mud brick $1\frac{1}{2}$ inches; all the other plaques are much smaller (B.M. 23556). A deposit from the south-west corner of the temple which Åāḥmes (Amasis II) built at Nabêshah included three models of bricks stamped  or , plaques of gold, silver, carnelian, lapis-lazuli, copper, lead and limestone (B.M. 23503).

The custom of placing foundation deposits under the corners of pyramids was adopted by kings of Nubia and the Northern Sûdân, and thanks to the munificence of the Sûdân Government, the British Museum possesses a valuable series of the foundation deposits which were excavated by Dr. Reisner at Nûrî, a famous pyramid field near the foot of the Fourth Cataract. The following is a description of three typical deposits:—The deposit of king **Ånlåmen** consisted of (1) Six blue faïence plaques, three stamped, and three moulded, containing the prenomen and nomen of the king—Ānkhkarā and Ånlåmen; (2) a blue-glazed faïence brick inscribed "Son of Rā, Ånlåmen, beloved of Hathor, giver of life"; (3) Rectangular plaques of gold, silver, copper and lead, inscribed with the king's prenomen, and models of slabs of mother-of-emerald, lapis-lazuli, alabaster, crystal and red stone similarly inscribed (B.M. 55562–63); (4) A faïence cartouche stamped 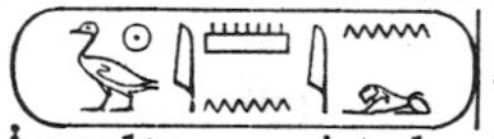.

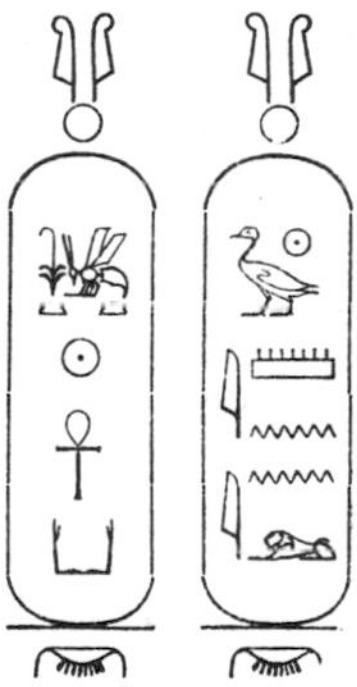

The deposit of king **Åspelta** consisted of—(1) Two faïence plaques inscribed with prenomen and nomen of the king; (2) Faïence models of two bricks inscribed 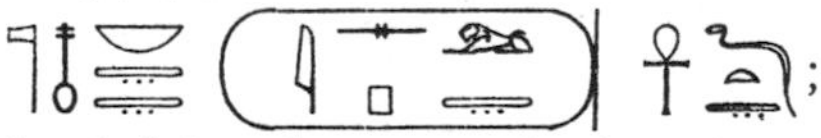; (3) Rectangular bricks of copper, lead, red stone, mother-of-emerald, lapis-lazuli, crystal, alabaster and faïence, each inscribed with one of the king's names; (4) a semi-circular piece of alabaster , inscribed Åspelta, and a piece of crystal $1\frac{1}{16}$ inches long, with a thread worked on it like a screw without point. These probably represent tools that were used in the construction of the pyramid (B.M. 55564). The deposit of **Mal-uaib-Åmen,** whose prenomen was 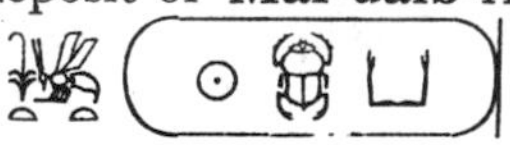, Kheperkarā, consisted

of (1) A faïence cartouche, coarsely shaped, stamped with his son-of-Rā name ; (2) a rectangular faïence plaque uninscribed; (3) Fifteen rectangular bricks of bronze, lead, mother-of-emerald, lapis-lazuli, haematite (?), etc., of different sizes; (4) a white stone , and bronze models of seven tools and other objects used in the construction of the pyramid (B.M. 55573). No object has been found among any set of foundation deposits which suggests that the deposit was other than purely commemorative—in other words, no deposit carried with it any magical protection of the building under which it was found.

OBELISKS

THOUGH the word obelisk is derived from the Greek ὀβελίσκος, a "little spear," the object itself is purely of Egyptian origin, and is called in the hieroglyphs *tekhen*, . The obelisk, or "sun-stone," as it is sometimes called, was assuredly connected with the worship of the sun, but whether it was actually worshipped as a god, or merely regarded as an earthly abode of the Sun-god or the solar spirit, is not clear. The oldest form of it is found in the tombs of the IVth dynasty. In these limestone obelisks are found in pairs, one standing on a small raised platform on each side of the stele, or the false door, through which the Ka of the deceased came from its tomb to enjoy the offerings made to it. Their presence was supposed to keep malignant spirits and influences from passing through the stele and down to the mummy chamber to harm the dead. In the great solar temple of User-en-Rā, or Nuserrā , a king of the Vth dynasty, the Sun-god Rā was represented by an obelisk standing on a sort of truncated pyramid, which in its turn stood on a sub-plinth. On its eastern side stood an alabaster altar, on which were sacrificed victims, probably captives taken in battle, whose blood was carried off by channels along the north side into alabaster bowls which were placed to receive it. As obelisks were used to protect the dead, so

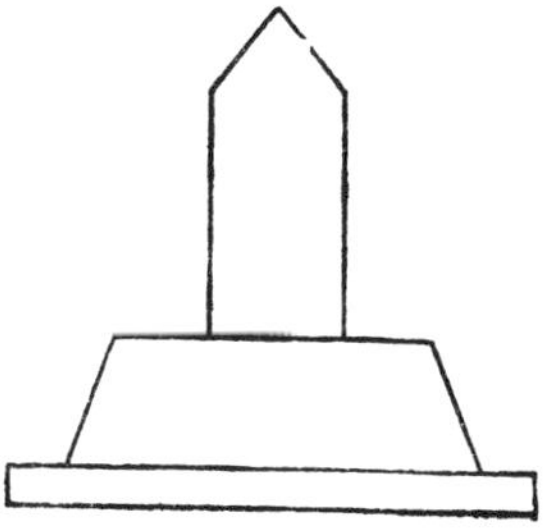

they were employed to protect the great buildings and temples which were built by some of the kings of the XIIth, XVIIIth and XIXth dynasties. The oldest survival of these is the obelisk which Usertsen (Senusert) I set up at Heliopolis; as the lowest part and its plinth are buried its exact height cannot be stated, but about 67 feet of it are visible.[1] This king set up a pair of granite obelisks, of which this obelisk is one, before the great " House of the Sun," which he rebuilt, and he covered their tops (pyramidions) with copper cases. Both were standing when 'Abd al-Laṭîf visited the site A.D. 1200. Usertsen I also set up a red granite obelisk of unusual type at Ebgig, or Begig, a place near the modern town Madînat al-Fayyûm. It was rectangular in shape with a rounded, not pointed, end, and judging from the ruins of it which are now lying there it must have been about 50 feet high. The obelisks set up by the kings of the XVIIIth dynasty taper gradually from base to pyramidion and are abundantly decorated with inscriptions and reliefs. Thothmes I set up obelisks at Elephantine, but only a fragment of one remains; he set up a pair at Karnak, but only one bears an inscription of his. Ḥatshepsut set up four obelisks, but only one of them is still standing; the upper part of its fellow lies near it. According to the inscription on its pedestal the queen caused the pair to be quarried at Aswân, brought to Cairo, and erected in the space of seven months—a marvellous achievement. The height of her obelisk now standing is said to be about 98 feet.[2] Thothmes III set up several obelisks at Karnak, but not one is to be seen there at the present day. The largest of these is probably that which now stands in the piazza of St. John Lateran in Rome. It was made by the command of Thothmes III, but was only set up several years later by Thothmes IV, who added his own inscription to the one which he had cut on it in the name of his grandfather. It was taken to Rome and set up in the Circus Maximus by Constantius, A.D. 357. It was thrown down and broke into three pieces, but was set up where it now is by Pope Sixtus V. It is a little more than 105 feet in height and is the highest Egyptian obelisk in the world. Thothmes III also set up a pair of obelisks in the great temple of Heliopolis, but they were removed to Alexandria and erected before the Roman temple (Caesarion) there when Barbarus[3] was eparch of Egypt, in the year B.C. 612.[4] One of these, which had fallen, and which was commonly known as Cleopatra's Needle, was given to the British by Muḥammad 'Alî early in the XIXth century. It was not removed from the place where it lay, near the railway station for Ramleh, until 1877, when, thanks to the munificence of Sir Erasmus Wilson, it was transported to England and set up on the Thames Embankment between Charing Cross

[1] A scale model of this obelisk made by Mr. J. Bonomi is exhibited in the Fifth Egyptian Room in the British Museum (55199).

[2] A scale model of this obelisk made by Mr. J. Bonomi is exhibited in the Fifth Egyptian Room of the British Museum (55198).

[3] *I.e.*, P. Rubrius Barbarus.

[4] See Merriam, *The Greek and Latin Inscriptions on the Obelisk Crab*, New York, 1873, p. 49; and Dittenberger, *Inscriptiones Selectae*, No. 656, Vol. I, p. 365.

Bridge and Waterloo Bridge.[1] The inscriptions of Thothmes III run down the centre of the sides, and those on both sides of them were added by Rameses II. The other obelisk was given to America and was removed by Gorringe to New York, where it was set up in the Central Park.[2] As was to be expected, Rameses II set up many obelisks at Tanis, and a pair at Karnak, and a pair at Luxor; one of the Luxor obelisks is still *in situ*, but the other is in Paris. As stated above he added bombastic inscriptions to an obelisk of Thothmes III, and he did not scruple to "usurp" the obelisks which his father Seti I set up at Heliopolis. With the end of the XIXth dynasty the custom of setting up massive obelisks of granite or basalt seems to have died out, and kings and officials contented themselves with pairs of comparatively small stone obelisks. Nekht-Ḥer-ḥeb, about B.C. 378, set up a pair of black basalt obelisks at the door of the sanctuary of the temple of "Thoth, the twice great," , to whom they were dedicated. Where the temple was situated is uncertain, but they were taken to Cairo towards the close of the XVIIIth century, and set up before one of the mosques. On the conclusion of the treaty made by General Hutchinson they passed into the possession of the British in 1801, and were sent to the British Museum by King George III in 1802 (B.M. 919, 920). Ȧmenḥetep II, the successor of Thothmes III, set up no large obelisks at Thebes, but it seems tolerably certain that he used obelisks to decorate the shrines of the small temples which he built in the Thebaïd. One of these still exists, and is now preserved in the Egyptian Collection at Alnwick Castle. It is one of a pair that this king dedicated to Khnem-Rā and was found in a village in the Thebaïd; it is made of red granite and is 7 feet 3 inches in height. It was given to Lord Prudhoe by Muḥammad 'Alî in 1838,[3] and when it arrived in England it was set up at Syon House, Brentford.

It is clear from what has been said above that: (1) From the Vth dynasty onwards obelisks were associated with the cult of Rā and other solar gods; (2) kings like Thothmes III regarded the dedication of obelisks to the gods as acts of worship that were acceptable to the gods; (3) in the minds of the Egyptians the idea of protection was associated with a pair of obelisks. But under the rule of the Ptolemies an obelisk was set up to commemorate some special event, as, for example, the granite obelisk that Mr. J. W. Bankes excavated on the Island of Philae in 1815. This obelisk is

[1] A handy popular account of this obelisk is given in King, *Cleopatra's Needle*, London, 1886. For Birch's description and translation of the texts on it see *Athenaeum*, October 27th and November 3rd, 1877. The story of its transport to England is given in *Engineering*, 1877–78.

[2] For the account of the transport see Gorringe, *Egyptian Obelisks*, New York, 1882.

[3] See Birch, *Catalogue*, p. 344.

about 21 feet high, and stands on a plinth, or pedestal, about 10 feet high; it was taken to Alexandria by Belzoni and thence to London, and it now stands in the park of the Bankes family at Kingston Hall in Dorsetshire, where it was "inaugurated" by F.M. the Duke of Wellington about 1840.[1] On each side of the obelisk is a hieroglyphic inscription recording the names and titles of Ptolemy IX Euergetes II, and those of Cleopatra his wife and Cleopatra his sister. On the pedestal are three Greek inscriptions containing (1) a complaint to Ptolemy IX to the effect that they (the priests) are unable to provide the necessary offerings to the gods, because they have to provide food for the throng of officials who visit the Island of Philae and force them to supply them with whatever they need; (2) a copy of the letter that Numenius sent to the priests telling them that the king had sent a letter to Lochus, the strategos of the Thebaïd, on the subject of their complaint, and giving them the king's permission to set up a stele; (3) a copy of Ptolemy's letter to Lochus, ordering him to prevent the priests from being annoyed by anyone in respect of the matters about which they had complained to him A special interest attaches to this obelisk, for it was from it that Mr. Bankes and Dr. Young identified the name of Cleopatra before 1818.[2]

The obelisk was also used as a funerary memorial stone in some cases, and took the place of the ordinary sepulchral stele. A good example of this is the little stone obelisk of Årȧ, , which tells us that the deceased was the Kher ḥeb, , of Heliopolis; he was a priest of Rā, and it is fitting that his memorial-stone should take the form of the famous "Sun-stone" of Heliopolis (B.M. 495). The upper part of the stone obelisk, B.M. 1512, is of interest, for it seems to have been dedicated to the Four Winds—Qebui, Shehbui, Henkhisenui and Hutchaiui; on the sides are the well-known symbols

[1] Copies of the Greek and Egyptian texts inscribed on this obelisk, with English translations of the same, will be found in my work on the Rosetta Stone, *The Decrees of Memphis and Canopus*, London, 1904, Vol. I, p. 135 ff. I visited the monument in Oct. 1914, with Mr. Basil Levett, and examined all the inscriptions that were within reach. The obelisk is handsomely mounted, but it stands in the park and is wholly unprotected from the abundant rains that fall in the winter and from frost. The side that faces the prevailing wind showed many signs of weathering, and the hieroglyphic inscriptions which are cut on the faces of the obelisk in perpendicular lines were much fainter than they were when Belzoni made his copy of them for Mr. Bankes. This copy was printed in a thin quarto volume, and from it I made the transcript that is printed in my Rosetta Stone. The late Lord Carnarvon, who had seen and examined the obelisk, was most anxious that it should be removed to some place under cover where it would be sheltered from rain and frost. I understood him to say that he had opened negotiations with its possessor, with the view of acquiring it by purchase or otherwise, but his death on April 5th, 1923, prevented him from achieving his wish.

[2] A scale model of the Bankes Obelisk is exhibited in the Sixth Egyptian Room of the British Museum (55204). It was given by Mrs. Mangles in 1878.

of the winds which were common in the Graeco-Roman Period. The obelisk as a sepulchral stele was also known in the Peninsula of Sinai, a fact which is proved by the obelisk with a rounded top (like the Obelisk of Ebgig in the Fayyûm) that was set up in Wâdî Maghârah as a memorial of Sebek-ḥer-ḥeb, , who died in the 44th year of the reign of Åmenemḥat III (B.M. 179, 180).[1]

The custom of erecting obelisks seems to have passed from Egypt to Axum in Ethiopia, but it is probable that in that country the native idea associated with the obelisk was different from that which was paramount in the Delta when the form of the worship of Rā that prevailed at Heliopolis was established there. The common word for obelisk in Ethiopic is *ḥawelet*, ሐወልት :, and the plural ሐወላት : *ḥawelât* = ὀβελίσκοι in Job xli, 21 (in the LXX). In Jer. l, 13 (LXX) στύλους Ἡλίου πόλεως is rendered by ዐምደ : ሀገረ : ፀሐይ : "pillars of the city of the Sun." The oldest obelisks at Axum are merely roughly hewn stones which seem to be connected with the primitive sun-worship of Ethiopia and Arabia, but the more modern are elaborately carved to represent forts or strong buildings of some kind, and some of them are 60 feet in height. A few years ago about forty obelisks were still standing, and about as many more had been overthrown and were lying where they had fallen. The great number of the obelisks at Axum suggests that they were sepulchral in character, and though some of them may have been set up in religious buildings, which are in ruins, many of them must be sepulchral or commemorative in character.[2]

The method employed by the ancient Egyptians in raising their great obelisks has formed the subject of many theories and speculations. Some have imagined that the Egyptians possessed powerful mechanical appliances which they used for the transport and raising of them, but it seems quite clear that such cannot have been the case. The evidence of the monuments does not support this view, and we are justified in assuming that both the tools used and the method employed were of the most primitive character. Both Sir John Aird and Sir Benjamin Baker thought that the method employed was this : The foundation for the obelisk and the pedestal on which it was to stand were first prepared, and then a huge mound of sand was heaped up on one side, the sand being kept from overflowing on to them by a low wall of mud bricks. The huge shaft of granite out of which the obelisk was to be cut was then dragged up on the mound of sand and laid in a horizontal position. The sand from the side of the mound near the pedestal was removed, and the

[1] A considerable amount of information about obelisks will be found in Zoega, *De Origine et Usu Obeliscorum*, Rome, 1797, fol.

[2] On the obelisks of Axum see Bent, *Sacred City of the Ethiopians*, London, 1893 ; Wylde, *Modern Abyssinia*, London, 1901 ; Glaser, *Die Abessinier in Arabien*, Munich, 1895 ; and Littman and Krencker, *Vorbericht*, Berlin, 1906.

end of the granite shaft allowed to descend gradually until it rested on the pedestal, when the shaft was pulled into an upright position by ropes. The shaping and polishing of the obelisk and the cutting of the inscriptions were carried out after the shaft in the rough was standing in position. Both these eminent engineering authorities were convinced that the Egyptians knew not the "jack," and the "crab" and the winch, and that they could never have made "sheers" long enough and strong enough to support the weight of any large obelisk. And both believed that only by the method outlined above could the obelisks have been set up. On a matter of this kind the practical engineer must be listened to with respect, for no living Egyptologist possesses sufficient technical knowledge to decide whether such a method is or is not possible.

Quite recently the question of the method by which the obelisks were set up in position has been raised by Mr. R. Engelbach, Chief Inspector of Antiquities of Upper Egypt, and in his recently published book[1] the theory which he propounds has much in common with that of Sir John Aird and Sir Benjamin Baker. His view is "that the obelisk was not let down over the edge of an embankment, but down a funnel-shaped pit *in* the end of it, the lowering being done by removing sand, with which the pit had been filled, from galleries leading into the bottom of it, and so allowing the obelisk to settle slowly down. Taking this as the basis of the method, the form of the pit resolves itself into a tapering square-sectioned funnel —rather like a petrol-funnel—fairly wide at the top, but very little larger than the base of the obelisk at the bottom. The obelisk is introduced into the funnel on a curved way leading gradually from the surface of the embankment until it engages smoothly with the hither wall of the funnel. The sand is removed by men with baskets through galleries leading from the bottom of the funnel to convenient places outside the embankment. . . . It is more than probable, therefore, that men would go down with the obelisk and, by digging, correct any tendency of the obelisk to lean sideways and to ensure—if necessary, by inserting baulks (struts) between the base of the obelisk and the opposite wall of the funnel—that it did not jam against it. . . . As soon as the obelisk had come down into its notch, men would enter through the gallery leading in from the end of the embankment, and clear every particle of sand from under the base, before it was pulled upright. Any tendency to rock after passing its dead-centre could be avoided by filling the space between the obelisk and the further wall of the funnel with coarse brushwood to act as a sort of cushion." Mr. Engelbach's text is illustrated by a number of excellent photographs of unusual interest.

[1] *The Problem of the Obelisks*, London, 1923, p. 67 ff.

THE TOMB STATUE OR KA FIGURE (?)

The Egyptians believed that every man possessed a spiritual duplicate of himself which lived within him from the moment of his birth to the moment of his death ; to this duplicate they gave the name KA (plural KAU) and the hieroglyph, 𓂓, which represents it is a conventional representation of a human breast with two outstretched arms. It was certainly believed to survive the death of the body to which it belonged, and it is assuming little to believe that it existed before the body to which it joined itself was born. When it joined the body it became its mental, moral and spiritual individuality and disposition, its rational guide, its far-seeing protector, and in some respects it acted as its guardian angel. What was supposed to happen to the Ka when the body died is not clear, but it is certain that it went on living, and the Egyptians, from the earliest times, made provision for its maintenance, because it was believed to be the most important of all man's immortal entities.[1] It seems as if in the Pre-dynastic and Early Archaïc Periods the Egyptians believed that the KA remained in the dead body, and lived on the offerings which were placed on the graves or in the little chambers above the pits which were dug in the hills under the early dynasties. But the primitive Egyptians came to the conclusion that a figure or statue must be provided for the Ka to dwell in, and that it was necessary to take almost as much care for its preservation as of the body itself. The oldest model of a human body known in the Valley of the Nile is B.M. 50945. It was found at Khizâm in Upper Egypt, together with the mud models of kneeling and standing steatopygous women with pendent breasts, which are exhibited in the Sixth Egyptian Room in the British Museum. It was found under a large earthenware covering, which seemed to have been built up piece by piece over it and the bones of a human body and a pot or two which were close to it.

In the later maṣṭabah tombs of the Old Kingdom at Ṣaḳḳârah and Gîzah, and the rock-hewn tombs at Aswân and other places, the Ka figure was formed of stone, and was made to represent the deceased as closely as possible. The features were most carefully modelled, the eyes were inlaid, and the colour and shape of the wig, necklace, dagger, tunic, etc., were reproduced with scrupulous accuracy. When small the Ka figure was set in a cavity in a wall of the tomb, and a large one was accommodated with a specially constructed enclosure formed of slabs of stone. In an enclosure of this kind an opening was provided, so that the Ka within the figure could enjoy the sight of the offerings and of his friends who were still living, and the smell of the incense. Examples of such figures are exhibited in the British Museum (Fourth Eg. Room). This

[1] See Maspero in *Memnon,* Vol. VI, p. 129.

wooden figure is 3 feet 8 inches in height, and was found in a cavity in the granite stele in the maṣṭabah of an official of king Khufu, whose name is not known. It was excavated at Ṣaḳḳârah under Mariette's direction by his foreman of works, called "Rubî," and the workmen, at once recognizing in it a striking likeness to the Shêkh al-Balad, or "Shêkh of the Village," then in authority at

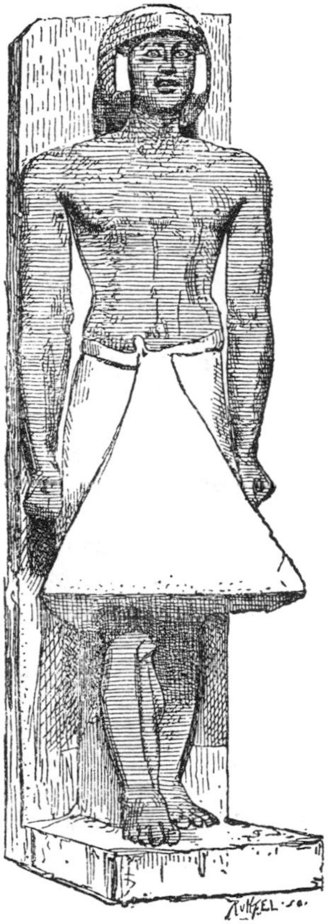

Statue of Ti. Vth dynasty.

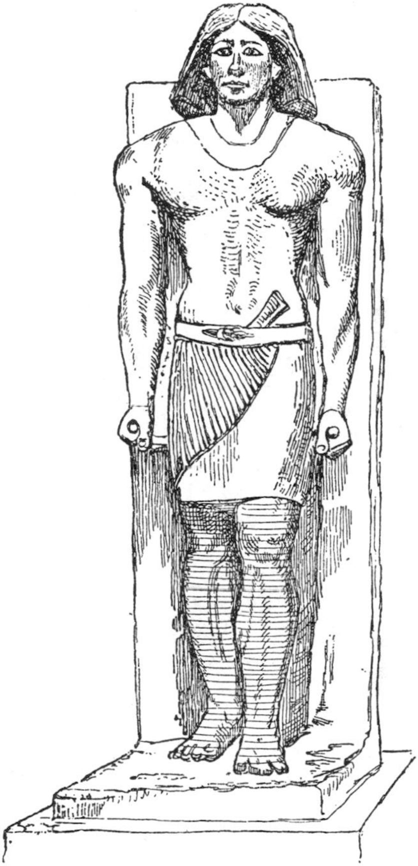

Statue of Rā-Nefer. Vth dynasty.

Ṣaḳḳârah, promptly called it "Shêkh al-Balad," and by this name it has been known ever since. The two illustrations above give a good idea of the Ka statues of the Vth dynasty at Ṣaḳḳârah.

When the Egyptians decided that a figure or statue must be made for the tomb, they found it convenient to provide a special table on which the offerings made to it were to be placed. This table was the Ḥetep, [hieroglyph], which has been described elsewhere. The necessity for giving offerings to the Ka regularly and continually, millions of times, , was impressed on every Egyptian from his childhood, for if a man failed in this duty the Ka might be compelled by hunger and thirst to drink dirty water and eat filth. In the Book of the Dead (Chapters LII and CLXXXIX) the deceased himself says, "Make me not eat what I abominate; filth is an abomination to me. Let it not touch my body, let me not be obliged to handle it or to walk on it with my sandals. Let my bread be made of white grain, and my beer from red grain. Let me not be sprinkled with filthy water (*i.e.*, urine)."

Under the XIth and XIIth dynasties Ka figures and statues were made of painted wood; typical examples of the XIth dynasty (or earlier) are B.M. 55583 and 55584. One of the finest examples known of the XIIth dynasty is that of king Auȧbrā Ḥer , which was found at Dahshûr by de Morgan. This figure had a model upon his head, and his head-dress, eyebrows and eyelids, beard-rest, neck-ornaments, nipples, and the nails of his hands and feet were covered with thin plates of gold. Round the waist was a thin girdle of gold, the ends of which reached half-way down his thighs.[1] This figure stood in a wooden shrine nearly 7 feet in height, and the inscriptions were painted in green upon thin plates of gold set in plaster. Under the New Kingdom Ka statues, made of wood and painted black, were placed in royal tombs; specimens of these are B.M. 854, the Ka statue of Seti I, B.M. 882, the Ka statue of Rameses II, and B.M. 883, the Ka statue of an unknown king. The Ka figures of private persons were made of gold, silver, bronze, wood, steatite, faïence and terra-cotta, and among the smaller examples B.M. 56842, 32743, 32732 and 32733 are worthy of note. The custom of placing a Ka figure in the tomb seems to have lasted until the Egyptians ceased to mummify their dead. The preservation of the body was necessary for the welfare and existence of the Ba, , or soul, and the provision of an abode and bread and beer was equally necessary for the life of the Ka. Unfortunately the ideas which the Neolithic Egyptians held about the Ka and its origin are unknown.[2]

[1] De Morgan, *Fouilles à Dahchour*, Vienna, 1895, p. 91, and pls. XXXIII and XXXIV.

[2] Some authorities hold the view that the figure or statue of the deceased in the tomb had nothing to do with the Ka.

Painted wooden tomb-figure of an official who flourished under the IXth or Xth dynasty. From a tomb at Asyuṭ. B.M. Fourth Egyptian Room.

Green stone statue of an official wearing a gold crown, mask, and chain of gold with a figure of the goddess Maāt. Date uncertain. From the Delta. B.M. Egyptian Gallery.

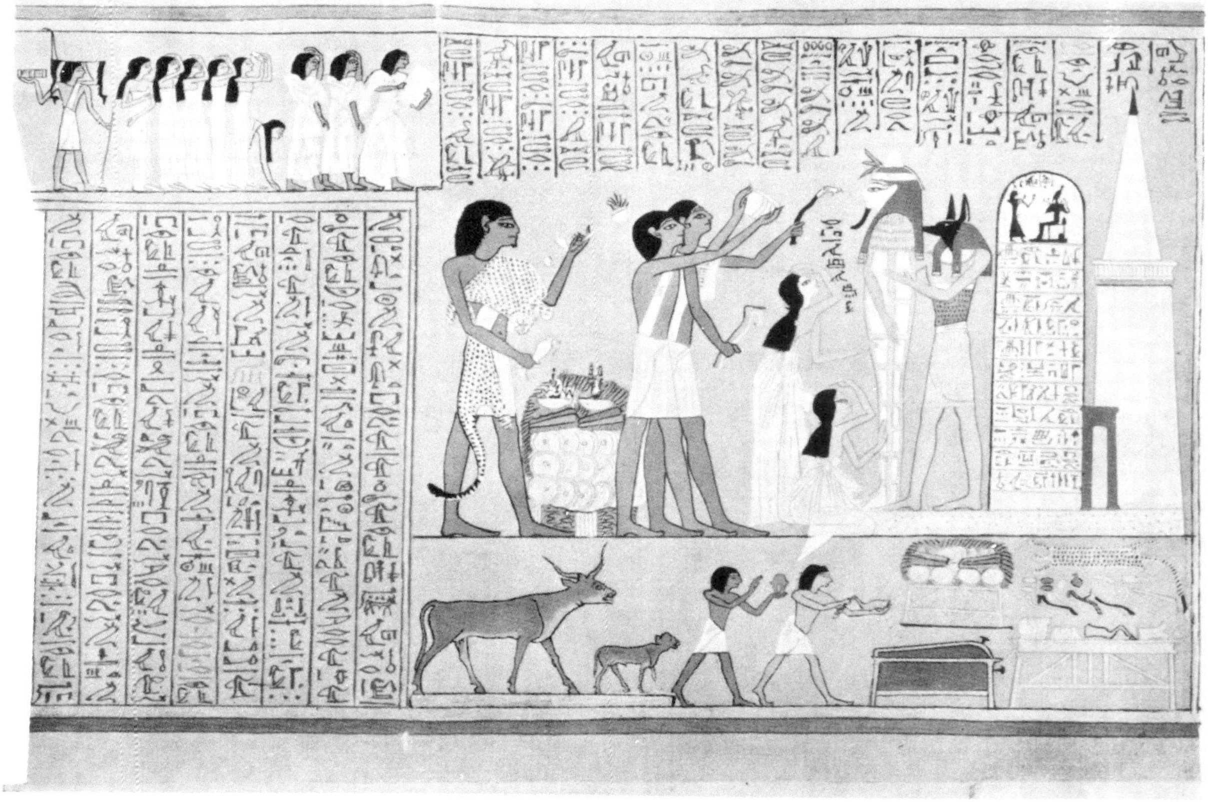

The Kher-ḥeb priest and his assistants performing the ceremony of "Opening the Mouth" on the mummy of Hu-nefer at the door of the tomb. Nasha, wife of the deceased, and her daughter before the mummy which is being received into the tomb by Anubis. XIXth dynasty. From the Papyrus of Hunefer in the British Museum (No. 9901).

MODELS OF OBJECTS USED AT THE OPENING OF THE MOUTH

A GOOD example of a set of such objects is B.M. 5526. Here in the face of a rectangular slab of limestone, with rounded back, are cut cavities to hold the PESH-EN-KEF instrument, , two stone knives, two bottles, and four vases for unguents. All the cavities save one, viz., that for a knife, contain the objects for which they were made. The Pesh-en-kef is $3\frac{3}{8}$ inches in length, the greyish green stone is $1\frac{5}{8}$ inches in length, the crystal and black stone bottles are $2\frac{1}{2}$ inches and $2\frac{1}{4}$ inches high respectively, and the four rock-crystal vases are each about $1\frac{1}{4}$ inches high, and only one of them is bored to a depth sufficient for use. The Pesh-en-kef was regarded as an object possessing magical powers even in Neolithic times, a fact which is proved by the example in flint (B.M. 37279). The two small stone knives (?) represent the " iron of the South " and the " iron of the North " respectively, or the two *neterti* instruments, . The white and black bottles are symbols of the purifying liquids of the South and North, and the four small crystal vases symbolize the four unguents.

A somewhat similar group of models in the British Museum (23222) is worthy of note ; in this group also one of the knives (?) is wanting. The objects are laid in hollows in a board measuring 6 inches by $4\frac{7}{8}$ inches, and the coarseness and irregularity of the work suggest that they belong to a very early period. Another group of models of this class is found fitted into the pedestal of a statue preserved at Alnwick Castle. Dr. Birch's description of them is as follows : " Figure of a man walking, wearing long striated hair, rude and coarse features, wearing a tunic, *shenti*, his left foot advanced, both hands pendent and clenched. He stands on a pedestal in shape of an altar of libations, rectangular, with rectangular spout ; on the pedestal are laid the following small models, two cylindroid jar-shaped vases, and a small one between two bottles like *prochooi* of dark stone, an object like an amulet of two ostrich feathers united of red material, and two other objects like knife-blades, the use and meaning of which are unknown. The figure is of veined alabaster (aragonite), and the pedestal, which is in the shape of a table of offerings, is of calcareous stone ; height of figure 15 inches, length of pedestal $14\frac{1}{2}$ inches, breadth $8\frac{1}{2}$ inches, depth $4\frac{1}{2}$ inches. From Abydos." Dr. Birch assigned the group[1] to the XIIth dynasty, but it undoubtedly belongs to the Old Kingdom. The object like " two ostrich feathers united " is, of course, the Pesh-en-kef, which has already been described.

[1] Birch, *Catalogue of the Collection of Egyptian Antiquities at Alnwick Castle*, London, 1880, No. 505, p. 64.

THE GRAIN BED OF OSIRIS

AMONG the objects of a miscellaneous character that are often seen heaped up in the outer rooms, or "offering chambers," of Theban tombs, excavators have frequently found a sort of "mattress," about 5 feet 4 inches long, and about 1 foot 10 inches in width, of much the same thickness as the thick padded quilt which is found in modern houses all over the East. This "mattress" usually lies within a rough rectangular wooden framework, which in a way suggests the upper part of a Sûdânî or Egyptian 'anḳarîb,' عَنْقَرِيب, or bedstead. When it is opened it is seen to consist of layers of papyrus and linen, and a large quantity of dust and dried grain, and it is now known that the object was a copy of the so-called "bed of Osiris," and that it was placed in the tomb to assist the resurrection of the deceased. The bed was made by sowing grain, probably barley, in a layer of moist earth which was laid upon a foundation of linen and papyrus matting; the grain was sown in the form of a figure of Osiris wearing the White Crown and having his usual attributes. In the darkness of the tomb the grain sprouted quickly, and when the shoots were a few inches high, layers of linen were laid over them, and linen cords, four or five in number, in imitation of the outer bands of a mummy, were tied round the whole bed,[1] which was left in the tomb. Now, Osiris had inherited the attributes of the old Grain-god Neper, , and had under the New Kingdom become the Grain-god of all Egypt, and not only the source of the harvest, but the harvest itself, and the food of his followers, living and dead. The barley which was placed in the tomb in the layer of earth symbolized the body of the deceased which, like the grain, contained a living germ. And the sprouting of the grain had the effect of making the dead body send forth from itself the germ of life that was in it in the form of the spirit body, which passed into the kingdom of Osiris, and lived henceforth with the gods and the spirits and souls of the blessed. The barley was the dead Osiris, and the sproutings from it were Osiris who, in the form of living plants, had risen from the dead.

The walls of the temple of Osiris at Denderah contain a long inscription[2] which deals with the festivals of the god, and describes at great length the making of a figure of Osiris of grain paste. The

[1] See Quibell, *Tomb of Yuaa and Thuiu*, p. 36; Daressy, *Catalogue*, No. 24661; Davis, *Tomb of Iouiya and Touiyou*, p. 45; and Wiedemann, *Museon*, N.S. IV, 1903, pp. 111–123.

[2] Portions of the text have been published by Brugsch and Dümichen (*Recueil*, I, 15, 16), Mariette, *Denderah*, tom. IV, pll. 35–39, and a summary of the contents of the first 32 lines by Lauth, *Aeg. Zeit.*, 1866, p. 66. The complete text, with a French translation, has been published by Loret, *Recueil de Travaux*, tom. III, IV and V.

grain was mixed with various substances and kneaded into a paste which was placed in a mould made in the form of a figure of the god. This mould was placed in the sanctuary, and on a certain day it was moistened with water, and a few days later the grain in the paste sprouted and sent forth shoots of young plants. The germination of the grain in the paste figure of Osiris in the mould was believed to produce the germination of all the grain sown in the fields in every part of Egypt, and also of the grain that was enclosed in the Osiris beds in the tombs. According to a text[1] in the tomb of Neferḥetep at Thebes, which has been translated by Gardiner,[2] the grain in the Osiris bed was moistened ceremonially on the eighteenth day of the fourth month of the season of Shemu,  (July–August), and the festival lasted until the twenty-fifth day, *i.e.*, from the eve of the eighteenth to the morning of the twenty-fifth—seven full days. This statement is followed by the ḥeka, or words of magical power, which had to be recited over the bed to make it fulfil its functions. The ḥeka consisted of an address to the deceased, who is identified with Osiris and Horus and his four sons, and he is adjured to rise up on his left side, as did Osiris, for Geb will open his eyes, and make rigid his legs, and he is assured that his heart, which is his mother, shall be given its right place in his breast. But the festival in connection with the sprouting of the grain in the figure of Osiris in the mould and the Lamentation for Osiris was celebrated in the fourth month of the season Akhet (November–December) and at Denderah lasted from the twenty-second to the twenty-sixth day. In the other great sanctuaries of Egypt, *e.g.*, Abydos, Memphis and Mendes, the festival was celebrated on days earlier in the month.

MODELS OF BOATS

THE primitive Egyptians believed that the abode of departed spirits was situated in a region which was remote from their country, and that the souls of the dead could travel thither both by land and by water. But the route by land was in one place or more interrupted by a river, which the dead had to cross, and the heaven that they hoped to reach was intersected by canals and streams. Therefore it was absolutely necessary to provide the dead with boats in the Other World. This was done by making models of boats and putting them in the tombs with the dead, so that when they arrived at the great river in the Ṭuat, or at the shore of the lake or sea in which the Island of the primitive god (and later of Osiris) was placed, the

[1] See Virey, *Sept Tombeaux Thébains*, Paris, 1891 (Vol. V of the *Mémoires de la Mission Archéologique Française au Caire*).

[2] *Tomb of Amenemhēt*, London, 1915, p. 115.

spirit of the boat might convey the soul to the place where it fain would be. In the Pyramid Texts souls were carried across the rivers by Ḥerefḥaf, , the ferryman of Osiris, who would, however, only ferry over to the Island of Osiris the souls of the righteous. And even the righteous man was not ferried over unless he knew the ḥeka, or word of power, that would set both the ferryman and the ferry-boat itself in motion. The custom of placing models of boats for the use of the dead in tombs is very old, certainly as old as the Neolithic Period in Egypt, as is proved by the light-brown mud boat painted with red lines that was found at Naḳâdah.[1] The custom was observed carefully under the Old and Middle Kingdoms, and models of boats, chiefly made of wood, were placed in the tombs until the end of the XIIth dynasty ; sometimes these models were so large that they could not be placed in the tomb, and they were therefore deposited near the tombs and covered over with sand. Thus three large boats were found buried in the sand near the Great Pyramid of Khufu, the largest being, according to M. Daressy,[2] about 195 feet long, 16 feet beam, and 16 feet deep. Such " models " were in truth veritable river-going boats, and would have carried a large crew. Another huge " model " of a river-boat was found near the tomb of Åmenḥetep II in the Valley of the Tombs of the Kings, but as it disappeared one night in a most mysterious fashion, no measurements of it, so far as I know, were taken. Few, if any, of the small wooden boats which we may assume to have been placed in the tombs of private individuals under the Old Kingdom have come down to us, but numerous examples of those of the Middle Kingdom are to be seen in national museums and in private collections. Some of these contain models of the mummy and a few attendants, and perhaps a priest also, and a bull for sacrifice. In others we see the deceased arrayed in white and seated in a small cabin, and the boat, having both a sail and oars, is supposed to be in motion. To place a model of a boat in a tomb was a simple matter, but to cause it to move over the river and lakes of the Other World it was necessary to sacrifice a bull, and without such a sacrifice it was hopeless to expect the boat to move. To prove to those who were concerned with such matters in the Other World that the bull had been sacrificed, the picture of the bull's hide was either painted on the walls of the cabin in which the figure of the deceased sits, or the cabin itself is actually covered over with the hide of the bull, which is fixed down around the edge by a row of studs.[3]

It is possible that the large boats found near the Great Pyramid were war-boats, and that it was actually believed that the king in

[1] See the description by Schäfer in *Aeg. Zeit.*, 1896, p. 161.
[2] *Bulletin de l'Institut Égypt.*, tom. V, Ser. 3, p. 37 ff.
[3] Garstang, *Burial Customs*, p. 84.

his journey towards the Other World might need an armed escort. Under the Middle Empire many of the small models of boats have on board armed figures. Thus in a wooden boat, about 3 feet 6 inches in length, found at Bani-Ḥasan in Upper Egypt, the crew proper consisted of eleven sailors, viz., a steersman, a look-out man, three sail-men and six rowers. These were protected by a Sûdânî man, who stands at the bows and holds in his right hand two arrows, and in his left a bow nearly as tall as himself. Near the stern is a small deck-house, on the outside of which hang two shields, and on the inside a case for spears; inside the deck-house are two figures of men, to whom the spears and shields belong, quietly seated playing draughts.[1] It is clear that these men had nothing to do with the working of the boat, and that they were amusing themselves until such time as their services were required in raiding a village for supplies or resisting an attack on the boat.

Though the placing of models of boats in the tombs of private persons ceased after the XIIth dynasty, the belief in the need of boats by the dead did not disappear with the dropping of the custom, and the priests endeavoured to provide them by magic and the use of words of power. They included in the Book of the Dead the "Chapter of bringing along (*i.e.*, providing) a boat in the Other World" (Chapter XCIX), and they drew above it a Vignette in which the deceased is seen standing in a boat with the sail hoisted. It is provided with two oars, which are attached to posts fixed near the stern, and as the deceased Nu is standing doing nothing, and the boat has no crew, we must suppose that the boat is moving by means of some power within itself. And this supposition is correct. The boat of Ḥerefḥaf, the celestial ferryman of the Pyramid Texts, refused to carry over to the Kingdom of Osiris any soul that was not righteous, and that could not prove its freedom from the taint of sin. But for the deceased who wished to sail in the boat depicted in the papyrus another test was prepared; he was obliged to know the names of the stream on which it sailed, and the banks on each side of it, and the landing-place, and the wind that moved it, and also the names of every part of the boat. When he approached the boat each part of it called upon him to declare its name, and when he had done so he was free to enter the boat and sail over to Sekhet-Åaru, where he would find meat and drink, and be at liberty to take any form he pleased, and go where he pleased. Other Chapters in the Theban Recension enabled him to enter the Boat of Rā and to sail over the heavens from east to west with the Sun-god. The Vignettes of the Sekhet-Åaru show that two boats were always ready for the use of the righteous; the larger one was moved by eight oars which worked themselves, and the motive power of the smaller was the Utchat, 𓂀, or Eye of Rā.

[1] This boat is figured in Garstang, *Burial Customs*, p. 156.

The idea that the souls of the dead were ferried over to the Land of the Blessed by a righteous ferryman passed from the Books of the Dead into the literature of the Christian Egyptians, or Copts. Thus St. John Chrysostom tells us that our Lord gave to John the Baptist a boat of gold, which he was to use in transporting the souls of the righteous over the river of fire in Åmente. This boat was provided with oars, to which lamps were attached. The oars, apparently, worked themselves under the direction of John the Baptist, and when the souls landed from the boat the lamps kindled themselves and lighted the paths over the roads of darkness until John brought the souls to the Third Heaven.[1]

THE SPIRIT HOUSE

THE religious literature of Egypt of all periods is full of statements concerning the occupation and enjoyments of the beatified, or "glorious spirits," in the Ṭuat, or Other World, but in spite of their celestial delights the souls of the dead wished to have a settled place of abode, or house, on the earth. Chapter CLII of the Book of the Dead is entitled "Chapter of building a house on the earth,"

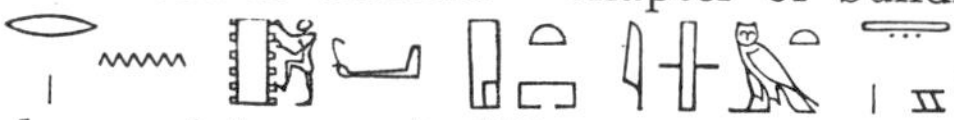

, and in the Vignette the deceased is seen building a rectangular house, with a door in one end. From the text we gather that the god Nebṭ and the goddess Sesheta assist the deceased to carry out the command, which Anubis gave him, to build the house, and that Osiris himself will take care that the "honourable spirit" is provided with provisions in his house. The craving for a house on earth existed at all periods, and the primitive Egyptians had buried with them earthenware models of the houses in which they hoped to live in the Other World. Some twenty years ago a number of these models were found in Upper Egypt, and several typical examples were acquired by the British Museum. In one of these (B.M. 32609) the house is rectangular and stands at one end of a rectangular courtyard, has two rooms, each with a doorway, and the roof is approached by a stairway on the left side of the courtyard, on each side of which is a low wall. On the right side of the courtyard, in the corner by the house, is a stand with water-pots on it, of much the same shape as the stands that hold the large *zîrs* (water-jars) in modern houses in Egypt. Lying on the ground in front of the house are models of joints of meat, bread-cakes, etc., and in front of these is a rectangular tank, which was emptied and filled by means of two small channels cut in the outside border. This "spirit-house" and courtyard measure 15⅛ inches by 14¼ inches by 7 inches.

[1] See Budge, *Coptic Apocrypha*, pp. 347–49.

Model of a boat with its sail hoisted. XIth or XIIth dynasty.

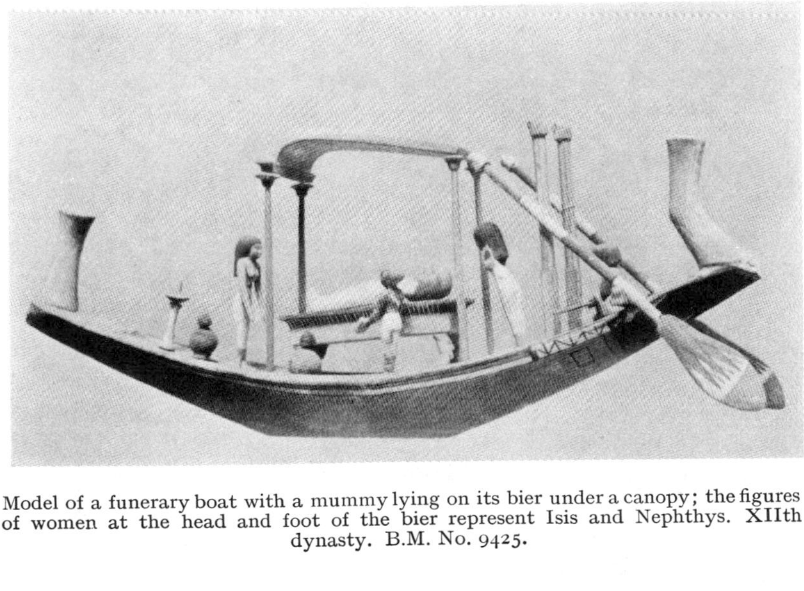

Model of a funerary boat with a mummy lying on its bier under a canopy; the figures of women at the head and foot of the bier represent Isis and Nephthys. XIIth dynasty. B.M. No. 9425.

Cippus of Horus. Ptolemaïc Period. B.M. No. 36250.

Another example (B.M. 32610) shows the house standing on a plot of ground which is rounded on one side. The house consists of a single room and is entered through a rounded doorway  ; on one side of it is a square opening divided into two parts by a pillar, and the upper part of the framework is decorated with little roundels. On the right is a stairway leading up to the roof, where there is a small chamber, which was probably used for sleeping in; it has a doorway, and part of its roof is open. The roof is surrounded by a wall which is as high as the sleeping chamber, and is pierced in one place by a circular hole. Below this hole is a spout, which suggests that the hole served as an escape, or drain, for rain-water. The upper part of the wall below the spout bulges outwards, so that the water running from the spout might drop on the ground away from the foundation, and not run down the wall itself. In the courtyard are models of an animal bound for roasting, joints of meat, a water-pot resting on a circular base, bread-cakes, and a number of other articles which would be eaten, presumably at a festival. The deceased wished to have not only a house of the kind that he approved of, but also a good supply of food. This example measures 16 inches by 14 inches by 7 inches.

Another model (B.M. 22783) represents what may be described as two one-storeyed houses, separated by a common party-wall; even the courtyard is divided by a low wall. Each house has one large, lofty room on the ground floor, with an opening, or window, in the back wall, and one upper room, with one opening in the front wall and another in the back wall. Before the rooms on the upper floor is a wide ledge like the floor of a balcony, supported on a pillar standing in the courtyard and divided by a wall the height of the rooms. Access to the upper floor and to the roof was obtained by two flights of stairs, one flight on each side of the girdle-wall, and thus the occupant of each of these semi-detached houses was in every way independent of his neighbour. On the floor of each half of the courtyard are laid out groups of articles of food, and against the wall of each of the lower rooms rest the same number of jars of wine (?). It is probable that, when these models were placed with the dead, words of power were recited on behalf of the deceased persons which would enable them to command them to turn into full-sized houses whenever they had need of them.

B.M. 32611 is a model of a different class of building. Here we have a small pylon-shaped edifice standing at the rounded end of a walled enclosure, and its general appearance suggests that it represents the sanctuary of some god. Above the doorway, the sides of which are adorned with two pillars, are two square openings. Inside the building, set against the back wall, is a seat of state, or throne, with raised sides, which are now partly broken away, and this was reached by means of three steps. The walls of the shrine rise above the level of the roof, and form a protecting wall, against which models of some kind of objects rest; a flight of stairs leads from the court-yard to the roof. In the centre of the courtyard is a rectangular garden (?), with a channel for water on all four sides; the water flowed into the channel on the right, and drained away by that on the left. On one side of the garden (?) lies an animal with large horns, and with his four feet tied together ready for sacrifice; on the other side are other offerings which I cannot identify. The front of the girdle-wall is adorned with four projections, two on each side of the lower portion of it, by which access to the enclosure might be obtained. This model measures 16 inches by 13 inches by 5½ inches.

WANDS AND OTHER OBJECTS IN IVORY

AMONG the objects found in 1887 at Ḳûrnah, in Western Thebes, was the mummy of a woman, who was buried in a plain rectangular wooden coffin of the XIth or XIIth dynasty, and in the coffin by her side lay the ivory object which is reproduced on p. 469. This object is semi-circular and slightly convex, and has rounded ends; it is 14⅜ inches in length and about 2⅞ inches wide in its widest part. On each side of it, cut in outline, is a series of figures of gods and fabulous and mythological creatures. On the obverse are: a lion couchant, a serpent with a knife in front of him, the hippopotamus-goddess holding a knife, a god, full-faced, with long hair, grasping in each hand a serpent, the symbol of fire, , and a knife, ; a hawk-headed leopard, with a pair of wings between which is a human head, the solar disk, , the figure of a woman or goddess, holding  in her right hand and a sceptre in her left, Ta-urt, a crocodile, a jackal-headed sceptre, with a knife, a cobra, , fire, , a hawk, the solar disk, , a knife, , Ta-urt holding in her left paw a knife which rests on , the Utchat, , and another knife and serpent. On the reverse are the figures of lions, serpents, knives, the full-faced god holding serpents, etc., and besides these we have: a serpent-headed god holding a serpent in each hand, the head of a ram, two crocodile heads, a beetle, the lion-god Aker (?), with a human head at each end of his body, a beetle, a lion with a greatly elongated neck, a frog, a lion with each of his four legs resting on an animal-headed sceptre with knife attached, and the goddess Ta-urt. A line of hieroglyphs on the obverse shows that this object belonged to "the lady of the house, Senbet,"  (B.M. 18175). Another example of this class of object is B.M. 24426, but it is only

11½ inches in length, and one end of it is pointed. The figures cut on it are in outline, and appear on one side only; on the pointed end is a fly, and on the rounded end a flower. In addition to the fabulous hawk-headed, winged, and human-headed lion and the hippopotamus, we have the Bull-god, with a head at each end of his body, a frog with a knife, seated on a bowl (?), and the head of a vulture, with two feathers on it, within a rectangle.[1] On a third example (B.M. 24425) the figures are in low relief, and both ends are rounded. Here we have a hippopotamus, a lion, a serpent,

a cat, , a ram-headed man, a beetle, a rope-work design, , a panther (or, leopard), the Ape of Thoth bringing back the Utchat, , a god, full-faced (the original of Bes ?), a ram-headed god with a sceptre, a frog on a stand, , a god carrying , a pair of serpents with legs, and a hippopotamus.

When the first of these objects arrived in the Museum, it was suggested by one archaeologist that it was a boomerang, and by another that it was a kind of collar which, by virtue of the figures cut upon it, possessed magical properties, and gave its wearer protection against the powers of evil. That it was supposed to *protect* its wearer is proved by the words *setep sa*, 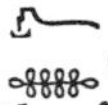, which occur on it just before Senbet, its owner's name. But the fact that the inscription

[1] See *Todtenbuch*, ed. Naville, Chapter CXLVB.

gives the name of Senbet, a married woman, disposes of the theory that it was a boomerang, and its size and shape make the theory that it was a collar impossible. The fact that the raised figures in the middle of B.M. 24425 are almost rubbed away, and that both B.M. 18175 and 24426 were broken in the middle in ancient days, suggests to me that these objects were frequently held in the hand and much used by their owners during their lifetime. As one of the three belonged to a woman it is probable that each of the others belonged to a woman, and we may assume that women carried and in some way used these objects at great religious festivals, and during times of great public rejoicings, *e.g.*, when hunters returned after a successful hunt, and soldiers after a victorious campaign came home laden with spoil. It is possible that B.M. 20778 is a portion of an object of this class, though it must date from the time of the Old Kingdom (VIth dynasty, or earlier). This object is of ivory and is 6 inches long, and the end that is left is rounded. On the convex side are cut in relief a lion's head, and the figures of a bull-headed god and another god, each holding ☥ in the right hand and a sceptre in the left, and standing on a serpent. Each of these figures has a bronze eye inlaid. The general appearance of these figures recalls that of the figures in the hunting scenes sculptured on the so-called "green slate palettes" of the Archaic Period, and the objects described above may be copies or imitations of objects which women carried under the early dynasties. Under the New Kingdom the wands which women waved in times of rejoicing were made in pairs, as we see from B.M. 20779, and they were in the form of human arms and hands. Each of these has the head of Hathor, *i.e.*, a woman's face with a cow's ears, wearing a heavy wig, the lappets of which curl outwards. Another pair of arms, cut from a small tusk, are only 7½ inches in length, and they are decorated with circles with dots inside them, ⊙⊙⊙ ⊙⊙⊙, and six lines across each wrist to represent a bracelet. They were acquired by the British Museum with the Anastasi Collection in 1839, and have been described as castanets.[1]

THE CIPPUS OF HORUS

DURING the rule of the last two or three native kings of Egypt, *i.e.*, in the IVth century B.C., the Egyptians endeavoured to protect their houses and courtyards and fields from the attacks of fiends and devils and their malign influences by setting up in their rooms and gardens little stone monuments, which Birch and the

[1] Descriptions and illustrations of a number of these objects were published by the late F. Legge in the *Proceedings of the Society of Biblical Archaeology*, Vol. XXVII, 1905, pp. 130–52, 297–303.

older Egyptologists called "Cippi of Horus." These pillars, or boundary-stones, or landmarks of Horus, are made of hard stone, frequently black in colour, and they usually have the form of a stele with a rounded top and a convex pedestal projecting in front. On this are sculptured in high relief a figure of Ḥerpakhraṭ (Harpokrates) standing with each foot resting on a crocodile, and the head of Bes, also in high relief, above his head. They vary in height from 2 or 3 to 20 inches; the small ones were carried or worn on the person as amulets, and the large ones were placed in the halls of houses, and probably at certain spots on roads and at the entrances to fields and vineyards. The largest known is the so-called "Metternich Stele," which was found in 1828 during the building of a cistern in a Franciscan Monastery at Alexandria and was presented by Muḥammad 'Alî Pâshâ to Prince Metternich.[1] As it bears on it the cartouches of Nektanebus I, who reigned from B.C. 378 to 360, it is clear that this extraordinary and wonderful object was made in the first half of the IVth century B.C. The reliefs and figures of the gods were believed to possess the power of driving away every devil, and noxious beast, and reptile from the persons and possessions of all those who were under their protection, and the inscriptions contained spells, or words of power, which Thoth himself had composed. The Cippus of Horus symbolized the triumph of light over darkness, of good over evil, of virtue over vice, and of order over chaos. Armed with the power of the "Aged God who renews his youth in his season, the Ancient of Days who makes himself a child again," and acting under his protection, the followers of the light were able to trample under foot serpents, snakes, vipers, and scorpions, and to destroy the crocodile, hippopotamus, lion, and the horned beast of the desert, the bodies of which were the abiding-places of monstrous devils. The arrows of light which Horus shot forth into the darkness scattered all the powers of night and evil. The figures of more than one hundred gods are cut on the Metternich Stele, and each had its specific work to do in protecting the man who through his uprightness of life was able to place himself under its charge.

The Cippus of Horus (B.M. 36250) in hard black basalt is a good typical example, and may be thus briefly described: The centre of the front of the cippus, which is 7½ inches in height, and is made of black basalt, is occupied by a figure of Ḥerpakhraṭ, *i.e.*, "Horus the Child," who wears on the right side of his head the lock of hair, 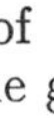, symbolic of youth. His arms hang by his sides and he grasps in his right hand two serpents, a scorpion by its tail, and a species of gazelle by its horns, and in his left he grasps another pair of serpents, a scorpion by its tail and a lion by its tail. Each foot of the god is planted on the head of a crocodile. Above his head is a head of Bes, and on the flat surface above it, within a disk,

[1] It was published by Golénischeff at Leipzig in 1877.

is cut a figure of the composite god who has a bird's body, human legs and arms, and the heads of four rams surmounted by the triple crown. He represents the fusion of the attributes of the Ram of Mendes and Osiris of Ṭeṭu. On the right of the god is a lotus sceptre with the hawk of Ḥer-Beḥuṭ, the great god, , standing upon it; on the left is a papyrus sceptre with plumes, and the name Tem-nefer-akhu-taui, . Above this are the words, "I am Horus Meḥen," , which may give the name of the Horus sculptured on the cippus. By the right leg of the god is a hawk-headed crocodile called "Horus, dweller in his towns (?)" , and by the left leg another hawk-headed crocodile wearing a pair of horns and a disk, , upon his head, and called Åmen-renf, .

On the flat surface on the right of the god are cut the names and figures of the following gods: (1) Horus, lord of Ḥeben, ; (2) Thoth, lord of Khemenu, lord of the words of the gods, ; (3) Ḥershef, ; (4) Ḥeka, lord of words of power, ; (5) Neith, lady of Saïs; (6) Khensu, lord of Smabeḥut, ; (7) Isis, with the body of a hippopotamus and holding a serpent and a scorpion; (8) Ptaḥ, in the form of a dwarf, standing upon ; (9) The scorpion-goddess Serqit, lady of life, ; (10) Nebt-ḥetep wearing and standing between two serpents, each hand grasping one of them.

On the flat surface on the left of the god are cut the names and figures of the following gods and goddesses: (1) The goddess Uritḥekau, , lady of , standing upon a crocodile, having a bird on its head. She wears on her head a disk to which two scorpions are attached; in her right hand she holds a serpent, and in her left a serpent and a scorpion; (2) the crocodile-god Meketh, ; (3) the lion-headed serpent Usrit, ; (4) the goddess Isis suckling Horus among the papyrus plants, . The serpent-goddesses Nekhebit and Uatchit form a canopy over her with their bodies, and on each side of her seat is a protective scorpion; (5) the crocodile-god Sebek, ; (6) Horus, son of Isis, carrying a serpent as a weapon; (7) the Golden Horus, , with the symbol of eternity, ; (8) the goddess Isis-Serqit, . She has horns and disk, , on her head, her body is that of a scorpion, the two (*sic*) tails of which form her legs; (9) a youthful god (Horus ?) holding a whip and seated on a crocodile under the protection of a serpent; he seems to be called "the vivifier of the gods," ; (10) the goddess Uatchit, , in the form of a serpent having the tail coiled round a papyrus plant: she wears the Crown of the North (the Red Crown); (11) the two gods Ḥu, , and Sȧa, , each of whom is seated and holds a knife. The front of the convex pedestal, the edges, and the back are covered with lines of hieroglyphs containing addresses to the gods, goddesses and sacred animals whose forms are cut upon the cippus, and adjurations to them to protect from evil hap, poison of all kinds, and noxious animals and reptiles, the body and soul of the person who had it made.

On the smaller cippi the sculptured figures vary in details, and the inscriptions are much abridged, only the opening words of the address to the gods being given (B.M. 30745). In this example Ȧmen-Rā is referred to as the creator of protection and life, (*sic*) . In B.M. 27373 Ḥerpakhraṭ is seen standing on three pairs of crocodiles, and his hands grasp the sceptres of the South and North as well as the serpents, scorpions, etc. On the reverse the god of chief importance is Thoth, who stands under a winged disk; on one side of him is Horus and on the other is Ȧnḥer. Below is a second scene representing Isis giving birth to Horus, and the attendant gods Horus the Elder and Anubis(?). This shows that the idea of resurrection and rebirth was associated with the cippus of Horus. In some cippi of Horus the head of Bes is so large that it stands above the top of the tablet, of which it becomes the chief feature. A good example is B.M. 958, which is 17 inches in height and is made of wood. The front of the cippus is uninscribed, and on the back, below a row of figures of gods, are eighteen lines of hieroglyphs written in yellow paint on a black ground, and containing magical prayers of a character different from those found on the cippi described above. Another cippus, which dates from the Ptolemaïc Period (B.M. 957), exhibits interesting peculiarities as regards the arrangement of reliefs and text. Horus wears an elaborate collar, and a pendent amulet of the heart, , hangs on his breast. On the back, cut in outline, we have: (1) Horus as a hawk, wearing the crowns of the North and South, perched in triumph on the back of an oryx (?), which symbolizes his victory over Āpep, , the personification of evil. In front of him is the god Menu, ithyphallic, and with raised arm, and by his side are figures of his special symbol and the circular hut which formed his original sanctuary. Behind Horus are figures of Thoth, the master-designer of the universe, and Khnemu, the chief craftsman. (2) A group of six gods and goddesses, among them being Rā and Horus, and the Beetle of Kheperȧ. (3) A dwarf with an Utchat, , above his head, a god spearing a serpent (compare the Vignettes to Chapters XXXV and XXXVII of the Saïte Recension of the Book of the Dead), an animal seated with a uraeus behind him, and a company of eight gods, four human-headed and four ibis-headed. These last probably represent the Ogdoad of the city of Khemenu, the home of the cult of Thoth. The inscription is mutilated, but sufficient of it remains to show that it contains an adjuration to all fiends and noxious creatures and reptiles to halt and make no attack upon those who are under the protection of the gods whose figures are cut on this cippus. For Horus defeated and slew the Arch-fiend Āpep, the Father of Evil, and the same fate must come upon every lesser fiend and devil. In the latter part of the Ptolemaïc and Roman periods models of the cippus of Horus were made of steatite, and were worn as amulets.

DRAUGHTS AND DRAUGHT-BOARDS

THE Egyptians called the **draught-board** , *senȧt*, or , , , , *sent*, and , meant "to play at draughts." Variant forms are , *stant* and , *sethent*. The **draughtsman** was called , *ȧb*, meaning perhaps the "thing that danced or was moved about," and the receptacle for the men (?) , *men*. The commonest hieroglyph for draught-board is , and as this sign occurs in the oldest inscriptions, it is clear that in some form or other the game of draughts was played under the earliest dynasties; it may even have been played in the predynastic period. A tradition preserved by a Greek writer attributes the invention of the game to the god Thoth. The oldest known draught-board was discovered by the late Mr. Ayrton (see his *Cemetery at El-Mahasna*, pl. 17); it is made of Nile mud, and on it are marked 12 squares, arranged in three rows, each row containing four squares. The pieces are in the form of little round stones. Draught-boards made of pieces of sandstone or bits of broken pottery, and having the same number of squares, may be seen in use in many parts of the Sûdân and Egypt at the present day. The oldest draught-boards were made of single blocks of wood, with the squares on one or both sides. Thus the specimen published by Prisse d'Avennes (*Mon. Ég.*, pl. 49) had thirty squares on one side and twenty on the other, arranged thus :

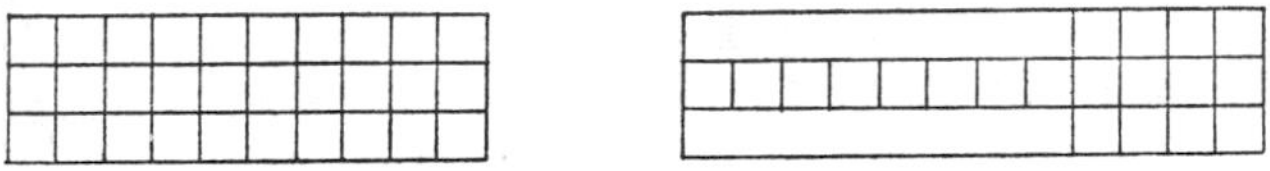

The larger specimens contain a drawer which holds the draughtsmen. The pieces of each of the two players were different in shape and size, as we may see from the drawings on the monuments. At first flat stones or bits of pottery, like counters, and small round stones served as pieces, but under the New Kingdom the pieces became symmetrical in shape, and their tops terminated in heads of men, lions, jackals, etc. Thus the draughtsmen which were made for Queen Ḥatshepsut were in the form of a lion's head,  ; one in ivory and several in wood are in the British Museum (Nos. 21580, 21592, etc.). When these were presented to the Museum by Mr. J. Haworth some authorities declared them to be modern forgeries, but beyond all doubt they are genuine. In another set of draughtsmen 10 have heads of Bes and 7 have heads of Ȧnpu (Anubis, B.M. No. 24668, etc.). Among royal draughtsmen may be mentioned those of Pharaoh Necho (about 650 B.C.), , made of limestone (B.M. No. 38254). The game of draughts was greatly beloved by all classes of Egyptians at all periods, and a draught-board with men was considered to be necessary for the happiness of the dead in the Other World. In the Papyrus of Ani we see him, with his wife Tutu by his side, seated in a bower moving the pieces on a draught-board. Who his opponent was is unknown, but we may assume that he had one, or perhaps many, from whom he expected to gain some advantage or possession. Two draught-boards were among the funerary equipment of Queen Ḥatshepsut ; one was made of acacia wood and ivory, and had a sliding drawer, and the other was inlaid with ivory and squares of blue-glazed Egyptian porcelain. In the former one of the squares is inscribed with , *nefer,* indicating probably that the player who succeeded in moving his piece on to it won the game. Both boards are in the British Museum (Nos. 21576, 21577). The "Satirical Papyrus" in the British Museum (No. 10016) shows us a picture of the lion and unicorn playing a game of draughts ; each has four pieces on the board and a piece in one paw, and the general appearance of the lion suggests that he is the victor. Much information about the game of Egyptian draughts will be found in Falkener, E., *Games Ancient and Oriental and How to Play Them,* London, 1892.

TOYS, BALLS, DOLLS, ETC.

THE **balls** with which women and men as well as children played were made of strips of linen rolled up tightly or cases of linen or leather filled with some substance like bran. Under the New Kingdom balls made of glazed Egyptian porcelain coloured blue and black were placed in the tombs as votive offerings. Games in which sticks or bats were used in playing with balls were apparently unknown. Many varieties of **dolls** are known. The commonest form is made of a piece of flat wood, in which the shape of the body is roughly outlined, painted with squares, triangles or lines in various colours ; a mass of short strings of mud beads represents the hair. Most of them are girl-dolls. Some are made of mud, others of stone and earthenware, and the bronze doll has sometimes movable arms (B.M. No. 37162). In a few cases the form and features are carefully cut, and such dolls might almost be regarded as portrait figures. **Toys** in the form of animals with movable limbs are tolerably common. Thus in the British Museum we have a man with a movable figure of a dog (No. 26254), an **elephant** that had movable legs (No. 17059), and a cat with inlaid eyes of crystal and movable jaw (No. 15671). In the Leyden Museum is a **crocodile** with a movable jaw.

HYPOCEPHALI

TOWARDS the end of the Saïte Recension of the Book of the Dead there is found a Chapter entitled " Chapter of making heat to be under the head of the deceased," and it contains a short series of spells, the recital of which, it was thought, would enable the head of a man to retain its natural heat in the tomb. The Rubric of the Chapter says that it must be " written upon a sheet of new papyrus and placed under the head of the deceased. Then great warmth shall be in every part of his body, even like that which was in him when he was upon earth." The Rubric goes on to say that the Chapter possesses very great power, because it was composed by the Cow-goddess, the mother of Rā, and that she recited it when he was about to set in the West, and that when she did so the god was immediately surrounded by fire which kept warmth in his body during the hours of the night. The Legend of the Cow and Rā is, no doubt, very ancient, but the custom of writing the Chapter upon papyrus and placing it under the head of the mummy in its coffin seems not to be older than the XXVIth dynasty. About that time the Egyptians began to write extracts from Chapter CLXII upon a circular sheet of papyrus, and to add to it several Vignettes, with descriptive texts, and a prayer to Åmen-Rā. This sheet was gummed on a piece of linen stiffened with plaster, and moulded to the back of the head of the mummy in the coffin ; it was trimmed into a circular form and was intended to represent the Eye of Shu, or the Eye of Rā, or the Eye of Horus. To this amulet the name of "hypocephalus" was given by P. J. F. de Horrack in 1862. Several **hypocephali** are known, and copies of most of them have been published, *e.g.*, by Birch (*Proceedings Soc. Bibl. Arch.*, vols. VI and VII), by de Horrack (*Rev. Arch.*, Paris, 1862; *Études Arch.*, Leyden, 1885; and *Proceedings Soc. Bibl. Arch.*, vol. VI), by Leemans ("Hypocéphale Égyptien" in the *Actes* of the Oriental Congress, Leyden, 1885), by Nash (*Proceedings Soc. Bibl. Arch.*, vol. XIX), and by Budge (*Catalogue of the Lady Meux Collection*, Second ed., London, 1896). Hypocephali vary from 4 in. to 7 in. in diameter, and the texts are usually written in black ink on a yellow ground, *e.g.*, B.M. Nos. 8445 *a-f*, but B.M. No. 8446 is written in yellow ink on a black ground. One example in bronze is known, viz., B.M. No. 37330; it was engraved for Tche-ḥer, the son of Utchat Shu, , and was found at Abydos. Strangely enough, almost the earliest publication of a hypocephalus is that given in a work by Joseph Smith, Jr. (1805–1844), the founder of the Church of Jesus Christ of Latter Day Saints, entitled *A Pearl of Great Price*, 1851, p. 7. The remarks made there about it have no archaeological value.

The texts and Vignettes found on hypocephali are to all intents and purposes the same, though in some they are fuller than in others. The following is a description of the Meux Hypocephalus, which is one of the best of this class of amulet known. A line of text runs round the outer edge and reads: "I am Åmen who is in the Shetat (Underworld). I am an honourable Spirit among the sailors of Rā. I come in and go out among the honourable ones. I am the Great Soul sparkling [in] his form. I come forth from the Ṭuat at his will. I come, I come forth from the Utchat (*i.e.*, Eye of Rā). I come forth from the Ṭuat with Rā, from the House of the Prince in Ånu (Heliopolis). I am a Spirit-Soul, , hastening from the Ṭuat. Give the things [needed] for his form! Give thou heaven to his soul, , and the Underworld to his Sāḥ,  (Spirit-body ?). I come forth from the Utchat." **Vignettes.** 1. A snake-god offering the Utchat, , to the god Menu. 2. An Utchat-headed goddess with a lotus, , and . 3. The Cow-goddess and the Four Sons of Horus, a lion and the ram of Åmen. 4. The Ogdoad of Åmen, Rā, , and . **Text.** "O Åmen, who hidest thyself, and concealest thy form, who illuminest the Two Lands (*i.e.*, Egypt) with thy Form in the Ṭuat! He shall make my soul to live for ever." **Vignettes.**

1. The Boat of Rā, with Horus in the bows spearing a serpent in the water. 2. Harpokrates seated and holding a whip and lotus. 3. The Boat of the Moon. An Ape-god restoring to the Moon-god his Eye. The deceased **Shainen**, , is working the boat. 4. A goddess falling prostrate and . **Vignettes.** 1. A god with two faces (like Janus), wearing and holding a jackal sceptre, , and . 2. Boat of Horus, Isis and Nephthys. 3. Boat of Kheperȧ, with an Ape-god (Thoth) restoring his Eye. 4. The Boat of Horus-Sepṭ (the Eastern Horus). 5. The god Ȧmen, with four ram's heads; on each side the Ape of Thoth, with paws raised in adoration. **Texts.** 1. "O Ba (*i.e.*, Soul), begetter of Forms, hiding thy body from thy children, destroy [every] obstacle to the light which can arise to the Two Utchats (*i.e.*, the Sun and Moon), and to his soul and body, Mut provides plans (?). Let him put the fear of himself into his enemies. Let Shainen enter into the Ṭuat of the gods, without repulse for ever and ever." 2. "O Ba, mighty one of terror, lord inspiring fear, greatly victorious one, who givest heat to the two august Utchats, whose Forms are august, to whom Mut has given his body, who hidest thy body in life! His Image becomes the emanation of the Lion, who is mightily victorious, and feeds the forms [of the dead]. Make to come forth and to go in the Osiris Shainen for ever."

TIME

THE hieroglyphic texts give the following divisions of time:— *ȧnt* = the "twinkling of an eye," *ḥat*, a second, *at*, a minute, , or , or *unut* (Copt. ⲟⲩⲛⲟⲩ), an hour, *hru* (Copt. ϩⲟⲟⲩ), day, , , *ȧbṭ* (Copt. ⲉⲃⲟⲧ), month, , , *renpit* (Copt. ⲣⲟⲙⲡⲉ), year. The day contained twenty-four hours, the calendar month thirty days, or three "weeks" of ten days ( ) each, and the year twelve calendar months. The Seṭ Period, , usually consisted of thirty years; the Ḥenuti Period, , of 120 years; a period of unlimited time was called Ḥeḥ, , and Tchet, , indicated Eternity. Classical writers say that the Egyptians during the Graeco-Roman

Period used the **Phoenix Period** and the **Sothic Period ;** the former containing 500, or 540, or 1,000, or 7,006 years, and the latter 1,461 years. In inscriptions in which the writers pray that the king may live for a very long time the following expressions are met with :—

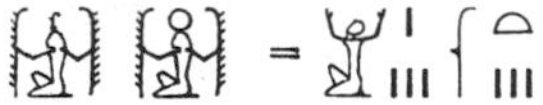 millions of years.

 ten millions of years.

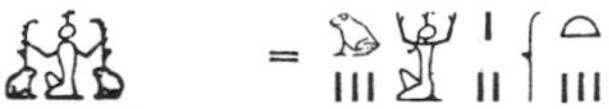 a hundred thousand millions of years.

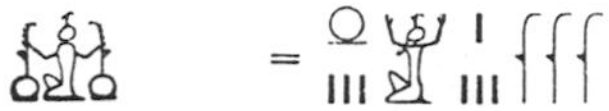 ten millions of millions of years.

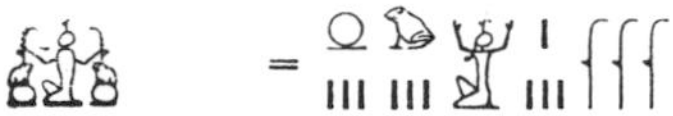 ten millions of periods of a hundred thousand millions of years.[1]

THE YEAR

The oldest year in Egypt consisted of twelve months, each containing thirty days, in all **360 days ;** the Calendar of Lucky and Unlucky Days given on the reverse of British Museum Papyrus 10474 represents the primitive Egyptian year. Very early in the Dynastic Period the Egyptians found that their year was too short, and so they added five days to the 360 days. These five days were called " the days over the year," , and the birthdays of Osiris, Horus, Set, Isis, and Nephthys, respectively, were celebrated on them. This year is generally known as the **vague** or **calendar year,** and was shorter than the true **solar year** of 365·2422 mean days by nearly a quarter of a day. This being so the vague year would be every fourth year nearly one day shorter than the solar year, and would in time work backward through all the months of the year, and after some hundreds of years the summer festivals would have to be celebrated in the winter. But the Egyptians must have had some means of checking the course of the vague year as it moved backwards, and it is possible that the annual rise of the Nile and the Inundation were sufficient guides to them in their agricultural operations. Ptolemy III Euergetes I attempted to bring the vague year in line with the solar year by ordering the addition of a sixth epagomenal day to the year every fourth year. Many writers have tried to show that

[1] See Devéria, *Notation des centaines de mille et des millions,* Paris, 1865 ; Brugsch, *Thesaurus* (*Astronomische und Astrologische*), p. 200 ff.

the Egyptians knew of and used the **Sothic year,** which began when the star Sepṭ (*i.e.*, Sothis, Sirius or the Dog-star) rose with the sun; this usually happened on July 19th or 20th. The Sothic year was a few minutes longer than the solar year, and the Sothic Period contained 1,460 Sothic years or 1,461 vague or Calendar years. In pre-dynastic times it is probable that the Egyptians only knew or recognized two seasons, **summer** and **winter,** which was the custom among many peoples in the Sûdân until comparatively recent times. But the dynastic Egyptians divided their year into **three seasons,** each containing four months: **Akhet,** , *i.e.*, the season of the sprouting, or bursting forth, of the crops, was the Egyptian Winter. **Pert,** , *i.e.*, the season for coming forth, or Summer, and **Shemut,** , *i.e.*, the hot, watery period of the Inundation. In the texts the months of each season are numbered from 1 to 4, thus the Annals of Rameses III are dated in , but

year 32nd, month third of Shemut, day sixth

it is certain that the Egyptians gave a name to each month, and that each name connected its month with a certain festival. Some of these names can be traced through the Coptic names of the twelve Egyptian months, which are as follows:—

ⲑⲟⲟⲩⲧ, ⲑⲟⲟⲩⲑ ⲡⲁⲁⲡⲉ, ⲡⲁⲱⲡⲉ ϩⲁⲑⲱⲣ, ⲁⲑⲱⲣ ⲭⲟⲓⲁϩⲕ, ⲭⲟⲓⲁⲕ	The four months of Akhet.
ⲧⲱⲃⲉ, ⲧⲱⲃⲓ ⲙ̅ϣⲓⲣ, ⲙⲉⲭⲓⲣ ⲡⲁⲣⲙ̅ϩⲟⲧⲡ, ⲫⲁⲙⲉⲛⲱⲑ ⲡⲁⲣⲙⲟⲩⲧⲉ, ⲫⲁⲣⲙⲟⲩⲑⲓ	The four months of Pert.
ⲡⲁϣⲟⲛⲥ̅ ⲡⲁⲱⲛⲉ, ⲡⲁⲱⲛⲓ ⲉⲡⲉⲡ, ⲉⲡⲏⲡ, ⲉⲡⲏⲫ ⲙⲉⲥⲱⲣⲏ	The four months of Shemut.

The name ⲑⲟⲟⲩⲧ =  or Thoth. Another name for the month was Tekhi, , which is also a title of Thoth; ϩⲁⲑⲱⲣ is clearly  or Hathor; and ⲭⲟⲓⲁϩⲕ represents 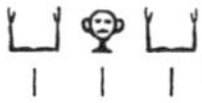,

Kaḥerka, which was the name of a festival. An ostrakon (B.M. 29560) transcribed by Erman (*Aeg. Zeit.,* Bd. XXXIX, p. 129) shows that ⲡⲁⲁⲡⲉ is derived from 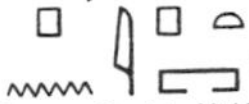, *Penȧpt,* and ⲙⲉⲭⲓⲣ or ⲙ̅ϣⲓⲣ from , *Penpa-Mekhir,* the month of the Mekhir festival, and ⲡⲁⲣⲙ̅ϩⲟⲧⲡ from 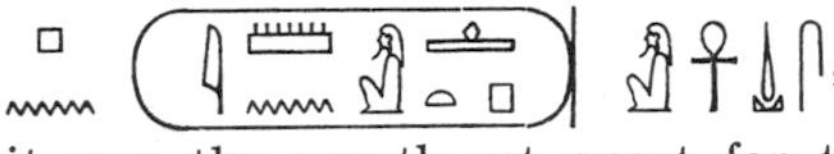, Pen-Ȧmenḥetep, meaning that it was the month set apart for the festivals ordered by Ȧmenḥetep III of the XVIIIth dynasty. The Copts reckon years by the **Era of Diocletian,** or the **Era of the Martyrs,** which began on the day equivalent to August 29th A.D. 284. The Coptic year consists of twelve months of thirty days each, with five additional days in a common year, to make up 365 days; an extra day is added every fourth year. The Julian Leap Years and the intercalary years of this Era fall together, and therefore the first day of Thoth always corresponds to August 29th. The Copts call the five (or six) additional days "the little month," ⲡⲓⲁⲃⲟⲧ ⲛ̅ⲕⲟⲩϫⲓ. Thus, though the Copts use forms of the ancient Egyptian names of the months for their months, they make their year begin on August 29th, though they make their New Year's Day to fall on September 10th or 11th. Some think that the days on which the months were to begin were fixed by the Romans at Alexandria about 30 B.C. If this be so, the explanation given by the Copts, that they decided to make August 29th the first day of their year from religious motives, must be regarded as a pious fiction which they promulgated about two and a half centuries later. One thing seems certain, viz., that their year does not begin when the ancient Egyptian year began. The **Shemut** season began with the rise of the Nile about June 15th, and ended with the final fall of the river about October 15th. The winter crops were sown and reaped in the season of **Akhet,** *i.e.,* during our months of November—February, and the summer crops were sown and reaped in the season of **Pert,** *i.e.,* during the months of March—June. The modern Egyptians do the same at the present time (see Lane, *Modern Egyptians,* Vol. II, p. 27). Egyptologists say that **Akhet** began on July 19th or 20th, **Pert** on November 15th, and **Shemut** on March 16th, and if they are correct it can only be concluded that the ancient Egyptians, like the Copts, did not make their year begin with the beginning of the season following that of the Inundations, as we should expect.

NUMBERS

		Hieroglyphic.			Coptic.	
1.	I	= 	*uāu*	(fem.)	ⲟⲩⲁ, ⲟⲩⲁⲓ, ⲟⲩⲁⲉ;	fem. ⲟⲩⲉⲓ
2.	II	= 	*seniu*	(,,)	ⲥⲛⲁⲩ	,, ⲥⲛ̀ⲧⲉ
3.	III	= 	*khmtu*	(,, *khmtt*)	ϣⲟⲙⲛ̄ⲧ, ϣⲟⲙⲧ	,, ϣⲟⲙⲧⲉ
4.	IIII	= 	*fṭu*	(,, *fṭt*)	ϥ̄ⲧⲟⲟⲩ	,, ϥ̄ⲧⲟ
5.	IIIII	= 	*ṭuu*	(,, *ṭut*)	ϯⲟⲩ	,, ϯⲉ
6.	IIIIII[1]	=  (?)	*sȧsu*	(,, *sȧst*)	ⲥⲟⲟⲩ	,, ⲥⲟ
7.	IIII III	= 	*skhfu*	(,, *skhft*)	ⲥⲁϣϥ̄	,, ⲥⲁϣϥⲉ
8.	IIII IIII	= 	*khmenu*	(,, *khment*)	ϣⲙⲟⲩⲛ	,, ϣⲙⲟⲩⲛⲉ
9.	III III III or III III III	= 	*pestchu*	(,, *pestcht*)	ⲯⲓⲧ	,, ⲯⲓⲧⲉ
10.	∩	= 	*metch*		ⲙⲏⲧ	,, ⲙⲏⲧⲉ
20.	∩∩	= 	*tchebāti*		ϫⲟⲩⲱⲧ	,, ϫⲟⲩⲱⲧⲉ
30.	∩∩∩	= 	*māba*		ⲙⲁⲁⲃ	

40.	𓎉	. . . .		ϩⲙⲉ	
50.	𓎊	[*ṭuiu*]		ⲧⲁⲓⲟⲩ	fem. ⲧⲁⲓⲟⲩⲉ
60.	𓎋	[*sȧsiu*]		ⲥⲉ	
70.	𓎌	[*skhfiu*]			
80.	𓎍	[*khmeniu*]		ϩⲙⲉⲛⲉ, ϧⲙⲉⲛⲉ	
90.	𓎎	[*pestchiu*]		ⲡⲥ̅ⲧⲁⲓⲟⲩ, ⲡⲓⲥⲧⲉⲟⲩⲓ	
100.	𓍢	[*shat* (?)]		ϣⲉ, ϣⲟⲩ	
200.	𓍢𓍢			ϣⲏⲧ	
1,000.	𓆼	*kha*		ϣⲁ, ϣⲟ, plur. ⲁⲛⲁⲛϣⲟ, thousands.	
10,000.	𓂭 or 𓂭 = 𓆓𓂭𓂝		*tchbā*	ⲧⲃⲁ, ⲑⲃⲁ, plur. ⲁⲛⲁⲛⲑⲃⲁ	
100,000.	𓆐 = 𓎛𓆑𓈖𓏌𓅱𓆐		*ḥefnu*	ϣⲉ ⲛ̅ϣⲟ, one hundred ten thousands; ⲙⲏⲧ ⲛ̅ⲧⲃⲁ, ten ten thousands.	
1,000,000.	𓁨 or 𓁨 = 𓎛𓎛		*ḥeḥ*	ϩⲁϩ. ϣⲟ ⲛ̅ϣⲟ, a thousand thousands.	

[1] The original form was *srs* 𓋴𓂋𓋴; see Jéquier, "Sur la prononciation de la lettre R," in *Recueil*, tom. XXXIV, p. 121.

Sethe[1] enumerates the following numerical abstracts :—, two-footed, biped, a pair ; , four-footed ; , four-sided ; , the gang of five ; , an eight, the eight-day week ;  or , the Company of Nine-gods ; , the Nine nations of the Sûdân who fought with bows and arrows.

Ordinal numbers are indicated by the addition of , ***nu***, to a number, *e.g.*, , four, , " fourth " ; also by prefixing  to the number, *e.g.*, , " eighth."

Fractions , *ges*, Copt. ϫoc, ϭoc $= \frac{1}{2}$;  $= \frac{1}{3}$,  $= \frac{1}{4}$,  $= \frac{1}{5}$,  $= \frac{1}{6}$,  $= \frac{1}{7}$,  $= \frac{1}{8}$,  $= \frac{1}{9}$,  $= \frac{1}{10}$,  $= \frac{1}{11}$,  $= \frac{1}{14}$,  $= \frac{1}{1\frac{1}{2}} = \frac{2}{3}$. For the land measures and dry and liquid measures see Möller, *Paläographie,* I., No. 679 ff. ; Brugsch, *Thesaurus* (*Geogr. Inschriften*), p. 597 ff. ; Sethe, *Von Zahlen*, p. 74 ff. ; Griffith, *Proc. Soc. Bibl. Arch.*, Vol. XIV, p. 410 ff.

[1] *Von Zahlen und Zahlworten*, Strassburg, 1916, p. 43.

INDEX

A CATALOG OF SELECTED

DOVER BOOKS

IN ALL FIELDS OF INTEREST

A CATALOG OF SELECTED DOVER BOOKS IN ALL FIELDS OF INTEREST

HOW TO WRITE, Gertrude Stein. Gertrude Stein claimed anyone could understand her unconventional writing—here are clues to help. Fascinating improvisations, language experiments, explanations illuminate Stein's craft and the art of writing. Total of 414pp. 4⅜ × 6⅜. 23144-5 Pa. $6.95

ADVENTURES AT SEA IN THE GREAT AGE OF SAIL: Five Firsthand Narratives, edited by Elliot Snow. Rare true accounts of exploration, whaling, shipwreck, fierce natives, trade, shipboard life, more. 33 illustrations. Introduction. 353pp. 5⅜ × 8½. 25177-2 Pa. $8.95

THE HERBAL OR GENERAL HISTORY OF PLANTS, John Gerard. Classic descriptions of about 2,850 plants—with over 2,700 illustrations—includes Latin and English names, physical descriptions, varieties, time and place of growth, more. 2,706 illustrations. xlv + 1,678pp. 8½ × 12¼. 23147-X Cloth. $75.00

DOROTHY AND THE WIZARD IN OZ, L. Frank Baum. Dorothy and the Wizard visit the center of the Earth, where people are vegetables, glass houses grow and Oz characters reappear. Classic sequel to *Wizard of Oz*. 256pp. 5⅜ × 8. 24714-7 Pa. $4.95

SONGS OF EXPERIENCE: Facsimile Reproduction with 26 Plates in Full Color, William Blake. This facsimile of Blake's original "Illuminated Book" reproduces 26 full-color plates from a rare 1826 edition. Includes "The Tyger," "London," "Holy Thursday," and other immortal poems. 26 color plates. Printed text of poems. 48pp. 5¼ × 7. 24636-1 Pa. $3.50

SONGS OF INNOCENCE, William Blake. The first and most popular of Blake's famous "Illuminated Books," in a facsimile edition reproducing all 31 brightly colored plates. Additional printed text of each poem. 64pp. 5¼ × 7. 22764-2 Pa. $3.50

PRECIOUS STONES, Max Bauer. Classic, thorough study of diamonds, rubies, emeralds, garnets, etc.: physical character, occurrence, properties, use, similar topics. 20 plates, 8 in color. 94 figures. 659pp. 6⅛ × 9¼. 21910-0, 21911-9 Pa., Two vol. set $15.90

ENCYCLOPEDIA OF VICTORIAN NEEDLEWORK, S. F. A. Caulfeild and Blanche Saward. Full, precise descriptions of stitches, techniques for dozens of needlecrafts—most exhaustive reference of its kind. Over 800 figures. Total of 679pp. 8⅛ × 11. Two volumes. Vol. 1 22800-2 Pa. $11.95
Vol. 2 22801-0 Pa. $11.95

THE MARVELOUS LAND OF OZ, L. Frank Baum. Second Oz book, the Scarecrow and Tin Woodman are back with hero named Tip, Oz magic. 136 illustrations. 287pp. 5⅜ × 8½. 20692-0 Pa. $5.95

WILD FOWL DECOYS, Joel Barber. Basic book on the subject, by foremost authority and collector. Reveals history of decoy making and rigging, place in American culture, different kinds of decoys, how to make them, and how to use them. 140 plates. 156pp. 7⅞ × 10¾. 20011-6 Pa. $8.95

HISTORY OF LACE, Mrs. Bury Palliser. Definitive, profusely illustrated chronicle of lace from earliest times to late 19th century. Laces of Italy, Greece, England, France, Belgium, etc. Landmark of needlework scholarship. 266 illustrations. 672pp. 6⅛ × 9¼. 24742-2 Pa. $14.95

ILLUSTRATED GUIDE TO SHAKER FURNITURE, Robert Meader. All furniture and appurtenances, with much on unknown local styles. 235 photos. 146pp. 9 × 12. 22819-3 Pa. $8.95

WHALE SHIPS AND WHALING: A Pictorial Survey, George Francis Dow. Over 200 vintage engravings, drawings, photographs of barks, brigs, cutters, other vessels. Also harpoons, lances, whaling guns, many other artifacts. Comprehensive text by foremost authority. 207 black-and-white illustrations. 288pp. 6 × 9. 24808-9 Pa. $8.95

THE BERTRAMS, Anthony Trollope. Powerful portrayal of blind self-will and thwarted ambition includes one of Trollope's most heartrending love stories. 497pp. 5⅜ × 8½. 25119-5 Pa. $9.95

ADVENTURES WITH A HAND LENS, Richard Headstrom. Clearly written guide to observing and studying flowers and grasses, fish scales, moth and insect wings, egg cases, buds, feathers, seeds, leaf scars, moss, molds, ferns, common crystals, etc.—all with an ordinary, inexpensive magnifying glass. 209 exact line drawings aid in your discoveries. 220pp. 5⅜ × 8½. 23330-8 Pa. $4.95

RODIN ON ART AND ARTISTS, Auguste Rodin. Great sculptor's candid, wide-ranging comments on meaning of art; great artists; relation of sculpture to poetry, painting, music; philosophy of life, more. 76 superb black-and-white illustrations of Rodin's sculpture, drawings and prints. 119pp. 8⅜ × 11¼. 24487-3 Pa. $7.95

FIFTY CLASSIC FRENCH FILMS, 1912-1982: A Pictorial Record, Anthony Slide. Memorable stills from Grand Illusion, Beauty and the Beast, Hiroshima, Mon Amour, many more. Credits, plot synopses, reviews, etc. 160pp. 8¼ × 11. 25256-6 Pa. $11.95

THE PRINCIPLES OF PSYCHOLOGY, William James. Famous long course complete, unabridged. Stream of thought, time perception, memory, experimental methods; great work decades ahead of its time. 94 figures. 1,391pp. 5⅜ × 8½. 20381-6, 20382-4 Pa., Two-vol. set $23.90

BODIES IN A BOOKSHOP, R. T. Campbell. Challenging mystery of blackmail and murder with ingenious plot and superbly drawn characters. In the best tradition of British suspense fiction. 192pp. 5⅜ × 8½. 24720-1 Pa. $3.95

CALLAS: PORTRAIT OF A PRIMA DONNA, George Jellinek. Renowned commentator on the musical scene chronicles incredible career and life of the most controversial, fascinating, influential operatic personality of our time. 64 black-and-white photographs. 416pp. 5⅜ × 8¼. 25047-4 Pa. $8.95

GEOMETRY, RELATIVITY AND THE FOURTH DIMENSION, Rudolph Rucker. Exposition of fourth dimension, concepts of relativity as Flatland characters continue adventures. Popular, easily followed yet accurate, profound. 141 illustrations. 133pp. 5⅜ × 8½. 23400-2 Pa. $3.95

HOUSEHOLD STORIES BY THE BROTHERS GRIMM, with pictures by Walter Crane. 53 classic stories—Rumpelstiltskin, Rapunzel, Hansel and Gretel, the Fisherman and his Wife, Snow White, Tom Thumb, Sleeping Beauty, Cinderella, and so much more—lavishly illustrated with original 19th century drawings. 114 illustrations. x + 269pp. 5⅜ × 8½. 21080-4 Pa. $4.95

A CONCISE HISTORY OF PHOTOGRAPHY: Third Revised Edition, Helmut Gernsheim. Best one-volume history—camera obscura, photochemistry, daguerreotypes, evolution of cameras, film, more. Also artistic aspects—landscape, portraits, fine art, etc. 281 black-and-white photographs. 26 in color. 176pp. 8⅜ × 11¼. 25128-4 Pa. $13.95

THE DORÉ BIBLE ILLUSTRATIONS, Gustave Doré. 241 detailed plates from the Bible: the Creation scenes, Adam and Eve, Flood, Babylon, battle sequences, life of Jesus, etc. Each plate is accompanied by the verses from the King James version of the Bible. 241pp. 9 × 12. 23004-X Pa. $9.95

HUGGER-MUGGER IN THE LOUVRE, Elliot Paul. Second Homer Evans mystery-comedy. Theft at the Louvre involves sleuth in hilarious, madcap caper. "A knockout."—Books. 336pp. 5⅜ × 8½. 25185-3 Pa. $5.95

FLATLAND, E. A. Abbott. Intriguing and enormously popular science-fiction classic explores the complexities of trying to survive as a two-dimensional being in a three-dimensional world. Amusingly illustrated by the author. 16 illustrations. 103pp. 5⅜ × 8½. 20001-9 Pa. $2.50

THE HISTORY OF THE LEWIS AND CLARK EXPEDITION, Meriwether Lewis and William Clark, edited by Elliott Coues. Classic edition of Lewis and Clark's day-by-day journals that later became the basis for U.S. claims to Oregon and the West. Accurate and invaluable geographical, botanical, biological, meteorological and anthropological material. Total of 1,508pp. 5⅜ × 8½.
21268-8, 21269-6, 21270-X Pa. Three-vol. set $26.85

LANGUAGE, TRUTH AND LOGIC, Alfred J. Ayer. Famous, clear introduction to Vienna, Cambridge schools of Logical Positivism. Role of philosophy, elimination of metaphysics, nature of analysis, etc. 160pp. 5⅜ × 8½. (Available in U.S. and Canada only) 20010-8 Pa. $3.95

MATHEMATICS FOR THE NONMATHEMATICIAN, Morris Kline. Detailed, college-level treatment of mathematics in cultural and historical context, with numerous exercises. For liberal arts students. Preface. Recommended Reading Lists. Tables. Index. Numerous black-and-white figures. xvi + 641pp. 5⅜ × 8½.
24823-2 Pa. $11.95

HANDBOOK OF PICTORIAL SYMBOLS, Rudolph Modley. 3,250 signs and symbols, many systems in full; official or heavy commercial use. Arranged by subject. Most in Pictorial Archive series. 143pp. 8⅛ × 11. 23357-X Pa. $6.95

INCIDENTS OF TRAVEL IN YUCATAN, John L. Stephens. Classic (1843) exploration of jungles of Yucatan, looking for evidences of Maya civilization. Travel adventures, Mexican and Indian culture, etc. Total of 669pp. 5⅜ × 8½.
20926-1, 20927-X Pa., Two-vol. set $11.90

THE ART NOUVEAU STYLE BOOK OF ALPHONSE MUCHA: All 72 Plates from "Documents Decoratifs" in Original Color, Alphonse Mucha. Rare copyright-free design portfolio by high priest of Art Nouveau. Jewelry, wallpaper, stained glass, furniture, figure studies, plant and animal motifs, etc. Only complete one-volume edition. 80pp. 9⅝ × 12¼. 24044-4 Pa. $9.95

ANIMALS: 1,419 COPYRIGHT-FREE ILLUSTRATIONS OF MAMMALS, BIRDS, FISH, INSECTS, ETC., edited by Jim Harter. Clear wood engravings present, in extremely lifelike poses, over 1,000 species of animals. One of the most extensive pictorial sourcebooks of its kind. Captions. Index. 284pp. 9 × 12. 23766-4 Pa. $9.95

OBELISTS FLY HIGH, C. Daly King. Masterpiece of American detective fiction, long out of print, involves murder on a 1935 transcontinental flight—"a very thrilling story"—NY Times. Unabridged and unaltered republication of the edition published by William Collins Sons & Co. Ltd., London, 1935. 288pp. 5⅜ × 8½. (Available in U.S. only) 25036-9 Pa. $5.95

VICTORIAN AND EDWARDIAN FASHION: A Photographic Survey, Alison Gernsheim. First fashion history completely illustrated by contemporary photographs. Full text plus 235 photos, 1840–1914, in which many celebrities appear. 240pp. 6½ × 9¼. 24205-6 Pa. $6.95

THE ART OF THE FRENCH ILLUSTRATED BOOK, 1700–1914, Gordon N. Ray. Over 630 superb book illustrations by Fragonard, Delacroix, Daumier, Doré, Grandville, Manet, Mucha, Steinlen, Toulouse-Lautrec and many others. Preface. Introduction. 633 halftones. Indices of artists, authors & titles, binders and provenances. Appendices. Bibliography. 608pp. 8⅜ × 11¼. 25086-5 Pa. $24.95

THE WONDERFUL WIZARD OF OZ, L. Frank Baum. Facsimile in full color of America's finest children's classic. 143 illustrations by W. W. Denslow. 267pp. 5⅜ × 8½. 20691-2 Pa. $7.95

FRONTIERS OF MODERN PHYSICS: New Perspectives on Cosmology, Relativity, Black Holes and Extraterrestrial Intelligence, Tony Rothman, et al. For the intelligent layman. Subjects include: cosmological models of the universe; black holes; the neutrino; the search for extraterrestrial intelligence. Introduction. 46 black-and-white illustrations. 192pp. 5⅜ × 8½. 24587-X Pa. $7.95

THE FRIENDLY STARS, Martha Evans Martin & Donald Howard Menzel. Classic text marshalls the stars together in an engaging, non-technical survey, presenting them as sources of beauty in night sky. 23 illustrations. Foreword. 2 star charts. Index. 147pp. 5⅜ × 8½. 21099-5 Pa. $3.95

FADS AND FALLACIES IN THE NAME OF SCIENCE, Martin Gardner. Fair, witty appraisal of cranks, quacks, and quackeries of science and pseudoscience: hollow earth, Velikovsky, orgone energy, Dianetics, flying saucers, Bridey Murphy, food and medical fads, etc. Revised, expanded In the Name of Science. "A very able and even-tempered presentation."—The New Yorker. 363pp. 5⅜ × 8. 20394-8 Pa. $6.95

ANCIENT EGYPT: ITS CULTURE AND HISTORY, J. E Manchip White. From pre-dynastics through Ptolemies: society, history, political structure, religion, daily life, literature, cultural heritage. 48 plates. 217pp. 5⅜ × 8½. 22548-8 Pa. $5.95

SIR HARRY HOTSPUR OF HUMBLETHWAITE, Anthony Trollope. Incisive, unconventional psychological study of a conflict between a wealthy baronet, his idealistic daughter, and their scapegrace cousin. The 1870 novel in its first inexpensive edition in years. 250pp. 5⅜ × 8½. 24953-0 Pa. $5.95

LASERS AND HOLOGRAPHY, Winston E. Kock. Sound introduction to burgeoning field, expanded (1981) for second edition. Wave patterns, coherence, lasers, diffraction, zone plates, properties of holograms, recent advances. 84 illustrations. 160pp. 5⅜ × 8¼. (Except in United Kingdom) 24041-X Pa. $3.95

INTRODUCTION TO ARTIFICIAL INTELLIGENCE: SECOND, ENLARGED EDITION, Philip C. Jackson, Jr. Comprehensive survey of artificial intelligence—the study of how machines (computers) can be made to act intelligently. Includes introductory and advanced material. Extensive notes updating the main text. 132 black-and-white illustrations. 512pp. 5⅜ × 8½. 24864-X Pa. $8.95

HISTORY OF INDIAN AND INDONESIAN ART, Ananda K. Coomaraswamy. Over 400 illustrations illuminate classic study of Indian art from earliest Harappa finds to early 20th century. Provides philosophical, religious and social insights. 304pp. 6⅝ × 9⅝. 25005-9 Pa. $9.95

THE GOLEM, Gustav Meyrink. Most famous supernatural novel in modern European literature, set in Ghetto of Old Prague around 1890. Compelling story of mystical experiences, strange transformations, profound terror. 13 black-and-white illustrations. 224pp. 5⅜ × 8½. (Available in U.S. only) 25025-3 Pa. $6.95

ARMADALE, Wilkie Collins. Third great mystery novel by the author of *The Woman in White* and *The Moonstone*. Original magazine version with 40 illustrations. 597pp. 5⅜ × 8½. 23429-0 Pa. $9.95

PICTORIAL ENCYCLOPEDIA OF HISTORIC ARCHITECTURAL PLANS, DETAILS AND ELEMENTS: With 1,880 Line Drawings of Arches, Domes, Doorways, Facades, Gables, Windows, etc., John Theodore Haneman. Sourcebook of inspiration for architects, designers, others. Bibliography. Captions. 141pp. 9 × 12. 24605-1 Pa. $7.95

BENCHLEY LOST AND FOUND, Robert Benchley. Finest humor from early 30's, about pet peeves, child psychologists, post office and others. Mostly unavailable elsewhere. 73 illustrations by Peter Arno and others. 183pp. 5⅜ × 8½. 22410-4 Pa. $4.95

ERTÉ GRAPHICS, Erté. Collection of striking color graphics: *Seasons, Alphabet, Numerals, Aces* and *Precious Stones*. 50 plates, including 4 on covers. 48pp. 9⅜ × 12¼. 23580-7 Pa. $6.95

THE JOURNAL OF HENRY D. THOREAU, edited by Bradford Torrey, F. H. Allen. Complete reprinting of 14 volumes, 1837–61, over two million words; the sourcebooks for *Walden*, etc. Definitive. All original sketches, plus 75 photographs. 1,804pp. 8½ × 12¼. 20312-3, 20313-1 Cloth., Two-vol. set $120.00

CASTLES: THEIR CONSTRUCTION AND HISTORY, Sidney Toy. Traces castle development from ancient roots. Nearly 200 photographs and drawings illustrate moats, keeps, baileys, many other features. Caernarvon, Dover Castles, Hadrian's Wall, Tower of London, dozens more. 256pp. 5⅜ × 8¼. 24898-4 Pa. $6.95